TOUR KEY MAP

# CALIFORNIA

*A Guide to the Golden State*

## NEW REVISED EDITION

HARRY HANSEN, *Editor*

*Originally Compiled by the Federal Writers' Project of
the Works Progress Administration for the
State of California*

## AMERICAN GUIDE SERIES

ILLUSTRATED

HASTINGS HOUSE · *Publishers* · New York

FIRST PUBLISHED IN MAY 1939

REVISED EDITION, 1954

COMPLETELY REVISED, 1967

# A Word About the New Edition

CALIFORNIA, A GUIDE TO THE GOLDEN STATE, was originally planned and carried out by the Federal Writers' Project of the Works Progress Administration for the State of California. First published in 1939, it is one of the distinguished AMERICAN GUIDE SERIES that comprises volumes on states, territories, regions and cities of the United States. The original edition was sponsored by Mabel R. Gillis, California State Librarian, and enlisted the energies of scores of editors and research workers, who brought together a record of California from the days of the first Spanish navigators to those of jet plane designers.

Thus it stands as one of the accomplishments of the WPA, which formed the Federal Writers' Project so that writers might find useful employment during the hard-bitten years of the 1930 decade. Henry G. Alsberg became director and outlined many of the patterns followed by the Series; James Hopper was director for Northern California and Leon Dorais for Southern California. The editorial staff comprised individuals already well known and a host of others who chronicled the lore of places and people. Among the writers were Robert C. Brownell, Miriam Allen DeFord, Alfred Frankenstein, Richard Hughes, Paul C. Johnson, Idwal Jones, Kenneth Rexroth, Nahum Sabsay and Amy Schechter.

The present revised volume is intended to record far-reaching changes that can be described only in superlatives. The huge migration to California has defied the energies of census takers and map makers. New cities have replaced crossroads hamlets; towns have obliterated woods and orange groves and industry has encroached on farms. Population figures estimated by pride-filled local organizations are sometimes considered unduly optimistic, but in California the population often outruns the estimates. Such figures in the following pages are based on reports of the U. S. Bureau of the Census, supplemented by returns of the State Department of Finance, local authorities, and, in the case of some unincorporated communities, post office circulation returns. Small camps and hamlets with a shifting population of from 50 to 200 remain largely as they were. The valuable historical material that made this book a mine of local and regional lore, has been retained.

v

# Contents

## Part I. California: From Past to Present

## Part II. Signposts to City Scenes

## Part III. Up and Down the State

## Part IV. Appendices

## Illustrations

# Maps

# Special Events in California

The following list of special events, based on a summary prepared by the Travel and Recreation Dept. of the California State Chamber of Commerce, San Francisco, is representative of the exhibitions, contests and festivals of more than local interest held annually in California. The dates are those of a current year, and while they change from year to year, will indicate approximately for what part of the month an event is scheduled. Regular commemorative events—St. Patrick's Day, Memorial Day, Independence Day, Labor Day, etc., are not listed.

## JANUARY

| | | |
|---|---|---|
| New Year's Day | Tournament of Roses Parade<br>Rose Bowl Football Game | Pasadena |
| 1-3 | National Dune Buggy Contest | Imperial Valley |
| 1-7 | New Year Regatta | San Diego |
| 9 | Rose Cutting, Mission San Antonio | King City |
| 20-23 | Bing Crosby National Pro-Amateur Championship Golf | Monterey |
| 21-29 | Chinese New Year's Celebration | San Francisco |
| 26-30 | Lucky International Golf Tournament | San Francisco |
| 29-30 | Mounted Police Annual Rodeo | Palm Springs |
| 29-30 | Winter Carnival with Sierra Dog Sled Races and Miss Sierra Snow-Flake Queen Contest | North Lake Tahoe |

## FEBRUARY

| | | |
|---|---|---|
| 2-6 | Bob Hope Desert Golf Classic | Palm Springs |
| 4-6 | Tomato Festival | Niland |
| 4-13 | Sports and Boat Show, Cow Palace | San Francisco |
| 5-6 | Sports Celebrity Dinner | Santa Rosa |
| 11-20 | Winter Festival | Laguna Beach |
| 16-20 | Imperial Valley Carrot Carnival | Holtville |
| 17-20 | Citrus Fair | Cloverdale |
| 18-27 | National Date Festival<br>Riverside County Fair | Indio |
| 18-27 | Southern California Boat Show, Pan Pacific Auditorium | Los Angeles |

| 19-22 | Whiskey Flat Days Celebration | Kernville |
| 24-26 | Almond Blossom Festival | Ripon |
| 25-27 | Camellia Festival and Parade | Temple City |
| 25-Mar. 6 | California Midwinter Fair | Imperial |
| 26-27 | Chinese Bomb Day Celebration | Marysville |

## MARCH

| 5-14 | Camellia Festival | Sacramento |
| 19 | Police Show | Palm Springs |

## APRIL

| 1-7 | Junior Grand National Livestock Exposition, Cow Palace | San Francisco |
| 4-9 | Macy's Flower Show | San Francisco |
| Easter | Sunrise Easter Service, Mt. Davidson | San Francisco |
| Easter | Sunrise Easter Service | Imperial Beach |
| Easter | Sunrise Easter Service | Hollywood Bowl |
| 15-30 | Festival of Arts | Pasadena |
| 18-24 | Pan American Festival | Lakewood |
| 20-24 | Gold Nugget Celebration | Paradise |
| 22 | Miss Sonoma County Contest | Santa Rosa |
| 23 | Cal-Aggie Picnic Day | Davis |
| 23-24 | Black Butte Sailing Regatta | Orland |
| 23-24 | Bass Derby | Rio Vista |

## MAY

| 1 | Loyalty Day Parade | Carpinteria |
| 1-2 | Wild Flower Show of Anderson Valley | Boonville |
| 5 | Cinco de Mayo | Indio |
| 6-8 | Road Races, Laguna Seca Race Track | Monterey |
| 12-22 | U. S. World Trade Fair, Brooks Hall & Civic Auditorium | San Francisco |
| 14 | Hi Neighbor Days | Alhambra |
| 16 | Fiesta, Mission of La Purisima Concepcion | Lompoc |
| – – – | Rose Festival | San Juan |
| 19-22 | La Fiesta | San Luis Obispo |
| 19-22 | Calaveras County Fair & Jumping Frog Jubilee | Angels Camp |
| 20-22 | Willows Lamb Derby | Willows |
| 20-22 | Fair Oaks Fiesta | Fair Oaks |
| 20-22 | Rose Festival and Parade | Santa Rosa |
| 23-29 | Rodeo Week | Redding |

| 26-30 | Sacramento County Fair | Sacramento |
| 28-29 | Hawaiian Festival | Palm Springs |

## JUNE

| 4 | Ram Sale and Sheep Dog Trials | Cloverdale |
| 9-12 | Conejo Valley Days | Thousand Oaks |
| 16-19 | U.S.G.A. National Open Golf Tournament, Olympic Club | San Francisco |
| 18-19 | Buckaroo Days | Boonville |
| 24-July 4 | San Diego County Fair | Del Mar |
| 26-27 | Flower Festival | Lompoc |
| – – – | All States Annual Outing | Los Angeles |

## JULY

| 1-4 | Freedom Season | Woodland Hills |
| 1-4 | Rodeo Fiesta | Folsom |
| 1-4 | Marin Art and Garden Fair | Ross |
| 4 | Cornique | Brentwood |
| 8-16 | National Horse Show | Santa Barbara |
| 21-24 | California Rodeo | Salinas |
| – – – | Fiesta de la Luna | Chula Vista |

## AUGUST

| 3-7 | Old Spanish Days Fiesta | Santa Barbara |
| 5-6 | Lion's Club Corn Festival | La Habra |
| 17-21 | San Luis Obispo County Fair | Paso Robles |
| 31-Sept. 11 | California State Fair | Sacramento |

## SEPTEMBER

| – – – | Wine and Grape Festival | Lodi |
| 16 | Mexico's Independence Day | Indio |
| 23-25 | Mendocino County Fair and Apple Show | Boonville |

## OCTOBER

| 1-3 | Desert Arabian Horse Assn. Show | Del Mar |
| 14-16 | Grand Prix, Laguna Seca Race Track | Monterey |
| 15 | Pioneer Day Parade | Paso Robles |

## NOVEMBER

| First week | Grand National Livestock Exposition, Horse Show and Rodeo, Cow Palace | San Francisco |
| – – – | Cattle Call and Imperial Valley Rodeo | Brawley |

## DECEMBER

| 3rd week | Great Western Livestock and Poultry Show | Los Angeles |
| 31 | East-West Football Game | San Francisco |

# A Guide to Recreation

## PLACES TO VISIT

*Aquariums, Marine Museums, and Submarine Gardens:* Submarine gardens, marine museum and aquarium at Avalon, Santa Catalina Island. Aquarium and marine museum, Scripps Institute of Oceanography at La Jolla. Submarine gardens, Municipal Museum, Hopkins Marine Biological Laboratory at Pacific Grove. Stillwater Cove submarine gardens at Pebble Beach. Steinhart Aquarium in Golden Gate Park at San Francisco, Cabrillo Beach Marine Museum at San Pedro. Aquarium at Venice. Marineland of the Pacific, Redondo Beach or San Pedro.

*Art Collections:* Carmel Art Association at Carmel. The Artists' Barn at Fillmore. Art Center, Fresno. Art Gallery, Pomona College, Claremont. Laguna Beach Art Association. Los Angeles County Museum of Art, City Hall Art Gallery, Municipal Gallery in Barnsdall Park, Art Gallery at UCLA, Los Angeles Art Assn. Long Beach Museum of Art. Keith Memorial Gallery in St. Mary's College at Moraga. Oakland Art Gallery and Mills College Art Gallery at Oakland. Richmond Art Center. Museum of Fine Arts and Thomas Welton Stanford Art Gallery in Stanford University at Palo Alto. Pasadena Art Institute at Pasadena. Mission Inn at Riverside. E. B. Crocker Art Gallery at Sacramento. Fine Arts Gallery in Balboa Park at San Diego. La Jolla Art Center (San Diego). San Francisco Museum of Art, San Francisco Art Association, California Palace of the Legion of Honor, and M. H. de Young Memorial Museum at San Francisco. Huntington Library and Art Gallery at San Marino. Faulkner Memorial Art Gallery in Public Library and Santa Barbara Museum of Art, Santa Barbara. Louis Terah Haggin Memorial Galleries, Victory Park, Stockton.

*Aviaries:* Santa Catalina Island Aviaries at Avalon. Roeding Park at Fresno. Griffith Park Bird Sanctuary at Los Angeles. Bird Shelter at Lake Merritt in Oakland. Balboa Park at San Diego. Golden Gate Park and Fleishhacker Playfield and Zoo at San Francisco.

*Museums and Special Exhibits:* Pony Express Museum at Arcadia. Herbarium and scientific collections at University of California at Berkeley.  Alligator Farm, Buena Park.  Knott's Berry Farm and Ghost Town, Buena Park.  Disneyland, Anaheim.  Naval Museum at Mare Island.  Los Angeles Museum of History and Science, and Southwest Museum at Los Angeles.  Municipal Museum and Snow Museum at Oakland.  Municipal Museum at Pacific Grove.  Leland Stanford Jr. Memorial Museum and Jordan Hall natural history collections, Stanford University, at Palo Alto.  Palace of Science, Museum of Anthropology, and Natural History Museum in Balboa Park and Junipero Serra Museum at San Diego.  M. H. de Young Memorial Museum and California Academy of Sciences Museum in Golden Gate Park at San Francisco.  Museum of Natural History at Santa Barbara.  Museum in Victory Park at Stockton.  Collections of pioneer relics at Columbia; Downieville; Fort Humboldt, Eureka; Independence; Customhouse, and First Theater, Monterey; William B. Ide Memorial Museum, Red Bluff; Mission Inn, Riverside; State Capitol and Sutter's Fort, Sacramento; Estudillo House, San Diego; Shasta; Mission San Francisco Solano and Vallejo Home, Sonoma; and Ventura.  Small natural history collections at Mae Loomis Memorial Museum, Lassen Volcanic tional Park.  Mineralogical collection, Ferry Building, San Francisco. Movieland Wax Museum, Buena Park.  Naval Training Center, San Diego.  Scotty's Castle, Death Valley National Monument.

*National Parks and Monuments:*  Cabrillo National Monument, Channel Islands National Monument, Death Valley National Monument, Devil's Postpile National Monument, Joshua Tree National Monument, Lava Beds National Monument, Muir Woods National Monument, Palm Canyon National Monument, Pinnacles National Monument, Kings Canyon National Park, Lassen Volcanic National Park, Sequoia National Park, Yosemite National Park.

*Observatories:*  Lick Observatory on Mount Hamilton near San Jose, Mount Wilson Observatory near Pasadena, Chabot Observatory at Oakland, California Institute of Technology Observatory on Palomar Mountain.  Observatory and Planetarium at Griffith Park, Los Angeles.

*Zoological Gardens:*  Deer enclosure, aviary, and duck ponds in Roeding Park at Fresno.  California Zoological Society Gardens, Lincoln Park; Bird Sanctuary and Zoo in Griffith Park at Los Angeles.  Oakland Zoo in Sequoia Park at Oakland.  William Land Park Zoo at Sacramento.  Zoological Society of San Diego Gardens in Balboa Park at San Diego.  Golden Gate Park and Fleishhacker Zoo at San Francisco. Applegate Zoo, Merced.

## SPORTS

*Athletic Stadiums:* California Memorial Stadium, University of California at Berkeley. Veterans' Memorial at Long Beach. Coliseum in Exposition Park at Los Angeles. Stanford University Stadium at Palo Alto. Rose Bowl at Pasadena. Balboa Park Stadium at San Diego. Kezar Stadium in Golden Gate Park at San Francisco. Los Angeles Memorial Sports Arena. Anaheim Stadium.

*Baseball:* Played year round throughout the State. San Francisco Giants, Candlestick Park, San Francisco. Los Angeles Dodgers, Dodger Stadium, Los Angeles, also used by Los Angeles Angels. Pacific Coast League plays in Los Angeles, Oakland, Sacramento, San Diego, and San Francisco.

*Football:* Played during fall and winter months throughout State by teams from universities, colleges, high schools, and independent clubs. Chief intercollegiate games are New Year's Day East-West games at Rose Bowl in Pasadena and Kezar Stadium in San Francisco.

*Golf:* Played year round throughout State at public and private club courses and many municipal links, including those in Griffith Park at Los Angeles, Lincoln and Harding Memorial Parks at San Francisco, and Balboa Park at San Diego.

*Horse Racing:* Continuous from fall until spring, with season divided among various tracks. Pari-mutuel betting at Bay Meadows and Tanforan, south of San Francisco; Santa Anita, near Arcadia; Hollywood Racetrack, Inglewood; and Del Mar, north of San Diego. Other tracks at Los Angeles County Fair Grounds in Pomona, State Fair Grounds in Sacramento, and various county fair grounds, operating during fairs.

## OUTDOOR RECREATION

*Boating:* Favorite yachting centers include San Francisco Bay, with yacht harbors at Black Point and San Francisco and clubhouses at Alameda, Alviso, Belvedere, Richmond, and Sausalito; Monterey Bay; Stillwater Cove yacht harbor at Pebble Beach; Santa Barbara yacht harbor in Santa Barbara; Terminal Island in Los Angeles Harbor; Alamitos Bay at Long Beach; Newport Bay; Coronado and San Diego. Accommodations for pleasure craft of other kinds at these and other seaside cities. Sailing in launches and sloops on lower Sacramento and San Joaquin and other rivers; canoeing, motor-boating, rowing on Russian River and other streams and lagoons. Boating of all kinds on Big Bear Lake, Clear Lake, Lake Arrowhead, and Lake Tahoe. Motorboat races on Lake Elsinore, Lake Merritt in Oakland, Alamitos Bay, Newport Bay, and Salton Sea.

*Camping:* Campgrounds, trailer camps, cabins, auto courts, motels, and tent cities at mountain, forest, desert, lake, river, and seaside resorts throughout State. Summer homesites in National Forests for rent from U. S. Forest Service. For details consult articles on specific National Parks.

*Fishing:* Trout fishing throughout the Sierra Nevada in Lake Tahoe, glacial lakes and their tributaries, and headwaters of Kern and Kings Rivers; in the north, upper Sacramento River and its tributaries, Klamath River, and streams of the Coast Range; in southern California, streams of the Sierra Madre and San Bernardino Mountains. Native varieties include rainbow (known as steelhead after going to sea), cutthroat, Dolly Varden, golden, and Tahoe; imported varieties, Loch Leven, Eastern brook, European brown. Lake shallows and riffles stocked with millions of trout fry from fish-hatcheries yearly. Other game fish imported from East include: black bass, found in Clear Lake, northern rivers, and lagoons south of Los Angeles; striped bass, in Suisun and San Pablo Bays; sunfish; and yellow perch. Giant king salmon caught in Monterey Bay in June, July, and August and in San Francisco Bay in August; quinnat and dog salmon caught off northern coast and during spawning season, in Klamath River and rivers of Coast Range. Best ocean fishing in Monterey Bay, where species from both northern and southern waters are found, and off southern California coast. South of Point Concepcion, most common ocean fish are albacore, barracuda, black sea bass, bonito, leaping tuna, sheepshead, swordfish, yellow-fin tuna; peculiar to southern California waters are corbina, croaker, flatfish, roncador and yellowfin. Piers for surf fishing at Long Beach, Ocean Park, Redondo, and Santa Monica. Best deep-sea fishing off Portuguese Bend, Redondo, and Coronado, Santa Catalina, San Clemente, and Santa Barbara Islands. Santa Catalina Island waters especially noted for sport with albacore, broadbill swordfish, dolphin, giant bass, leaping tuna, marlin swordfish, white sea bass, and yellowtail. Shellfish, especially abalone clams, and mussels, are dug at many points along coast. See *Regulations.*

*Hiking:* Well-marked trails lead through national parks and forests and radiate from resorts in Sierra Nevada, Coast Range, and southern California ranges. Horses, pack animals, and guides available at mountain resorts throughout State. Camps and lodges make wilder mountainous regions accessible to skilled mountaineers. All trails open in July and August; southern trails from May to November. Easy trails lead into Sierra Madre Mountains from Big Pines, Camp Baldy, Crystal Lake, and Mount Wilson; into San Bernardino Mountains from Big Bear Lake and Lake Arrowhead; San Jacinto Mountains from Idyllwild and Kenn Camp; Santa Ynez Mountains from Santa Barbara; Mount Hamilton Range from Alum Rock Park near San Jose; Santa Cruz Mountains from California Redwoods State Park; Berkeley Hills from Berkeley; Mount Diablo Range from Danville or Walnut Creek; Mount Tamalpais region from Mill Valley; Bear Valley forest and Tomales Ridge from Inverness, Olema, or Point Reyes; Castle Crags State Park from Castella; and into redwood groves from resorts along Redwood Highway. Short trails to points of interest in Kings Canyon, Lassen Volcanic, Sequoia, and Yosemite National Parks are well marked. Among peaks easily climbed by amateur hikers are Mount San Antonio, Mount Wilson, Mount Lowe, Mount Diablo, Mount Tamalpais, and Lassen Peak. Mount Shasta is climbed from late June until early October. Trails into Trinity-Salmon Alps lead from Cecilville and Trinity Center, into Marble Mountain primitive area from camps along State 96. For skilled mountaineers, trails radiate into High Sierra from Lake Tahoe, Tuolumne Meadows, Yosemite Valley, Kings Canyon and Sequoia National Parks, Kings River Camp in Kings River Canyon, Huntington Lake, and Bishop, Lone Pine, and Independence in Owens Valley. Pacific Crest Trail, traversing main divides of highest ranges in Pacific Coast States, has five sections in California: Lava Crest Trail, 330 miles; Tahoe Yosemite Trail, 260 miles; John Muir Trail, 185 miles; Sierra Trail, 160 miles; and Desert Crest Trail, 475 miles. For information about the northern recreation area generally address the chambers of commerce of the adjacent cities.

*Hunting:* Deer, most common large game animal, are of three varieties: blacktail, mule, and white-tail. Found in Sierra Nevada north of Lake Tahoe, in northeast above Alturas, and in coast Range from Oregon to Mexican border. Open season varies according to region, beginning August 1 in Coast Range and ending October 15 in Sierra Nevada. Bears hunted with aid of guides and trained dogs in Sierra Nevada, parts of Coast Range, and San Bernardino Mountains. Cougars, fair game at any season (bounty on scalps), hunted with dogs in regions where deer are found. Foxes common, especially in Coast Range; gray wolf and wildcat (red lynx) sometimes hunted. Smaller game animals include badgers, cottontails and jackrabbits, gray and Douglas squirrels, porcupines, raccoons, and woodchucks. Most hunted game fowl are wild ducks, including bluebill, canvasback, gad-

wall, mallard, ruddy, spoonbill, sprig (pintail), teal, and widgeon.
Open season usually October 15 to January 31. Chief duck hunting
grounds are Suisun marshes to north and Alviso marshes to south of
San Francisco Bay; "tule lands" along Sacramento, San Joaquin, and
other rivers of Central Valley; marshlands back of beaches at Alamitos
Bay, Newport Bay, and lagoons in southern California; and scattered
regions in Imperial Valley, around Monterey Bay, and in Klamath
River country. Characteristic method is shooting in marshes from
"tule splitter" boats, but bay blinds and baited ponds are also employed. Wild geese and brant are fair game in duck season. Also
hunted in autumn and winter are mountain quail, chiefly in higher
Sierra and counties north of San Francisco Bay, and valley quail, in
lowlands and foothills. Blue grouse, sage-fowl, and Wilson snipe are
hunted frequently; also avocet, band-tailed pigeon, golden and upland
plover, ruffed grouse, sandhill crane, and wild dove.

*Motoring:* Among favorite scenic drives for automobilists are Red-
wood Highway through redwood groves of Humboldt County (*see
Tour 1a*), Victory· Highway over Donner Pass and down Yuba
Bottoms (*see Tour 9a*), Feather River Highway through gorge of
Feather River (*see Tour 6B*), Skyline Boulevard along crest of the
Sierra Moreno south of San Francisco (*see Tour 1b*), Seventeen-
Mile Drive around Monterey Peninsula (*see Tour 1c*), Carmel-
San Simeon Highway along coast (*see Tour 1c*), and Rim-of-the-
World Drive through San Bernardino Mountains (*see Tour 12b*).
Good highways scale Sierra Nevada, Coast Range, and southern Cali-
fornia Mountains. Among peaks climbed to summit by highways are
Mount Wilson, from Pasadena; Mount Hamilton, from San Jose;
Mount Diablo, from Danville; Mount Tamalpais, from Mill Valley.

*Ocean Bathing:* Sheltered bathing beaches along coast from Trinidad
to San Diego and at Avalon, Santa Catalina Island. Among favored
beaches in north are Neptune Beach at Alameda, Ocean Beach at San
Francisco, and the beach at Santa Cruz; in south, beaches at Malibu,
Santa Monica, Ocean Park, Venice, Redondo Beach, San Pedro, Long
Beach, Seal Beach, Newport, and San Diego. Favorite season for
bathing extends from June to September, but hardy swimmers take dips
the year around. Amusement zones at Neptune Beach, Ocean Beach,
Santa Cruz, Ocean Park, Venice, Redondo, Long Beach, and Seal
Beach; many others easy to reach from Freeways.

*Riding:* Scenic equestrian trails in foothill, mountain, and desert
regions, especially in Griffith Park, Los Angeles, and Golden Gate Park,
San Francisco; Del Monte Forest, and Sierra Nevada resorts.

# Hunting, Fishing and Driving Regulations

HUNTING AND SPORT FISHING are carefully regulated and controlled by the Fish and Game Commission, appointed by the Governor and getting authority from the Legislature. The Department of Fish and Game is responsible for the administration and enforcement of the Fish and Game Code. It is supported by the sale of hunting and fishing licenses, fines for violations and commercial fishing taxes, one-half of which goes into the Preservation Fund, the other half to the county affected, which must use the proceeds for propagation and conservation of fish and game. Fishing in the National Parks needs no license.

*Licenses for Hunting:* A state license is required for taking any bird or mammal except a non-protected animal. In addition a Federal duck stamp is needed for taking migratory waterfowl; deer tags for deer, bear tags for bear, pheasant tags for pheasants. The license year is from July 1 to June 30. Hunters under 18 may get a license only on presentation of a California license from a prior year, or a certificate of competence from a safety training course.

*Fees for Hunting:* Resident under 16, $1; resident, $4; nonresident, $25. Resident deer tag, $2. A resident is one who has lived in California six months prior to his application, or who is on active military duty in the U. S. Armed Forces or auxiliaries. Nonresident deer tag, $10; bear tag, $1; not issued to anyone under 12. Pheasant tags, $2. Trapping, $1; no license required for anyone under 18.

*Licenses for Fishing:* A sport fishing license is required of any person 16 years of age or over, including members of the Armed Forces, for taking any kind of fish, mollusk, amphibian or crustacean in California waters, except for persons fishing from a public pier in the open sea adjacent to the coast or islands or in waters of bays contiguous to the ocean. No license stamp is required for taking frogs. One stamp is required for fish in inland waters, excluding trout but including steelheads. Two stamps are required for trout. The license is for the calendar year.

*Fees for Fishing:* Resident license, $3; nonresident, $10; special 10-day nonresident, $3; special 3-day, waters of Pacific Ocean, $1; sport fishing license stamps, each $1; Colorado River special use stamp, $2. Persons 16 years old and over fishing in Lake Tahoe and Topaz Lake must have a California license with stamps or a Nevada license. Any person fishing from a boat or other floating device in the Colorado River must have a California license plus an Arizona use stamp, or vice versa.

Complete details of regulations for the ensuing year are published annually in July by the Department of Fish and Game, 1416 Ninth St., Sacramento 95814, in two pamphlets: *Hunting Regulations* and *Sport Fishing Regulations*. These give the seasons, limitations of species and size of bag, protected areas and game, permissible firearms and angling methods, and descriptions of how and when fish may be taken from any body of water, from mountain stream to the Pacific Ocean. National Parks enforce rules of their own in addition to the California regulations. Federal laws prohibiting certain types of firearms also apply.

*Hunting Regulations:*   It is unlawful to carry a loaded rifle or shotgun in a vehicle on any road open to the public; to hunt while intoxicated; to use a light to take a bird or mammal, except raccoon; to fail to fill out and attach the game tag after taking deer, bear or pheasant; to discharge a firearm within 150 feet of a dwelling; to use a shotgun larger than 10 gauge; to shoot from a public road; to possess a machine gun, silencer, shotgun with barrel less than 18 inches long, or rifle with barrel less than 16 inches. Hunters may not kill at any time condors, bold eagles, white-tailed kites, trumpeter swans, mountain sheep, spotted fawns, sea otters, sea elephants, and Guadalupe fur seals. Hunters should obtain permission from landowners before entering private property. Campfires should be attended and put out on leaving; refuse should be burned if fires are allowed, and tins and bottles should be carried away.

Shooting hours for big game, including but not limited to bear, deer, antelope, and European wild pigs, are limited to one-half hour before sunrise to one-half hour after sunset. No more than one dog per hunter may be used for taking deer or bear, and dogs are prohibited during the archery season for deer and bear.

*Driving Regulations:*   Drivers over 21 may use out-of-state licenses for one year. A man who takes a job in California needs a California license for driving. Drivers between 16 and 21 must obtain a California license within 10 days of entering state. A new resident my operate his passenger car without registration until his home state registration expires. Military personnel may carry license plates from home state or place where they served. A person who buys an automobile from a dealer out of state for use in California must pay a use tax of 4% of the purchase price. Fees: $8 plus $2 for each $100 of value of vehicle, estimated by Dept. of Motor Vehicles, Sacramento. Registrations expire Dec. 31; renewal deadline next Feb. 4. Dept. of Motor Vehicles, Sacramento, California.

Speed regulations are enforced. On Freeways and expressways the maximum is 65 mph. Slower speeds are often indicated for merging traffic. Inside cities maximum generally is 25 mph.

# Winter Sports in California

A Digest from *Winter Sports Guide* of the Travel & Recreation Dept., California State Chamber of Commerce, San Francisco, Sacramento, Los Angeles.

RECREATION IN WINTER is calling many tourists from adjoining states to California. As the State Chamber of Commerce expresses it: "Nowhere else can you hop in a car, romp in the snow, and return home to mow the lawn, all in the same day." It is the place for "shirt-sleeve skiing," with a long season, usually from December to April, in some cases even until July. More than 55 resorts of varying sizes are active.

*Transportation:* Southern Pacific Railway, with the Cascade streamliner between San Francisco and Portland, serves the Mount Shasta Ski Bowl through connecting bus service from Dunsmuir. City of San Francisco streamliner from San Francisco has direct or connecting service to all Donner Summit, North Lake Tahoe, and California-Nevada ski areas. San Joaquin Daylight streamliner connects with buses at Merced for side trips to ski areas in Yosemite National Park. Transportation from Tulare to Sequoia-Kings Canyon National Park is available by special arrangement. Consult local Southern Pacific agents. The Western Pacific serves the Feather River area. Santa Fe Railway operates train and bus service from San Francisco through Stockton, Merced and the San Joaquin Valley to Los Angeles, reaching snow sports areas by bus, and same service north from Los Angeles.

Bus lines reach all popular sports areas. Greyhound Lines reach Reno, Stateline, Bijou, Strawberry and points on State 40 and State 50, Dunsmuir and Mount Shasta; also between Los Angeles and Reno via US 395, with two schedules daily each way to the Inyo-Mono areas. Group transport by chartered bus can be arranged. Continental Trailways has service between San Francisco and Merced, with connections to Yosemite, also charter service.

*Information for Motorists:* California State Chamber of Commerce issues a bulletin on road conditions to news media every Wednesday. It is compiled from reports of the U. S. Forest Service, National Park Service, local chambers of commerce, highway maintenance and patrol agencies. Automobile associations keep members informed of daily conditions. Motorists are advised to carry tire chains and attach them before entering snow areas; also to have anti-freeze in radiator.

Make reservations in advance, especially for holidays. Many resorts offer reduced rates for midweek stay. Pack arrangements can include room, meals, ski instruction and use of tows. Useful are the Learn-to-Ski Weeks. Many resorts will rent ski equipment. Ski lessons before skiing are advised to increase safety and pleasure. The Far West Ski Assn., of the U. S. Ski Assn., provides its members with a number of advantages, including discounts, insurance, advice on resorts, etc. Headquarters, 812 Howard St., San Francisco, and 6404 Hollywood Blvd. (Hollywood), Los Angeles.

## HOW TO REACH WINTER SPORTS AREAS
### Name of Area, Location, Mailing Address, Nearest Highway

Alpine Meadow, 1 m. s. of Squaw Valley. Box 865, Tahoe City. State 89.

Badger Pass, Yosemite National Park, 22 m. s. of Valley. State 140, 41.

Blue Ridge, near Wrightwood. Box 82, Wrightwood. State 2.

Calaveras Big Trees State Park, 3 m. e. of Arnold. State 4.

Cedar Pass, 19 m. e. of Alturas. Modoc Ski Club, Alturas. US 299.

Cerro Noroeste-Mt. Abel, 30 m. s. of Maricopa. R. R. Bin, The Fort, Taft. US 399.

China Peak, Huntington Lake, 68 m. e. of Fresno. Box 128 Shaver Lake. State 168.

Coppervale, 5 m. e. of Westwood. 140 S. Gilman, Susanville. State 36.

Dodge Ridge, 3.7 m. e. of Pinecrest. Box 513, Long Barn. State 108.

Donner Ski Ranch, Donner Summit. Box 66, Norden. US 80, State 89.

Echo Summit. S. Lake Tahoe. Box 96, Stateline. US 50.

Granlibakken, 1 m. s. of Tahoe City. Box 22, Tahoe City. US 80, State 89.

Greenhorn Mtn., Shirley Meadows. Via Glenville, 50 m. ne. of Bakersfield. Box 245, Wofford Heights.

Green Valley, Bear Lake area. 10125 Lynrose St., Temple City. State 18 & 30.

Happy Hill, Bear Lake area. 1 m. w. of Village. Box 162, Big Bear Lake. State 18 & 30.

Heavenly Valley, Bijou. Box 237, Stateline. US 50.

Holiday Hill, Wrightwood area. Box 327, Wrightwood. State 2.

Horse Mountain, 40 m. e. of Eureka. 3154 C St., Eureka. US 299.

Inyo Basin, Onion Valley. 15 m. w. of Independence. How Villa, Lone Pine. US 395.

June Mountain, 56 m. n. of Bishop. Box 22, June Lake. US 395.

Kratka Ridge, Angeles Crest Area. 1015 E. 16th St., Los Angeles. State 2.

Laing's, Lake Tahoe area. Laing's, Emigrant Gap. US 80, State 89.

Lassen National Park, 9 m. ne. of Mineral.    Mineral Lodge.    State 36, & 89.

Mammoth Mountain, Minaret Rd.    Box 24, Mammoth Lakes.    US 395.

Mescal, Wrightwood area.    Box 338.    State 2.

Moonridge, 3 m. e. of Village.    Big Bear Lake.    State 18 & 30.

Mount Baldy, 11 m. n. of Upland.    Ski Lifts, Mt. Baldy.    State 30.

Mount Pinos, 20 m. w. of Lebac.    Box 338, Wrightwood.    US 99.

Mount Rose, 12 m. ne. of Lake Tahoe.    Box 2958, Reno, Nev.    State 27.

Mount Shasta, 12 m. ne. of Mt. Shasta Ski Bowl, Mt. Shasta.    US 99.

Mount Waterman, 32 m. ne. of La Canada.    817 Lynnhaven Lane, La Canada.    State 2.

Papoose, Squaw Valley.    Drawer A, Olympic Valley.    US 80, State 89.

Peddler Hill, 38 m. ne. of Jackson.    1127 Dolores Way, Sacramento. State 88.

Phillips Pow Wow Lodge, Twin Bridges.    State 50.

Pla-Vada, near Kingvale.    Box 195, Soda Springs.    US 80, State 89.

Plumas Eureka, 5 m. e. of Westwood.    680 Colorado St., Portola. US 80, State 89.

Powder Bowl, Deer Park, 1 m. s. of Squaw Valley.    Box 864, Tahoe City.    US 80, State 89.

Rainbow, Box 55, Soda Springs.    US 80, State 89.

Rebel Ridge, 3 m. e. of Village.    Box 159, Big Bear Lake.    State 18 & 30.

Sierra Ski Ranch, Twin Bridges.    US 50.

Slide Mountain, 13 m. ne. of Lake Tahoe.    Box 706, Crystal Bay, Lake Tahoe, Nev.    State 27.

Snow Forest, Big Bear.    140 S. Wilbur Ave., Covina.    State 18 & 30.

Snow Summit, 1½ m. e. of Village.    Box 77, Big Bear Lake.    State 18 & 30.

Snow Valley, Keller Peak.    Box 8, Running Springs.    State 18 & 30.

Soda Springs, 3 m. w. of Donner Summit.    Box 5, Soda Springs.    US 40.

Squaw Valley, 7 m. n. of Tahoe City.    Box 27, Tahoe City.    State 89 off US 40.

Strawberry Lodge, 40 m. e. of Placerville.    US 50.

Sugar Bowl, 1 m. w. of Donner Summit.    Box 5, Norden.    US 80.

Sugar Loaf, 6 m. e. of Posey via Granite Sta.    Bin 5B, Posey.

Table Mountain, Wrightwood area.    Box 57, Wrightwood.    State 2.

Tahoe Ski Bowl, 7 m. s. of Tahoe City.    Box 305, Homewood.    State 89.

Wolverton Ski Bowl, Sequoia National Park.    52 m. e. of Visalia.    Address Park.    State 198.

Yuba Ski Land, 12 m. e. of Sierra City.    520 Cascade Dr., Fairfax. State 49.

# Annual Competitive Ski Events

Following are the schedules for competitions held annually under the auspices of the Far West Ski Association. Dates are those of the 1964-1965 season and can be used as guides to subsequent years; the months will remain the same and the days will be adjusted as needed; consult announcements in local newspapers.

Abbreviations: *CC—Cross Country; D—Downhill; GS—Giant Slalom; J—Jump; S—Slalom.*

## SENIOR COMPETITION

| | | | |
|---|---|---|---|
| Nov. 29 | GS | Turkey Trophy | Squaw Valley |
| Dec. 6 | GS | – – – – – | June Lake |
| Jan. 10 | S | Birthday Slalom | Squaw Valley |
| Jan. 31 | S | La Velle Cup | Kratka Ridge |
| Feb. 7 | GS | Frank Campbell & Avalanche | Mt. Waterman |
| Feb. 14 | GS | Avalanche Inferno | Snow Summit |
| Feb. 20-21 | DS | Arizona Snow Cup | Arizona Ski Bowl |
| Mar. 6-7 | S-D | Far West Kandahar | Alpine |
| Apr. 4 | S | Alexander McFadden | Squaw Valley |
| Apr. 4 | GS | San Gorgonio | San Gorgonio |
| Apr. 25 | S | Dick Springer Memorial | Mammoth Mountain |
| May 30 | GS | Memorial Day Race | Squaw Valley |
| July 4 | GS | Midsummer Derby | Squaw Valley |

## JUNIOR COMPETITION

| | | | |
|---|---|---|---|
| Jan. 9-10 | D-S | Point Race | Sugar Bowl |
| Jan. 17 | GS | San Gorgonio | Kratka Ridge |
| Jan. 23-24 | GS-S | Point Race | Slide Mountain |
| Feb. 6-7 | D-GS | Point Race Div. Champ | Mammoth Mountain |
| Feb. 7 | GS | Fresno Bee Silver Ski | Yosemite |
| Feb. 14 | S | Lions Club Jr. Slalom | Yosemite |
| Feb. 27-28 | S-D | Point Race | June Mountain |
| Mar. 7 | GS | Schrader Memorial | Mt. Shasta |
| Mar. 27-28 | GS | Sacramento Bee | Heavenly Valley |
| Apr. 4 | GS | Soda Springs | Soda Springs |
| Apr. 11 | GS | American Legion | Yosemite |
| Apr. 12 | GS | Levi Ski Rodeo | Soda Springs |
| Apr. 16-17 | – – – | Yosemite Jr. Trophy | Yosemite |
| Apr. 17 | D-GS | Sugar Bowl | Sugar Bowl |
| Apr. 18 | – – – | Disney Race | Sugar Bowl |

# PART I
# California: From Past to Present

# Where the Dream Comes True

NOW MORE than ever before California is the rainbow's end for great numbers of Americans. For more than one hundred years the people of the Cis-Sierra have turned their eyes with longing toward the Pacific foreshore. Farmers from the black soil of Iowa, from the little towns of the Mississippi and Ohio basins, wearied by the harsh winters, sold their holdings and followed the transcontinental trail to the Coast. Less fortunate but no less hopeful were the survivors of the dust storms of the Great Plains, who packed their ramshackle cars with household goods and children and struck out for the place where the dust no longer blew. Then came the stream of the more prosperous, ready to "retire," who chose California because even in the middle of the twentieth century it still had the promise of Paradise. Within recent years they have made California the most populous state of the nation.

Always the nation's playground, the objective of those wishing to prolong their lives in leisure and comfort, California is today a greater host than ever. It entertains in the course of a year more than six and a half millions who arrive by plane and train, by bus and private motor car, and deploy to the hills and valleys, the beaches and resort towns. To accommodate them there has come about a proliferation of motels, golf courses, air lifts, ski runs, regattas and parades, and such luxurious retreats as Palm Springs have attained the allurement of European spas. Good fortune, too, has smiled upon lagging enterprise. When the motion picture mills of Hollywood seemed to have exhausted their lode, there came the talkies; when the popularity of the talkies diminished, there came a revival of cash and customers with television. And to delight the imagination with fantasy in tangible form, the world's most elaborate amusement park sprouted in the midst of the orange groves.

It pays to be first at a scene, for firstcomers invariably are heralds of identification.   The explorers and navigators who first laid eyes on *Alta California* bequeathed their names, and today more millions than existed in their own nations make daily use of them.   Juan Rodriguez Cabrillo never sailed far beyond the Channel Islands, but his name is fastened forever on California's southernmost borders.   Sir Francis Drake tarried briefly on his marathon around the world, but his place on the signboards of hotels, roads and pleasure boats remains secure.   Every schoolboy has heard about Portola, who missed Monterey Bay, and Vizcaino, who found it, and now that most of the ancient Spanish Missions are restored the fame of Father Junipero Serra is known to all.

The newcomer, drawn by the mild climate, quickly becomes aware that California is a Spanish legacy, quite different from the land of the Puritans.   He can hardly move around without meeting evidence that once the hospitable Spaniards cultivated these farms—pardon, ranchos and haciendas.   And although California was overrun by tough characters who called their diggins Black Gulch Camp, Greenhorn Creek, Fiddletown and Railroad Flat, preference obviously has been given the Spanish, even if the melodious terminology is only a land salesman's shoptalk.   But who would wish to change alamos to poplars, robles to oaks, nogales to walnuts, fresno to mountain ash?   True, there are the General Sherman Tree, the Douglas MacArthur Park and the Nimitz Freeway, but they have not displaced the saints and the feast days that constitute a garland of names for cities and towns.

---

Here one may traverse the dense wilderness, primitive and uncontrolled.   Here is seclusion, a refuge far from the road of city traffic, the fumes of motor exhausts.   Hunter, camper and fisherman penetrate the wild country of the northern ranges and lose themselves in the dark, dank woods, but with a difference—they have the confidence, unknown to the pioneer, that the highways are within easy reach.   The wilderness is an unkempt place, but accessible and controlled.   It stretches for miles and miles, especially in the vast terrain of the Cascades, the Six Rivers, Shasta and Marble Mountains, in the High Sierras, Inyo, Mendocino and Trinity, and farther south into the wild areas of San Bernardino National Forest.   Men have hacked at these formidable barriers for ages, but the protecting arms of the nation and the State have kept them wild for the good of civilized man.

Those who do not yield to the mountains, surrender to the everlasting phenomena of the sea.   There it stretches for more than twelve hundred miles of coastline, within easy reach from all the towns of the Pacific slope.   Over and over again it arouses feelings of aspiration in the beholder; he takes its fresh air deep into his lungs and moves to wrestle with its waves or enjoy its satisfactions from a sheltered spot.   To many the sea is a never-failing source of wonder and refreshment.   In the northern counties it can be a raging surf that breaks upon the sharp, craggy rocks.   In the south it rolls up on the long sandy slope, inviting the swimmer and the surf rider.   In between it may remind the visitor of its suffocating strength when it sends long lines of mist swirling through the Golden Gate, wiping out visibility beyond ten paces.   Great areas of the coastline have been set aside for public use, some providing the cool background of trees saved from the lumberman's axe.   Yet within the decades under review more acres of incomparable redwoods have fallen to provide commercial lumber, and despite the hosannahs sung to the glory of the trees, the legacy of the past shrinks, never to be recovered.

Robert Louis Stevenson was the most literate, and possibly the most eloquent of those who have recorded their sensations on viewing the physical grandeur that is California, although we will be everlastingly grateful for the keen observation of John Muir.   High on the slope of Mount St. Helena, in what is now the Stevenson Memorial Park, Robert Louis was occupying a rustic cabin with his bride.   Below the mountain lay parts of three counties—Napa, Lake and Sonoma; from its summit Stevenson could see the Bay, Mount Diablo, the open ocean, the cornlands and tule swamps of the Sacramento Valley, "to where the Central Pacific Railroad begins to climb the sides of the Sierras."   From his airy height he observes the morning fog coming in from the sea, not as a stiffling enemy that clutches at the throat, but as a spectacle.   The impression is caught forever in *The Silverado Squatters:*

"Napa Valley was gone; gone were all the lower slopes and the woody foothills of the range; and in their place, not a thousand feet below me, rolled a great level ocean.   It was as though I had gone to bed the night before, safe in a nook of inland mountains, and had awakened in a bay upon the coast. . . .   Far away were hilltops like little islands. I began to observe that this sea was not so level as at first sight it appeared to be.   Away in the extreme south, a little hill of fog arose against the sky above the general surface, and as it had already caught the sun, it shone on the horizon like the topsails of some gaunt ship.   There were huge waves, stationary, as it seemed, like waves in a frozen sea; and yet, as I looked again, I was not sure but they were moving after all, with a slow and august advance.   And while I was yet doubting, a promontory of the hills, some four or five miles away, conspicuous by a bouquet of tall pines, was in a single instance overtaken and swallowed up.   It reappeared in a little, with its pines, but this time on an islet, and only to be swallowed up once more and then for good.   This set me looking nearer, and I saw that in every cove along the line of mountains, the fog was being piled in higher and higher, as though by some wind that was inaudible to me. I could trace its progress, one pine tree first growing hazy and then disappearing after another; although sometimes there was none of this forerunning haze, but the whole opaque white ocean gave a start and swallowed a piece of mountain at a gulp. It was to flee these poisonous fogs that I had left the seaboard, and climbed so high among the mountains. And now, behold, here came the fog to besiege me in my chosen altitudes, and yet came so beautifully that my first thought was of welcome."

Sometimes it is not fog but the billowing clouds of smoke that blot out landscapes. Within weeks whole mountain sides have been denuded. Even the habitations that men built close to the green cover to savor the rich aromatics of the woods are swept away when the flames come down from the hills. Here nature seems in league with men to whom great trees are merely so many feet of lumber. From prehistoric times down to today fires from numerous causes have taken toll of the State's heritage.

---

There are fewer orange groves today than there were twenty years ago, but there are more steel mills, aircraft factories, makers of electronic devices, builders of bridges, skyscrapers, missiles and space craft. As the pool of labor widened industry cut the long haul from the eastern seaboard and came to California to tap it. More workers meant more houses; the little towns crowded upon the orchards for citrus fruits and the fields of garden truck; the orchards shrank and the townsmen considered themselves benefited as shippers of manufactured goods. The average Californian accepts the change as the price paid for more prosperous living, but there are thoughtful persons who feel saddened at the swift decline of agriculture, and ask themselves: "How long?" "How far?"

On the surface there is sunshine and prosperity, but underneath the smiling aspects of California life there is the tension of competition, the rush of youthful energy, the dormant threat of the unsatisfied. The frequent violence that marked the decades of the gold-seekers, the period of political corruption, the labor wars, has not ended in California. There is nothing static in California's civilization; it is everywhere in process of adjustment to needs and demands. One season it is a battle between longshoremen and shippers at the docks; another it is the riotous frenzy of desperate minorities; in its mildest form it is the political intransigence of students shouting dozens of conflicting demands under the privilege of free speech. Such turbulent acts are California's legacy; they are possibly more urgent, more noisy, than those of other states of the Union, but they are part of the great vitality that expresses itself in violent eruptions as well as peaceful undertakings, and they are not ignored.

More prosaic, but no less imposing, is the record of California's provision for the prosperity and wellbeing of its citizens. The hundreds of thousands that pour across its boundaries from other states come to a land that has legal safeguards for all who choose to remain there. This does not mean that all who swarm into the State immediately find themselves free from economic anxieties. The State can ameliorate, but it cannot remove, all the drawbacks to individual welfare that stem from vocational incapacity in highly competitive fields. But it can apply a formidable number of laws protecting the worker's interest, and point to the advantages gained by collective bargaining, the steady increase in the earnings of women as well as men; the usefulness of workmen's compensation, unemployment insurance, health care, and vocational and general education on a grand scale.

The skyscrapers are the latest symbolic interpretation of man's reach for freedom exemplified by the tall sequoia on the Stanford seal. The piercing pinnacles of fifty-four stories are emerging above the rooftops of the cities as if to dwarf the redwoods and compete with the hills. They were inevitable in a closely organized business economy where offices must be concentrated in the most populous areas. They throw into shadow images of more modest construction in days when life was less departmentalized. Limited at present to the bulging metropolis, they do not impinge on the orderly vistas of smaller cities that still preserve the uniformity of an urban skyline. The plain, well-proportioned, brightly-lighted structures that house both municipal and industrial undertakings in California provide a new basis for civic beauty.

# Natural Setting and Conservation

"IF CALIFORNIA lies beyond those mountains we shall never be able to reach it," wrote John Bidwell, leader of the first overland emigrant train, in his journal on October 29, 1841. But on the next day he set down: "We had gone about three miles this morning, when lo! to our great delight we beheld a wide valley. . . . Rivers evidently meandered through it, for timber was seen in long extended lines as far as the eye could reach." The day after he continued: "Joyful sight to us poor, famished wretches! Hundreds of antelope in view! Elk tracks, thousands! The valley of the river was very fertile, and the young, tender grass covered it like a field of wheat in May."

Thousands of later emigrants who struggled to the crest of the Sierra Nevada, towering like a massive wall along the State's eastern border, were equally overjoyed at their first glimpse of El Dorado. As they stood at the summit, the dry wilderness of the Great Basin lay behind them. To north and south rose the rock-ribbed flanks of the huge Sierra Nevada, about 385 miles long and with an average width of about 80 miles. Westward they looked toward the Great Valley of California, a vast elliptical bowl averaging 50 miles in width and more than 400 miles long, larger in area than Vermont and New Hampshire combined. Beyond the valley stood the dim blue peaks of the Coast Range, skirting the ocean and parallel to the Sierra in chains from 20 to 40 miles wide and 500 miles long. Far to the north, beyond their vision, the rugged Cascade Range and Klamath Mountains closed in on the valley's northern rim; and far to the south, the Tehachapi Mountains thrust their barrier from east to west across its southern end.

California, with a total area of 158,297 square miles, is the Union's second largest State. In the language of the geographer, its latitude extends from 32° 30′ to 42° N., and its longitude from 114° to 124° 29′ W. Its medial line, from Oregon to the Mexican border, is 780 miles long. Its width varies from 150 to 350 miles. Its coastline is approximately 1,200 miles—somewhat less than one-tenth of the total coastline of the United States. So pronounced is the eastward curve of the State's southern coast that San Diego lies farther east than Reno in Nevada, although Eureka, a northern port, is the most westward city in the United States. On the east the State is bordered by Nevada and by the Colorado River, which separates its southeastern corner from Arizona.

Beyond each end of the mountain-walled Great Valley, which is California's most distinctive topographic feature, the terrain is broken and rugged. Northward lie the Siskiyou Mountains, a natural barrier between California and Oregon. In the northwest, wild timbered slopes reach to the Pacific; in the northeast, mountain spurs hem in barren lava-bed plateaus. South of the Tehachapis' dividing line lies southern California comprising one-third of the State's area. Here the complex network of the Sierra Madre, the San Bernardino, and other ranges separates the so-called Valley of Southern California, a broad strip of broken country near the coast, from the arid wastes of the Mojave and Colorado Deserts in the hinterland. From Point Concepcion, where the Coast Range breaks into numerous ridges and the coast swings in sharply to the east, the Valley of Southern California, which includes the V-shaped coastal plain of the Los Angeles Basin, stretches southward to the Mexican border.

These chief geographical districts—the Sierra and Coast Range regions and the Central (Sacramento-San Joaquin) Valley in the north, the coastal lowlands, the mountains, and the desert country in the south—present startling physiographic contrasts and extremes, from active volcano to glacier, from arctic flora on mountain tops to cotton plantations below sea level. From the peak of Mount Whitney, the highest point in the United States, it is but 60 miles to Death Valley, the continent's lowest area. Human activities range from fur-trapping in the snows of the Klamath region to prospecting for minerals in the furnace-like heat of the southeastern deserts.

California's contour is marked by lofty mountain peaks towering above precipitous gorges and canyons. Of the 41 peaks that exceed 10,000 feet in height, the tallest is Mount Whitney (14,496 alt.) in the southern Sierra. The Sierra's abrupt eastern slope has one of the steepest general gradients on the North American continent. Over a

160-mile stretch the lowest pass is at an altitude of 9,000 feet, while Kearsage, the most frequently used pack horse pass on this stretch, is 12,050 feet; in this area the peaks range from 13,000 to 14,000 feet in height. Although there is a gradual decline in altitude to the north, other isolated peaks of the Sierra rise above 14,000 feet. Northward the western slopes are gashed by river canyons sometimes half a mile deep.

The Sierra's sculptured splendor is in part the work of glaciers which carved deep valleys, expanses of polished rock, and towering granite walls over which roar great waterfalls, glacial lakes and meadows. Most beautiful of the valleys is Yosemite, in the midsection of the Sierra; loveliest of the lakes is Tahoe (6,225 alt.), cupped between the main Sierra and the basin ranges at the angle of the Nevada-California boundary. A few glaciers even now survive on the highest summits, the finest of them being a group of five supported by Mount Shasta (14,161 alt.).

Dominating the northern end of the Sacramento Valley is Mount Shasta, the most striking of the many extinct or dormant volcanoes in the northern California mountains. Lassen Peak (10,435 alt.), 85 miles southeast of Mount Shasta, is a mildly active volcano—the only one in the United States that has had a generally observed eruption. Although traces of volcanic action are most abundant in the State's northeastern sector, where lava beds spread over vast tracts, there are also extinct or dormant volcanoes in Owens Valley and the Mojave Desert, and numerous hot springs in the Coast Range.

The Coast Range, more complex than the Sierra, includes numerous indistinct chains from 2,000 to 7,000 feet high. Each chain is broken down into forested spurs and ridges enclosing small pleasant valleys and plains drained by rapid streams.

The Santa Ynez, San Barnardino, and San Gabriel Mountains bound the lowland of southern California on the north and northeast, and subdivide it into more or less distinct valleys or basins. Farther south the coastal lowland is bounded by the Santa Ana and San Jacinto Ranges, an elevation that extends into Mexico. The southern California ranges are marked by the lofty peaks (more than 10,000 feet high) of San Bernardino, San Jacinto, and San Antonio and by the well-defined passes of Soledad, Cajon, and San Gorgonio.

Among the mountain-walled valleys between the southern end of the Sierra and the border of Nevada is the long and narrow Owens Valley, bordered by granite walls. About 40 miles east of dry Owens Lake, along the California-Nevada border, lies Death Valley, its lowest point 276 feet below sea level. It stretches between the sheer rocky walls of the Panamint Range on the east and the Amargosa Range on the west—130 miles long and from 6 to 14 miles wide—a region of stark simplicity, majestic silence, and spectacular desolation. South of Death Valley spread the Mojave and Colorado Deserts. The Mojave is an expanse of ancient dried lake bottoms, short rugged ranges, and immense sandy valleys. Parts of the Colorado Desert lie below sea level—250 feet below at its lowest point. In its southern end is the fertile Imperial Valley, largely reclaimed from the desert for agricultural use by irrigation, where the Salton Sea, formed when the Colorado River broke its banks in 1905, floods an ancient lake bottom.

In addition to the Great Valley in the north and the coastal district (including the rich Los Angeles Basin and Santa Clara and San Fernando Valleys) in the south, cultivated lowlands occur elsewhere in the State. Below San Francisco Bay stretches another Santa Clara Valley; and southeast of Monterey Bay, between the Santa Lucia and Gabilan Ranges, lies the long Salinas Valley. North of San Francisco in Sonoma, Mendocino, and Humboldt Counties are similar areas. The northeast corner of the State, hemmed in by steep ranges, is suitable for cattle raising and restricted agriculture despite its lava beds and sagebrush.

In the whole 400-mile length of the Great Valley there is only one break in the mountain walls through which the waters of the interior can escape to the sea. Behind the Golden Gate at San Francisco, cutting across the full width of the Coast Range, is a great gap through which passes almost the entire drainage of the Great Valley. Into Suisun Bay pour the waters of the Sacramento and San Joaquin Rivers; they empty through Carquinez Strait into San Pablo and San Francisco Bays, and through the Golden Gate into the Pacific Ocean.

The scantily forested eastern flanks of the Coast Range contribute no stream lasting enough to reach either the Sacramento or the San Joaquin in the dry season; but down the western slopes of the Sierra, tributaries pour through precipitous canyons to the great rivers at each end of the valley. Fed by Mount Shasta's melting snows, the Sacramento, California's largest river, is joined by the Pit, McCloud, Feather, Indian, Yuba, and American Rivers as it flows southward 350 miles to its confluence with the San Joaquin in the Delta region. The Sacramento's lower course is through a marshy plain partly inundated yearly. The San Joaquin, whose valley comprises more than three-fifths of the central basin, flows northward from its headwaters in the mountains of Fresno County. Into it drain the waters of the Fresno, Merced, Tuolumne, Stanislaus, Calaveras, Mokelumne, and Consumnes Rivers, together with many smaller streams.

The seaward slopes of the Coast Range are drained by the Klamath (joined by the Scott and Trinity), Mad, Eel, and Russian Rivers north of San Francisco, and south of it by the Salinas, Santa Maria, Santa Ynez, Santa Clara and other secondary rivers, many of them intermittently dry. Southern California's so-called rivers—the Ventura, Los

Angeles, San Gabriel, Santa Ana, San Luis Rey, Santa Margarita, and San Diego—are for the most part dry creek beds except during spring floods.

A peculiarity of the State's drainage system is its many river "sinks" where the waters either dry up from evaporation or, like the Amargosa River in Death Valley, disappear beneath the surface. Through Modoc and Lassen Counties, in the far northeast, stretches a chain of alkaline "lakes"—Goose, Upper and Middle, and Honey Lakes. They are all without drainage to the sea, and the spring run-off rapidly evaporates. In the Central Valley, south of the area drained by the San Joaquin, the Kings, Kaweah, and Kern Rivers, fed by the melting snows of the high Sierra, formerly emptied into shallow marsh-girt lakes. But with the impounding of water for irrigation these lakes have dried up, and the old lake beds have become farm lands. The Mojave Desert, in whose sandy wastes the Mojave River is swallowed up, is dotted with glistening alkaline-incrusted dry lake beds. In Riverside, San Diego, and Imperial Counties, many creeks (so-called rivers whose beds are normally dry) run toward the desert sink of the Salton Sea region.

California has two magnificent natural harbors, San Francisco and San Diego Bays, both landlocked; and one great artificially built harbor, the port of Los Angeles. San Francisco Bay, entered through the Golden Gate, is among the world's finest; here, besides the port of San Francisco itself, are those of Oakland, Alameda, and Richmond. San Diego Bay, safe at all seasons, is sheltered from ocean winds by Point Loma, a promontory seven miles in length. The Los Angeles harbor, fronting on open San Pedro Bay, 20 miles from the city, is protected by a breakwater. California's best minor harbors are those of Monterey and Santa Cruz, on Monterey Bay, and Eureka, on Humboldt Bay, some 280 miles north of San Francisco.

There are two groups of islands off the California coast. The Santa Barbara Islands, nine in number, lie between Point Concepcion and San Diego, 20 to 60 miles from the mainland. From San Miguel Island in the north to San Clemente Island in the south they are scattered over a distance of 155 miles. The best known island of the group is rugged Santa Catalina, 25 miles long with an average width of four miles, which stands 20 miles south of San Pedro. The Farallones, a group of six small rocky islands, lie about 28 miles west of the entrance to San Francisco Bay.

## CLIMATE

The first American writer to describe California's natural features refrained from the rhapsody which has characterized most of the subsequent discussion of the State's far-famed weather. "The climate of

California," wrote Captain William Shaler, "generally is dry and temperate, and remarkably healthy; on the western coast the sky is generally obscured by fogs and haze, but on the opposite side it is constantly clear; not a cloud is to be seen, night or day. The northwest winds blow very strong eight months in the year, on the western coast, with very little interruption; the land breezes at that time are hardly perceptible; but in the winter months they are stronger and regular. In the months of January, February, and March there are at times very high gales from the southeast, which render most of the bays and harbours on the coast unsafe at that season."

California's climate is characterized by certain peculiar features: the temperature of the entire Pacific Coast is milder and more uniform than that of regions in corresponding latitudes east of the mountains; the year divides, in general, into two seasons—wet and dry—instead of into the usual four seasons; and where extreme summer heat occurs, its discomfort is lessened by the dryness of the air.

Despite these general characteristics the State is a place of many climates, due to distance from the ocean, situation in reference to mountains, and, above all, altitude. Thus there are sharp climatic contrasts within a single limited area. One may go sleighing within sight of blossoming orchards, or view snow-clad peaks while bathing in the sea. A winter traveler in the high Sierra will be reminded of the Alps, while anyone venturing into the scorching inland valleys in midsummer will conclude that whoever labeled California "semitropical" was a master of understatement.

The term, however, is applied with good reason to the strip of land between the coastal mountains and the ocean. For those who have never visited this area the most restrained account of its climate is likely to seem hyperbole. The year-round weather is more equable than that of any other part of the United States; and from San Francisco southward to Monterey, the difference between the average summer and winter temperatures is seldom more than 10 degrees. In this coastal region frost heavy enough to halt the greening of the hills under winter rains is as rare as thunder and lightning; and always some flowers are in bloom. Sea breezes and fogs tend to stabilize the temperature without extremes of heat or cold.

The annual mean temperature of San Francisco is 56°; the summer mean is less than 60°, the winter 51°, and the lowest recorded temperature 27°. In San Diego the winter mean temperature is 54°, the summer 68°. In Monterey the difference between January and August mean temperatures is from 10° to 14°; in Los Angeles 14° to 16°. Because of the California current and the marine air from the Pacific anticyclone, summer in San Francisco is actually cooler than fall. These same factors induce fogs, night and morning, in that region and all along the California coast during the greater part of the summer. So dense and persistent are these coastal fogs that great areas south of San Francisco devoted to truck gardening require no other moisture during the summer months. The Coast redwood, as well as the plants which grow beneath it, is watered by the fog that condenses on its foliage.

In the southern part of the Central Valley, temperatures are often very high. Although the annual mean temperature of the inland is 64°, in Fresno and Bakersfield the mercury occasionally soars above 110°. The desert temperatures are still higher, the summer mean in Fort Yuma being 92°. In Death Valley, the average daily minimum for July, the hottest month, is 87.6°. But on July 10, 1913, it reached 134°, only slightly less than the highest natural air temperature hitherto accurately measured. In the mountain regions, on the other hand, summer temperatures are much lower and the winters are very severe. At the top of Mount Lassen, in the winter of 1932-33, the mercury registered 56° below zero.

Annual rainfall in the State varies from about 80 inches at Crescent City in the extreme north to about 10 inches at San Diego in the extreme south. At San Francisco the annual average is about 22 inches; at Los Angeles, 16 inches. The northern half of the Sierra and the northwest counties are covered by a heavy rain belt. In the high mountains precipitation, almost entirely in the form of snow, provides most of the run-off which supplies water for the cities and for irrigation. In the high Sierra the average annual snowfall is from 300 to 400 inches. At Tamarack in Alpine County the snowfall during the winter of 1906-7 was 844 inches, the greatest ever recorded for a single season anywhere in the United States. The belt of heavy rain shades off to a region of lighter rainfall which covers all the rest of the State except Inyo, Kern, San Bernardino, and Imperial Counties, and the eastern portion of Riverside County. The limits of this third region may, in dry years, include all of the State below Fresno and the entire Central Valley.

In general, rains occur in California only in the months from October to May. Even during this rainy season, the valley districts usually have no more than from 25 to 35 rainy days. Throughout the rest of the year excursions may be planned everywhere, except in some parts of the mountains, with considerable confidence that no rain will dampen the occasion.

## GEOLOGY AND PALEONTOLOGY

Every major division of geologic time is represented in California by marine sediments, and many of them by continental deposits as well.

As the Pacific Ocean on the west and the ancient Great Basin Sea on the east alternately encroached on the California region, each supplied that part of the record which the other omitted. In formations of the last two periods, the Tertiary and the Quaternary, California is particularly rich.

Structurally the Sierra Nevada is a single colossal block of earth's crust lifted along its eastern edge to a height of more than 11,000 feet above the adjoining blocks, and gently tilted westward. The oldest known rocks making up these mountains are intrusions of molten rock (magma) and limestones, cherts, shales, and sandstones, all sedimentary, and nearly all changed into their metamorphic equivalents in the process of mountain building. These older sedimentary rocks were deposited in ancient seas of shifting extent and depth, which during the second half of the Paleozoic and the first two periods of the Mesozoic era, covered now one part, now another, of the Pacific Coast. Toward the close of the Jurassic period, the lands that were eventually to become the ancestral Sierra Nevada, the Cascades, and the Klamath Mountains began to emerge from the sea.

During the Cretaceous period the Sierra's whole block tilted westward. This process of tilting and folding wrenched open leaves of slates, once shales; heated mineral-bearing solutions escaped from the magma that was cooling and solidifying below and filled the slate openings with gold-bearing quartz. The Eocene epoch of the Tertiary period was comparatively quiet. The Sierra slowly underwent additional elevations and subsidences accompanied by active erosion of the surface rocks. Meanwhile the rivers were cutting their channels down the western slope and carrying the products of erosion to the inland sea. There was further release of gold from the bedrock, and the formation of rich placers. In the Oligocene epoch following, there was volcanic activity, and the Sierra gold-bearing stream channels were dammed and filled with rhyolite ash.

Volcanic activity continued during the Miocene age, and in addition to lava there were extensive mud flows and tuffs. In the Pliocene epoch the volcanoes were far less active, and in the Pleistocene the volcanic cover was removed in part by erosion. The veins and buried stream channels were cut into, and gold-bearing gravels were washed from their ancient channels and redistributed along new streams. This is the origin of so-called free gold. The Sierra had been greatly worn down in late Tertiary times, but the Pleistocene epoch of the Quaternary period was an era of re-elevation. There was much faulting, and a new period of volcanic activity began which is not quite ended today.

In the early Tertiary period the Sierra slopes were luxuriant with vegetation, but toward the end of that period the climate became much cooler. The slopes and summits were encased in thick ice and snow, which kept them captive. The glacial periods of the Pleistocene were relieved by intervals during which the ice fields retreated toward the crests, yielding to climates even milder than that of California today. But when the ice of the last glacial age had finally retreated (traces of this epoch still linger in various glaciers such as those on Shasta), the Sierra crest stood stripped of vegetation and soil, exposing those bare expanses of whitish granites and schists that now give it its dazzling beauty. Yosemite and other extraordinary Sierra valleys and canyons are also glacial legacies, as are the numerous lakes in the high Sierra. Tahoe, lovely lake and the deepest in the United States, was made partially by glaciation and partly by faulting, erosion, and volcanic damming.

The volcanic activity of Miocene times was especially great in the Cascade Range, where a number of volcanic peaks rose in a comparatively short time. Mount Shasta was one; the still active Mount Lassen was another, and the volcanic range extends north into Oregon and Washington. Eastward from the range extends one of the largest lava fields in the world, covering 200,000 square miles to depths of from 200 to 2,000 feet. This lava plateau, generally decomposed on the surface, which stretches beyond California into Oregon and across into Idaho and Wyoming, did not for the most part erupt through typical volcanic vents, but flooded up through great cracks or fissures. The Pit River, flowing through the Cascades, has cut deep into the series of volcanic rocks (andesites) some 7,500 feet in thickness, and the thin but widespread basalts. Because of the depth of this covering, the pre-Miocene history of the region is uncertain.

The oldest of the accessible formations of the Klamath Mountains are pre-Cambrian metamorphic rocks including schists, quartzites, and crystalline limestones—the last named consisting partly of sedimentary, partly of igneous rocks, both metamorphosed. The first two periods of the Mesozoic are represented by smaller proportions of sedimentary rocks which are covered by remnants of once extensive beds of sandstones, shales, and conglomerates of the Cretaceous period. There were also periods when volcanoes were active, especially the early Devonian period and the greater part of the Mesozoic era. The mass had been uplifted during the Jurassic period, but erosion and subsidence brought the ancestral Klamath mountains to below sea level in the Cretaceous period. This oscillation continued more or less quietly, except for an outburst of great volcanic activity in the middle of the Miocene. The most recent re-elevation, like that of the Sierra, was at the beginning of the Quaternary period. At approximately the same time, gold-bearing gravels were carried down along the sides of many canyons by erosion.

There are no Paleozoic (old life) rocks in the northern Coast Range, but crystalline limestone and schist, probably of this age, are found in the Santa Cruz, Gabilan, and Santa Lucia Ranges. Of the next era, the Mesozoic, Triassic period remains are lacking, but from the Jurassic come most of that complex series of Coast Range rocks known as the Franciscan. These are sedimentary rocks of several types: conglomerate, sandstone, shale, variegated chert, and (rarely) limestone. With them is embedded a great series of volcanic and plutonic rocks of the same age.

Cretaceous rocks in the Coast Range are abundant. They make up considerable parts of the Santa Lucia, the Temblor, and Diablo Ranges, and they become even more widespread north of San Francisco. The rocks consist chiefly of shale, siltstone and sandstone, with some small streaks of coal, and—near Coalinga—shale, which is the source of the oil in overlying Tertiary beds. The Cretaceous sea covered considerable parts of what is now the north Coast Range, but the region that now comprises the Santa Lucia Range and the Salinas Valley was relatively higher than at present, and formed Salinia, a long narrow peninsula running out to the northwest. The Eocene strata are relatively uncommon except in the eastern foothills near Coalinga and in the Mount Diablo region. The rocks are similar to those of the Cretaceous. There are considerable beds of coal, but the latter is of poor quality. Salinia had become an island, and there was a similar island whose axis ran along what are now the Gabilan and Mount Hamilton Ranges northwest to Marin County.

The Oligocene formations in the Coast Range are chiefly of red sandstone; there are also certain organic shales, which seem to be the source rocks for the oil of Kettleman Hills. The seas had become less widespread. Salinia extended farther north and west, but the San Joaquin Valley still formed an arm of the sea into which drained the rivers of Mohavia—a name given to the region now covered by the Mojave Desert, Death Valley, and the Owens River Valley. In the early Miocene there was much volcanic activity in the Coast Range, and this ultimately cut off the sedimentary deposits from Mohavia and prevented their reaching the sea. There followed in the late Miocene another period of widespread shallow seas and many coastal islands. Much organic siliceous shale was laid down, and this is the source of the oil in the Santa Barbara and Ventura coast region as well as elsewhere. Of Pliocene origin are calcareous and feldspathic sandstones and thick beds of brown and blue sandy clay. As elsewhere in California, the climate became cooler. There was still a series of islands and peninsulas along the entire coast.

In the Pleistocene epoch most of the old interior seas and bays disappeared. This was a period of violent deformation of structure, with foldings and bendings of the strata and a series of faults. Of these latter, the San Andreas fault, which was responsible for the earthquake of 1906, extends from Tomales Bay, 40 miles north of San Francisco, to the Mojave Desert, 600 miles southeast. In contrast to the more common type of vertical movement, it has a horizontal drift. The extent of its movement during Tertiary times was at least 700 feet, and according to some estimates as much as 10 or 20 miles. The Hayward fault, which runs sub-parallel to the San Andreas across San Francisco Bay and through Berkeley, is also important; and the Coast Range is cut by several smaller faults.

The Great Valley is an immense trough formed late in the Jurassic period when the mountain ranges inclosing it began to rise from the water. Unlike most valleys in the United States, which were cut by streams, it came into being through the sinking of the earth's crust. From that time on it remained an inland basin. For long periods it was flooded with salt water, as the sea flowed in through gaps in its intermittently rising barriers. The upward thrust of the Coast Range in the middle of the Tertiary period made it a nearly landlocked and shallow inland sea. Finally, in early Pleistocene times, the streams of the Sierra and the Coast Range, steadily carrying down their loads of sediment, caused a recession of the sea and laid down the flat valley floor. Although the valley is probably still sinking, it has filled with alluvium as fast as it has sunk. In some places drillings to depths of more than 3,000 feet fail to reveal bedrock.

The Transverse Ranges, comprising the San Bernardino, San Gabriel, Santa Monica, Santa Inez, and Santa Susana Mountains, have a general east-west trend, but differ only slightly in their geology from the chains of the Coast Range. Some of their Tertiary sedimentary rocks are more than 30,000 feet thick, exceeding in thickness any other such rocks in North America. They are remarkably rich in fossils.

Extending southeast of the Los Angeles Basin to a point beyond the Mexican border, the Peninsular Ranges include the San Jacinto, Santa Ana, Santa Rosa, and Coyote Mountains, with plateaus and valleys in between. Their geology has been but little studied, but they seem to belong to the fault-block type of mountains. While the faults are branches of the San Andreas, their general geology is rather like that of the Sierra, the dominating rocks being granitic.

The Great Basin comprises all that part of California lying southeast of the Sierra and east of the Peninsular Ranges, including the Colorado Desert, the Mojave Desert, and the Basin Ranges. Except for the Imperial Valley and some smaller areas under irrigation, the section is today a complete desert. The Colorado Desert, in part 245 feet below sea level, is a depressed block between active branches of the alluvium covered San Andreas fault in the Peninsular Ranges and the Mojave Desert to the north and east. The Mojave Desert region has isolated mountain ranges rising abruptly from desert plains. Farther north the Basin Ranges, of typical fault-block structure, run roughly parallel from north to south and are separated by deep basins or troughs. Death Valley, the most famous of the basins, is the bed of a lake of Pleistocene times and shows distinct sets of shore lines. The Great Basin had a number of such lakes in recent geologic time, although the region as a whole has been a land area since Cretaceous times. In the Panamint and Amargosa Ranges, which fence in Death Valley on the east and west, are formations from as far back as the Paleozoic era, but the valley, as such, is recent. The Mojave Desert's many short mountain ranges of various trends are largely of ancient volcanic and metamorphosed Tertiary rocks. The rest of the Mojave is an expanse of great sandy valleys and of dry lakes holding deposits of dead seas—salt, gypsum, soda, and borax. The last named was formed when the red-hot lava streams flowed into the saline lakes. The Colorado Desert is underlaid with Tertiary volcanic flows and coarse conglomerates, above which lie Quaternary fresh-water silts and sandstones.

With the rise of the mountains to the north and west in the early Miocene epoch, the sea that covered them was cut off and inland drainage systems were created. Rainfall decreased and the region slowly dried up. However, lakes of considerable extent have existed in the basin of the Colorado River within the period of the occupation of the country by the Indians, whose old camps may still be found on the margins of what are now salt flats.

A number of regions in California, particularly in the Coast Range and the Los Angeles Basin, are rich in fossils. Numerous fossil radiolaria found in the Franciscan cherts show their marine origin, and the north Coast Ranges have yielded fossil ferns, cyads, and conifers, as well as several kinds of mollusks and smaller marine organisms of the Cretaceous period. The types of marine organism found in the Eocene rocks indicate a much warmer surface water than exists on the California coast at present, and consequently a warmer climate.

From the Sespe beds between Los Angeles and Ventura have come bones of a variety of mammals of Oligocene times: the rhinoceros, the oreodont, the miohippus, the camelid, primitive carnivores, rodents, and insectivores. At a number of places the remains of primitive horses, peccaries, and camels have been found in Miocene formations. In the Pliocene strata there are primitive horses close in form to the modern horse.

The best-known paleontological area in California, and one of the richest in the world, is La Brea Pits in Los Angeles County. Since Tertiary times the quaking and sticky area of the La Brea asphalt beds has been a death trap for unwary animals. Beneath it have been preserved the skeletons of a prehistoric menagerie, including the imperial elephants, largest of all land mammals, whose domain extended from eastern Nebraska to Mexico City, hideous great ground sloths and little ground sloths, sabre-tooth tigers, giant wolves, camels and horses, llamas, wide-front bison, and numerous smaller species such as turtles, snakes, beetles, and birds. Well-preserved forms of vegetation, which show the evolution of plant life, have also been unearthed here. Noteworthy among these is a complete eight-foot cypress of the McNab species, which was discovered standing upright, buttressed by bones. This species is now found only rarely on the dry hills and flats of the Coast Range in northern California.

The Mojave and Death Valley Deserts of southern California have yielded fossils of the Oligocene and Miocene epochs, deposited as long as 25,000,000 years ago. In a narrow canyon near Barstow, where layers of breccia in dazzling colors were thrust up by an ancient volcanic upheaval, scientists have discovered during the past twenty years the remains of three-toed horses, several varieties of camels, antelope, and smaller animals, and an animal almost identical with the desert coyote of today. The complete skeleton of an Ice Age elephant (terrabeladon), similar to fossils discovered in the Gobi Desert, was found in 1938 near Saltdale, Kern County, in the northern part of the Mojave Desert. Death Valley's Tertiary beds have yielded the remains—including a skull three feet long—of a titanotherium, a large mammal that somewhat resembled the rhinoceros, found in red sandstone formations of the Oligocene epoch near Leadfield.

The fossils of Inyo County's "oldest muds in the world" are so abundant that, in geologist G. D. Bailey's words, they "are hauled away by carloads to fill the museums of the East." In Fresno County, less rich paleontologically, submammalian fossils have been found near Coalinga, a Pliocene mastodon skull at the north end of the Kettleman Hills, and fossil mastodon bones near Fresno. A rare find, uncovered in the Coast Range west of Fresno in 1937, was a fossil of eight vertebrae of a mesasaurus, huge sea lizard of the upper Cretaceous epoch. Kern County has yielded fossil animal bones of Tertiary and earlier ages and exceptionally rich marine fossils of the mollusca phylum, among them some highly ornamented forms showing a considerable degree of advancement in racial development.

The first dinosaur remains ever uncovered on the west coast of America were found in 1936 in the hills west of Patterson, Stanislaus County, by a high school student. The remains consisted of the tail and one hind foot. In other mountain counties of northern California, ancient caves—including Hawver's Cave on the North Fork of the American River in Eldorado County, and Potter and Samwell Caves on the McCloud River in Shasta County—have proved to be veritable storehouses of the bones of mammals swept in by river floods in the remote past. Remains of the giant ground sloth (megalonyx) have turned up in the earth fan at the entrance to Mercer's, or Murphy's Cave in Calaveras County.

The State's most unexpected paleontological discovery was dredged from the mud of San Francisco Bay during construction of the island site of the 1939 Golden Gate International Exposition. From sandstone strata 45 feet below the bay level, a tooth and a section of the ivory tusk of a Columbian mammoth (*elephas Columbia*) of the middle Pleistocene epoch were scooped up and pumped through 17,000 feet of pipe line. On the Peninsula, near Menlo Park Station, San Mateo County, remains of a mastodon skeleton were found in June 1927, buried in the plain formed by the coalescent fans that fringe the Bay. The discovery included a molar tooth, preserved without even discoloration of the enamel, three sections of a tusk, and fragments of ribs and other bones.

The most complete quarry in California for specimens of the Tertiary period was discovered in 1926 near Moraga, Contra Costa County, on the site of an ancient fresh-water lake. The fossils so far recovered are not so well preserved as those of the La Brea Pits, but they are believed to be more complete and to predate the La Brea remains by about 9,000,000 years. A three-toed giant horse and a three-footed antelope, a camel much larger than any known today, and the most primitive dog of its type yet found are among the species. Other discoveries include fossils of mastodons, hyenalike dogs, sabretooth cats, oreodons, peccaries, and a host of smaller creatures. At Irvington, in Alameda County, remnants of a prehistoric horse, an antelope, a mammoth, and a horned toad—all more than 500,000 years old—were found in 1936 and turned over to the University of California department of paleontology, which discovered the beds.

## PLANT AND ANIMAL LIFE

California's plant and animal life is as diverse as its environment. Since its climate ranges from subtropical to Arctic, its terrain from arid, below sea level deserts in the south to moist, forested mountains in the north and from icy Sierra ridges on the east to foggy coastal slopes on the west, the State embraces a wide variety of flora and fauna. All the life zones of North America, except the tropical, are represented, their distribution depending not so much on latitude, as in most regions, as on altitude. California's plant and animal life, virtually isolated from the rest of the continent, is frequently distinctive and sometimes unique. While some species have migrated into the mountain slopes and coastal fog belt of the north from Oregon, and into the semiarid deserts, plains, and mountains of the south from Mexico, only a few eastern species have had the hardihood to cross the inhospitable deserts of the Great Basin and scale the barrier of the Sierra. These have undergone striking transformation in their migration.

Botanically, California is notable in particular for the unusual number of its annuals, both species and individuals, and for its numerous rare species of the lily family. More evergreens, especially the conifers, and fewer deciduous trees are found here than in most other States. Notable also are the many species of trees surviving only in limited localities from past ages, of which the best known are the Monterey pine and Monterey cypress and the two Sequoias (the coast redwood and the "big tree"), representing a family extinct elsewhere since the Ice Age. Still another distinctive feature is the chaparral—extensive pigmy forests of shrubs, stunted trees, and associated herbaceous plants —which covers the hillsides of the Upper Sonoran zone in dense thickets. It remains dormant throughout the hot dry summer, but becomes active with the rains of late winter and early spring.

The eucalyptus and acacia of Australia, the pepper tree of Peru, and the palm tree of the tropics flourish in both rural and urban areas; the eucalyptus (*eucalyptus globulus*) especially has been so widely planted in groves and roadside lanes both along the coast and in the Great Valley as to seem like a native. The wild yellow mustard, that covers orchard lands and hillsides in season with a yellow-green tide, was planted by the earliest Spanish settlers, as was the wild radish. The geranium and fuchsia both grow to extraordinary size in all the coast counties, where there are no extremes of heat and cold. In a number of places in the Sierra foothills, Scotch broom (*cystisus scoparius*) more than holds its own as an "escape" in the chaparral; and a species of filarese (*erodium macrophyllum*), a valuable forage crop, has become widely distributed.

The animals of the State are also distinctive, though less conspicuously so than the vegetation. The birds as a whole tend to be grayer, paler, and of slighter build than their eastern relatives. There are fewer species of snakes and more of lizards. Except for several species of trout, few fresh-water fish are native to the State, although some interesting indigenous species are found among the fauna of the tidal strip.

The streams were once abundantly supplied with sturgeon, but this magnificent fish has practically disappeared save in the least accessible rivers of the State's northwest coast. The icy lakes and streams of the Sierra favor many species of native and introduced trout. The former include the rainbow trout, or steel head, the Tahoe trout, the golden, the cutthroat, and Dolly Varden. Salmon, migrating from the ocean to their upstream spawning beds, are found in the northern coastal rivers in the spring. Dog salmon and quinnat salmon frequent coastal waters and the great king salmon enters the Bay of Monterey during the summer months. Other deep-sea fishes are the black and white sea bass, the yellowtail, the sheepshead, the "tonno," the albacore, the leaping and the yellowfin tuna, the bonito (the *Sardo chilensis* of the Pacific), the voracious barracuda (*Sphyraena barracuda*), and the battling swordfish.

Marine life of every kind is prolific and variegated. The California lobster, though large, lacks the huge pinchers of his eastern cousin. The pilchard or sardine (*Sardinia caerulea*) is found in such numbers during its run as to comprise 20 percent of the annual value of the State's fisheries. Herds of sea lions roar from the rocks off San Francisco, and elsewhere the leopard seal is occasionally seen. The abalone, most noted of California's shellfish, is a table delicacy and its shell is of use in manufacture. Oysters are plentiful but smaller than eastern varieties.

California is divided by biologists into six life zones, in each of which the altitude and climatic conditions are roughly uniform throughout the zone (*see accompanying map*). These are designated the Lower Sonoran, Upper Sonoran, Transition, Canadian, Hudsonian, and Arctic zones. The first is the lowest in altitude, and the warmest; the last is the highest and coldest. The Lower Sonoran zone includes the larger part of the Great Valley from Red Bluff to Bakersfield, all of the great arid and desert regions southeast of the Sierra to the Nevada and Arizona lines, and several long narrow strips extending from the Salinas Valley south. The Upper Sonoran takes in all the foothill country of the Sierra Nevada, the lava plateaus of Modoc and Lassen Counties, the western slopes of the Sacramento Valley, the inner chains of the Coast Range and Valleys from Mendocino County to San Francisco Bay, and all of the coastal region south of San Francisco except the Santa Cruz Mountains and the higher elevations of the Santa Lucias. These latter belong to the Transition zone, which also includes all of the coast country north of San Francisco, the heavily watered northeastern counties and a long belt, between 2500 and 5000 feet high in the Sierra. The Canadian, Hudsonian, and Arctic zones lie in the higher elevations of the Siskiyous, the Trinity Mountains, the Sierra, the San Bernardino and San Jacinto ranges.

It is possible to mention here only a few of the commoner or more characteristic inhabitants of these biologic zones, as a brief indication of the extraordinary range and variety of California's plant and animal life.

In the Colorado Desert section of the Lower Sonoran zone are found the California fan palm; the cylindrical cacti, echinocactus, and bigelovia; the mesquite, screwbean, and palo verde; and in the rainy season, among other flowers, the dwarf desert poppy and several diminutive asters. The most famous of plants peculiar to the Mojave Desert is the Joshua tree (*Yucca arborescens*). Along the river bottoms of the Great Valley grow Fremont cottonwoods and valley oaks. The mammalian life, mostly nocturnal in its habits, includes jack rabbits, kit foxes, kangaroo rats, pocket mice, and white-footed mice. Few animals besides the various species of chipmunks and ground squirrels appear in the daytime. In recent years the San Joaquin and Tulare basins have been overrun by Texas opossum, all originating from imported animals which either escaped or were liberated. The birds of the Lower Sonoran include Texas nighthawks, mocking-birds, blue grosbeaks, road runners, phainopeplas, cactus wrens, hooded orioles, verdins, and LeConte thrashers. Because of the large number of rodents, hawks and owls are unusually common. The tule elk once roamed over the marshes and sloughs of the Tulare Basin and San Joaquin River; today the last herd can be seen at the State park west of Bakersfield. The reptiles include the sidewinder (a small rattlesnake), the desert tortoise, and the horned toad.

The Upper Sonoran zone includes the State's great chaparral belt. This was the home of the now extinct California grizzly; it is still the haunt of the rapidly disappearing California condor, largest flying bird of the northern hemisphere. Here are found Digger pines, blue and scrub oaks, California buckeyes, many species of manzanita and ceanothus, certain kinds of yucca, and a host of other shrubs. Some of its distinctive species of birds are the California jay, stellar jay, California thrasher, bush tit, Anna hummingbird, bell sparrow, house finch, dusky poorwill, valley quail, mourning dove, and yellow-billed magpie. Among the animals are the brown-footed woodrat, brush rabbit, antelope, and ring-tailed cat (a relative of the raccoon).

This is a region rich in flowers. Early travelers in the State were eloquent in their descriptions of the continuous garden that once blanketed the plains and lower slopes. At a later time John Muir wrote, "For a distance of four hundred miles, your foot crushed a hundred flowers at every step." Most of this land is under cultivation now, and much of the rest is heavily grazed; but on fallow lands, in spite of the ravages of careless tourists in well-traveled regions, wild flowers still flourish in surprising abundance and soon recapture abandoned fields and ranges. Among the most common genera are gilia, nemophila, mint, mimulus, godetia, phacelia, lupine, orthocarpus, castilleia, dodecathon, viola, and calochortus. The State flower, the California poppy, or eschscholtzia, is most abundant in this zone. In the spring it colors hills and fields and roadsides with great masses of brilliant orange. It acquired its generic name from Adelbert von Chamisso, a German poet and naturalist, who saw it in bloom at San Francisco in 1816 and named it for a college friend who accompanied him—the German naturalist Johann Friedrich Eschscholtz. Though the eschscholtzia is widely distributed, it is not found in the densely wooded regions or at high elevations. A plant that is common to all parts of California and that occurs in a greater number of species here than anywhere else in the world is the lupine. As herb or shrub it varies from dwarf kinds in the high Sierra to the arborescent varieties growing close to the ocean. The pea-shaped flowers are of many colors, ranging from white through pale yellow, pink, and lavender to deep blue and purple.

In the Transition zone, which includes most of the State's great forests and therefore supplies most of its commercially valuable timber, are the redwood (*Sequoia sempervirens*) forests of the Coast Range, extending from the Oregon border on the north to the coastal canyons below Monterey on the south and as far as the inner limit of the summer fogs on the east. The redwood is one of the tallest trees in the world, commonly growing more than 200 feet high, and sometimes more than 300 feet. Trunks are often 15 to 20 feet in diameter, and occasionally from 20 to 25 feet. One of the peculiarities of the redwood is its shallow root system, though the trunks are strongly buttressed at the base. Because of the spongy, fire-resistant bark, these trees survived the annual fires set by the Indians of the region to clear out the underbrush and make hunting easier. The gently tapering shafts are almost bare of branches for a hundred feet or more above the ground. The bark is a deep purplish red, massively fluted; the foliage is delicate and feathery. A virgin redwood forest, with the light filtering through the treetops and falling in diagonal beams between the great columns, is one of the most beautiful sights in the world.

Beneath the trees, watered by the fog which they have trapped and precipitated, is an extraordinarily luxuriant growth. Swordferns, woodwardia ferns, alumroot, fringecups, barrenwort, fetid adderstongue, erythronium and violas, trillium and fritillaria carpet the floor. In almost impenetrable thickets grow the huckleberry, Oregon grape, rhododendron, azalea, California buckthorn, salmonberry, elder, and wild currant. The trees most commonly found in association with the redwood are the broad-leaved maple, madroña, tanbark oak, California laurel, and (usually in separate stands) the somber Douglas fir. Of these Coast Range trees the most picturesque is the madroña, a species of arbutus, which moved Bret Harte to write:

Captain of the western wood
Thou that apest Robin Hood!
Green above thy scarlet hose,
How thy velvet mantle shows!
Never tree like thee arrayed,
O thou gallant of the glade!

The Transition zone is particularly rich in animal life. It is the home of the Columbian black-tailed deer, black bear, Pacific coon, marten, mink weasel, skunk, fox, packrat, and mountain beaver. The California ring-tailed cat, common in both the Upper Sonoran and the Transition zones, is one of the handsomest animals peculiar to the West; it is often tamed and kept as a pet. Cougars and bobcats are fairly common. A few small herds of Roosevelt elk survive in the extreme northwest. Of the few reptiles, gopher snakes, garter snakes, and the rattlers are commonest. Amphibia are numerous, as is to be expected in so moist a region. The streams abound in water-puppies, and the woods in big mottled redwood salamanders which thrive on the abundant yellow groundslugs. In the depths of the Transition zone forests the birds are neither very numerous nor very conspicuous. Kingfishers, chickadees, various warblers, towhees, varied and hermit thrushes, robins, juncos, mountain quail, and hummingbirds are the most common.

East of the redwood belt, on the slopes of the Klamaths, the Cascades, and the northern Sierra, is a mixed forest of coniferous and deciduous trees, with the former predominating. Yellow pine, Douglas fir, sugar pine, white fir, incense cedar, western yew, mountain birch, and white oak are the important trees of this region. The herbaceous flora resembles that of the southern Sierra and the drier portions of the redwood belt. This is the home of the white Washington lily, the orange *Lilium pardalinum,* the erythronium, western azaleas of white or pink, several lupines, and the curious darlingtonia, which traps unwary insects in its hoodlike leaves. The Klamath Mountains, marking the border line between the Oregonian and Californian floras, are of great interest to botanists. With the exception of the antelope of the Modoc lava beds, the mule deer, the eastern kingbird, and an occasional eastern bobolink, the fauna of this area is much like that of the coastal region.

South of Lake Tahoe lies the characteristic Sierran forest. Here at an average elevation of about 3,500 feet is found the "big tree" (*Sequoia gigantea*). Unlike the redwood (*Sequoia sempervirens*), it does not form great belts of continuous forest but stands in about 35 isolated groves, scattered from the American River to the Tule. These trees are probably the oldest living things in the world—some of them have been shown by ring counts to be not less than 4,000 years old. In diameter they average from 15 to 20 feet; their average height is about 250 feet. The "big tree" is bulkier than the redwood, with cinnamon-colored bark and foliage similar to that of its coast cousin. The two Sequoias, with the ginkgo tree and the marestail, are survivals from a flora that was nearly destroyed in the glacial period. In Miocene times, Sequoias of various species were common over much of the northern hemisphere. In spite of their great age, both individually and as a species, the "big trees" are not dying out, but rather are increasing with the aid of the reforestation work of the United States Forest Service and office of National Parks. The "big tree" is found on the edge of the Transition and Canadian zones, usually close to stands of fir. Below it, in the Transition zone, stretch extensive forests of yellow and sugar pine, incense cedar, golden and black oak, California laurel, and broadleaved maple. In this Sierran forest, the most common wild flowers are pentstemons, gilias, mariposa tulips, pussypaws, mimulus, lappulas (wild forget-me-nots), collinsias, tiger and leopard lilies, buttercups, and the omnipresent lupines.

As one enters the Canadian zone, a change is immediately noticeable. The yellow pine gives way to the related Jeffrey pine. As one ascends, mountain pines and red firs and (higher still) lodgepole pines dominate the forest. Brushy areas are covered with dwarf manzanita and ceanothus. Under the firs grows some herbaceous vegetation, mostly living on the decayed wood common in fir forests. Notable in this vegetation are the brilliant snowplant, several species of corallorrhiza, and the cancerroot. This is also the home of the unique Sierra puffball. Some of the more conspicuous birds are the blue-fronted jay, Sierra junco, western chipping sparrow, Sierra hermit thrush, water ouzel, evening grosbeak, Sierra grouse, and Townsend solitaire. Among the animals are the mountain weasel, yellow-haired porcupine, snowshoe rabbit, golden-mantled ground squirrel, Sierra chickaree, and certain species of chipmunks.

The Hudsonian zone is the belt of forest immediately below timber line. With the Canadian zone it shares the lodgepole pine, which is here the dominant cover. Usually associated with, or above the level of, the lodgepole are the white bark, foxtail, and silver pines. These latter trees, with the mountain hemlock, form the stunted and twisted growth of the timber line. Birds become scarcer in this zone, though mammals remain plentiful; some of the species extend up from the zones below. The California pine grosbeak, mountain bluebird, white-crowned sparrow, alpine chipmunk, Sierra marmot, Sierra cony, pine marten, Sierra least weasel, and wolverine are typical of the region.

The Arctic-Alpine zone, the highest of all, is a treeless area stretching from an elevation of about 10,500 feet to the summits of the loftiest peaks. Here are found the Sierra primrose, the blue and fragrant polemonium, the yellow columbine, the alpine buttercup, the steershead, and the alpine shootingstar. Only one species of bird is native to the zone, the Sierra rosy finch; but many others visit it, notably flocks of migrating hummingbirds and, in the summer, gray and white Clark nutcrackers. The principal mammals are visitants from lower elevations; however, the Sierra cony is often found in these heights and the Sierra white-tailed jackrabbit makes its home here. The Sierra Nevada bighorn sheep are seen occasionally in the White Mountains east of Owens Valley and in some of the southeastern ranges. A small band remains in the Mount Whitney region, survivors of those described by John Muir, which in his day ranged along the Sierran crest to the vicinity of Sonora Pass.

Certain animals range through several zones, particularly the mule deer, the coyote, and the cougar or mountain lion; as do a number of birds notably the blue-fronted jay, the Sierra junco, the redshafted flicker, certain hawks, and some of the sparrows. The flowers and trees are generally confined within the limits of their native zones, although various similar forms, distinguishable only by botanists, occur at several elevations. Thus, the Jeffrey and western yellow pines can be differentiated with certainty only by a chemical analysis of their sap; while the Compositae generally, and particularly the asters, are the despair of all but highly trained specialists.

Gone now from most sections of the country is Nature's intricately organized population of bear, marten, beaver, otter, elk, deer, and badger. Tilled fields have replaced the natural haunts of fox, lynx, bobcat, and fisher. But in California these animals still possess the sunny chaparral and the green shade of forests. The United States Forest Service estimates that in the 18 national forests of California, covering nearly one-fifth of the State's area, there are 111,000 blacktail deer, 148,000 mule deer, 7,000 bear, 2,800 antelope, 24,000 foxes, and 1,230 mountain lions. Man's encroachments have not yet driven out all the mountain sheep, weasels, badgers, raccoons, muskrat, beaver, and otter. Over vast areas of the California wilderness, human footprints seldom obliterate the tracks of paw and hoof.

## NATURAL RESOURCES AND THEIR CONSERVATION

In no state is the conservation of natural resources being pursued as energetically as in California. Local, county and State organizations are thoroughly aware that the great natural heritage can be eroded and lost unless positive efforts are made, through legislation, to save the legacy of the past. The pressure of private interests to use the natural bounty for their own profit is accepted as part of the economy, but safeguards have been established in many fields to overcome misuse, waste and exhaustion and provide for replacement.

In 1961 the State took a big step forward in establishing the Resources Agency of California, bringing together a number of bodies that had been working independently. Headquarters were located in a new Resources Building at 1416 Ninth St., Sacramento. The Department of Conservation is a major unit of the Agency. Under the Department were placed four administrative divisions: Forestry, Mines and Geology, Soil Conservation and Oil and Gas. These have specific responsibilities in supervising the use of lands and natural products, which are protected by a series of laws.

California has a land area of 100,314,000 acres, of which about 47,000,000 acres are owned by the Federal Government, approximately 3,000,000 acres are owned by the State, and about 50,000,000 acres are in private hands. In preserving natural resources the Department of Conservation often works with all three groups of land owners.

## CONSERVATION OF FORESTS

In recent decades the people of California have become aware that fires can sweep away great areas of the finest trees. Forest fires not only have denuded many hills but have leveled dwellings in wooded places, as in the case of the Bel Air section of Hollywood and Santa Barbara. Once fires have started in the dry brush they can not be stopped without leveling wide spaces and even then a high wind may carry embers a long way. Thus the emphasis has to be on prevention, and toward that both federal and state agencies bend their efforts.

The Division of Forestry of the Department of Conservation has the job of preventing and controlling forest fires on about 39,000,000 acres of forest, range and watershed lands. During the forest-fire season it adds nearly 2,000 fire-fighters and lookouts. It is endlessly engaged in removing fire hazards, such as rubbish dumps, and littering, building fire breaks, and controlling the practices of campers and other users of forests. The Division also manages eight state forests containing 70,238 acres of land, demonstrating proper use of the areas. The largest, Jackson, in Mendocino County, has 52,042 acres. Others are Latour in Shasta County, Mountain Home in Tulare, Boggs Mountain in Lake, Las Posadas in Napa, Mount Zion in Amador, Ellen Pickett in Trinity and Loghry in Santa Clara-Santa Cruz. Removal of timber resulted in the sale of 22,400,000 board feet in 1963. Damage to trees from deer and epidemics of insects are subject of studies.

Training centers for men who wish to enter the service is conducted at two centers. There is emphasis on training for fire-fighting, for there is no other way of recruiting leaders. Another educational practice of the Division is the Conservation Camp Program, under which it conducts 37 camps, where about 2,500 men annually learn forest practices under the custody of the departments of Youth and Adult Corrections.

Timber is one of the great commercial assets of California. The manufacture of wood products is the State's fourth major industry. Plywood factories are multiplying. Value by manufacture now exceeds that of New York and Oregon, the second and third states in this category. Wood has so many uses today that every inch of a tree is converted into a valuable product. What used to be considered waste is now the basis for pulp, paper, paperboard, hardboard, insulating board, charcoal, chemicals, compressed fuel logs, rayon and particleboard. The bark is used for soil mulch and other purposes.

It is estimated that only 17,300,000 acres of forest land are open for commercial use, the rest being a protected public domain. Yet the commercial interests demand more terrain and trees 1,000 or more years old are marked for destruction if some of the plans succeed. California legislators have faced two such efforts recently, both associated with straightening of roads and boundaries. Nor are the business interests always to blame. A proposal to run a highway along the coast through a grove of redwoods, necessitating cutting down many patriarchal trees, brought protests from many places outside of California.

## OIL AND GAS

The Division of Oil and Gas of the Department of Conservation supervises drilling, operation, maintenance and abandonment of oil and gas wells in California. Its object is to prevent waste and damage in oil and gas deposits and natural gas, to protect fresh water from contamination and direct repressuring operations to overcome land surface subsidence. Notices of intentions to drill or abandon wells must be filed with the Division, which also issues statistics and maps relating to the industry and geology. Producing areas are divided into six districts with offices at Inglewood, Santa Paula, Santa Maria, Bakersfield, Taft, Coalinga and Woodland.

A vast treasure in oil lies under the waters of the Pacific Ocean adjacent to the coast of California. An attempt by the State to establish ownership beyond the traditional limits was defeated by the United States Supreme Court in 1965. The decision was an outcome of a controversy that began when modern apparatus for drilling under the sea was proved practicable.

In 1945 the Supreme Court decided that the Federal government owns everything under the water from the California shoreline to three miles out to sea. In 1952 Congress passed a law reversing this decision and President Truman vetoed it. In 1953 the Submerged Lands Act, signed by President Eisenhower, gave California all rights from the coast three miles out and to the "seaward limit of inland waters." In 1963

California interpreted this to mean three miles beyond the shoreline of the Catalina Channel and other islands, considering these as extensions of the main shoreline. This would extend its ownership many miles out to sea, according to the Federal government. It was this contention that was denied by the Supreme Court. The rights given California under the Submerged Lands Act still stand.

California produces about 725,000 barrels of oil a day from land wells, a decline from the 1,000,000 barrels a day reached in 1953. At the same time it produces about 110,000 barrels a day from offshore drilling. The increased demand for petroleum products and the decline in production from land wells has caused intensive exploration for offshore wells. In 1965, 996 offshore wells were producing, and operators were paying the State royalties and rent amounting to millions of dollars. The greatest offshore development has taken place since the Tidelands Act of 1955 authorized drilling in submerged lands and offshore.

## WATER DEVELOPMENT AND USE

Irrigation is at the base of California's agricultural prosperity. Access to water, proper use of it, and drainage to protect the soil after use, are three stages in successful irrigation of California's 9,000,000 acres. California also needs water in huge quantities for its people. More than 70% of its water flows in rivers in the northern third of the State, while 77% of the need for water is in the southern two-thirds. An average of 29,000,000 acre-feet of water annually flows unused to the ocean from streams in the north Coastal region, more than the net use of the entire state.

This is the situation that has brought about prodigious efforts to divert fresh water to reservoirs and carry it to the dry sections. Local districts were authorized in 1887, but the first state-wide water plan was not published before 1921. In the early decades of this century cities began to go far afield to procure water. These projects included the 238-mile long Owens River Aqueduct carrying water all the way from the Sierra Nevada to the San Fernando Reservoir of Los Angeles and the Colorado River Aqueduct of the Metropolitan Water District of Southern California, completed in 1941 and increased in volume 1952-61. This aqueduct delivers an immense quantity of water, but to conserve the Colorado River flow for other states the U. S. Supreme Court has decided that Southern California must reduce its demands by about one-half after it gets an alternative supply from the State Water Project up north. Colorado River water also passes into the San Diego aqueduct, and the All American Canal and Coachella Canal, which supply the Imperial Valley.

In the north there is the Hetch Hetchy system of San Francisco and the East Bay Municipal Utility Aqueduct from the Tuolumne River. In 1921 voters authorized bonds for the Central Valley Project, which irrigates land, supplies water to municipalities and turns turbines in hydroelectric power plants. It has been built by the Bureau of Reclamation and stores water at Friant Dam, Shasta Dam, Keswick Dam, Folsom Dam, Nimbus Dam and Sly Park Dam. The water is delivered as far as Kern County by large canals.

The California Water Plan, first state-wide plan in the country, was adopted in 1957 and in 1960 the electorate approved $1,750,000,000 in bonds to start it. Governor Edmund G. Brown urged immediate construction of the Oroville Dam to make impossible floods as devastating as that of Christmas, 1955, when Marysville and Yuba City were badly damaged. Although incomplete the Oroville Dam substantially held back the flood waters of 1964 reducing the flow.

All water projects are now supervised by the State Department of Water Resources, which coordinates its activities with these of the United States government. A joint State-Federal project is the Peripheral Canal, intended to carry surplus water from northern California around the Sacramento-San Joaquin delta for transportation southward. There also will be joint use of the Federal San Luis unit of the Central Valley Project and of the California Aqueduct of the State Water Project. The government also is expected to cooperate with the State in building a nuclear pumping plant and in testing desalination processes.

The Census of 1960 reported 33,017,822 acres of irrigated farmland in the United States and 7,386,748 acres in California.

The northern 30% area of the State produces more than 70% of the water, and the lower two-thirds of the State uses 77% of the water supply. According to a 1961 summary 8,516,000 acres were being irrigated and 13,126,000 of land capable of being irrigated were not getting the water. The largest storage reservoirs are in these counties: Fresno, Kern, Lake, Modoc, Napa, Plumas, Placer, San Bernardino, Shasta, Trinity and Tuolumne.

About 21,000,000 acre-feet of water are now being used. An acre-foot of water covers one acre one foot deep. According to the Extension Service of the California Agricultural Experiment Station, University of California, half of this amount is pumped from underground sources, some of which are being depleted; 70% of the annual runoff is north of the latitude of Sacramento and 80% of the ultimate estimated need is south of that line. The annual runoff within the State, according to the Department of Water Resources, is 71,000,000 acre-feet. This, plus the State's right to Colorado River water can provide 51,-000,000 acre-feet of water for future needs, sufficient to irrigate 20,000,000 acres and provide also for 3,600,000 acres of urban, suburban and industrial development.

# The First Californians

WHEN on June 17, 1579 "it pleased God" to send Francis Drake's *Golden Hind* into the "faire and good bay" north of the Golden Gate, he encountered "the people of the country, having their houses close by the water's edge." Overawed, they supposed the bearded, white-skinned sailors who bestowed on them "necessary things to cover their nakedness" to be gods and "would not be persuaded to the contrary." The men, their faces painted in all colors, left their bows behind on a hill and came down to the shore bearing presents of feathers and tobacco. The women remained on the hill, "tormenting themselves" in some sacrificial frenzy and "tearing the flesh from their cheeks." Their king, "clad with conie skins and other skins," arrived with a retinue of "tall and warlike men," bearing a sceptre. After much singing, dancing, and speech making, they begged Drake to "take their province and kingdom into his hand and become their king."

In the interior Drake's men found other villages. Up and down California, if they had traveled farther, they would have discovered others, for the Indians of California were widely but unevenly scattered over the State's fertile regions. The estimated native population of almost one inhabitant to each square mile was comparatively large; the Central Valley was probably more densely populated than any other part of North America at that time.

For an unknown age before the white man first stumbled upon them in the sixteenth century, the Indians of California had dwelt in their scattered bands, walled off from the rest of the aboriginal world by mountains and deserts. On the shores of San Francisco Bay, along the southern California and Humboldt Bay seacoasts and in the San Joaquin Valley, evidence has been unearthed from their shell mounds—huge kitchen middens of shell, ash, and earth, piled up layer by layer from the refuse of daily living over the centuries—indicating a culture which remained almost unchanged over a period of perhaps three or four thousand years. It was probably the simplest culture in all aboriginal North America.

The scattered bands dwelt in isolation one from another, each fishing in its own creek, catching game in its own preserves, gathering nuts, seeds, and berries in its own forests. The village, composed of groups of kin and relatives by marriage, was the unit of society, its members holding rights in common to a specific tract of land; seldom was it united with other villages by tribal ties. Even among the semi-organized tribes of northern central California, the village was the real social unit. The Maidu of central California, although united in language and customs, distinguished their local groups into Hill Maidu, Valley Maidu, and Mountain Maidu. The only exceptions were the Mojave and Yuma in the far southeast, who displayed aggressive tribal unity against outsiders.

In customs and in culture the isolated villages varied widely, but in nothing so widely as in language. Over most of the State a villager needed to travel little more than 50 miles to encounter other Indians whose language he could not speak; in a 50-mile journey through many regions he might pass the boundaries of three or four distinct language groups. More than 100 dialects of 21 distinct language stocks were spoken. Of all the many language groups, only three larger language families from outside the State were represented in California: the Hupa and their neighbors in the far northwest belonged to the Athabascan; many groups in the south to the Shoshonean, and the Mojave and Yuma along the Colorado to the Yuman linguistic stock.

Drake's men discovered tribes living in conical, dome-shaped, or round huts. In the northwest part of the State they were covered with light planks or poles; towards the south with bark, brush, or thatch; in the Sacramento Valley, with sod. The ceremonial center for most villages was the *temescal* (sweat house), round and earth-covered, almost airtight. Confinement in its steam-vapored interior, followed by a plunge into icy water, was considered an effective remedy for illness and a pleasant cleanly habit.

California's great stands of oak provided the Indians with their staple food in most parts of the State. Acorns were dried, ground with pestles in stone or wooden mortars, and leached with repeated soakings in hot water to remove their tannic acid. This acorn meal, seasoned with salt or wood ashes, was eaten as it was, baked in unleavened cakes, or boiled in a gruel. In the southwestern desert country the Indians gathered mesquite beans and on the eastern Sierra slopes, piñon nuts; only near the Colorado River did they cultivate plants for food. Often they ground or roasted grass seeds, berries, roots, and nuts, and stored them in baskets. Lacking pottery, which only the Indians in the extreme southeast near the Colorado River knew how to make, most of the California natives boiled their food in close-woven baskets, into which they dropped hot stones. They hunted small game with snares, sticks and nets, or bows and arrows; larger game with the aid of pits and traps, and, in the north, dogs. Deer-hunters often donned deer-skins and stuffed deer's heads to approach their game. Grasshoppers and caterpillars were also eaten. Everywhere fish were caught with hook, net, or spear; by the seashore clams and mussels were gathered, and along the rivers of the north, salmon were speared during the spawning season.

The California Indians perfected basketry and thus supplied themselves with utensils for gathering and winnowing grain, cooking and storing water. Into their weaving went sedge, bulrush, redbud, willow, diggerpine, juniper, bracken, grape, or tule. With strands stained with vegetable dyes in clear blues, deep reds, warm yellows, and luminous pinks, the weavers worked fine geometric patterns. The Pomo families of Lake, Sonoma, and Mendocino Counties sometimes wove into their baskets the downy, many-colored feathers of birds.

The California Indian's other possessions were few and crude. Out of bone, shell, or stone he carved his arrowheads, awls, pestles and mortars, pots, charm stones, beads, and pendants. For money he used dentalium or clamshell disk beads, ground, bored, and strung, and valued according to size, thickness, and polish. His musical instruments were varied; most widespread was the rattle, made of split clap-sticks, gravel-filled cocoon bunches, bundles of deer hoofs, or turtle shells and gourds; in addition there were bone whistles, flutes, musical bows, and drums.

He built two kinds of vessels for navigation: the balsa, a raft or float made of tule rushes for use in quiet waters, sometimes replaced by huge woven baskets in which goods or human beings were ferried across streams; and the wooden canoe, hollowed out of a log, for use on the ocean. The Canalino Indians living along the Santa Barbara Channel made boats of lashed planks, craft found nowhere else in North America.

Most village groups were headed by a chief, who held the office more often by virtue of wealth than heredity; he was privileged only to advise, not to command. Within the village group, scarcely any distinctions, either of social status or vocation, were drawn, except in the northwest, where social classes based on the possession of wealth tended to form. In the absence of any coherent tribal organization warfare as practised in eastern North America was unknown, although sporadic feuds broke out between kin or local groups.

The only other tribal functionaries besides the chief were the shamans. The shaman, might be either a man or a woman, who acquired supposedly supernatural powers through consultation with spirits in a dream. Sometimes he cured illness by "sucking the pain object" from the patient's body, sometimes by bringing back his wandering soul, sometimes by blowing tobacco smoke on the affected part, by chanting incantations, or by inducing a trance. Supposedly he could kill, as well as cure. Among these shamans were specialists, the rain, rattlesnake, and grizzly bear doctors. Most feared of all in northern California were the grizzly bear shamans, who either dressed in bearskin robes, or were credited with the power of turning themselves into ferocious grizzlies in order to destroy their enemies.

Birth, puberty, marriage, and death called for religious observances. In most localities the husband kept to his house for several days (usually four) after the birth of a child, abstaining with his wife from meat and salt. Among the Achomawi and Shasta in the northeast, boys at the age of puberty were initiated into the life of the group with simple ceremonies by fasting, whipping with a bowstring, and the piercing of their ears. The initiation of girls was more elaborate: hidden away, sometimes in a separate hut, they were instructed in womanly duties, meanwhile eating no meat, bathing frequently, and scratching themselves with special carved sticks (since scratching with the hands was taboo). Marriage was a somewhat loosely defined institution except in the northwest, where the bridegroom presented gifts in proportion to the social standing of his bride's family. In most parts of the State the dead were forgotten as soon as their bodies had been buried or cremated; to speak their names was commonly taboo. Among the southern California group, however, the chief public demonstrations were mourning ceremonies, celebrated at annual or semi-annual memorials by burning the piled-up effigies of all the recent deceased, to the accompaniment of sad wailing.

The only organized religious cults which gained a foothold in California were the *kuksu* (big-head) and *toloache* (Jimsonweed) cults. The *kuksu* rites, practised in the southern Sacramento Valley, were celebrated, almost always in winter, by dancers representing gods. Their faces painted and disguised by curtains of feathers, grass, or shredded rushes, they danced in earth-covered, dome-roofed dance houses to the accompaniment of stamping on a hollow-slab foot drum. The cult trained the adolescent boys and girls (initiating the boys with puberty rites), organized the male members of the community, and focused the activities of the shaman. The *toloache* cult, practised in the San Joaquin Valley and in southern California, centered about the taking of the narcotic Jimsonweed plant to induce hallucinations. Its practitioners used sand paintings to picture the cosmos. The *toloache,* like the *kuksu* cult, conducted puberty rites, some groups extending them to girls as well as boys, with the intention of making the initiate strong, fortunate, and successful. Some groups celebrated with ceremonial rites such events as the first fire-making or acorn-gathering of the new year or the first catch of salmon in the spawning season. In the northwest, the exhibition of prized possessions like prepared deerskins was celebrated by dancers decked out in all their valuable goods. The groups of the southeast and desert performed ritual dances to accompany song cycles in celebration of mythical events.

In 1769, nearly two centuries after Drake's brief visit, Franciscan friars trudged into the country to convert the "heathen." Cross or sword, the Indians had to choose. On several occasions bloody struggles broke out, in which the Indians were usually defeated. Only the groups in the mountains escaped missionary efforts: those who submitted were baptized. Almost all the natives in the coastal regions were brought to live in and around the 21 Franciscan missions, established from San Diego to Sonoma between 1769 and 1823. From 4,000 in 1783, the Mission Indian population was increased to 7,500 by 1790, to 13,500 by 1800, and to 20,355 by 1805. The monotonous round of work and prayer, the rigid moral regulations, the cramped and prisonlike housing made life unbearable for many. They ran away, although they faced whipping if caught, or they died.

The resentment against the missions flared several times into open rebellion. On November 4, 1775, some 800 rebels swept down from the hills and set fire to San Diego Mission. The year after, San Luis Obispo was burned. The Yumas in 1781 destroyed their mission and freed themselves, arousing the spirit of revolt among the Indians of San Diego and San Juan Capistrano. During the last two decades of the century there were conflicts at Santa Barbara, at most of the southern missions, and at San Juan Bautista. In February 1824 the neophytes at Purisima Concepcion, Santa Ines, and Santa Barbara revolted simultaneously, killing several people and burning the buildings at Santa Ines. In 1829 secular authorities waged a campaign against the forces of Chief Estanislao (for whom Stanislaus River and County are named). A fugitive from Misión San José, Estanislao led a band of other escaped neophytes and wild Indians of the San Joaquin Valley in an uprising that was crushed only by a force of 100 Spaniards with muskets and cannon.

When the Mexican Government broke the mission system's land monopoly with its secularization decrees of 1833-34, the Indians were suddenly freed. Well-meaning in their despotism as the mission fathers may have been, they had degraded their converts into dependent slaves, unable to shift for themselves. In theory, secularization was to grant rights of citizenship to the Indians and restore to them one-half of all mission land, livestock, and farm tools. In practice, the neophytes relapsed into helpless vagrancy, too demoralized to work their own lands, if indeed they had not been dispossessed of them by crooked administrators. The mission population fell off rapidly, decreasing from 24,634 in 1830 to 6,000 in 1840. The Indians took up their old life in the wilds, if luck was with them; if not, they fell into wretched peonage on the vast private ranchos.

On the ranchos the Indians were never paid, and in the small industrial establishments of the later Mexican period they were paid only with glass beads, parched corn, or homemade brandy. The raw, poisonous liquor, drunk with greediness, killed many of them; scarlet fever, smallpox, tuberculosis, and syphilis killed many more.

From an estimated total of 133,000 in 1770 the Indian population had already fallen by 1852 to 85,000, and continued to decline at an accelerated rate under the American regime. The drop in Indian population between 1849 and 1856 has been estimated at 50,000. One of John C. Frémont's men reported in 1847: "We killed plenty of game and an occasional Indian. We made it a rule to spare none of the bucks." As Americans acquired the Mexican grants, they drove the ranch Indians off; the squatters who staked off so-called Government lands pushed the aboriginal inhabitants back into the mountains and deserts. Their salmon waters muddied by mining operations, acorn groves cut down for firewood, hunting lands confiscated, the Indians were left to starve. In the towns and cities, where they were paid only half the wages of whites, they were cut down by disease and drink.

When the less submissive of the Indians resisted starvation by depredations on American property or livestock or retaliated for outrages by killing white men, they were massacred without mercy. For nearly three decades after American occupation of California, "Indian wars" continued—the Klamath War of 1851-52, Kern River War of 1856, Pit River massacres of 1867, and the Modoc War of 1873. During the campaign of 1855-59 in the north, soldiers killed more than 100 Indians, while settlers of the Mad and Eel River regions put at least 200 to death in a series of massacres. Up to December 1854 the State had spent $1,030,530 on Indian campaigns; during the next six years it spent twice that amount. The cattle raids and attacks on emigrant trains of the Yumas and Mojaves were answered in the Owens Lake incident of 1865, when the settlers drove 100 Indians to a terrible death in the corroding waters of an alkaline lake. The Pit River Valley massacre of 10 or 15 white men in 1867 was followed by the destruction of a whole village. During the troubles in the far north which eventually culminated in the last and bloodiest of the Indian "wars," the Modoc War of 1873, a company under Captain Ben Wright fell upon the Indians when they laid down their arms to make a treaty and murdered so many that Wright could boast of making a "permanent" treaty with at least 1,000 Indians.

The Indian, his affairs entrusted to special agents who seldom interfered in his behalf, had no spokesman before the Government of a people who wanted only to steal his land. The white man found it easy to support almost any charges against him. According to Helen Hunt Jackson, early champion of the Indian, " 'Papers from Washington' seemed to give the white man the right to deprive any Indian of the land of his forefathers—so the Indian gradually disappeared, 'hunted down, driven out.' The United States Government took over all the Indian holdings, and grants to white people could be obtained on application without any consideration for the right of occupancy by the Indian. To betray sympathy with the Indian was more than any man's 'political' head was worth."

As early as 1849 the Federal Government had commissioned agents to collect data on Indian rights and land titles. In the following year it appointed a commission of three which eventually succeeded in signing 18 treaties with chiefs of more than 100 groups, representing most of the State's Indian population. In return for their promise to recognize United States sovereignty, keep the peace, settle on reservations—18 in number, aggregating 7,500,000 acres—and cede their land rights to the Government; they were to receive farm implements and goods, instructors in blacksmithing, woodwork, and farming, and maintenance of permanent reservations. The treaties were transmitted to the Senate but never ratified; for over half a century they remained hidden in Senate archives. Meanwhile the Indians of California, having fulfilled their part of the bargain, remained uncompensated for their losses, seeing their promised 7,500,000 acres dwindle to 500,000.

Beginning in 1853, the Indians were gradually gathered together on reservations. The first one was established at Tejon; others were established later on the Klamath River south of Crescent City, at the mouth of the Noyo River on the Mendocino coast, and at Nome Lake in the Sacramento foothills. The results at first were far from happy, since bands of diverse origin and speech were lumped together indiscriminately. Under a system of education which forced the white man's ways upon the Indian, aboriginal culture disintegrated rapidly. As the natives ran away faster than they died, one reservation after another was abandoned. Little by little the reservations were robbed of their more valuable lands. The ones that exist today, as well as the land allotments made to individuals, are located chiefly in unproductive hill country. Here the Indians, housed and clothed much like their white neighbors, practice farming, stockraising, and handicrafts, on some reservations under the guidance of Indian Bureau agents. The children attend either Indian schools, such as the Sherman Institute near Arlington, Riverside County, or public schools to which the Indian Bureau makes tuition payments.

For every seven or eight Indians living in California before the white man came to stay, only one remained 14 decades later. The Indian population, including half and mixed bloods (nearly 30 percent of the total), had fallen by 1910 to 16,371—a decline of about 90 percent. The 1950 census counted 19,947, but this number had increased to 39,014 in the census of 1960, partly by migration.

The Bureau of Indian Affairs supervises lands held in trust by Indians, improves economic conditions, directs vocational training and helps move Indians from bare subsistence areas in the Midwest to locations in California that provide better living conditions. Much of its work is being transferred to State and local agencies, which extend welfare and public health services without discrimination as to race. The principal office of the Bureau is in Sacramento, and there are ten additional administrative offices. Some of the reservations in the southeastern corner of the State are administered by the Phoenix, Arizona, office. The State has 113 reservations and ranches allotted to Indians; the largest is the Hoopa Valley Reservation of 87,500 acres in Humboldt County. Indians in California have the same freedom of action as non-Indians; they are citizens before the law, and only when they live on trust land, for which they pay no taxes, are they subject to the Bureau's property regulations.

# California's Last Four Centuries

WITHIN the half century after Christopher Columbus discovered the new world, Europeans discovered and named California. In 1513 Vasco Núñez de Balboa reached the Pacific coast at Panama; twenty-two years later another Spaniard, Hernando Cortés, discovered a land he named California; and in 1542 Juan Rodríguez Cabrillo, a Portuguese navigator, rode at anchor in San Diego Bay, the first white man to see any part of the region now known as California.

The chain of events that led to California started with the search by Columbus in the Caribbean in 1493 for the island Mantinino, which he had been told "was peopled merely by women." Columbus thought this might be Marco Polo's Amazonian island "near the coast of Asia." He failed in his search, but the fabulous isle fascinated other navigators during the next decade. After Garcia Ordóñez de Montalvo published his romance *Las Sergas de Esplandián* in 1510, Spanish navigators were familiar with both the legend and with the name California. A passage reads: "Know that, on the right hand of the Indies, there is an island called California, very near to the Terrestrial Paradise, which was peopled with black women. . . . Their arms were all of gold."

Spain's dominion in the new world was extended to the western coast of Mexico by Cortés' conquest of the empire of Montezuma. In an attempt to push it farther west and north Cortés sent two ships commanded by his kinsman Diego Hurtado de Mendoza on a "voyage of discovery" in 1532. Mendoza got as far north into the Gulf of California as 27° N. before a mutinous crew compelled him to send back one of the ships; of his own vessel, nothing but vague rumor was ever heard again. Fortuno Ximenes, pilot of an expedition sent to search for Mendoza, anchored in a small bay "near the 23rd degree of latitude," landed, and was killed by natives, along with 20 of his men. The survivors reported the discovery of an island, said to "abound in the finest pearls." On May 5, 1535, Cortés entered the little bay Ximenes had found (possibly the present La Paz) called it Santa Cruz, landed and named the supposed island California. He was convinced that it lay "on the right side of the Indies," if not "near to the Terrestrial Paradise."

For more than a year Cortés stayed in the new land, a desolate sandy waste, while the mutinous soldiers cursed him, "his island, bay, and his discovery." Clinging tenaciously to his search for the "seven cities of Cibola" in the north, he sent three ships, under command of Francisco de Ulloa, to begin a thorough survey of the coast line in 1539. Ulloa examined both shores of what he called "The Sea of Cortés," now known as the Gulf of California, discovered that Cortés' island was really a peninsula. Later in the same year, it is said, he sailed around Cape San Lucas and surveyed the Pacific coast line of the peninsula, getting as far as the 28th degree—some say as far as "Cape Engano, near the 30th degree." By this time, however, Cortés had gone back to Spain, never to return.

The new viceroy, Don Antonio de Mendoza sent Cabrillo, in command of the ships *San Salvador* and *La Victoria* "to examine the western side of California as far northward as possible, seeking particularly for rich countries and for passages leading towards the Atlantic." Cabrillo sailed from Navidad, a small port in Xalisco, on June 27, 1542. Slowed by adverse winds, he finally entered "a very good closed port" on September 28, which he named San Miguel—the bay of San Diego. He discovered Santa Monica Bay and the three large islands of the Santa Barbara group, rounded Cabo Galera (Point Concepcion) and Cabo de los Reyes (Point Reyes). The ships passed the Golden Gate without seeing it. On the way back they found the harbor in the island of the Santa Barbara group which they named *La Posesion*. There Cabrillo, who had been suffering from a broken arm, died on January 3, 1543, and the command passed to his pilot, Bartolomé Ferrelo. Sailing north again, the ships reached a promontory on February 26, probably Cape Mendocino, which Ferrelo named Cabo de Fortunas (Cape of Perils or Stormy Cape). Turning back, they eventually came into their home port, Navidad.

Disappointed by the reports of the expedition, Spanish officials became more and more convinced that north of Mexico the New World contained "neither wealthy nations, nor navigable passage . . . between the Atlantic and Pacific Oceans." Later, when the treasures of the Orient began to come into the port of Acapulco from the Philippines and from China, Spain found in the long continental mainland the best protection of its inland sea—the Pacific. England's sea rovers had no way into the Pacific except by rounding Cape Horn. This Francis Drake did in his 100-ton schooner, the *Golden Hinde;* he anchored on June 17, 1579, in what became Drake's Bay and named the region New Albion.

Drake's visit seems to have aroused Spain's dormant interest in California. In 1584 Francisco Gali made a much more thorough examination of the California coast than Cabrillo had done 42 years before, and 11 years later Sebastián Cermeno was directed, while returning from Manila to Acapulco, to examine the California coast, "in search of harbors in which galleons might take refuge." Losing his own ship, somewhere "near San Francisco Bay south of Cape Mendocino," he sailed southward along the coast in a small boat and sighted the Bay of Monterey, which he named "San Pedro Bay."

With three ships "well officered," Sebastián Vizcaíno made a second attempt in 1602 to explore the coast, sailing as far as Cape Mendocino, naming the first harbor he reached, "the best in all the South Sea," San Diego. On November 12, Carmelite friars of his party celebrated Holy Mass ashore—the first time in Upper California. Vizcaíno spent almost a year in the survey, but like Cabrillo he missed the Golden Gate. He renamed many places named in 1542 by Cabrillo, among them San Diego, Santa Catalina, Santa Barbara, Point Concepcion, the Carmel River, Point Reges, and Monterey Bay—in honor of the viceroy, Gasper de Zunigay Acebedo, who was the Count of Monterey.

After Vizcaíno's visit Spain's efforts were largely spent in attempts to colonize New Mexico rather than Upper California, though recurrent attempts were made to keep alive the pearl-fishing industry on the eastern coast of the Gulf of California. The most pretentious of these was in 1683, when Don Isidro de Atondo, placing settlers, soldiers and Jesuits at different points, planned a steady penetration of California. But the project lagged, and not until 1697 did Jesuits receive royal warrants to enter upon the reduction of California at their own expense. In that year the first permanent colony was planted in Baja California —at Loreto by Father Juan Maria Salvatierra. Father Kino, in 1701, crossed the Colorado near Yuma and entered Alta California, working among the Indians of "Pimeria Alta."

By 1734 Vitus Bering was pushing his exploration of Alaska, and Spain began to fear the colonizing activities of Russia along the Pacific coast. Twenty years later a new peril arose, when France was swept from sovereignty in America by Britain. Spain could put off no longer the settlement of Alta California.

A high officer of the Spanish "Council of the Indies," José de Gálvez, was sent to Mexico as *visitador-géneral* and arrived in Mexico City in 1766. Early in the following year Carlos III of Spain issued a decree banishing all Jesuits from Spanish territories. Franciscans were to take over the mission at Loreto, which was to be the base of the operations, both military and pastoral.

Captain Gaspar de Portolá was appointed Governor of Baja California and ordered to proceed to Loreto to superintend the transfer of mission property. He reached Loreto with an escort of fifty soldiers, accompanied by fifteen Franciscan monks, and was joined by Father Junípero Serra, who was made president of the missions in California, and Gálvez. The king had ordered Gálvez "to send an expedition by sea to rediscover and people the bays of San Diego and Monterey." Gálvez thought it would be well to send a land expedition also and Father Serra concurred with this plan. Three missions in Alta California—at San Diego, Monterey and at an intermediate point—were to be established, also two presidios or military posts.

On January 9, 1769, one of the ships, the *San Carlos*, left La Paz; two days later the *San Antonio* sailed from San Lucas, and the *Señor San José*, from Loreto soon after. The vessels were loaded with ornaments, sacred vases, church vestments, household utensils, field implements, seeds, and other settlement needs. The *San Antonio*, under Captain Juan Pérez, reached its destination, San Diego Bay, on April 11; the *San Carlos* on April 29. Scurvy had swept both vessels, but its ravages on the *San Carlos* had so prostrated the crew that not even a boat could be lowered. The *San Antonio's* boats carried the sick ashore, where they convalesced behind a temporary stockade.

The march by land was no less long and painful. The forces divided into two columns, one under an army captain, Fernando de Rivera, and the other under Portolá. With the latter went Father Serra. The columns took different routes, each driving a herd of cattle. Rivera's party reached San Diego on May 15; Portolá's route was more difficult and his party did not arrive until July 1.

The expedition lost no time in putting its plans into action. Misión San Diego de Alcalá was dedicated on July 16, two days after Portolá had led sixty-four members of the expedition away to the north to find the Bay of Monterey. Through country described by Portolá as "rocks, brushwood and rugged mountains" wound these newcomers—Spanish officers in brilliant uniforms, monks in gray-brown cowls, leather-clad soldiers, Indians on foot. On October 2 they reached Monterey, failed to recognize it, and pushed on. In Father Crespi's words: "The expedition strove to reach the Punta de los Reyes, but some immense arms of the sea which penetrate into the mainland in an extraordinary fashion would have made it necessary to take a long, circuitous detour." Those arms of the sea, first seen by Sergeant Ortega and his band of scouts, were the reaches of San Francisco Bay. Curiously inept at foraging for food, the company would have starved except for their pack animals. They ate twelve in as many days.

At last, on January 24, 1770, they returned to San Diego, "smelling frightfully of mules." At San Diego there was so much suffering from illness and hunger that Portolá decided to abandon the expedition and return to Baja California if help did not come from Gálvez by March 20. But at dusk on March 19 they sighted a sail on the horizon—and less than a month later were on their way back to Monterey.

This time they recognized the Bay, and on June 3, 1770, dedicated the sites of the mission and the presidio. Serra felt that they were dedicating themselves to the task of civilizing the natives and winning them for God. To Portolá, the planting of royal standards and crosses in the name of King Carlos III of Spain, signified the assertion of Spain's rights in California. During the next half century nineteen more missions were established, and near some of them presidios and pueblos. The last mission—San Francisco Solano—was founded north of San Francisco Bay on July 4, 1823.

The missions formed a chain of civilized outposts along the coast, spaced a day's journey apart. Each had its herd of cattle, its fields and vegetable gardens, tended by the Indian neophytes. The Indians were taught by the padres to build irrigation systems and they became weavers, masons, carpenters, and blacksmiths. Thus the missions could be nearly self-sustaining, though they did receive clothing, furniture, implements, and tools from New Spain, in exchange for their surplus of meal, wine, oil, hemp, hides, and tallow.

The work of the padres, measured by the number of Indians reclaimed from their free life in the wilderness and put to tilling fields, was for a time successful. But even in 1786—at a time when the future of the missions was most promising—a discerning French scientist, Jean François Galaup de la Pérouse, visited California and wrote that he was not impressed with what the padres were accomplishing. He doubted whether the mission system would ever develop self-reliance in the aborigines.

The presidios, with their small military staffs, were established to protect the missions from hostile natives and possible invaders. Their military equipment was meager and antiquated, but fortunately the soldiers had little use for it. They occupied themselves with explorations, bear hunts, capture of run-away neophytes, carrying of the mails, and providing their own food supply. Like the padres, the soldiers were supposed to receive regular wages from New Spain, but more often than not the money failed to come, and they were forced to become more self-reliant than most subjects of the paternal Spanish Government.

Gradually small towns began to grow. Some of them, like San Diego, San Francisco, Santa Barbara, and Monterey, spread around the edges of the presidios, and were at first under military rule. Others sprang up near the missions; among these were Sonoma, San Juan Bautista, San Juan Capistrano, and San Luis Obispo. Los Angeles and San José began as independent towns, with civic governments, and San Francisco, although an adjunct to the Presidio, was definitely planned by the Spanish authorities as a civic enterprise. Its first settlers were 240 immigrants brought from Sonoma, and Tubac, Mexico, by Juan Bautista de Anza. Leaving Tubac in October 1775, he led them over the present Arizona desert and the snows of the high Sierra, and arrived with his company, almost intact; only one person, a woman, died on the way, and eight children were born. (The Spanish Government had supplied every anticipated need.) On March 28, 1776, Anza located a presidio along the Golden Gate. The settlers, who had stopped in Monterey, arrived on June 27.

Although Portolá had hoped to establish the authority of Spain in California, his successors could not even repel the small company of Russian fur traders who landed in 1812 and boldly built a stockade, Fort Ross, in the Spanish province. The Spaniards made polite protests but the intruders stayed as long as was convenient to them. Because of their military weakness, the presidio commanders were also forced to receive respectfully the visits of British, French, South American, and *Yanqui* ships—all of which were technically forbidden to enter the California harbors. The captains of these vessels carried home eloquent reports of life in California . . . and it was inevitable that one or another covetous nation would snap the weakening Spanish rule.

After Mexico won its independence from Spain in 1821 and California settlers had their first taste of self-government, their dissatisfaction with the patriarchal mission authority crystallized. The Indians were virtual slaves—who could not be sold, but could be pursued if they left the mission grounds, brought back, whipped, and locked up, and when penitent allowed to go to work again. Though unhappy enough to plan two or three revolts—the worst occurring in 1824— the Indians were not very articulate about their plight, but the "young Californians"—a party of progressive Castilians—took up the Indians' cause. Their efforts, added to the republican sentiment in Mexico, resulted in a decree issued by the Mexican Congress in 1833 removing the missions from Franciscan management. California's Mexican Governor, José Figueroa, had made a careful plan for the secularization of the missions, but he died before it could be carried out and the impatient *Californios* made the change unwisely and with too much haste.

One-half of the mission land and livestock was to have been given to the Indian neophytes who had developed it and to whom it had belonged before the coming of the Spaniards. Since they had never been taught self-discipline, they were to be forbidden to sell or mortgage their holdings. But when the missions were finally dismembered colonists helped themselves to mission lands and the cattle. The Indians received little cash for what they were able to sell, and that little they quickly squandered.

*The Good Life:* A few years after Portolá's earnest little company struggled up from Baja California, there rode into the new province a new kind of Spanish immigrants. Travelers returning to New Spain had told how the mission herds were thriving on the virgin pastures of Alta California. Castilian colonists, attempting to raise their cattle on the stonier soil of Mexican ranchos, were tempted to move on up the coast. The viceroy encouraged them with generous land grants. Although mission authorities opposed such colonizing by individuals, in 1786 Lieutenant Colonel Fages, Governor of Alta California, was empowered to make private grants and to outfit each *ranchero* with a storehouse and at least 2,000 head of cattle. By 1824 the colonist was also guaranteed security of person and property and freedom from taxes for five years.

The ranch houses, built of sun-dried adobe brick were plain but comfortable. Fields, worked by Indian labor, surrounded the house and beyond these were the vast pasture lands for the family's herds. The *rancheros* and their wives worked from dawn to sunset as industriously as the people who labored for them. The individual ranchos had to be self-sustaining, for the arrival of the supply ship was uncertain. All visitors praised their hospitality. "If I must be cast in sickness or destitution on the care of the stranger," wrote Walter Colton, "let it be in California; but let it be before American avarice has hardened the heart and made a God of gold."

It was the younger sons of these families who led the progressive factions when the *Californios* were forced into politics. As long as Spain's American colonies remained loyal, even California, the remotest of them, looked to Madrid for guidance and assistance. The *Californios* took no part in the struggle to sever Spanish dominance in the New World but, when they learned early in 1822 that an independent government had been set up in Mexico City, they suddenly became conscious of their republican rights. On April 9, 1822, Governor Pablo Vicente de Sola and ten delegates—eight presidio *comandantes* and military officers and two priests—met at Monterey, recognized California "from this time . . . as a dependent alone of . . . the Empire of Mexico and independent of the dominion of Spain." On November 9, 1822, California set up her own legislative body, the *Diputación,* composed of six *vocales,* or representatives, one from each presidio and pueblo district. During this first brief period of independence, the province acted decisively. It declared the Indians free citizens, opened the ports to trade, levied import and export duties, and taxes on crops and cattle, and established a military force and militia, and a judiciary.

California in March 1825 formally became a Territory of the Republic of Mexico. Under the Republic, California government consisted of: a governor, appointed by the national government; a secretary; a territorial legislature; a superior court; a prefect and sub-prefect (sheriffs); district judges; *alcaldes* (minor judges); justices of the peace; and *ayuntamientos,* or town councils. The Territory of California could send one *diputado* to represent it in the Mexican Congress but had no vote.

In November 1825 Luís Antonio Arguello's provisional governorship (1822-25) was ended by the arrival of a Mexican governor, José Maria de Echeandía. Echeandía's troubles began at once. The soldiers struck and marched against some of his Mexican troops, when he was not immediately able to pay their wages. But as generally happened in the local rebellions of this period, no blood was spilled. Although Echeandía rescinded some of the measures put into effect during Arguello's term, on the whole he was liberal and just. But in March 1830 he was replaced by a dictatorial governor, Manuel Victoria, who did not, however, take office until February 1831. Victoria opposed secularization of the missions, ordered the death penalty for small misdemeanors, and refused to convoke the *Diputación* or to give the *Californios* more voice in their affairs, although urged to do so by prominent *diputados.* The *Californios,* led by Pío Pico, Juan Bandini, and José Carrillo, seized the presidio at San Diego and advanced towards Los Angeles. On December 5, 1831, they clashed with Government troops near Cahuenga Pass. The fight was not severe, for there was only one fatality, but Victoria was convinced that he probably could never subdue the independent spirit of these provincials, and he returned to Mexico.

Into the *rancheros'* lives of gentlemanly leisure had come a new sense of political responsibility. Although they had no heritage of democratic ideals, as a class the *caballeros* acquired quite suddenly a natural desire to take their own government into their own hands. This they did in 1836, revolting against Mexico to proclaim the "Free and Sovereign State of Alta California." But the Republic of Mexico made concessions which brought California back into the Union.

During this transitional period, 1830 to 1846, a number of "battles" were fought which usually settled the current controversy. But the *Californios* had such an aversion to shedding blood that the opposing forces generally were careful not to shoot if the enemy was within range of their guns. Most of the decisions were won by oratory and *pronunciamentos.* Some of the *Californios'* controversies were with the

Mexicans, some with each other. When they had an unpopular Mexican governor to oust, they united fervently, but between times they indulged in just as violent local disputes. Jealous from the beginning were Los Angeles and Monterey, each wanting to be the capital. The balance of power between customhouse and legislature was never settled. One of the most bitter of the many individual rivalries involved two of California's respected citizens—Juan Bautista Alvarado, a spellbinding young leader who became civil governor at 27, and his uncle, Mariano Guadalupe Vallejo, Alvarado's co-ruler as military chief. Their disagreement brought down upon them Mexican authority, in the person of General Manuel Micheltorena who arrived with an army of convict soldiers in August 1842. Micheltorena, the last of the Mexican governors, stayed in the province for three years. He was driven out by the *Californios* under Castro and Alvarado in March 1845, 15 months before the Americans took command at Monterey.

*Yankee Bargain:* The tide of American pioneer families that flooded California in the 1840's was preceded a generation earlier by a smaller migration of skippers, traders, and trappers who came on brief commercial missions. True to their reputation for driving a good bargain, they secured wives, estates, and finally control of the province and its gracious people. The visitors were welcomed by the *Californios,* but not by their rulers in Mexico City or Madrid. Even before 1800 the Spanish Court had instructed the colonists that no foreigners were to land at California's ports or cross its borders.

Since the Court had neglected, however, to send regular supply ships to the colonists, the *Californios* seldom turned away the *Yanqui* skippers when they arrived with shiploads of such essentials as skillets, needles, cotton cloth, and plows. The captain of an American vessel wrote in 1817: "We served to clothe the naked soldiers of the king, when for lack of raiment they could not attend mass, and when the most reverend fathers had neither vestments nor vessels fit for the church, nor implements wherewith to till the soil." The first United States ship, the *Otter* of Boston, docked at Monterey in 1796. In 1799 the *Eliza* stopped at San Francisco, and in 1800 the *Betsy* at San Diego. In addition to the regular traders, storm-battered whalers bound home from the North Pacific stopped at California harbors for repairs and supplies, paying for them with household goods brought from New England. Gradually, in spite of Spain's embargo, California hides and tallow began to find their way to Atlantic coast markets.

While Yankee skippers were breaking into the California ports, Yankee trappers climbed the barrier of the Sierra and descended the canyons into the Sacramento and San Joaquin Valleys. They explored many parts of California the Spaniards had never reached and took away a fortune in furs.  On the whole, since they offered the Spaniards little and threatened much, they were not received as well as were the sea-faring traders.  But one trapper, James Ohio Pattie, assured himself a welcome by bringing smallpox vaccine.

Before foreigners settled among the *Californios* there had been little commercial enterprise in the province, but the newcomers immediately started to organize its business life.  One ambitious firm, McCullough & Hartnell—called "Macala and Arnell" by the soft-spoken Spaniards —contracted to dispose of the entire mission output of hides for a yearly shipload of supplies.  While the foreigners aided California financially in this period, they held it back politically; in most cases they supported the despotic Mexican governors against the rebellious *Californios* because they feared that revolution would endanger their commercial interests.

The influence of the Americans after the arrival of the first United States immigrant train, the Bidwell-Bartleson company, in 1841 rose steadily.  They had not yet declared any intention of raising the United States flag over the presidios, pueblos, and ranchos, but that purpose was stirring in their minds, as the *Californios* must have realized after October 19, 1842.  On that day two American vessels sailed into Monterey Bay and their commander, Commodore Thomas Ap Catesby Jones, ordered the port to surrender to the United States.  Stationed at Peru, the Commodore had heard a rumor that the United States and Mexico were at war and had hurried north to annex California.  When he learned that no war had been declared, he retired from Monterey on October 20 with elaborate apologies . . . leaving the *Californios* something to think about.

Quieter but more significant was the arrival of Captain John C. Frémont, the U. S. topographical engineer later honored as "The Pathfinder," who came to California in 1844 on a scientific expedition.  The next year he came again, this time visiting Monterey for several weeks as the guest of the United States Consul, Thomas O. Larkin.  José Castro, the prefect, met Frémont and entertained him—but in January 1846 Castro learned that Frémont, en route to Monterey, had left two detachments of soldiers behind him in the back country.  Upon Frémont's assurance that his party were interested only in scientific data, Castro gave them permission to spend the winter in California, with the express provision that they remain away from the coast settlements.  Frémont left Monterey to rejoin his soldiers.  Six weeks later the prefect learned that Frémont's band were camped at his back door, in the Salinas Valley, and demanded that they leave California at once.  Then Frémont, acting perhaps under secret orders from Washington (the whole question of Frémont's official instructions remains a controversy), fortified a little hill, Gabilan (Hawk's Peak), and raised the American flag. His force was so small that it seems fantastic to regard this gesture as the first maneuver in the annexation of a great territory—but so it was. It came to nothing. When General José Castro made some not very effective military advances, Frémont withdrew up the Sacramento Valley, and after spending a week at the fort of Johann August Sutter, the Swiss immigrant who welcomed overland caravans at his colony of New Helvetia on the Sacramento River, retreated northward toward Oregon.

The retreat was made without haste, however. On the shores of Klamath Lake, Frémont was overtaken by two men from Sutter's Fort with the message that Lieut. A. N. Gillespie was following his trail with dispatches for him from the United States Government. Frémont and his company broke camp and retraced their steps. When he had read Gillespie's dispatches, he knew, as he wrote later, "that at last the time had come when England must not get a foothold; that we *must be first.* I was to *act,* discreetly but positively." Soon afterwards all the American ranchers north of San Francisco Bay were informed by an anonymous paper that a band of Californians were on their way north to destroy the crops, cattle, and houses of the Americans. What followed remains largely conjecture, since Frémont withheld most of the story. Probably the Americans, when they reported to Frémont for aid, were advised to provoke the Californians into an act of overt hostility. At any rate, they struck first when a small band headed by Ezekiel Merritt captured 250 horses which a group of *vaqueros* were driving southward to Castro's camp in the Santa Clara Valley.

As dawn was breaking on June 14, 1846, in the pueblo of Sonoma, the northern frontier, a little band of Yankees who had surrounded the house of the comandante of the presidio, General Mariano G. Vallejo, seized him and the other officers. The presidio, ungarrisoned, was taken without a shot. The rebels, led by farmer William B. Ide, hauled down the Mexican flag and raised a new one of their own, fashioned of homespun with a strip of red flannel and decorated in brown paint with a star, the figure of a grizzly bear, and the words "California Republic." Although war had begun between the United States and Mexico on May 13, neither the rebels nor Frémont knew it. Despite the provocation of the Americans, the *Californios* remained strangely reluctant to make reprisals, even when the force at Sonoma grew to 130 and Frémont marched to join them at the head of 72 mounted riflemen.

Although the intentions of the Americans must have been thoroughly revealed to the *Californios,* by July 1, their two ranking officials, Governor Pio Pico in Los Angeles and General José Castro in Monterey, were so absorbed in a private dispute that they made no preparations to defend the province. While they were arguing with each other in Los Angeles, Commodore John D. Sloat sailed into Monterey Bay and on July 7, raised the American flag on the custom-house, and claimed California for the United States. Two days later the flag was flying over San Francisco and Sonoma.

In alarm, Castro and Pico combined at last to resist the invasion. Mustering a hundred men, they were ready when the American forces —350 strong—landed in San Pedro under Commodore Robert F. Stockton, who had arrived in Monterey on July 15 to succeed Commodore Sloat. But before a shot was fired, both Castro and Pico had fled to Mexico, and on August 13 Stockton entered Los Angeles. Leaving Capt. Archibald Gillespie in charge, he returned northward. On September 23 the *Californios* attacked the small garrison. John Brown (California's Paul Revere) carried an appeal for help to San Francisco on horseback, covering more than 500 miles in less than five days. But, by the time Captain Mervine had reached Los Angeles with reinforcements on the *Savannah,* Los Angeles had been recaptured. On October 6 the *Californios* met and defeated Mervine and his sailors in a battle at the Domingues Rancho and drove them back to their ship in San Pedro Bay. At Santa Barbara and at San Diego the American flags so recently raised were hauled down again.

Meanwhile the *Californios,* skirmishing with the Americans led by Frémont and Thomas O. Larkin in the Salinas Valley, seemed to be getting the better of it, until late in the fall assistance arrived for the Americans. An expeditionary force sent overland from Santa Fe by the War Department, under command of Colonel Stephen W. Kearny, arrived on December 5 and engaged with General Pico's forces the day following in an indecisive skirmish. Kearny's men, when combined with Stockton's and the resident Americans, now made an army of 600, equal to the *Californios'* forces. The two "armies" met in the battle of San Gabriel and of La Mesa on January 8 and 9, 1847. So decisive were the American victories, that the *Californios* surrendered. On January 10 General Kearny and Commander Stockton once more raised the American flag over Los Angeles, and on the 13th hostilities finally ended with the signing of articles of capitulation by General Andres Pico and Frémont at a ranch house near Cahuenga Pass. The incident was like the patching up of a quarrel by old friends, for the Americans required of the *Californios* only that they give up their artillery and pledge to obey the laws of the United States. On February 2, 1848, when the Treaty of Guadalupe Hidalgo was signed, California was formally relinquished by Mexico.

California's adopted sons had one more job to do. Although the United States now owned California, Congress made no satisfactory provision for its civil government because the Congressional slavery and anti-slavery factions could not come to an agreement on these questions. After a confused period in which military law, Spanish law, and American law were simultaneously administered in California, Brigadier-General Bennet Riley, U.S.A., military Governor, took official action on June 3, 1849, when he issued a proclamation "recommending the formation of a State constitution, or a plan for a Territorial government." When the convention met in Colton Hall, Monterey, on September 1, 48 delegates were admitted to seats. On October 10 they adopted a constitution, which was ratified by people on November 13, 1849. It remained in force until 1879.

On the day of ratification (as provided by the constitution) the people elected a Governor, Lieutenant Governor, 16 State senators, and 36 assemblymen. On December 15, 1849, the State legislature convened and on the 20th inaugurated Peter H. Burnett as Governor, and John McDougal as Lieutenant Governor. On the same day the legislature elected two United States Senators, John C. Frémont and William M. Gwin, and on December 22 most of the State officials and the supreme court judges.

On December 20, 1849, the military Governor, General Riley, issued a remarkable proclamation: "A new executive having been elected and installed into office in accordance with the provisions of the Constitution of the State, the undersigned hereby resigns his powers as Governor of California." The proclamation constituted a recognition by the highest United States agent in California that California had declared itself to be a State, although legally, of course, it had no right to do so without Federal permission. Its action precipitated an eight months' argument in Congress, prolonged by pro-slavery Congressmen who fought to prevent the admission of a new non-slavery State. Finally on September 9, 1850, California was admitted to the Union as a free State.

*Flood Tide:* Hundreds of reports describing California as "a perfect paradise, a perpetual spring" had started eastern families building prairie schooners several years before California became American territory. The first pioneer train, organized largely by John Bidwell, left Independence, Missouri, May 19, 1841 and reached the San Joaquin Valley on November 4. The first to travel in wagons, the Chiles-Walker Party, came in 1843. By 1846 thousands, including the tragic Donner party, almost half of whom died of exposure and starvation en route, were on the westward trails. It was in that year that immigrants also started to come around the Horn, one group of 200 Mormons arriving at San Francisco on the ship *Brooklyn* on July 31.

A member of one of the overland trains in 1845 was a young New Jersey wagon builder, James Wilson Marshall, who went to work for Sutter, building a saw mill on the south fork of the American River near the site of Coloma. While inspecting the tail race there, one morning late in January 1848, Marshall picked out of the water a piece of shining metal half the size of a pea. At first he thought it was iron pyrites, but when he pounded it between stones and found it soft, he knew that what he held in his hand was gold. Alone in the upland forest Marshall "sat down and began to think right hard," as he wrote in his diary. It is doubtful whether he guessed that his discovery would start the greatest mass movement of people since the Crusades.

Less than six months later Walter Colton, *alcalde* of Monterey, wrote: "The blacksmith dropped his hammer, the carpenter his plane, the mason his trowel, the farmer his sickle, the baker his loaf, and the tapster his bottle. All were off for the mines, some on horses, some on carts, and some on crutches, and one went in a litter." By June 1848 scarcely a male remained in Monterey, San Francisco, San Jose, or Santa Cruz. Soldiers deserted, and so did the detachments sent to capture them. Hundreds of ships lay at anchor in San Francisco Bay, their crews gone to the foothills. Fields of wheat went unharvested, homes and shops were abandoned, newspapers suspended publication, and city officials closed their desks.

The gold fever spread almost as quickly throughout the Nation and the world. At one time westbound wagon trains passed between Missouri and Fort Laramie in an unbroken stream for two months. By March 1849, 17,000 had embarked for California from eastern ports. Within its first 10 years as one of the United States, California became generously populated—not only with Americans, but with the adventurous of all nations. Between 1847 and 1850 the population of California increased from 15,000 to 92,497 and a decade later the Federal Census enumerated 379,994 persons in the State. Substantial pioneer families were among the Argonauts who danced and played games on the crowded little ships, while gales, scurvy, and starvation threatened them. Others trudged courageously over trails so bordered with the wreckage of previous parties that one immigrant, James Abbey, counted in 15 miles 362 abandoned wagons and the bleaching bones of 350 horses, 280 oxen, and 120 mules.

> Oh! Californy!
> That's the land for me!
> I'm bound for Sacramento
> With the washbowl on my knee.

In the boisterous shanty-towns of gold rush days—Git-up-and-git, Bogus Thunder, Angel's Camp, You Bet, Shinbone Creek, Red Dog, Lazy Man's Canyon—the average return was up to $50 a day, though many made much more. From one panful of dirt $1,500 was washed, and a trench 100 feet long yielded its two owners $17,000 in 7 days.

Sometimes gold was picked out of the rock "as fast as one can pick kernels out of a lot of well-cracked shell barks." Fully as much was made by those who served the miners. Many a tent-store took in $1,000 a day. Owners of river steamers and stage coaches, conveyors of water, innkeepers, entertainers gathered in copious wealth. They supplied the elementary needs; amenities were nonexistent. One of the "best hotels," described by Hinton R. Helper, was a canvas structure, floored with dirt. It consisted of an undivided room were guests ate, drank, and slept in tiered bunks. "When we creep into one of these nests it is optional with us whether we unboot or uncoat ourselves; but it would be looked upon as an act of ill-breeding to go to bed with one's hat on."

The colorful ruffians of the times have been so immortalized as to create the impression that the camps were lawless. As a matter of fact, the mining camps, in distinction to the cities, stand as one of the world's best examples of men's spontaneous ability to govern themselves. With no formal legal setup, the miners, extremely diverse in background and nationality, established a society with a high degree of justice and democracy—particularly in the early years. Later, when "loose fish" and "bad whites" came to California in increasing numbers, crime became more difficult to control, both in the camps and in the feeder-town, San Francisco.

Gold seekers, disembarked after a nine-month trip around the Horn or down from the camps with bags of gold, wanted the lustiest entertainment imagination could provide. They got it. Visitors gambled around the roulette tables—residents gambled in real estate, nails, cork, calico, rice, whatever commodities could be cornered—all gambled with their lives, for it is said that during the years from 1849 to 1856 more than a thousand murders were committed in San Francisco, with but a single execution. Of city government there was practically none. An alarmed official addressed his fellow citizens in 1849: "We are without a dollar in the public treasury. . . . You have neither an office for your magistrate, nor any other public edifice. You are without a single police officer or watchman, and have not the means of confining a prisoner for an hour." To remedy the situation the citizens formed the vigilance committees of 1851 and 1856. The former drove out the "Hounds," a gang that attacked various racial minorities, and the latter dispersed more "reputable" crooks in league with bankers and politicians. Both groups sprang from a widespread desire for democratic control, representing the community as a whole. Less clearly characterized by a sense of responsibility for its actions was the similar sort of spontaneous government that arose in Los Angeles, where voluntary citizens' committees broke up the bandit organizations of Salomon Pico, Juan Flores, and Pancho Daniel.

In 1854 the Great Bonanza suddenly slackened. Fortunes large and small collapsed. Disillusioned miners drifted up and down the State. Added to their numbers were the wagon trains and boatloads of immigrants arriving, now, to homestead on Uncle Sam's new fertile acres. They came not realizing that most of this vast land had been apportioned long before to the *Californios,* who had been guaranteed their property rights at the end of the Mexican war. The Americans simply moved onto the ranchos and dared the owners to put them off. What to do with these squatters became the question of the hour. Unfortunately the boundaries of the ranchos had never been fixed exactly. "Professional squatters" were hired by land-grabbing corporations. Unscrupulous legislators defended the squatters in order to court their votes. When at last riots and bloodshed forced the Federal Government to take action, a survey of the State was ordered and a land commission formed to adjust disputes. In the end many of the Spanish families were reduced to comparative poverty. They were remarkably patient. General Vallejo, one of them, wrote, "The inhabitants of California have no reason to complain of the change of government, for if the rich have lost thousands of horses and cattle, the poor have been bettered in condition."

The admission of California into the Union had not satisfied all Californians. In 1850 Walter Colton had predicted that an independent nation would spring up on the Pacific unless Congress built a railroad to the Coast, for without it, California would easily have become self-sufficient. The cry for independence was soon taken up by southern sympathizers, the followers of pro-slavery Senator William S. Gwin, who overran southern California, especially San Bernardino County. The Democratic Party, which controlled the State legislature in every session but one from 1851 to 1860, was torn by the struggle between the Gwin faction and the anti-slavery faction headed by David C. Broderick, who was elected to the Senate in 1857. When Broderick was slain in a duel by Gwin's henchman, David S. Terry, in September 1859, his successor in the Senate, Milton S. Latham, joined Gwin in the demand for a republic on the Pacific. He declared in 1860 that if civil war should break out, California would declare its independence. In 1860 the pro-slavery Democrats had gained overwhelming strength in both houses of the legislature, but in the year following they split, and Abraham Lincoln carried the State—by less than a thousand votes. In the nick of time a plot to seize Federal strongholds in California and raise Confederate forces was frustrated. When news of the fall of Fort Sumter came on May 17, California pledged its loyalty to the Union, and in the next session of the legislature Republicans controlled the assembly. Gold from California's mines began traveling eastward to help win the war for the North.

*Steel Rails to Sunny Shores:* When the first transcontinental railroad was completed in May 1869, new multitudes of pioneers traveled westward. Although two decades had passed since the first Argonauts set out across the plains, California had still not absorbed its surplus population. The new pioneers found their promised land in a state of poverty and strife—wages low and unemployment widespread, capital scarce and interest rates prohibitive, land titles uncertain, freight rates exorbitant, and water rights held by monopolies. They found the labor movement restless, anti-Chinese agitation rampant, and the whole people in an uproar against a government corrupted by railroad control.

Following collapse of a wild frenzy of speculation in wildcat mining and oil company stocks in the 1860's had come an even wilder boom in Nevada silver mining stocks, set off by exploitation of the Comstock Lode's Bonanza mines in 1872. The California Stock Exchange Board, organized in that year, became the scene of such violent excitement that the flush days of forty-nine paled in comparison. Throughout the State people invested in stocks every cent they could borrow, beg, or steal. A few made millions; most lost all they had. For on August 27, 1875, the Bank of California crashed—and California was shaken to its foundations.

The hard times that followed the bank panic bore down on people in town and country alike. The farmers of the interior valleys, already oppressed by inequable mortgage and taxation laws, the railroad's high freight rates, monopoly of land and water rights by the railroad and land companies, and finally by the ravages of a severe drought in 1876, took with ill grace the added burdens of an economic depression. In the cities wages fell and breadlines grew as thousands were thrown out of work—and hungry men walking the streets began to resent the Bonanza kings' ostentatious display of their newly found wealth.

Meanwhile the long-smouldering hostility against the Chinese, who had been thronging in since 1848 as miners, truck gardeners, laundrymen, fishermen, and workers on the railroad, had begun to break out in flames. It was incited by politicians, among them Governor Henry Haight, who had said in December 1869: "The Chinese are a stream of filth and prostitution pouring in from Asia, whose servile competition tends to cheapen and degrade labor." As workingmen, under artful urging, began to blame the Chinese for all their wrongs, the anti-Chinese feeling spread throughout the State. In 1871 a lawless gang looted and pillaged Los Angeles' Chinatown and lynched nineteen Chinese. The labor movement took up the cry: "The Chinese must go!" On July 23-24, 1877, several thousand rioters burned and sacked Chinese laundries in San Francisco and fired the Pacific Mail Steamship docks where Chinese immigrants landed. Elsewhere there were sporadic outbreaks of violence.

Despairing of redress for their difficulties from the railroad controlled State government, city and farm workers, and even some small businessmen and small landholders organized the Workingmen's Party of California, promptly nicknamed the Sand-Lot Party for its Sunday afternoon meetings on San Francisco's vacant sand lots harangued by the Irish spellbinder, Dennis Kearney. The party vowed "to wrest the government from the hands of the rich and place it in those of the people, where it properly belongs; to rid the country of cheap Chinese labor as soon as possible; to destroy the great money power of the rich . . . to destroy land monopoly in our state by a system of taxation that will make great wealth impossible in the future."

For a solution to their problems, the people looked to the legislature. The authors of California's first constitution, framed in the idealistic days of the Gold Rush, had given the legislators sweeping powers—to levy taxes, make appropriations, grant franchises, and give away public lands—of which the legislators of the seventies took full advantage. By 1878 the Workingmen's Party had grown so strong that it forced the legislature to adopt an act calling a constitutional convention. Of the 152 members of the convention who came together on September 28, 1878, 51 were members of the Workingmen's Party and 78 were nonpartisan; they included mechanics, miners, farmers, and even a cook, as well as lawyers, doctors, journalists, and teachers.

The constitution which they adopted was ratified by the voters May 7, 1879. It was termed reactionary by some, radical by others. It remodeled the judiciary department, improved prison regulations and prohibited convict labor, and passed a law instituting the eight-hour working day. In general, it differed little from the organic law common in most States of the Union, but when compared with the constitution of 1849, it marked a distinct advance toward popular control. The power of the legislature was everywhere curtailed. "Lobbying" was made a felony. Provisions to tax and control common carriers and corporations, and to regulate public utilities and services were inserted. A two-thirds vote in both houses and ratification by the people were required to pass a constitutional amendment. Suffrage was extended to "every male citizen," 21 years or more old who had lived in California for a year, "provided *no native of China*," and no idiot, lunatic, convicted criminal, or illiterate "shall ever exercise the privileges of an elector." The legislature was to consist of 40 senators and 80 assemblymen, meeting biennially. The Governor, Lieutenant Governor, secretary of state, controller, treasurer, attorney general and surveyor general were to be elected by the people for four-year terms. A two-thirds vote of each house could overcome the Governor's veto. Judicial powers were confined to a supreme court (a chief justice and six associate justices), three district courts of appeal, a superior court for each county, and also minor courts (as amended Nov. 8, 1904).

The Workingmen's Party was driven out of existence in 1880 by a fusion of Democrats and Republicans—but not before its anti-Chinese agitation had led to a vote by the people of the State (154,638 to 883) against further immigration from China. On March 20, 1879, the national Congress passed an exclusion bill, killed by the veto of President Rutherford B. Hayes. Two years later a treaty with China giving the United States the power to "regulate, limit, or suspend" Chinese immigration was ratified by the Senate.

Although the State's population had increased 54 percent during the 1870's, its professional boosters—fast becoming a familiar type—discovered soon after 1880 that promotion would bring still more new settlers. For the first time California went afield to bid for immigrants with advertisements, books, magazine and newspaper articles telling about the extraordinary climate and resources of "the Coast." Typical was this from B. F. Taylor's *Between the Gates:* "Whoever asks where Los Angeles is, to him I shall say: across a desert without wearying, beyond a mountain without climbing . . . where the flowers catch fire with beauty . . . where the pomegranates wear calyx crowns . . . where the bananas of Honolulu are blossoming; where the chestnuts of Italy are dropping; where Sicilian lemons are ripening; where the almond trees are shining . . . in the midst of a garden of thirty-six square miles—there is Los Angeles." The inducements were so convincing that by 1884 the Southern Pacific was doing a rushing passenger business at fares of $125 from the Midwest to Los Angeles. When the Santa Fe was completed the following year, the two roads entered on a rate war that reduced fares to $5 and even, at one time, to $1. Multitudes climbed on the trains and started West, savings in their pockets, bound as they thought for a sort of South Sea paradise.

A real estate boom began, legitimate enough in that it originated in a sudden influx of buyers. But the shrewd encouragement of swindlers led most of the citizens to believe that the 1885 boom was only the prelude to another that was to "outclass the present activity as thunder to the crack of a hickory-nut." Prices of Los Angeles lots rose from $500 to $5,000 within a year. Truck gardens and outlying vineyards worth $350 an acre were squared off into lots and sold for $10,000 an acre. Networks of sidewalks ran mile after mile out into the sagebrush. Elaborate hotels were built on desert tracts—and never occupied except on the opening day.

The newcomers, many of them unsophisticated farmers and small tradespeople from the Middle West, grew hysterical when the boom got really under way. The wealthier among them paid $20,000 to $50,000 for waterfront lots on a lonely stretch of shore, "Redondo-by-the-Sea," because "engineers" had declared that a submarine oil well off Redondo kept the water smooth and made an ideal harbor. Smaller savings were invested in Widneyville-by-the-Desert, a wasteland covered with Joshua trees, spiny and tortuous. Since the grotesque trees failed to give the site a homelike atmosphere, the promoters stuck oranges on the spines—and sold a citrus grove! To Widneyville, as to the other boom towns, prospective buyers were carried in tallyhoes and stages, accompanied with bands, to be greeted on the grounds by the smoothest of high-pressure salesmen and plied with free chicken dinners and all the liquor they could drink. "Millionaires of a day," to quote Theodore C. Van Dyke, "went about sunning their teeth with checkbooks in their outside pockets."

In 1887 many of those millionaires were suicides, as syndicates collapsed, banks closed, individuals and business firms went bankrupt, and the bands, the tallyhoes, and the oratory disappeared from the sunny scene. Once more the bubble had burst. The hard times of the early 1890's lay ahead, breadlines once more lengthened, unemployed men mustered to join Coxey's Army in a hunger march on Washington, and the cities put their jobless thousands to work on public works projects. The influx of new settlers dwindled.

*Twentieth Century:* But the tide of immigration once more rose and new multitudes flocked in, swelling the population by 60 percent in the decade from 1900 to 1910. "A new century—a new order" became the slogan. The new century began with prosperity, marked by rising wages and industrial expansion, the development of the petroleum and hydroelectric industries, and of intensive fruit growing on a big scale. But the newcomers, mostly people from the Midwest who brought with them a long tradition of active participation in community affairs, found much in California to challenge—corruption in municipal politics, machine control of government by corporations, industrial strife, and anti-Oriental agitation.

For once more the outcry against the "yellow peril" had broken out. The Japanese, imported in increasing numbers by large agriculturists to take the place of the Chinese as farm workers, had begun to settle as farmers and tradesmen, managing their small holdings so thriftily that soon they were displacing white workers and farmers. Although they numbered but 14,243 in 1906—and for many years had been excluded along with other Orientals from the privilege of naturalization—military and patriotic groups, merchants' associations, and labor organizations combined to raise the cry: "California shall not become the Caucasian graveyard." In 1906 the San Francisco Board of Education passed an order segregating the 93 Japanese pupils in the city schools in an Oriental public school. When Japan protested that the action was a violation of her treaty with the United States, the

Federal Government persuaded the board to rescind its order. The result of the diplomatic controversy was the "Gentlemen's Agreement" of 1907, by which the United States agreed to admit Japanese children below the age of 16 to the regular public schools, while Japan contracted to prevent the emigration of laborers to the United States. But anti-Japanese feeling persisted and grew in California.

One of the first evils that challenged the attention of California's civic-minded newcomers in the early years of the century was corruption in city politics. The prosecution of San Francisco's "City Hall graft ring" led the way in a series of exposures of municipal scandals that introduced the muckraking era in California. From 1906 to 1908 the whole State followed with eager interest the prosecutions of political boss Abraham Ruef, Mayor Eugene Schmitz, and Patrick Calhoun, United Railroads head, pushed by Fremont Older, Rudolph Spreckels, and James D. Phelan; attorneys Francis J. Heney and Hiram Johnson; and detective William Burns. In Los Angeles the reform movement was taken up in 1909 when the editor of the *Herald,* T. R. Gibbon, accused Mayor A. C. Harper and his associates of enriching themselves through forcing owners of vice dens to buy stock in fictitious sugar companies by promising police protection. The municipal clean-up campaign, soon joined by the editors of the *Evening Express* and various citizens' committees, succeeded in defeating Harper in the next election.

In State politics the battle against control by corporation lobbyists, fought so ardently in the 1870's, was still to be won. As early as 1905-06, resolutions demanding Government ownership of railroads were passed at Bakersfield and Fresno, aimed against the Southern Pacific. The demand for public ownership was linked with demands for other reforms. The Independence League, a group of liberal Democrats meeting in Oakland in September 1906, came out for equal suffrage, the eight-hour working day, and State arbitration of industrial disputes, as well as for public ownership. At the same time a demand for direct primary legislation to reform the election laws was arising out of charges of fraud at the State party conventions. When a new economic depression shook the whole financial and business structure of the State in 1907, the reform movement gathered sudden strength.

The outcome was a political revolt which took form in a coalition of liberal Republicans, organized in Oakland in August 1907 as the Lincoln-Roosevelt League. It proposed to give the people of the State a direct voice in government by freeing the Republican Party from domination by "Vested Interests." Its platform included such planks as the direct primary, popular election of Senators, and institution of the initiative, referendum, and recall. It promised to elect "a free, honest, and capable legislature, truly representative of the common interests of the people of California." As leading newspapers throughout the State swung to the support of the Lincoln-Roosevelt League, it rallied enough votes in 1908 to elect a legislature which passed a direct primary law, soon ratified by the people. When it gained control of the Republican Party in 1910 by electing its candidates to nearly every State and Congressional office, the State was shaken by a political upheaval.

The Lincoln-Roosevelt League's candidate for Governor, Hiram Johnson, took office in 1911. The new legislature which convened at the same time fulfilled its platform promises by approving a long series of legislative reforms. The 22 amendments to the Constitution of 1879, which it adopted and the people ratified, included provisions for woman suffrage, a new railroad commission, the initiative, referendum, and recall, and workingmen's compensation for industrial accidents. Theodore Roosevelt called its enactments "the most comprehensive programme of constructive legislation ever passed at a single session of an American legislature." When the Roosevelt Republicans bolted the Republican National Convention of 1912, they nominated Hiram Johnson as Theodore Roosevelt's running mate on the progressive "Bull Moose" ticket, which carried the State in the national elections.

A concession to anti-Japanese agitation was the 1911 legislature's alien land law. It was supplemented in 1913 by the Webb Act, forbidding aliens ineligible to citizenship to own agricultural land in the State, which the legislature passed over President Woodrow Wilson's protests. The Japanese evaded its operation by forming land corporations or by transferring ownership to their American-born children, but the hue and cry forced enactment in 1920 of the Asiatic Land Law, forbidding such evasions. Despite Japan's protests, the United States Supreme Court upheld in 1923 the constitutionality of the Webb Act. And in 1924 Congress revised the immigration law to exclude Japanese.

The reform wave continued into the early years of the World War. In December 1913 the Republican State Central Committee, announcing that it foresaw no hope of progress within the Republican Party, recommended the formation of the Progressive Party. The new party, formally launched on December 6 of that year, attracted a mass of former Republican voters. In the elections of November 1914, when Hiram Johnson was returned to office, the Progressives won more decisively than in any previous election. But in 1916, the year in which Johnson was elected to the Senate, the bitter feud between Republicans and Progressives gave California to Woodrow Wilson by the narrow—and history-making—margin of 3,773 votes.

Already California had embarked on the feverish expansionist period of the World War boom years, as wages, industrial output, and

# Agriculture

ALMOND TREES IN BLOSSOM, PASO ROBLES

PIONEER WINERY, BUENA VISTA, SONOMA

AGING WINE IN 30,000 BARRELS, CIENAGA

VINEYARDS NEAR CUCAMONGA

COTTON UNDER IRRIGATION, SAN JOAQUIN VALLEY

COTTON HARVEST, COACHELLA VALLEY

COTTON GIN, IMPERIAL VALLEY

ORANGE GROVE NEAR COASTAL RANGE, UPLAND

YOUNG ORCHARD PROTECTED BY SMUDGE POTS

DATE PALMS, NEAR INDIO

FIGS IN THE DRYING YARD

GRAPEFRUIT ORCHARD, COACHELLA VALLEY

A SEA OF LETTUCE, CENTRAL CALIFORNIA

LOGS FOR MILL AND MOUNT SHASTA, McCLOUD

the number of wage earners and industrial plants soared dizzily. Between 1910 and 1920 the assessed value of real and personal property doubled. The opening of the Panama Canal in 1914, celebrated the following year by the Panama-California Exposition at San Diego and the Panama-Pacific International Exposition at San Francisco, seemed to promise unlimited growth of California's maritime trade. The reform movement was soon forgotten. In southern California the unexpected plea of guilty by J. B. and J. J. McNamara, on trial in 1911 for the dynamiting of the Times building, had crushed the labor movement and turned the tide of a municipal election against the socialist candidate. When the bombing of San Francisco's Preparedness Day parade July 22, 1916, was followed by the swift arrest of labor organizers Thomas Mooney and Warren K. Billings, a controversy that created much ill feeling among labor groups for years had begun.

By 1930 the population had grown to 5,677,251, an increase of 65 per cent in ten years, giving California sixth place in population in the Union. When the financial crash was followed by the depression of the 1930's, many newcomers found themselves jobless and without income. Plans to revitalize the economy led to a succession of political schemes. One known as EPIC, for End Poverty in California, became the platform on which Upton Sinclair ran for governor on the Democratic ticket and lost. It comprised plans for exemption of small homes and farms from taxation, pensions for the aged and disabled, and graduated taxes on incomes, inheritances, corporations and unused property. The Townsend Plan, promoted by Dr. Frances E. Townsend of Long Beach, advocated payment of $200 a month to everyone over 60. In 1938 another plan, known as the "Ham and Eggs Plan," proposed paying aged persons $30 weekly from the proceeds of a 2 per cent state sales tax. These projects were an indication that the public conscience demanded support in old age, finally written into the social security and similar welfare acts.

In the late 1930's California was the objective of the thousands of farmers impoverished by the drought in the Dust Bowl of the Plains States. Once again the migrants filled the roads and improvised crude wayside camps, hoping for work, in farm areas where Japanese, Mexicans and Filipinos were competing at the lowest wages. The industrial upswing during World War II helped revive the economy. But the need for reforms and welfare projects brought out a protest vote that elected Culbert L. Olson governor, the first Democrat to hold this office in 43 years. The Democrats were unable to repeat their victory and Earl Warren, Republican, won in 1942. When Governor Warren resigned to become Chief Justice of the United States Lieut. Governor Goodwin J. Knight succeeded him; Knight was elected governor in 1954 and served until November, 1958, when the Democrats recaptured the office under the leadership of Edmund G. Brown.

*Migration to the Golden State:* A great human tidal wave is inundating California, in the words of Edmund G. Brown. Every day newcomers arrive with their household goods and often with their bank accounts to swell a population total that now exceeds every state in the Union. The Census of 1960 gave California 15,717,204 inhabitants. On July 1, 1965, the Bureau of the Census made an estimate of 18,602,000, and allotted New York 18,073,000. These totals were not made by counting noses, as is done in the decennial census, but by sampling methods established by the Bureau, which has found them a fair measure of the actual returns.

Again using its provisional figures of 1965, the Bureau estimated that the civilian resident population was 309,000 less than the population total, whereas only 44,000 were non-resident civilians in New York state. Statistics based on the decennial census of 1940 to 1960 showed that California had increased by 129 per cent. California statisticians estimate, quite conservatively they say, that the state will have 22,000,000 in 1970, with the help of the natural increase—excess of births over deaths.

Immigrants from other states have numbered about 350,000 a year in the 1960's, but a tapering off to 300,000 by 1970 has been forecast, still a sizable block. In 1963 the natural increase by births was nearly 240,000 and estimates place it at 300,000 in 1970. The cities get the largest number of newcomers from outside the state, but many retired persons choose small communities in the periphery. Of the total population, 61 per cent lives in the metropolitan areas of San Francisco and Los Angeles; 24 per cent lives in seven other urban areas—Bakersfield, Fresno, Ontario-Riverside-Bernardino (not too remote from the magnetic pull of Los Angeles); Sacramento, San Diego, Santa Barbara and San Jose.

The non-white part of California's citizenry is small when compared with the rest, but the statistics disclose some surprises. The American Indian is supposed to be dying out, but in California there were 19,647 in 1950 and 39,014 in 1960, some, possibly, having come from other states. In 1950 there were 462,172 Negroes; in 1960, 883,861. The state still attracts Japanese and Chinese; in 1950 it had 84,956 Japanese; in 1960, 151,317, of whom 38,332 were foreign-born. In 1950 it had 58,324 Chinese; in 1960, 95,600, of whom 40,796 were foreign-born.

Of the great expanding areas in California, San Francisco in the north and Los Angeles in the south, the San Francisco Bay Area of nine counties accounted for 62% of the State's increase in population from new residents from 1950 to 1960. The latest estimate of people in the Bay Area, that of July, 1963, numbered 4,078,000, a gain of nearly 12%

since the Census of 1960. Civilian employment in the Bay Area was
1,584,000 in 1963. As of 1965 it is estimated that about 11,279 persons are added to the population every month and nearly 1,000 new or
expanded industries are recorded annually. Factors in this development
are the great harbor at San Francisco, the access of shipping to such
ports as Richmond, Oakland, Redwood City and as far inland as Sacramento and Stockton; the quick communication between central cities and
suburban counties by means of freeways, railroads, buses and airways,
and the cultural facilities. The latter include opera, symphonic music,
twenty colleges and universities and scores of smaller institutions, and
more than 500 research agencies.

What the weekly addition between 11,000 and 12,000 persons means
in terms of needs was dramatically illustrated by Milton M. Teague,
president of the California State Chamber of Commerce at Sacramento
in 1963, when he said that every week California needs 4,200 new housing units, 6,780 new motor car registrations, 120 new classrooms for
3,000 new pupils, 122 additional retail outlets, 6,000 more telephones.

While the rise in population is usually cited with pride State officials
and scientists are watching the relation of people to food production and
consumption and foreseeing some difficult adjustments. Whether California will have 40,000,000 or 70,000,000 people in A.D. 2000, it will
have a much harder time raising food for them inside the State. As the
Dean of Agriculture of the University of California, Dr. Maurice L.
Peterson, said, California makes room for people by taking farmland,
often the very best, and covering it with houses and factories. "By 1975
we may drop around 13,500,000 acres of farming land. How can we
keep this equation from spelling disaster? Only by raising the amount of
food we can produce per acre." It will not be simple to achieve, he
explains, for it will take lots of research, which costs money, but which
must be provided now lest the consequences be disastrous.

# Riches From the Soil

WITHIN the rock wall formed by California's two great mountain ranges lies the long level stretch of the Sacramento-San Joaquin or Central Valley, also known as the Long Valley. It has been called the world's most fertile growing region, which contains about two-thirds of the State's acres of productive agricultural lands. Other major growing areas are the coastal valleys, the intensely developed farm area south of the Tehachapis, center of the citrus industry, and the arid but potentially highly productive desert region in the southeastern corner of the State, which includes the profitably irrigated Imperial Valley.

The wide range of topography, soil, and climate makes it possible to produce every species of temperate zone and subtropical fruit, vegetable, and field crop within the limits of the State. Pears grow on the cool mountain slopes to the north; asparagus, celery, beans, onions, and rice in the black soil of the Sacramento-San Joaquin delta area; lettuce in Salinas Valley, called "the Valley of Green Gold"; grapes for dry wines on the sunny foothills of Napa and Sonoma Counties; prunes —most of America's supply—in the sheltered orchards of Santa Clara Valley; table, wine and raisin grapes, peaches, apricots, plums, olives, and a fabulous yield of cotton in the brown silted loam of San Joaquin Valley; oranges, lemons, limes, pomegranates, figs, avocados, loquats, guavas, almonds, and walnuts to the south; dates far out in the desert to the southeast beyond Indio.

The State is ideally adapted to the modern, industrialized, mass-production type of specialized intensive farming. The dominant unit in the agricultural pattern is the large-scale, mechanized, irrigated "ranch," operated with the precision of a Ford factory, employing hundreds of workers and turning out specialized crops for eastern and foreign markets or for California's fruit and vegetable canning and preserving industry.

A typical large-scale fruit ranch in the extreme southern end of San Joaquin Valley—6,000 acres devoted exclusively to the production of "green" or fresh fruit—ships more than two dozen carloads of peaches, plums, and grapes daily at the peak season and employs 2,500 men and women in orchards, vineyards, and packing sheds. Hidden by the gentle, scarcely perceptible swell of the plain is the heart of the ranch: the cluster of administrative buildings, the white staff bungalows on a miniature Main Street with gay little gardens and tennis courts, the packing-sheds and refrigeration plant and railroad siding, the schoolhouse and store. Beyond lie the separate labor camps for the groups of seasonal workers.

The elaborate irrigation system is equipped with 18 pumps, run by 125- to 250-horsepower deepwell turbines. They draw the ranch's water supply from subterranean springs, fed by melting snow in the mountains. Farm machinery includes 15 caterpillar tractors, 43 trucks and trailers, over 50 company-owned automobiles, and 22 mules—apparently still indispensable to farming even in this ultra-modern form. The carpenter shop puts together a reserve supply of 300,000 crates before the season opens; 60,000 crates can be stored in the refrigerating plant when they are packed with fruit.

Ranch personnel includes the ranch manager, his assistants and office staff, a physician, an electrician, a blacksmith and five assistants, a cook and 11 assistants for the single men's cook houses. The labor force of men and women engaged in irrigating, tractor driving, and picking, packing, and shipping fruit ranges from 700 at the lowest point in December to 2,500 at the highest in the summer, averaging 2,200 from April through December. At peak season, in the packing sheds alone, 450 workers pack plums and about 325 pack grapes. The conveyor system is used from the time the crated fruit is brought in on trucks for sorting and packing until the finished, boxed, scientifically pre-cooled product glides out on the belt to the refrigerator cars, waiting on the siding of the ranch's special branch line.

Agriculture is the basic industry. Its income outstrips the combined income of oil and mining. In addition, more than one-fourth of the total value of products from manufacturing industries is in industries directly allied to agriculture, such as milling, canning, packing, and preserving. In 1963 California was first of the states in cash receipts from farm marketing, surpassing Texas in gross farm income. It produces nearly one-half of the country's fresh fruit output, as well as 95%

of its dried fruit, a third of its truck crops, and nearly a third of its canned fruits and vegetables.   California holds first place in many of the country's most important fruit and truck crops and some field crops. In many crops, such as lemons, dates, figs, and olives, the State has a monopoly of commercial production.

Farm production in California has risen greatly by intensive cultivation.   Since about 1885, the tendency has been to concentrate on increasing output, with an accompanying expenditure of money and labor per acre which today has reached a point probably unequalled anywhere else in the world.   The huge outlays for power, irrigation, water rights, fertilizer, machinery, labor, and transportation have necessarily developed California's intensive agriculture into an extremely complex industrial and commercial enterprise, far removed from the simplicities of farming in the familiar sense of the word.

The old family-size farm, run by the farmer and his family and a few hired hands, is steadily declining in importance and in number. Those that remain are increasingly operated, not as self-sufficing family units, but as commercial enterprises, imitating on a miniature scale the big "outdoor factories."   Many are direct adjuncts of fruit and vegetable packing corporations, for which they produce selected crops according to company specifications under supervision of the company's fieldmen and, in many cases, with funds advanced by the company.

Farm land is shrinking; it is estimated that for each increase of ten people in the state one acre of land is converted to non-agricultural use. The total of 99,260 farms represents a decline of almost 18,000 farms, or about 15%, since 1954, not including about 6,000 eliminated from the statistical tables because the definition of a farm changed.   The average California farm is now 371 acres.   Sixty-nine per cent of farm operators are full owners of their farms.

California crops brought an income of $3,463,698,000 in 1963, according to the U. S. Dept. of Agriculture.   Total government payments reached $32,181,000.   The government payments were allocated to the following programs: conservation, $5,782,000; sugar, $11,667,000; wool, $2,372,000; soil bank, $2,313,000; feed grains, $8,337,000; wheat, $1,710,000.

California leads the United States in agriculture, including livestock, with more than 300 products and a gross annual income of approximately $3.4 billion.   It raises one-fourth of the nation's fruits, nuts and vegetables, and takes first place in production of almonds, apricots, grapes, lemons, lettuce, peaches, pears, prunes, sugar beets, tomatoes and walnuts. There are 118 different types of farming, including specialty crops not raised elsewhere.

Making the desert bloom is almost a bred-in-the-bone ambition, and with the help of irrigation California farm operators have maintained the highest gross and net income in the United States. Only 37 percent of California's land is in farms, with 13 percent crop land. Livestock, dairy and poultry industries are large, cotton production ranking first in income, grapes second, hay third, tomatoes fourth, oranges fifth, potatoes sixth, lettuce seventh, barley eighth and rice ninth. California growers harvested 1,950,000 bales of cotton on 944,000 acres in 1960. In 1963 farm value was estimated at $311,056,000 and the value of cottonseed at $40,404,000. Only Texas exceeded California in cotton production.

Farm output has increased more rapidly in the Pacific region than in any other areas of the country, according to studies of the U. S. Bureau of the Census. The reasons are improved varieties, fertilization, irrigation, use of pesticides, soil improvement and weed control. Output also has been increased by mechanization; trucks and tractors have replaced the horse; draft horses are rarely used and most of the horses counted in statistics are saddle horses. The average California farm was estimated in 1963 as having 400 acres, value at $168,000 with buildings. The average farm size in the nation was 325 acres, valued at $42,000.

The great growth in population has brought new consumers to the California market, but it forecasts a change in farming, both in quantity and in location. The expanding cities are infringing on the farms, especially in southern California; orange groves have been destroyed to make place for subdivisions. About 50,000 acres are lost annually to urban expansion. Industry also is taking farmland as decentralization becomes possible through rapid transportation and lower taxation. The leading agricultural counties in the United States are Fresno, Kern and Tulare, all in the San Joaquin Valley. In terms of cash farm sales the Valley leads. It raised 96% of all raisin grapes, 78% of freestone peaches, 60% of plums, 50% of cherries, 37% of walnuts and 53% of the navel oranges of the country.

*Friars as Farmers:* The large-scale pattern for agriculture was set in the opening days of California agriculture by the Spanish-Mexican mission and rancho. The mission padres used their Indian neophytes to cultivate large tracts of desert land, and experimented boldly with a variety of vegetables and fruits. Today mission olives and grapes, planted 150 years ago by the Spanish padres, are still among the most favored varieties of these fruits. From the end of the eighteenth century until the secularization of the missions (1834-37), mission agriculture developed with amazing rapidity. A maximum Indian labor force of 20,000 to 30,000 was said to have been reached in 1804. In 1834, according to the historian, Duflot de Mofras, the 21 missions existing in California territory had under cultivation a total of 70,000 hectares (a hectare equals 2.471 acres) of wheat, corn, barley, and beans and possessed 242,000 cattle, 65,000 horses, and 321,500 sheep.

When the Spanish monarchy under King Carlos III occupied Alta California in 1769, only usufructuary title of various grades was granted to individuals, since absolute title in all lands was vested in the king. Theoretically the Indians were recognized as natural owners of lands sufficient for their subsistence, and the missions, therefore, held the vast grants ceded them in trust for their Indian wards. Few large grants were made under the Spanish regime except to missions, for the padres strenuously opposed secular grants. When Mexico proclaimed her independence from Spain in 1823, only 20 secular grants existed in California. Ten years later the number increased to about 50 and by 1845, to 700 or 800.

The padres' bitter opposition to Mexican secession from Spain rose to a climax when the Mexican Congress issued its decree of August 17, 1833, ordering the division of mission properties in Alta California. With the Indians deprived of most of the land that was theirs, the *rancheros* assumed prominence in the State's agricultural development.

*Cattle on the Range:* The era of the Spanish-Mexican land grant was a purely pastoral period. The cattle ranch with its tens of thousands of acres of wild range land was the dominant form, farming being conducted only to raise sufficient produce for the immediate needs of the individual ranch. Cattle were raised largely for their hides and tallow, the principal export articles, which the *rancheros* exchanged with the Yankee traders for flour and various luxury and other manufactured articles. For half a century California was considered a major source of tallow and hides.

The bigger *rancheros* lived like feudal lords with scores of retainers and servants. Their vast herds, roaming the valleys and foothills, were rounded up yearly at rodeo season and driven into home pastures. Don Manuel Nieto, recipient in 1784 of the second grant given in California, sixteen square leagues (71,016 acres) including the site of Long Beach, ran 100,000 head of cattle on his tract. Don José Domingo Peralta, owner of the Rancho Cañada del Corte de Madera, in Santa Clara Valley, had his private embarcadero, chapel, bull ring, and fleet of boats to transport his hides and tallow. On a *rancho* in the San Luis Obispo district, there was said to be a room filled with baskets of silver and gold and huge chests brought by galleon from China stuffed with rare silken shawls, satins, laces, embroideries, and jewels.

The American conquest opened a new market for agricultural products even before the discovery of gold. The period is graphically described in the diary of John Sutter, the great adventurer-agriculturist and first white man to settle the interior, who combined a longing to live in the grand style with an intensely practical passion for farming. In California Sutter achieved all his dreams, raising fine crops and cattle on the immense grant he received from Governor Alvarado—22 square leagues (97,648 acres) including the present site of Sacramento. He ruled his domain, called New Helvetia for his native Switzerland, in the manner of an independent fortified kingdom "with 24 pieces of ordnance available," until the discovery of gold on his land ruined instead of enriched him.

"I found a good market for my products among the new-comers and the people in the Bay district" Sutter wrote of the period immediately following the American occupation. "Agriculture increased until I had several hundred men working in the harvest fields, and to feed them I had to kill four or sometimes five oxen daily. I could raise 40,000 bushels of wheat without trouble, reap the crops with sickles, thrash it with bones, and winnow it in the wind. There were thirty plows running with fresh oxen every morning. The Russians were the chief customers for my agricultural products. I had at the time twelve thousand head of cattle, two thousand horses and mules, between ten and fifteen thousand sheep, and a thousand hogs. My best days were just before the discovery of gold."

The wave of wild speculation, rising in the wake of discovery of gold in 1849, affected agriculture along with every other phase of California life. A huge new population had to be fed—93,000 in 1850 as against 15,000 in 1848. Gold was plentiful, meat and vegetables scarce. Prices reached astronomical heights. The return from 150 acres planted to onions, tomatoes, and potatoes near San Jose is said to have been $200,000 in one season. Near Sacramento four men made $40,000 from 16 acres of potatoes. The price of cattle rose from $6 a head in 1846 to $300 a head by the close of 1849, with sales as high as $500 a head recorded in Sacramento. Stock raising, like every other phase of activity in California, went through an artificial forced growth.

When the gold rush passed its crest, agriculture began to take over the dominant role in the economic life of the State as thousands of ex-miners settled on the land or went to work on the big cattle or wheat ranches. The number of miners in the State rose from 57,797 to 82,573 in the fifties; the number of farmers rose from 1,486 to 20,836.

The stock raising industry advanced rapidly as measures were taken to improve the breed of cattle, previously bred for hide and tallow, in order to suit them for eating and dairy purposes. Spanish cattle were interbred with American stock which settlers drove hundreds of miles across the plains. Stock raising had reached its highest point when the great drought of 1862 hit the "cow country" that stretched from the Monterey area to San Diego, burning up thousands of acres of range land, killing over a million cattle and horses, ruining and driving off the land thousands of ranchers. The drought delivered the death blow to the Mexican cattlemen, whose California grants, already insecure, now passed almost entirely into the hands of Americans, largely land speculators.

The forced sales of those years, when land prices fell to from 25 to 50 cents an acre, precipitated the first genuine California land boom. A syndicate of San Francisco financiers, incorporated as the Los Angeles and San Bernardino Land Company, bought up Don Abel Stearn's *rancho* of 200,000 acres south of the Tehachapis, placed it on the market in 1868 in tracts of 40 acres and up, and put on a high-pressure advertising campaign that brought in a flood of buyers from the East and the North. As land values rose, the syndicate cleaned up a $2,000,000 profit. In the late sixties and the seventies the railroads received immense land grants from the Government—the Central Pacific alone received 1,349,000 acres—and brought in settlers by the thousand with similar boom methods.

The public domain in California was rapidly disappearing. The *Pacific Rural Press* showed in 1875 that 45 men held 4,000,000 acres of land. The struggle against absentee ownership and the evils of landlordism became a major political concern, and the Constitutional Convention of 1879 stressed the need for legislation curbing the great land companies and railroads. The California State Grange, today an important organization of the family-farm type of farmer, was formed as a protective organization against the big interests that were becoming the decisive influence in agriculture. In the seventies, at the peak of its early growth, the Grange demanded a Government curb on grain speculation; taxation of uncultivated land held for speculation at the same rate as cultivated land; Government control of irrigation, then in its beginnings; and railroad freight rates.

*The Epoch of Wheat:* In the 1870's California became the second wheat State in the Union. In addition to the sudden decline in stock raising, after the great drought, there were other basic causes for the rapid rise of wheat. Rates for shipment by water were low. Wheat was a staple commodity in international trade, and it could be shipped long distances without deterioration. The huge bonanza wheat farms, celebrated by Frank Norris in *The Octopus,* became the outstanding feature of the eighties. The Central Valley became a world granary. On these wheat ranches the process of mechanization, which has played such an important role in California's trend towards large-scale farming, was first developed.

This era was short-lived, however. Although wheat, barley, and other extensive crops continued increasing in value up to 1919, fruit, vegetables, and other intensive crops had begun to supplant them in importance by the turn of the century. The exorbitant railroad freight rates which raised land prices and cut wheat profits, the competition of new grain fields in the Mississippi Valley and Russia, and the rapid growth of population were factors in forcing all farmers to raise crops promising higher returns from a given area. The development of irrigation projects, begun in 1872 along the San Joaquin and Kings Rivers and rapidly pushed after 1885, spurred the change from extensive farming. Meanwhile the construction of new railroad lines and introduction of the refrigerator car facilitated transportation of fruit and vegetables.

*Mass Production in the Orchard:* Although the accomplishments of mission agriculture had pointed the way, the real development of present-day California farming began with the conscious efforts of the "fruit pioneers" of the early American period. Many of the early settlers who sailed around the Horn or toiled across the plains showed their deep faith in the brave new land by bringing along seeds and slips and even trees from their former homes. In more recent years the United States Department of Agriculture has sent its men to scour four continents in search of valuable fruits and plants adapted to growing conditions in the State.

The work of Luther Burbank contributed materially to the agricultural pre-eminence of intensive fruit growing in the State. When as a young man Burbank arrived in 1875 from Worcester, Massachusetts, to carry on his experimental work in California, he wrote of the Sonoma Valley: "I firmly believe from what I have seen that it is the chosen spot of all this earth as far as nature is concerned. . . . I cannot describe it! I almost have to cry for joy when I look upon the lovely valley from the hillsides." Among the new plant varieties which he originated were 60 varieties of plums and prunes, the result of 40 years of experimentation. He also introduced important varieties of peaches, nectarines, quinces, and apples, and his experimentation with berries resulted in the origination and introduction of 10 new varieties. In addition to the famous Burbank potato, he introduced varieties of asparagus, tomato, squash, and corn.

The establishment of orange growing on a commercial basis drew the attention of farmers all over the country to the financial possibilities of irrigated intensive fruit growing in California. The exotic picture of orange groves set in hot valleys surrounded by snow-capped mountains, of trees with their glossy green foliage hung heavily with golden globes, fitted into the California legend, caught men's imaginations almost as strongly as the gold of '49, and brought California before the Nation as an agricultural Eldorado.

The first orange grove was set out at the San Gabriel Mission near Los Angeles in 1804, although the orange had been introduced into California about 1770 and was reported as flourishing at Mission Buena Ventura in 1792. The first commercial grove was planted in 1841 by the Kentucky trapper, William Wolfskill, with trees from the

San Gabriel Mission; his success stimulated a number of other farmers to experiment with the fruit. The present great citrus industry was mainly developed from two seedless orange trees, sent to the pioneer Eliza C. Tibbetts at the newly established Riverisde farming colony, by the U. S. Department of Agriculture in 1873. The trees belonged to the "Washington Navel" variety, originally imported from Bahia in Brazil. The introduction of the navel orange by the U. S. Department of Agriculture initiated an industry. Lemon growing, too, was gradually developed to a point where it could meet European competition.

*Vineyards and Wineries:* The expansion of the wine industry has been highly important to the agricultural economy of California. Until World War II many of the vineyards remained in the possession of the families that had planted them, the third generation carrying on the wine industry. This had faltered during the Prohibition years, when the vineyards produced large crops of raisins, still a major agricultural product.

The climate and the soil have proved most beneficial for raising grapes and California wines have been so well established nationally that they dominate the market. New avenues for California wine are constantly being opened, and such gestures as limiting wines served at political dinners to American brands have helped concentrate attention on domestic products.

In a typical year, 1963, California had 477,400 acres in forty-eight counties devoted to vineyards, providing more than 5 billion pounds of grapes a year and earning an annual income of around $150,000,000. The larger part of the acreage, 259,463 acres, was devoted to raisins, for California produces practically the whole raisin crop of the United States. Of the remaining area, 86,749 acres were devoted to grapes for table use and 131,188 acres of grapes were used to produce wine.

The Franciscans set out the first California vineyard at Misión San Diego de Alcalá about 1770. Each of the missions had its vineyard and its winery. The industry in its later developments was pioneered by vineyardists and wine producers from France, Italy, Hungary, and Germany. The noted Hungarian viticulturist, Agoston Haraszthy, brought cuttings of the Muscat Alexandria grape in 1851, founded California's huge raisin-growing industry, introduced the Zinfandel red wine grape, and later imported 200,000 vine cuttings including all the most important European varieties. The finest dry wines come from the coast area, especially Sonoma, Napa, and Alameda Counties.

The Central Valley has wineries that specialize in dessert wines. Vineyards are almost contiguous along US 99 near Fresno, Madera, Cutley, Sanger, Tulare, Delano and Dinuba. Modesto, Escalon and Lodi, near Sacramento, have many vineyards. Lodi, home of twenty wineries, has a grape festival and national wine show in September. South of San Francisco the Santa Clara valley is most productive. In the San Diego area vineyards cluster around Escondido (US 395). The San Bernardino Mountains rise above the Cucamonga-Etiwanda-Ontario-Guasti vineyards. From Los Angeles to Palm Springs vineyards are lined up beside US 60 and US 70.

Peaches had grown in California from early mission days, but it was the trees, seeds, and seedlings brought in by settlers from the East that laid the basis for the present great industry which today supplies 98 percent of the country's canned peach crop, all of its dried peaches, and a fresh fruit crop exceeded only by Georgia. Although peaches are produced on uplands and plains in most parts of the State, the most concentrated production is in the "peach bowl" of San Joaquin Valley.

Santa Clara County is the largest dried fruit packing and fruit canning center of the world. The Santa Clara Valley grows 70,000 acres of prunes, producing over 40 percent of California's total crop, and 20,000 acres of apricots. Fifty percent of California's fancy canned fruit is packed in the valley, and 30 percent of its general canned fruit, amounting to over 72,000,000 quart cans.

Among California's more exotic products are olives, dates, and avocados—all, except avocados, monopoly crops. The gray-green olive groves are scattered over the State from the Mexican border almost up to Mount Shasta in the north. Among leading varieties are the Mission from Mexico, the large Manzillo and Sevillano from Spain, the Ascalano from Italy. Dates are practically all grown within a 25-mile radius from Indio, where the California Date Growers Association processes most of the crop. In order to find the best varieties of avocado for commercial cultivation in California and Florida, the Office for Foreign Plant Introduction of the U. S. Department of Agriculture spent nine years exploring the avocado districts of Mexico and South and Central America.

Walnuts, leading nut crop, in 1963 produced a crop valued at $35,562,000. Two-thirds of the State acreage is in southern California. The California Walnut Growers Association, to which 90% of the growers belong, has central warehouses where the nuts are scientifically treated, handled, and marketed.

*Field, Farm, and Vegetable Garden:* California typically combines age-old methods of cultivating its "stoop" crops—as field hands classify truck and field crops that need intensive hand cultivation—with the most modern machine farming technique. The airplane seeding of rice fields was first tried in the Sacramento rice area, where over 90% of the California crop is raised. Pilots flying within 25 feet of the ground, plant in 5 minutes eight 100-pound sacks of rice. From 30 to 40 acres can be planted in an hour. Before seeding in early spring, tractor-drawn fleets of giant gang plows and scrapers construct the levees around the rice fields. For five months after seeding, levees are used to maintain water on the field at a level of 6 inches in depth.   Nine gallons of water per minute must be pumped to each acre.   In October big threshers harvest the crop.

The development of California's extensive dairy industry has been largely dependent on the State's high production of tame hay.   The value of the tame hay crop in 1963 was $134,514,000, topped only by the value of cotton and grapes.   This figure includes the value for alfalfa, which flourishes even in semi-arid districts.   In the areas where alfalfa is grown as an irrigated crop, it yields up to seven and eight cuttings a year; sometimes there is a new crop every 30 days.   In the old days, settlers coming around the Horn found the dark green alfalfa fields of Chile so attractive that they took along cargoes of hay and seed.   Henry Miller, landowner and cattle rancher, who is said to have boasted that he could drive his herds from Oregon to Mexico on his own land, initiated California's commercial production of alfalfa in the San Joaquin Valley, sending to Chile in the seventies for shipments of the seed.   His alfalfa holdings became the largest in the United States.

Cotton in this State, largely a speculative crop, has been subject to booms like those that formerly plagued the citrus industry.   The 1963 cash farm income from cotton (lint and seed) was $325,001,000.   Cotton became an important crop in 1917, when representatives of the Department of Agriculture were sent to California to experiment in production of the tough-fibred type of cotton urgently needed for tire fabric and airplane wing coverings.   The State's cotton production is only about two percent of the national total, but the crop is significant for its concentration on a single quality variety, Alcalá, rare and in great demand in this country.

The development of the "lettuce bowls" in the Imperial Valley and Salinas-Watsonville areas has come almost entirely since World War I.   Effective advertising, health and diet concepts stimulated the demand, and the rise of lettuce from a small truck crop to a mass-produced commodity within the past few years has been spectacular. A large part of the lettuce crop is produced by "migratory" farming. In 1963 lettuce was the second largest earner among vegetable crops, returning $110,276,000, better than potatoes and melons, but behind tomatoes, which earned $54,259,000.   Asparagus flourishes in the delta area.   Peas are big business, calling for shipments in carload lots at the top of the season.   Only Colorado exceeds California in sugar beet production per acre, which conformed for years from the wage standards set by the Federal government.   Artichokes, introduced by the Italians of California and the French of Louisiana, are grown in the coastal strip from Marina to San Luis Obispo.

Peak demands for labor in California are usually reached in September; seasonal lows occur in February and March. Of the 544,000 workers on California farms in September, 1959, 156,000 were farmers and family workers, 122,000 were year-round workers; 182,000 were temporary domestic workers and 84,000 were foreign contract workers. The average age of all farm operators in California in 1960 was 51 years, with about 17 percent 65 or older. As elsewhere in the United States young people are leaving farms in greater proportion than any other age group. This means that those who remain behind must have better training and education than before, more knowledge, skill and managerial ability to make farm operation profitable.

The fruit and garden truck industry faced a crisis in 1965 because a law enacted by Congress in 1963 terminated the use of seasonal labor from Mexico as of December 31, 1964. The braceros were laborers who came with their families to harevst crops when they were ripe and ready for shipment. The 88th Congress, First Session, passed the law forbidding the import of seasonal farm labor.

The principal pressure to enact the law came from labor organizations and welfare groups that contended the Mexican laborers were paid wages too low for American laborers to accept and thus abetted unemployment. A study by the University of California established that unemployed Americans who were recipients of welfare benefits were not willing to work in the fields. Mechanization was not sufficiently advanced to make up the difference and competitive factors made it impossible to increase wages or pass the increase on to the consumer. As a result growers of perishable crops cut down acreage planted, in expectation of a labor shortage. Tomato growers planted 116,000 acres instead of 143,000 the year before; the crop was down about 500,000 tons. There were 40,600 fewer farm workers in 1965 than in 1964.

California growers made a determined effort to recruit seasonal workers, bringing bus loads from as far away as the Middle West. Their experience was disheartening, for the workers were either inefficient or unstable. Some attempts have been made to take advantage of the temporary labor obtained under the Immigration & Naturalization Act, which annually permits about 60,000 workers to come into the United States.

Changes in agricultural procedures in recent decades have been too numerous to list; many of them were aided by the University of California Agricultural Extension Service, established in 1914 to give aid to the farmer. Herbert Hoover called it "the greatest adult education effort in the world." Some of the improvements in which it has a part are: Control of mastitis in dairy cattle, saving an estimated $2,000,000 annually; increase of alfalfa yield in Tulare County 1.5 tons per acre by fertilization studies; artificial insemination for heavy-type turkeys; control of the rice leaf miller and increase of rice yield by 80% in eight years, 1954-1962; the Dairy Herd Improvement Program, with 327,000 dairy cows enrolled, adding millions in value because of higher output; control of an aphid that had cost growers a $12,000,000 loss annually; developing pure lettuce seed for growers in Monterey County to restore abandoned areas.

Changes of the last twenty years include: (1) Packaging for consumer use. Formerly only 3 percent of fresh fruits and vegetables for the retail market were consumer packaged; now about 50 percent are. (2) Extension of concentrated and frozen products. Thirty years ago strawberries packed in barrels were about the only fruit commercially frozen. In 1960 a plane load of strawberries was flown from Orange County to London, England. (3) Rapid farm-to-consumer service via airplanes, piggybacks, interstate trucks. Cut flowers flown daily to Chicago and New York.

In describing the complexity of California farm production, the Extension Service stresses the importance of the farmer as a consumer. In 1959 he bought $486,000,000 worth of feed, $87,000,000 worth of petroleum products, $40,000,000 in seeds, not to mention fertilizers, lime and gypsum. Today machinery and motor vehicles cost much more than the oldtime draft horses and heavy-duty farm wagons. From the farms, the products extend to the processing and canning plants, where 30,000 are employed the year around and 90,000 at the peak of the season. Dairying accounts for about 16 percent of farm income. The retail value of milk is twice its value at the farm, but in the meantime the wages of 300,000 people involved in production, processing and distribution are counted in.

# Industry and Finance

FOR HALF a century the first outposts of Spanish rule, the missions, were the centers of economic life in California's shut-in feudal world. They grew into industrial institutions, each with its weaving room, blacksmith shop, tannery, wine press, and warehouses. The Indian neophytes, held in subjection by the energetic, practical Franciscan friars, learned to tan leather, weave coarse cloth, bake bricks and pottery, make soap and candles, and grind corn. When the missions were secularized (1834-37), however, their industrial activities disappeared rapidly as the skilled neophytes, now free but most of them robbed of their land rights, either worked on the ranchos or took to the wilds.

Hardly had secularization been accomplished when the 1840's heralded an economic revolution. Canny, ambitious foreigners, most of them Americans, pushed into the sleepy province. They harnessed the streams to run the wheels of gristmills and sawmills that soon supplanted the household *metates* (mortars) and the crude mule- and ox-power mills of the Californians. In 1843 an American trapper, Stephen Smith, set up California's first steam gristmill and sawmill at Bodega. John Augustus Sutter, a Swiss emigrant, built a flour mill, set up a distillery, and began the weaving of coarse woolen blankets at his colony of New Helvetia (now Sacramento). On the eve of the American conquest, according to Thomas O. Larkin, United States Consul, California was exporting enormous amounts of lumber, soap, and brandy.

The treaty of Guadalupe Hidalgo, recognizing the American conquest, had not yet been signed when gold was discovered in the tail-race of Sutter's sawmill at Coloma. Although a small scale gold rush had sprung up in the San Fernando Hills back of Los Angeles six years earlier, the enormous riches of the California Hills had remained unsuspected. Virtually every enterprise but mining now stopped. Larkin later wrote: "Every blacksmith, carpenter, and lawyer is leaving; brick-yards, saw-mills, and ranches are left perfectly alone." Another writer reported: "Every bowl, warming pan, and piggin has gone to the mines. Everything in short that has a scoop in it that will hold sand and water. All the iron has been worked up into crowbars, pick axes and spades."

During the first three years of the rush, placer miners took out the surface "pay dirt" from the "diggin's" with pick, shovel, crowbar, and tin pan. Other contrivances replaced the pan: the washing rocker or "cradle," a criblike wooden box mounted on rockers, with a "riddle" or sieve; the "Long Tom," a wooden trough with a riddle at one end over a riffle box; and the "board-sluice," a long open flume with riffle-bars across the bottom. Even with such primitive tools as these, fabulous amounts of gold were mined—in 1849, approximately $10,-000,000 worth; in 1850, more than $41,000,000; and in 1852, the year of largest production, more than $81,000,000.

The demand for money far outstripped the supply. Californians scorned paper money. Gold dust, a "pinch" to the dollar, substituted for currency. Silver coins of many nations crept into circulation: Mexican dollars, German marks, French 5-franc pieces. Private assayers coined gold pieces of widely varying denominations for profit. Not until April 1854, when the new San Francisco mint began operations, did Government minted coins circulate in needed quantities.

Merchants received gold dust and specie for safe-keeping in their vaults; soon they were buying and selling gold, loaning funds, dealing in exchange. Stephen A. Wright opened his "Miners' Bank" in San Francisco late in 1848, Naglee and Sinton their "Exchange and Deposit Office," and the Rothschilds of London their San Francisco branch early in 1849. The Wells Fargo Bank and Union Trust Company of today, founded as an express company, entered banking in 1852. By the close of 1853, San Francisco had nineteen banks, carrying on business in cramped offices and shacks. Few of these, however, survived the depression following the bank panic of Black Friday, February 23, 1855. For nearly a decade afterwards, banking continued to be marked by instability.

As the "flush days" of mining drew to a close, machines began to replace men. In 1851 the first mill for crushing quartz was erected in Grass Valley, Yuba County; by 1857, more than 150 quartz mills had been built for working the lode. In 1852 placer mining was revolutionized when hydraulic methods were introduced at American Hill in Nevada County. By the seventies, millions of tons of gold bearing sand had been washed down under powerful jets of water and flushed into the Yuba and Feather Rivers. The destruction of valley farm lands by the debris precipitated a struggle between farmers and miners which finally led to prohibition of hydraulic mining by injunction in 1880.

Mining remained the chief industry throughout the first decade of the American regime, absorbing almost 60 percent of the inhabitants. After 1859, however, the annual output of gold began to decrease, falling to $18,000,000 by 1870. Meanwhile, a population increase from 92,597 in 1850 to 379,994 a decade later, gave manufacturing its first great impetus.

By the winter of 1849-50 San Francisco had grown into a lively manufacturing center of shipbuilding yards, foundries, flour mills, and workshops. To supply tools and machinery for the mines, Donahue Brothers established their foundry (later the Union Iron Works) in 1849; other foundries were soon opened. The wool of California's sheep was utilized in the weaving of cloth; the hides of its cattle in the tanning of leather. A sugar refinery, using raw sugar from the Hawaiian Islands, was established on the Bay in 1860. In that year there were close to a hundred gristmills throughout the State, while about three times as many sawmills were making lumber of its ponderosa pine, its redwood, and Douglas fir. The gold mines still held first place in 1860, with a $45,000,000 production, but manufactures assumed growing importance, with an output valued at $24,000,000.

During the middle 1860's a prospecting mania swept the State, recalling the feverish "flush days." Prospectors wandered into California's most isolated regions, hunting for gold, copper, silver, quicksilver. So many amazing discoveries were reported that a thousand new companies began to peddle mining stock. Frenzied financiers extended their efforts to a new field, oil wells. From Humboldt County to San Diego, wildcat wells were drilled as more than 60 companies entered the field. The San Francisco *Bulletin* reported that from 40,000 to 50,000 gallons of oil had been produced in 1865. But the bubble soon burst. The wildcat mining companies began to collapse and by the end of the decade the oil companies, too, wound up in practical failure when their product was pronounced of no value.

None the less, the growth of industry continued. When the Civil War interrupted normal communications, goods once imported from the Atlantic Seaboard, shoes and clothing, chemicals and drugs, furniture, iron and steel, distilled liquors, soaps and candles, and tobacco were produced within the State. As cities grew, gas plants, planing mills, foundries, brick and pottery works were built, and banking institutions sprang up. Four years after the legislature had provided for incorporation of Savings and Loan Societies in 1862, there were five savings banks with total deposits of $8,650,000. In southern California, remote from the gold fields of the populous north, I. W. Hellman in 1865 hung up his sign, "I. W. Hellman, Banker"; three years later Alvinza Hayward and Company opened, with a capitalization of $100,000.

Even after two decades of industrial development, California was not yet a manufacturing State in 1870. Industry still labored under some of its original handicaps: lack of fuel for power, of facilities for transporting goods to markets, of an adequate banking and credit system. A further setback was the financial panic of 1875, which followed the eastern panic of two years before, and was itself aggravated by the collapse of wild speculation in mining stocks. It broke with startling suddenness when the Bank of California, a financial power since 1864, closed its doors because of the speculations of its president, William C. Ralston. Banks collapsed throughout the State; in Los Angeles all closed, two permanently.

A widespread demand for Government regulation of banking forced the legislature in 1878 to pass the Banking Act, under which "a board of three bank commissioners was appointed with power to call for statements from the banks, make examinations of their affairs, regulate the conduct of their business, and to close insolvent concerns." Of the 84 banks then in existence, five were forced into liquidation. In spite of this temporary slump, bank deposits by 1890 had grown to $230,000,000, representing an 88 percent increase in 10 years, while the number of banks increased from 120 to 232.

Industrial expansion kept pace with banking. The growth of agriculture called for farm implement and wagon factories and for mills and factories to process its goods for market. The influx of inhabitants during the Great Boom of 1887-88 widened the local market, furnished needed capital, and increased the labor supply. By 1890 the number of manufacturing establishments was nearly twice that of 1870, the value of manufactured products more than three times as great, and the capital invested nearly four times as great.

The Nation-wide panic of 1893 rocked industry and banking to their foundations once more. On June 14, the Riverside Banking Company crashed. Two banks closed in San Francisco, four in Los Angeles, and several others throughout the State. After 1898, as the business trend turned upward again, banking resources were more than doubled. But again in 1907, as another national depression hit California, bank failures shook the State. One consequence was the Bank

Act of 1909, imposing more stringent regulations, which brought greater stability to California banking.

Industrial production, meanwhile, had risen. By 1899 California had 4,997 manufacturing establishments, representing an estimated capital investment of $175,000,000, which produced goods valued at $257,000,000. The chief industries were, in the order of their importance, sugar and molasses refineries, meat-packing plants, lumber mills and brickyards, flour and gristmills, fruit and vegetable canneries, foundries and machine shops. Manufacturing had far outgrown mining, which produced $29,313,460 of mineral products in 1899. Handicapped by lack of fuel, it was still little more than an adjunct to agriculture. But by this time manufacturing had begun to draw upon new resources of power—petroleum and hydroelectric energy.

In 1893 E. L. Doheny and C. A. Canfield sank a shaft with pick, shovel and windlass on a plot of ground at the corner of Patton and West State Streets in Los Angeles. A little oil oozed up, the first trickle from a vast reservoir which numberless derricks in the Los Angeles field would soon begin to drain. Years before, the early Spanish settlers, whose cattle sometimes got mired in surface oil pools, had plastered the sticky *brea* (Sp., tar) on the roofs of their adobe houses. As early as 1855 or 1856, Andres Pico had distilled small quantities of oil for use at Mission San Fernando. Wildcat companies were drilling wells throughout the State in the 1860's. In 1874 the California Star Oil Company established the first refinery near Newhall. During the next decade fields were being worked in the Puente Hills, Whittier, Summerland, Newhall, Ventura, and Los Gatos districts. By 1888 annual production had risen to 690,000 barrels. The Coalinga, McKittrick, and Midway-Sunset fields in the San Joaquin Basin were producing by 1890 or 1891, the Los Angeles-Salt Lake field by 1893. Production had risen in 1900 to 4,319,950 barrels and this was but a fraction of the yearly output to follow.

In 1882 George Chaffey began to operate a small power plant near Etiwanda. When the San Antonio Light and Power Company was formed, just a decade later, to transmit electricity from its power station in San Antonio Canyon near Pomona, only two other commercial plants, one in Oregon and the other in Colorado, were producing hydroelectric power. A year later the Redlands Electric and Power Company was operating its plant on Mill Creek in the San Bernardino Mountains. By 1900 the hydroelectric industry, grown to a producing capacity of 30,500 kilowatt hours, was developing speedily to meet the demands for electricity of railroad, mine, factory, home, and farm.

The new century saw a marked increase in the industrial development of the State. The value of manufactured products increased nearly tenfold in the first quarter of the century, from the $257,000,000 of 1899 to $2,443,000,000 in 1925. During World War I period of forced expansion, industrial output rose 170 percent in value and after the abrupt decline of post-war deflation, industrial growth continued rapidly. From 1919 to 1925 the increase in value of manufactured products was 1.5 percent for the country as a whole but 28 percent for California. Industry, as it expanded, became more evenly distributed. Los Angeles, like San Francisco, became a foremost manufacturing center; Oakland, Richmond, San Jose, Berkeley, and Fresno outstripped Sacramento, their former leader.

After World War II industry expanded at a rapid pace. With the increase in steel mills and airplane plants durable goods had a big upswing. By 1960 transportation equipment, which includes vehicles, airplanes and their parts, was leading in production, payrolls and employees, adding more than $2.5 billion value by manufacture and paying out more than $1.6 billion to 240,000 workers. The second largest manufacturing industry was food and kindred products, which includes fruit and vegetable canneries, which added $2.1 billion annually by manufacture. California brands were widely sold in every American city and had international acceptance. Sea-food canning was still important in the southwest, especially for tuna, although the sardine crop in the Monterey area had faltered. Wine-making had doubled and tripled its investment and in 1966 was reported to sell more than 143,000,000 gallons a year.

Next to food products the third leading industry in California is electrical machinery, followed by ordnance, fabricated metal products, nonelectrical machinery, printing and publishing, chemicals and allied products, stone, clay and glass products. Some of the most important missiles and space exploration devices used by the Federal government are manufactured in California.

Oil production has been first among the State's industries since 1919. The era of greatest productivity began in 1920, with the opening of such fields as Huntington Beach, Santa Fe Springs, and Signal Hill. From 1920 to 1926 California produced 1,300,000,000 barrels, more oil than in previous history. During boom period the industry had more than its share of unscrupulous promoters and in 1927, the year of the startling Julian Petroleum Corporation scandal in Los Angeles, the department of natural resources took over State regulation of oil production. Today in the oil fields that dot Los Angeles, Ventura, Kern, Fresno, Orange, and Santa Barbara Counties, the passerby may see enormous forests of oil derricks sucking black gold from the earth night and day.

California's mineral production continues to rise. In 1963 mineral production was valued at $1,525,000,000, an increase of $58,000,000 over that of 1962. The mineral fuels group (petroleum, natural gas, natural gas liquids) accounted for 66 percent of the total, nonmetallic minerals for 31 percent and metals for 3 percent. The value of mineral fuels rose above $1 billion for the first time in five years. Although two states produce more petroleum, California consumes more petroleum products than any other state. Five states had a large natural gas yield in 1963 but only Texas consumed more.

A large consumption of gasoline is by vehicles. California had nearly 10,000,000 motor vehicles registered in 1963 and a total of 21,207 retail service stations. About 16 percent of the State's total revenue came from fuels used in motor transportation.

Exploration for oil continues successfully. In 1962 the large Asphalto oil field in Kern County was discovered and by the end of 1963 it was producing 15,000 barrels of crude a day. This was found in an area where the oil fields were approaching full development. Kern County has the largest petroleum production, with Los Angeles County second. The discovery of commercial oil in the Brentwood Field, Conta Costa County, extended the northern limit of oil production about 40 miles into what was hitherto considered a dry natural gas area.

The remarkable record of Kern County was enhanced by production in 1963, when it yielded 95,257,000 bbl. of crude petroleum, and more than 117 billion cubic feet of natural gas. Some of the county's important products are boron minerals and compounds produced from crude borates taken from a large open pit mine at Boron by the U. S. Borax & Chemical Corp. Borates in Kern and Inyo counties and brines from Searles Lake were the source of all U. S. production and most of the world supply.

Los Angeles County obtains more than 78,000,000 barrels of petroleum annually, and more than 85 billion cubic feet of natural gas. This county is the State's petroleum refining center, with 16 operating refineries with a capacity of 789,140 barrels daily, 58 percent of the State's capacity.

Mining is still carried on in a score or more of counties, but gold, silver, copper, lead and zinc are produced in much smaller quantities than formerly. Copper is generally obtained in small quantities where gold, silver and lead are mined, or as a byproduct in processing tungsten ore in Inyo County. In 1962 the Bureau of Mines reported 86,867 troy ounces of gold valued at $3,040,345 and 156,528 troy ounces of silver, valued at $200,218. Gold recovered from placers represented 95 percent of the total. One bucket-line dredging operation with four dredges scooping gravel out of river beds; three dragline excavating and sluicing operations and nineteen nonfloating washer plants recovered 96 percent on the placer gold. Lode gold has been diminishing and the Original 16 to 1 mine at Alleghany in Sierra County, in operation for more than fifty years, has closed down.

California has good reason for believing that "the broad shift of the

United States is westward," as Melvin H. Baker, chairman of the board of National Gypsum Co., expressed it when locating a new $5,000,000 plant at Richmond. The presence of a great reservoir of labor and a huge Pacific Coast demand for manufactured products caused numerous leading corporations of the United States to locate in the Golden State. Expansion of facilities by United States Steel Corp., Bethlehem Steel Co., Soule Steel Co. and Kaiser Steel Corporation has increased output of different steel products many times within the last five years. Bethlehem Steel acquird 1,875 acres at Pinole Point in Richmond for development of a new steel fabricating plant, capable of 30,000 tons a year of steel for bridges and building construction, at the same time continuing its three rolling mills at South San Francisco and enlarging its cold-headed quality steel facilities and wire mill at Vernon in the Los Angeles area. Kaiser Steel has been adding facilities at Fontana and Napa and contributed construction steel to the Hartford Building of 33 stories in San Francisco, the Vincent Thomas Bridge at San Pedro, the Pacific Telephone Bay Area headquarters in San Francisco, and steel work on the San Mateo-Hayward Bridge across lower San Francisco Bay. California's steel production was less than 1,000,000 ingot tons of steel in 1941 but had reached 3,800,000 tons by 1964. The three major and six smaller steel companies employed 21,500, with a $160,000,000 payroll and shipped 3,700,000 tons of finished products worth $350,000,000.

California is in the lead in the application of nuclear power. Dr. Ernest O. Lawrence built the cyclotron or atom smasher and with Glenn T. Seaborg and associates at the University of California discovered plutonium, fission of plutonium-239, and scores of radioactive isotopes, used in medicine and industry. Reactors have been built at La Jolla, Canoga Park, San Jose, Pleasanton and near Los Angeles. Electricity is being generated with nuclear powered plants by Pacific Gas & Electric, San Diego Gas & Electric and Southern California Edison. The AEC has granted 10% of its licenses to California, and about 1,000 licenses for the use of radioactive materials in gauging devices and tracers in the oil industry. About 23,500 persons in California are in nuclear work. A 500-watt nuclear power system was built by Atomics International at Canoga Park for SNAP-10A, sent into space in April, 1966, from Vandenburg Air Force Base, the first nuclear reactor to operate in outer space.

# From Clipper Ship to Jet Plane

"TOO SWIFT arrives as tardy as too slow" might have been the motto in Spanish California. The pack mules of the padres ambled from one mission to another. There was no reason for speed nor was speed possible in a *carreta* (cart), squeaking with its ponderous wheels of solid oak over roads little more than trails. The trail from San Francisco to San Diego had a formal name, *El Camino Real,* the King's Highway, which generally followed what is now US 101 but often turned aside to reach the Missions. Couriers carried the mail along the hot, dry way to Loreto in Lower California, whence letters went across the gulf of San Blas and on to Mexico City. There was no urgent need for swift delivery.

Trade was no less leisurely. Although the Spanish government prohibited trade with other than Spanish ships, American and British ships successfully smuggled their goods into California long before the Mexican government removed this restriction. Californians needed too many products to resist the temptation of dealing with smugglers, while the profits which awaited the Yankee sea captains from trading their manufactured wares for seal and sea otter pelts, hides, tallow, and lumber were enough to induce them to risk capture of their ships and confiscation of their cargoes. Their illicit trade grew to the point where a hide came to be called a "California bank note," substituting for money as the common medium of exchange.

When gold was discovered in 1848 the sudden mass movement taxed intercoastal transportation facilities to the utmost. By March 1849, 17,000 persons had sailed from Atlantic and Gulf coast cities for

California; in the same year fully 35,000 traveled the tortuous overland routes. With such mushroom growth came an extraordinary demand for goods, so that freight rates rose to $50 and even $60 a ton. The Pacific Mail Steamship Company, established when the gold rush began, speeded construction of its three 1,000-ton steamers for the New York-to-San Francisco run. The first of these, the *California,* arrived at San Francisco February 28, 1849, laden to the water's edge with 400 Argonauts taken aboard at Panama. The company rapidly built up a combined Atlantic and Pacific fleet of 29 steamships. Aided by the Panama Railroad and a government subsidy for carrying mail, it did an enormous business, bringing some 175,000 passengers to California and taking back $200,000,000 in gold within ten years.

The New England shipbuilders, too, rose to the emergency. Soon that most beautiful of sailing ships, "the knife-edged clipper with her ruffled spar," was cutting the sailing time around the Horn to little more than three months. The *Flying Cloud* and the *Andrew Jackson* made the trip in 89 days. All this record-breaking bustle meant enormous profits to the owners. In one passage the *Samuel Russell,* carrying a 1200-ton cargo, earned a gross revenue of $72,000, or more than the cost of building the ship.

From San Francisco, travelers continued by horseback or steamer to the mines. The first river steamer to make regular runs from San Francisco to Sacramento was a little launch named the *Pioneer,* imported in sections on the deck of a sailing ship, which began puffing and blowing up the river in the summer of 1849. A number of other vessels of not too great draft were pressed into service on the Sacramento and San Joaquin, where rivalry for speed led sometimes to forcing of the boilers and terrific explosions. Since there were not enough steamers of light draft to handle the traffic, the high fares—2 ounces of gold or its cash equivalent—and the freight rates of $50 per ton from San Francisco to Sacramento led the owners of medium-sized sailing vessels to attempt the trip. Once the master had got his craft out of the tangle of shipping in the harbor of San Francisco, the bay breezes made the passage up through San Pablo and Suisun Bays easy enough. If his destination was Stockton, he could still count on a little breeze, his chief trouble being to keep to the main channel through a circuitous course in the San Joaquin delta. But if he began to sail up the Sacramento, his troubles were manifold, as Captain Coffin of the *Sophronia* complained in his account of "fifteen days' labour, boiling and roasting" en route to Sacramento. The river banks were "so overgrown with oaks and sycamores that we lay becalmed. . . . The only way to advance was to warp and tie." Before a year was out, however, several steamers suitable for the river run had made the trip around the Horn or through the Straits of Magellan. The most famous of these was the *Senator,* of which it was later said that she carried enough gold to sink her had it been carried all in one load.

From Stockton, Sacramento and Marysville, focal points on the river routes, *carreta,* calash, and spring wagon carried men and supplies to an ever growing number of new mining camps. Driven by Mexican *arrieros* (mule drivers), each animal with a load of 300 pounds, mule teams set out not only with bacon and beans and shovels, but with plows, barrels of whisky, pianos, and printing presses. Later, as roads took the place of trails, the stage coach and the heavy freighter were pressed into service. The first Concord Coach reached California in 1850. With its steer-hide springs, its stout ash spokes, its landscaped panels, and damask-lined curtains, it was, by comparison with the *carreta,* a model of beauty and comfort.

In June 1851 there were but 34 post offices in all California. With gold or high wages beckoning, no one would carry the mail at Government pay; hence the rise of the expressman who carried mail independently from San Francisco, Sacramento, or Stockton, charging at first the fantastic price of $4 a letter. If the post rider was shrewd, he presently became a treasure carrier, or even a banker—if he could get hold of a safe. Within another year the business of carrying gold from the mines had attracted a number of far-sighted Easterners. The Adams Express Company established itself, and in May 1852, Wells, Fargo and Company announced, "We are now prepared to forward gold dust, bullion, specie, packages, parcels, and freight to and from New York and San Francisco, thence to Sacramento, Marysville, Nevada, Shasta, Stockton, Sonora, and all the principal towns of California and Oregon."

In 1858 Congress gave the Butterfield Overland Mail an annual subsidy of $600,000. Their stages went across the old Santa Fe Trail from San Francisco to St. Joseph in 23 days. When the Civil War interrupted service on the Butterfield line, the stages used the middle or California trail route via Colfax and Truckee, across the Nevada desert to Salt Lake City. Stages also ran north to the mines in Trinity and Shasta Counties and across the Siskiyous into Oregon. In 1862 the discovery of the rich Comstock silver mines in Nevada brought about a kind of reversal of the emigrant trail. As a rival to the California Route, a toll road was built from Placerville over the summit of the Sierra Nevada down the steep drop to Tahoe Valley and thence into Nevada. Over it ran the stages of the Pioneer Line.

Far swifter than the best stages were the riders of the Pony Express, who for a brief period carried a fast mail service from Missouri to California each week. Riding a horse bred for the race track, carrying no arms, even wearing clothes and boots as light as possible, the rider sped across some 1,900 miles in eight days. With the opening of telegraph service across the continent in 1861, the Pony Express was discontinued, but it had already blazed the way for the first trans-continental railroad.

In striking contrast was another brief experiment. In 1852 Jefferson Davis urged, in Congress, the use of the camel on the Great American Desert. The California press became naively eloquent. Why not "a dromedary express to carry the fast mail"? Congress made a small appropriation and two caravans of camels were shipped to Texas. Some of these or their offspring eventually reached California and the Army used them between Fort Tejon and Los Angeles. Unfortunately the camels frightened horses and mules. The teamsters and mule skinners and *vaqueros* swore in two languages that they would have no trek with these strange beasts. The Army drivers could not pack or manage the camels properly and were unwilling to learn. In the end the camels were auctioned off: some to end their days in circuses, others to carry salt to the Comstock mines, still others to be set adrift on the desert.

California's first railroad was the modest little Sacramento Valley line which in 1856 began running east 22 miles from the capital to Folsom, reducing considerably the time to the mines. It had a wood-burning locomotive, as did the line which joined San Francisco and San Jose in 1864. In Southern California, over a line from Los Angeles to Wilmington, ran a vainglorious black and gold locomotive called the *San Gabriel,* alongside of which the *vaqueros* used to race, shouting at it derisively and profanely in Spanish.

As early as 1836 there had been talk of a transcontinental railroad, but partisan rivalry over the slavery question between North and South held up action by Congress until 1862. In that year Theodore Judah, who had been chief engineer for the Sacramento Valley Railroad and agent of the Pacific Railroad Convention in Washington, returned to California to announce that he had found a practicable railway route across the Sierra Nevada. His enthusiasm and vision were such that he was able to fire the imaginations of four wealthy, hard-headed Sacramento merchants: Leland Stanford, a grocer, Charles Crocker, a dry-goods man, and Collis Huntington and Mark Hopkins, partners in a hardware establishment. These became the "Big Four."

In 1863 the Union Pacific began to build west from Omaha, the Central Pacific east from Sacramento. Men were scarce; money was short; labor troubles halted construction until Crocker imported Chinese coolies. There were no power tools in the 1860's and no explosives but black powder. With pick and shovel, steel and jack, the crews dug and blasted through the granite of the Sierras. It became a race with the Union Pacific which ended in May 1869 at Promontory, in

Utah, where Stanford drove in the golden spike. The Southern Pacific completed its line to Los Angeles in 1876 and a year later to Texas tidewater, connecting southern California directly with the South and East.

The first coach trains to cross the continent, for all their red plush and polished brass, were none too comfortable. In winter a stove at one end of the coach gave very uneven heat, and in summer there was no ventilation without dust and cinders. However, the coaches were palaces on wheels compared to the emigrant trains that brought to the west the hopeful tide of Europe's poor. The discomfort and squalor of these trains was described in detail by Robert Louis Stevenson in *The Amateur Emigrant*. Provisions for sanitation were quite inadequate; the journey long. "Haste," we learn from this account, "is not a foible of the emigrant train. It gets through on suffrance, running the gauntlet among its more considerable brethren."

The enthusiasm which had greeted the Southern Pacific in 1869 fell to a low ebb in the eighties, when this railroad and the Santa Fe entered into an agreement with the Pacific Mail Steamship Company and formed the Transcontinental Association with the purpose of keeping up freight rates. The farmers and businessmen in the interior of the State complained bitterly at paying rates which were not only high but also fluctuating. The board of railroad commissioners, controlled by the railways, refused relief; it permitted tariffs which were grossly discriminative. The struggle between the Southern Pacific and the farmers was long and bitter, leading even to bloodshed in Tulare County.

Also chafing under the burden of the freight rates charged by the Transcontinental Association, San Francisco merchants in 1891 organized the Atlantic and Pacific Steamship Line with six steamers designed to compete with the Pacific Mail. In the same period businessmen of the interior towns and cities joined San Franciscans in forming the Merchants' Traffic Association. The new organization, besides sponsoring the new Atlantic and Pacific Steamship Line, enabled the Panama Railway Company to establish a competitive line between New York and San Francisco via the Isthmus of Panama. It was chiefly responsible for the building in 1895-6 of the San Francisco and San Joaquin Valley Railroad from Stockton to Bakersfield.

On the coast line from San Francisco to Los Angeles, the Southern Pacific did not complete the section between Lompoc and Santa Barbara until 1901, and the Northwestern Pacific road to Eureka was not completed until 1914. Even with these lines constructed there were (and still are) a number of fair sized towns which have never been served by any railroad. In addition to these, many places popular for vacations—the Geysers, Tassajara Springs, even Yosemite until 1907—could be reached only by coach and six.

The coast country, inaccessible by both sea and land, has remained largely cut off from the rest of the State. Santa Monica, Santa Barbara, Port San Luis, Monterey, Drake's Bay, Fort Bragg—none of these has deep water facilities or even very safe anchorage in stormy weather. Indeed, apart from the superb bay of San Francisco, only San Diego and Eureka have good natural harbors. To overcome the lack of safe anchorages along the rocky coast, shippers have resorted to the ingenious device of the "high line," lowering their goods with block and tackle over hawsers strung from the cliffs to waiting vessels offshore. Up and down the northern coast are lumber towns where lumber has been shipped in this fashion since the 1870's.

For years Los Angeles was handicapped by the lack of an adequate harbor. The final selection of San Pedro ended the long "Free Harbor Fight" between the people of Los Angeles and the Southern Pacific, which had greatly favored the plan for a harbor at Santa Monica. The choice also greatly benefited the new San Pedro, Los Angeles and Salt Lake Railroad, which followed the old Mormon trail across southern Nevada to its western terminus at San Pedro. San Pedro's open bay, protected only on the west by a headland, seemed not too promising until the completion of a nine-mile long breakwater protecting the outer harbor and the excavation of a spacious inner harbor from shallow tidal areas.

Since the opening of the Panama Canal, intercoastal vessels, tramp steamers, naval craft, luxury liners in round-the-world service—all have made California harbors regular ports of call. Today the flags of every maritime nation flutter in the winds. During the first quarter of the century San Francisco's foreign commerce increased fourfold, while traffic in cargo destined to the region west of the Rockies, for which both San Francisco and Oakland harbors are particularly designed, swelled the volume of trade. During the 1920's, growing fleets of lumber freighters and oil tankers passed in and out of Los Angeles harbor until it became one of the greatest lumber-importing and oil-exporting harbors. In 1964 the Port of Los Angeles and the adjoining harbor of Long Beach handled 32,423,036 net tons of shipping. The San Francisco Bay area, including more than ten principal ports, in 1962 handled 44,642,357 comparable tons; one of the units, Richmond, outlet for products of heavy industry, handled 14,596,376 tons in 1964.

The ferryboats which for so many years have been as much a feature of San Francisco Bay as the islands of Yerba Buena, Angel, and Alcatraz, had as their forerunner a whale boat named by some flight of the imagination the *Pirouette*. In 1851 she began running as a ferry to San Antonio (now East Oakland) with a tariff of $1 per person, $3 per horse, $3 per wagon, $5 per two-horse wagon, $3 per head of meat cattle, $1 per sheep, and $1 per hog. The appearance of competitors cut these rates in half within a few years. The ferries, which eventually achieved the luxurious air of great floating palaces, continued to serve the Bay until completion of the San Francisco-Oakland Bay Bridge in November 1936 and the Golden Gate Bridge in May 1937. As traffic poured across the two bridges, the ferry lines, one by one, began gradually to suspend service.

The development of urban and interurban street railways began in 1861, when San Francisco acquired its first street cars, drawn by horses, in one street up to 1913. When people built homes on steep hills, a transportation problem arose. It was ingeniously solved by Andrew Halladie, who in 1873 produced the world's first cable cars.

The considerable distance from San Francisco and Los Angeles to other centers of population has made California an important State in the short but dramatic history of the airplane. In 1883 John J. Montgomery, professor of physics at the University of Santa Clara, built a glider which soared some 600 feet, but this was only one of many abortive attempts to fly in heavier-than-air craft. Among the memorable pioneer flights with which California has been associated were Silas Christofferson's first non-stop flight from San Francisco to Los Angeles in 1914; Lindbergh's preliminary flight from San Diego to New York in 1927; the first non-stop flight over the Pacific to Hawaii by Lts. Maitland and Hegenberger in 1927; and the 7,800-mile flight from Oakland to Australia by way of Hawaii and the Pacific Islands of Kingsford-Smith, Ulm, and Lyon in 1928. From the California shore the Pacific was first bridged commercially by air. Climaxing six years of intensive preparation by the Pan-American Airway system, the world's first trans-Pacific commercial service opened in October 1936, when the China Clipper made a round-trip passenger flight between San Francisco and Manila. In July 1937 the Philippine Clipper, arriving at Cavite Bay, Manila, completed the first 1,000,000 miles of commercial flight over the big water.

Jet propulsion grew up with World War II. Although there is no single name attached to the device, it is quite certain that the first experiments were made under supervision of California Institute of Technology (CALTECH) of Pasadena. The Guggenheim Aeronautical Laboratories moved its tests to the mountains beyond Pasadena. During the war this section concentrated on rocket engines. This developed into the Jet Propulsion Laboratory of the Institute, now operated for the National Aeronautics and Space Administration.

The Laboratory designs and builds space-craft systems that are used in space explorations, maintains two-way communications with spacecraft and analyzes scientific data obtained from flights. Explorer I, the first satellite, was a product of this Laboratory and its major achievement was discovery of the Van Allen Belt of radioactive particles in the earth's magnetic field. The most important recent event was the journey of Mariner IV in July, 1965, when this gave data and photographs of Mars. In between these dates the Laboratory has contributed much scientific information concerning space. It has measured the solar wind that affects the earth's magnetic field, the temperature of the atmosphere and the surface of Venus, established new data about the magnetic field and rotation of Venus. It also has been active in lunar probes.

Since 1929 the Guggenheim Foundation has aided the work in aeronautical science at Caltech. What the research workers discovered was vital to the technology of flight and aircraft design. Many engineers trained at Caltech joined the numerous aircraft manufacturers that established themselves in California. One of the largest is the Lockheed Missile & Space Company, which employs 23,000 persons in California alone. It has been developing the Agena Satellite, the Polaris and Poseidon Missiles, and working on a large number of programs associated with defense. It also develops craft used for meteorological work, such as the Tiros and Nimbus satellites for accurately predicting the weather, of vital importance to agriculture. This firm also is engaged in studying a water desalinization plant for the U. S. Dept. of the Interior, and has developed a 50-ton research submarine for developing the technology of undersea investigation.

In the 1960s California's airports and airstrips exceeded 1,800 in number and the State had approximately 14% of the nation's pilots and airports. By the middle of the 1960-70 decade approximately 600 heliport sites were in use, and of this total 110 helistops were in the Los Angeles area. The number increases annually.

Control is vested in the State Aeronautics Board of five, appointed by the governor, a policy-making body, and the Division of Aeronautics, a division of the Public Works Department, which applies regulations and acts to increase the use of aviation, public and private, and insure safe operation of airports. One of its current activities is the application of zoning rules, for "zoning is the act of protecting airspace from hazards on the ground." The Division cooperates actively with school districts and colleges in flight instruction and encourages courses in aviation.

# *Workingmen*

"THERE is no state in the Union, no place on earth, where labor is so honored and so well rewarded," David C. Broderick told the United States Senate in his maiden speech in 1858, "no time and place since the Almighty doomed the sons of Adam to toil, where the curse, if it be a curse, rests so lightly as now upon the people of California."

The vigorous independence of the pioneer has persisted until present times as a characteristic of the State's labor movement. Of the men who had the hardihood to make the long westward trek in Gold Rush days, many were skilled workingmen from trades in which unions were being organized. Among the European-born immigrants were English Chartists, Irish nationalists, French and German political exiles of 1848—men schooled in the labor movement, in struggles for national independence, or for democratic liberties. In the new-born camps and towns of California, they found no feudal tradition to influence social relationships. To people who saw men in overalls win or lose fortunes overnight, there was no place for concepts of the superiority or special privileges of the wealthy.

The State's labor movement began in its first big city, San Francisco, since early days the trade-union center of California and, until later years, of the whole region west of the Rocky Mountains. The second great metropolitan center, Los Angeles, remained an open-shop stronghold for half a century, the lower labor standards of its competing industries threatening the gains won by labor in the north. But, as Los Angeles outstripped San Francisco in population, the disparity between labor conditions in the two cities began to diminish, for San Francisco trade unionists came to realize that labor in the north could hold its gains only with the aid of labor in the south. During the 1930's the organized labor movements of both cities began to pool their strength in an effort to overcome the sharp contrast between urban and rural working conditions and attempted to organize the vast numbers of underprivileged migratory workers in the State's dominant industry, agriculture.

The swift tempo of San Francisco's growth from village to metropolis characterized the development of its labor movement. The printers organized in 1850; teamsters, draymen, lightermen, riggers and stevedores in 1851; bakers and bricklayers in 1852; calkers, carpenters, plasterers, brickmasons, blacksmiths, and shipwrights in 1853; and musicians in 1856. Although most of these organizations had to make several starts before they achieved stability, they gained better working conditions for their members, kept wages balanced with the wildly rocketing cost of living, and launched the movement for progressive labor legislation. Of the labor laws pushed through in two decades, 1850-70, by these infant labor unions, the most important were provisions for payment of wages, a mechanics' lien, and an eight-hour day. In no other city in the country, it is said, did so many workers enjoy the eight-hour day as in San Francisco during these years.

The outstanding labor struggle of the 1860's, the molders' and boilermakers' strike of 1864, was conducted along lines typical of those spacious days. The strikers were opposed by a newly formed ironworks employers' association, which threatened to levy a fine of $1,000 on the first employer to grant the strikers' demands. The association wired Portland, New York, Boston, and Providence for strikebreakers and paid their fare West. When the strikebreakers arrived at Panama, however, they were greeted by a delegation of representatives from the striking unions and the San Francisco Trades Union, the city's first central labor body. All arrived at San Francisco on friendly terms as fellow union members.

The organization of the first effective State federated labor body, the Mechanics' State Council, was the labor movement's defense against employers' opposition to the eight-hour day. Forming the "Ten Hour League" (1867) to counter labor's "Eight Hour League," the employers, following the shipowners' action in discharging all who worked on the eight-hour basis on the chief steamship lines, pledged themselves to hire no one for less than a ten-hour day. "By so doing," they stated, "we believe that we are working for the best interest of the journeymen mechanics as well as for the best interests of the city and state at large." The Mechanics' State Council, organized in the Los Angeles as well as the San Francisco area, responded by affiliating with the National Labor Union, America's first great national labor federation.

An era of comparative protection for labor came abruptly to its end with completion of the first transcontinental railroad in 1869. Labor, hard hit by the falling wages and the rising unemployment of the depression-ridden decade that followed, began to lay the blame for its misfortunes on the thousands of Chinese coolie railroad workers suddenly turned loose on the labor market. For the next two decades the campaign against the use of Chinese labor, pushed to the limit by politicians and demagogues, diverted the energies of the trade union movement. But labor's fear of being reduced to servitude was well founded. Still fresh in men's minds was the struggle against the efforts of pro-slavery officials and landowners to introduce slavery to California; this had first been brought to the fore in 1852 when railroad and landowning interests were prevented, by protest meetings of miners and city workers, from forcing a law permitting importation of contract labor through the legislature. The anti-Chinese movement, although accompanied by racial discrimination which gave rise to outbreaks of brutal violence, was primarily based on economic interest. In ever greater numbers the Chinese were taking over work in the fields, in the service trades, in the light manufacturing industries—until by 1872 they comprised half of all the factory workers in San Francisco. The wages paid them were far below wages of American workers. And when Americans refused to have their wages lowered to the pay levels of the Chinese, employers threatened to hire Chinese workers instead. On the other hand, the builders of the Central Pacific had threatened to hire American workers when Chinese construction hands struck against $30 monthly for a 12-hour day (1867).

"The Chinese Must Go!" was the slogan that carried Dennis Kearney, one of the most widely known figures in the early California labor movement, to prominence. Until he appeared on the scene in 1877 as a saviour of the masses, he had been vociferously anti-labor. Joining the "law and order" group formed by nervous businessmen in July 1877 when rioters roamed the city denouncing Chinese and capitalists, he suddenly left it to lead the rioters. Refused admission to the Workingmen's Party of the United States, he set up in October 1877 a rival organization, the Workingmen's Party of California. At Sunday afternoon meetings of workers and unemployed on vacant sand lots, where he delivered incendiary speeches, his favorite pose was with a noosed rope in his hand. This he declared was his platform. He was jailed for advising every man "to own a musket and a hundred rounds of ammunition" but was soon released. Eventually, as opposition arose within the Workingmen's Party, an investigating committee charged him with being a "dictator . . . more than suspected of selling out to the enemy"—the enemy in this case being railroad and banking interests.  Discredited, Kearney went back to the draying business he had left and devoted himself to getting rich.

The man who headed the opposition to Kearney, Frank Roney, remained an outstanding figure in the State's labor movement long after Kearney's retirement.  Active as a young man in the movement for Irish independence, he had emigrated to the United States to become a national figure in the iron molder's union.  He arrived in San Francisco in 1875, wrote the constitution and platform of the Workingmen's Party, and soon took his place as a leader in the labor organization drive of the 1880's.  Following the disappearance of the Workingmen's Party from the political scene, he was elected president of the Federated Trades and Labor Unions of the Pacific Coast, later the San Francisco Central Labor Council.  To Roney was entrusted the job of organizing the seamen of the port of San Francisco, twice previously attempted with no more than short-lived success.

In what was known as the world's worst shanghaiing port, the Seamen's Protective Association, headed by Roney as president, took up the fight against wages so low and shipboard conditions so brutal that crews could be filled only by kidnapping.  The association faced the opposition of shipowners, crimps, and underworld elements who preyed on sailors.  During one meeting held in 1880, according to the union's minute book, "there were constant interruptions by the boarding-house sharks and their whiskey-brought bummers, going even so far as to throw valuable eggs, that did not have time to get the proper age and odor, at the agitators; but they made a bad failure, for the superior intelligence and calmness of the speakers entirely discomforted their enemies."  The union fought for seamen's civil rights by preferring charges against brutal ships' officers in Federal courts. It won the backing of progressive San Franciscans, chief among them Henry George, single-tax proponent, editor of the San Francisco *Post,* and a consistent supporter of the labor movement.  The fight to improve seamen's working conditions was extended into the legislative field when Roney drew up and presented to Congress two laws, one embodying the union's demand for punishment of brutal officers and the other specifying that two-thirds of the crew of every American vessel should be American citizens.  The legislative struggle was later taken up and carried on for some thirty years by Andrew Furuseth, as secretary of the Sailors' Union of the Pacific and (from 1908) of the International Seamen's Union of America.

As a result of the struggle against a sharp wage cut in 1885 a stable organization, the Coast Seamen's Union, was at last set up with the aid of officers of the Knights of Labor, then at the peak of its growth in California, and Socialists from the International Workingmen's Association, of whom five served on the union's original advisory committee. The union halted the drive for wage cuts, organized branches at leading ports up and down the Pacific Coast, and launched (1887) the *Coast Seamen's Journal,* for years the Coast's most important labor paper. In 1891 the Coast Seamen's Union and the deep-sea steamship sailors' union dropped their jurisdictional differences and merged as the present Sailors' Union of the Pacific.

Following organization of the seamen, the waterfront unions became an important factor in San Francisco's labor movement, for longshoremen, ship calkers, pile drivers, and other waterfront workers had already been organized for a period of years. Feeling a bond of common interest, the maritime unions made repeated efforts to achieve joint organization. The Wharf and Wave Federation (1888), the City Front Labor Council (1891), and the Waterfront Federation (1914-1923) were predecessors of the present Maritime Federation of the Pacific.

The City Front Federation of 1901, reputed to have been the strongest trade federation in the country at the time, grew out of the intense organizational drive in all crafts that accompanied the great industrial boom at the turn of the century. During the two decades that followed its organization, the trade union movement grew at such a pace that San Francisco took first place among the unionized cities of the United States. But labor's gains were not achieved without opposition. To meet what they considered the threat of union domination, employers organized on a broader and more effective basis than in the past. A complicated and tense situation developed, which culminated in the building trades strike of 1900 and the City Front Federation strike of 1901. The successful conclusion of the building trades strike was followed by organization of the Building Trades Council, which became the most powerful factor in the labor movement. The City Front Federation strike, in which the waterfront unions went out in support of locked-out teamsters, was bitterly fought because both labor and employers knew that the question of establishing the open shop in San Francisco was at stake. Although the unions partially lost the strike, they checked the open-shop drive and survived.

Out of the City Front Federation strike grew the Union Labor Party, supported by the San Francisco Central Labor Council because of its resentment over Mayor James D. Phelan's use of police to protect strikebreakers brought into the city. The Union Labor Party's candidate for mayor, Eugene Schmitz, was elected in 1902 to succeed Phelan. The story of how an alleged alliance of politicians, utilities, and vice interests won control of the party has been told by Fremont Older, editor of the San Francisco *Bulletin,* who helped lead the reform movement that culminated in the graft prosecutions initiated against Schmitz, Abraham Ruef, and a long list of municipal office-holders in 1906. Older's story deals, too, with the activities of Patrick Calhoun, political boss and United Railroads head, who, it is said, precipitated the 1907 traction strike in an effort to halt the prosecution, by diverting public attention. Having aroused public indignation against labor, on the ground that the strike was holding up reconstruction of the earthquake-wrecked city, Calhoun melodramatically broke the strike. Those in control of the Union Labor Party had by this time been denounced by the San Francisco Central Labor Council in an emphatic statement published May 30, 1906, which said, in part: "We declare every corruptionist, briber and bribed, should be prosecuted and punished according to law and hereby pledge our cooperation to that end." In the end Calhoun was brought to trial, but acquitted.

Despite the rapid growth of the labor movement in San Francisco, Los Angeles remained largely a non-union town. The employers of San Francisco had stated flatly that unless the unions acted to level competition with the south by organizing Los Angeles they would begin a new drive for open-shop conditions in the Bay area. Taking up the challenge, labor sent a corps of organizers south in June 1910. In Los Angeles the Founders and Employers Association was refusing to meet with union representatives of some 1,200 workers idle in a metal-trades lockout covering all plants in the city. The International Molders Union sent its national organizer, George Gunray, to aid the Los Angeles drive. As the organizing drive got underway, the public began to develop a sympathetic attitude toward unionism.

And then occurred the disaster that for many years was to delay labor organization in Los Angeles. At one o'clock in the morning of October 1, 1910, an explosion shattered the plant of the Los Angeles *Times*, owned by General Gray Otis, leader of the city's anti-union forces. Twenty-one of the workers in the building were killed and many injured.

Intense excitement followed and while the Labor Council, investigating, announced that the explosion had been a gas explosion, the police, the grand jury, the Mayor's committee, civic bodies, the City Council, also investigating, declared that the explosion had been caused by dynamite. Otis offered a reward of $300,000 for the finding of those responsible. Three groups of detectives began the search.

On April 14, 1911, James B. McNamara and Ortie McManigal were arrested in Detroit by the detective William J. Burns. Ortie McManigal in a confession implicated, among others, James McNamara's brother John J. McNamara, Secretary of the International Association of Bridge and Structural Iron Workers' Union. J. J. McNamara was arrested on April 22 in Indianapolis. The Mc-

Namaras were taken to the Los Angeles jail and held; McManigal was taken along as prosecution witness.

Labor, convinced of the innocence of the McNamaras, rose to their defense. According to Perlman and Taft (*History of Labor in the United States 1896-1932,* Volume IV) "Los Angeles was at the time the battlefield of several simultaneous labor wars. . . . The explosion in the morning of October 1, 1910 . . . came as a climax in these hard fought battles." The American Federation of Labor raised a quarter of a million dollar fund, and the famous advocate, Clarence Darrow, was retained to defend the men.

The trial dragged on slowly with labor—still certain of the men's innocence—engaged in a veritable crusade. But Clarence Darrow apparently became convinced of the great strength of the State's case. Through the journalist Lincoln Steffens, he began to negotiate with the authorities. In retrospect, Steffens wrote in his autobiography that his newspaper report of the case "began by saying that both capital and labor had pleaded guilty, and showed that the McNamaras had made no confession which involved other persons but had entered into an agreement by which, without force, the labor problem was to be reconsidered in the most anti-labor city in America."

The details of the agreement made with the prosecution have remained a source of argument. According to Perlman and Taft, "The agreement with the prosecution stipulated that both brothers would plead guilty, and that J. B. McNamara would receive life imprisonment but John J. McNamara a less severe sentence, and that all other prosecutions would be dropped." Influential people of Los Angeles and the court officers were won over, and so finally were the McNamaras. On December 1, 1911, Attorney Darrow rose in court and stated that his clients wished to change their plea from "not guilty" to "guilty as charged." Four days later James B. McNamara was sentenced to life imprisonment and John J. McNamara to a term of 15 years. In passing sentence the judge verbally castigated the men: which action, it is alleged, was against the agreement. Later that part of the stipulation concerned with the prosecution of others was also disregarded.

The decade that followed saw a rapid growth in the influence on California's labor movement of the Industrial Workers of the World, central organizing agency in Northwest logging camps and Midwest wheat fields, as it began extending its work to the mines, lumber camps, ports, and agricultural areas of the State. It came into prominence in California at the time of the Wheatland hop field riots of 1913, which brought before the Nation for the first time the intolerable conditions of field labor in the State and prompted an investigation leading to the first Government action in cleaning up these conditions. The situation that prompted the riots at the Wheatland hop ranch, said to belong to the State's largest single employer of field labor at the time, was later described by Carleton W. Parker, executive secretary of the State Commission of Immigration and Housing: "Twenty-eight hundred pickers were camped on a treeless hill . . . Some were in tents, some in topless squares of sacking . . . there was no provision for sanitation, no garbage disposal. The temperature during the week of the riot remained near 105 degrees, and though the wells were a mile from where the men, women and children were picking . . . no water was sent into the fields . . . It developed in the state investigation that the owner of the ranch received half of the net profit earned by an alleged independent grocery store, which had been given the grocery concession and was located in the center of the camp grounds." The overcrowding of the camp was found to have been aggravated by the fact that the ranch owner had followed the common practice of advertising for twice the necessary number of pickers in order to keep down wage levels. In the rioting that began when a sheriff's posse broke up a protest meeting, four were killed. A week after the riot, the first act regulating California labor camps went into effect.

The I. W. W. continued to play an important part in the labor movement until the early post-war period. Among the causes contributing to its decline were the anti-union drive and the prosecution of many of its members under the State's newly passed criminal syndicalism laws. Its last important appearance in the State was in the 1923 seamen's strike at San Pedro, when Upton Sinclair was arrested for publicly reading the Declaration of Independence.

A prominent defender of the two I. W. W. leaders, Richard Ford and Herman Suhr, who were arrested in the Wheatland disturbance and convicted after a long-fought trial, was a young Irish member of the molders' union, Thomas Mooney. The leading part that he played in the electrical workers' strike of 1913 and in the attempted organization of United Railroads workers in 1916 also brought him to the fore in northern California as an aggressive trade unionist. He was a leading member of the group that began preparing a new organizational drive in southern California to counter a new open-shop campaign in the north organized by employers. As such he came particularly to the attention of the "law and order" committee formed by the San Francisco Chamber of Commerce to promote adoption of an anti-picketing ordinance.

The newspaper files of the period reveal the combination of anti-union and wartime preparedness propaganda in an attempt to label as disloyal labor's determination to maintain its organizational lines. In the tense atmosphere of the growing struggle a bomb exploded, killing ten persons, on the route of the Preparedness Day parade staged in San

Francisco July 22, 1916. Among those arrested were Mooney, his wife Rena, and his friend, Warren K. Billings. Found guilty, Mooney was sentenced to be hanged and Billings to life imprisonment. After world-wide protests, Governor William D. Stephens, at the behest of President Woodrow Wilson, commuted Mooney's sentence to life imprisonment in November 1918.

The case soon became one of the most celebrated labor controversies of modern times. In the course of repeated State hearings and Federal inquiries, a picture of corruption was revealed that strengthened the conviction held by many people that the case had been a frame-up. On the basis of new evidence soon uncovered, and of confessions and other evidence exposing the perjury of key prosecution witnesses, the jurors who found Mooney guilty and the judge who sentenced him publicly reversed their positions. As the years went by, more and more evidence indicating Mooney's innocence came to light. In August 1928 every living person connected with the prosecution, except District Attorney Charles Fickert and an assistant, recommended Mooney's pardon. The trial judge, Judge Griffin, declared in a public address in February 1929: "The Mooney case is one of the dirtiest jobs ever put over and I resent the fact that my court was used for such a contemptible piece of work." But for 22 years, Mooney remained in San Quentin penitentiary while successive Governors resisted appeals for a pardon. Throughout these years the case was carried through State and Federal Courts as Mooney's defense attorneys asked for a review of new evidence and opening of a new trial. Finally in October 1938, after lengthy hearings in San Francisco before a referee, the United States Supreme Court, passing on the case a second time, found itself compelled on legal grounds to deny a requested review of the case. A month later Culbert L. Olson, who had expressed his firm belief in Mooney's innocence while still a State senator, was elected Governor of California. One of his first steps on taking office in January 1939 was to issue an unconditional pardon.

In the meantime the wartime anti-union campaign had driven ahead to success, initiating a period of open-shop domination that lasted throughout the 1920's. It reached its climax in 1921, when the newly formed Industrial Association of San Francisco raised a war chest of $1,250,000 to break the building trades strike of that year. With the collapse of the building trades unions, too weakened to resist when the Industrial Association's wage board cut wages twice within a year, the strongest single force in the labor movement of that period was rendered helpless. At about the same time, the Metal Trades Council was defeated, losing agreements it had held with the employers since 1907. The seamen's unions, too, went down to defeat in 1921. The loss of the dock strike of 1919, called in protest against alleged endangerment of life and limb by speed-up and excessive loads, had already caused the collapse of the riggers' and stevedores' union. In the succeeding decade, the "American Plan," substituting individual for collective bargaining, prevailed throughout the State.

The resurgence of the labor movement following enactment of the National Industrial Recovery Act in 1933 was marked especially by the outburst of latent protest against long-standing grievances on San Francisco's waterfront. The conditions that prompted the 1919 strike had continued under the agreement signed in December 1919 between the Waterfront Employers' Association and the Longshoremen's Association of the Pacific, organized by longshore gang bosses, which longshoremen designated a "company" union, calling it the Blue Book Union (for the color of the membership book); the agreement made every dock worker who refused to join ineligible for employment. Another basic grievance was the "shape-up" system of hiring from the docks, which longshoremen claimed forced them to wait without compensation for hours at a time, fostered corrupt control of employment by hiring agents from whom men had to buy their jobs, and resulted in some men working 24 and 36 hours and longer without sleep, while others starved for lack of work. As a leader in protests against abuses, the lanky young Australian, Harry Bridges, who had been working on the docks ever since he had come ashore as a sailor 12 years before, was coming to the fore; among longshoremen he was known as "Limo Harry," a first-class winch driver and a man who stood up for his rights. Within a few weeks after a charter had been secured from the International Longshoremen's Association in September 1933, about 90 per cent of the men on the front had joined the new union. At a coastwise convention held in the spring of 1934, the longshoremen formulated demands to correct the abuses on the docks. When hearings led to no definite result, they took a strike vote on March 7. The seamen's unions, likewise showing a new vitality, had also been refused when they presented demands to the shipowners. On May 15, 1934, they voted to join the strike; and the ship clerks and licensed officers' organizations followed suit.

The killing of two waterfront picketers and the clubbing and gassing of a hundred others by police on Thursday, July 5, 1934—afterwards known as "Bloody Thursday"—was the incident that swept nearly every union in the Bay area into the second important general strike up to that time in the Nation's history. From July 17 to July 19 stores closed, shops and factories shut down, and trucks and street cars stopped running in San Francisco as 127,000 workers left their jobs. The strike aroused the emphatically expressed opposition of many newspapers, individuals, and organizations throughout the Nation. The NRA Administrator, General Hugh S. Johnson, appeared on the scene to denounce it in a public address. Only July 20 the strikers began returning to their jobs. The waterfront unions, however, after mediation of the dispute, won agreements with the shipowners which still serve as the basis of labor relations in the maritime industry. They were enabled to organize in 1935 the Maritime Federation of the Pacific, first attempt to apply the principle of joint organization on a coastwise basis.

California would feel proud to boast that there is no unemployment in the State, but unfortunately it, too, has men out of work. The reason, however, differs from that of most other states; the vast shift of population to the Pacific Coast makes available more workers than industry can absorb. The California State Chamber of Commerce estimated in 1964 that to close the gap between jobs and people industry must hire 200,000 more men than it did. If the rate of increases continued this would be 1,200,000 by 1970.

Much of the excess labor, however, is not ready to fill the many technical jobs of specialized industries, which thereupon import craftsmen from other states. To obviate this the State's Division of Apprenticeship Standards of the Department of Industrial Relations encourages training of young men in apprenticeship programs. The State looks to private industry to help train apprentices for the skilled work it offers, and there has been a notable response, although 24,000 apprentices registered in June, 1964, were considered too few for the needs. The California Conference on Apprenticeship, a voluntary organization of representatives of labor and managment that meets biennially, has been encouraging industries to train apprentices for specialized work. The State Chamber of Commerce estimates that more than 3,500,000 young people will enter the labor market in the 1960-1970 decade, two-thirds with a high school education or less. To see that these arrivals have skills to make a proper living is not only helpful to the economy but to the stability of society.

In Los Angeles the trade union movement had advanced despite the continued open-shop stand of employers, who in 1938 pushed through a drastic anti-picketing ordinance. Although a number of industries remain largely unorganized, the disparity between labor conditions in the State's two larger cities no longer exists. A basic factor in bringing about this change was the rapid growth of unionization in such mass production industries as aircraft, auto, rubber, and oil. Intensive organizational drives have been staged among musicians, teamsters, workers in the building trades, and in the motion-picture and other industries. The almost complete organization of all trades in the harbor district, San Pedro, has given the city's growing labor movement solid backing. A force to be reckoned with has been the rise of unions in the motion-picture industry. To the surprise of many who believed that movie people would never step out of their make-believe world, screen actors, writers, and directors became union members, though not without studio strikes of some duration.

The two big sections of the labor movement, AFL and CIO merged in 1955. The California State Federation of Labor and the State's CIO Council united in 1958 to form the California Labor Federation. Labor was considerably strengthened; the Federation has about 1,500,000 members and with the addition of the International Brotherhood of Teamsters and the International Brotherhood of Longshoremen's and Warehousemen's unions, both independent, union membership surpassed 1,800,000. The San Francisco Employers' Council was formed in 1938 and the Associated Farmers, Inc., at about the same time.

After the dislocation of workers by World War II had been overcome union labor extended its memberships and made steady gains in better wages, vacations with pay and fringe benefits. In the late 1950's and early 1960's there was a steady advance in memberships and benefits. Contracts providing vacations with pay covered 94% of California union workers in 1964, compared with 86% in 1961. The increase was due principally to vacation agreements in the construction industry. The largest groups of construction workers covered by contracts without paid vacations are the Teamsters, Laborers, and Electrical Workers in most southern counties. Most of the other union workers without paid vacations are fishermen, fruit and vegetable packers, actors, extras and other talent groups in motion pictures, and barbers. Of the workers 67% have contracts for three-week vacations, and 31% have four-week vacations, as against 19% in 1961. Eligibility (based on number of years served) also has been lowered. Five-week vacations have been obtained by more than 20,000 workers, especially in petroleum refining and rubber industries, and a small group obtained six-week vacations. With a few exceptions the agreements call for vacations with full pay.

By July, 1965, labor unions had reached a record high of 1,871,700 members, as reported by Ernest B. Webb, director of the Dept. of Industrial Relations. The year's gain was 47,600 members, a 2% jump that nearly matched the 2.7% rise in nonfarm employment. Manufacturing unions had picked up 13,400 members, despite a loss of 2,600 in food processing. Advances were most conspicuous in transportation equipment and ordnance, metals and machinery and paper and allied products. Membership in non-manufacturing locals sustained an 11-year advance, adding 34,200 to a high of 1,315,000. Only transportation and warehousing did not gain. Biggest increases were in government (up 11,200) and trade (up 7,500). The increase in government workers reflected the escalation in Vietnam and affected unions of Federal civilian employees in shipyards, depots and military hospitals.

Nearly one-fifth of the union members in industry are women— 359,200 out of 1,871,700. The largest proportion (244,300) is in non-manufacturing, such as trade, which has 60,300, and hotels and eating places, which have 54,700. There are 114,900 unionized women in manufacturing; the largest proportion, 36,100, in food and kindred products. Government work, which is attractive to women, has 27,200 union workers, about one-fifth of the total in this category.

The situation in the 1960 decade is reflected in these reports of the Division of Labor Statistics of the State Dept. of Industrial Relations:

In the five-county San Francisco-Oakland Metropolitan Area, union membership totaled 465,800 in July, 1965, 7,900 more than in the previous July. The membership rise of 1.7% took place while the non-agricultural work force rose 2.5%. Most of the added members, 7,400, were picked up in non-manufacturing industries. Building trades locals gained 3,600 members, and locals in trade, service industries, and government also recorded sizable gains.

Los Angeles County unions had 745,900 members in mid-1965, up 26,100 from mid-1964. The membership increase of 3.6% substantially exceeded a 1.9% rise in non-farm employment in the same period. Union gains were about equally divided between manufacturing and non-manufacturing industries. Factory locals added 13,300 members, with aircraft and ordnance accounting for two-thirds of the rise. Non-manufacturing locals gained 12,800 additional members, most of them in government, wholesale and retail trade, and motion picture production, theaters, and other entertainment.

Despite a 4.5% increase in non-farm employment, labor union membership in Orange County declined from 80,500 in July, 1964 to 79,600 in July, 1965. Building trades locals reported a net loss of 2,000 members, which was partially offset by moderate gains in public utilities, government, and other industries. Membership losses in the building trades were probably the result of cut-backs in residential construction. Orange County comprises the Anaheim-Santa Ana-Garden Grove Metropolitan Area.

Union membership in Santa Clara County (San Jose) stood at 90,800 in July, 1965, unchanged from 1964. Employment in the area rose 4.5% over the year. Unions lost 1,200 members in manufacturing, primarily in canning and in metals and machinery. Gains by non-manufacturing locals made up for the loss, with public utilities, trade, and government registering the biggest increases.

Membership in San Diego County labor unions totaled 74,800 in July, 1965, up 900 from the previous July. The 1.2% rise in membership was the first increase reported in this area in five years. Non-farm employment rose 3.3% during the period. Most of the membership gain was concentrated in non-manufacturing industries, with locals in government leading the way.

In manufacturing, there was a slight drop in the number of members.

Most of the loss took place in aircraft and ordnance, where employment also declined.

During the 1960's employment rose to a record of more than 7,000,000 persons, with unemployed around 350,000 and diminishing. The largest labor force, in manufacturing, accounted for one out of every ten jobs added in 1965. Manufacturing employed 1,408,000 in 1965, about 19,000 more wage and salary workers than in 1964. This was accounted for by a spurt in electronics, aircraft, missiles and instruments, and a revival of aerospace activities, which had been curtailed for two years.

Non-agricultural wage and salary workers averaged 5,774,500 during 1965, an increase of 189,900 jobs, or 3.4% over 1964. The 1964 gain was 3.3%. Government work, trade and services accounted for 80% of the new jobs. The growth of goverment jobs exceeded all other categories. With an average of 1,106,000 on the public payrolls, the increase had been 62,000, or about 6% in one year. One-half of the growth in public jobs represented expansion of public school staffs to cope with the larger enrollments. The Economic Opportunity Act of 1964 also was influential in this increase by supporting the Neighborhood Youth Corps and the Work-Study Program. The war in Vietnam halted the downtrend in Federal defense employment that had prevailed for two years.

Of durable manufacturing in California, one-fifth of the labor force is engaged in transportation equipment, in which aircraft leads. Food and kindred products top the non-durable manufacturing total. Vocational enrollment is moving up; in a recent tabulation the U. S. Dept. of Commerce counted 455,419 in California, 398,750 in Texas and 194,821 in New York. Aerospace research and development increased in 1965 after a two-year glide. In 1963 the National Science Foundation counted 172,800 scientists and engineers in California.

The sharpest conflicts since the revival of the West Coast labor movement in 1933-34 have developed out of what employers have termed the "inland march" of city trade unions. To meet it, the forces opposing unionism have systematized and extended their organization. Led by the Associated Farmers, Inc., representing the corporative farm interests of the State, they have induced a number of the valley towns to adopt anti-picketing ordinances. The Farmers' Transportation Association of Southern California, organized in 1938 in nine southern counties under the auspices of the Associated Farmers, announced its intention to maintain "the right of every man to work without being coerced into joining or not joining a union."

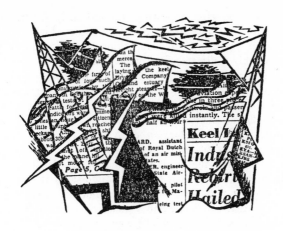

# Press, Radio and Television

"**T**RUE with his rifle, ready with his pen, and quick at the type case"—thus Walter Colton, American *alcalde* at Monterey, described California's pioneer journalist, Dr. Robert Semple, a buckskin-clad Kentucky emigrant, who stood 6 feet 8 inches in his stockings. On August 15, 1846, only a month after the American flag was raised at Monterey, Semple and Colton printed news of the United States' declaration of war on Mexico in the *Californian,* the first newspaper published within the State. "A crowd was waiting when the first sheet was thrown from the press," wrote Colton. "Never was a bank run upon harder; not, however, by people with paper to get specie, but exactly the reverse." For twelve and a half cents the customers got a single sheet a little larger than foolscap, printed half in English and half in Spanish.

A wooden, hand-operated Ramage press ran off this first issue. It had been manufactured in New York about 1800, shipped to Mexico City for use in the Mexican government printing office, and packed on mule-back to Monterey about 1834. Colton described the equipment as "old enough to be preserved as a curiosity; the mice had burrowed in the balls, there were no rules, no leads, and the types were rusty and all in pie." When he and Semple had cleaned the type, cut rules and leads out of a sheet of tin with a jack-knife, and hunted up part of a keg of ink, they were still faced by their worst problem—lack of paper. All that could be found was a small supply of the coarse stuff used to wrap cigarettes on board a coastwise sailing ship. It had to serve.

The *Californian,* after appearing intermittently for nearly a year, was moved, old press and all, to San Francisco. There, on May 22, 1847, the paper reappeared in competition with San Francisco's first journal, the weekly *California Star,* which the Mormon pioneer, Samuel Brannan, had established on January 9 of the same year.

Neither paper displayed any interest in what was perhaps the biggest news story in California history—James Marshall's discovery of gold at Coloma. "Great chances here for scientific capitalists," wrote Dr. Robert Semple in the *Californian* of March 15, 1848, seven weeks after the event, in a 67-word paragraph which chilled any possible excitement. Although the rival *Star* occasionally devoted its columns to unenthusiastic and somewhat technical discussions of gold during the next few weeks, it was word-of-mouth rumors of prospectors having "struck it rich" that convinced San Francisco's unscientific non-capitalists that Marshall's discovery might concern them too.

"All sham—a superb (*sic*) take-in, as was ever got up to guzzle the gullible," wrote the *Star's* acting editor, E. C. Kemble, on his return from a trip to the mines in April. Unluckily for Kemble, his boss, Sam Brannon, who had also gone out to investigate, appeared one day on Portsmouth Square flourishing a whisky flask full of gold dust and shouting, "Gold! Gold from the American Fork!" Even the most apathetic citizens were so fired by Brannan's dramatic proclamation that hundreds followed him back to the mine.

Before the stampede of readers—and even printers—San Francisco's two infant newspapers were helpless. The *Californian* suspended publication May 29. Two days earlier the *Star* had urged its readers: "Pay up before you go—everybody knows where. Papers can be forwarded to Sutter's Fort with all regularity. But pay the printer, if you please, all you in arrears." On June 4 it, too, ceased publication, and again California was without a single newspaper.

The gold rush, however, far from stifling journalism, fostered its growth. By August 1848 the *Californian* had resumed its career. It was bought the following month, together with the *Star,* by Kemble, who merged the two papers into one which he introduced November 18, 1848, as the *Star and Californian,* soon to be renamed the *Alta Californian.* So rapid was its growth that two years later it became a daily, and soon its publishers were printing it on a steam press. Enlisting the services of Mark Twain as a contributor and Bret Harte as an editor, it became—and for more than a generation continued to be—one of California's leading papers.

Meanwhile the creaking old Ramage press which had printed the original *Californian* had continued on its travels. Together with an assortment of old type and a lot of Spanish foolscap, it was shipped by Kemble up the Sacramento River to the settlement of New Helvetia (now Sacramento). It was set up in a makeshift office of adobe, wood, and cotton cloth, and on April 28, 1849 ran off the first weekly issue of the *Placer Times,* the Sacramento Valley's pioneer paper. Kemble soon lost his monopoly of the Sacramento news market, for on April 1, 1850 the Sacramento *Transcript* appeared and on August 3 of the same year the *Settler's and Miner's Tribune.* After a two-months championship of the Squatter's Association, however, the *Tribune* was buried in Sacramento's newspaper graveyard, the first of some 70 or 80 short-lived papers which started and discontinued publication during a period of 30 years.

Still farther into the interior, the pioneer Ramage press was packed to continue its newspaper-founding exploits. On July 4, 1850 it printed the Mother Lode's first paper, the Sonora *Herald.* It went on running off news of fights and gold until the fall of 1851, when it was moved to Columbia to print the Columbia *Star.* In most of the larger mining towns, newspapers were soon flourishing. Within ten years after the discovery of gold, Jackson and Marysville each had seven papers; Columbia, five; and Sonora, Mariposa, and San Andreas, three. Nor did all these die with the gold rush. Auburn's *Placer Herald* has been issued ever since 1852, and Downieville's *Mountain Messenger* since 1853.

Even in the sun-baked adobe village of Los Angeles, newspapers were making a place for themselves. The first paper was run off May 17, 1851 on a hand press brought around the Horn in a windjammer. This was the Los Angeles *Star* or *La Estrella de Los Angeles,* a four-page weekly, printed half in Spanish and half in English. So isolated was the sleepy pueblo that the *Star's* news, which often appeared as late as six weeks after the event, was news to nobody when it finally saw print. The uncertainties of waiting for the mail—once delivered as late as 52 days after leaving San Francisco—so disgusted the editor that eventually he gave up his job. The publishers of the *Southern Californian,* founded July 20, 1854, inherited an old font of Spanish type. They struggled along with it, substituting two "V's" for the missing letter "W" until a sailor who had heard of their hardships strolled in one day with news of a fine font of English type which he had seen in the Sandwich Islands (Hawaiian Islands). Overjoyed, they solved their difficulties by sending for it. An all-Spanish paper, *El Clamor Público,* began competing for the Spanish-speaking readers in June 1855.

San Diego, too, was by this time reading its pioneer paper, the *Herald,* established in May 1851. Many a chuckle must have escaped its subscribers when they read the writings of "John Phoenix," as the irrepressible wag and practical joker, Lieut. George H. Derby, called himself. This young Army officer, assigned to the job of diverting the San Diego River, which was silting up the bay, found San Diego such a dreary hamlet that he began writing for the *Herald* to relieve his boredom.    Derby perpetrated his most famous exploit when the paper's editor, confident of the victory of the Democratic ticket he had been supporting, entrusted Derby with the management of the paper while he spent a fortnight in San Francisco.    "John Phoenix" promptly reversed the *Herald's* politics.    Not content with attacking all the candidates his editor had been boosting, he eloquently sang the virtues of the rival Whigs.    His counter-campaign was so effective that the Whigs carried the election in San Diego County by a four-to-three majority—although the Democrats managed to carry the State.

Within eight years of the *Californian's* first appearance, 57 newspapers and periodicals within the State were serving an average total of 290,000 readers.    The dreams of sudden riches, with which the gold rush had fired men's minds everywhere had transformed California into one of the most important news markets of the world.    Now, as the scramble to lay hands on her wealth bred graft and political skulduggery, many of California's newly-born papers became the mouthpieces of the law-and-order citizenry and took the lead in crusades against corruption.    Their editors needed courage, for in those turbulent days the Colt revolver was deemed mightier than the pen.

Into the turmoil of San Francisco's early political strife stepped the most influential of the fighting editors, James King of William, who used that signature to distinguish himself from another James King. On October 8, 1855, he published the first number of his *Daily Evening Bulletin*.    He found much to attack, for San Francisco, after the spasmodic outburst of indignation which brought into being the Viligance Committee of 1851, had slipped back into lawlessness.    King's editorials slashed mercilessly at the unholy coalition of grafting officials, financial magnates, and gang leaders who were swindling the people through political power.    These were the forces, as King soon pointed out in his stinging attacks, that maintained a reign of terror, encouraging robbery and murder, in order to continue stuffing ballot boxes, fixing the courts, and plundering the treasury.    Not hesitating to print names, King boldly exposed a rogue's gallery of public enemies in high places. Within a year the *Bulletin* had out-stripped all other papers in the city, winning recognition as the foremost champion of the people's right.

The *Bulletin* charged, on May 14, 1856, that political boss James P. Casey was an ex-inmate of Sing Sing prison who "had stuffed himself through the ballot box . . . to the board of supervisors." On the afternoon of the same day, Casey shot and mortally wounded King.    Without hesitation Casey gave himself up at the police station, confident that his friends would protect him.    As King lingered between life and death, a second Vigilance Committee, led by some of the active members

1887 when young William Randoph Hearst took over his father's chaste and ultra-conservative San Francisco *Daily Examiner,* installed some of his college classmates on the staff, and began to publish California's first eight-page daily. Introducing to the Pacific Coast the "human interest" style popularized by Joseph Pulitzer's *World,* the *Examiner* not only presented in vivid prose the news of the day but investigated officials and spotlighted abuses. Its reporters were assigned to such spectacular stunts as testing the ferryboats' life-saving devices; one of them "fell" overboard, while others stood by with stop watches to time the rescue. Signed stories made their writers nationally famous. Circulation boomed, and the *Examiner* became the nucleus of the nation-wide Hearst chain. The *Examiner* in 1965 printed 300,000 copies mornings and 430,000 Sundays.

The fighting traditions of James King of William seemed to be reviving when Fremont Older, whom Oswald Garrison Villard called "one of the two first-rate journalists of the Pacific Slope," became editor of the San Francisco *Bulletin* in 1895. Entering vigorously into the struggle to oust the all-powerful Southern Pacific Railroad Co. from political control of the State, Older became one of the star figures —along with his famous fellow-Californian, Lincoln Steffens—of the muckraking era. In 1906 he joined the campaign to expose the graft ring headed by Mayor Eugene E. Schmitz and political boss Abraham Ruef which ruled from the City Hall. At the height of the campaign, when most of the other newspapers were attacking the graft prosecution with bitter invective, Older waged his fight so aggressively in the *Bulletin* that his enemies kidnaped him and carried him to Santa Barbara. A decade later, when he became convinced that District Attorney Fickert had used perjured evidence to convict Thomas J. Mooney and Warren K. Billings of the Preparedness Day bombing in 1916, Older published an extra edition of the *Bulletin* with the headline charging a frame-up in the case. This was the first time that the charge had been made by any disinterested person.

In 1909 the Los Angeles *Herald* began a reform crusade with a series of red-bordered articles entitled "Is Vice Protected in Los Angeles?" The movement thus initiated, which was soon joined by the Los Angeles *Evening Express,* the Fresno *Republican,* the Sacramento *Bee,* and the Oakland *Tribune,* strengthened a political revolt leading to formation of the anti-monopolist Lincoln-Roosevelt League. But in Los Angeles the crusade was suddenly swept into the background by the dynamiting of the *Times* building, on October 1, 1910. J. B. McNamara, secretary of the Structural Bridge and Iron Workers, and his brother were arrested and tried in a long-drawn-out court case which ended in the McNamaras' sudden and unexpected plea of guilty.

Although labor disavowed violence, Governor James N. Gillett said, "Whether guilty or not, labor unionists will have to be blamed for the crime until it is shown they are not guilty." The San Francisco *Daily News* vehemently sprang to the defense of the unions. This little four-page penny paper was started in 1903 in a shabby wooden house "south of the slot." The equipment was of the humblest—a few old chairs and tables, a decrepit linotype machine, and a press purchased from a Chinese newspaper. From the start it was a workingman's paper, costing but 25 cents a month. The guiding principle of the editor, William Wasson, to "cut every item to the bone but increase the number of items," made the writing admirably succinct. Greatly expanded, it became in 1921 a part of the Scripps-Howard chain.

Rising costs and sharper competition led to a consolidation of San Francisco newspapers. The *News* was combined with the *Call-Bulletin* in August, 1959, with both the Hearst and the Scripps-Howard interests represented in the *News-Call Bulletin*. On June 2, 1962, Scripps-Howard sold its share to Hearst Publications. The newspaper has a circulation of 180,000 copies.

The De Young family remains represented in the ownership of the San Francisco *Chronicle,* of which Charles de Young Thieriot is editor. It has a morning circulation of more than 350,000 and a Sunday edition of more than 370,000 copies. The Knowland family is in control of the Oakland *Tribune.* Joseph R. Knowland was president and publisher until his death, February 1, 1966, at the age of 92. William F. Knowland, former U. S. senator is editor and general manager, and J. W. Knowland is vice president. It has evening and Sunday editions and a weekday circulation of more than 200,000.

Los Angeles is the city of large circulations. The *Times* leads the field with more than 800,000 morning and 1,000,000 Sunday copies distributed. Its nearest competitor is Hearst Publications, with the *Herald Examiner*'s evening edition circulating 730,000 copies, and the Sunday edition 719,000.

In the 1960s five major Negro newspapers were published in California. The oldest is the Los Angeles *Eagle,* dating from 1879, and circulating more than 27,000 copies. Next largest is the Los Angeles *Sentinel,* with 12,500. The *Sun Reporter* of San Francisco prints 8,762 copies. Smaller organs are the Oakland *Voice* and the San Diego *Voice.* San Francisco Chinese began publishing the *Gold Hill News* in 1854 and citizens of Chinese background ever since have published their own news organs.

# RADIO

The first California radio station to broadcast the human voice, KQW of San Jose, was pioneering for the world, as well as for California, when it initiated in 1912 regular broadcasts of speech and music. KQW, operated by the Herrold Wireless Laboratories, had begun its experiments in 1909, broadcasting from a "carpet" antenna —11,000 feet of wire strung between two seven-story office buildings—connected with a crude arc transmitter. Three years later it again took the lead in the use of radio as an entertainment medium, when it began sending out the songs and ukelele tunes of two high school boys, Al and Clarence Pearce. The Government license granted KQW in 1912 was reputedly the first to be issued for actual radio telephony.

KQW was also a pioneer in developing the mechanics of radio. Dr. Charles D. Herrold's arc transmitter, the first improvement made on Marconi's equipment, was too high-powered for any microphone then in use; so Herrold constructed a microphone by hooking six telephone transmitter units to a single diaphragm. Using the antenna at Mare Island near San Francisco, Herrold's transmitter established in 1913 what was at the time a world's record for long-distance radio transmission, when its broadcast was tuned in by the army transport *Sherman,* 950 miles at sea. In the same year two-way communication over a distance of 250 miles was established between Mare Island and Point Arguello. Visitors to the Panama-Pacific Exposition at San Francisco in 1915 were thrilled at listening through ear phones to music broadcast by KQW from San Jose. Soon afterward, this station established two-way communication with KDN in San Francisco and opened a studio for the reception of daily concerts broadcast from the Fairmont Hotel—the first such receiving studio in the world.

Californians have been contributing their share of radio inventions ever since the days when crystal detectors and loose-coupler tuners comprised radio receiving equipment. The so-called "Father of Radio," Dr. Lee de Forest, began experimenting in 1912, at his laboratory in Palo Alto, with Audion tube "cascade" amplifiers. His success in amplifying signal strength led to perfection of the amplifying systems used in present-day transmission and reception. Ten years later the Magnavox loudspeaker, developed in Oakland, introduced for the first time the dynamic principle (moving coil in a magnetic field) which were adapted to loud-speakers on receiving sets.

Since 1922 many of radio's most popular forms of entertainment have been developed in California. The earliest "audience show" was KFRC's *Blue Monday Jamboree*, presented as an experiment to determine how the song-and-patter show could be given appeal for an air audience; its variety technique is still considered to have a more predictable popularity than any other type of radio entertainment. *One Man's Family*, inaugurated on KGO in 1932 was the first program to adapt radio's particularly intimate facilities to drama by using casual dialogue, unhurriedly delivered, to lend verisimilitude to the characters. One of the earliest of the hillbilly folk programs, *Mac's Haywire Orchestry*, was put together by a California cowboy, "Mac" McClintick, who assembled a quartet of guitar, harmonica, fiddle, and banjo ukelele. The latter was played by San Francisco's book critic, Joseph Henry Jackson, who began reviewing on the air in 1922 and has been succeeded by William Hogan. The first broadcast from an airplane was made in a Martin bomber, loaned by the U. S. Army, over Crissey Field, San Francisco. In July, 1925, KJBS pioneered mobile short-wave radiophone transmission by relaying the band music of California's Diamond Jubilee celebration. Broadcasts from the *Malolo* in 1931 were the first regularly scheduled programs from a ship at sea.

Since 1933 radio has leaned more and more heavily on motion picture personalities, a change that has emphasized the star system in radio entertainment and caused a westward shift in production. The shift began in 1933, when Rudy Vallee broadcast from an improvised studio on the RKO lot between scenes in his first motion picture. Commercial shows, though often financed, planned, and written in the East, were transferred to Hollywood because of its abundant facilities.

## TELEVISION

The coming of television in the 1940s was the next great change to affect radio. It linked radio with film and opened up an entirely new field for development. Technicians had talked about it for several decades and the principal patents had been obtained in 1934 by Philo Farnsworth and Vladimir Zworykin, Americans who had been working independently. When experiments indicated that it would prove to be practical radio corporations were dismayed at the estimates of costs, which seemed to be excessive. But the possibilities of television were so tremendous that American business turned to the new medium with confidence and allocated sums larger than any earmarked for publications or radio when the quick response of television audiences became evident.

The Federal Communications Commission authorized television

July 1, 1941, and about 10,000 sets were in use before Pearl Harbor. Commercial television was serviced from the Empire State Building, New York City. By 1944 color tubes were almost ready; Columbia Broadcasting System and Radio Corporation of America (NBC) were in hot competition and had practical results by 1946 and 1947. Columbia pioneered with a one-hour color program in 1951.

At first television programs originated in New York and it was believed that this immense new business of acting for TV would develop there. It was soon discovered that the facilities of Hollywood were superior and after video tape was introduced in 1955 it became the principal production center for television.

Closed-circuit television was introduced in 1947, when the world series baseball games in New York were sold to networks, which then charged a fee for showing in halls and bars. The original impact on small movie theaters was marked by lowered attendance. By 1965, when the Clay-Patterson boxing match at Las Vegas was thus exhibited interference with other programs was negligible. Closed-circuit television is used profitably for restricted routines such as surgery performed in a hospital. The proposal to sell programs free from advertising to the household has not made much progress.

National Educational Television (NET) feeds programs to three stations in San Francisco, Sacramento and Los Angeles. The Los Angeles station, KCET, opened in 1964 with auspicious backing, including grants from the Department of Health, Education & Welfare, the Ford Foundation, Metromedia, NBC and CBS. Educational television also is sponsored by colleges in San Bernardino, San Mateo, Santa Clara and San Jose.

Once means had been found to flash television across the nation its growth became phenomenal. The presence of cameras at horse races, national conventions, inaugurations, and disasters provided an immediacy in reporting that smashed all competitive efforts. Even the Aeronautics & Space Administration worked for the networks by making possible the Early Bird communications satellite. Advertising billing in 1965 reached approximately $1.6 billion. Columbia Broadcasting System in 1964 reported net earnings of $49,655,739. Unimagined wealth poured into the pockets of popular stars who often had their own producing units. Television studios in Hollywood became an object of pilgrimage and more than 1,000,000 persons visited a single center annually. Commercially Hollywood outranked any entertainment producing center in the world and one commentator described it as a bonanza second only to oil.

# The Movies

I T all began so suddenly—decorous suburban Hollywood must have felt that a strange new race had descended from the sky. One actress did alight from on high, unintentionally. She was Pearl White, heroine of thriller serials, who had been performing in a "prop" balloon before the cameras when it broke its moorings. She was rapidly drifting seaward until she pulled the rope that deflated it, landing herself—and so demonstrating the resourcefulness demanded of movie actresses in 1912.

Hazardous though life might be for performers in the "flickers," the trek to Hollywood had started. Any girl could get a job if she would ride along in the cab of a runaway locomotive—any man if he could shoot a rabbit from the back of a galloping horse. The next best thing, in 1912, was to be very tall or short or weigh 300 pounds or 30 or, at the very least, to resemble a tramp or a colonel or a duchess. The thrillers of those hectic days told their stories in the main titles: *The Outlaw and the Child, True Love Never Dies, Mary's Stratagem, A Good Turn, Her First False Step.* Most of them were advertised as having "a strong moral tone." They were expected to have, as well, plenty of excitement. As a director of the time expressed it: "Never mind the acting—we want *action!*"

The producers, working at the same speed as the characters in their dramas, never stopped to build a stage if they could rent a barn, or a dressing room if they could buy a tent. Behind the flimsy walls of the mushroom studios, Tom Mix and his director were vying with each other to invent stunts dangerous enough for their thrill-fed fans.

Custard pies were flying between Mack Sennett and Ford Sterling. Mae Marsh, in a voluminous grass skirt, was tempting Bobby Herron. Hollywood in 1912—a small town carnival!

A decade and a half before, the cinema industry had got under way on the other side of the continent in New York, where Thomas Alva Edison's kinetoscope made its first appearance on April 14, 1894. The spectators dropped a nickel in the slot and peeped into a cabinet. Two years later the first modern screen projector, Thomas Armat's vitascope, liberating the moving images from Edison's peepshow, began its commercial career at Koster & Bial's music hall in New York. To curious spectators the vitascope showed picture sequences of simple incidents: a snowstorm raging through a city, a policeman chasing a hapless tramp, a fire engine racing to a midnight alarm. Its audiences were amused, but as soon as the novelty wore off, they dropped away.

An Edison cameraman, Edwin S. Porter, had an idea: the motion picture should tell a story. The overwhelming success of his first film, *The Life of an American Fireman,* encouraged him to make others, of which *The Great Train Robbery,* released in 1903, was the classic. At first the films were exhibited by itinerant showmen on portable projectors, but on Thanksgiving Day, 1905, the first theater devoted exclusively to the showing of motion pictures opened in a Pittsburgh storeroom. The price of admission for the 15-minute program was a nickel, which gave rise to the name "nickelodeon." Soon scores of Bijoux, White Ways, Fairylands, and Lyrics appeared in eastern cities.

As the "flickers" grew in popularity the chief producers found it necessary to safeguard their claims to the promised profits. Since 1897 Edison had been suing them for pirating his patents. In defense they formed, in January 1909, the Motion Picture Patents Company, soon widely known as the "movie trust." Their airtight monopoly was threatened, however, by the small producers, exhibitors, and exchanges excluded from the trust, who began importing bootleg equipment and filming their pictures in obscure hide-outs. Against them the trust launched a battle of suits and injunctions, raids and riots. They fled— from one loft to another, to Florida, to Cuba, and finally, to California.

California had been claimed for the movies when William Selig, one of the "patent pirates" fought by Edison, skipped to Los Angeles in 1908 to complete a film began in his Chicago studio. His picture, *The Count of Monte Cristo,* was the first commercial film produced in the State. Two years passed before another picture was made in the West. By that time, the patents group were hounding the independent New York Motion Picture Company. The flight of this company to Los Angeles began a westward movement of independents and, eventually, of the trust companies themselves. They opened their studios in Los Angeles, Santa Monica, Glendale, and, finally, in Hollywood—where

David Horseley's Nestor Film Company of New Jersey settled in the autumn of 1911 to make Hollywood's first movie in a studio at Sunset Boulevard and Gower Street.

The arrival of the trust companies on the Coast brought the war with the independents to a new battleground—where the independents found two weapons which won them victory. The first was the "feature" picture; the second was the "star" system.

The "feature" picture—a film of more than one or two reels—was revolutionary in 1912. While France, Italy, and Germany were experimenting with the long film, the monopolistic Motion Picture Patents Company, controlled by financiers, had limited American pictures to two-reel elementary treatments of elementary concepts. There was no room in this production scheme for artistic experimentation. The independents, on the other hand—many of whom had been old-clothing, jewelry, and junk dealers—proved to be better showmen.

Adolph Zukor imported the first multi-reel picture, *Queen Elizabeth,* made in France in 1911 by Louis Mercanton with Sarah Bernhardt and Lou Tellegen. The enthusiasm of American audiences proved that they were ready for picture drama in the grand style. While other European features were being imported, American producers began getting their own long films ready for the market. The first gallant attempts included James Young's *Cardinal Wolsey* with Clara Kimball Young, and D. W. Griffith's *Judith of Bethulia* with Blanche Sweet. Within six years appeared other films that critics still remember with respect: Griffith's *The Birth of a Nation, Broken Blossoms,* and *Intolerance;* Sennett's *Tillie's Punctured Romance;* Lubitsch's *Carmen* starring Pola Negri; *The Squawman;* and Chaplin's *A Dog's Life.* In *The Birth of a Nation*—America's first super-feature—Griffith revolutionized production technique, creating a picture which attracted the attention of the intelligentsia to the cinema for the first time in this country. The picture rolled up an astounding box-office record; though the validity of its characterization has since been questioned, it still plays occasionally in the world's out-of-the-way places. During this period the trust, persisting on the whole with mass-produced short films, languished.

As Zukor, onetime furrier, introduced the full length picture, so Carl Laemmle, onetime clothing dealer, introduced the star system. The patents trust, pursuing a mass production policy, had paid the screen player very low wages, assuming that the public would let him remain as anonymous as a bookkeeper. But Carl Laemmle, one of the trust's shrewdest foes, noted that patrons were asking at the box office when "the cute little girl with the curls" would appear again; and so he hired the cute little girl from Biograph at double her former salary. She was Gladys Smith—better known by the name of the character she had played in Biograph pictures, "Little Mary." As Mary Pickford, she was presently receiving $10,000 a week in salary and half the profits on her pictures.

At about the time the little girl with the curls was attracting notice, a young player deserted an English music hall company to work in Mack Sennett's Keystone Comedies at $150 a week. His shoes and small moustache, his talent for getting into pathetically funny situations, and his genius for expressing himself through simple gestures soon made Charlie Chaplin a universally beloved character. Producers scrambled for him, the successful bidder paying him $150,000 for signing a contract which guaranteed him $10,000 a week.

Now picture patrons were demanding not only feature pictures, but "stars." The names of Marguerite Clarke, Blanche Sweet, Pauline Frederick, Theda Bara, William Farnum, Tom Mix, Anita Stewart, Alice Joyce, Earle Williams, William S. Hart, Norma and Constance Talmadge, Lillian and Dorothy Gish, Mae Marsh, Harold Lockwood, and May Allison went up in marquee lights. Many of these players came to the films from the shipping rooms and offices of large cities, others from small town beauty contests and midwestern farms. Many had no previous dramatic training of any sort, and some never found it necessary to acquire any. Some built hillside mansions with swimming pools, and Japanese gardens; hired armies of servants, agents, and secretaries; gave parties which lasted for days, stirring the talk of the Nation. Some saved their money, helped their relatives, and retired wealthy and happy; others died early of drink and drugs; others faded back into obscurity. All of them in their hour of glory were sent fan mail by the carload and mobbed by hysterical crowds at docks and railroad stations.

The introduction of movie cycles accompanied the rise of movie stars. *Traffic in Souls* inspired a series of "daring" exposés; *The Miracle Man* was responsible for a cycle of heavily moralistic pictures; *The Spoilers,* for two-fisted Northwesterns; *Passion,* for costume films. *Over the Hill* started a race for the profits to be made on mother love. While critics pleaded for originality—and continued pleading for two decades—successive themes were milked: desert love, crime, war, aeronautics, exploration, the private lives of royalty and geniuses, the gaiety of the nineties. The 1930's brought in cycles of adaptations of Victorian novels, Shakespearean dramas, musical farces, and comedies.

The years from 1912 to 1920 passed without radical improvements in mechanical methods—although cameramen perfected the dissolve, the fade, double exposure, and the close-up—but not without an important change in the industry's financial structure. The World War had ended the competition of European film companies, leaving the huge and growing market to the American producers. The conservative patents trust let this opportunity escape, and the independents through superior showmanship won by 1930 control of the industry—an industry of world-wide proportions which had grown in a single decade into one of the United States' ten largest.

The independent producers began at once to exhibit imagination and initiative—as well as partiality for the grandiloquent. They enlarged the studios and gave them ornate facades. Dozens of new stages were constructed, many vast enough to house skating rinks in one end and ballrooms in the other. Outgrowing the informality of the early years—when householders were generally glad to lend their fishponds for the swimming party in Mabel Normand's latest farce—they built their own sets. One producer erected a range of lath-and-plaster mountains, and another, a canvas desert diorama half-a-mile in length, while Paramount built a full-size steamship to lie forever at anchor on the lot. Million-dollar "prop" and wardrobe departments were organized. Every studio amassed its library. One acquired a zoo. And each opened a laboratory for developing a new art—that of illusion. Here ingenious craftsmen built miniature models of clippers and cathedrals, painted foregrounds on glass, engineered filming of underwater scenes on dry land through a thin tank of moving water, and discovered an effective imitation fog in sprayed mineral oil. Studio staffs were augmented by architects, decorators, gag men, publicity writers, script girls, couturiers, research directors, and technical experts.

As expansion of the industry attracted new thousands to Hollywood, until the crowds outside the casting offices overflowed the streets and "still pictures" overflowed the files inside, the studios formed the Central Casting Bureau. Within a short time 10,000 would-be stars had applied. A clearing house for extras, "Central Casting" began filling the studios' daily talent needs. For each registered applicant was assembled a record of physical characteristics—height, weight, color and type of hair, color of eyes, and health; abilities—driving a car, swimming, diving, dancing, riding; history—former residence, marital status, court record (if any), income from other sources. A complete inventory of the applicant's wardrobe with the interviewer's critical comments went into the file, and finally the answer to the question: Can the applicant act? Only a few dozen were able to make an adequate living. In 1928 and 1929, with production at its height, but 194 registered extras worked two days or more a week. Fifty-four of these were women, whose incomes averaged $14.25 weekly. The men earned $14.52 weekly.

Meanwhile the industry's expenditures, if not the wages paid the extras, were mounting dizzily. Salaries kept pace with expansion as studio executives paid themselves up to $500,000 a year and their top flight stars even more. If Hollywood in 1912 was a carnival, by 1925

# Education

UNIVERSITY OF CALIFORNIA, BERKELEY
New Student Union and Sproul Hall (Administration Building) in foreground; University Library, center; Sather Tower and Berkeley Hills

BERKELEY CAMPUS, UNIVERSITY OF CALIFORNIA, AT DUSK
LeConte Hall (Physics) and Campbell Hall (Mathematics-Astronomy)
in foreground. San Francisco Bay in distance.

MAIN REFERENCE ROOM, UNIVERSITY LIBRARY, BERKELEY

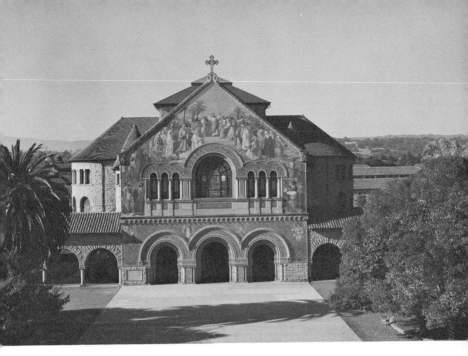

MEMORIAL CHURCH, STANFORD UNIVERSITY

TRESIDDER MEMORIAL UNION, STANFORD UNIVERSITY

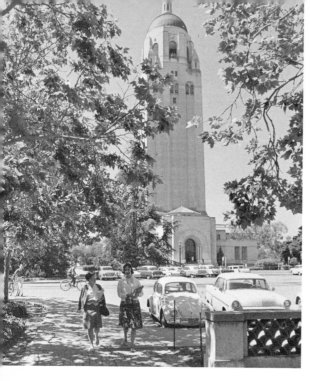

HOOVER INSTITUTION ON WAR, REVOLUTION AND
PEACE, STANFORD UNIVERSITY

PHYSICS LECTURE HALL, STANFORD UNIVERSITY

BEVATRON, LAWRENCE RADIATION LABORATORY, BERKELEY

ION LINEAR ACCELERATOR,
LAWRENCE RADIATION LABORATORY, BERKELEY

MUSIC HALL, POMONA COLLEGE, CLAREMONT

OCCIDENTAL COLLEGE, LOS ANGELES

OBSERVATORY DOME, PALOMAR MOUNTAIN,

STATE COLLEGE AT FULLERTON, ARCHITECT'S DRAWING

OLD SCHOOLHOUSE, RESTORED, CALICO

it resembled an extravaganza, mad and merry. In one picture the star wore a $30,000 chinchilla coat; since it could never be used again, of course, the fur was cut up and sewed on bathing suits. Greta Garbo was reported to be getting 90,000 fan letters every month.

Lavish too were the pictures of this decade in conception, plot, and background. In 1920 audiences were impressed by *Way Down East* and in 1921 by *The Three Musketeers.* In the five years following they were successively staggered by *Robin Hood, The Covered Wagon, Scaramouche, The Hunchback of Notre Dame, The Iron Horse, The Ten Commandments, The Merry Widow, Beau Geste,* and by *Ben Hur,* which took three years to film and cost more than $4,000,000. Producers hoped the public would be staggered. Actually, there were dawning signs of boredom. The public was giving unanimous approval to an unpretentious little film called *Nanook of the North,* to the slow-paced, realistic *A Woman of Paris,* and—strangest of all—to the German film *The Last Laugh,* a simple story about the heartbreak of a doorman.

During these years the producers were expanding in still another direction, the ownership of theaters. Chains were organized and battles fought for the control of first-run houses. In an effort to eliminate all competition, the producers bought hundreds of legitimate theaters and either dismantled them or remodeled them for screen showings. A public that had been devoted to its stock, its big and small time vaudeville, and its weekly visits from touring companies began making its choice in theatrical entertainment among the productions of Universal, Paramount, Fox, Warner Brothers, Metro-Goldwyn-Mayer.

The general extravagance required money, money required bankers, bankers demanded boards of hard-headed directors. And so it happened that the one-time independents, grown powerful (Adolph Zukor, Carl Laemmle, William Fox, Sam Goldwyn, and others), now found themselves taking orders from Wall Street. Under banker control began an effort to wed efficiency and showmanship. Stage producers had always recognized it as the very essence of harlequinade to be spontaneous, unpredictable—but now Pierrot was regimented. Sharp eyes in New York grew very sharp indeed when they read that Erich von Stroheim kept 5,000 extras waiting all day in a square while he rehearsed an actress in the grand manner of royalty descending from a coach. Over the stages hung the smoke of the battle between showmen and efficiency experts.

In this decade it was a mechanical invention that caused the inevitable upheaval. Agents of the Bell laboratories were knocking on producers' doors in 1925 with a device for synchronizing the images of the projector with the sounds of a talking machine, but with box office returns bad and getting worse, the picture executives shook their heads.

Finally the salesmen took their device to Warner Brothers, a second-string studio which had fallen behind in the theater-building race. The Warners were desperately interested and, after a demonstration, hopeful. In April 1926 they formed the Vitaphone Corporation for sound experimentation and production. *Don Juan,* their first full-length picture with recorded musical accompaniment, caused a stir. Soon after the release in 1927 of *The Jazz Singer,* starring Al Jolson, the public began to demand sound films.

By autumn of 1929 the talkie trend had become a stampede. In the scramble to revamp production methods, First National was absorbed by Warner Brothers, and William Fox—himself a pioneer in the talkie field—was forced into retirement. Other major producers survived, but not all their studio personnel. Writers and directors of "silent days" were scrapped along with equipment and techniques, while strange new faces—song writers and musicians hustled out from New York's Tin Pan Alley—began appearing on the lots. Old acting favorites who lacked the pleasing voice which talkies demanded quietly disappeared, and new stars rose in their places.

From the talkie revolution the movie industry went into the depression of the 1930's, a crisis that affected mechanical techniques, production methods, financial structures, and even the type of entertainment.

In the effort to attract depression audiences, perfection of the color process was speeded. *The Toll of the Sea,* one of the early experiments in color, was filmed in 1921, though not very satisfactorily, since the blues failed to register. Later Jack Warner had experimented with color somewhat more successfully in *The Desert Song* and *On With the Show. Becky Sharp,* produced by an affiliate of the Technicolor Corporation, demonstrated the possibilities in color movies but was itself a failure. But the appeal of color in films continued, especially after the experimenters realized that it would become the next commercial asset. The Technicolor Corporation held the principal patents and so perfected its product that motion picture studios leased its methods for their big features. Production of color films is complicated by the necessity of shooting them on three negatives. Besides the color cameras, a staff of experts is required to harmonize settings and costumes and plan lighting. Actors must be found who are handsome even without much makeup.

Walt Disney, the most resourceful figure in the development of the animated cartoon, contracted with the corporation in 1934 to make his Mickey Mouse and Silly Symphonies cartoon films in color. He began work the same year on the first feature-length animated cartoons, *Snow White and the Seven Dwarfs.* A new type $75,000 camera was employed to lend a three-dimensional illusion to the 250,000 separate paintings which went into the making of the film. Three years later, when *Snow White* was released, audiences delighted in the large surfaces of rich, clear color. In no previous cartoon film had there been such successful treatment of running water, clouds, dust, steam, and the glint of sunlight on a steel blade. The success of *Snow White* and *Bambi* demonstrated the possibilities in the color medium. An experimenter with a genius for making a success of innovations, Walt Disney built an organization that poured vitality into motion pictures. From cartoons he moved to extravaganza, studies of animal life, voyaging far afield. Building on romance and fantasy he gave substantial form to make-believe.

The end of the fourth decade finds the industry's use of illusion developed to extraordinary lengths. Window glass is generally made of rock candy; stones of tar paper, balsa wood, and cork; snow of gypsum and bleached corn flakes; icicles of fibre hair dipped in plaster of Paris. Strawberry gelatine is the usual substitute for blood. Since about 80 percent of all pictures are shot indoors on the studio stages, the prop shop must stock many sorts of artificial flowers and trees. (One studio had enough daisies to cover a ranch meadow and apple blossoms for 28 trees.) Each studio has a library of sound effects and the equipment for producing them.

The studio lots of today combine the efficiency of the factory with the irrationality of the theater. A small town in itself, each studio has its network of paved streets, lined with stucco buildings that house the various departments—the huge stages, the prop warehouses, the carpenter and machine shops. In the shadow of a planing mill may stand a star's "quaint" dressing room, and behind the barnlike structure that houses the wardrobe, a piece of Venice, complete with canal, gondolas, and flower-strewn balconies.

Perfection of mechanical technique and streamlining of picture production are two of the industry's answers to depression problems. Another answer has been the general improvement in the quality of entertainment.

Some producers, believing that audiences wanted to forget their troubles, gave them farces; others became aware of a plea, grown more insistent, for realism. "Authentic," "natural," "unexaggerated"—during the thirties these adjectives were heard, almost for the first time, at studio conferences. As a result, fans have had the pleasure of giving box-office laurels to such lifelike films as *I Am a Fugitive from a Chain Gang, Of Human Bondage, The Informer, Dead End,* and *It Happened One Night.* And even the romantic films have achieved greater fidelity to essential truth and significance of theme.

During World War II the movie industry quickly seized the opportunity to exploit patriotism and courage, portray the rapacity of the enemy and report, with greater freedom than ever before, the work of the enlisted men and the activities of the home front. The Goverment welcomed the cooperation of the industry and opened channels for reporting the war. Activities of the Army, Navy, Marines, Air Corps and Coast Guard were shown.

Of films based on incidents of the war *Mrs. Miniver* won an Academy award for Greer Garson and MGM. Others relating to the war were Chaplin's *The Great Dictator, Mission to Moscow, Days of Glory, From Here to Eternity, This Land of Mine, The Story of GI Joe, A Walk in the Sun,* and *The Diary of Ann Frank.* In 1946 Fredric March and Sam Goldwyn (RKO) won an Academy award with *The Best Years of Our Lives.* But audiences will never forget two outstanding films based on war themes: James Michener's *South Pacific* as interpreted by Rodgers and Hammerstein, and *The Bridge on the River Kwai.*

During the war writers had a choice of villains among Nazi Germans and Japanese, but anti-discrimination laws and the need for markets abroad limited the use of foreign types; the studios had to fall back on the average American-born white for skulduggery. Communists were still fair game, especially when detective stories, always popular, gained a new impetus with *The Spy Who Came in from the Cold.* The exploits of Ian Fleming's resourceful James Bond in spectacular splashes of color in *Doctor No, From Russia With Love, Goldfinger* and *Thunderball,* in which melodrama was mixed with pulchritude, proved to have tremendous box-office appeal in the 1960 decade and rolled up millions for their producers. They started dozens of imitations on screen and television. Next to Cinderella the sleuth is the most popular character in motion pictures, and the spy is simply the detective in international intrigue, making use of violence far surpassing that of a western desperado.

Movie scenarios continued to find themes in topical events, but by the 1960s they dealt more frequently than ever with abnormal human behavior. The rise in prestige of Italian and Swedish film makers encouraged exploitation of marital and extra-marital situations and soon Hollywood, encouraged by court decisions in favor of free speech, was making films about dope addicts, libertines and sexual frustration. The Will Hays code, which the producers had established for their own protection against boards of censorship, was losing force. When the U. S. Supreme Court denied the right of New York State to ban *The Miracle,* restrictions on religious themes were practically eliminated.

Some of the films that dealt with aberrations of human conduct were *The Snake Pit, The Man With the Golden Arm, Baby Doll, Blackboard Jungle, Rebel Without a Cause* and *The Moon Is Blue.* Writers hit anti-Semitism in *Gentlemen's Agreement;* politics was a base for *State of the Nation* and the award-winning *All the King's Men;* the psychopathic detective appeared in the writings of Dashiell Hammett and

Raymond Chandler. Dick Powell became a national favorite in portraying the lackadaisical sleuth in *The Thin Man,* a characterization that was still on television in 1966, as was a watered down version of Sherlock Holmes. There was a psychological thriller in *Angel Street* and psychopathic evidence in *The Lost Weekend.* Among the earliest films to deal with discrimination against the Negro were *Home of the Brave* and *Lost Boundaries.*

At the same time films depicting more conventional forms of entertainment had commendable successes, among them *The King and I, The Pajama Game,* and *The Solid Gold Cadillac.*

During these post-war decades the authority of the studio, with its hordes of consultants and advisers, was weakened by the rise of independent producers and the impact of strong-minded individuals on their productions—men like Elia Kazan, John Huston and Otto Preminger. The need to economize had something to do with this, for much of the high cost was the result of oversized staffs. In 1948 a great many employees had been dropped, but top executives and popular actors were not affected; the saying went that only those earning less than $1,500 a week were fired. In this year financing experienced a setback; the Federal Government enforced the Sherman Anti-Trust Act and ordered producing corporations to divest themselves of their theaters.

When television became practical families discovered that they did not need to leave their own living rooms for entertainment. As a result thousands of neighborhood theaters closed. For a time it appeared that the golden age of motion pictures was over. Then producers decided to compete with the musicals and dramas of the living stage. It took courage and costly financing, but proved profitable in one of the most famous of long-run pictures in color, *Gone With the Wind,* which won an Academy award in 1939. Selznick International found itself well compensated for its daring, for the film made the rounds of the earth numerous times and wiped out its huge expenses. This also was one of the successful tests of Technicolor.

Producers now concentrated on long, expensive films such as Metro-Goldwyn-Mayer's *Ben Hur* and Cecil B. DeMille's *Ten Commandments.* With the aid of color the camera swung over oceans, mountains and lands with strange habitations and startling customs. *Around the World in Eighty Days* and *Cleopatra* proved successful despite an unprecedented outlay; *Mutiny on the Bounty,* a new version of an older story, had hard going, chiefly because MGM had subsidized a whole colony of actors and technicians in remote places. But the immense popularity of the Academy-award winner, *The Sound of Music,* which cost far less, proved that a film story, properly presented, could compete with both television and live theater. This was further proved by that international bonanza, *My Fair Lady.*

Hollywood passed another milestone in 1952 when Cinerama arrived, using Fred Waller's triple camera effects, followed quickly by other experiments. The attempt to realize three dimensions by providing spectators with colored eyeglasses failed, but Twentieth Century-Fox scored when *The Robe* was shown on wide screen by CinemaScope, and Todd-AO added to the success of *Around the World in Eighty Days*.

Popular comedians and singers held their popularity through the changing decades. Jack Benny, Bob Hope, Bing Crosby, Frank Sinatra, Groucho Marx, Lucille Ball and many others grew wealthier with the decades. Huge salaries were earned by actresses such as Elizabeth Taylor; only death stopped the dazzling career of Marilyn Monroe. By 1966 Cecil B. DeMille, Clark Gable, Humphrey Bogart and Louis B. Mayer were gone from the Hollywood scene, but the golden moon with the dollar sign shone more brightly than ever.

# *Education*

FRANCISCAN friars, the first white settlers who plodded northward into California, came with books in their hands, for the
purpose of their pilgrimage was to educate the heathen Indians.
Their pioneer successors—fur trappers and gold miners—were often
men of action rather than learning, but they had an extraordinary
respect for the wealth bound between the covers of books. With
first-hand knowledge of the many miles from California to the older
institutions of learning in New England and Europe, they voted generous expenditures for schools.

For California's native Indians, five decades of rigorous training—
planned to make them civilized tax-paying subjects of the Spanish
king—were in store when the Franciscan missionaries arrived in the
spring of 1769. Beyond manual and religious training they did not
aspire, however. Mission authorities feared the growth of learning
among the Spanish, as well as the Indian population, claiming that
education had no purpose but to breed discontent in the common people.
They excommunicated two of the province's most illustrious citizens,
Juan Bautista Alvarado and Mariano G. Vallejo, for reading Jean
Jacques Rousseau.

The first efforts to found secular schools were made by the Spanish
Governor, Diego de Borica (1794-1800). During his administration,
schoolmasters—mostly retired soldiers who could wield the *disciplinas*
(cat-o'-nine-tails) began teaching reading, writing, and figuring in
one-room schools at San Jose, Santa Barbara, San Francisco, San Diego,
and Monterey· No sooner had Borica left the territory, however, than

his educational system collapsed. The schools established during the next thirty years were also short-lived.

Governor José Figueroa (1833-1835) reported, soon after his arrival, that only three schools were in existence, taught by incompetent and ill-paid teachers; he established six more schools and ordered higher salaries for the teachers. Juan Bautista Alvarado (1836-1842) imported teachers from Mexico to give instruction in reading, writing, arithmetic, and the catechism; girls were also taught needlework and boys typesetting and printing. Attendance was compulsory for children between the ages of six and eleven. The schools were handicapped by their lack of funds and equipment. Despite the meager opportunities and the opposition of most of the clergy, some of the more ambitious sons of the land-owning families acquired a fair classical education, but only with the private tutoring of educated military officers, foreigners, or priests.

The American immigrants of the 1840's followed eastern and mid-western rather than Californian precedents in education. In December 1864 California's first American school was founded—in a dilapidated structure, once a stable, on the grounds of Mission Santa Clara. Here an overland immigrant, Mrs. Olive Mann Isbell, taught two dozen pupils, sitting on boxes around a fire in the center of the earthen floor. In the following year a schoolroom was equipped with desks and benches in the Monterey customhouse, and Mrs. Isbell tried to teach 56 scholars, although she could speak no Spanish and they no English. San Francisco's first American school was opened April 3, 1848 in a redwood schoolhouse on Portsmouth Square. The building was also used for town hall, court house, church and jail. The schoolmaster, Thomas Douglass, a Yale graduate, began with a class of six pupils which soon increased to 38, but six weeks later the gold rush excitement swept him off to the mines. On April 8, 1850 the first free public schools were established by an ordinance of the city council in San Francisco. This was California's first public school ordinance.

The educational needs of children in mining towns, lumber camps, ports, and rural villages were recognized by the State when California's first constitution provided, that a school "be kept up in every school district at least three months in every year." Fabulous revenues were expected from the sale of Federal Government land grants, "inviolably appropriated to the support of the common schools"; but since the total proceeds from grants of 500,000 acres were only about $250,000, that early ambition had to be curtailed. Gradually State school legislation was extended until by 1860 it provided for levying of city and school district taxes, appointment or election of county and city school superintendents and city boards of education, and authorization of boards of examination to grant teachers' certificates. Finally, in 1866, California's legislators adopted the Revised School Law, drafted by the far-seeing superintendent of public instruction, John Swett, which fixed State and county school taxes at adequate levels and established district school libraries, county teachers' institutes, and city boards of examination. For the first time in the State's history, public schools—in rural as well as urban areas—were free for every child.

The State's first colleges were established almost as early as its first public schools. Santa Clara College (now the University of Santa Clara), founded by Jesuit Fathers Giovanni Noboli and Michele Accolti, and California Wesleyan College (now the College of the Pacific at Stockton), founded by the Reverend Isaac Owen of the Methodist Episcopal Church, were both opened at Santa Clara in 1851. A year later the town of Benicia welcomed girls, who came to attend opening classes of the Young Ladies' Seminary. Southern California's first institution of higher learning, St. Vincent's College (now Loyola University), was opened in Don Vincente Lugo's adobe home on the Los Angeles Plaza in 1865 by Fathers of the St. Vincent de Paul Mission.

The first State constitution called for establishment of a State university to promote "literature, the arts, and sciences." But the nucleus of the University of California was a private institution, known at first as Contra Costa Academy and later as the College of California. Opened by the Reverend Henry Durant at Oakland in 1853, it began collegiate instruction in 1860. On March 23, 1868, Governor Henry H. Haight signed the legislative act creating the University of California. The institution was formally opened September 23 of the next year on the College of California's campus. In 1873, the year in which the first 12 graduates ("the twelve disciples") received their diplomas, the university moved to its present site on the slopes of the Berkeley hills.

Although the first public high school was opened in San Francisco in 1856, the legislature declined to support secondary institutions for more than half a century. The more thickly settled communities were obliged to conduct high schools at their own expense. In 1884 the University of California inaugurated the "accrediting system," which admits pupils with excellent high school records to the university without examination. The result of university supervision under this system was to raise secondary school standards to a uniformly high level. Finally, in 1903, the legislature amended the school law by passage of an act providing for State support of high schools.

The legislature in 1907 authorized high school boards to prescribe postgraduate courses of study. First to take advantage of the new regulation was Fresno, followed soon by Los Angeles and Santa Barbara. By 1910 the number of these "upward extensions of high schools" had grown to ten. A law enacted in 1917 recognized junior colleges as an integral part of the State's secondary school system. Today California has 76 such institutions.

Colleges as well as high schools multiplied in the late nineteenth century. The University of Southern California, founded under the auspices of the Methodist Episcopal Church in 1880, has grown into an institution with 18,000 students and 1,000 teachers. Others in Southern California were Pomona College (now a unit of Claremont Colleges, Inc.), Occidental College, Whittier College, the University of Redlands, and the California Institute of Technology. Leland Stanford Junior University, wealthiest privately endowed university in the West, was opened at Palo Alto in 1891. It is now called Stanford University. Public normal schools were established in 1862.

The State Superintendent of Public Instruction is elected every four years and is not allied with any political party. He is chief administrative officer of the State Dept. of Education and executive officer of the State Board of Education. The State Board has charge of educational policies for all schools except the University of California, State Colleges and private schools. Its members are appointed by the Governor and confirmed by the Senate and it determines the policies of the State Dept. of Education. Among other tasks, it selects the textbooks that are distributed free in the elementary schools. The State Department controls the public school system, except for the University and the State colleges.

The enactments of 1927 established the State Dept. of Education in a form modified in 1947 and 1961. It has six administrative units: (1) the Division of Libraries, headed by the State Librarian, appointed by the Governor; (2) the Division of Special Schools and Services, providing support for the residential schools for the deaf, blind and cerebral palsied, and programs for the handicapped; (3) the Division of Higher Education, which supervises junior college and adult education, and post-high school education in private schools, looks after teacher education and supply and combats discrimination; (4) the Division of Instruction, which coordinates and improves instruction and deals with specialized subjects and State-Federal vocational programs—it administers the National Defense Education Act, to stimulate education in science, mathematics and foreign languages, teacher education and research; (5) the Division of Public School Administration, which looks after material interests such as buildings, textbooks, lunch programs, training and finance—in 1962-63 it apportioned $761,000,000 in state funds to elementary and secondary schools; (6) the Division of Departmental Administration, which provides executive, accounting, research and legal services to the Department; it also supervises the California Maritime Academy.

On October 31, 1964, enrollment in all regular grades and special classes was 4,925,615, an increase of 224,579 (4.8 percent) over the year before. This was slightly below the increase of 1962, which was 250,503 (5.6 percent). Enrollment in grades nine through twelve also showed a slight change; in the 1963 report they increased 8.8 percent, but in 1964 grew 4.8 percent. Junior colleges showed an increase of 15 percent in 1964, as against 11.8 in 1963. There were 60,697 pupils on half-day sessions, a drop of 11,876 from the previous year.

In 1938 the State was spending $135,000,000 on its public schools. In 1960-61 it appropriated $1,518,184,029 for this purpose; in 1962-63 the appropriation had risen to $1,800,196,193.

An indication of the task facing boards of education in the large cities is the attendance figures for their public schools. The Los Angeles School System, which takes in almost twice as much territory as the City of Los Angeles, in a recent year enrolled 756,510 students, 356,988 of them in the elementary grades. It spends $35,000,000 a year for new schools and additions to existing schools.

In accepting and applying the newer conceptions of education, California has kept pace with the rest of the country and in some respects stepped ahead. Even in early days, the California high school teacher of mathematics was likely to stress the value of original demonstrations, while California high schools led from the beginning in adoption of laboratory methods in teaching natural sciences. Today California's public schools teach scientific subjects integrated into the social studies unit in the elementary grades. Groups of high school students have built and are operating a seismological station, school weather stations, astronomical observatories, radio stations, and recording studios.

The general tendency to emphasize functional knowledge has been marked in the State. The department of education's commission for vocational education directs an extensive vocational training program in agriculture, business, homemaking, trade and industry, and vocational rehabilitation. Its bureau of agricultural education, in 1935-36, was supervising 137 vocational agricultural departments in the schools and a teacher-training course. The bureau of business education oversees courses of training adjusted to the needs of merchants and businessmen, in which specially selected students are taught. Among the many practical subjects taught in high schools are classes in homemaking, for boys as well as girls, under supervision of the bureau of homemaking education. The bureau of trade and industrial education supervises apprentice training programs, organizes trade advisory committees of employer, employee, and public school representatives in many communities, and conducts State-wide conferences of foremen, personnel managers, sales managers, and other executives.

In the California Polytechnical Institute at San Luis Obispo, established in 1901, agriculture students conduct their own farm enterprises and aeronautics students operate a Government-approved commercial airplane repair station. The California Maritime Academy trains personnel for the coast's merchant marine. Three months nautical courses have been given in the past on such well-known sailing vessels as the *Tusitala* and the *Joseph Conrad*.

In carrying out the new curriculum, California schools have taken advantage of the State's many opportunities for outdoor play to stress their physical training and recreation programs. During the four depression years, 1932-1936, more gymnasiums, tennis courts, playgrounds, and swimming pools were constructed than in any previous four-year period. The recreation program is supplemented in many schools by health supervision. Both the construction and the recreation programs were conducted largely with the aid of the Government's Works Progress Administration before World War II.

The Co-ordinating Council has been operating in California cities for nearly fifty years. The plan sets up a voluntary board of members from school, police, health, and recreation departments, welfare societies, and research and guidance bureaus, to pool ideas, information, and mutual support in all matters pertaining to the welfare of youth. Not only are problem children given understanding aid, but also the gifted are sought out and provided with special opportunities. The work of California's coordinating councils, particularly those in Berkeley, San Francisco, and Los Angeles, has so materially decreased juvenile delinquency that scores of communities in other States have organized similar bodies. In fact the National Committee on Crime Prevention reported: "Your Committee believes that there is no other single step that could be put into operation that would be as far-reaching and as quickly beneficial as the widespread use of the coordinating council."

The handicapped child in California, if completely disabled, is taught at home or in a hospital or preventorium; if crippled, he is transported to special classes; if handicapped by vision, hearing, or speech defects he receives remedial instruction. California was one of the first states with a program of speech correction.

The growth of the University of California is an example not merely of students crowding into its halls but of an enlightened plan to meet educational needs of the future. In 1938 the University had 25,806 students; in 1965 and 1966 it had more than 60,000 full-time students and a faculty of more than 13,000; part-time students were more than 36,000, raising the total of those attending this educational system to nearly 100,000. The University confers nearly 12,000 degrees on all levels, about two-thirds of them baccalaureate. With Berkeley as its base, the University has developed its great plant at Los Angeles (UCLA) attended by more than 20,000 students. It started as the Southern Branch in 1919, received its present title in 1927 and added the Medical Center there in 1946. The original Medical Department in San Francisco has been developed since 1873 and is now the San Francisco Medical Center. The Davis campus, a farm in 1905 and then part of the College of Agriculture, became a rounded institution in 1959. The Citrus Experiment Station at Riverside (1907) had a College of Letters and Science added in 1954 and became a general campus in 1959. The Scripps Institution at La Jolla, with a School of Science and Engineering added in 1959 was opened to undergraduates in 1964. The Santa Barbara College was taken over in 1944 and was made a general campus in 1959. The newest additions, Irvine and Santa Cruz, demonstrate the adaptation of the theory that form follows function in architecture; gone are attempts to relate college buildings to classical or romantic themes; the new study halls are built for light, ventilation, economy of movement and accessibility, with dormitories close by. Such new colleges start with libraries of between 75,000 and 100,000 volumes, and are planned to expand in order to serve 25,000 students in the coming decades.

Although numbers are a measure of usefulness, they do not disclose the University's immense contribution to culture and life. The University goes where needed. It operates 70 research and extension centers. The Ernest O. Lawrence Radiation Laboratory at Berkeley is world renowned; besides the University operates two off-campus installations for atomic research, at Livermore, Calif., and Los Alamos, N. M. Other scientific research is done at Lick Observatory on Mt. Hamilton, in the high altitudes of White Mountain and in forest economy at Richmond. There are nine field stations of the Agricultural Experiment Station. The Agricultural Extension Service has fifty farm and home advisor offices. University Extension conducts classes in 175 California communities. Such facilities indicate the scope of higher education in the middle of the twentieth century.

Another impressive development in higher education is the system of California State Colleges, which numbered eighteen by 1966. In the 1963-64 year, when sixteen were in operation, the colleges had reached an enrollment of 135,000, from 120,000 the year before. The trustees then began planning for 250,000 by 1970. The State Colleges are supported by State appropriations and special funds and offer tuition-free courses to qualified students. While the rising tide of students must be provided for, the concern of the trustees is to keep a high level of education. As the Chancellor, Glenn S. Dumke, said: "This nation and this state have no choice between education for numbers and education at a high level of quality. If we over-commit ourselves in terms of size, we may under-commit ourselves in terms of quality." The colleges look to the Coordinating Council for Higher Education to support their master plan.

In order to get the best qualified students the master plan calls for close examination of the records of high school students who are eligible for admission.   The plan has reduced the number of such eligible students from the top 40 percent to the top 33⅓ percent.   Some of those not fully qualified have been diverted to junior colleges.   Considerable building is being carried out, especially of new residence halls.   An experimental 500-student "college within a college," intended to cut degree requirements by one year, is being conducted at Palos Verdes. Student Unions are being erected at some of the colleges from revenue bonds and not with state funds.   State appropriations for support expenditures run around $100,000,000 a year.

Opportunities for studying abroad have been extended to California colleges.   In 1963-64 the State Colleges started the plan and more than 100 students were able to study in Europe and Taiwan for a year and to live either in dormitories or in private homes.   Preference is given to upper division students with high grade point averages.   In the 1965 school year Japan was added.   The numbers participating will be limited; the Chancellor of the State Colleges explained: "We are not establishing American academic colonies abroad."

Junior colleges have been growing proportionately and many communities now offer high school graduates opportunities to complete their freshman and sophomore college courses before entering a university, or to take vocational training for business and industrial employment. Business administration, home economics, industrial arts, pre-architecture, pre-dental, pre-medical, teaching, and other skills are taught.   The student may live at home and yet take part in all student activities. Afternoon and evening classes are available.   Some of the junior colleges have large enrollments; El Camino has nearly 12,000 students, Cerritos, at Norwalk, more than 7,000; American River at Sacramento, more than 7,000; Long Beach as many as 24,000.   The seven junior colleges in Los Angeles have between 5,000 and 12,000 students each.   Los Angeles offers the student a choice among 200 occupational curricula. Anyone completing any of the two-year courses is eligible for an associate-in-arts degree and can transfer easily to a four-year college.

# The Arts

I LEARNED that there were a number of artists in the city who had sought to try Dame Fortune in the gold-fields, but with such scant success that they returned to the harbor . . . to seek patrons in . . . gilded temples of chance," wrote Prince Paul of Wurttemberg in his unpublished account (in the Stuttgart Archives) of his visit to the gambling halls of brawling, new-grown San Francisco in 1850. "Here we were regaled with very good music," he wrote. "In order to allure the public the owners of these gambling places employed musicians, among these many real orchestral artists and singers." He found the walls covered with a "great number of copper prints and oil paintings." And through the open doorways of saloons and public houses he saw "Mexicans dancing old California steps to the tunes of their national airs. The dancers carried out many very different movements and steps, and all with a certain haunting charm of grace and rhythm. . . ."

An earlier visitor to California would have gone to the mission churches to satisfy an interest in the arts, for the mission fathers were the first art patrons, decorating their chapels with paintings, instructing their Indian neophytes in music and church drama, and writing accounts of their missionary labors. But in 1850, Prince Paul mapped the best itinerary for the art lover when he visited San Francisco's "gilded temples of chance." If he had come later, he might have visited the cramped newspaper and magazine offices where Bret Harte and Mark Twain worked or the crude gas-lit theaters where Lotta Crabtree and Lola Montez performed. Later still, he might have paid calls to the art galleries and grand opera houses founded and endowed by the millionaire "bonanza kings." Today the arts flourish in so many places throughout California—in seaside artists' colonies, in big city garrets and studios, "little" theaters and concert halls, and in the sound-proofed stages of Hollywood lots—that Prince Paul, if he were visiting California now, would find it much more difficult to decide where to go. Perhaps he would find it more difficult still to understand how all the many activities of California's artists, musicians, painters, and writers arose from humble beginnings in gambling halls only ninety years ago.

## LITERATURE

The history of California letters begins long before the gold rush and Bret Harte and Mark Twain. During the Spanish and Mexican periods a number of able men, to whom authorship was but one of many tasks, were recording their experiences and observations, with little reward in money or fame. Their writing consists mostly of diaries and reports, with detailed descriptions of the country; but much of it bears the impress of unconscious artistry.

When in 1542 Juan Rodríguez Cabrillo explored the coast of California, one of the members of his expedition, Juan Paez, wrote a *Relación* or narrative of the voyage. Later in the same century, Chaplain Francis Fletcher and others accompanying Francis Drake, the dashing English buccaneer, wrote of the northwest coast of California and its red-skinned inhabitants near whose primitive villages Drake anchored his ship, the *Golden Hind*. These accounts were included in *The World Encompassed* (1628), compiled by Drake's nephew. The expeditions organized by Sebastián Vizcaíno in 1602 were described in journals kept by Father Antonio de la Ascensión and an unknown scrivener. From these journals the history of the Vizcaíno expeditions was retold by Father Juan de Torquemada in his *Monarquía indiana* (1615) and later by Martín Fernández de Navarrete and Jerónimo Martín Palacios in their collected accounts of voyages of discovery, published a few years later.

The true father of California literature, however, did not appear until after the middle of the eighteenth century. Junípero Serra was then president of the new missions in upper California, and Francisco

Palóu was his most highly-valued associate. Out of devotion to the Father President, Palóu wrote the memorable *Life and Apostolic Labors of the Venerable Father Junípero Serra* (1787); and during his ten years at Mission Carmel and Mission Dolores, he wrote his *Historical Memoirs of New California* (1857), recording the work of the Franciscans in the new province and describing with dramatic power the gradual conquest of a wild land.

The expeditions of Juan Bautista de Anza, trail-maker and the founder of San Francisco, had several chroniclers, foremost of whom was Father Pedro Font, astronomer with the expedition of 1775-76. Font's complete diary, which he compiled at leisure from notes written during his laborious 3,000-mile journey from Mexico to Monterey and to the site of present San Francisco, was published in 1930 in an English translation by Herbert Eugene Bolton. The journals of Juan Crespi and Pedro Fages also depict faithfully the new land as it appeared in the latter half of the eighteenth century.

In 1798 two books containing descriptions of California during the mission period were published in London—*A Voyage Round the World,* from the French of Jean François de Galup, Comte de la Pérouse, the distinguished navigator, and *A Voyage of Discovery,* by Capt. George Vancouver, the English explorer. Other seafaring travelers who wrote on Spanish California were George von Langsdorff and Otto von Kotzebue, who came on behalf of the Russian Government. When Kotzebue visited San Francisco in 1816, he was accompanied by the German poet and naturalist, Adelbert von Chamisso, who wrote a curiously gloomy description of the presidio.

California's first printing press was brought to Monterey by Governor José Figueroa in 1833 and taken over by Augustin V. Zamorano, California's first printer, who in 1834 issued the *Reglamento provincial*. The 55 separate items published by this press were mostly Hispano-Californian official documents, but they also included proclamations of the United States officials, a commercial paper, and at least two catechisms.

Several accounts of the province were written by foreigners during the Mexican period. The *History of Upper and Lower California* (1839) by Alexander Forbes, a British merchant in Mexico, was the first book in English dealing exclusively with California. *Explorations du territoire de l'Oregon, des Californies, etc.* (1844) by Duflot de Mofras reflects much enjoyment found in the province by a young French traveler. Alfred Robinson, an American trader who arrived in California in 1829 and married into the aristocratic De la Guerra family, wrote *Life in California* (1846), a pleasant and informative work. Richard Henry Dana, then a young sailor on the *Alert,* was in Santa Barbara at the time of Robinson's marriage, and he described the wedding in his famous *Two Years Before the Mast* (1840), other parts of which throw a vivid light on contemporary Monterey, San Francisco, and San Diego.

Of all early American accounts of the region during· this period the journal of the indefatigable explorer and fur scout, Jedediah Strang Smith, is the most entertaining. His journeys through California in 1826 and 1828 were faithfully recorded in sketches and diaries, thought to have been burned in San Francisco until they were discovered, edited by Maurice Sullivan, and published in 1934.

*Sixty Years in California* (1889) by William Heath Davis, another Yankee who married into an important California family, is an excellent account of experiences in the new country before and after the gold rush. Other books by early American arrivals in the territory are James O. Pattie's *A Personal Narrative* (1833) and David H. Coyner's *The Lost Trappers* (1847). John Charles Frémont, who played such a conspicuous role in the American occupation of California, wrote several books dealing in part with the late pastoral era, which ended with the discovery of gold.

Most of the chronicles written in California during the Spanish and Mexican periods remain unpublished; many of the manuscripts, however, survive in various collections—notably the Bancroft Library at the University of California, which contains the lengthy *Historias* of Antonio Mario Osio, Juan Bautista Alvarado, and Gen. Mariano Guadalupe Vallejo, the *Memorías* of José María Amador, and the *Reminiscencías* of Estevén de la Torre.

Within the new society created by the gold rush, journalists, story writers, and verse makers soon began to flourish. Among the many enthusiastic commentators of this period was Bayard Taylor, poet and globe-trotter, whose California ballads and high-flown prose work, *Eldorado, or Adventures in the Path of Empire* (1850), gave easterners an idealized picture of life in the gold fields.

Meanwhile the grotesque humor peculiar to the West was making its appearance in southern California, where Lieutenant (later Colonel) George H. Derby, writing in the San Diego *Herald,* spun his webs of satirical nonsense under the pen names of "John P. Squibob" and "John Phoenix." Derby's hilarious and often vitriolic commentaries, some of which were later compiled in the two volumes, *Phoenixiana* (1856) and *The Squibob Papers* (1859), have remained dear to the hearts of many Californians to this day.

But the literature of American California did not begin officially, so to speak, until 1852. In that year J. Macdonough Foard and Rollin M. Daggett founded the *Golden Era,* a journal devoted to mining, commerce, education, agriculture, local and foreign news, fine arts, and literature. It attained a large circulation not only in San Francisco, its place of publication, but also throughout the mining districts, and acquired many contributors who later became famous. The *Pioneer,* established in the same city two years later, was more strictly a literary magazine, but it lasted only two years, while the *Golden Era* survived until 1882. The *Pioneer* is remembered for the brilliant series of papers contributed to it by Colonel Derby and for the letters of "Shirley" (Mrs. Laura A. K. Clapp). The *Illustrated California Magazine* and the *Hesperian* were other short-lived periodicals established in the 1850's.

In 1857 the *Golden Era* printed a few verses signed "Bret"; and three years later their author, Francis Bret Harte, a young man from Albany, New York, found a badly needed job in the *Era's* composing room. Many of his early sketches were published in the journal. Another contributor to the *Era* was Samuel L. Clemens, a young eagle-eyed Missourian with a skeptical drawl, who had recently quitted Nevada to become a reporter on the San Francisco *Call.* In 1864 Clemens met Bret Harte, by this time a clerk in the local United States Branch Mint and star contributor to a new literary magazine, the *Californian.* A little later, when Harte was temporarily in editorial charge of the *Californian,* he engaged his new acquaintance as a regular contributor. Clemens' first sketch for the magazine was "A Notable Conundrum," signed with his usual pen-name of "Mark Twain." It was through Harte's influence and encouragement that Mark Twain, according to his own testimony, was changed "from an awkward utterer of coarse grotesqueries to a writer of paragraphs and chapters that have found a certain favor." Besides these two, the *Californian* numbered among its contributors Charles Warren Stoddard and Ina D. Coolbrith, both destined to more than local literary fame.

Mark Twain's first book, *The Celebrated Jumping Frog of Calaveras County and Other Sketches,* published in 1867, marked the true beginning of the California school. Twain soon became known outside the borders of the State. He visited the Sandwich Islands and then made a journey to Europe and the Holy Land, which he described in 50 letters to the *Alta Californian,* one of the oldest of San Francisco newspapers. These letters later became *Innocents Abroad,* which together with *Roughing It* (based upon his experiences in Nevada) established his reputation throughout the English-speaking world.

In 1868 Bret Harte became the editor of the *Overland Monthly,* which had just been established in San Francisco. In the second issue he published, after considerable hesitation, "The Luck of Roaring Camp." With the exception of "The Work on Red Mountain" (later rewritten and called "M'liss"), which lay forgotten in the *Golden Era,* the fastidious Harte had previously ignored the mining camps as background for his fiction. Many Californians now derided the story as unworthy of the author and of their home State.   But when the comments of the eastern critics began to arrive, Harte knew that, like some of his miners and gamblers, he had struck it rich.   This, with such subsequent stories as "The Outcasts of Poker Flat" and "Tennessee's Partner," made Bret Harte and the *Overland Monthly* household words among readers at home and abroad.   Harte was embarrassed by the fame of his "Heathen Chinee" and other humorous verse, but gratified by the success of his stories.   He left the Coast in a blaze of glory, never to return.   His later years were spent abroad, chiefly in England.

Before Harte's arrival in London, another California writer, "Joaquin" (Cincinnatus Heine) Miller, had created a sensation there, both as a poet and as a picturesque personality, addicted to high top-boots and long flowing hair.   Born in Indiana, Miller had been an Oregon editor and judge and a gold-miner before becoming a poet.   The poems that brought him fame were written mostly on the Pacific Coast and published in England in 1871.   After extensive wanderings abroad, he settled down in Oakland in 1885 and died there in 1913.   His *Songs of the Sierras* (1871) and *Songs of the Sunlands* (1873) deal for the most part with the turbulent exploits of pioneers, outlaws, and Indians, and with the scenic marvels of the West.

Henry George came to California in 1858, and for more than two decades made a precarious living through his work for Sacramento and San Francisco newspapers.   Here he wrote his famous treatise on the single tax, *Progress and Poverty* (1879).   Other, though less distinguished, California authors of the same general period were Prentice Mulford, the humorist; Noah Brooks, journalist, historian, and writer of books for boys; and John Vance Cheney, poet and essayist.

None of the outstanding writers of the pioneering days was born in the State; few of them became permanent residents there.   Reflecting the excitement and shifting character of the period, much of their fiction and poetry consists of broad caricature and sentimental melodrama; but the regionalism expressed in their work was complete, self-contained, and solidly founded.   Their humor, irreverent and lusty, was characteristically American.

On the cover of Harte's *Overland Monthly* a grizzly bear stands on a railroad track, apparently defying an approaching train.   But the strongest grizzly is no match for a locomotive; neither could the sectional character of California's culture long resist the influences that came with the completion of the railroad.   Nevertheless, in the closing decades of the nineteenth century, California literature partly retained its regional character.   A new literary magazine, the *Argonaut,* established in 1877 by Frank M. Pixley, had numerous able contributors and long maintained high standards.   Many literary works produced in the State still dealt with the local scene.   Helen Hunt Jackson's well-known romance of southern California, *Ramona* (1884), presented a touching picture of the interrelations of the whites and the Indians. Gertrude Atherton, who was born in San Francisco in 1857 and began her literary career in the late 1880's, gathered material for her early novels by visiting old towns and talking to the descendants of old Spanish settlers. In *The Doomswoman* (1892), *The Californians* (1898), *The Splendid Idle Forties* (1902), and *Rezanov* (1906), she embodied her knowledge of the Spanish era. Her *California—an Intimate History* (1914) is an unconventional treatment of the subject.

Ina Coolbrith, still retaining the lyrical fervor that had impressed Bret Harte, published *A Perfect Day and Other Poems* (1884), *The Singer of the Sea* (1894), and *Songs of the Golden Gate* (1895), all three full of local color. *The Mountains of California* (1894), the first book to appear from the pen of John Muir, scientist and prose poet, was permeated by a deep love for nature in the spectacular aspects that she displays in California. A less gifted nature-lover, George Wharton James, published his *Picturesque Southern California* and *Nature Sermons.*

Southern California and its Spanish and Indian backgrounds was the *milieu* of Charles Fletcher Lummis, who died in 1928. Author of such charming studies as *The Enchanted Burro, The Land of Poco Tiempo,* and the collected *Spanish Songs of Old California,* he is lovingly remembered for his long editorship of the California magazine *Out West.*

But the work of Ambrose Bierce, acknowledged leader of California letters during this period, is in no sense regional. His stories deal with the corpse-strewn battlefields of the Civil War, the nameless places of morbid fancy. They are meticulously finished; and in them, as in his other writings, his satire stings like the scorpion. In connection with the brilliant tales collected in *Black Beetles in Amber* (1892), *Can Such Things Be!* (1893), and *In the Midst of Life* (1898), Gertrude Atherton said that Bierce had "the best brutal imagination of any man in the English-speaking race." Through his columns in the *Wasp,* the *Argonaut,* and the San Francisco *Examiner,* Bierce became a power in California journalism. Some of his stories are still reprinted, while his invective has by no means lost its biting force. The strange disappearance of Bierce in Mexico, just before the World War, lent a dramatic touch to his career.

Charles Warren Stoddard, continuing the literary labors begun in company with Bret Harte, Mark Twain, and Ina Coolbrith for the *Californian,* added the Pacific and the South Seas to his domain. One of his last books deals with the California missions. Edward Rowland Sill, author of *The Hermitage* (1868) and other volumes of verse, taught for a number of years at the University of California. His "Opportunity" and "The Fool's Prayer" are still often reprinted.

Gelett Burgess, that friendly humorist, lived in California for several years before and after the turn of the century. In 1895-97 he edited *The Lark* for a San Francisco publisher, gaining renown that was later to embarrass him with his "Purple Cow":

> I never saw a PURPLE COW,
> I never hope to see one;
> But I can tell you, anyhow,
> I'd rather SEE than BE one!

Hubert Howe Bancroft collected a library of 60,000 books, maps, and manuscripts (now lodged in the Bancroft Library of the University of California), and working with a large corps of assistants produced in 30 years nearly 40 volumes of history, biography, and essays, including a *History of the Pacific States of North America* (1882-90) in 28 volumes. Bancroft has been accused of "factory" methods in writing history and of perpetrating many errors as a result, yet some authorities consider the *History of the Pacific States* to be the greatest feat of historiography in modern times. No serious student of Western history can wisely ignore it, and many general readers find it enjoyable. The four-volume *History of California* (1885-97) by Theodore Hittell, however, holds a greater fascination for the lay reader.

Notable in the literary annals of California was the visit in 1879-80 of Robert Louis Stevenson, then on the threshold of his literary career. He lived for a while in Monterey and later in San Francisco, where his marriage to Mrs. Osbourne took place. *The Silverado Squatters* (1883), *The Wrecker* (1892), *The Amateur Emigrant* (1894), and many of his published letters have to do in whole or part with the California scene. Ten years later a young British journalist named Rudyard Kipling paid a brief visit to San Francisco, and endeavored without success to sell some of his writings to the editors of that city.

With the beginning of the present century came a third period in California literature. Increased facility of communication and increased centralization of cultural activities on the eastern seaboard had finally broken down the old regionalism. The local scene was no longer the chief source of inspiration. Many young Westerners, dreaming of a career in literature, yearned to reverse Horace Greeley's dictum and go East in search of fame and fortune. The work of some of these writers bespoke an awakening social consciousness. Edwin Markham, a fervent champion of democracy, stands at the threshold of the new era. "The Man with the Hoe," a poem published in a San Francisco newspaper near the turn of the century, made Markham famous in a single day.

Of principal importance in this pre-war period were Frank Norris and Jack London and the literary colony founded at Carmel by the poet George Sterling in 1905. Norris, leaving the University of California, had studied art in Paris and there had fallen under the influence of Zola and the naturalistic school. Abandoning the brush for the pen and returning to California, he began to write novels conceived on a gigantic scale. The unforgettable *McTeague* (1899) was followed by *The Octopus* (1901) and *The Pit* (1903)—the first two volumes of a trilogy the "epic of wheat." Norris died at the age of 32, with the trilogy unfinished; but in *McTeague* and *The Octopus* he left two pioneering books that, despite their extravagance of expression, remain distinguished landmarks in American fiction.

In the Carmel group, besides George Sterling, were: James Hopper, a short-story writer of distinction; Mary Austin, author of *The Land of Little Rain* (1903) and several other notable books; Nora May French, a young lyric poet; and Frederick R. Bechdoldt, a writer of western stories. Jack London and Herman Scheffauer were regular visitors. Sinclair Lewis came a little later and with William Rose Benet spent a year there, as did Upton Sinclair. Michael Williams, author of *The Book of the High Romance* (1918), lived at Carmel for several years, as did Harry Leon Wilson, who wrote *Ruggles of Red Gap* and many other popular stories.

Rupert Hughes lived in Los Angeles until his death in 1956. Both Will and Wallace Irwin studied at Stanford, were editors in San Francisco, and celebrated before-the-fire Chinatown, Wallace in *Chinatown Ballads* (1905) and Will in *Old Chinatown* (1908). Stewart Edward White is known in California chiefly for his *Story of California* (a trilogy, 1927) and for his novels of the gold rush and vigilante days, *The Gray Dawn* and *The Forty-Niners.* Jack London, born in San Francisco in 1876, gained instant popularity with *The Call of the Wild* and *The Sea Wolf,* and in subsequent books described strong men in battles with fate, while he preached the virtues of socialism. Before he died in 1916 he had become as much a romantic California hero as Robert Louis Stevenson.

An "oyster pirate" and longshoreman, London turned to literature in his teens. After an arduous apprenticeship, he began to produce short stories, novels, autobiographical and sociological works that were enthusiastically received throughout the western world. As a fiction writer he glorified the elemental in men; as a socialist he foresaw a merciless war of the classes. Supermen and superwomen stalk through his stories, many of which are based upon his own experience, interpreted through an intensely romantic imagination. London's peregrinations took him to many places, and even on his great ranch in Sonoma County he managed to live dramatically, with an air of grandeur. London has written the best accounts of hardships suffered by men who joined the gold rush to the Klondike. Although he understood the lot of the underdogs he was too eager to tell stories to become a good propagandist for radicalism, and he is read today mainly for the tales he tells.

George Sterling was a poet whose brilliant imagination and poignant sense of beauty were held tightly within classic forms. His poetic dramas, odes, and sonnets are now somewhat at variance with the prevailing taste. But *The Testimony of the Suns* (1903), several of the sonnets, and certain shorter poems such as "Autumn in Carmel," possess enduring beauty. Sterling, for many years well known in Carmel and San Francisco, has become an almost legendary figure since his death in 1927. Herman Scheffauer, like Sterling a disciple of Ambrose Bierce, was another lyric poet of similar talent and expression.

Gertrude Atherton (1857-1948) became nationally famous as a novelist but remained a resident of California all her years. Her *Adventures of a Novelist* appeared in 1932. Kathleen Norris likewise lived in California; she had written more than 80 novels when she died in 1966, aged 85. Her husband, Charles Norris, who wrote *Brass* and other novels, was a brother of Frank Norris. Charles Caldwell Dobie used San Francisco in his short stories and in *San Francisco, A Pageant*. Robert Frost was born in California in 1875, but lived principally in New England. Lincoln Steffens, reform journalist, was born in Sacramento in 1866 and made his home in California in his later years, when he wrote his *Autobiography*. Most prolific writer about social and political issues has been Upton Sinclair. His famous novel, *The Jungle* (1906), was written before he came to Pasadena, and later Monrovia, to live. In addition to novels of social criticism such as *The Brass Check* (1919) and *The Goose Step* (1923) he put his comment on world affairs into the the popular form of Lanny Budd's adventures. He was active in anti-poverty campaigns and won the Democratic nomination for governor in 1934. He then wrote *I, Governor of California and How I Got Licked*. He won the Pulitzer Prize for *Dragon's Teeth* in 1943; published *My Life and Letters* in 1960, and *Autobiography* in 1962. Southern California and its Spanish and Indian backgrounds were used by Charles Fletcher Lummis, long editor of *Out West,* in *The Enchanted Burro, The Land of Poco Tiempo,* and *Spanish Songs of Old California*.

At Big Sur, near Carmel, Robinson Jeffers, poet (1887-1962), built his stone tower. His dramatic poems are filled with feeling for the non-human world and express admiration for the natural beauty of the Monterey Bay area. Another poet, Yvor Winters, has been a member of the faculty at Stanford University, as has the novelist Wallace Stegner.

California's people and places have given authenticity to John Steinbeck's novels. He was born in Salinas, briefly attended Stanford University and found some of his best themes in the canning area of Monterey. He described life there in *Cannery Row,* and wrote sympathetically about the *paisanos* in *Tortilla Flat*. He won the Pulitzer

Prize in 1940 for *The Grapes of Wrath,* a novel about the plight of the Dust Bowl migrants who came to California. He also has written about unemployed laborers in *Of Mice and Men* and *In Dubious Battle.* In 1962 he won the international honor of the Nobel Prize for Literature. More recently his *Travels With Charley,* a story about a dog, won wide popularity. Steinbeck now lives in New York.

Irving Stone, whose novels are based on historical characters, was born in San Francisco, graduated from the University of California in 1923 and holds a master's degree from the University of Southern California. He taught economics in both universities before his *Lust for Life,* a tale of Van Gogh, became a bestseller in 1934. His *Sailor on Horseback* deals with the life of Jack London. His most recent success is *The Agony and the Ecstacy.* William Saroyan, who began his career with a collection of short stories, *The Daring Young Man on the Flying Trapeze,* was born of Armenian parents in the San Joaquin Valley; he has written many short stories and plays. Hamlin Garland ended his days in California, as did Jim Tully, author of *Beggars of Life* and *Jarnegan,* who wrote scenarios in Hollywood. Max Miller, author of *I Cover the Waterfront,* also lives in the State.

In the 1950's San Francisco incubated a literary movement best characterized as a verbal explosion. Writers who became known as the Beat Generation used much energy and some talent to advertise their conviction that post-war American politics and society had alienated them. They briefly shocked and irritated the more reserved authors and critics. Kenneth Rexroth, San Francisco poet and critic, born in Indiana, called them "the disaffiliated." Most outspoken were Allen Ginsberg, poet, and Jack Kerouac, novelist, who were not native San Franciscans but hailed from New York and Massachusetts. Ginsberg produced *Howl!,* a vituperative blast, described by one critic as an "individual experience in negatives." In 1957 the San Francisco police vainly tried to suppress its sale because it contained words the police judged obscene. In 1958 Kerouac published *On the Road,* a story about fevered motoring across country with no apparent rational object. His later books dealt with slum life and one with Negro-white entanglement. Critical of his own time he studied Zen Buddhism. He gained some followers but most of the young were in a combative rather than a contemplative mood. The Beats had their historian in Lawrence Lipton, another midwesterner, who predicted in *The Holy Barbarians* that they would inherit the earth.

San Francisco became a hothouse for poetry during these decades. Groups first met in the Bagel Shop, since closed, and rallied to poetry readings started by Kenneth Rexroth in the City Lights Bookshop, 201 Columbus Avenue, and participated in by Kenneth Patchen, Robert Duncan and William Everson, now a Dominican lay brother. The shop was owned by Lawrence Ferlinghetti, himself a poet and patron of poets.

Poetry also was seriously practiced at the San Francisco State College, the University of California, and Stanford University. At the latter institution Thom Gunn represented the younger poets in the faculty and Yvor Winters the older. There was much study and making of poetry in all the colleges up and down the coast.

The frustration and defiance in the work of young writers was reflected also in a disregard of conventional attire and behavior by extreme types, called beatniks. They lived in "pads," usually an ill-furnished room, smoked "pot," experimented with drugs, grew beards and often used profanity. The inability of a rich America to solve the tensions of the hour was blamed for their "alienation." But the literary impact of the Beats faded when their message was seen to be wholly nihilistic in a society that was energetically working to solve its difficulties. Critic Rexroth asserted the poets had won their fight against formal patterns and schools and were successors of the revolt of the 1920's, but that "the literature of violent alienation not only still exists but has become very popular amongst the young." In the colleges, notably at Berkeley, youths were active in demonstrations for a variety of causes, including free (and uninhibited) speech, desegregation, sexual freedom, socialism, spiritual regeneration, and abolition of nuclear weapons. A professor of sociology at the University of California (Davis) Edgar Z. Friedenberg, is the author of sympathetic studies of the younger generation in *Coming of Age in America* and *The Dignity of Youth and Other Atavisms.*

While fiction and poetry get primary attention in literary valuation, there is impressive authorship in the historical and scientific fields, and the faculties of California colleges are filled with authors of national and international repute. At one time California Institute of Technology (Pasadena) had many Nobel Prize winners among its alumni and faculty, and today UC and Stanford share similar honors. The coming of Allan Nevins, American historian and Pulitzer prize-winner, to the Huntington Library as historical consultant was only one example of the cultural migration from the East to California.

## MUSIC

With the coming of the Franciscan friars in 1769, the Indians heard a new kind of music—the thousand-year-old music of the Roman Catholic mass. A great illuminated vellum volume of Gregorian chants, brought from Spain, may still be seen at the Mission of San Juan Bautista. The notes for the tenor, bass, and baritone were written in different colored inks in some of the scores, to help the natives distinguish their parts. Patiently the California Indians were taught to sing the sacred melodies. When Robert Louis Stevenson was living in

Monterey, toward the end of the ninteenth century, he went to the annual festival in honor of San Carlos, held in the ruins of the Mission San Carlos Borromeo, and heard aged Indians, who had come many miles to attend the ceremony, sing the Latin words and music with good accent. Even today some Indians in San Diego County assist in church services by chanting medieval Latin hymns.

The appearance of Spanish-Mexican folk music in California brought to pueblo and rancho the passionate rhythms of the fandango, piquant serenades, Andalusian ditties, and ballads. Troubadours from Monterey and Santa Barbara used to wander northward to visit the great hospitable ranchos around the village of Yerba Buena.

No sooner had American conquest put an end to the slow, feudal life of the ranchos than the Forty-niners began swarming into the new El Dorado from all over the world. On the long journey overland across the plains or by sea around the Horn, they whiled the time away with song and dance. The chorus of "Oh! Susanna!" sung on the way, runs:

> "I'm going to California,
> With my banjo on my knee!"

In the "diggin's," around the camp fire at night, the miners sang pre-Civil War songs—"Ben Bolt," "The Last Rose of Summer," "Pop Goes the Weasel"—often improvising new words for the old airs, or making up new melodies.

Opera—French, German, and Italian—made its appearance in California almost as early as the Forty-niners. Regular performances were given in San Francisco in 1851. In Los Angeles traveling companies that wandered up from Mexico gave performances. Often these companies came to grief, leaving their stranded artists to settle where luck had left them. The famous old Tivoli Opera House was a result of their congregating in San Francisco. Starting as a public beer garden in 1877, where citizens drank to the strains of the Vienna Ladies' Orchestra, the establishment decided to put on Gilbert and Sullivan's *H.M.S. Pinafore* in 1879. The Tivoli continued until 1906 with an unbroken run of comic and grand opera. Its contemporary, the Grand Opera House, was built in 1876 as "a new and elegant temple of the drama" seating over 3,000, with a handsome proscenium and mezzanine boxes. Here a long line of famous singers appeared in an operatic career culminating in a brilliant performance of *Carmen* with Sembrich and Fremstad, Scotti and Caruso, on the night before that memorable date in the history of San Francisco, April 18, 1906. Among the singers who began their careers in California were Emma Nevada, Luisa Tetrazzini, and Lawrence Tibbett.

The San Francisco Opera Company is a most distinguished member of the four major professional opera organizations of the United States. Its typical season averages forty performances of sixteen operas, and in addition to classic repertory it mounts revivals and premieres of original work. Its roster includes the most eminent artists from the United States and abroad. It gives an average of twenty-one performances annually in Los Angeles and appears also in Berkeley, Sacramento and San Diego.

San Francisco and the Bay Area have access to other opera performances besides those of its premier organization. The Spring Opera has developed admirably with support from the Ford and San Francisco Foundations. Opera West performs in the Palace of the Legion of Honor. The West Bay Opera gives three operas a year at the Palo Alto Community Theater. There is also encouragement for new artists in the competition sponsored by the Merola Opera Fund, which provides contracts for winners.

Some local opera groups rehearse most of the year in order to give a few performances, and others give programs without scenery or choruses. All hope to enlarge their schedules as support increases. The Riverside Opera Company gives operas in English six times a year. The Redlands Community Opera gives six free performances of four operas annually in Redlands Bowl. The Goldovsky organization is a small but well-trained singing company that tours the state. The Opera Festival at Laguna Beach, the Ojai Music Festival and the Fresno Fine Arts Festival attract large audiences. The Santa Barbara Civic Opera and the West End Opera at Upland provide annual programs.

Many opera groups hope for better facilities and more adequate theaters. The Los Angeles Opera Company, which customarily gives four to six performances, has moved to the new Pavilion of the Civic Theater and expects to expand. The San Diego Opera Guild is sponsoring a local opera organization to use the new theater in the Civic Center, which seats 3,000. The California Arts Commission recommends state subsidies and larger private donations for the arts.

When celluloid became audible in Hollywood, composers began to move West. Theme song inventors and modernist orchestrators were at a premium. The early history of jazz is closely connected with San Francisco. "They've got a dance out there, they call the grizzly bear" —so went the lyric. One of the original popularizers of the jazz tempo was Art Hickman, whose first contact with ragtime had been on the Barbary Coast. In the early days of the talkies most musical scores were patchworks of themes from familiar classics. Then Hollywood began importing the better composers of popular songs—men like Irving Berlin and George Gershwin—to write melodies which were inserted with infinite labor into film drama plots.

Since then many composers have been hired by Hollywood to write especially for sound films. The roster of those employed in the last twenty-five years includes Frank Loesser, Frederick Lowe, Kurt Weill, Werner Janssen, George Antheil, Ferde Grofe, Jerome Kern, and Erich Korngold.

California composers include Ernst Bacon, whose *Symphony in D Minor* won the 1932 Pulitzer Prize; Charles Wakefield Cadman, noted for his use of Indian themes, and William Grant Still, conductor as well as composer. Henry Hadley, for some years conductor of the San Francisco Symphony, did much of his work in the State; Ernest Bloch wrote his symphonic suite *America* in the hills of Marin County; and Arnold Schoenberg became chairman of the department of music at the University of California at Los Angeles. Among the moderns are Gerald Strang, Roy Harris, Frederick Jacobi, and Henry Cowell.

There is wide appreciation of symphonic music in California, and cities that cannot afford professional orchestras organize amateur groups with professional leadership. The State has 164 such orchestras, exclusive of high schools, but only five are all-professional: San Francisco, Los Angeles, Oakland, San Jose and Santa Clara. Numerous orchestras from out-of-state come annually, and artists of national reputation are often headliners at annual music festivals. The San Francisco Symphony and the Los Angeles Philharmonic are supported by donations, and the former appropriates as much as $1,000,000 annually. The Doctors Symphony Orchestra of San Francisco is an example of how well-qualified amateurs can form a group for enjoyment and musical appreciation. The City of Los Angeles helps support its Philharmonic and Hollywood Bowl seasons and the County aids the nineteen community orchestras inside its boundaries.

Symphony orchestras with half or more professional musicians are active in Long Beach, Marin County, Pasadena and Claremont. Programs of high quality are given with fewer professionals in San Diego, Fresno, Sacramento, San Bernardino and Monterey. In citing the cultural activities of the Fresno Philharmonic, the California Arts Commission says that "in addition to its six home concerts each season, it also tours at least one of its programs, presents several youth concerts, and sponsors a junior Philharmonic orchestra, several youth training programs and three chamber music concerts."

Since 1956 the American Symphony Orchestra League has been giving the Summer Institute of Orchestral Studies at Asilomar on Monterey Peninsula. Its six-week study program for conductors, composers and orchestra members enrolls about 1,500 musicians annually.

Appreciation of chamber music has been growing in recent years and groups playing it have been multiplying, but their audiences are naturally limited in size. The Carmel Bach Festival has been an inspiring influence, but it also includes choral works. Some groups reach wider audiences when they perform for television.   Most colleges encourage chamber music.   The Southern California Chamber Music Society now performs its twelve annual programs in a new 600-seat hall at the County Museum of Art, Los Angeles.   The San Francisco Chamber Music Society gives programs in the Hall of Flowers in Golden Gate Park. There are active groups in San Rafael and Pasadena.

The Monterey Jazz Festival, held annually since 1957 in the Fair Grounds, gets wide attention from fans not likely to favor chamber music.   Duke Ellington, Louis Armstrong, Earl Hines and Miles Davis have participated.   Some of the proceeds have been donated to Monterey Peninsula College for the study of jazz, and a $5,000 scholarship has been established for the same purpose.

## PAINTING AND SCULPTURE

In the days before the Civil War, the Rocky Mountains were a favored subject among American landscape painters. The artists who came to the Western territories were stirred by the magnificence, grandeur, and sheer size of the new country. To them, as to the gold seekers, America had suddenly opened extravagant possibilities. Here was a land of prodigies: mountains, precipices, cataracts, dead craters, snowy ascents, vertiginous cliffs. It seemed to the pioneer artists that this wild country was prepared to yield limitless esthetic rewards.

California art of this period succeeded in exciting eastern imaginations and in disclosing the scenic marvels of the virgin territory. Artistically, however, it overshot its mark in attempting to reproduce in pictorial terms the gigantic proportions of the mountains, canyons, and forests of the West. Many of the huge canvases of that time, technically weak and devoid of emotional content, today seem of dubious value.

The painters of spectacular scenery were not, however, the first artists to reach California. Before their arrival, a unique artistic development had taken place in connection with the Spanish Missions which administered California territory for the larger part of a century. The Indians whom the padres found in the locality had practiced handicrafts and pictorial art according to traditions extending back to prehistoric times—the "rock paintings" discovered in California mountains and caves are evidence of this early skill. The missions, which exploited the labor of the natives, brought them under the influence of Spanish teachings in religion and the crafts. The indigenous art, with its motifs and symbols representing the sun, men, animals, and nature mysteries, thus became oddly intermingled with the old World tradition. For example, in the "Stations of the Cross" series painted on sail-cloth at the San Gabriel Mission before 1779, Indian neophytes working under direction of their Spanish masters repeated a centuries-old Christian theme. Most of the early mission murals were later covered with whitewash and plaster; they are being reclaimed today, chiefly through the efforts of the Index of American Design division of the Federal Art Project. Indian craftsmen, and on occasion the padres themselves, also produced carved and painted statues and figurines, plaques, iron grille work, church implements, costumes, stamped and colored leatherwork, textiles, metalwork, and embroideries. An exceptionally rich and varied "folk art" was thus contributed to early California.

During this era numerous paintings and sculptures were brought into California from Spain and Mexico, and wandering artists from those countries painted panels and altarpieces and portraits of the Spanish gentry.  While somewhat primitive technically, the unsigned portraits, a few of which are still owned by descendants of the haciendados and by California museums, are often charming and esthetically satisfying in their direct, literal treatment.

By the end of the eighteenth century books of travel and exploration began to include illustrations of California.  Perhaps the first of these is Vancouver's *A Voyage of Discovery,* published in London in 1798, which contains two sketches of mission and presidio buildings "taken on the spot" by J. Sykes.  Interesting aquatints of California scenes are to be found in other volumes of the first half of the nineteenth century.  The first painter to remain and practice in California, whose name is known, is W. S. Jewett.  Early in 1850 he executed a large oil, which, according to the first issue of the famous *Overland Monthly,* July 1868, "properly ought to begin the record of California art production."  The painting represents a newly arrived immigrant family on a summit of the Sierra Nevada.

The discovery of gold brought, along with members of the other professions, a few painters, and for some 30 years their chief aim was to reproduce the California scene.  One of the most successful was Charles C. Nahl, born in Germany of a family of accomplished artists.  His work, little known outside of California, shows a familiarity with European traditions.  His *The Fandango* and *Sunday in the Mines* are excellent pictorial documents.

Of the school of heroic landscape, Albert Bierstadt (1830-1902), Thomas Hill (1829-1913) and Thomas Moran (1837-1926) achieved the widest popularity both at home and abroad.  Bierstadt, born in Düsseldorf, was brought to America as a child.  His *Landers' Peak,* drew an enthusiastic response from his contemporaries.  Bierstadt spent much time in California among the natural wonders of the Yosemite Valley, the Sierra, and the great valleys of the Sacramento and San Joaquin.

Thomas Hill started his career as a coach painter.  His canvases, like those of Bierstadt, were enormous panoramic views of mountain ranges, which seemed in their day to express the "magnificent scenery of that marvelous region, where the roar of the whirlwind and the roll of thunder reverberate like the tread of countless millions who evermore march westward."  Later generations, however, have found less substance in Hill's paintings.

Thomas Moran, a man of extraordinary versatility, had profited from study abroad.  The influence of Turner enriched his canvases, and though in his own time he was less eagerly acclaimed than Bierstadt or

Hill, his solid talent has since given him a higher rank. Like others of the California group, Moran devoted much of his work to the dramatic scenery of the West; he also was considered one of the best etchers of his day. Moran painted with ease and fluency, and his composition was masterly; yet, on the whole, his work lacks subtlety of handling and is too solid and inert for modern taste.

Notable among the many lesser painters who followed Bierstadt, Hill, and Moran, are Raymond A. Yelland, marine painter and art educator; Jules Tavernier, whose work includes numerous paintings of Indian life as well as many landscapes; Thaddeus Welch, painter of the Mount Tamalpais region; and Charles D. Robinson, who celebrated the scenic marvels of the Yosemite Valley.

Of special distinction among California landscapists was William Keith (1838-1911), who came to California in 1859. Like the painters of the French Barbizon school and his friend George Inness, Keith sought subjective harmony and poetic mood in his painting. He avoided the grandiose, and in his work the theatrical naturalism of Moran and Bierstadt gave way to brooding and tranquil scenes—serene groves of live oak, clearings in the interior of woods, hillsides, brooks—remarkable for their play of light and shade. Toby Edward Rosenthal (1848-1917), a native of Connecticut, was brought as a child to San Francisco, where he studied under the Mexican painter, Fortunato Arriola. Rosenthal spent much time in Europe, maintaining a studio in Munich. In its literary themes and scrupulous craftsmanship, his work reflected the styles of the Munich and older Düsseldorf schools. His method was laborious and scholarly; it was not exceptional for him to spend three years in research, travel, and sketching, to produce a single canvas like *The Trial of Constance of Beverley,* now owned by Stanford University. Rosenthal's documentary paintings brought to his studio many admirers and buyers, while lithographers bid against one another for permission to reproduce them, even before they were dry.

With the decline of the heroic school new influences from the East and from abroad began to affect California painting and sculpture. In the last quarter of the nineteenth century, the currents of impressionism, Munich genre painting, eclecticism, and French romanticism mingled with the local development. Public interest in art during this period was stimulated by the organization of the San Francisco Institute of Arts in 1874; the founding of the E. B. Crocker Art Gallery in Sacramento in 1884; the exhibition of 60 local artists at the World's Columbian Exposition in Chicago in 1893; the establishment of the M. H. de Young Memorial Museum in San Francisco in 1895, and of the Southwest Museum in Los Angeles in 1903.

The Bohemian Club of San Francisco, founded in 1872, reflected the diversity of interests animating the newer art. Among its members during the decades that followed were Arthur Matthews, painter, architect, and decorator, examples of whose works may be seen on the walls of many public buildings in the State; Bruce Porter who executed stained glass and mural paintings for California churches and public buildings; Gottardo Piazzoni, landscapist, who contributed the murals at the San Francisco Public Library; Xavier Martinez, born in Mexico, who has lived for many years in the Bay region, where many of his works are in the possession of the Oakland Art Gallery; Charles Dickman, painter of landscapes and marines; and Henry Joseph Breuer, landscapist. Arthur Atkins, who despite his early death left a number of excellent landscapes, was close to the Bohemian Club.

Having moved to Monterey in 1895 Francis McComas, Bohemian Club painter of oils, water colors, and murals, became one of the Monterey-Carmel group which included Charles Rollo Peters, widely known as the painter of the "nocturnal witchery and glamour of California," and Armin Hansen, colorist and etcher. William Ritschel painted many landscapes of the Monterey-Carmel coast line.

By the turn of the century notable artists were working in Los Angeles, where the painting of William Wendt exerted an early influence. The hills of this region, drenched in sunlight for the greater part of the year, furnish the subject matter of most Southern California landscapists. Soon Los Angeles was no longer the only Southern California art center: groups were formed in Santa Barbara, Laguna Beach, San Diego, La Jolla, and other localities.

California's first eminent sculptor was Douglas Tilden, born in 1860. He received his early education at Berkeley and later studied sculpture in Paris. Among his best known works are *The Football Players* in Berkeley and the *Mechanics' Fountain* in San Francisco. Robert I. Aitken, whose many monuments in the State have received high praise, was one of Tilden's pupils. Edgar Walter and Earl Cummings were also influenced by Tilden. Other California sculptors of the period are Roger Noble Burnham, Frank Happersburger, Marion F. Wells, Chester Beach, and Haig Patigian. The figures of wild life executed by Arthur Putnam, who died in 1930, received wide appreciation.

The San Francisco Exposition of 1915 brought the work of the French moderns to the attention of a considerable number of Californians. As elsewhere, the immediate response to this new art was mainly one of bewilderment and irritation. In the next decades, however, the aims of Cezanne, Van Gogh, Seurat, Gaugin, and their twentieth century followers gradually became more intelligible both to California artists and to the public. Modern influences entered the California School of Fine Arts, founded in 1874, through courses by Arnold Blanch and Maurice Sterne. New decorative and experimental techniques began to be applied by an increasing number of local artists. Abstract and surrealist art, regionalism, and social realism became major trends. The Mexicans, Rivera, Orozco, and Siqueiros, inspired in many artists of the San Francisco and Los Angeles areas a new interest in the problems of mural painting.

Today there are so many artists in California, working in such a profusion of styles and aims, that the State has become one of the leading centers of art activity in the Nation. It is, unfortunately, impossible to describe here the scores of personalities and accomplishments that merit attention.

In sculpture, too, new possibilities were explored: the massive figures of workmen produced by the social realists; the archaic formalism favored in architectural ornament; the suggestive shapes of the abstractionists; and the controversial experiments of the pioneers of new media.

Important museums and galleries have appeared in California since the beginning of the twentieth century. Among these are: the Los Angeles County Museum of Art, founded 1961, new building, 1965; Los Angeles Art Association, organized in 1925; the Fine Arts Society of San Diego, 1925; the Henry E. Huntington Art Gallery at San Marino, opened in 1928; the Louis Terah Haggin Memorial Galleries at Stockton, 1928. After World War II and especially after 1950 there was great multiplication of art galleries, museums of natural history, and preservation of historical houses. These included the J. Paul Getty Art Museum in Malibu, the San Diego Aerospace Museum, the Kern County Museum at Bakersfield with its pioneer village restoration projects; the Judah L. Magnes Memorial Museum of Oakland, commemorating Jewish history in the West; the Palm Springs Desert Museum; the Los Angeles State and County Arboretum at Arcadia, which also preserves historical houses; the Museum Center at Oakland, which was planned to include three separate museums; the San Bernardino County Museum at Bloomington, and such ambitious building projects as the restoration of Old Sacramento of the days of 1849.

The Federal Arts Projects of the WPA before 1940 carried out an ambitious program. Murals, sculpture, easel painting, and graphic work executed under its auspices have been allocated to public buildings throughout the State. Its Index of Design Division and art teaching staffs performed broad services in popular education. Another Federal Agency, the Treasury Department Art Project, commissioned murals for government buildings on a competitive basis.

At the Golden Gate International Exposition of 1939 California painters and sculptors, including representatives of the newer styles, reached a larger public with murals and sculptures for the fair grounds. The vast exhibition of old masters assembled at the Palace of Fine Arts comprised examples of the Italian, Flemish, Dutch and English schools.

Whether it will be possible, or even desirable, to distinguish in the future a distinct "California style" no one can state with assurance. In the meantime, art in the State has discovered in such essentially public genres as mural painting and reliefs, sculptured monuments, and government-sponsored exhibitions a deeper orientation with respect to the social life of the community.

<<<<<<<<<<<<<<<<<<<<<<<<<<<<<<<<<<<<<<<<<<<<<<<<<<<<<<<<<<<<<<<<<<<<<<<<<<<<<<<<<<<<<<<<<<<<<>>>>>>>>>>>>>>>>>>>>>>>>>>>>>>>>>>>>>>>>>>>>>>>>>>>>>>>>>>>>>>>>>>>>

# THE THEATER

The fiesta, the pageant, and the outdoor theater were natural developments in California, where people have always spent much of their time in the open. When Americans first came to California, they found a people who amused themselves with singing and dancing, and on fiesta days watched the fandango danced to the accompaniment of choruses. This essentially Mediterranean type of entertainment has survived in such diverse forms as the Ramona Pageant, La Fiesta de Los Angeles, the Bohemian Club's "high jinks" and the Mt. Tamalpais Mountain Play. But for fifty years after the influx of Americans California was, in general, not very conscious of its Spanish heritage, and the theater as elsewhere in the United States, followed the British and French tradition.

In 1846 the wing of an adobe house in Monterey, surviving today as the oldest theater in California, became an amusement hall for Stevenson's New York Regiment. Minstrel shows, old English farces, and even Shakespearean plays were produced. American soldiers at the Sonoma garrison played Benjamin Webster's *The Golden Farmer* in an improvised theater for four months in the following year, and minstrel shows were given by the American soldiers in Santa Barbara.

The forty niners—most of them without families—were enthusiastic and generous patrons of any kind of entertainment. The gold rush brought actors from the Mississippi showboats; from the theaters of New Orleans, Galveston, Mobile, and New York; from Europe and Australia. Dramatic actors, "Ethiopian serenaders," minstrels, circus clowns, acrobats, performed in tents and crudely contrived temporary halls, or in the gambling rooms of the hotels and saloons, surrounded by French mirrors, French pictures, and blazing chandeliers, while faro, monte, rouge et noir, vingt-et-un, ronda, and roulette games went on night and day. Female performers, who were extremely rare at first, met with sure success. Home melodies sung by women had a powerful effect on the miners, who frequently showered the performer with nuggets and small pouches of gold dust.

In Sacramento *The Bandit Chief* was performed by professionals at the Eagle Theater, the first building erected in California especially for theatrical performances. It was a wooden frame with canvas walls and a roof of tin and sheet iron. Estimates of its cost ranged from $30,000 to $85,000. It was formally opened October 18, 1849, although the "Stockton Minstrels" had played in it to a full house the month before.

Driven from Sacramento by floods, the Eagle Theater Company went to San Francisco in January 1850, and in a second-floor hall performed *The Wife,* a touching tale in blank verse. San Francisco had already, on June 22, 1849, witnessed its first theatrical performance. In a rickety schoolroom, crowded to suffocation, Stephen C. Massett, a stout, red-faced little Englishman, with a great mop of curls, sang original ditties and burlesqued famous singers of the day. The front seats were reserved for ladies, of whom there were four present. Rowe's Olympic Circus and several minstrel companies appeared during the same year. Most of the halls erected in San Francisco were destroyed by the fires of 1850 and 1851, but new theaters were rapidly built, including the Museum and the famous Jenny Lind. The Museum's first play, *Seeing the Elephant,* ridiculed the gold rush, and, in general, performances at this theater had local flavor. The Jenny Lind, twice burned to the ground and rebuilt by Tom Maguire, was more ambitious and gave many Shakespearean plays. In 1853 there were seven theaters in San Francisco, among them the American, the Adelphi (built by the French), and the costly and massive Metropolitan.

Junius Brutus Booth, the elder, came to San Francisco with his 19-year-old son, Edwin, in 1852; on the death of his father young Edwin remained for a while in California laying a firm foundation for his later fame. Kate Hayes, "the willowy swan of Erin," arrived in the same year, "fresh from triumphs at the Covent Garden." Other actors came—James Stark, Anna Thillon, Signora Elise Biscaccianti— and many more. Shortly afterwards Lotta Crabtree, aged nine, made her first dramatic appearance, in Petaluma as Gertrude in *A Loan of a Lover.* Breaking into an occasional jig and roll in the midst of the performance, she won her audience; thereafter, whether playing her banjo, dancing, and making merry, or acting scenes of overwhelming pathos as "Little Nell," Lotta could do no wrong. She attained extraordinary popularity throughout northern California,

> "Because in Lotta we can see
> Artistic concentration
> Of sweetness, strength and piquancy,
> A pungent combination."

and to many Californians her legend remains alive to this day. The celebrated Lola Montez, favorite of kings, made her home for a time at Grass Valley, and danced there and at other camps and slumgullion centers.

In San Francisco the opening of the California Theater in 1869, under the joint direction of the two great actors, Lawrence Barrett and John McCullough, dimmed the glory of the Metropolitan. The first plays were Bulwer-Lytton's *Money*, followed by *Marie Antoinette* and *Richelieu*. In 1877 Hélène Modjeska, the Polish actress, came from the southern California bee ranch where she and her husband had spent several months in political exile, and appeared at the California in *Adrienne Lecouvreur*, the first of her successes on the English-speaking stage. The California, rebuilt in 1888, remained a popular playhouse until destroyed by the fire in 1906. Among its competitors was the Baldwin Theater, for a time managed by young David Belasco, later to become a world-famous actor-manager and producer.

While accepting the Broadway diet, Californians can boast of the stars who began their careers in the old Coast theaters. The roll includes Nance O'Neill, Maude Allan, Isadora Duncan, Minnie Maddern Fiske, Maude Adams, Marjorie Rambeau, Holbrook Blinn, Blanche Bates, Pauline Lord, and Edna Wallace Hopper. Mary Anderson was a native of Sacramento; Frank Mayo made his debut in San Francisco; David Warfield first worked as an usher in a San Francisco theater. Like Belasco, William A. Brady was born in California and had his first professional experience in San Francisco, as did Morris Mayerfeld, who built the Orpheum circuit.

There has been a large upswing of interest in the theater in recent decades and although resident performing companies are few, there are numerous groups, professional and amateur, that produce intermittently. Two of the best-known are the Actor's Workshop of San Francisco, founded and until recently directed by Herbert Blau and Jules Irving, who were succeeded by John Hancock, and the Theater Group of UCLA, associated with University Extension, both of which have had Ford Foundation grants and toured the State. Also active are the International Repertory Theater of San Francisco and the Actor's Theater Freeway Circuit of Los Angeles. The California Arts Commission, which is trying to build State and voluntary support for theaters, found that some professional organizations in Los Angeles County had considerable "stability and continuity," and as examples named Players Ring Gallery, the Stage Society, the Los Angeles Theater Arts Foundation, the Pasadena Playhouse, the Magnolia Theater of Long Beach, Seiden & Bufan productions, Equity Library Theater West, Ray Bradbury's Pandemonium Theater and Frank Silver's acting group.

Active in the San Francisco Bay Area are the Festival Theater of San

Anselmo and the Gate Theater in Sausalito, the Regional Arts Council reported that the International Repertory, the Cathedral Civic and the Aldridge Players—a new Negro theater group, "all have a considerable sense of mission." Some professional productions are staged in Hollywood under arrangements with Actors' Equity Assn., whereby actors temporarily on the sidelines act to keep in practice. No admission is charged; sometimes actors even pay a fee to participate. Best-known of the Los Angeles enterprises are Theater West, Projects '58 and the Professional Theater Center at Desilu Studios. Twelve theaters give week-end performances charging admission under an "Off-Broadway" contract with Equity.

Long Beach has been commended for its Council of Living Theater, composed of representatives of its six community theaters, colleges and schools, who cooperate on civic productions. The Glendale Center Theater is considered a stable and successful enterprise. Community theaters flourish in many cities. They are served by volunteers without pay and average three to four annual productions on two week-ends. Their audiences prefer comedy to experimental plays.

The California Arts Commission, in its report to the Governor and Legislature, pointed to San Diego as an example of progress in the performing arts. It has its annual Old Globe Shakespeare Festival, the Circle Arts Musical Theater, the Civic Light Opera Assn., the Mission Playhouse in Old Town, Actors' Quarter, an avant-garde group, and La Jolla Playhouse, which has summer productions with professional stars. With the help of the Theater & Arts Foundation and the University of California at San Diego the Playhouse has been planning a $3,000,000 theater for a professional resident company and the University. Professional and amateur actors also join hands in the Sacramento Festival of the Arts, which gives seven different productions during ten days.

Although one caustic critic wrote, "It has been difficult to stem the tide of quantity versus quality," others have viewed the growing interest in the theater as a healthy cultural stimulant.

# Highways Into the Future

CALIFORNIA'S FREEWAY and Expressway System can justifiably be called one of the wonders of the modern world. These strips of concrete that bind together the habitations of the people from the Oregon border to Mexico are as truly agencies of communication as the telephone and the airplane. The first freeway, the Pasadena, was opened January 1, 1941, after the California legislature had authorized the Department of Public Works to apply freeway standards to any new or old portion of the State Highway System. In 1956 the U. S. Congress enacted the Federal Aid Highway Act to finance the National System of Interstate and Defense Highways, of which California was to receive 2,174 miles, all to be included in the freeway system. By this time the State legislature recognized the tremendous impetus given the growth of the State by easily accessible roads capable of handling immense traffic without hindrance, and in 1959 it voted the Freeway and Expressway System, the most ambitious building program of any state in the nation.

The master plan contemplated connecting all primary centers of industry and natural resources with depots of labor and materials and major shipping points, also providing continuity of travel. The State had built 2,940 miles of multilane divided highways by 1965, 1,589 miles of them freeways and 733 miles expressways. Construction continued on more than 500 projects for which contracts valued at $402,980,400 were awarded in the 1963-1964 fiscal year. In the following year more than $600,000,000 was allocated for surveys, planning, acquisition of land and construction. Work also continued on the routes of the Interstate System, which has to be completed in 1972. California profits to the extent of $2,275,000,000 in Interstate funds, expended, obligated or budgeted.

When completed in 1980 there would be a 12,000-mile network of roads connecting practically everything. The prospect has not been pleasing to many Californians, who abhor the congested traffic lanes. A proposal to cut through a forest of redwoods brought protests from inside and outside the State. In 1966 San Franciscans held up—at least temporarily—official plans to add new freeways in the County.

Highway needs and proposals are carefully screened by the California State Chamber of Commerce before being recommended to the Division of Highways. The system is reviewed by the Legislature every four years to keep up with possible changes in traffic conditions. The Legislature designates routes as state highways and fixes the terminals. Sometimes it designates general control points through which they must pass. The Highway Commission determines specific routings.

After planning comes financing. The State has suffered no monetary stringency because highway building and maintenance are based on pay-as-you-go highway use. Predictable funds come from gasoline and diesel fuel taxes, registration fees and drivers licenses, weight fees on commercial vehicles and taxes on for-hire trucking. The constitution requires that revenues from highways be used for road construction and maintenance, and the administration of the Division of Highways, the Department of Motor Vehicles and the Highway Patrol. The Federal government returns to the state the taxes it collects from the user of highways. More than 91 percent of the coast of building the state's portion of the Interstate System comes from Federal funds, as does 58 percent of the amount spent on certain primary, secondary and urban highways that are entitled to Federal aid. The law requires the Highway Commission to allocate 55 percent of construction funds to the thirteen southern counties and 45 percent to the remaining forty-five counties each year. It also determines the minimum expenditures for each highway district. There are eleven districts with 16,500 employees. Construction goes to private contractors with competitive bidding.

Building roadways can be as spectacular as erecting fortresses was in medieval times. Huge hills have been moved aside by bulldozers to make possible easy grades for the motorist. Rock-breaking machinery has bitten into what poets call the eternal hills and opened new arteries for travel. Where an interchange of roads is necessary two and three-story structures of steel and concrete have risen to carry the swift-moving vehicles of commerce over possible obstacles.

The state-wide radio system consists of more than 1,500 mobile units, 200 radio stations, 52 microwave stations and 125 hand-carry units. The first phase of the microwave circuit was completed on US 50 between Sacramento and Echo Summit. Radio is used on construction projects and bridge maintenance, and teletype for administrative functions. Even television has a place in supervision of traffic. As an example, a television camera mounted to command the two-lane Caldecott Tunnel entrance on State 24 can keep maintenance personnel posted on traffic. In the case of congestion switching on of additional fans and blowers would be signified.

California roads are clearly marked. There are four principal designations: U. S. Interstate and Defense highways have a shield with a narrow red section separated by a white line from a deeper blue section on which the numerals appear. These highways move across the country, with even numbers for east-west routes and odd numbers for north-south routes. When Interstate goes directly through a city or around it the marker has three digits, the first an even number. When the first figure of three is odd it indicates a spur. U.S. highways have numerals on a shield without embellishments; state roads have numerals inside a plain circle; county roads in California have numerals inside a plain square.

Speed regulations are posted; maximum speed on highways is 65 mph and if 70 is allowed on freeways it is posted.

Good roads and motor cars interact; with easier access comes a steady increase in vehicles. California leads the nation in the number of vehicles registered, which in 1965 was slightly under 10,000,000. The rate of increase is larger than that of the United States as a whole, when both trucks and passenger cars are counted; the passenger car rate of increase is slightly below that of the nation.

Bridges are a part of highway communication and their design, construction and maintenance comes properly under the supervision of the Bridge Department of the Division of Highways. Every form of bridge, viaduct and tunnel construction is to be found in California. So easily do many of them merge into the landscape that the driver of a passenger car or truck running smoothly over the concrete and asphalt roadways frequently does not realize that he is indebted to an intricate piece of engineering that supports his road.

Until 1964 the Golden Gate Bridge had the longest suspension span in the United States and the Transbay to Oakland was not far behind. The third largest suspension bridge in California is the superstructure of the Vincent Thomas Bridge between San Pedro and Terminal Island, with a central span of 1,500 ft., opened 1963. In 1964 the California Toll Bridge Authority authorized the Department of Public Works to proceed with the design and acquisition of right-of-way for a toll bridge from San Diego to Coronado. Studies were begun for financing and constructing additional toll crossings of San Francisco Bay south of the Transbay Bridge. A new approach to the Benicia-Martinez Bridge from Interstate 80 at Cordelia to the north end of the Bridge also was authorized. Many new bridges spanned rivers, creeks and canyons.

A new Sacramento River Bridge carries Interstate 80 from Jefferson Blvd. in West Sacramento to Fifth St. in Sacramento; the river spans are 275 ft. long. The Caldecott Tunnel for vehicles through the Berkeley Hills, adjacent to two older tunnels, is 3,300 ft. long, 28 ft. wide between curbs, lined with tile and provided with fluorescent lighting. It cost $11,050,000. Also lately opened was new Route 154 carried over Cold Springs Canyon between Santa Barbara and Santa Ynez by a 700-ft. steel arch span. A new bridge carrying Interstate 40 across the Colorado River at Topock was being constructed at a cost of $2,400,000, of which Arizona paid half. A new bridge across the Klamath River at Klamath, to cost $1,500,000, will carry Interstate 101. A view of the work carried on by the Highway Department in cities is given by the completion in San Francisco of a third unit of Route 82 freeway at a cost of $7,500,000 and a $4,000,000 construction project on State 280 at the San Francisco-San Mateo county line, comprising a three-level interchange and thirteen bridges.

# *Architecture*

THE EARLIEST architecture in California was that of the Spanish Franciscans. These missionary friars, led by Fra Junípero
Serra, founded 21 missions along the coastwise *Camino Real*
between 1769 and 1823—the first at San Diego, the last at Sonoma.
It has been said that the poverty to which the Franciscan monks were
pledged is the virtue of their mission churches. In comparison with
eighteenth century Spanish Colonial architecture in Mexico and the
Southwest, they exhibit simplicity of form and humility in treatment.
The relative austerity of the missions was due mainly to the limited
resources in materials and skilled labor.

There are three general types of plans in mission churches: those
having only a simple nave without side aisles, as San Miguel and
Dolores; those of rectangular plan with a single bell tower on the
front, as San Buenaventura and San Luís Rey de Francia; and those
with two belfried towers, as admirably exemplified by Mission Santa
Barbara. Typically, the missions were planned around a patio quadrangle, usually enclosed by the church and minor buildings—the cells
of the friars, quarters for the Indian workmen, servants and soldiers,
guest rooms, work shops, refectory, kitchen, and convent for young
Indian women. These minor buildings were arranged in two and
sometimes three rows of chambers with arcaded cloisters fronting the
patio and sometimes the outer plaza. The arches were carried on heavy
piers rather than columns.

The missions were constructed of stone and adobe, finished inside
and out with mud plaster and frequently strengthened on the outside

with heavy buttresses. The whitewashed exterior walls, with their simple architectural adornments and deeply recessed wall openings, are in striking contrast to contemporary Churrigueresque style of vice-regal Mexico. They were relieved only by the typical grouping of detail around the doors and windows--pilasters, classic trim, paneling, and an occasional iron or wooden grille. The most characteristic features, however, are the pitched roofs of hewn timber covered with red tile; the square towers with their domed and arched belfries, usually in two stages; and the curvilinear gables rising above the peak of the roof to give a more elaborate silhouette and added height to the facade. Frequently the gable ends were adorned with a niched figure of a saint or pierced with arched belfries, as at Mission San Gabriel. Occasionally they were designed in the form of a classic pediment. Perhaps the most notable mission church in California is Santa Barbara. The design of its strictly classic facade with columns and pediments, based upon a drawing in the Spanish edition of Vitruvius, is entirely in keeping with the earliest phase of the Spanish Renaissance. The restored San Juan Capistrano Mission with its ruined sanctuary and cloistered arcades is architecturally one of the most pretentious of the chain. Other notable missions in California are San Carlos de Borromeo at Carmel, San Gabriel Arcangel near Los Angeles, San Diego Alcalá in San Diego, and San Antonio de Padua near Jolon.

Generally free of the emotionalism and excesses of the Spanish baroque, the interiors of the missions reflect the simple taste of the Franciscan order. They are characterized by long narrow naves with whitewashed walls and painted ornaments, low dados, slender pilasters naively rendered in imitation of marble, occasional festoons and draperies, and timber ceilings with dark hand-carved, stenciled beams supported at the walls by scrolled brackets. Forming the focal point at one end is the sanctuary with its high altar, decorative reredos and wine glass pulpit. The altar and reredos were often freely embellished with colorful paintings, draped figures and gilded carvings executed by the padres and Indian craftsmen in the manner of both the Plateresque and Churrigueresque Spanish tradition. The fine detail of the facade of San Carlos near Monterey, the delicately carved reredos of San Juan Capistrano and the ornate retable of the mortuary chapel of San Luís Rey de Francia are striking but not isolated examples of Franciscan decoration. The monks also acquired ornate and gilded furnishings from Mexico and Spain and enriched their walls with paintings, as exemplified by the elaborate reredos of the Mission Dolores and the murals at San Miguel.

Within a few years of the coming of the Franciscans the Spanish Government made vast grants of land, where the Spanish and Mexican *rancheros* built their homes and established themselves with their families, their *vaqueros,* and their herds. Like the builders of the missions they used adobe, but whereas the monks wished to put up churches as nearly as possible in a style traditionally ecclesiastical, the Spanish dons were concerned only with comfort and convenience. The charm of these adobe houses lies in their simplicity, their admirable proportions, and their fitness with the landscape.

Many Spanish Colonial houses are still standing. In southern California they are usually one story in height and rectangular in plan, occasionally with a wing forming an "L." Their timber roofs, covered with hand-riven shingles or tile, frequently extend over a long veranda supported by wooden posts along one or sometimes three sides of the house. The interiors are planned with and without corridors; circulation from one room to another in the case of the latter is provided by way of the veranda. The thick adobe walls are covered with white-washed mud plaster and pierced with small double-hung windows, set flush with the outside wall surface and frequently protected by simple iron or wooden grilles. The interiors, also finished in plaster, have tile and wooden floors, ceilings with exposed hewn beams of pine or redwood, and deep splayed and paneled windows, often having seats and inner shutters.

Farther north the houses are frequently two stories in height with massive first story walls, three feet thick, and thinner second-story walls generally offset from the inside. The two-story dwellings have balconies at the front and rear, occasionally extending around the entire house. The balconies are generally of two types: two storied, with posts extending from ground to roof of upper gallery; and cantilevered, with posts at the second story supporting an overhanging roof. Due to the weight of tile roofing, the balconies are frequently covered with wood shakes or hand-split shingles.

Numerous adobe structures erected by the Spanish dons during the prosperous 1830's and 1840's are still found along the streets of small coast towns, in the old sections of the large cities, and scattered over the valleys and plains. By far the greatest number are in Monterey. Among the most notable of these Colonial structures in this historic town are the Larkin house, the Old Customs House, the Pacific Building (one of the early hotels), the Eldorado House, the Escolas House, and the Old Whaling Station. Perhaps one of the most picturesque ranch houses is the Olivos House near Ventura with its two-story porch, outer stairway and belfried gate. Other notable examples are found in the Paseo de la Guerra in Santa Barbara, on Olvera Street in Los Angeles, and along the picturesque streets of Old Town in San Diego.

Many of the first American settlers were from New England and they brought with them the stern architectural traditions of that

region.   Even before 1850 an architectural fusion had begun.   The
Americans combined their sound workmanship and feeling for good
design with the traditions of Spanish California.   In the coast counties
already settled by the Spanish, they frequently used adobe, but added
early nineteenth-century American detail in the form of clapboard siding, green blinds and double-hung windows and paneled doors flanked
by small side lights.   Some of the intrepid pioneers from the East dismantled the homes they had occupied, brought the material with them
around the Horn, and reconstructed their dwellings in California.   One
of these structures, erected in 1852, is on the Sherwood ranch near
Salinas.

During the eighteen thirties and eighteen forties, while the first
overland immigrants were arriving in the Sacramento Valley, Russian
pioneers were also attempting to establish a permanent settlement in
Sonoma County.   Little remains of the pioneer structures of these two
groups except the quaint timbered Russian church at Fort Ross with
its two silo-like cupolas and adjoining stockade, and the Old Bale Mill
in Napa County, built in 1846.   The latter, covered with narrow clapboards, is a notable example of American pioneer architecture with its
high "false front" and huge mill wheel.

With the discovery of gold in 1848 and the mushroom growth of
the older cities (especially in the north) and of the mining towns, the
orderly development of the Spanish-American style of architecture was
pushed into the background.   The older inhabitants in the south and
in the rural districts continued to build in the traditional manner,
sometimes crudely imitated by the newcomers.   But most of the buildings of the mining towns in Sierra, Amador, El Dorado, and Tuolumne Counties, many of which are still in use today, frankly record
the restless and temporary aspects of the era.   Here are found numerous dilapidated structures of frame, brick, and stone, one and two
stories in height; some with steep gable roofs and overhanging eaves,
others with front porches with rickety plank floors, slender wood posts
and sagging shed roofs, while many are characterized by their "false
fronts" with straight and saw-tooth silhouettes.   Answering the needs
of these mushroom towns countless general stores, makeshift hotels,
rooming houses, banks, and saloons were erected.   Many of these
buildings may be seen in the vicinity of Downieville, El Dorado, Columbia, Knight's Ferry, and Weaverville.   With their iron doors and
window shutters, they still stand—sometimes gutted with fire as at El
Dorado; sometimes deserted as in the ghost towns of Old Shasta or
Hornitos; but sometimes, as at Sonora or Angels Camp, they continue
to serve the purposes for which they were built.

Until the building of the transcontinental railroad in 1869, new
fashions in architecture, as in other spheres, came slowly across the

plains or around the Horn. The railroad was not an unmixed blessing, architecturally, for not only did it bring the lumber mill closer to every town, it brought the silver of the fabulous Comstock Lode, which meant wealth—and wealth meant ever larger buildings with more and more fantastic architectural elements. An epidemic of the Victorian pestilence in aggravated form seized California. Whether it was the American version of Victorian Gothic with its pointed arches, battlements, and crestings or the vagaries of the French style of Napoleon III with its mansard roofs and cupolas, bracketed pediments, iron crestings, and the addition of interminable jigsaw work, the results were lamentable and are obvious enough in all the older towns and cities. In San Francisco thousands of Victorian horrors were destroyed in the earthquake of 1906; but many remain, their lines sometimes a little softened by shrubs and vines, sometimes stark and bare in their shabby decay. The architecture of San Francisco, prior to the great fire and earthquake, was predominantly a product of this period and taste. Notable among the city's remaining mid-nineteenth century buildings are the Octagon House near the corner of Union and Gough Streets, the Hoataling Store on Jackson Street, standing among a number of earlier structures, and Fort Winfield Scott in the Presidio. Other examples of this era are the old schoolhouse at Almaden; a quaint hillside house with a broad veranda adorned with jigsaw ornaments, at the corner of Dodge and Stuart Streets in Sonora; and the pretentious gabled and bracketed Carson House, built by a wealthy lumberman in Eureka.

During the late nineties a number of buildings were erected along more academic lines: the State Capitol in Sacramento with its Italian Renaissance dome and Corinthian porticos, the Fresno County Courthouse, and the Ferry Terminal Building in San Francisco, with its slender tower pleasantly recalling the Giralda in Seville. At this time the architecture of California was influenced in a relatively minor way by the Romanesque Revival of H. H. Richardson. At Palo Alto the buildings for Stanford University afforded a group of his followers a fine opportunity to adapt the massive stonework, arcades, and mosaics of the Romanesque style to the design of the Memorial Church and the adjoining quadrangle. Other examples of this stylistic phase are the Mills Building in San Francisco, designed by Daniel Burnham, and the old Santa Fe Station in Los Angeles.

At the turn of the century an improved but somewhat eclectic taste became manifest in California as elsewhere. The Neoclassic and Italian Renaissance styles, popularized in the East by McKim, Mead and White and by the grandiose buildings of the Chicago World's Fair in 1893, were freely adapted to the designs of monumental public buildings. In 1915 the buildings of the Panama Pacific Exposition in San

Francisco contributed a lasting impetus to these traditional and stylistic trends.

More recent adaptations of classic architecture are the buildings of the formal civic group in San Francisco: the Renaissance City Hall by Bakewell and Brown, the Opera House, and the War Memorial Building. The Neoclassic California Palace of the Legion of Honor, by George Applegarth and H. Guillaume, is another example of formal design in this city. The Public Library, the State Building and the new Federal Building, with its long colonnade leading up to the plaza, all show the academic training of their architects in the Beaux-Arts tradition. In Berkeley the buildings of the University of California are of white granite in the Neoclassic style. Correct and academic, they indicate a high order of talent, but perhaps only the tall campanile and the highly stylized Life Sciences Building by Arthur Brown show a touch of genius. The United States Post Office at Sacramento, enriched by a fine Doric colonnade, follows the classic tradition with a rugged modern simplicity. At San Marino is the Huntington Library, by Myron Hunt, suggesting a more feminine rendering with coupled Ionic columns, and enhanced by formal landscaping. Perhaps the most modern adaptations of the Neoclassic style in civic buildings are the massive new Civic Center in San Diego, and the lofty Los Angeles City Hall, by Parkinson, Martin, and Austin, with its skyscraper tower and crowning pyramidal roof.

Bertram Goodhue's California Building erected in San Diego (1915) displays a masterly handling of the highly ornate Spanish Churrigueresque style of old Mexico and has been a guiding influence in the development of the modern California Mission style. Of the modern Spanish Colonial buildings, many are frankly reminiscent, direct copies or close modifications of existing Spanish or Mexican structures, while others show considerable change and development. One of the most consistent examples of the former is the palatial City Hall of Santa Barbara, the work of Thomas Mooser, Jr. Other instances are to be found in the numerous buildings of Morgan, Walls and Clements. Although there exists no rule or ordinance governing architectural design in the city of Santa Barbara, the art commission and the county regional planning board have encouraged and regulated the use of Spanish designs throughout the city. Various college buildings, including those at Occidental, Mills, and Scripps, display an admirable use of Spanish forms. The buildings making up the Pasadena Civic Center, the most notable of which is the library by Myron Hunt, are grouped about a terraced square. Their style is a formal expression of the Spanish Renaissance, florid in its detail but admirable in its unity and mass. The individual buildings, held together by a consistent handling of the architectural elements, are dominated by the reddish gold dome of the City Hall.   Several buildings of the California Institute of Technology in Pasadena, the Henry Data House and the Country Club in Montecito, the W. K. Kellogg Ranch buildings near Pomona, and in San Diego the Serra Museum, the permanent buildings of the Panama-California Exposition, the U. S. Marine Corps Base, and the U. S. Naval Air Station demonstrate the validity of the style to all but extremists.

In recent years a number of outstanding works have been designed in a more modern version of the Romanesque style than that of H. H. Richardson.   The University of California at Los Angeles has a fine group of buildings designed in this manner.   Smaller but no less admirable Romanesque designs are seen in the junior college building and Sacred Heart Church in Sacramento, the Church of the Precious Blood and St. John's Church in Los Angeles, and, surprisingly enough, in the tower of a wholesale coffee establishment near the San Francisco waterfront.   Splendid examples of the ecclesiastical Gothic tradition, all adapted with a freshness and vigor of style, are St. Dominic's in San Francisco, the First Presbyterian Church in Oakland, Emanuel Presbyterian Church in Los Angeles, and the unfinished Grace Cathedral in San Francisco.   There are also occasional examples of the more colorful Byzantine style in such buildings as the Temple Emanuel in San Francisco and the B'nai B'rith Temple in Los Angeles.

Since the beginning of the twentieth century one of the chief developments in California domestic architecture has been the bungalow, which derives its name, and, rather remotely, its structure from the domestic architecture of the white population of southeast Asia.   The bungalow was first developed in southern California, where its wide overhanging eaves, flat pitched roof extending over broad porches, and low windows were admirably adapted to the climate.   Cheap and easy to build, the type soon swept the State and later the country.   Well-to-do clients demanded two- and even three-story bungalows, and these buildings are often handsome as well as homelike.   Berkeley and the residential areas of Los Angeles, which were most fashionable prior to the World War, contain many fine examples.

The truly encouraging element in contemporary domestic architecture is the return to a simple interpretation of the Spanish Colonial type of house.   The fusion of the Spanish adobe with the early eighteenth and nineteenth century traditional American wooden types with the addition of such modern features as corner windows, has come to be called the "Monterey" style.   It is admirably suited to modest living and today, for the first time since 1870, great numbers of well-designed houses are being erected in this manner.  The David Selznick House in Beverly Hills and the Edward Heath House in San Marino, both by Roland E. Coate, and the Gregory Farm, near Santa Cruz, by William W. Wurster, are excellent examples of this modification of a traditional style.

The development of modern domestic architecture in California stems from the International Style, established immediately after the World War in France, Holland, and Germany by such men as Le Corbusier, Gropius, Van der Rohe, and Oud, as well as from the highly radical innovations of Frank Lloyd Wright.  The international phase has been enthusiastically adapted in California by Richard Neutra, William Lescaze, R. M. Schindler and others.  Independently, both Wright and Neutra follow the dictum, "Form follows function." Both have envisaged a new architecture designed to conform with twentieth century industrial society.  Following the epigram of Le Corbusier, "A house is a machine for living," the work of the ultra-modern practitioners demands the use of both modern building materials and engineering methods: the use of synthetic plastics, ferro-concrete, cantilevers; the blending of interior and exterior construction, and, subsequently, built-in furniture; and finally the complete lack of applied ornament and decoration.

Wright, however, developed from the earlier Chicago School of Louis Sullivan in a direction of his own.  His work, recognized in Europe before it was widely accepted at home, is romantic, full of imaginative flights, very daring structurally, and highly personal. Among his finest homes in California are the Freeman House in Los Angeles, and the home of George Millard in Pasadena, both with low massive exterior walls constructed of decorated blocks; the Aline Barnsdall House in Hollywood, with its tapering walls and its geometric ornaments suggesting an Aztec or Mayan temple; and the Dr. Paul Hanna House at Stanford.

Perhaps no one has been more courageous in carrying the principles of functionalism to their final conclusions than Richard Neutra.  His earlier work in Los Angeles, including his Garden Apartments, the Lovell House, the All-Plywood House, and his own Research House has been the subject of wide discussion.  Because of his rigorous engineering training and his awareness of social issues, he has stressed the use of prefabricated building materials, engineering devices derived from utilitarian structures, economy and efficiency of construction, and constant emphasis on the relation of the house to the movement of its occupants.  He has dealt admirably with the problems of mass housing and community planning.  R. M. Schindler, another exponent of this modern school, has designed many "outdoor" houses of prefabricated materials, revealing the mingling of interior and exterior in his "garden with walls and roof," his use of disjunct planes, sun walls, and open areas.   The beach house of Professor Alexander Kaun at Richmond and the V. McAlmon House on Waverly Drive, Los Angeles, are notable examples of his domestic work.

No survey of the contemporary architectural scene is complete without mention of the steady growth and improvement of commercial buildings.   The office building exhibits a development from the steel skeleton structure embellished with various stylistic forms to the modern version of the skyscraper, with its simple mass and emphasis upon vertical and horizontal lines.   Splendid examples of the latter are Timothy Fleuger's Four-Fifty Sutter, the Russ Building, and the Empire Hotel, originally built to house the Temple Methodist Episcopal Church and the William Taylor Hotel, in San Francisco.   The Kaiser Center in Oakland (360 ft., 28 stories) looks twice its height as it rises above Lake Merritt.   The United States Post Office in Stockton, the Los Angeles County Hospital and the new San Francisco Mint are both modern and monumental.   The Los Angeles Public Library by Goodhue—a towering buttressed structure of modern design, set in a beautifully landscaped tract—is a noteworthy example of highly stylized traditional architecture.

Up to World War II there was no general movement in California to erect tall buildings such as took place in New York City and other cities of the eastern seaboard.   The "earthquake proviso" of 150 ft. was widely observed.   With a few exceptions office buildings in San Francisco did not exceed 30 stories in height and one of the streamlined structures, No. 450 Sutter St., had only 26.   The 435 ft. height was reached by both the Russ Building and the Telephone Building; the Hardford went up 465 ft. and had 33 stories.   The new Wells Fargo Building, with 561 ft. and 43 stories, was expected to become the tallest on the West Coast, but construction had hardly begun when the Bank of America published plans to erect more than 50 stories of glass and steel and thus have the tallest man-made landmark on the Coast.

Los Angeles, able to expand laterally, removed its limitation of 150 ft. in 1957, but builders made no effort to push beyond 30 stories. The office spire of the City Hall dominated down town, and although it had only 28 stories to the 32 of Occidental Life Building, at 454 ft. it was two feet taller than the latter.   By 1965 Los Angeles builders were ready to go skyward and Bunker Hill became the area for major reconstruction.   The huge monolith of the Union Bank in 1966 rose 42 stories and more than 500 feet, and with its facilities for accommodating motor cars underground set a fashion in business building.   The Crocker-Citizens Building followed the same pattern, but its cruciform tower of 40 stories above a four-story base was an innovation.

The trim, rambling, well-lighted experimental public schools in Santa Monica and Los Angeles, with their outdoor classrooms and ample play areas, ably illustrate the principles of modern planning. Other notable examples of efficient and economical planning are the Emerson junior and the Corona senior high schools in Los Angeles, by Richard Neutra, and the John Adams junior high school in Santa Monica, by Marsh, Smith and Powell. While the so-called neo-Mediterranean style was favored by some colleges, the University of California, engaged in planning for its new campuses, wholeheartedly embraced the structures of glass and steel that left no dark corners anywhere.

The mild climate of southern California affords unusual opportunities for the construction of numerous outdoor theaters and stadia. Among the most notable of these are the huge Hollywood Bowl, the Spreckels outdoor organ and amphitheater in Balboa Park at San Diego, the Los Angeles Memorial Coliseum, and the celebrated Rose Bowl in Pasadena.

Two great bridges add their graceful lines to the horizon of the Bay. The San Francisco-Oakland Bay Bridge, opened in 1936, was designed by C. H. Purcell of the State Dept. of Public Works. The Golden Gate Bridge, opened in 1937, was designed by Joseph B. Strauss. The latter was the world's longest single-span suspension bridge until November, 1964, when its 4,200 ft. span was surpassed by the fifty-foot larger span of the Narrows-Verrazano Bridge in New York.

Great changes in architecture were impending by 1940. It seemed that the last big effort of the romantics was the Golden Gate International Exposition on Treasure Island in San Francisco Bay in 1939-40. The two expositions at San Diego, 1915-16 and 1935-36, left a legacy of decorative neo-Spanish architecture that still inspires students. After the San Francisco Fair closed its gates architects turned to the new schools of functional design. When the Pavilion of the Music Center of Los Angeles and the new Los Angeles County Museum of Art opened in 1965, the West Coast was completely in step with modern style.

# PART II
## Signposts to City Scenes

# Berkeley

*Transportation:* Southern Pacific, University Ave. and Third St.; Santa Fe, University Ave. and West St. Pacific Greyhound Bus Lines and National Trailways, University and San Pablo Aves. Electric transit, Shattuck Square, regular services to San Francisco and environs. Principal highway connections, US 4 (Interstate 80), also same direct across Bay via San Francisco-Oakland Bay Bridge. Flying services at Metropolitan Oakland International Airport, 15 *m.*

*Accommodations:* Berkeley has several modern hotels within one block of the University campus, and well-equipped motels, especially on University Ave. Hotel Claremont, in 22 acres of landscaped grounds is a widely known resort hotel.

*Community Facilities:* Berkeley has two general hospitals with 449 beds. Medical facilities include 330 physicians and surgeons, and 114 dentists. Educational facilities include 17 elementary schools, 2 junior high schools and one high school on 2 campuses, one adult day school, one evening school, one trade and technical college; the University of California, State Schools for Blind and Deaf and 5 Divinity Schools. There are 94 churches, 5 libraries, 2 newspapers and 5 banks.

Research institutions in the area include Hillcone Steamship Co., Hyman Laboratories, Inc., Institute for Clinical Pharmacology and Medical Research, Laboratory for Science and Solano laboratories.

*Recreation:* Facilities include 11 theaters, one summer musical theater, 21 parks, 9 playgrounds and a Yacht Harbor. Nearby are Charles Lee Tilden Regional Park, Temescal Regional Park and Round Top Regional Park. Four city recreation centers conduct social, physical and creative activities for all ages throughout the year. Dance, gymnastics, drama, arts and crafts, judo, fencing, folk dance, bridge, physical fitness programs are open to all. Learn-to-sail classes at Aquatic Park 80-acre lake. Fireplace barbecue, outdoor amphitheater in John Hinkel Park. Harbor, foot of University Ave., offers boating, fishing in the Bay or from the pier (no license). Swim centers have classes and competitive and diving programs. Tennis class for youths and adults in the following parks: Codornices, Grove, James Kenny, Live Oak and San Pablo. Berkeley Recreation & Parks Dept., 1835 Allston Way.

BERKELEY (0-1,300 alt., 111,268 pop., 1960, 120,300 Oct., 1964), on a wide plain below a low range of hills, borders on the east shore of San Francisco Bay, facing the Golden Gate. At the upper edge of the city, against protective hills and wooded canyons, stand the buildings of the University of California. Viewed from the bay, the city seems to radiate from the white campus buildings.

Berkeley, however, is more than a college town. It is an industrial center, a business city, a suburban home for thousands of workers. Upward from the industrial waterfront extend myriads of small homes occupied by those who man the factories in East Bay cities and San Francisco. Office workers whose jobs are in San Francisco reside chiefly in north and southeast Berkeley. It is a unit in the expanding Alameda County which had 908,209 pop. in 1960 and over 1,000,000 in 1964.

The two main shopping districts exemplify characteristic differences between the two parts of town. The Shattuck Avenue district, just west of the university campus, bears all the signs of ordinary commercial development. The Telegraph Avenue shopping area, extending southward from the main campus entrance, is full of young people and of shops reflecting their needs and interests.

South of the campus is a residential section with old homes of an architecture peculiar to Berkeley. The early inhabitants, aware of the corrosive effect of sea air on paint, utilized pitched roofs, walls of unpainted shingles, and vines to cover them, and built rustic houses that blended with a background of hills overgrown with oak, boxwood, manzanita, and bay. Bordering the campus on three sides are fraternity and sorority houses, some in the old tradition of Berkeley architecture, some designed in modern fashion. Vying with them in importance as student dwellings are modern stucco apartment buildings and old-fashioned boarding houses. On steep hills to the north, rising above the campus, cling those homes which have given Berkeley the right to be compared to Amalfi and Naples. Here every residence has a prospect of the bay, and some have canyon views as well; gardens hang to the edge of rock banks or trail in terraces down the hillside.

Along the waterfront is Berkeley's factory district where industrial plants produce toilet articles, drugs, inks, printing material and structural aluminum products. Largest employer in non-manufacturing enterprises is the University of California, 12,162.

Berkeley took its name from George Berkeley, Bishop of Cloyne (1685-1753), the Irish philosopher who crossed the Atlantic to found an institution for evangelizing and educating the Indians, and who wrote "Westward, the course of empire takes it way." Henry Durant, one of the trustees of the College of California, hailed the words as prophetic. Bishop Berkeley's ideals were thought so proper for a young college town that the trustees adopted his name.

Originally, Berkeley was part of the 46,800-acre Rancho San Antonio granted to the Peralta family in 1820 by the Spanish Governor de Sola. American squatters had a false survey made in the 1850's, cutting off 7,000 acres of redwood timber and all the waterfront. They drove off

Peralta cattle, and had José Domingo Peralta jailed for trying to eject them from his land. In 1853, title to what is now Berkeley was purchased by American speculators for $82,000. The first American building in Berkeley was a roadhouse erected in 1853 near San Pablo Avenue and Delaware Street.

Foundation of the university gave impetus to Berkeley's growth, but other factors contributed. In 1874 there were only a few residences south of the campus, and two years later the population was only 948. Following 1884, however, when a large reservoir was built and water pipes were laid, growth was rapid. By 1906 streets were paved and huge residential tracts had been opened; the Santa Fe built a station, and the Key Route established 38-minute service to San Francisco, opening the way for large scale commuting. A determined effort failed to make Berkeley the State capital, but attracted notice to the town. Following the San Francisco earthquake and fire in 1906, many refugees moved permanently to Berkeley. In 1905 the population was 23,378; in 1907 it was 38,117.

A fire, starting in the hills and fanned by a strong wind, destroyed most of the city north of the campus in September, 1923. The disaster resulted in the creation of one of the most efficient fire-prevention systems in the United States and in a Disaster-Preparedness Plan. A deputy fire warden is on duty day and night in a Berkeley hills tower to insure against a repetition of the fire.

Berkeley's civic pride expresses itself in municipal administration, law enforcement, and education. In 1923 the city adopted the council-manager form of government and since has been regarded as a model in municipal administration. Among the Bay cities Berkeley ranks seventh in manufacturing, with about 8,000 employed in industry that dispenses an annual payroll of $39,000,000. Besides the University Berkeley has the Pacific School of Religion, the Baptist Divinity School, the Church Divinity School of the Pacific and the Armstrong College of Business Administration.

## THE UNIVERSITY OF CALIFORNIA

The spacious University of California campus extends across Berkeley from Oxford St. east to the hills and from Hearst Ave. south to Bancroft Way, on rising land that affords a splendid view of San Francisco Bay. The campus, originally a plain of oaks cut through by Strawberry Canyon, is now a beautifully landscaped park, with roomy white buildings, groves of eucalyptus, oak, and pine, lawns planted with shrubs and flowering trees, and brilliant gardens. The central campus has 178 acres; with outlying acreage, 1,500.

In 1896 Mrs. Phoebe Apperson Hearst financed an international competition for a comprehensive university building plan. The winning plan by Emile Benard was subsequently modified by himself and by John Galen Howard, brought from New York as university architect. The Hellenic style of architecture and the main lines and vistas, with modifications, were determined by the original plan.   Gaunt old South Hall, one of the first two campus buildings, was built before the plan. It still survives.

The State constitution of 1849 provided for the university, but it owes its inception largely to the efforts of two zealous educators and clergymen.   The founding of the university was delayed for two decades by legislative disagreement, but Henry Durant and Samuel Hopkins Willey prepared privately for its coming.   In 1853 Mr. Durant opened the Contra Costa Academy in Oakland, grandparent of the unborn institution; in 1860 the academy became the College of California under Mr. Willey's leadership; and finally in 1869 the college became the nucleus of the new university.

A charter was granted in 1868, but the College of California carried on instruction for 18 months until the work of organization was complete.   By that time a faculty of 10 was ready to serve 40 students entering the new university.   Registration and public interest increased in 1870 when a co-education plan was adopted.

By 1873 two halls, North and South, had been built on the Berkeley campus and 167 men and 22 women enrolled there.   This was the nucleus for the great institution that has achieved many distinguished goals.   It is governed by a Board of Regents of twenty-four members, sixteen appointed to sixteen-year terms by the Governor, and eight holding office ex-officio.   The President of the University, appointed by the Regents, is administrative office of all campuses.   The California Alumni Association has about 50,000 members.

In nearly 100 years the University not only has increased the facilities for education at its home base in Berkeley, but has reached out to meet students more than halfway by building on eight other campuses, a feat of organization that has set the pace for higher education in the United States.   The other centers are Los Angeles, Davis, Riverside, San Francisco Medical Center, Santa Barbara, San Diego (1964), Santa Cruz (1965) and Irvine (1965).   At Berkeley the enrollment for 1963-64 was 26,756, which included 10,327 undergraduate men and 7,344 undergraduate women; 6,854 graduate men and 2,221 graduate women.   The extension division enrolled 47,528 in Northern California.   There were 2,477 foreign students.   The teaching staff numbered 3,235, the research staff, 1,394.

The University in 1965 had 15 schools and colleges, 72 departments of instruction, 43 bureaus and laboratories; 15 centers for research and 3 teaching museums.   The Main Library has 20 specialized branches and a total of 2,900,000 books and regularly received 36,000 different periodicals.   The Bancroft Library, with historical collections, possesses the plate of brass that has been identified as having been left by Sir Francis Drake in 1579.

The University supervises housing of students and gives special attention to their welfare.   There are 8 residence halls for men with 1,664 occupants and 10 for women with 1,669 occupants; 4 student cooperatives for men and 5 for women, and 919 apartments are provided in

Albany Village for married students. When an undergraduate registers he automatically becomes a member of the Associated Students of the University of California (ASUC), which sponsors student activities. Especially useful is the STUDENT UNION, completed in 1961, one of a Student Center Complex including the Commons for dining, and the Student Office Building, erected 1965. INTERNATIONAL HOUSE is a residential and social center for foreign and American students and visiting scholars and has quarters for 530. More than 60 countries are represented.

## LOWER CAMPUS

SATHER GATE, built of bronze and concrete above a bridge and roadway was erected with funds provided by Jane K. Sather in memory of Peder Sather. College meetings and rallies are often held here.

WHEELER HALL, housing classrooms and auditorium of the College of Arts and Sciences, is a neo-classic structure of white granite, adorned with Ionic colonnades, built in 1917 and named for Benjamin Ide Wheeler, university president from 1899 to 1919.

The LIFE SCIENCES BUILDING, a majestic neo-Classic structure with rusticated base, modified Corinthian columns, high attic story and fine bronze grilles, was completed in 1930 under the supervision of Arthur Brown. In addition to the life sciences and their allied departments, it contains the MUSEUM OF VERTEBRATE ZOOLOGY (*open to students only*), the Institute of Experimental Biology, the Laboratory of the State Board of Health, and the HERBARIUM (*open 8:30-12, 1-5 Mon.-Fri.; 8:30-12 Sat.*)

The AGRICULTURE GROUP consists of Hilgard Hall, Giannini Hall, and Agriculture Hall, all of modified Italian Renaissance design, with corner quoins and tile roofs. In the greenhouses (*not open*) nearby experiments are conducted in plant breeding.

The ART GALLERY, facing Bancroft Lane (*open noon to 6 p.m.*), has examples of all the fine arts. The DECORATIVE ARTS BUILDING, east of the Gallery, has student and professional works. DWINELLE HALL, opposite the Life Sciences Bldg., has Chinese jade, sculpture and ceramics. Kroeber Hall, east of the Hearst Gymnasium for Women on Bancroft Way, has contemporary art, with the Lowie Museum of Anthropology adjoining.

HAVILAND HALL, the School of Education, contains the Alexis F. Lange Educational Library and an exhibition of photography, handicraft, and etchings.

LEUSCHNER OBSERVATORY (*open 8-10 p.m. first Sat. each month*) is a group of domed buildings completely equipped for the study of astronomy. It contains 5- and 8-inch refracting telescopes. The university's main astronomical work, however, is done at Lick Observatory (*see TOUR 2b*).

The SCHOOL OF ARCHITECTURE BUILDING, contains laboratories, drawing and modeling rooms, and architectural exhibition rooms.

The ENGINEERING GROUP comprises the Engineering Laboratory, the Engineering Design Building, Hesse Hall, and the Mechanics' Building. In the Materials Testing Laboratory is a huge testing machine (capacity 4,000,000 pounds) for trial of structural members. Materials for Hoover Dam, the San Francisco-Oakland Bay Bridge, and other important public projects were tested here.

The HEARST MEMORIAL MINING BUILDING, of Italian Renaissance design, was given in 1907 by Phoebe Apperson Hearst in memory of her husband, Senator George Hearst. It has classrooms for mining engineering students and exhibits. The EARTH SCIENCES BUILDING, opposite Leuschner Observatory, has a seismograph recorder on the first floor, a rock collection on the third and charts and maps on the upper floors. *Open 8 to 5 Mon. through Sat.*

The CHEMISTRY GROUP includes Gilman Hall, built in 1918 and named for Daniel Coit Gilman, the university's second president, who organized the chemistry department in 1872.

The LIBRARY of the University has a central location near the Sather Tower. (*Open weekdays, 8-10, except Saturdays, 8-5; Sundays, 1-10*). It is the center of twenty branch libraries and a number of smaller departmental collections. With about 3,000,000 volumes and many periodicals it is one of the best equipped libraries anywhere. The Library has the Bacon Art and Library Collections, the Library of French Thought, the Alexander F. Morrison Library for recreational reading, and the Bancroft Library, based on the collection of the historian Hubert Howe Bancroft, the last housed in a building adjoining. It includes more than 100,000 volumes on Spanish-American history and has the 1579 brass plate attributed to Sir Francis Drake.

SATHER TOWER, popularly called the Campanile, designed by John Galen Howard, was built in 1914 through a bequest by Jane K. Sather. Designed in the Italian Renaissance style, with pyramidal roof, belfry, and pinnacles, it recalls the lofty campanile in St. Mark's square in Venice. It is constructed of granite, 307 feet high, 36 feet square, with a clock on its four sides, and an observation platform at the top. The belfry contains 12 bells, cast in England. A Gutzon Borglum bust of Lincoln stands at the south base.

ESHLEMAN HALL, on Bancroft Way, houses the student publications. It was built in 1930 and named for John Martin Eshleman, an alumnus and former Lieutenant Governor of California.

## UPPER CAMPUS

The HEARST GREEK THEATER is designed in the manner of an ancient amphitheater. Built of concrete, it has a semicircular auditorium seating 7,154 persons, and a stage adorned with Doric columns and pilasters. The theater was presented by William Randolph Hearst in 1903. Classic dramas are occasionally given.

LAWRENCE RADIATION LABORATORY, on a hill east of the campus, was established in 1936 as part of the University's Department of Physics. It is named for its former director, Dr. Ernest O.

Lawrence, who invented the cyclotron in 1930 and received the Nobel prize for physics in 1939. The Laboratory is operated under contract with the U. S. Atomic Energy Commission by the University of California. Dr. Glenn T. Seaborg, former chancellor of the University and associate director of the Laboratory, also a Nobel prize winner, is chairman of the Atomic Energy Commission. During World War II the Laboratory was engaged under Manhattan Engineer District in an electromagnetic isotope separation process, which led to the establishing of the federal Oak Ridge plant. Work at Berkeley is devoted primarily to basic research into the nature of the atomic nucleus, with associated research into biology and medicine. In 1952 the AEC asked Dr. Lawrence to form a second nuclear weapons laboratory and this was established at Livermore. It is operated by the University as also is the Los Alamos Scientific Laboratory in New Mexico, which the University founded in 1943. *See also page 86.*

Room 307 of Gilman Hall has been made a national historic landmark because here on February 24, 1941, Glenn T. Seaborg, chemistry instructor, and two associates established the presence of element 94, which they called plutonium. The next step, in which Emilio Segré, now head of the Department of Physics, took part, was the creation of isotope plutonium-239 and its fission, a powerful source of atomic energy. A year later Enrico Fermi and associates established control of the first chain reaction at Chicago. Previously Edwin M. McMillan, now director of Lawrence Radiation Laboratory, with P. H. Abelson transmuted Uranium-238 into element 93, which he called neptunium.

The release of atomic energy was made possible by the invention of the cyclotron, or atom-smasher, by Ernest O. Lawrence. This led to the creation of radioactive isotopes from such elements as phosphorous and sodium, opening new prospects for diagnosis and treatment of disease. Today the Bevatron atom-smasher accelerates protons to 6.2 billion volts (BeV.). In 1963 McMillan was authorized by the AEC to design a 200 BeV. machine, location to be determined by Congress. It is expected to cost around $348,000,000.

Space has been allocated on the hills above the campus for the new LAWRENCE HALL OF SCIENCE, named for the great physicist who invented the cyclotron here. The purpose of the Hall, in the words of the University announcement is "the stimulation and improvement of science education for youth. Laboratories, workshops, seminars, classrooms, and special exhibits are to provide exceptional educational opportunities for teachers, students and the public."

Among the many achievements at Berkeley are the first isolation of a virus, including the one causing human poliomyelitis; discovery of a number of pituitary hormones, among them the human growth ACTH; discovery of all eleven artificial elements heavier than uranium; first use of radioactive tracers in the study of a cell; discovery of the anti-proton and other elementary particles that form the basis for all matter; the first breakdown and reconstitution of a virus, with the discovery that nucleic acid carries the vital infectious properties, and first demonstration of permanent chemical changes in the brain as the result of learning. Berkeley also is the center for studies and research in physical development, behavior and aging; the effect of social environment on the physical and psychological adult human behavior and personality. Computers are used for many operations, including the translation of languages, seventy-nine of which are taught at Berkeley.

ATHLETICS and PHYSICAL TRAINING headquarters are located near Bancroft Way on the south side of the campus. HARMON GYMNASIUM FOR MEN on Dana St. has a basketball arena and two swimming pools, and rooms for boxing, wrestling, fencing and gymnastics and courts for squash and handball. North of the Gymnasium is the EDWARDS FIELD AND TRACK STADIUM. More than 700 men compete in intercollegiate athletics annually, and in a typical year of the 1960's 973 intramural teams entered competition in twenty-two different sports, from riflery to rugby. National fame was won by Andy Smith's team of the 1920's, Clint Evans' NCCA basketball winners of 1947, Pete Newell's national basketball champions of 1959 and Ky Ebright's three Olympic championship crews. Dan Bowden was the first American to run the four-minute mile, and Leamon King and Jack Yerman won gold medals at recent Olympic Games. All-American football teams have included Brick Muller, Vic Bottari, Jackie Jensen and Joe Kapp; baseball victors have included George Dixon, Andy Wolfe and Darrell Imhoff. Farther east on Bancroft Way is the HEARST GYMNASIUM FOR WOMEN and its adjoining athletic field. It has three swimming pools and rooms for sports, exercising and dancing. The Women's Athletic Assn. sponsors sports clubs and conducts intramural sports programs.

CALIFORNIA MEMORIAL STADIUM, seating capacity 76,-780, was built in 1923 at a cost of $1,750,000, in memory of students who died in World War I. Football, soccer, and rugby games are held here.

BOTANICAL GARDEN (*open 9-4 daily*), in Strawberry Canyon above the Memorial Stadium, is a 35-acre tract devoted to plant culture. The collection includes 5,000 rare rhododendrons, and 2,000 cacti and succulents, growing in natural settings of sand and stone. There is an open-air theater, a memorial to Stephen Mather, first director of the National Park Service, in a five-acre tract of pine and redwood. STRAWBERRY CANYON RECREATIONAL AREA has a pool, tennis courts and playing fields. Clubhouse and pool may be used by permit, April-October.

## OTHER BERKELEY FEATURES

The PACIFIC SCHOOL OF RELIGION (*open by appointments, guides*), 1798 Scenic Ave., is a graduate theological school, interdenominational and co-educational. An A.B. degree is a prerequisite for entrance, and the school trains for all branches of religious work. There are three buildings, the Administration Building of Gothic archi-

# Cities

THE MALL, FRESNO

TELEGRAPH HILL WITH COIT TOWER, SAN FRANCISCO

FISHERMAN'S WHARF AND RUSSIAN HILL, SAN FRANCISCO

SAN FRANCISCO CABLE CAR

EASTER SERVICES,
HOLLYWOOD BOWL

STARS' PRINTS IN
CONCRETE,
GRAUMAN'S THEATER,
HOLLYWOOD

CITY HALL AND CIVIC CENTER, LOS ANGELES

MacARTHUR PARK, LOS ANGELES

STATE CAPITOL AND ANNEX, SACRAMENTO

LONG BEACH, WITH MUNICIPAL AUDITORIUM.
OIL WELLS IN BACKGROUND

DISNEYLAND, ANAHEIM

KAISER CENTER OFFICE BUILDING, OAKLAND

OLVERA STREET, MEXICAN VILLAGE, LOS ANGELES

tecture in gray cut stone; the gray stucco Dormitory, of Tudor design; and the HOLBROOK MEMORIAL LIBRARY (*open 8-6 Mon., 7-6 Tues.-Fri., 9-12 Sat.*), the twin of the Administration Building in structure. The library houses a collection of 30,000 volumes, including a "Breeches" Bible, Geneva, 1560; Babylonian cuneiform tablets; fourth century Biblical inscriptions on papyrus; and an extremely rare copy of the inscription on the Nestorian Monument in China. An archeological exhibit has relics dating from 3500 B.C. to the beginning of the Christian era.

TILDEN PARK, in Wildcat Canyon over the hills from Berkeley, is a part of the 10,000-acre East Bay Regional Park. Lately a rough, hilly country of manzanita and scrub oaks, and abounding in birds and small mammals, the park, improved with WPA labor, includes a golf course, scenic drives, and three camp districts.

CRAGMONT ROCK PARK, Regal Rd. and Hillside Ave., a neatly landscaped four-acre plot, rises from the lawns around it to the abrupt outcropping of rock that gives the park its name, and at 800 feet altitude has a lookout station with a fine view of San Francisco Bay, the bridges, and Golden Gate directly opposite.

BERKELEY AQUATIC PARK, flanked for more than a mile by the Berkeley bayshore and US 40, is built in the bay, and is composed largely of the lagoon thus formed. Water depth ranges from 3 to 15 feet and is controlled by floodgates. Small boats can be rented at the boathouse, there are facilities for model yacht racing, and the lagoon is a wildfowl sanctuary.

# *Fresno*

*Communications:* Fresno is located almost midway between San Francisco and Los Angeles, 185 *m.* from San Francisco, 219 *m.* from Los Angeles by freeways. It is served by the Southern Pacific and Santa Fe railways and Greyhound Bus lines. Its principal north-south highway is US 99, which has a bypass at Fresno. Other major routes are State 41, 168 and 180. Fresno Airport has direct connections with international airports in California. Fresno Travel-Tour, via Municipal Line Bus, starts at 9:30-10 a.m. from principal hotels.

*Information:* Tourist Information Center, operated by the Chamber of Commerce at Belmont Ave., on State 99, open daily. Fresno County and City Chamber of Commerce, 2331 Fresno St.

*Recreation:* Fresno is the focal point in Central California giving access to a large number of major sites for scenic drives, hunting, fishing, camping, following trails. Public and private golf courses dot the area, including Airways, Belmont, Fig Garden, Municipal, Fort Washington Country and San Joaquin Country clubs. Within a short drive are Millerton Lake and Pine Flat Lake, both with an all-year trout season, with a limit of five trout unless special rules apply; also the San Joaquin River for trout and salmon, which is closed from November 1 to opening day of the general season; for night fishing regulations for specific species consult information agencies or Fish & Game Commission, Sacramento; same for hunting. State 41 leads northeast direct to Mariposa Giant Redwoods of Yosemite National Park, 97 *m.;* State 180 goes southeast entering Sequoia National Park at General Grant Grove and King's River Canyon, 52 *m.* State 168, connecting with State 41, leads to Shaver, Huntington and Florence Lakes.

*Accommodations:* Fresno's Convention Center can accommodate associations up to 7,000 members. Principal hotels, Californian, Del Webb's Townehouse. Numerous motels especially along State 99, including Fresno Hascienda, Clinton Ave., with 347 rooms.

*Events:* Raisin Day, second Saturday in May. West Coast Relays, same day in May, Fresno State College. Fresno District Fair, September.

FRESNO (292 alt., 60,685 pop., 1940; 133,929, 1960; in 1965 local authorities estimated it had 154,000). It is the world's raisin center and principal marketing, shipping and purchasing point for the fertile San Joaquin Valley.

Tall modern buildings rise abruptly from the flat valley floor, surrounded by residential sections planted with trees to provide shade in the sweltering heat of summer. The business district, in the central and oldest part of town, grew around the railroad station, with the streets parallel to the tracks and diagonal to the cardinal points. Later streets were squared with the compass, and a set of 45-degree intersections resulted, all around the original square.

From the city limits the vineyards radiate in seemingly endless rows, set exactly 10 feet apart. The grapes ripen in August, September, and October, and are placed on trays to dry in the sun. With these agricultural environs, and with the country's largest fig gardens only four miles away, Fresno naturally is predominantly a farming community, despite its skyscrapers, neon lights, modern store fronts, and busy traffic. Farm markets are held on Fresno Street alongside Courthouse Park on Tuesday, Thursdays, and Saturdays, and fresh vegetables, fruits, and flowers are sold direct to the consumer. Farm workers and growers throng the streets on Saturday nights, and the Fresno District Fair in September is an event of major local importance.

Fresno has profited by the great prosperity of the San Joaquin Valley, which is served with abundant water from the high Sierras, impounded in numerous reservoirs of which Friant, Pine Flat and Huntington are notable examples. The city is bisected by the Southern Pacific Ry. and US 99, which parallels the railroad. The Santa Fe also enters Fresno. On the southern boundary of the city is LEMOORE NAVAL AIR BASE. To the northeast in the County, are SIERRA NATIONAL FOREST, with peaks rising to 10,000 ft.; SEQUOIA NATIONAL FOREST and KING'S CANYON NATIONAL PARK. The great sequoias extend across the county line into Tulare County. Fresno County in 1964 had 43,825 employed in agriculture, 30,475 in trade, 22,050 in services, 20,150 in government work and 15,125 in manufacturing.

Fresno was one of the first California cities to contract for a plan of development. This was drawn up in 1918 by Gilbert Cheney, San Francisco architect; but not activated. The dream persisted and in 1964 Victor Gruen produced the first segment of the new Fresno plan when THE MALL was opened. It extends down the center of Fulton St., is closed to vehicles, and has trees, fountains, benches and flowers that are changed seasonally. Formerly choked with traffic, the Mall now invites pedestrians. It is connected with the development and modernization of 19 square blocks on 85 acres in the heart of the city, sponsored by the Downtown Association of Fresno. An underpass will connect West Fresno with the downtown area. The city engaged in building garages with a $15,000,000 bond issue.

Fresno, unlike many California cities, is purely an American growth. Spanish and Mexican expeditions passed up the site as desolate and barren. Indian troubles scared away settlers of the period preceding the gold rush, and the Forty-Niners, bound for the Sierra foothills, hurried across the valley to the diggings. After the gold rush, the Americans turned to stock raising, and the site of Fresno supported thousands of cattle. The first settlement is supposed to have been made in the 1860's by A. J. Manssen, a Hollander.

A few families joined Manssen, but the place remained "the sorriest and most woe-begone little settlement on the map" until 1872, when it became a station on the Central Pacific Railroad, which pushed through the valley that year. The railroad builders staked out a town, which they called Fresno (Sp., ash tree) Station, for the name of the county. The ash trees were in the foothills, and not near the town.

In 1874 Millerton, the only important settlement in the area, voted to relinquish the county seat to Fresno Station; and soon after, practically the whole population of Millerton moved to the new county seat in order to be on the railroad line. The town is now covered by MIL-LERTON LAKE, the waters of which were impounded by Friant Dam of the San Joaquin River and which is also in MILLERTON LAKE STATE PARK (State 41 and 145). The countryside was so bare that boys had to play hide-and-seek in the graveyard. Cows, horses, dogs, and pigs wandered about in the streets, and flocks of sheep were driven through the town.

With the spread of controlled irrigation and the realization that the soil was extremely fertile, new crops were developed and the town grew fast. Partly through the efforts of Agoston Haraszthy, Hungarian financier and investor, grape raising was popularized in California (*see AGRICULTURE*). Americans planted vines in their wheat fields. Italians, French, and Swiss started growing grapes on 20-acre parcels acquired for that purpose.

The dry white wine made by foreign growers was of indifferent quality, but the continuous sunlight led naturally, after about 1874, to the preparation of raisins. An output of 103,000,000 pounds in 1894 overloaded the market, and the price dropped to two cents a pound. The Raisin Growers Association, a co-operative group organized in 1898 for the protection and efficient handling of the raisin industry, still controls the bulk of the crop. During World War I profits were large because raisins were a convenient food to pack and ship. When it was discovered that raisins are rich in iron, an advertising campaign was launched with the slogan "Have you had your iron today?" and raisins sold in five-cent packages at candy counters. Today 60 per cent of the United States raisin production comes from the Fresno district.

In 1886, Frank Roeding and his son had begun experiments with Smyrna fig culture at their own expense and in the face of open ridicule from other horticulturists. In June, 1889, they learned the secret of caprification (cross-fertilization of the Smyrna fig by the fig wasp), and the industry was at last able to compete with foreign importations.

With a population of 12,470 in 1900, Fresno adopted its first city charter. Agriculture progressed rapidly in the next ten years. Cotton growing was introduced in the valley and cotton is now a leading product. Manufacture of sweet wines supplanted that of the dry wines.

Manufacturing kept pace with agricultural growth, and Fresno now ranks fifth among California cities as an industrial center. Its many manufacturing establishments include flour and lumber mills, machine shops and foundries, potteries, brickwork, and soap factories.

## POINTS OF INTEREST

COURTHOUSE SQUARE, Van Ness Ave. at Mariposa St., a central park two blocks square, is dominated by the neo-Classic FRESNO COUNTY COURTHOUSE, a symmetrical three-story edifice with flat balustraded roof, pedimented Corinthian entrance portico, and a dome and cupola. A fountain, the BOY WITH THE LEAKING BOOT, the figure of a lad holding a worn shoe was given by the Salvation Army in 1895.

ACADEMY OF CALIFORNIA CHURCH HISTORY, 1530 N. Fresno, has the archives of the Spanish Missions.

FRESNO COUNTY FREE LIBRARY occupies a new building at 2420 Mariposa St., in the Civic Center. It operates 41 branch libraries and an extensive bookmobile service in city and county.

FRESNO MEMORIAL AUDITORIUM, 2435 Fresno St., was erected by the city in 1932 in memory of the war dead.

FRESNO MUSEUM, 1944 N. Winery Ave., is a natural history museum with dioramas showing the San Joaquin Valley. It has an Indian Room, cactus and fern gardens, a duck pond with native birds and a collection of live animals of the area. (*Tuesday through Friday, 10-5, free*)

FRESNO STATE COLLEGE, near State 168, estab. 1921, enrolled 8,404 students in 1965. FRESNO CITY COLLEGE (Junior) had 6,328 students in 1965.

KEARNEY MANSION in Kearney Park was opened in 1962 as a museum of late 19th century with furnishings by the Fresno County Historical Society. It is a two-story and dormer house erected by Martin T. Kearney, wealthy landowner and president of the first California Raisin Growers Assn. (1898-1904). He used it as his office, 1900-1906. In May, 1906, he died while returning from Europe. His Fruit Vale Estate was given to the University of California. In 1949 the University gave the building and adjoining land to Fresno County for a park. (*Open Thursday through Sunday afternoons and holidays*)

FORT MILLER BLOCKHOUSE, built 1851 at Rootville, later Millerton, was removed to Roeding Park in 1944 when Friant Dam flooded the site. It contains a museum of historical objects. (*Open Saturday and Sunday afternoons*).

ROEDING PARK, Belmont and Thorne Aves. has been planted with hundreds of different trees and shrubs. Its ZOO (*open daily, 10-5*) has a sea lion show Wednesday through Sunday at 2:30 p.m. Guided tours by the Fresno Zoological Society.

ROMA WINERY of the Roma Wine Co., owned since 1942 by Schenley Industries, Inc., on Church Ave., east of State 99 is the world's largest winery. It covers 55 acres, can handle 80,000 tons of grapes a season, and has storage capacity for 16,700,000 gallons of wine. (*Tours from 9 a.m. on*) Roma Winery at Kingsburg, East on Sierra St., off State 99, has a capacity of 7,800,000 gallons.

The SUN MAID RAISIN PLANT (*open 8:30-4:30 weekdays, July-Jan.; guides*), Butler Ave. and Hazlewood Blvd., the largest raisin-packing plant in the world, occupies many-windowed gray concrete buildings that cover several acres.

# *Hollywood*

*How to Get There:*  Hollywood is a district of the City of Los Angeles, approx. 8 *m.* west of the Civic Center.  Its boundary starts at Western Ave., No. 5400 on Hollywood Ave., reached by bus.  From the Union Station by cab or motor car take the Hollywood Freeway, which runs northwest and has ramps at principal Hollywood intersections.  From the northwest by way of US 101 and Ventura Freeway.  Sunset Blvd., south of Hollywood Blvd., runs west past Sunset Strip, through Beverly Hills toward Santa Monica.

*Accommodations:*  Hollywood proper is well supplied with hotels and motels at prices moderate to expensive.  The influx of transients is so large that early reservation of lodgings is recommended.  Luxury hotels are found chiefly in Beverly Hills.  In Hollywood the Hollywood Knickerbocker, 1714 N. Ivar Ave., has 400 rooms; Hollywood Roosevelt, 7000 Hollywood Blvd., 450 rooms; Gene Autry's Continental, 8401 Sunset Blvd., 300 rooms; Hollywood Plaza, at Hollywood & Vine (1637 N. Vine St.) 200 rooms.  A number of hotels provide kitchenette facilities and apartments.  Motels include Carlton Inn, 2011 N. Highland Ave., 82 units; Coronet Motel, 5410 Hollywood Blvd., 60 units; Hallmark House, 7023 Sunset Blvd., 75 units; The Players, 777 N. Vine St., 43 units; Town & Country, 2111 Cahuenga Blvd., 20 units; numerous others.

*Homes of the Stars:*  These are scattered through a wide area of winding streets in Beverly Hills, Bel Air, and adjoining communities, many accessible from Sunset Blvd.  Folders giving locations are available at bookshops and at All-Year Club of Southern California, 705 W. Seventh St., Los Angeles 17.  Visitors should remember that stars change homes frequently.

*Annual Events:*  Easter Sunrise Services, Hollywood Bowl; Symphonies under the Stars, same place, all summer, see newspapers for dates; Pilgrimage Play, Amphitheater, July and August.

## MOTION PICTURE, RADIO AND TELEVISION STUDIOS

The large television studios of the networks welcome visitors for touring and as audiences.  Motion picture studios are not generally open to the public, but some are partially visible via Tanner Gray Line.  Exceptions are Universal City, which provides tours and entrance fee, and Warner Bros., Burbank.

ALLIED ARTISTS PRODUCTION STUDIOS, 4376 Sunset Dr.

AMERICAN BROADCASTING CO.  Radio Sta. KABC, 3321 S. La Cienaga.  Television, KABC-TV, Channel 7, Television Center, 4151 Prospect St., at Talmadge, Hollywood 27, NO 3-3311.  Address: Guest Relations, Tickets.  Pick up at 1539 N. Vine St.

BING CROSBY PRODUCTIONS, 780 Gower St.

CINERAMA, INC., 4050 W. Pico St.

COLUMBIA BROADCASTING SYSTEM.  Radio Div., 6121 Sunset Blvd.  KNXT, Channel 2, Television City, 7800 Beverly Blvd. at Fairfax, Los Angeles 35, HO 9-1212.  Free daily tours, 1 p.m. to 5 p.m.  No children under 12 admitted.  Address Guest Relations, Tickets.  Pick up TV tickets at Radio Center, 6121 Sunset Blvd.

COLUMBIA PICTURES CORP., 1438 Gower St.

DESILU STUDIOS, 780 Gower St.

EDUCATIONAL TELEVISION, 1313 Vine St.  KCET, Channel 28.

GOLDEN WEST TELEVISION PRODUCTIONS, INC.  KTLA, Channel 5, 5800 Sunset Blvd., HO 9-3181.  Address: Guest Relations, Tickets.  Group studio tours arranged on request.

KCOP TELEVISION, INC. Channel 13, 915 N. La Brea, Hollywood. OL 6-6050. Address: Guest Relations, Tickets.
KTTV TELEVISION STA. Channel 11, 5746 Sunset Blvd.
METRO-GOLDWYN-MAYER (MGM), 10202 W. Washington Blvd., Culver City.
NATIONAL BROADCASTING CO. KNBC, Channel 4. Radio and Television at Color City, 3000 W. Alameda Ave., Burbank.
MUTUAL BROADCASTING SYSTEM. KHJ-TC, Channel 9. Radio and Television, 5515 Melrose Ave., Hollywood 38, HO 2-2133.
PARAMOUNT PICTURES CORP., 5451 Marathon Ave.
REPUBLIC CORP., and REPUBLIC PICTURES INTERNATIONAL, 4024 Radford Ave., North Hollywood.
RKO GENERAL Broadcasting-Television Sta. KHJ-TV, 5515 Melrose.
SAMUEL GOLDWYN STUDIOS, 1041 N. Formosa.
TECHNICOLOR STUDIOS, 6311 Romaine.
TWENTIETH CENTURY-FOX FILM CORP., 10201 W. Pico Blvd. Television, 1417 N. Western Ave., Culver City.
TIMES MIRROR BROADCASTING CO. KTTV, Channel 11, 5746 Sunset Blvd., HO 9-3181. Address Guest Relations, Tickets, for studio tour.
UNITED ARTISTS, 1041 N. Las Palmas Ave.
UNITED PICTURES, INC., 6725 Sunset Blvd.
UNIVERSAL STUDIOS (MCA), University City, 3900 Lankershim Blvd.
WALT DISNEY PRODUCTIONS, 500 S. Buena Vista, Burbank.
WARNER BROS. PICTURES, 4000 Warner Ave., Burbank.


HOLLYWOOD (385 alt.) motion picture capital of the world and a name that has become synonymous with extravagant entertainment, is not a city but an integral district of the city of Los Angeles, with a population that varies according to the definition of how far it extends. The City Planning Commission places its area at 14.5 square miles and in 1963 counted 138,100 inhabitants. The Hollywood Chamber of Commerce reported Hollywood's 1963 population as 187,891, and its 1964 count as 192,441, indicating its steady growth. If the Los Angeles districts of North Hollywood and West Hollywood are included, the official population is 269,500.

The center of Hollywood's business district, is Hollywood Blvd. and Vine St., made known nationally by radio comedians. This is eight miles from the Civic Center of Los Angeles and twelve miles from the coast. On Hollywood Blvd. are located GRAUMAN'S CHINESE THEATER, at 6925, home of film premieres, and the EGYPTIAN THEATER, at 6712; also the HOLLYWOOD ROOSEVELT HOTEL, at 7000. The buildings at Hollywood and Vine are undistinguished, but one block north on Vine is the dominating office structure of Capitol Records, CAPITOL TOWER, entirely circular. South of Hollywood Blvd. is the famous SUNSET BLVD., which runs all the way to Santa Monica. The Hollywood Freeway extends in a northeasterly direction from the center of Los Angeles to the Ventura Freeway, US 101. The Hollywood district is bounded on the east by Silver Lake and Griffith Park, on the south by Wilshire, on the north by North Hollywood and the city of Burbank and on the west by West Hollywood and the city of Beverly Hills. Included in Movieland are the independent cities of Burbank, Beverly Hills and Culver City. North of Hollywood a network of winding roads leads into the foothills of the Santa Monica Mountains, (known locally as the Hollywood Hills), which constitute a natural boundary in that direction. Hyperion Avenue and Riverside Drive, along the Los Angeles River, mark the eastern limits. To the south, at Melrose Avenue, Hollywood merges into Los Angeles. Sunset Blvd. and Hollywood Blvd. lead straight to Beverly Hills.

Farther west on Sunset Boulevard, toward Beverly Hills, is a section popularly known as "the Strip." Here are restaurants and other movie colony night spots, high-priced antique shops, salons, gift shops. On Sunset the visitor will find attractive interiors and specialized cuisine, for instance: Ciro's (French), Cafe de Paris (French), Abruzzi (Italian), Bit of Sweden (Swedish), La Rue (cosmopolitan), The Marquis (cosmopolitan), Moulin Rouge (French), Scandia (Scandinavian).

Motion picture influence is visible in another purely Hollywood contribution: drive-in barbecue stands, restaurants, and bars, built of papier-mache to represent fairy-story castles, tumble-down houses, gargantuan fish, ice cream cones, and lop-eared puppies. Each stands on a large parking area, and waitresses in slacks and brass-buttoned jackets hook trays over open car windows to serve the customers in their automobiles.

Hollywood probably attracts more types and nationalities than any city of its size in the world. Here are the nobility, ex-nobility, and pseudo-nobility of a dozen countries; the artistically inclined from every corner of the world who aspire to movie jobs; and average Americans who live here because they like the climate, or were born here. Precocious children from all over the country are brought to Hollywood in hope of breaking into motion pictures. Dozens of dance studios and dramatic schools attempt to train children and adults for screen careers. About 75 percent of the population is connected with the motion picture industry, the studios employ between 35,000 and 40,000.

Many actors and extras still live in Hollywood, but most of the stars prefer Beverly Hills, Bel Air, Brentwood, and ranches in the San Fernando Valley. In the first flush of cinema prosperity Hollywood society went in for extravagance and informality, evidenced by carefree parties and sporty cars. Now top-flight movie society affects white ties and evening gowns, with the accent on dignity and position, but the yardstick of eminence is still the number of digits in the salary.

The first habitation on the site of Hollywood was an adobe dwelling built by Don Tomás Urquidez in 1853. In the sixties and early seventies much of the valley was laid out in 160-acre farms, and families of immigrants from all over the world settled here. The present name dates from the boom of 1887 when Horace H. Wilcox opened a real estate subdivision, which his wife christened Hollywood.

In 1896, the year T. L. Tally opened his "Phonograph and Vitascope Parlor" in Los Angeles, with four peep holes for spectators, Hollywood was still a crossroads where the arrival of the Toluca stage to San Fernando Valley was the event of the day. In 1910, when it had a population of 4,000, Hollywood traded its civic independence for a share in Los Angeles' water supply, but held tenaciously to its identity.

At about this time an ironic fate selected this ultra-respectable, church-going village as headquarters for a new form of amusement: the motion picture. Independent film companies, trying to escape a monopoly in the East, took refuge in Hollywood and under its almost continuous sun began shooting scenes in orange grove and canyon, ranch house and barn.

The Horsley brothers, operating under the name of the Nestor Company, were the first producers to settle in Hollywood; they leased the old Blondeau Tavern and barn at Sunset Boulevard and Gower Street in October, 1911, converted it into a studio, and made the first Hollywood picture, *The Law of the Range.* Wilcox had opened the original subdivision as a temperance colony, and the sudden appearance of boisterous show people and cowboys parading the hitherto quiet streets in the best wild-west fashion came as a rude shock to the inhabitants. The villagers at first considered the "fillums" and those who made them disreputable and somewhat sinful, and resented their intrusion. But the pioneers were followed by other independents, and eventually members of the eastern producers' trust took advantage of the climate and low rents in Hollywood. When Cecil B. De Mille moved his troupe west, he is said to have had tickets for Flagstaff, Arizona. Deciding that Flagstaff didn't "look western enough" he too went on to Hollywood.

The town boomed. In the 1920's motion pictures became a billion dollar industry. Sound films necessitated better writing, direction, acting, and management. There was an increasing trek westward from Broadway and other centers. While "Hollywood" is commonly used to designate the motion picture industry as a whole, most of the major studios are located in its periphery.

Hollywood was faced with the loss of a large segment of picture production when actors and producers turned to foreign locations. The lower costs of making films there, as well as the advantage at first of income tax deductions for residence abroad, combined to make Rome and other foreign cities profitable for Americans. For a time Hollywood faced loss of employment and curtailment of its prosperity. The situation changed in its favor when television fortuitously turned to Hollywood. Today TELEVISION CITY, COLOR CITY and similar major headquarters of networks have made it a new center of employment and tourist interest.

Hollywood has its own newspaper services, despite full coverage by the big Los Angeles dailies. The *Reporter* gives news of the studios. The *Citizen-News,* 1545 N. Wilcox, circulates throughout the contiguous communities.

## POINTS OF INTEREST

HOLLYWOOD BOWL (*always open; adm. prices vary during season*) end of Bolton Rd., 1 block S. of Highland Ave. and Cahuenga Blvd. intersection, is a 60-acre natural amphitheater framed by chaparral-covered hills. The white-walled platform is surmounted by a removable sounding shell, designed by Lloyd Wright, and the acoustics are such that an unaided voice on the stage can be heard in the back row. "Symphonies under the Stars," held yearly since 1922, grand opera, and the Easter Sunrise Service are presented here. The bowl has more than 20,000 seats, and the sloping runways provide standing room for 10,000. Near the entrance is a large bowl for voluntary contributions. The top is covered with wire netting and the accumulated coins are removed only at the end of the season, according to a carefully cultivated legend.

The PILGRIMAGE PLAY AMPHITHEATER (*open during performances; adm. 50¢-$1.50*), 2580 Highland Ave., is a natural amphitheater where a play based on the life of Christ is enacted nightly during July and August. The Pilgrimage Play was written by Mrs. Christine Wetherill Stevenson in collaboration with H. Ellis Reed, and first produced in 1920. A large wooden cross on the hillside, lighted at night, is a guidepost to the theater.

The JAPANESE GARDENS (*open 10-6 daily; adm. 25¢, children with adults free*), Orchid and N. Sycamore Aves. (also known as the California Scenic Gardens and Home), were built and decorated at a cost of $2,000,000 by Adolph and Eugene Bernheimer in 1913. The elaborately landscaped hillside estate contains more than 30,000 trees, many rare tropical shrubs, several goldfish pools, and a Japanese shrine. Overlooking the Japanese terraces is the 14-room Yama Shiro, (castle on the hill), designed in the manner of a Buddhist Temple of the ancient Shoguns. It is filled with rare objects of Japanese and Buddhist art. There is also a miniature garden with dwarf trees, canals, waterfalls and reproductions of ancient dwellings.

GRAUMAN'S CHINESE THEATER, 6925 Hollywood Blvd., a spectacular adaptation of the Chinese style of architecture, designed by Meyer and Haller, is the scene of Hollywood's major premieres, where stars and film moguls attend opening performances of new films with the ballyhoo of searchlights, floodlights, microphones and loudspeakers, and roped-off aisles covered with carpet.

The facade, in the form of a U-shaped forecourt with a Chinese gate, set between terminal piers, suggests the approach to an ancient temple garden. Four large obelisks, embellished with oriental decorations, surmount the two colossal piers. In the forecourt is a grove of palm trees and other shrubs, and concrete slabs bearing the hand and foot prints of stars and their messages of congratulation. At the end of the forecourt a colorful pagoda forms the entrance to the theater, roofed in bronze aged to the color of jade green, and supported by two coral-red octagonal columns mounted with wrought-iron masks. Under the curved roof, and deeply set between the flanking piers, is a great stone dragon, modeled in relief on a slab 30 feet high.

The EGYPTIAN THEATER, 6712 Hollywood Blvd., which shows motion pictures, is the spot where the Hollywood premieres originated as a scintillating social event, with the showing of *Robin Hood* in 1922. An Egyptian god in the forecourt bears out the motif of the building.

FARMERS' MARKET, Third St. and Fairfax Ave., a shopping center of popular service and visitors' interest is noted for its opulent display of fresh fruits and garden truck, as well as for shops, snack bars and restaurants. (*Open 9 a.m. to 7 p.m., closed Sundays.*)

DE LONGPRE PARK, De Longpre and Cherokee Aves., with landscaped lawns, bamboo, and palms, is named for the celebrated French painter, long a Hollywood resident. In the center of the park is a bronze statue *Aspiration,* a nude male surmounting a globe, by Roger Noble Burnham, erected as a memorial to Rudolph Valentino, super-lover of the silent screen, who died in 1926.

CAMPO DE CAHUENGA, north of Hollywood to Lankershim Blvd., one-half block north of Ventura Blvd., is the spot where Mexican General Andres Pico signed the treaty of surrender of his forces to Lt. Col. John C. Fremont, Jan. 13, 1847, after the Jan. 9 battle of La Mesa.

COLUMBIA BROADCASTING SYSTEM RADIO DIVISION has its headquarters in the extensive building complex at 6121 Sunset Blvd., erected in 1938. The work of William Lescaze, the building is entirely modern in design. It has a five-story central unit of concrete and glass, with long horizontal lines and corner fenestrations, and lower, outflung studio sections. Visitors can watch rehearsals and some of the 14 weekly broadcasts that originate in the seven "streamlined" studios, peer behind the scenes at the master control, and see the laboratory for sound effects.

HOLLYWOOD CEMETERY, 6076 Santa Monica Blvd., is the flower-bordered and elaborately landscaped resting place of many Hollywood notables, including Rudolph Valentino, John Gilbert, and William Desmond Taylor. Harrison Gray Otis, long-time publisher of the Los Angeles *Times,* and William Andrews Clark, Jr., patron of the Los Angeles Philharmonic Orchestra, are also buried here.

In the CENTRAL CASTING OFFICE, 8480 Beverly Blvd., many actors, bit players, and extras are registered. On short notice it can supply types of actors ranging from Siberian Samoyeds to British Members of Parliament.

BARNSDALL PARK, Hollywood Blvd. and Vermont Ave., with an area of 10 acres, has a wading pool for children, picnic tables, and cooking conveniences. The Arts and Crafts Center offers instruction in painting, sculpture, weaving, copper enameling and other crafts. Classes adults on weekday evenings; for children on Saturdays.

TELEVISION CITY, 7800 Beverly Blvd., is the imposing center of the Columbia Broadcasting System television networks. It was the first of the facilities planned exclusively for television when the major networks realized that this was about to become the most profitable part of their investment. CBS assembled twenty-five acres for a site far from its already imposing radio headquarters at 6121 Sunset Blvd. Its architects, Pereira & Luckman, produced a master plan for a television center costing upwards of $35,000,000, announced as "the biggest urban business development since Rockefeller Center was built around radio."

The object was to transfer all the CBS television activities from New York City, and to include not only studios but an office building 600 ft. long, intended to shelter some of the multitudinous radio and television concerns of Hollywood.    Until now the master plan has proved a bit too ambitious for immediate needs and is in abeyance.

Television City, completed in 1952, today covers 360,000 sq. ft., which is quite an expanse in itself.    It has four studios and three rehearsal halls.    Only live programs are produced here, some with audiences contributing their uninhibited laughter and approval.    The personnel, including stage hands and temporary employees, is about 675. The main building rests on 1,673 concrete piles and has been constructed so that new sections can easily be added.    All dressing rooms and storage spaces for scenery and properties are on the lowest level, easily accessible from the place where the performers park their cars.    On the main level is the high studio space and a central corridor.    The top level is the rehearsal hall.    Audiences can circulate around the building, thus keeping clear of the movement of performers to the studios.    Important to construction are the demountable end walls, facilitating expansion of studios.    Special provision is made for audiences, usually 350 seats to a studio, sunk below the performing floor level.    Since three cameras are trained on most television shows, a middle runway has been constructed, dividing the audience, but so built that spectators will not turn their interest from the performers to the cameras, or get in the way of the apparatus.    Studio roofs are supported by trusses 130 ft. long.    From them are hung a batten system, mechanical and electrical equipment and air conditioning supply ducts.

> Tours lasting 40 minutes are conducted through Television City, Monday through Saturday, no admission charge.    Large groups must make reservations through the Guest Relations Dept., Television City, Los Angeles 90036, which also acts on requests for tickets to shows.    Size of party and alternate dates should be mentioned with self-addressed reply envelope.    Children must be at least 12 years old.

COLOR CITY is the great color television production center of National Broadcasting System, at 3000 West Alameda Ave., Burbank, which is contiguous with Hollywood's northern limits.    Until 1950 the studios were located in the center of Hollywood, at Sunset Blvd. and Vine St., in a building completed only in 1938.    The need for more room for both broadcasting and film processing led NBC to acquire fifty acres in Burbank, where construction was begun in 1952.    In 1960 NBC opened the first all-color plant in the country, an investment of $16,000,000.    It also opened the only news color film processing plant. Of the 980 persons employed, about 600 are technicians.    Many well-known television programs originate at Color City and are put on video tape.    They include especially those of Bob Hope, Danny Thomas and Dean Martin, as well as appearances by Frank Sinatra, Julie Andrews, Fred Astaire, Judy Garland and other top-ranking performers.    Hope and Thomas are their own producers.    NBC produces television programs for independent managements and its Telesales Department has an annual income of $1,000,000. The performances are given before audiences and guides are available for visitors.

METRO-GOLDWYN-MAYER STUDIOS are not contiguous to Hollywood but are located to the southwest beyond Beverly Hills in CULVER CITY, an incorporated municipality in Los Angeles County. The City is about 10 miles west of the Civic Center of Los Angeles and had an estimated population of 33,163 in 1963. The town was platted in 1913 by Harry H. Culver, a Nebraska investor, on land originally part of the La Ballona Rancho of Macedonio Aguilar. In 1915 Culver induced Thomas Ince to buy land for motion picture production which, by 1924, became the seat of Metro-Goldwyn-Mayer.

In 1966 MGM occupied 185 acres and 195 buildings fronting on West Washington Blvd. and extending into the hills. It had 28 sound stages, 19 man-made lakes and rivers, and many permanent sets, including European villages and streets of the old West. More than 2,500 were employed there. The music library contains 4,000,000 items.

Part of the MGM acreage in Culver City is considered enormously valuable because of the presence of oil. Removal of the studios to a new site in the Canejo Valley has been proposed but not yet carried out.

Although Culver City advertises itself as California's Film Capital it also invites industries other than picture-making and has 900 small and large corporations, employing more than 50,000. Industries include Hughes Aircraft Co., which has its own airport, Ampex Computer Products and Avnet Corp. San Diego Freeway crosses the city from the north, and Washington Blvd. is its chief artery, reaching with Venice Blvd. to the beaches at Venice. Immediately south of Washington Blvd. is the MARINA DEL REY small-craft harbor of Venice, which was begun in 1958 and is expected to become a major resort.

WARNER BROS. STUDIOS, described as "the largest and most modern motion picture and television film production center in the world," occupies 102 acres a short distance north of the Hollywood district line in the independent municipality of Burbank. Warner Bros. made their first Hollywood film in 1918, operating a studio on Sunset Blvd. In 1928 they bought the First National Studio in Burbank and moved there. Of the four Warner brothers Jack is president of the corporation. They began showing films in a remodeled store in New Castle, Pa., in 1906; in 1912, when they owned five theaters and two film exchanges, they began making their own films in Brooklyn. Their first Hollywood production was *My Four Years in Germany,* based on the memoirs of James W. Gerard.

Warner Bros. Studios has a center group of 24 sound stages, large arch-roofed buildings. The highest has a clearance of 72 ft. from floor to rafters. Stages vary in size from 133 by 236 ft. to 133 by 160 ft. The television operations building, erected 1958, contains 130 office suites, 26 film editing rooms and four projection rooms. The crafts building employs 400. A building devoted to Frank Sinatra and his office and production staff is said to have cost $500,000. One building is devoted to the making of Bugs Bunny and other cartoons.

Sound pictures were introduced August 6, 1926, when *Don Juan* was released with a synchronized musical score. The first major picture with sound was *The Jazz Singer,* released in October, 1927.

The most spectacular success to come from the Warner Studios is the motion picture version of *My Fair Lady,* with Audrey Hepburn, Rex Harrison and Stanley Holloway in the leading roles and George Cukor directing. Warner paid $5,500,000 for the screen rights to the play that had 2,717 performances between March, 1956, and September, 1962, in New York alone and 2,090 performances in London. It is being performed regularly in many foreign cities. On Stage No. 7, the largest on the lot, the studio built Higgins' four-story house, the portico of St. Paul's and the flower and vegetable markets of Covent Garden.

UNIVERSAL CITY STUDIOS, which welcome tourists rather than lock them out, can be reached by a short bus ride from Hollywood and Vine north to Ventura Blvd. and Lankershim Blvd., or via Hollywood Freeway to the Lankershim Off-ramp. From downtown Los Angeles, use MTA bus No. 93. Fronting on Lankershim is UNIVERSAL CITY, an independent municipality of 410 acres, seat of Universal Pictures Corp., established there in 1915 by Carl Laemmle. Now a subsidiary of MCA, Inc., Universal asserts it has the largest aggregation of facilities for films, radio and television in the Hollywood area. The Plaza, where the principal buildings are grouped, is dominated by the 11-story MCA Tower, filled with executive offices, and also has the basic units for pictures and television, the Studio Commissary, which can serve 2,000; the City's U. S. Postoffice and the Production Bldg., which supplies casting, art and research.

In July, 1965, Universal started conducted studio tours on a scale never before attempted in Movieland. On an 11-acre hill site on the "Back Lot" it began erecting a Visitors Village, with the object of eventually providing for 5,000 tourists daily. Among the many exhibits is the Phantom Stage, one of the 37 sound stages, containing the theater and huge chandelier used in *The Phantom of the Opera* in 1925 (with Lon Chaney), 1930 and 1943. Here also can be seen New York Street (*87th Precinct, M-Squad, Going My Way*); Courthouse Square (*Inherit the Wind, To Kill a Mockingbird*); Five Points (*The Virginian, The Tall Man, Tales of Wells Fargo, Wagon Train,* dozens of westerns); Falls Lake, built in 1926 for *Uncle Tom's Cabin* and used as recently as *The Ugly American;* the facade of Notre Dame de Paris (*The Hunchback*) Mockingbird Lane of *The Munsters;* Park Lane (*McHale's Navy*); Tower Park (*The Birds*) and numerous streets—Brownstone, Southern, Mexican, Denver, European—all used in films and television shows. The visitors learn that movie sets may be used repeatedly with slight changes. In the Hacienda, where executives and stars live, visitors may see Cary Grant, Glenn Ford, Richard Boone, Sandra Dee and many others. The tour includes an inspection of a star's "dressing room," actually a well-equipped house. (*For reservations phone Studios Tour, Universal City, Triangle 7-1311; fee, adults $2.50, children 12 and under, $1.25*)

# Long Beach

*Communications:* Long Beach Municipal Airport, Spring St. and Cherry Ave., and San Diego Freeway. Connections with Santa Fe, Union Pacific and Southern Pacific and all Los Angeles facilities. Greyhound Bus Lines. Santa Fe Trailways.

*Freeways:* Seven freeways give quick access to Long Beach from all parts of Los Angeles County and City. Travel time to center of Los Angeles 30 min. Harbor Freeway (State 11) from Los Angeles to San Pedro connects with San Diego Freeway (Interstate 405). Long Beach Freeway (State 7) north-south, connects with San Diego Freeway, Santa Ana Freeway (US 101, Interstate 5) and San Bernardino Freeway (US 60, Interstate 10). Pacific Coast Highway (State 1) comes into Long Beach from Wilmington (west). At Los Alamitos Circle it connects with Lakewood Blvd. (State 19).

*Fishing:* Pier fishing at Belmont Pier, Rainbow Pier, Alamitos Bay Pier and on outer harbor breakwater. Tackle and live bait may be purchased and rented at Belmont Pier and Pierpont Landing. For deep sea fishing Pierpoint Landing and Belmont Pier have chartered boats. For grunion fishing the grunion run only at night at high tide and frequently wiggle upon the beach in such numbers that fish and game laws prohibit catching them in any other way except scooping them up by hand. The exact times and dates of grunion runs are published in newspapers.

*Golf:* Six public courses: Recreation Park, Lakewood Country Club, El Dorado Park, Skylinks, Heartwell Park, Three-Par (night lighted). *Miniature Golf:* Shady Acres, 5555 Long Beach Boulevard, open 10 a.m. to midnight daily. *Pitch and Putt:* (driving links) Circle Golf Fairway, 2300 Redondo Ave., open 7 days 8 a.m. to 10 p.m. GA 7-9187; El Dorado, night-lighted, open 7 a.m. to 11 p.m. daily, 2400 Studebaker Road, 430-3089; Heartwell Golf Course, 6700 E. Carson, 421-8921, open 7 a.m. to 11 p.m. daily.

*Public Facilities:* 227 churches; 46 denominations; 72 hotels and motels; 10 hospitals; main library, 10 branches; 4 local radio stations; 1 state college, 1 junior college, 15 junior high schools, 55 elementary schools.

*Sea Adventures:* Sea-lane tour of the Port, from Wharfinger's Office, Pier A. Take Ocean Blvd. to bridge, turn off at Port sign. Follow Harbor Scenic Dr. to Wharfinger's Office. Harbor cruise, 20 miles, daily; call HE 2-0408 or HE 2-1116. Visits to ships of U. S. Navy: open Saturday and Sunday, 1 p.m.-4 p.m. Call HE 5-5377 for directions.

LONG BEACH (47 alt., 250,767 pop., 1950; 344,168, U. S. Census 1960, of which 34,242 by city growth, 59,159 by annexation; 370,251, est., Regional Planning Comm., 1965; Greater Long Beach area, 453,629 est., 1965) is California's fifth largest city, the second largest in Los Angeles County, the third largest port in the state, after Los Angeles and Richmond. It spreads over a level plain to the edge of sandy bluffs overlooking the 8-mile long crescent-shaped beach of San Pedro Bay. From the shore it stretches north to surround the oil derricks of Signal Hill, an independent community, and the areas of North

Long Beach; it is bisected by the San Diego Freeway (US 405) and at Carson St. in the northeast adjoins Lakewood (67,126 pop., 1960). On the east it crosses the San Gabriel River to the limits of Alamitos and Orange County.

Shipping is one of the major items in Long Beach prosperity, for the Port of Long Beach handles up to 12,000,000 tons of cargo annually. In a typical year of the 1960s nearly 2,000 vessels (62 steamship lines) used the port, including the P. & O. liner *Canberra*. The Port occupies the Harbor protected by made land that juts out into San Pedro Bay west of Los Angeles River estuary. There are 47 deep-water berths and 25 new berths were to be operating by 1968. The Belt Line railroad has 34 miles of tracks serving wharves and storage sheds. The bulk grain terminal on Pier A is as tall as a 24-story building and can load ships at 1,000 tons per hour. Its capacity is 1,871,500 bu. The bulk oil terminal can accommodate the largest tankers, such as the 940-ft. *Manhattan,* which carries 754,000 bbl. of crude oil.

The income from Port operations is greatly enhanced by the recovery of oil from Harbor and City tidelands. Out of a total income of $46,758,580 in fiscal 1963-64 $40,924,847 was derived from oil operations, and only $4,876,680, or 10.5%, from the Port itself. The State received 18%, the City 17½% and the Port retained 15%.

Land subsidence caused by the removal of oil from the Wilmington field, which affected the U. S. Naval Shipyard and downtown Long Beach has been halted by the injection of salt water into the sands.

The HARBOR SEA SCOUT BASE is located on the east bank of the land and the Southern Pacific spur runs down to the harbor entrance. The entrance channel separates Long Beach from Terminal Island, part of which is occupied by LONG BEACH NAVAL SHIPYARD and the U. S. NAVAL STATION. In the station area is the eastern approach to the VINCENT THOMAS BRIDGE (toll), which crosses the main channel to San Pedro. The sum of $12,700,000 was appropriated for the new GERALD DESMOND BRIDGE across the harbor entrance.

Long Beach is several towns in one—a seaside resort, a haven for elderly retired persons, and an industrial center drawing its income from oil, shipping, and manufacturing. Although many people depend on the city's industrial payroll for their living, the city still has many retired residents from the Middle West, especially Iowa, attracted here by the sunny climate, the seaside location, and the low cost of living. It was in Long Beach that Dr. Francis Townsend, a local physician, first won support for his old-age pension movement.

The strip of mud and sand on which Long Beach was built, long the bartering place of Indians from Santa Catalina Island and the mainland, was part of the vast 200,000-acre tract granted in 1784 by the King of Spain to Manuel Nieto in payment for his services in the royal army. Divided into Rancho los Alamitos (little cottonwoods) and Rancho los Cerritos (little hills), it passed in 1840, after Nieto's death, into the hands of John Temple and Abel Stearns, both Massachusetts Yankees who married into Spanish families, and became Mexican citizens and wealthy landowners. Around their homes centered the social life of the region, marked by bull fights, horse races, and rodeos in which the two families and their servants carried on a friendly rivalry, the winner sponsoring a celebration at which casks of wine were opened, an ox was barbecued, and dancing and merrymaking lasted far into the night. The drought of 1863-64 killed off so many of their sheep, cattle, and horses that the owners lost their land through foreclosures. It was bought by Llewellyn Bixby and Benjamin and Dr. Thomas Flint.

Home owners were first attracted in 1881 when W. E. Willmore subdivided 10,000 acres of barley field and sold it for $12.50 to $25 an acre, naming his community Willmore City. The only connection with the outside world was a horse and buggy and later a four-horse stage coach to Wilmington, until a wooden car track was laid for a horse-car line known as the "Get Off and Push Railroad" because the passengers had to supply locomotive power when the horses balked. When Willmore City went bankrupt in 1888, it was re-named Long Beach—just in time to advertise itself as a seaside resort to the throngs of new settlers attracted by the southern California real estate boom of the same year. Its later growth was slower and steadier. The development of the surrounding territory (54 towns, including Los Angeles) led to the establishment of small industries supplying the increasing demand for manufactured articles. Not until discovery of the Signal Hill oil field in 1921, however, did Long Beach acquire large industries.

Long Beach is closely associated with developing East Wilmington, considered a major underwater oil reserve. Arrangements for drilling in submerged areas have been made by the State and City of Long Beach with the THUMS Long Beach Co., the title signifying the component companies—Texaco, Humble, Union, Mobil, and Shell.

In March, 1933, an earthquake of major proportions leveled buildings throughout the city, including most of the Long Beach schools, killed 120 persons and destroyed property valued at $40,000,000. The extent of the destruction was attributed largely to lax building standards. A widespread rebuilding program was immediately undertaken under more rigid restrictions.

The oil industry still plays the dominant role in the Long Beach industrial scene. Second in importance is canning of tuna and mackerel. The city's largest manufacturing plants produce motor cars, soap, and airplanes.

## POINTS OF INTEREST

The new CIVIC CENTER became a reality by 1965 when two huge structures of glass and steel, standing parallel, joined the Long Beach skyline. They are the COUNTY BLDG., which houses Municipal and Superior Court rooms and other branch offices of the County of Los Angeles, and the PUBLIC SAFETY BLDG., headquarters for Police and Fire departments and other protective agencies located in the block bounded by Broadway, Ocean Blvd. and Chestnut and Magnolia Aves.

Older buildings, but no less modern concrete structures, are the CITY HALL, MUNICIPAL UTILITIES BLDG., and VETERANS' MEMORIAL BLDG.

The CENTRAL PUBLIC LIBRARY (*open 9-9 weekdays*), in the center of the park, erected 1909, was damaged in the 1933 earthquake and repaired 1937. The first floor hall has a mural by Suzanne Miller giving scenes from English and American literature. The Long Beach Public Library System includes the Main Library, 10 branch libraries and a bookmobile and 499,447 volumes. The Main Library has collections of phonograph records, 16mm films and foreign books. It files 10,034 periodicals and 58 newspapers.

CALIFORNIA STATE COLLEGE AT LONG BEACH, 6201 E. 7th St., opened in 1945 with 160 students; in 1965 it had nearly 30,000. LONG BEACH CITY COLLEGE (junior) 4901 E. Carson St., has more than 16,000 students annually and a library of 76,000 volumes.

The PIKE and NU-PIKE, on the beach at Seaside, are flanked by theaters, reptile exhibits, dance pavilions, side shows, curiosity shops, shooting galleries, "oriental stores," penny arcades, and cafes. Here, against a flamboyant background of flags and posters, side-show barkers spiel incessantly. Here the MAGNOLIA PIER extends into the ocean. West of this area at the estuary of Los Angeles River is the LONG BEACH HELIPORT.

The MUNICIPAL AUDITORIUM, S. of Long Beach Blvd., stands on a landscaped square of filled-in land in the placid 32-acre lagoon sheltered from the ocean by the horseshoe-shaped rock embankment of RAINBOW PIER. The 3,800-foot pier has a motor driveway and pedestrian promenade. A massive neo-classic structure, nine stories in height, with a two-story arcaded gallery in the rear suggesting the Coliseum in Rome, the auditorium contains three assembly halls, the largest of which seats 4,875. On its facade is an immense tile mosaic mural, the work of the Federal Art Project. The Long Beach Municipal Band presents its concerts here (*3:30 and 7:30 Tues., Sat.; 2:30 Sun.*). The lagoon is the scene of year-round bathing and boating, of water carnivals and fireworks displays on festive occasions.

LONG BEACH HARBOR is visited annually by thousands of tourists and one of its major attractions is the Sea-Lane Tour. The modern POST ADMINISTRATION BLDG. (1960) is an 8-story structure, with a sightseeing gallery. Of interest is the 74-ft. ceramic mural fronting the building, which portrays incidents since Cabrillo's arrival in 1542. (*Open 8 a.m. to 5 p.m. on weekdays, except holidays*)

BIXBY PARK, Ocean Blvd. and Cherry Ave., 10 acres in area, is primarily a picnic park, noted as the site of State society picnics. Wide, slightly rolling lawns, shaded by groups of oak, pine, cypress, sycamore, and palms, overlook the boulevard and ocean. The Federation of State Societies estimates that 100,000 people have attended the Iowa picnic.

ALAMITOS BAY, S.E. end of Second St., has a popular beach for still-water swimming, boating, and water sports. From the bay a labyrinth of canals branch into the residential section of Naples and a long arm runs inland to Recreation Park. ALAMITOS STATE PARK, at the tip of the peninsula sheltering Alamitos Bay from the ocean, is a 34-acre recreation park with facilities for picnicking and swimming (*overnight camping prohibited*). On the bay side is a sandy beach protected from high tides by a rubble wall.

RECREATION PARK, entrance 7th St. and West Blvd., has picnic facilities, playgrounds, a salt-water swimming pool, an artificial lagoon, and the MARINE STADIUM, which was constructed for the rowing races of the 1932 Olympiad. The stadium, bordered by public beaches, is the scene of national inter-collegiate regattas. The park also has workshops where children learn to build toy boats.

SIGNAL HILL, climbed by Panorama Dr., overlooks the spreading city blocks of Long Beach, the curving shoreline, and the ocean. On its slopes is the independent community of SIGNAL HILL (4,627 pop.), an island of tanks, steel and wooden oil derricks, and stucco bungalows shaded by pepper-trees. The town government levies taxes only on oil wells. The hill, once an Indian signal post and later a lookout point for signaling incoming ships, was sold by "Don Juan" Temple in 1866 for 74¢ an acre. It was a quiet residential suburb when discovery of oil in 1921 transformed it into a booming oil field that reached a maximum production of 268,000 bbl. per day.

The LONG BEACH MUNICIPAL AIRPORT, Cherry Ave. and Spring St., was the starting point for Douglas Corrigan's "wrong-way" flight to New York and back by way of Ireland in 1938. A bronze plaque commemorates the flight. There are more than 422,000 takeoffs and landings annually. A modernization program costing $6,500,000 was undertaken in 1965. The Airport is the center of the city's industrial complex, where Douglas Aircraft maintains one of its principal plants.

## POINTS OF INTEREST IN ENVIRONS

Northeast of Long Beach a number of residential communities, some recently incorporated, are filling the open spaces. On State 35 is LOS ALAMITOS, with a U. S. Naval Station and a race track. Farther north are HAWAIIAN GARDENS (3,356 pop., incor. 1964); DAIRY VALLEY (3,505 pop., incor. 1956); and ARTESIA (12,865 pop., incor. 1959), named for the artesian wells that existed here on the Rancho de Los Coyotes.

SOUTH GATE (120 alt., 58,100 pop., est. 1964) in the Los Angeles-Long Beach area is 9 *m*. s. of Los Angeles on the Long Beach Freeway and State 10.

SANTA CATALINA ISLAND, 25 *m. See Tour 2c.*

# Los Angeles

## INFORMATION

Los Angeles County Chamber of Commerce, 1151 S. Broadway. Los Angeles Chamber of Commerce, 404 S. Bixel St. Also Chambers of Commerce in the communities of the city and the independent cities and towns of the county. *California Travel Guide,* Travel & Recreation Dept., California State Chamber of Commerce, 1000 Wilshire Blvd. Automobile Club of Southern California, 2601 S. Figueroa St., and National Automobile Club, 618 West Olympic Blvd., both affiliated with the American Automobile Assn. (for members). All Year Club of Southern California, 628 W. 6th St. Mission Trails Assn., 25 W. Anapamu St., Santa Barbara. Associated Chambers of Commerce of Orange County, Inc., Anaheim (Disneyland, San Juan Capistrano, Knott's Berry Farm, Laguna Beach).

## TRANSPORTATION

*Railroads:* Union Pacific Railroad, Southern Pacific Lines, Atchison, Topeka & Santa Fe Railway, at Union Passenger Terminal, 800 N. Alameda St., Madison 7171. Pacific Electric Railway (freight), 610 S. Main St., Tucker 7272. Harbor Belt Line Railroad (freight).

*Bus Lines:* American Bus Lines, 629 S. Main St., Trinity 0951; Burlington Trailways, same address; Continental Santa Fe Trailways, 601 S. Main St., Trinity 3403; Greyhound Bus Lines, Sixth and Los Angeles Sts., Trinity 9781; Gray Line Motor Tours, MA 8-3111. Rapid Transit District (tours). Call Transit Information, 747-4455. Los Angeles Transit Lines, 1061 S. Broadway, Prospect 7211 Tanner Motor Tours, 1207 W. Third St.

*Air Traffic:* Los Angeles International Airport, 1 World Way, Aeronaves de Mexico; Air France, American, BOAC, Bonanza, Continental, Delta, Flying Tiger, Japan, KLM, Lufthansa, Mexicana, Pan American, Pacific, Pacific Southwest, Slick, Scandinavian, United, UTA. Helicopter Service: Los Angeles Airways, four-county area; Helicab to downtown hotels; Inter-City Airways serves City of Commerce, Paramount and Down Town; Copter Transit Inc., air freight from Cargo City. Van Nuys Airport, with heliport, in San Fernando Valley.

## SPORTS AND RECREATION

*Baseball:* American League in Dodger Stadium, Chavez Ravine, used also by Los Angeles Angels. Pacific Coast League at Wrigley Field, 4100 S. Avalon Blvd. Hollywood Angels at Hollywood Baseball Park, 100 N. Fairfax Ave.

*Boating:* Echo Park, Glendale Blvd., Bellevue Ave. Hansen Dam Park, 11170 Foothill Blvd. Hollenbeck Park, Cummings and Fourth Sts. Lincoln Park, Mission Rd. and Alhambra Ave. MacArthur Park, Alvarado and 7th Sts. Reseda Park, 18411 Victory Blvd. Cabrillo Beach, including ride around harbor. *(Half hour and hourly fees).*

*Boxing and Wrestling:* Olympic Auditorium, 1801 S. Grand Ave. Hollywood Legion Stadium, 1628 N. El Centro Ave.

*Fishing:* Hansen Dam Lake, continuous open season for bass, blue gill, crappie. Echo Park Lake, open to children up to 15 years of age, Saturday mornings; also Wednesday mornings during summer. Crowley Lake, part of Los Angeles Power & Water Dept. system, 310 *m.* north, has city-operated motor boats or row boats available. Open May through July for trout; fly fishing with barbless hooks Sept. 15-Oct. 31 from Los Angeles north landing to mouth of Convict Creek.

*Football:*  National League, Los Angeles Memorial Coliseum, Exposition Park, Figueroa St. and Santa Barbara Ave.  Collegiate games, Coliseum, September-December.  New Year's Day East-West game, Rose Bowl, Pasadena.

*Golf:*  Fox Hills and Baldwin Hills Club, 5800 W. Slauson Ave., Culver City. Griffith Park Municipal Course, Los Feliz Ave. and Riverside Dr.  Hansen Dam Park, 11770 Foothill Blvd.  Holmby Park, 601 Club View Dr.  Inglewood Country Club, 3424 W. Manchester Blvd.  Los Feliz Park, 3207 Los Feliz Blvd. Sepulva Dam Park, 16821 Burbank Blvd., Encino.  Western Avenue Course. *For advance telephonic reservation privilege ($1) write Recreation & Park Dept., 305 City Hall, Los Angeles.  Fees on regulation 18-hole courses $2 per round and 50¢ per person for reservations.  After 3 p.m. in winter and 4 p.m. in summer daily fees are $1.  Nine-hole courses, $1 per round plus 50¢ per person for reservations.*

*Horse Racing:*  Hollywood Turf Club, Hollywood Park, Inglewood; fifty days, May-July.  Los Angeles Turf Club, Santa Anita Park, Arcadia, 14 *m.* east on Huntington Dr.; December-mid-March.

*Ice Skating:*  Polar Ice Palace, 615 N. Van Ness Ave.

*Swimming:*  The City of Los Angeles (Dept. of Recreation & Parks) operates 42 municipal swimming pools, 13 miles of public beaches, six lakes and facilities at Hansen Dam in San Fernando Valley.  Learn-to-swim classes for boys and girls and small craft training, with life guard service are provided.  Major beaches are in Will Rogers Beach State Park, north from Santa Monica; Venice Beach, from Ocean Park boundary south to Marina del Rey Channel; Dockweiler Beach State Park, south to El Segundo; Cabrillo Beach, at Los Angeles harbor breakwater, San Pedro (overnight camping).  Also swimming in Hansen Dam Park, Osborne Ave., between Glenoaks and Foothill Blvds., with boating and picnic facilities. *(Parking 25¢ weekdays, 50¢ Saturdays, Sundays, holidays; $1 additional for boats and trailers)*.  Municipal pools are open daily from 9 a.m. to 12 noon, and 1 p.m. to 5 p.m., except Sundays, 1 p.m. to 5 p.m.  Lessons mornings, Mondays through Fridays.  Children under 12, 20¢; 12 to 17, 30¢; 18 and over, 40¢.  Swimming pools at Downey, Fernangeles and Verdugo are shallow pools for children, free.  Most pools have Saturday morning splash sessions for ages 7 to 17, free.  Los Angeles Swimming Stadium contains the Olympic Pool, built 1932 to Olympic competitive requirements, seats 5,000, has a pool 50 meters long, 20 meters wide; has diving, water polo, programs.

LOS ANGELES (286 alt., 2,481,595 pop., 1960; 2,731,700, est., 1965 by City Planning Dept. and authorities) is the largest city in California and third largest in the United States.  It covers an area of 458.2 square miles or 293,251 acres, generally termed the largest municipal area in the country, although challenged lately by Oklahoma City, Okla. (324,253 pop., 1960).  The population of Los Angeles would be much larger if numerous independent communities in Los Angeles County, contiguous to the city, were counted in, these including such populous places as Long Beach, Pasadena, Glendale, Beverly Hills, Burbank, Culver City, Huntington Park, Inglewood, El Segundo and Santa Monica. The big city has so many near neighbors that the 1960 Census reported 6,038,771 in the whole County, or 4,559,956 outside city limits, of which 344,168 were credited to Long Beach.  There is still land available for annexation; the latest took place March 30, 1965, when the Porter Ranch in the San Fernando Valley was added to the city.

Population is therefore a major topic of interest in Los Angeles, alternating with the baseball exploits of the Dodgers and the Angels, the Freeways and the smog.  The City Planning Department estimated that the city added 50,000 persons annually in the five years, 1960-1965.  While all sections of the city gained, the San Fernando Valley led with an increase of 22% in the five years, indicating the drift to the environs of large cities observed in other parts of the country. This was partly explained by the size of San Fernando Valley as a statistical area, for it occupies 215 square miles out of the city's 458.

Los Angeles is governed by a Mayor and a City Council of 15, elected every four years. The City Attorney and the City Controller are elected for the same period. For salaries the Mayor received $25,000; City Attorney, $23,000; Controller, $18,000; Councilmen, each $12,000. Of the 28 departments, 19 are controlled by boards or commissions, the heads of which are appointed by the mayor and confirmed by the Council. The Board of Education is elected. The City Clerk has major responsibilities of liaison between officials and public, and is really secretary of the city. He keeps the records of legislation, supervises the Tax and Permit Division, which collects taxes, and the Land Records Division and the Election Division.

INDEPENDENT SCHOOL SYSTEM. One of the monumental accomplishments of Los Angeles is not visible in one piece—it is called the Los Angeles City Schools, a term that covers a system twice as large as the area of the city, serving other independent municipalities in the county as well. In administration it is independent of city and county. The seven junior colleges, which offer freshman and sophomore courses of a four-year college curriculum, are in a separate district, but all are governed by the Board of Education of seven members, who are elected for four-year terms every other year. The Superintendent of Schools is the chief executive officer of the Board and the school system.

Fall enrollment for a typical year, 1964, showed 756,510 pupils in the system's 596 schools. Of this total 356,988 were in the elementary schools, from kindergarten through sixth grade; 127,584 were in junior high schools; 122,538 in senior high schools; 69,359 in day and evening junior college classes and 80,041 in adult education high schools. There are 27 adult schools and 13 schools for the handicapped. To operate these schools, pay the 30,000 teachers and the 15,000 non-teaching employees, the 1964-1965 budget called for $440,000,000. The tax rate for the school district was $4.22 for each $100 of assessed property valuation. Nearly 66% of the money needed came from taxing real and personal property; 32% came from State funds. As about 30,000 new pupils enter Los Angeles schools every year the system is currently spending about $35,000,000 a year for new schools and additions, paid for by bond issues approved by popular vote.

NEW CULTURAL CENTERS. With the 1960s came a resurgence of efforts to provide Los Angeles with cultural centers commensurable with its civic importance. Public-spirited donors provided the basic financial aid. By 1965 Los Angeles had ready the new COUNTY MUSEUM OF ART and the MUSIC CENTER OF THE PERFORMING ARTS, both of which were welcomed with enthusiasm by residents from the mountains to the sea.

LOS ANGELES COUNTY MUSEUM OF ART, Hancock

Park on Wilshire Blvd., opened Mar. 31, 1965, is the largest art museum built in the United States since the National Gallery of Art was opened in Washington 24 years before. It consists of three pavilion-like structures arranged on a central raised plaza that is 600 ft. long and set beside a reflecting pool. The buildings were designed in the Mediterranean style of southern California by William L. Pereira & Associates, with Jas. H. Langheim partner in charge. The main pavilion, the AHMANSON GALLERY, houses the permanent collections in galleries around a four-story, 85-ft. high central atrium. The Great Hall on the main level rises two stories and shows major large-scale paintings and tapestries. The galleries show continental paintings from the 14th through the 18th centuries. The third level has paintings from western Europe and the United States of the 19th and 20th centuries and the fourth level is devoted to decorative arts, textiles and costumes, prints and drawings. At the northeast side of the plaza is the LYTTON GALLERY, devoted to changing exhibitions. The third pavilion, the LEO S. BING CENTER, has a theater seating 602, the Children's Gallery and Workshop, lecture rooms and a research library of 45,000 volumes. The buildings are surrounded by colonnades of slender concrete columns. Covered walks between the buildings and over the outdoor dining area are made of aluminum frame topped with clear plastic domes. In the center of the pool is a fountain sculpture by Norbert Kricke. The land was donated by the County Board of Supervisors and the cost of the museum, $11,500,000, was raised by private donations. The annual budget for salaries and maintenance is $1,000,000.

Among the many citizens who have made the new County Museum possible is Norton Simon, industrialist, who acquired international renown when he bought *Titus* by Rembrandt in London for $2,234,000, with the object of showing it at the Museum.

The MUSIC CENTER FOR THE PERFORMING ARTS is a rallying point of the greatest importance to the cultural growth of Southern California. It occupies a seven-acre site at the top of the Civic Center, bounded by First, Temple and Hope Sts., and Grand Ave. There are three buildings, the first of which, the DOROTHY CHANDLER PAVILION, a symphony hall and opera house seating 3,250, was completed December 6, 1964, while work was progressing on the AHMANSON THEATER, a 2,100-seat auditorium, and the MARK TAPER FORUM, a circular theater seating 750. The MALL PLAZA and GARAGE also were completed in 1964. The LOS ANGELES PHILHARMONIC ORCHESTRA gave a full season of performances from Dec. 2, 1965, through April 15, 1966, under the direction of Zubin Mehta, Charles Munch, Antal Dorati, and other great conductors.

The cost of the Music Center is placed at $33,500,000, of which $18,300,000 was raised by volunteers headed by Mrs. Norman Chandler. It is operated for the County of Los Angeles by a nonprofit organization of which William Severns is general manager. The architects are Welton Becket & Associates. Structural engineers are Stacy & Skinner. Consultants on acoustics are Paul Veneklasen, Dr. Vern O. Knudsen, Dr.

Robert Leonard; on stage engineering, William P. Nolan; on lighting, Jean Rosenthal and Jo Mielziner; on seating, Ben Schlanger.

The Pavilion has curved sides faced with dark granite and glass, fluted columns faced with textured white concrete panels extending to the full height of the building and around its periphery. A wide outdoor promenade surrounds it on two levels. From the Mall Plaza the visitor enters a foyer with a grand staircase rising four stories, and serving the Grand Hall and the Terraces. The Terraces open on the Grand Hall, which is three floors high. The Hall has three 17-ft. tall crystal chandeliers suspended from a ceiling set with diamond-shaped mirrors. Patterned green and beige carpeting harmonizes with the onyx walls. The Hall opens on the terrazzo-covered upper promenade. The Pavilion is 330 ft. long, 252 ft. wide and 92 ft. tall. The main orchestra floor is nearly square and the last row of seats only 98 ft. from the stage. There is a Founders Circle and an area for wheelchairs.

The stage is described as extremely large and flexible. The proscenium can vary from 36 ft. to 58 ft. in width with a maximum height of 30 ft. The playing stage is 64 ft. deep and 169 ft. wide, and the rear wall is 104 ft. from the curtain line. There is a demountable orchestra shell and an acoustical canopy capable of adjustment for different types of performance, using direct sound radiation for the symphonic and operatic concerts and electro-acoustical reinforcement for light opera. The Pavilion is especially well equipped to provide for the casts. The dressing rooms are numerous, equipped with lounges, lockers, showers, and besides principals can accommodate 100 ballet and 100 chorus members.

The decor of the auditorium emphasizes the elegance of the whole structure. The curtain has a sunburst pattern in shades of gold. Deep coral carpeting and seats contrast with the curtain. The front part of the room is patterned in butternut wood, the rear covered with beige silk vinyl.

On the Grand Avenue side of the Pavilion is the CURTAIN CALL RESTAURANT with cocktail lounge and coffee shop. It is decorated in walnut with beige, rust and brown accents and is intended to recall a music hall of the early 1900s. The PAVILION RESTAURANT on the fifth floor has a rich decor in blue, white and gold, seats 170, and provides a view of the city. The top floor also has two rooms for banquets.

Two other units were designed to fit gracefully into the Music Center. The MARK TAPER FORUM, a circular structure, and the AHMANSON THEATER, almost square, were to be joined by a 48-ft. tall colonnade surrounding both. The Forum has been designed for drama, chamber music, recitals, lectures and meetings. The plans called for a structure 140 ft. in diameter, rising from a reflecting pool 175 ft. square, which must be crossed on a bridge to the main foyer. The main entry foyer is beneath the seating and a stair leads to the upper floor. A novel stage effect is produced by a cyclorama screen at the rear of the stage, a movable open metal screen 10 ft. in front of it, and a movable floor section between the two for prop changes and effects. A curtain of light is used to wall off the darkened stage during changes of scene.  The color scheme for the auditorium walls is light gray vinyl at the rear becoming darker toward the front, while seat colors range from plum in front, blue in the center and turquoise at the rear.  The foyer wall holds abalone shell cut into small mosaics.

The AHMANSON THEATER to the north of the Forum, contains numerous innovations.  Stage and auditorium are 155 by 175 ft., 73 ft. high, with the wall facing the Forum entirely of glass enclosing the main lobby and two upper floors.  This theater, seating 2,100 on three levels, has the first 13 rows of 1,000 seats arranged as a dress circle.  One level up the Parquet Terrace provides 600 loge seats entered from a promenade. A proscenium that extends to the ceiling, a fore-stage, an adjustable orchestra pit.  The design for the decor calls for three stages of red, from brilliant red of the velvet curtain to dark burgundy of the carpet, with walls of pewter gray textured vinyl and a small-scale design resembling cut velvet, light at the rear, dark at the stage.  The Music Center Mall Plaza forms a formal courtyard at the western end of the main Civic Center Mall, and provides a promenade with a view of the entire Civic Center.  It has a 75 ft. square reflecting pool with fountains, benches and arcades of trees.  Entrance to the Mall Plaza from Grand Ave. is by a monumental stairway.  Entrance to parking under the Mall is from Grand Ave., with elevator service to the Pavilion.

PORT OF LOS ANGELES on the Pacific Ocean is the great shipping faciiity that accounts for a large share of the commercial prosperity of Los Angeles.  In 1909 the city extended its jurisdiction to the harbor area and voted bond issues for development.  When the Panama Canal was reopened in 1921 the Port moved 7,700 miles and 21 days closer by water to the eastern seaboard.  In 1929 the value of commerce there passed the $1 billion mark; exports were reaching 87 different countries. The building of docks, warehouses, storage tanks, berths since World War II has been of such extent that by 1964 the Port was first on the west coast in tonnage handled and tenth in the United States, with more than 24,494,049 net tons handled by 3,751 ships.  Bulk petroleum led the tonnage, with 16,839,000 tons.  San Francisco exceeded the Port in general cargo.

The Immigration & Naturalization Service of the Dept. of Justice reported 230,584 persons arrived and departed from the Port of Los Angeles and San Pedro in 1964; 131,813 were United States citizens and 98,771 aliens.  In 1963 imports reached 5,639,000 short tons and exports 2,961,000.  Coastwise receipts were 4,130,000 tons and shipments 6,868,000 tons.

Large passenger liners using the Port included ships of the Grace Line, Holland America, Johnson, Matson, Moore-McCormack and P. & O.  Japan led all other flag ships calling at the Port.  In fiscal 1963-64 construction was begun on a vast array of improvements.  They included new cargo terminals, a 10-story administration center, a bulk loader to cost $4,750,000, a new Catalina terminal, and the Cabrillo Beach Marina, with berths for 3,100 private craft and restaurant and apartment facilities. In 1963 a $16,000,000 cargo-passenger terminal was dedicated. Dredging of the West Basin deepened the area to 35 ft. and added 96 acres to Terminal Island. At the Supertanker Terminal oil carriers from the Persian Gulf are unloaded by push-button controls at a rate of 35,000 bbl. per hour. Aluminum containers for general cargo holding 23 tons are similarly handled in loading. A new recreational area is Ports o' Call, a small village with exotic merchandise. The Fisherman's Fiesta, in late October, draws 250,000 visitors annually. The Port is protected by a nine-mile breakwater at the end of which shines Angel's Gate Lighthouse, with a beam visible 15 miles.

LOS ANGELES INTERNATIONAL AIRPORT represents the most modern adaptation to jet-age needs. It has 1,000 landings and takeoffs daily and 9,914,785 passengers used its facilities in fiscal 1964. The main airport, at 1 World Way, has for landmarks 135-ft. parabolic arches of steel that support a restaurant and observation deck and a 172-ft. control tower. The latter houses the air traffic control of the Federal Aviation Agency and administrative offices of the Department of Airports. Trams carry passengers from the parking area to ticket offices and terminal buildings. The first moving sidewalk, 420 ft. long, was installed in the American Airlines terminal. There are two parallel runways 12,000 ft. long, and one 8,000 ft. long. The parking space accommodates 5,000 cars and a 3½ story garage will add space for 750 more. The newest physical development is the large CARGO CITY, with facilities for handling many times the freight and cargo now received. This amounted in 1964 to 159,000 tons of freight and 44,000 tons of air mail.

The Department of Airports also manages the VAN NUYS AIRPORT, which has more than 150,000 private and business airplane flights annually, with a heliport on Woodley Avenue, Van Nuys, for local services for San Fernando Valley residents. Los Angeles County operates four airports, all devoted to general aviation. These are Compton, El Monte, Brackett Field at Pomona, and Fox Field at Lancaster, in the Antelope Valley. Several of the smaller cities within Los Angeles County have municipal airports, namely Torrance, Santa Monica, and Hawthorne, all for general aviation.

Reflecting its rapid expansion, the city's population is largely a transplanted one. From census to census a steady flow of newcomers has created virtually a new city; in only one decade since 1870 has Los Angeles failed at least to double its population. Many of the recent arrivals are from the Middle West and the East, elderly folk who have retired on a moderate income. Others have been drawn by the business opportunities offered by a growing community. Others, driven from their homes by depression, droughts and dust storms, have come seeking a new start in the City of the Angels.

Several large racial and language groups add contrast and color to the vast mosaic of the city. With more than 100,000 Mexicans originally brought in to work on farms and in canneries, Los Angeles is the fifth largest Mexican city in the world. Living almost wholly to themselves, many of them speak only their mother tongue. Negroes comprise the next largest group, many employed in industries and some found in almost every business and professional field.

The local Japanese, many of them American citizens, have their own shops, restaurants, native-language schools and newspapers, chamber of commerce, and American Legion post, in the district centering on E. First Street, between Los Angeles Street and Central Avenue. Many of the Japanese are engaged in trade, particularly in the fruit and vegetable markets. Old Chinatown along Alameda Street near the Union Passenger Terminal has changed and many Chinese have moved to New Chinatown, north of Main Street. The Filipino colony, approximately equal in number to the Chinese, is almost entirely male, employed for the most part in household services.

HISTORY. The growth of the modern city dates roughly from 1880, almost a century after its founding. In 1769 a party of explorers and missionaries under Capt. Gaspar de Portolá discovered an Indian village named Yang-na here, and impressed with the fertile river valley, named the spot Porciuncula for a chapel in Italy beloved by St. Francis. When Franciscan padres returned two years later, they selected a site nine miles northeast on which to build San Gabriel Mission and begin their work of converting the Indians and cultivating farms, orchards, and vineyards, but settlement did not really begin for another decade. On September 4, 1781, as the American Revolution was drawing to a close on the other side of the continent, Don Felipe de Neve, Governor of California, marched from San Gabriel with a handful of soldiers and eleven families from Mexico, chiefly Indians, Negroes, and mulattoes. A few priests from San Gabriel Mission assisted him as with solemn rites and ceremonies he founded El Pueblo de Nuestra Señora la Reina de Los Angeles de Porciuncula (The Town of Our Lady the Queen of the Angels of Porciuncula).

Each of the First Families of Los Angeles was given a plot to cultivate and a lot facing the Plaza, the large square that for a century remained the hub of community life. It took three years for the straggling village to acquire a small adobe church on the Plaza. For seven years the reins of government were in the hands of a corporal, Vicente Felix, a Spaniard in command of an "army" of four or five Mexican soldiers. Discharged soldiers and colonists from Mexico drifted in from time to time; by 1800 the settlement numbered 70 families, living in some 30 adobe dwellings and engaged chiefly in raising grain and cattle.

Intruders from the outside world were rare. In 1805 the *Lelia Byrd* touched at San Pedro, the first American vessel to anchor here in defiance of the Spanish law prohibiting trade with foreign ships. The master of the ship carried back to the United States along with a cargo of hogs and sheep, a glowing account of the wealth of California, a report that brought an increasing number of American ships to these shores in the next few years. Captured as a "pirate" in 1818, Joseph (rebaptized José) Chapman became the first English-speaking settler. Held prisoner for a time, he was set to work, being a skilled carpenter, and later erected the church, since remodeled, that still stands facing the Plaza; he capped his career by marrying into one of the pioneer families. After the secularization of the missions (1834-37), more American traders, miners, and adventurers drifted in, embraced the Roman Catholic religion, married Mexican heiresses and became Yankee dons. During the storied rancho period all of southern California was held under the virtual feudal sway of a handful of Mexican cattle barons —Pico, Figueroa, Sepulveda, Bandini, and others, whose wealth and power are still recalled by the names of streets and places.

In 1846, at the outbreak of the Mexican War, the sleepy pueblo was a nondescript village of less than 3,000, but with the seizure of California by the United States it suddenly became a rip-roaring frontier town. Times were good after 1849 when the rush of gold-hunters into the country to the north created an insatiable market for southern California cattle. Los Angeles' reputation for violence was almost unmatched even in those rough-and-ready days; its lawlessness was such that many referred to it as Los Diablos (the devils). In 1871 after the accidental killing of a white man by a Chinese, a mob attacked Chinatown, and slaughtered 19 Chinese. For the first time Los Angeles was front-page news. The town was shocked into sudden sobriety.

The Southern Pacific Railroad reached Los Angeles in 1876 and the Santa Fe in 1885. Immediately one of the bitterest railroad rate wars in history broke out. The Santa Fe reduced the fare from the Mississippi Valley from $100 to $95; the Southern Pacific reduced it to $90. Passengers scurried from one railroad office to the other to obtain the latest bargain. At the height of hostilities the fare dropped to $15, then to $5, and for one day in the spring of 1886 the Santa Fe advertised "Kansas City to Los Angeles for a dollar!" Train after train rumbled into Los Angeles, packed to the doors, and the first and gaudiest of its real estate booms was under way.

Within little more than two years the population swelled from 12,000 to 50,000. Many swept in on the tidal wave were homeseekers, but most came to make a fortune in real estate, and to make it quick. At first the little town scarcely knew what was happening. Buildings went up overnight. Land speculation reached fantastic proportions. Lots around the Plaza sold at $1,000 a front foot; subdivisions were laid out from Santa Monica to San Bernardino, a distance of 70 miles; promoters paid cash in advance for full-page advertisements to spur the dilatory.

By 1892 the population was 50,000. A well drilled in the front yard of a private home by E. L. Doheny and C. A. Canfield had struck oil. Soon the city was dotted with 1,400 derricks, in chicken yards, back gardens, and front lawns. Children of a generation ago rode up and down on the slow-moving walking beams, as on a teeter-totter. The wells within the city were gradually depleted, but oil production in the vicinity jumped to new heights with the discovery in 1921 of the huge Signal field at Long Beach.

Meanwhile Los Angeles businessmen were agitating for the development of an adequate harbor at San Pedro, but not without bitter opposition. Ocean frontage at Santa Monica was controlled by Collis P. Huntington, president of the Southern Pacific, who sought to have Congress appropriate $4,000,000 to build a breakwater and harbor there. The Santa Fe Railway, a majority of the Chamber of Commerce, and other business groups sent lobbyists to Congress, which in the end selected San Pedro and appropriated $2,900,000 to start the work that has since created the huge artificial harbor.

The want of an adequate water supply, always a vital need in this land of much sunshine and little rain, inspired a gigantic project to pipe in the entire flow of the Owens River, 238 miles distant in the High Sierra. A $22,500,000 bond issue to finance construction was proposed; as part of the campaign, the existing supply of water was reduced by running it into sewers; strict prohibitions were issued against watering lawns and gardens; with the hot sun burning and baking the ground, the vote on the bond issue was a foregone conclusion. In 1913 the Owens River was on its way to Los Angeles, but it did not arrive. The enormous pipeline had been built only as far as the arid San Fernando Valley, which, it transpired, had been taken over by a small group, who meanwhile had persuaded the city to annex its 108,000 desert acres. The bond issue had stipulated that the water be brought to the city; the stipulation was ingeniously met by extending Los Angeles to the water, to the great profit of those who then subdivided and sold the new annex to the city for as much as $1,000 an acre. With the diversion of the river, the once fertile and prosperous Owens Valley became, in Will Rogers' phrase, "a valley of desolation."

In the face of bitter opposition from open-shop industrial interests organized into the powerful Merchants and Manufacturers Association, led by Gen. Harrison Gray Otis, publisher of the *Times,* labor unions had long struggled to gain a foothold in Los Angeles. A feud of twenty years standing had been precipitated when Otis locked out the paper's typographers in 1890. The climax came early in the morning of October 1, 1910, when an explosion wrecked the *Times* building, killing 20 men.

During the now fabulous 1920's the city's population of approximately 600,000 more than doubled; a phenomenal building boom resulted, with contractors working vainly to meet the great need of housing. Subdivisions sprang up like mushrooms all over the metropolitan area; office buildings, apartment houses, and theaters were rapidly erected until the sole reminders of the town of Spanish and early American days were a few adobe houses and buildings tucked away here and there.

Architecturally, modern Los Angeles is a potpourri of styles, reflecting its different periods of almost convulsive growth. There are many survivors of the post-Civil War area, with their cupolas and curlicues; many brownstones of the 1880's, with elaborate ornament and great bay windows with colored glass; a large number of frame bungalows and box-like office structures of the first two decades of the century. The booming 1920's contributed the stucco dwellings and apartment houses, many pseudo-Spanish in style, as well as the skyscrapers, the movie "cathedrals," and the restaurants of bizarre design—one like a hat, another like a rabbit, a third like an old shoe, another a fish. In striking contrast with all of these are the extremely modern houses and buildings of concrete, steel, and glass. Today the forty-odd story office towers are rising to pierce the upper air and change the skyline.

Socially, too, Los Angeles is a medley of many philosophies and ways of life. To the newcomer southern California is a curiously exciting combination of massive mountains, blue sea, Spanish romance, and Hollywood glamor, offering many of them a welcome change from the stereotyped patterns of the old home town. Here is a spirit of live and let live that encourages the transplanted Iowan or Bostonian to experiment with the unconventional in dress, houses, ideas, and religions. Countless movements flourish in Los Angeles, from the crusades of such religious sects as the Rosicrucians, and the Church of the Four Square Gospel, founded by the late evangelist Aimee Semple McPherson, to groups organized to promote a score of economic and political doctrines.

## POINTS OF INTEREST

### PLAZA AND CIVIC CENTER

PUEBLO DE LOS ANGELES is a State Historical Monument comprising structures in and around the old SPANISH PLAZA, rebuilt or restored, located near Main and Los Angeles Sts., and Sunset Blvd. The Plaza lies southeast of the first plaza, laid out in 1781 by Gov. Felipe de Neve, founder of the city, whose statue stands on the circular fountain in the center of the park. Long ago floods forced the abandonment of the original adobe houses clustered about the first square. Around the present plaza laid out between 1800 and 1812, the pueblo's aristocracy built their homes. Under the American regime the square was transformed into a round park with paths radiating from the center, occupied until 1873 by a water tank.

The PLAZA CHURCH (*open every day*), 100 Sunset Blvd., also known as the Church of Our Lady the Queen of the Angels, the oldest in the city, was constructed in 1818-22 under the supervision of José Chapman, California's first Yankee. The mission padres at San Gabriel donated several barrels of brandy to raise the funds. Its historic bronze bells in the squat corner tower still chime the Angelus above the noise of the city streets, as they did over a century ago.

OLVERA STREET (El Paseo de los Angeles; Span., the walk of the angels), a brick-paved lane running from Marchessault St. north to Macy St., named for Don Agustin Olvera, who fought against Frémont, has been restored in the manner of an old Mexican street. Work began in 1929, with prison labor, and the street was dedicated in 1930.

A carved wooden cross at the entrance commemorates the founding of the pueblo of Los Angeles in 1781. On the street are 70 shops; a line of stalls runs down the center. The street is at its best in the evening, when cafes are gay with music, and colored lanters light the shops.   Every year from December 16 to 24 the colorful ceremony of Los Posados (the lodgings), telling the story of Mary's journey to Bethlehem in search of a birthplace for Jesus, is enacted.   Another rite, on the Saturday before Ash Wednesday, is the Blessing of the Animals, when a varied assortment of beasts is led through the street to receive a priest's blessing.

The AVILA ADOBE (*open 9 a.m.-11 p.m. daily; small fee*), 14 Olvera St., now a private museum, was the home of Don Francisco Avila, *alcalde* of the pueblo in the early nineteenth century.   After Avila's death in 1831, it passed into the hands of his widow, Doña Encarnación. Occupied by Commodore Robert F. Stockton in 1847, it was damaged by an earthquake in 1857 and restored along with Olvera Street in 1929. Today, only one wing remains of the L-shaped 18-room mansion.

LA GOLONDRINA, 35 Olvera Street, a two-story brick house, was built before 1865, when Antonio Pelanconi purchased it for use as a winery, one of the first in Los Angeles.   Only the hand-grooved balcony, the beams, and the fireplace of the original structure remain.

LA ZANJA MADRE FOUNTAIN (the mother ditch), opposite 35 Olvera St., is an unpretentious stucco monument commemorating the great open ditch that in early days supplied the pueblo with water from the Los Angeles River.   A diagonal band of brick in the paving of Olvera Street marks the line of the ancient canal.

The LUGO HOUSE, 516-22 N. Los Angeles Street, one of the first two-story adobe buildings in the city, and the only one remaining, was built in 1840 by Don Vicente Lugo.   In 1865 it housed St. Vincent's College, the first college in southern California, now Loyola University.   The building with its hip roof, dormers, and frame siding retains little of its original appearance, and is now occupied by a Chinese curio shop.

The OLD PICO HOUSE, 430 N. Main Street, a hotel built in 1869 by Pío Pico, who was the last Mexican Governor of the State, became the rendezvous of the elite of the Southwest because it had bathtubs and gaslight.   Both the corner restaurant and the poolroom on Plaza Street lead to a small patio.

BAKER BUILDING, N. Main and Arcadia Streets, a broad threestory structure, designed in the manner of the French second Empire, with classic arcades, central tower, and corner turrets, mansard roof and large dormers, was built in the late nineteenth century by Col. R. S. Baker.

DODGER STADIUM, on part of 5 acres in Chavez Ravine, north of Civic Center, is the home of the Los Angeles baseball team of the American League.   It is a cantilevered arena with four tiers, also used by the Los Angeles Angels.   When the Dodgers came west they first used the MEMORIAL COLISEUM, 3911 S. Figueroa St., seating 105,000.   At 3939 S. Figueroa St. is the MEMORIAL SPORTS ARENA, commemorating the heroes of World War II and the Korean War.

The LOS ANGELES UNION PASSENGER TERMINAL, N. Alameda St. between Aliso and Macy Sts., designed under the supervision of Donald B. Parkinson, is a T-shaped group of 30 low, white-stucco, red-tile-roofed buildings of modified mission architecture, topped with a 135-foot clock tower. The terminal of the Southern Pacific, Union Pacific, and Santa Fe railroads; the large main structure and the smaller buildings are separated by narrow areas designed to absorb earthquake shock. The plan of the main building includes a vestibule, a concourse, a large arcade, and a waiting room. Flanking the waiting room are two large patios; east of the south patio is the reception hall adjoining the departure and arrival lobby. Leading from this lobby is a passenger tunnel with ramps giving access to tracks. It was completed 1939 at a cost of $11,000,000.

LITTLE TOKYO ("Lil' Tokyo") First St., E. of Main St., is an area where Japanese shops offer oriental wares.

CHINATOWN, similarly an oriental headquarters, North Broadway and College St. has restaurants with exotic appeal for westerners.

CATHEDRAL OF ST. VIBIANA (*open 6 a.m.-8 p.m.*), Second and Main Sts., was Los Angeles' first Roman Catholic cathedral, opened in 1876. It was made the seat of the Archdiocese of Southern California in the fall of 1936. Cruciform in plan, the design of the classic edifice is based upon that of the church of San Miguel del Puerto, Barcelona, Spain. A relic of St. Vibiana, the child saint, allegedly recovered from the Roman catacombs, reposes in its original brass-bound casket in a niche in the upper part of the main altar.

THE STACK is the name popularly given to the Freeway Interchange some blocks north of the Civic Center, practically a monument to modern highway engineering. It is a 4-level crossing of 6 and 8 lane motor freeways—the Harbor, Hollywood, Pasadena, San Bernardino, Santa Ana and their connections.

The LOS ANGELES TIMES BUILDING, Times-Mirror Square, is the home of Los Angeles' largest morning and Sunday newspapers. The modern setback structure (1935) has a lofty central section flanked with massive buttress piers and low four-story wings. On a base of polished black granite rises pinkish granite to the second floor, above which the walls are of cream-colored limestone, with dark metal window frames. On the face of the towering section is a large clock, illuminated with red and blue neon lights, and surmounting the roof is the bronze eagle that survived the dynamiting of the old First-and-Broadway plant in 1910. With a circulation of more than 800,000 mornings and 1,100,000 Sundays, they reach all parts of southern California. The Times-Mirror Co. has expanded into other newspaper and book publishing and owns the New American Library of New York and the World Publishing Co. of Cleveland, O.

The CIVIC CENTER (*all buildings open 8-5 weekdays*) is bounded by Alameda on the east, Grand Ave. on the west, First St. on the south and Ord St. on the north. It is an irregular area where official buildings have been multiplying since 1949, necessitating the removal of many familiar landmarks. It includes the City Hall, County Hall of Justice, Post Office and Federal Court Bldg., Municipal Court Bldg., Superior Court Bldg., California State Bldg., State Public Works Bldg., Health Administration Bldg., Police Administration Bldg. and other official structures.

The CITY HALL (*top-floor observation balcony open 9-3; guides, free*), 200 N. Spring St., the city's tallest building, rising from its block-square grounds to a height of 464 feet, is visible for miles around. Designed by Parkins, Martin, and Austin, it is dominated by a buttressed skyscraper tower, capped with a stepped pyramid dome resting on a square colonnaded base. The Lindbergh airplane beacon is at the apex. The central tower soars above a four-story base and flanking wings. The exterior is finished in granite and glazed terra cotta. Notable among its rooms are the basilica type city council chamber, with beamed ceiling and Italian marble columns; the session room of the board of public works, with blue, green, and gold arcades at each end; and the mayor's reception room, with teakwood floor and redwood ceiling, adorned with coats of arms.

U. S. POST OFFICE AND COURT HOUSE, 312 N. Spring St., designed by G. Stanley Underwood, is an 18-story structure of neo-Classic design, opened in January 1939. The building houses the main post office, Government departments and bureaus, and Federal courts.

The exterior, finished in white ceramics with a granite base, is entirely without embellishment. The central section rises above a broad three- and four-story base. Its dark metal windows and white piers emphasize the vertical lines of the exterior. On either side of both the Main and Spring Street entrances are two flagpoles with bronze bases and four Doric columns. Ceramic medallions adorned with eagles flank the doors, and between the columns are aluminum grills bearing the seals of various Federal departments. Walls of the public lobbies are lined with rose marble and sienna travertine.

The LOS ANGELES COUNTY HALL OF JUSTICE, Temple St. between Broadway and Spring Sts., occupying a city block and rising 14 stories in height is a massive limestone and granite structure. The building erected in 1925 is designed in the Italian Renaissance style with rusticated stonework, heavy cornices, and crowning two-story colonnade. The building houses the County Jail in its five upper stories.

The HALL OF RECORDS between First and Court Sts., the oldest of Los Angeles County public buildings, was erected in 1909. A gray sandstone and marble structure, 11 stories high, it is topped with corner turrets and dormers. Here are the offices of the county government divisions, and more than 400,000 volumes in the County Law Library. In the office of the Board of Supervisors on the 11th floor are old prints picturing Los Angeles as it was in 1854, 1857, and later.

The modern steel and concrete STATE BUILDING, First and Spring Sts., consists of a massive main section, rising above two nine-story wings. The interior is finished with gleaming marble.

## DOWNTOWN

ANGEL'S FLIGHT, a short cable railway, built 1901, starts from a pavilion at Third and Hill Sts. and carries passengers up the steep slope between Hill and Olive Sts. on Bunker Hill. An observation tower 110 ft. tall gives a view as far as the San Gabriel Mountains.

The BILTMORE HOTEL, Fifth and Olive Sts., opened 1923, is a modified Italian Renaissance building of 12 stories, with a lobby on two floors. Exit on the upper floor is to Grand Ave. Two blocks south the newly built NUMBER ONE WILSHIRE BUILDING, 30 stories tall, fronting on Grand, stands at the start of the famous WILSHIRE BOULEVARD.

The EDISON BUILDING, Fifth St. and Grand Ave., 13 stories tall, is headquarters of the Southern California Edison organization. It is built of granite, limestone and terra cotta in cream-colored hues. A corner octagonal entrance pavilion leads to a huge marble lobby decorated with an allegorical mural, *Power,* by Hugo Ballin.

PERSHING SQUARE, bounded by Fifth, Sixth, Hill and Olive Sts., has walks lined with coco palms and an ornamental fountain surrounded by banana plants. Cars are parked in an underground garage. In the park are memorials of World War I and the Spanish-American War. A statue of Beethoven faces the hall formerly used by the Philharmonic Orchestra, now church property.

The LOS ANGELES PUBLIC LIBRARY, 630 West Fifth St., is the largest public library west of the Mississippi River. Established 1872, it is a department of the city government and has been tax-supported since 1878, receiving 7¢ of each $100 of assessed valuation on all real and personal property, as well as annual appropriations from special funds. It had 59 branches and a stock of 2,977,034 books in 1964, when 767,755 persons made use of its extensive services. It has an operating budget of $7,237,472. The Library building was designed by Bertram Goodhue and has sculptures by Lee Lawrie and murals by Albert Herter and Dean Cornwell.

> Next in size to the city Library stands the LOS ANGELES COUNTY PUBLIC LIBRARY, 320 W. Temple St., which has 230 outlets. In 1964 it reported a stock of 2,087,133 volumes, including 578,100 juvenile books, and an operating budget of $5,854,411. Other major libraries in city and county include the LOS ANGELES COUNTY LAW LIBRARY, 301 West First St. (401,357 vols.); the COUNTY MEDICAL ASSN. LIBRARY, 634 S. Westlake Ave. (89,579 vols.); the COUNTY MUSEUM LIBRARY, Exposition Park (50,000 volt.); the PHILOSOPHICAL RESEARCH SOCIETY LIBRARY, 3910 Los Feliz Blvd. (40,000 vols.); PARAMOUNT PICTURES RESEARCH LIBRARY, 5451 Marathon St. (35,000 vols.); the WM. ANDREWS CLARK MEMORIAL LIBRARY, 2205 W. Adams Blvd. (65,000 vols), and about 100 more.

CALIFORNIA INSTITUTE OF THE ARTS (CAL ARTS) was formed in 1962 by a merger of the Los Angeles Conservatory of Music (1883) and the Chouinard Art School (1921). In 1966 it prepared to move from Downtown Los Angeles to VALENCIA, a residential project to be built by 1968 on 44,000 acres 30 miles north. CAL ARTS has been given a 38-acre campus by Walt Disney and will add theater arts to its curriculum. A large endowment has been raised from Federal grants and private donations.

UNION BANK SQUARE, bounded by Fifth, Fourth and Figueroa Sts. and the Harbor Freeway in Downtown Los Angeles, is the site of the tallest office structure, 42 stories, in the City and Southern California. Erected 1966 this huge rectangle of steel and glass is the first structure of the BUNKER HILL URBAN RENEWAL PROJECT, which is expected to cost $350,000,000 before completion. The skyscraper is financed by the Connecticut General Life Insurance Co. and the Galbreath-Ruffin Corp., and the Union Bank has leased fourteen floors. The building and contiguous area occupy 3.7 acres, for which the owners paid $3,200,-000. There are four levels below the plaza for parking cars, accessible to the Harbor Freeway. The high lobby extends through the first floor and carries elevators and escalators. Columns stand free of the walls on the four sides of the building.

The CROCKER-CITIZENS BUILDING, Sixth St. and Grand Ave., another 42-story giant, was designed in 1966 by William L. Pereira & Associates. It was to cost $30,000,000, have nine levels for parking, and rise as a cruciform tower above a four-story base.

UNITED CALIFORNIA BANK, Sixth and Spring Sts., led the parade of tall buildings when the City Council removed the 150-ft. limit in height in 1957.

SUNKIST BUILDING, 705 W. Fifth St., Bunker Hill, is head-quarters of Sunkist Growers, Inc. It has a marble and aluminum entrance and a lobby with decorated ceiling beams.

BRADBURY BUILDING, Broadway and Third Sts., built 1893 by Col. Lewis Bradbury of Bunker Hill, is notable for its large five-story interior well with galleries protected by wrought-iron railings.

RICHFIELD BUILDING, 555 S. Flower St. is a setback structure, 371 ft. tall, with black masonry and gold terra cotta trim.

The PACIFIC COAST STOCK EXCHANGE, Los Angeles Division, is a modern 12-story structure, completed in 1930. The granite facade, with fluted pylons and bronze reliefs, is practically windowless.

## NORTH AND EAST

ELYSIAN PARK (*open 5 a.m. to 9 p.m. daily*), entrance N. Broadway and Los Angeles River, is a 600-acre municipal park, with seven miles of paved roads twisting in hairpin curves through arroyo-gashed hills, a matted tangle of wild roses, creepers, blue gum eucalyptus trees, drooping pepper trees, and gnarled live oaks. Ten miles of foot trails lead through canyons and up steep hills. From Point Grand View, a rustic lookout, is a view of the city and mountains beyond. Elysian Park was established in 1886. A landslide in 1938 revealed a forgotten tunnel that provided an auxiliary water supply for the city in the 1870's. The PORTOLA-CRESPI MONUMENT, left of the park entrance, is a granite boulder. Here, on August 2, 1769, Don Gaspar de Portola and Padre Juan Crespi, leading the first overland exploration of California, pitched camp.

EL ALISAL (*open on application at the Southwest Museum*), a large house on the west side of the Arroyo Seco at Avenue 43, is named for the giant sycamore tree around which it was built and which still towers from the patio high above the Spanish roof of the very un-Spanish stone building. Charles F. ("Don Carlos") Lummis, who arrived in Los Angeles in the 1880's after a 3,507-mile marathon hike, built the house with his own hands, aided only by a young Indian boy.  He is remembered not only for his Promethean cultural activities but for his prolific publicity of the region.

SYCAMORE GROVE, N. Figueroa St. and Pasadena Freeway is a 20-acre plot of lawns studded with giant sycamores.  Since its establishment as a park in 1905, it has been used frequently for those State picnics so typical of Los Angeles, at which the city's adopted citizens congregate to reminisce about days "back home."  The park provides free stoves, firewood, tables, tennis courts, and playground equipment for children.

CASA DE ADOBE (*open 2 to 5 p.m. Wed., Sun.*), 4605 N. Figueroa St., built by the Southwest Museum, is a replica of a typical California dwelling of the early nineteenth century.  One room contains a display of numerous household articles; the others are arranged and furnished in keeping with the period.  Walks shaded with grapevines divide the gardens, which contain many varieties of cactus.

The SOUTHWEST MUSEUM (*open 1 p.m. to 4:45 p.m. daily except Mondays and important holidays, and last two weeks in August and first two weeks in September*), Marmion Way and Museum Drive, overlooks the Arroyo Seco and Sycamore Grove.  Opened in 1914, the white concrete building, without ornamentation, has a tile-roofed tower at one end and a high square tower at the other.  The museum contains relics and art of the primitive peoples of Western America, collected by the Southwest Society of the Archaeological Society of America, founded in 1903.

A bright MAYAN PORTAL, designed in the manner of the portal of the House of Nuns at Chichen Itza, in Yucatan, forms the entrance to a 260-foot tunnel leading into the base of the hill on which the building stands.  Dioramas on the sides of the tunnel depict the history of the primitive Asian men who settled the Western American coast.

An elevator runs to the LOWER LOBBY, 108 feet above, containing American Indian exhibits.  In the south wing is the SOUTHWESTERN INDIANS ROOM, with relics and modern handicraft of the "sky-dwelling" Pueblos, and of the nomadic Navajo and Mojave.  In the NORTHWESTERN INDIANS ROOM, are displays of Alaska and British Columbia handicraft—carved ivory and totem poles.

From the lower lobby the center stairway leads to the PLAINS INDIANS ROOM, displaying a tepee of tanned skins, clothing and weapons of Blackfeet, Cheyenne, Crow and Arapaho.  The adjoining room on the north is the PREHISTORIC PUEBLO INDIANS TOWER, containing relics from Southwestern cliff dwellings—fabrics woven from yucca and turkey feathers, and colored with brilliant vegetable dyes.

THE AMERICAN INDIAN BASKETRY WING, built 1940-41, contains the Catherine Boeing Poole Collection of 2,446 specimens made by tribes in Washington, British Columbia, California and the Southwest, including baskets made by the Pomo Indians.

In the south wing of the same floor is the AUDITORIUM.  West of the Auditorium is the TORRANCE TOWER, which contains the Library of the Southwest, a collection of works on archaeology, ethnology, and primitive art of the Southwest and Spanish-America.

Since 1927 the Museum has supported archaeological expeditions that have uncovered many prehistoric sites and artifacts in the Southwest. Since 1942 they have made discoveries at Black Dog Cave, Nevada, Big Tujunga Wash, Calif., Pinto Basin near Little Lake, Calif., Tule Springs, Nev., Manix Lake, Calif., San Nicolas Island, Calif., Dyck House Ruins, Ariz., San Clemente Isl., Calif.

OCCIDENTAL COLLEGE occupies a 120-acre site on the northeastern rim of Los Angeles. Founded in 1888 by the Presbyterian denomination, it became non-sectarian in 1910 and is coeducational, with students limited to 1,450, of whom 850 are men. It has three eleven-week terms in which each student takes no more than three courses per term. It offers premedical, predental and pre-engineering courses, a program in diplomacy and world affairs, and enables qualified students to study in foreign countries for six months. Of the student body 85 per cent lives on campus. The buildings range from modified Spanish Renaissance to modern. The Mary Norton Clapp Library has more than 190,000 volumes (1965) and contains the Robinson Jeffers Collection (the poet was a 1905 graduate), a 500-book Lincoln collection, and a section of mystery-detective fiction. A five-week Drama Festival is held in the summer; students also act in the Playmill Theatre. The Hillside Theatre, outdoors, seats 5,000. Tuition costs $1,500 a year; room and board, $990 to $1,050 a year, with other fees added the basic annual cost is approx. $2,600.

LINCOLN PARK, bounded by Mission Road and Alhambra Ave., containing eucalyptus-shaded picnic grounds and a six-acre lake for boating, has two tennis courts, a merry-go-round, children's play apparatus, four horseshoe courts, and a conservatory of rare tropical plants.

LOS ANGELES COUNTY GENERAL HOSPITAL, 1200 N. State St. (Mission Road, Marengo & De Soto Sts.), occupies 123 structures on a 56-acre site. The ACUTE UNIT, the main building, is a massive, set-back structure with soaring vertical lines rising 20 stories from a slight eminence. It is visible from most of the hilly eastern section of the city. The building is constructed of steel and reinforced concrete with ample fenestration, 31 acres of floor space, a large kitchen, 75 wards, 16 major surgeries and 4 maternity delivery suites. The unit, designed by 60 local architects, was completed in 1932.

Among the other hospital units, on the western section of the grounds, are the OSTEOPATHIC BUILDING, the PSYCHOPATHIC BUILDING, the COMMUNICABLE DISEASES BUILDING, and the INTERNES' HOME. The hospital's capacity is 4,000 patients.

The institution was founded in an adobe house on North Main Street in 1858 and operated by the Sisters of Charity. A two-story frame hospital was erected on the present site in 1878.

CHURCH OF OUR LADY OF LOURDES (*open at all hours*), 3772 E. 3rd St., designed by L. G. Scherer in the form of a Spanish mission church but highly stylized in its modern treatment of traditional architecture, is dominated by a lofty corner tower.  The building is notable for its fine metal and stone grills and the gleaming metal cap of the tower.  The traditional beamed ceiling of the nave contrasts with the modern peaked arches bordering the side aisles and the stepped silhouette of the chancel arch.  Over the altar is a slender baldachino.

## WILSHIRE AND NORTHWEST

ECHO PARK, a 26-acre area at Bellevue Ave. and Echo Park Ave., encloses a willow-fringed lake that up to 1891 furnished power for an early woolen mill.  In the park are a community building, four-and-one-half-acre playground along Bellevue Avenue, two outdoor gymnasiums, and a wading pool for children.

ANGELUS TEMPLE, 1100 Glendale Blvd., north of Echo Park, is a huge domed auditorium seating 5,300, and offices, built for the Four Square Gospel, founded by Aimee Semple McPherson (died 1944).

GRIFFITH PARK, largest of the 112 parks operated by the Recreation and Parks Department of the City of Los Angeles, and with its 4,043 acres the largest park area within the limits of any American city, extends along the eastern line of the Hollywood District at Western Ave. into the foothills of the Santa Monica Mountains.  Its principal entrances are at Los Feliz Blvd. at Riverside Drive, the off-ramp of the Golden State Freeway, Vermont Ave., and Western Ave.  Its expanse can accommodate many thousands of citizens bent on recreation, for it offers golf, tennis, baseball, softball, camping, picnics, riding, pools, theater, a zoo and star study.  The land was originally a part of the Los Feliz ranch and was donated to the City in 1898 by Col. Griffith J. Griffith.

The most ambitious development yet undertaken is the GREATER LOS ANGELES ZOO, for which ground was broken Mar. 23, 1964.  It replaces an outmoded zoo that cared for 1,200 wild animals and can house more than twice that number.  It is supported by the City and a nonprofit association of civic leaders.  The new installations include an administration building, a CHILDREN'S ZOO, an animal hospital, commissary and maintenance buildings, and parking for 3,600 motor cars.  With the help of the association the City has acquired many unusual specimens.  Among these are a male and a female hippopotamus, a rare maned wolf from the Amazon, a pair of white kangaroos and two Tasmanian greys; three yellow baboons from the Somali Republic; raccoon dogs from Japan, and a two-toed sloth from the Canal Zone.  The kangaroos were obtained in exchange for the skeleton of a saber-tooth tiger, dug from the Le Brea tar pits.

GRIFFITH OBSERVATORY, opened 1935, is located on a spur of the foothills.  An obelisk before the entrance, designed by Archibald Garner, commemorates the great astronomers.  On top of the shaft rests an astrolabe.  The Observatory has a HALL OF SCIENCE, where exhibits of the moon are currently most popular; it demonstrates lunar phases by means of a small model that revolves around the observer.  Other exhibits cover the fields of electricity, optics, spectroscopy, geology, chemistry and electronics. A twin refracting telescope with a 12-inch and a 9½-inch lens is used at night. Most important is the PLANETARIUM, in which a new Zeiss projector was installed in 1964. The attendance here is often 20,000 a month during the summer, while the Hall of Science has up to 775,000 a year. (*Observatory, open free weekdays, 11 a.m. to 10 p.m., Sundays, 2 to 10 p.m., free; Planetarium shows 3 and 8:30 p.m., adm. 60¢ for adults, 30¢ for students under 18.*)

TRAVEL TOWN, an exhibit of vehicular development, is one of the Park's most educational installations. Exhibits include a 104-ton locomotive, a Japanese airplane, a San Francisco cable car, a trolley car, a historic depot, and a section where the members of the Live Steamers Club operate small-scale trains. Entrance at 5200 Hollingsworth Drive. (*Open 10 a.m. to 5 p.m., free*)

FERN DELL NATURE MUSEUM, Western Ave. Canyon, offers a nature study program for youths and adults, and free movies on Saturdays and Sundays, 1 to 5 p.m. Displays of bird, animal and plant life are open 1 to 5 p.m., Wednesday through Sunday. Girls and boys 8 to 12 years old may join the Junior Zoological Society (*50¢ a year*). Picnic sites are located in FERN DELL by the sides of a mountain brook.

The GREEK THEATER in Vermont Canyon is an outdoor auditorium of Doric design with 5,000 seats. It is used for plays, light opera and meetings.

BOYS' CAMP of Griffith Park makes use of the mountain terrain and is open to boys 8 to 12 years old. It includes a lodge, cabins, dining facilities, swimming pool and overnight outdoor camping. Rates for week and weekend set by Recreation & Parks Dept. HOLLYWOODLAND GIRLS' CAMP in the canyons of Griffith Park has similar facilities for girls 8 years old and over.

DOUGLAS MacARTHUR PARK, entrance Wilshire Blvd. and Alvarado St., is cut in two by the Wilshire Boulevard causeway. This 32-acre park in the heart of one of Los Angeles' most densely populated sections is shady and landscaped, and fringes a small artificial lake. Free band concerts are given on Sunday afternoons. The park contains a monument with an 8-ft. bronze figure of General Douglas MacArthur, dedicated Jan. 26, 1955. Also a bronze statue of General Harrison Gray Otis, former publisher of the Los Angeles *Times*.

OTIS ART INSTITUTE (*open 3 to 4 p.m. weekdays; guides*), Wilshire Blvd. and Park View St., is a two-story stucco building of Mission architecture, with Corinthian columns at its portal. In the side yard, visible from the boulevard, is a stone miniature of the old Los Angeles *Times* building, dynamited in 1910 as the climax to a labor dispute that had national repercussions. Formerly the home of General Otis, the Institute is now an adjunct to the Los Angeles County Museum of History and Science.

IMMANUEL PRESBYTERIAN CHURCH (*admission by application at office*), Wilshire Blvd. and Berendo St., designed with the Germanic serenity of a northern Gothic cathedral, has a 207-foot tower.

Five lancet windows rise to the immense rose window portraying the Nativity in stained glass. Within, the Gothic hammer-beam trusses of the ceiling, columns and arches, oak furnishings, and huge Gothic chandeliers harmonize with the massive dignity of the exterior.

The AMBASSADOR HOTEL, 3400 Wilshire Blvd., a roomy rambling structure with spreading tile-roofed wings, sits far back from the street in a huge expanse of lawn. The hotel has its own swimming pool, playground, shopping center, and movie theater.

The WILSHIRE BOULEVARD CHRISTIAN CHURCH (*admission by application at office*), Wilshire Blvd. and Normandie Ave., designed by Robert H. Orr, is distinguished by its west facade cartwheel window, based upon that of the Rheims Cathedral in France. Romanesque in style, with basilica type auditorium and soaring campanile, the church recalls the churches of northern Italy.

B'NAI B'RITH TEMPLE (*open for services 7:30 p.m. Friday, 10 a.m. Sat.*), Wilshire and Hobart Blvds., is the city's largest Jewish temple. Dominating it is a dome 135 ft. in diameter, inlaid with mosaic, surrounded with the minaretlike pinnacles of the octagonal main auditorium. Broad stone steps lead to three arched entrances, above which is a huge rose window. Within, Byzantine columns of black Belgian marble rise to the majestic domed ceiling, finished in dull gold, from which hang chandeliers of bronze. The altar, ark, and choir screen are of carved, inlaid, dark walnut, and framed in marble and mosaic. The walls are enriched by Hugo Ballin's Warner Memorial paintings, depicting Biblical and post-Biblical themes.

The WILSHIRE METHODIST EPISCOPAL CHURCH (*admission by application at office*), Wilshire and Plymouth Blvds., is of modified Spanish Romanesque architecture. The design of the interior is dominated by a large rose window and a tall corner tower with buttressed and pinnacled belfry.

HANCOCK PARK, entrance at Wilshire Blvd. and Curson Ave., a 32-acre preserve, is known chiefly for the LA BREA PITS, near the center of the park. They are ugly bogs with subterranean oil and tar bubbling slowly to the surface. A film of water camouflages the sticky quagmire, forming a trap for the unwary, as it did in ages past when prehistoric animals gathered here to drink and were caught in the preservative tar. Birds of prey and carrion-eaters fed on the sinking animals and were themselves caught in the pitch. The pits are the richest source of Pleistocene or Ice Age remains in the world. Skeletal remains of the only American peacock ever found, of sabre-tooth tigers, Imperial elephants, woolly mammoths, giant ground sloths, small early camels, condors, Great American lions, and other prehistoric species have been removed from the pits. There is an exhibit of La Brea fossils at the Los Angeles Museum of History and Science in Exposition Park. A restoration of Ice Age animals floundering in the tar, by Charles R. Knight, hangs in the Field Museum, Chicago. Prehistoric skeletons were first discovered in 1906. G. Allen Hancock, last private owner, donated the site to the City in 1916.

The CARTHAY CIRCLE THEATER, 6316 West San Vicente Blvd., designed by Dwight Gibbs in early Spanish style, dominated by a high tower, is headquarters of Fox West Coast Theatres Division of National General Corp. Representative scenes of early California provide the decorative motif.

Carthay Center bears a corruption of the name of Daniel O. McCarthy, pioneer of '49, whose San Francisco paper, the *American Flag*, helped keep California within the Union at the outbreak of the Civil War. The McCARTHY MEMORIAL FOUNTAIN, Vista and San Vicente Blvd., a bronze basin surmounted with the figure of a miner panning the gold, bears a tablet inscribed to "The Gallant Pioneers of '49." Nearby is a stump from the Petrified Forest north of San Francisco, dedicated by the Native Sons of the Golden West to Galen Clark's discovery of the Mariposa Big Trees. At the end of the parkway, across Commodore Sloat Drive, is a boulder inscribed to the memory of "Snowshoe" Thompson, pioneer hero, who for twenty years carried the mails over California's mountains and rescued lost travelers.

The UNIVERSITY OF CALIFORNIA AT LOS ANGELES (UCLA), campus entrance at Westwood Blvd. and Le Conte Ave., occupies a 383-acre grassy campus on a terraced knoll overlooking the center of the village of Westwood, which lies between Beverly Hills and Santa Monica. On a low hilltop stand the university's terra cotta, brick and tile central buildings of Lombardic Romanesque design, grouped about a central esplanade. On the north side of the esplanade is JOSIAH ROYCE HALL, housing the auditorium, classrooms, and faculty offices, named for the eminent American philosopher, a graduate of the university. Across the green on the south side is the large red brick LIBRARY BUILDING dominated by its enormous arcaded octagonal tower. It is designed in the early Italian Romanesque style with rich brick and stone ornamentations of Byzantine Romanesque.

Simpler in detail and more modern in treatment are the lesser buildings grouped to the east and south: Haines Hall (chemistry), Physics-Biology, Administration, and Education Buildings. Westward from the esplanade, an imposing brick stairway with terra cotta balustrades descends the hill to the men's and women's Gymnasium Buildings.

Before 1940 the university had 14 buildings; in 1965 it needed 74 and had invested $177,648,000 in construction. It comprises 14 schools and colleges, including agriculture, business administration, fine arts, education, engineering, dentistry, law, library service, medicine, nursing, public health and social welfare. The School of Medicine, established 1946, is the nucleus of the Medical Center, which occupies 30 acres on the campus and has another 34-acre site nearby. Among special installations are the Computing Facility, equipped with a highspeed IBM 7090, a low-kilowatt Argonaut training nuclear reactor in the Department of Engineering, and a spiral ridge cyclotron developed by the Department of Physics. Students may participate in choral groups, glee clubs, opera, symphonic and chamber music, six bands, and in stage, motion picture and television activities.

An integral part of the University of California, the University of California at Los Angeles grew out of the old Los Angeles State Normal School, founded in 1881. In 1919 the institution became the University of California, Southern Branch, and in 1927 the University of California at Los Angeles. It outgrew its original campus and in 1925 a new site in Westwood Hills was presented to the Regents by the cities of Los Angeles, Santa Monica, Venice, and Beverly Hills. The new campus was dedicated in September 1929.

Enrollment, 1965, was 21,043; faculty, 1,324. The Library has 1,753,000 volumes and plans for 4,000,000.

CALIFORNIA STATE COLLEGE, 5151 State College Dr., one of the eighteen State colleges, enrolls more than 20,000 students annually, and has a faculty of 1,000.

The U. S. SOLDIERS' HOME (*open 3-4 daily*), entrance Wilshire Blvd. and Veteran Ave., provides free hospitalization for veterans of the Civil, Spanish-American, and World Wars. On the rolling, wooded, 700-acre estate are almost 170 buildings. Modern buildings were constructed in 1939-1940. Here are located the headquarters and large hospital of the VETERANS ADMINISTRATION.

## SOUTH AND SOUTHWEST

ST. VINCENT DE PAUL ROMAN CATHOLIC CHURCH (*always open*), Figueroa St. and W. Adams Blvd., designed by Albert C. Martin, is an imposing white edifice in the Churrigueresque style, embellished with a wealth of exterior carvings and statuary in Indiana limestone. Its ornate façade is topped with a 125-foot corner tower, and a tile-inlaid dome, rising majestically from the crossing.

ST. JOHN'S EPISCOPAL CHURCH (*open 7-5 daily*), 514 W. Adams Blvd., recalls the eleventh century church at Toscanella, Italy. The interior is distinguished by its elaborate beamed ceiling, copied from that of the Church of San Minato in Florence.

HELMS HALL, 8760 Venice Blvd., opened 1948, is the home of Helms Athletic Foundation, founded 1936 by Paul H. Helms to honor athletes in all categories of sports. Here are displayed trophies and momentoes of famous athletes and events. Among its activities are the Helms World Trophy, Sports Hall of Fame, Athlete of the Year and many other distinctions; there also is a comprehensive sports library. (*Open daily except Sunday; free*)

The UNIVERSITY OF SOUTHERN CALIFORNIA, University Ave., between 34th St. and Exposition Ave., had eight acres when founded in 1880 on land donated by a Catholic, a Jew and a Protestant. At that time Los Angeles had 11,000 people. The campus has grown to more than 100 acres and the SCHOOL OF MEDICINE occupies twelve acres adjoining the County Hospital. The University was sponsored by the Methodist Conference of Southern California but has been nonsectarian since 1926. The original building, Widney Hall, cost $5,000. It is used by the SCHOOL OF MUSIC and is a State Historical Monument.

USC has a faculty of 1,013 and enrolled 18,800 students in 1965, nearly 9,000 in graduate study.

Since 1961 USC has been financing a master plan of $106,000,000, to be completed in twenty years. By 1966 USC had finished new construction costing $14,000,000 and had plans drawn for another $26,000,000 investment. The Ford Foundation gave $7,500,000 conditional on the university's raising $22,500,000 by the end of 1967.

Among the older structures are the GEORGE FINLEY BOVARD ADMINISTRATION BUILDING, of red brick with a red tile roof, in early Italian Renaissance style. At the entrance stands the Trojan Warrior, the university's symbol, 8 ft. tall on a 10-ft. pedestal, by Roger Noble Burnham; The EDWARD L. DOHENY, JR., MEMORIAL LIBRARY (1932), in modified Italian Romanesque; the STUDENT UNION, an Italian Renaissance *palazzo;* and the SEELEY WINTERSMITH MUDD MEMORIAL BUILDING, with architecture based on Byzantine and Lombard Romanesque. Above it rises a clock tower with chimes. Across the front of the court extends an open cloister forming a quadrangle.

EXPOSITION PARK, bounded by Figueroa Street, Menlo Ave., Exposition Blvd., and South Park Drive, known in early days as Agricultural Park, was the scene of Los Angeles' first agricultural fairs. The 114-acre tract acquired by city, county, and State near the turn of the century, was improved and opened as Exposition Park in 1910.

On the Exposition Boulevard side is the MEMORIAL GATEWAY, flanked by massive pylons commemorating the Tenth International Olympiad of 1932, held in the park's Memorial Coliseum. Broad bench-lined walks lead to the seven-acre SUNKEN GARDEN, planted with 15,000 rose bushes of 118 different varieties, and marked at each corner by white marble statuettes. Paralleling the Sunken Garden on the east is the red brick Armory, headquarters and training barracks for the 160th Infantry, California National Guard.

The LOS ANGELES COUNTY MUSEUM OF HISTORY AND SCIENCE (*open 10-5 weekdays, 2-5 Sun. and holidays*), west side of Sunken Garden, is a repository of artifacts, scientific exhibitions, and relics. The original T-shaped, glass-domed building of red brick was formally opened Nov. 6, 1913. Two units of a new building have been added.

The LOS ANGELES MEMORIAL COLISEUM, designed by John and Donald Parkinson, is at the end of The Mall, a 1,065-foot oblong stretch of green bordered by young deodars. A huge peristyle with a 400-foot arcade and a 70-foot central arch, topped with a pedestaled urn, forms the main gateway. Within, rising in vast tiers above the circular field of turf, are 79 rows of seats accommodating 105,000 people. A fifth of a mile long and three-fifths of a mile in circumference, the stadium covers 17 acres; its walls, 106 feet high, enclose a five-acre playing field, the scene of major football games, track meets, rodeos, pageants, religious ceremonies, and civic gatherings.

SIMON RODIA TOWERS, 1765 E. 107th St., Watts, are three metal-concrete structures decorated with bits of china and glass, tallest 100 ft., built by a tilesetter, 1921 to 1954. Watts (34,800 pop., 1963), is the predominantly Negro section where rioting in August, 1965, took 34 lives.

# Monterey

*Transportation:* Del Monte Express of Southern Pacific Ry., daily. Greyhound Bus Lines, daily service.

*Airport:* Community Airport, 3 *m.* east on State 68, used jointly by military and civilian aircraft.

*Accommodations:* City and County have many motels with picturesque locations, swimming pools, some with fireplaces. Rates average $8 to $12.

*Information:* Visitors & Convention Bureau, Monterey Peninsula Chamber of Commerce, P. O. Box 489. Area code 408 375-2252.

*Golf:* Monterey is in an area that has some of the finest courses in the West. They are strung along the coast and include some spectacular hazards. They are Pebble Beach, at Del Monte Lodge; Cypress Point (private); Monterey Peninsula Country Club (private); Del Monte, opposite the former Del Monte Hotel; Pacific Grove. The Bing Crosby National Pro-Amateur Golf Championship games are played in January at Pebble Beach, Monterey Peninsula CC and Cypress Point.

*Fishing:* Boats for deep-sea fishing leave daily from Fisherman's Wharf. Fishing for red rock, ling, blue, sea trout, red snapper. Trolling for king salmon, silverside salmon, sea bass and halibut. Limit, 3 salmon per person. In ocean waters north of Yankee Point in Monterey County Scuba diving apparatus may be used only for rock scallops. South of Yankee Point mollusks and crustaceans may be taken in similar fashion. Open season for abalones is March 16 to January 14. Open season for clams (pismo), in Monterey County September 1 to April 30.

*Licenses:* The State requires a sport fishing license of anyone 16 years old or over, including members of the Armed Forces, excepting persons fishing from a public pier in the ocean. No license stamp is required for ocean fishing. Fees: For resident of 6 mos. or more, $3; for nonresident $10; for 10-day nonresident, $3; for 3 days, $1. The Dept. of Fish & Game, Sacramento, provides booklet of regulations.

*Special Events, Monterey Peninsula (a selection):* January—Bing Crosby National Pro-Amateur Golf Championship, Pebble Beach, Monterey Peninsula Country Club, Cypress Point. February—Point-to-Point race meeting & hunt, Pebble Beach Stables. Spring Orchid Show, Carmel and Monterey Bay Orchid societies, Fair Grounds. March—International Open Chess Tournament, Hotel San Carlos, Monterey; Invitational Skeet Shoot, Pebble Beach Gun Club. April—Annual wildflower show, Pacific Grove Museum; Miss Monterey County Contest, Junior Chamber of Commerce. May—Road races, Laguna Seca Race Track; Pony Club Horse show, Pebble Beach Stables; Stuart Haldorn Regatta, Stillwater Yacht Club. June—Monterey Merienda, commemorating Monterey's birthday; North-South Team matches, Pebble Beach, Cypress Point golf courses; California Amateur Gold Championships, Pebble Beach, Cypress Point, Monterey Peninsula Country Club, Del Monte courses. July—Sloat Landing commemoration, Customs House; Invitational Interclub Tennis, Pebble Beach; California Junior Girls State Golf Championships, Del Monte; Feast of Lanterns, Pacific Grove. August—Carmel Valley Horsemen's Assn. annual roundup; Summer horse show, Pebble Beach; Junior Tennis Championships, Pebble Beach. September—California Seniors golf tournament, Monterey Peninsula Country Club; Annual Monterey Jazz Festival, Fairgrounds. October—S. F. B. Morse Regatta,

Stillwater Cove; Monterey Grand Prix, Laguna Seca Race Track; Annual Butterfly Parade, Pacific Grove. November—Air Defense Command golf tournament, Pebble Beach.

MONTEREY (0–600 alt., 22,618 pop. 1960), lies at the southern end of Monterey Bay, within the northward curve of Point Pinos, which protects the harbor from heavy seas and high winds. At Monterey *El Camino Real* returns to the coast. After leaving San Luis Obispo Gaspar de Portola and the padres had turned inland to avoid the mountain barrier of the Santa Lucia Sierra.

Richard Henry Dana, arriving at Monterey on the brig *Pilgrim* in 1834, thought the town made a "very pretty appearance" with its redroofed, white stucco houses, the white sand beach, green pines, and deep blue bay. The city gives the same impression today.

In 1890 Monterey still looked like a Mexican town; adobe buildings with red tile roofs were numerous. The march of commerce removed many of these, and the adobe structures standing today are the result of a tardily awakened interest in the city's colorful past. Some of them have been preserved by descendants of the original builders; some were bought by appreciative "Americanos"; a few have been made State monuments.

To the north the shore sweeps in a curving line toward Santa Cruz. To the east are the convolutions of the Santa Lucia Range, covered with oak and pine, beyond which rise the bare heights of the Gabilan Range. The near hills and pines of Point Pinos block the view to the south, where the coast abruptly changes to stone crags topped with weirdly-shaped trees, and small deep coves and sheltered beaches. Monterey cypress along the shoreline and Monterey pine, both named for the city, are indigenous to a limited area in the vicinity.

Alvarado Street, running north and south, is the town's main artery. Starting from the weather-beaten Fisherman's Wharf that puts out into the bay, passing the Old Customhouse, flanked at first by stores selling fishermen's supplies and small restaurants specializing in sea food and Mexican dishes, it crosses the center of the town with its more choice shops, banks, hotels, office buildings, and finally comes to an end at the old Cooper mansion. To the west of Alvarado the business district soon yields to a residential section, which climbs steep hills block after block to wooded heights where its gardens mingle with a semi-wilderness of trees and shrubs high above the port.

At the northern limits of the city is the Presidio of Monterey, the United States Army post. Its rolling 396 acres cover territory reaching from the bay to the hills; here the old Spanish works once put up a show of protecting California with eight or ten cannon, even then obsolete. Stretching along the shore is the row of fish canneries that represented Monterey's major industry before the supply of sardines diminished, and became widely known through John Steinbeck's novels.

Cabrillo, exploring the unknown coast in 1542, saw Point Pinos. Sebastian Vizcaíno, merchant-explorer, sailing into the bay in 1602, named it Monterey for the Count of Monte-Rey, Viceroy of Mexico, and described it in such superlatives that those who came after him could not recognize it for 167 years. Gaspar de Portolá's "sacred expedition" of 1769 worked its way overland to find and settle it, twice camped near without recognizing it, passed by, discovered San Francisco Bay, returned, and only on another expedition in the spring of 1770 realized that they were on the stubbornly sought spot. Father Crespi and Father Junípero Serra took formal possession of the land, established the Presidio, and founded the Mission San Carlos de Monterey. In 1775 the King of Spain formally recognized Monterey as the capital of California.

From that time until 1822, when, through the Mexican revolution, California became part of the Mexican republic, Monterey had five different governors. They tried, without much success, to develop Alta California and to pour gold into the coffers of Spain (see *CALIFORNIA'S FIRST FOUR CENTURIES*). In 1818 Hypolite Bouchard, the French pirate, raided the town, chased the residents inland, and pillaged for a week before sailing south. After the revolution, the first legislature met in Monterey to draw up California's first constitution. Meanwhile Yankees were learning of tremendous profits to be made in sea otter and whales. Their ships anchored off the Old Customhouse and the town traded for silks, shoes, spices, mirrors, and cartwheels.

Under the Mexican flag there were endless squabbles and bickering, and Monterey was the seat of intrigue and plotting even up to the time Commodore Sloat raised the American flag over the Customhouse in 1846. In 1836 Juan Bautista Alvarado, assisted by Isaac Graham, an American trapper, attacked Monterey. Governor Gutiérrez fled to Mexico after the insurgents landed one cannon ball near his house. A subsequent compromise made Alvarado governor, with headquarters at Monterey. The population of Monterey increased slowly under governors with such resonant names as Figueroa, Arguello, Micheltorena, Castro, Pío Pico. Secularization of the missions in the 1830's increased the number of rancheros and Monterey achieved an impressive social life.

In 1849 Bayard Taylor visited Monterey to observe the last of the old Spanish mode of life, and found that "the native population possesses a natural refinement of manner which would grace the most polished society." William H. Brewer in 1861 found Monterey Bay "a great place for whale hunting," and saw that the beach was white with whale bones; "hundreds of carcasses there decayed, fattening clouds of vultures."

Monterey began to lose its drowsy Mexican ways as specialized agriculture began to supplant cattle raising, and as the fisheries and the allied canning industry developed. Its natural beauty drew artists and writers: Robert Louis Stevenson passed some time here; Charles Warren Stoddard retired and died here; and by the late 1800's many landscape painters had settled in Monterey.

Once the leading industry of Monterey was fishing; today its best income comes from the military establishments of the area and from the hundreds of thousands of annual visitors. Sardines, once the main catch, no longer abound; the record catch of 234,000 tons dropped to 142,282 tons in 1946 and the next year barely 26,800 tons were obtained. In 1965 only one cannery was operating in the area made famous by John Steinbeck's novels, *Cannery Row, Sweet Thursday* and *Tortilla Flat.*

## POINTS OF INTEREST

*There are many points of interest in Monterey worthy of notice. These lie along a Path of History, charted by the city and marked by an orange checkered line in the middle of the street. This route starts at the Royal Presidio Chapel and loops through the city back to its starting point. Each historic building and site has an explanatory sign. Good maps are available locally. The following list includes outstanding points along the route.*

ROYAL PRESIDIO CHAPEL of SAN CARLOS DE BOR-ROMEO (*open 9-5 daily*), Church St. between Camino El Estero and Figueroa St., founded in 1770 by Father Junipero Serra, was the second in the California system of missions. To keep his acolytes away from the soldiers of the presidio, Father Serra moved the mission in 1771 into the Carmel Valley, where its church stands today (*see TOUR 1C*). The Monterey building remained as the presidio chapel. Damaged by fire in 1789, it was reconstructed and dedicated in 1795. It has been in continuous use since, and is the only presidio chapel remaining in California.

The facade, perhaps the most ornate among California missions, rises higher than the roof of the church in the form of a carved gable, and is covered with cream-colored stucco. The arched entrance with its heavy paneled doors is flanked by Doric pilasters and topped with a classic entablature. In the upper gable is a shell-headed niche bearing a statue of Our Lady of Guadalupe. A wide square tower and belfry, roofed in red tile, rises at the left of the facade. In it are two old bells. There are fine vestments, holy vessels, and ornaments in the building.

CASA ABREGO (*private*), 592 Abrego St., built by Don José Abrego in the late 1830's, is a long one-story white adobe building with a narrow porch. The walls of the upper gables are of vertical boards. Abrego brought the first full-length mirror to California. When his daughter saw her reflection in it she asked: "Who is that lovely girl?" Since 1956 it has been the home of Casa Abrego Club, a women's club.

ROBERT LOUIS STEVENSON HOUSE, Houston St., between Webster and Pearl Sts., now a State monument, is a small two-story house with adobe walls, white plaster finish, and shingle roof. Stevenson lived here for three months in 1879 while working on *Amateur Immigrant* and *Vendetta of the West.*

GENERAL JOSE CASTRO'S HEADQUARTERS (*private*), NW. corner Pearl and Tyler Sts., houses a Spanish handcraft forge and cabinet-making shop. CASA DE CASTRO (*private*), at Del Monte Fairways, was the general's home.

The COOPER HOUSE (*private*), 508 Munras Ave., a long two-story adobe finished in pinkish plaster, was built by Capt. John Bautista Rogers Cooper in 1829.  In its day it was a *casa grande,* or "big house," bespeaking its owner's wealth and importance.

CASA AMESTI (*private*), 516 Polk St., a two-story, white-plastered adobe with a balcony, was built in the 1830's by José Amesti as a gift for his daughter.

The STOKES HOUSE (*private*), 500 Hartnell St., built by Dr. James Stokes in the 1840's, is a two-story white-plastered adobe structure with two-story porches, front and rear.  A well-preserved pottery kiln is in the back courtyard.

HOUSE OF THE FOUR WINDS (*private*), Main St. between Jefferson and Madison Sts., is a small, white-plastered adobe, built in the late 1830's by Thomas O. Larkin.  Its windows and doors are painted green, and just under the roof a hand-hewn beam can be seen. The building was named for a weather vane on the roof.

SHERMAN'S QUARTERS (*open*), Main St. between Jefferson and Madison Sts., is a one-story house, roofed in red tile, its peeling plaster showing the adobe brick beneath.  William Tecumseh Sherman lived here from 1847 to 1849 when a lieutenant, U.S.A.

The LARKIN HOUSE (*open*), 462 Main St., was built in 1835 by Thomas Oliver Larkin, first and only United States consul to California, and used as a consulate from 1844 to 1846.  It is a two-story hip-roofed house of adobe construction, finished in soft pink plaster, with a two-story gallery running around the front and two sides.

FRIENDLY PLAZA, Pacific St. between Jefferson and Madison Sts., Civic Center of Monterey, covers two blocks.  This house became the pattern for the Monterey style of architecture.  A Larkin grand-daughter bought it in 1922, lived here 35 years and in 1957 gave it to the state.  (*Guided tours, Wednesday through Sunday*)

COLTON HALL (*open 9-5 weekdays*), west side of Friendly Plaza, is a two-story stone building finished in plaster, designed in the New England post-Colonial style by the Rev. Walter Colton, Yankee alcalde (mayor) from 1846 to 1849.  Used for city offices.

MONTEREY JAIL, flanking Colton Hall on the south, a one-story buff sandstone building erected in 1854, is no longer used but open to the public.  Former tenants included Tiburcio Vasquez, the gentle-man bandit who could kill with a smile; Anastacia García, the killer who "went to God on a rope" pulled by his friends; Matt Tarpey, taken from his cell by vigilantes and strung up for the murder of a woman; and highwaymen of stage-coach days.

FEW MEMORIAL CITY HALL, Friendly Plaza, S. of the jail, is a one-story, L-shaped structure built in 1934.  The foot of the "L" incorporates an adobe house, built in 1843.

CASA VASQUEZ (*private*), Dutra St., between Madison and Jefferson Sts., is a white adobe half hidden by shrubbery and a large Monterey cypress, and set behind a cactus hedge and picket fence.  It is said to be the birthplace and home of the bandit, Tiburcio Vásquez.

CASA ALVARADO (*private*), 510 Dutra St., a long, low adobe

with a red brick front porch, was the home of Juan Bautista Alvarado, revolutionist, patriot, and governor of California from 1836 to 1842. He was so busy with politics that he could not attend his own wedding; a friend stood proxy at the ceremony in Mission Santa Clara and brought the bride home.

FIRST AMERICAN THEATER IN CALIFORNIA (*open 1-5 weekdays*), SW. corner Pacific and Scott Sts., a long, rectangular adobe with a frame shack at one end, was built in 1843 as a boarding house and saloon. In 1847 the New York Volunteer Regt. produced *Putnam the Iron Son of '76* and packed the house—at $5 a seat. A large wooden door, raised like the lid of a box, served as curtain. Footlights were candles and whale oil lamps. A State Monument since 1906, it has occasional historical plays by a local organization.

The FIRST BRICK HOUSE IN CALIFORNIA, 351 Decatur St., a small two-story house, now a restaurant, was built by the Dickinson family in 1847 of red brick kilned in Monterey.

The OLD WHALING STATION (*private*), 391 Decatur St., is a restored two-story adobe structure, with a shingle roof and a second story balcony across the front. A white-washed frame lean-to extends across the rear in the manner of a New England "salt box." It was built for Portuguese whalers in 1855 when there were 500 whaling vessels in Pacific waters, most of them out of the Sandwich Islands. The diamond-patterned walk and the patio are paved with whale vertebrae.

The PRESIDIO OF MONTEREY, entrance Pacific St. N. of Decatur St., covers 396 acres, running from the shore back into the pine-covered hills. It is now the site of the DEFENSE LANGUAGE INSTITUTE of the U. S. Naval Postgraduate School, of which the central school occupies the former Del Monte Hotel. On a hill above the entrance is a STATUE OF FATHER SERRA, a life-size figure standing in a boat, a gift of Mrs. Leland Stanford, 1901. Vizcaíno landed here in 1602, and Father Serra said mass on the same spot in 1770. Near the entrance is a STATUE OF JOHN DRAKE SLOAT, commander of the American forces that took Monterey. The Presidio was developed in 1902, as a cantonment for troops returning from the Spanish-American War.

CANNERY ROW, symbol of modern industry rather than old Monterey, is that area between David and Reeside Avenues once filled with busy canneries processing sardines. It became a literary landmark through the Monterey novels of John Steinbeck. Today its principal attraction is Neil de Vaughn's Fish and Steak House, 654 Cannery Row. Numerous seafood restaurants are concentrated at Fisherman's Wharf.

OLD CUSTOMHOUSE (*open 10-5 daily*), N. end of Alvarado St., consists of a low central section of plastered adobe and frame built by the Spanish in 1814 and higher additions built in 1823 and 1846. On the front of the building, facing the bay, runs a full-length porch covered by the sloping tile roof. The end sections have second-story galleries. Low walls enclose a garden. Here Commodore Sloat raised the U. S. flag July 7, 1846.

A STATE MUSEUM in the building preserves a $1,000 Parisian lace dress worn by Doña Escolástica de Dye, a famous beauty of the time. Other historic exhibits include a burro cart with solid wood wheels, and a woman's wedding dress of the Mexican period. Upstairs is the BOHEMIAN MEMORY ROOM, containing the Albert W. Bender collection of original letters and manuscripts of Robert Louis Stevenson, Ambrose Bierce, and George Sterling.

FISHERMEN'S WHARF, N. end of Main St., is a collection of weather-beaten wooden sheds and buildings built on a complicated pattern of piers. Seafood restaurants and fresh fish shops line the first pier. There is always noisy activity on the wharf: the foreign tones of Italian and Japanese fishermen, the creak of the wooden piles as heavy trucks pull out loaded with fish, the shouts of skippers docking their boats; the croaking of sea gulls. Inside the sheds lie great piles of fish. Japanese abalone divers hang their rubber suits out to dry, and Japanese girls prepare abalone steaks for shipment. When the albacore run, there is real excitement on the wharf. Boats go out empty and come back loaded to the gunwales with the game fish, each one caught by a hook and lure. The fish are cleaned and packed on the wharf.

The SANCHEZ ADOBE, 412 Alvarado St., built by Gil Sánchez in 1829 and now housing shops and a bar, is the only house on the street with a balcony.

MONTEREY PENINSULA COLLEGE was opened 1948 as a junior college on an 87-acre campus at Fremont Ave. and State 1. It enrolled 3,800 students in 1964.

FORT ORD is 6 miles north of Monterey. Other military facilities are the U. S. COAST GUARD STATION, the U. S. NAVAL AIR FACILITY, and the COMBAT DEVELOPMENT COMMAND EXPERIMENTATION CENTER.

The SEVENTEEN MILE DRIVE is a major scenic attraction for tourists. It is a toll road ($2 per motor car) extending along the Pacific Coast and touches Carmel, Pebble Beach, Seaside, Cypress Point, Seal Rock, Midway Point, with its lone cypress, a favorite camera subject; Pacific Grove, where thousands of Monarch butterflies stay during the winter and where a pageant for children is held in October. *See Tour 1, Section C, Monterey to Las Cruces, p. 340, et. seq.*

# Oakland

*Information:* Oakland Tribune, 401 13th St. Oakland Chamber of Commerce, 1320 Webster St. State Dept. of Motor Vehicles, 5300 Claremont Ave. State Dept. of Employment, 235 12th St.

*Transportation:* Southern Pacific, Western Pacific, Santa Fe railroads. American, Pacific, Pacific Southwest, Trans World, United, West Coast, Western, and San Francisco-Oakland Helicopter air lines at Metropolitan Oakland International Airport, 12 minutes from center of city. Bus lines, including Greyhound, Continental Trailways, Peerless Stages, Gray Line Tours. Alameda-Contra Costa Transit.

*Highways:* Nimitz and Eastshore Freeways, multilane, from San Jose to Sacramento. MacArthur Freeway from San Francisco-Oakland Bay Bridge to San Leandro and beyond. Warren Freeway from upper Berkeley to south of Oakland along the foothills. Tunnels connecting Oakland with Orinda, Walnut Creek areas northeast; Grove-Shafter Freeway (in part) connecting Caldecott Tunnels with Nimitz Freeway in Oakland.

*Bridge:* San Francisco-Oakland Bay Bridge. Approaches: 38th and Market Sts., 8th and Cypress Sts.

*Marine Terminals:* The Port of Oakland has more than two miles of berthing space, three marine terminals for general cargo, 800,000 sq. ft. of transit sheds and 1,000,000 sq. ft. of outside storage space.

*Motor Vehicle Fees:* Out-of-state license fees are honored in California until expiration date or until nonresident is employed. A service fee of $5 is charged for the first registration in California of a vehicle that previously has been registered elsewhere, in addition to any registration fee or use tax that may be applicable. Vehicle license fees are $8 yearly plus 2% of market value of vehicle in lieu of local personal property taxes. The application fee for license or instruction permit is $3. A visitor over 21 with a driver's license issued by his home state may drive as long as the license remains valid.

*Recreation:* Lake Merritt, 160-acres of tidal salt water in the center of Oakland, surrounded by Lakeside Park, including Children's Fairyland, and Peralta Playland, both scaled to youth-size; Natural Science Center, wild game refuge and flower gardens. Also Jack London Square and Morcom Rose Garden. The City maintains 31 parks; the East Bay area has 15,000 acres of Regional Parks and two state parks; Jos. R. Knowland Arboretum with a new zoo in Oakland and Alameda State Beach Park, opposite the city.

*Annual Events:* California Spring Garden Show, Exposition Bldg., 10th and Fallon Sts., April; I.A.A. Sports Carnival, Municipal Auditorium, 12th and Fallon Sts., Winter and Spring; Mills College Horse Show, May; Festival of the Holy Ghost (Portuguese), Pentecostal week, Exposition Bldg., 10th and Fallon Sts.; East Bay Gladiolus Society Exhibition, June; Boys' Smelt Derby, Lake Merritt, July; Bowling Green Contests, Lakeside Park, Sept.; Outboard Motorboat Races, Lake Merritt, Sept.; Columbus Day Celebration, Lakeside Park; Christmas Pageant, Municipal Auditorium, 12th and Fallon Sts.

OAKLAND (0–1,600 alt., 367,548 pop., 1960; 385,900, 1965 est.) is the metropolis of the industrial and residential East Bay area and the county seat of Alameda County, which has approx. 1,000,000 population. It is the fourth largest city in California. The city of Alameda lies on an island separated from Oakland only by a narrow waterway. Oakland is connected with San Francisco by the 8¼ mile San Francisco-Oakland Bay Bridge (*auto toll 25¢*). It covers a land area of 53.4 sq. mi., a water area of 25.7 sq. mi., total, 79 sq. mi.

Oakland and its sister communities, Berkeley, San Leandro, Hayward, Emeryville, Piedmont, and Alameda, are framed by the relatively low Berkeley Hills (up to 1,900 feet), which parallel the shoreline of the Bay. Eastward beyond these wooded slopes appear the higher elevations of the Contra Costa Hills, culminating in Mount Diablo (3,800 feet) some 30 miles east of the city. Southward the hills drop to the level East Bay shore permitting the city to expand without hindrance in that direction. Five miles to the west, across the bay, is San Francisco. Of the many thousands transported daily between the cities, the majority are Oakland commuters.

The port of Oakland has facilities to accommodate any vessel in the Pacific trade. The Oakland Estuary, formerly a shallow slough, is called the inner harbor, and the open bay portion to the north is the outer harbor. Three transcontinental railroads enter the city.

The modern Oakland home is of light stucco, tile-roofed, studio-windowed, with arches and patios. Built on hillsides, flats, and knolls, these houses show, in construction and landscaping, the benefits of a mild climate. Here and there, however, are sharp-gabled, high-ceilinged, full-basemented, weathertight houses built by pioneers who did not realize they had come to a moderate climate. City parks and private gardens contain many varieties of semitropical trees—camphor, acacia, pepper, dracena, eucalyptus and palm.

Along the ridge of the Berkeley Hills winds the Skyline Boulevard, offering a view to the east of the dry, tawny hills of Contra Costa; to the west spreads the thickly settled marginal plain and the glowing bay, rimmed by the jagged silhouette of San Francisco. Below is the metropolitan cluster of downtown Oakland, dominated by the 17-story CITY HALL (319 ft.) and the 28-story KAISER CENTER (390 ft.).

An upsurge of civic and economic activity began in 1955 with the erection of the Kaiser Center, costing $50,000,000, headquarters for the Kaiser industrial empire, and the later development of Metropolitan Oakland International Airport for jet-age accommodations. For completion in the 1960-70 decade Oakland authorized a Coliseum complex, to cost $25,000,000, including a stadium with 49,000 seats and a covered arena, with parking for 9,000 cars. A cultural center to cost $7,000,000 was authorized by the voters and the design drawn by Eero Saarinen & Associates.

Lake Merritt, a salt-water lake, is a few blocks from the Oakland business district. Until 1898 it was an unsightly tidal basin fed by waters from the Estuary; today it is a 155-acre, Y-shaped lake with grassy banks, the water level controlled by hydraulic gates. Encircling the lake are a hiking path, a park strip, and a high-speed boulevard, and in the crotch of the "Y" is 53-acre Lakeside Park. At the base of the "Y" is Peralta Park, reclaimed from the mud flats.

Of Oakland's ethnic groups the most numerous is the Negro community, concentrated in West Oakland near the railroad shops and yards, which provide their chief employment. On the outskirts of the city live many of the Portuguese dairy farmers who have settled in great numbers in Alameda County. Other minor groups are Italians, Chinese, Japanese, Filipino, and Mexicans.

The first white men to see what is now Oakland were Spaniards—Lieutenant Fages and Father Crespi, who headed an expedition in 1772. The expedition pushed as far north as Antioch, and active developments took place across the Bay, but it was nearly half a century before the site of Oakland was colonized.

Cavalry Sergt. Luís María Peralta, as a worthy soldier of the royal Spanish army, received title in 1820 to a 48,000-acre domain, named it Rancho San Antonio, added "Don" to his name, and lived as befitted a gentleman of leisure. His grant included the entire East Bay area.

For twenty years Rancho San Antonio played an important part in the commercial, religious, and social life of California. In 1842, the sergeant divided the ranch among his four sons, and Vincente Peralta was given the area where Oakland now stands. They owned great herds of cattle, maintained a large retinue of *vaqueros* (cowboys), and pursued the Spanish life of "fiesta and siesta." The American victory over Mexico in 1848 ended the era of the Spanish landowner in California, and the discovery of gold in the same year hastened the rout. Mobs of gold seekers came to the flourishing town of San Francisco, many of whom tramped to the diggings through the Peralta holdings. Some of them visualized greater riches from these acres than from the Mother Lode. They squatted on the rancho, built shacks and fences, and ran off cattle, and resisted every effort of the owners to evict them.

Moses Chase, however, who came to Oakland in 1849, was of a more ethical turn of mind. He became associated with the three Patten brothers in a lease of 460 acres from Antonio Peralta. They were the first farmers of the district, raising good crops of grain and hay. The early town of Clinton took form on their acreage. The Patten brothers soon entered the lumbering business in the Peralta Redwoods, a stand of giant trees that extended from the top of the range midway to the Oakland estuary. In the middle 1850's more than 400 men were employed in the mills, cutting lumber for the building of San Francisco, Oakland and their environs.

In 1851, the Rancho San Antonio was well spotted with squatters and purchasers, and in that year there appeared a man who gave the Latin owners, and the Americanos, a lesson in plain and fancy financing. Horace W. Carpentier had a degree from an eastern university, a keen sense of values, and more than one man's share of vision. He acquired a townsite in the present downtown Oakland, imported a few "residents" from the redwoods, and in 1852 incorporated the Town of Oakland, with himself in the mayor's chair. The name he selected from the numerous stands of *encinas* (evergreen oaks) that dotted the landscape. Two years later Mr. Carpentier incorporated the town as a city, and by that time had acquired the entire Oakland waterfront in exchange for building three tiny wharves and a frame schoolhouse. Thus began the "battle of the waterfront," which was terminated in 1910 when the assigns of Carpentier agreed with the city to waive title to their properties in exchange for long term leases.

The first ferry across the bay began operating in 1850; first train chugged through Oakland in 1863; and overland service was established in 1869. In 1906, when San Francisco fell victim to earthquake and fire, 50,000 refugees moved to Oakland. There was a building boom to provide housing for refugees who became permanent East Bay residents. The city annexed all hamlets and towns to the southeast and in 1907 the population reached 147,000. The industrial stimulation that followed this influx moved Oakland into third place among California manufacturing cities as early as 1910, and by 1920 its population increased to 216,000.

OAKLAND NAVAL SUPPLY CENTER provides material needs for all ships of the U. S. Navy in the Pacific and Far East areas. OAKLAND ARMY TERMINAL transports U. S. Army personnel and materials overseas. U. S. NAVAL AIR STATION is located across the waterway in Alameda. OAK KNOLL NAVAL HOSPITAL is a large Oakland facility.

## POINTS OF INTEREST

1. OAKLAND CITY HALL, Washington St. between 14th and 15th Sts., designed by Palmer, Hornbostle and Jones, and completed in 1914, was the highest building for decades, its 17 floors rising 319 feet and towering in three set-back sections embellished with classic colonnades and arches and topped with a baroque cupola.

2. The SNOW MUSEUM OF NATURAL SCIENCE (*open daily 10-5*), 274 19th St., a white frame structure with a columned portico, is one of three components of the new OAKLAND MUSEUM, fronting Lake Merritt at 1,000 Oak St., which scheduled its formal opening for Spring, 1968. The others are OAKLAND PUBLIC MUSEUM (page 242) and OAKLAND ART MUSEUM. The new museum, designed by Eero Saarinen & Associates, will have available four city blocks and cost $7,000,000. The Snow Museum has a large exhibit of mammals collected by Henry A. Snow and his son Sidney.

3. LAKESIDE PARK, irregularly bordering the N. shore of Lake Merritt, threaded by Bellevue Ave., has facilities for tennis, bowling-on-the-green, and horseshoe pitching, and a municipal bandstand where free outdoor concerts are given on Sundays, August to October, 2-4 p.m.

4. LAKE MERRITT WILDFOWL SANCTUARY is a game refuge administered by the United States Biological Survey, which maintains a banding station near the Canoe House. Ducks and other wildfowl, which make their headquarters here from November to March, are fed at 10 a.m. and 3:30 p.m.

5. The EMBARCADERO (landing place), on the NE. tip of Lake Merritt, is a horseshoe-shaped walk bordered by concrete columns.

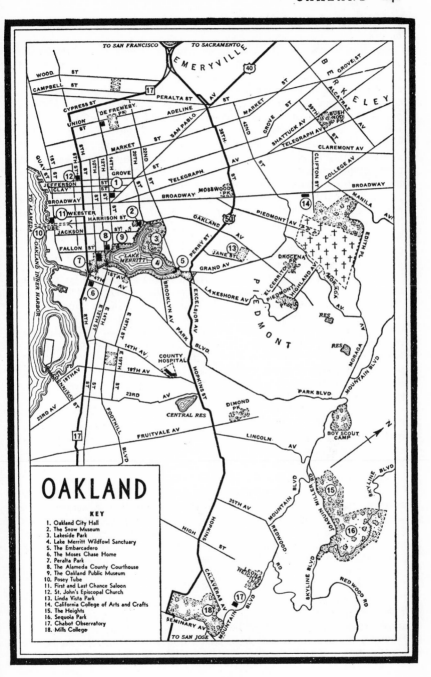

# OAKLAND

### KEY
1. Oakland City Hall
2. The Snow Museum
3. Lakeside Park
4. Lake Merritt Wildfowl Sanctuary
5. The Embarcadero
6. The Moses Chase Home
7. Peralta Park
8. The Alameda County Courthouse
9. The Oakland Public Museum
10. Posey Tube
11. First and Last Chance Saloon
12. St. John's Episcopal Church
13. Linda Vista Park
14. California College of Arts and Crafts
15. The Heights
16. Sequoia Park
17. Chabot Observatory
18. Mills College

The Spaniards shipped hides and tallow from here in flat-bottomed barges.

6. The OAKLAND PUBLIC MUSEUM (*open 9:30-5 weekdays, 10-5 Sun. and holidays*), 1426 Oak St., is a two-story brown frame house containing exhibits in natural science, ethnology, and history. In the Natural Science Section are birds, mammals, insects, and butterflies; the Ethnology Department displays artifacts of Alaska, British Columbia, California, and Pacific Islands. The History Section contains relics of the War of 1812, Civil War, Spanish-American War, and the World War; the California Room has relics of Indian, Spanish and pioneer days. In the two Colonial Rooms are reproductions, including a "whatnot" once the property of Abraham Lincoln. The museum also houses displays of old coins, firearms, medals, and currency.

7. The MOSES CHASE HOME (*private*), NE. corner 4th Ave. and E. 8th St., the oldest dwelling in Oakland, was built about 1850. The four original rooms are still intact, and serve as a nucleus for the white-painted 14-room house with its gable roof and green shutters, and its porch extending across the front. Chase was Oakland's first American settler, arriving via Cape Horn from Massachusetts in 1849.

8. PERALTA PARK is a landscaped tract on the S. shore of Lake Merritt between 8th and 12th Sts. The MUNICIPAL AUDITORIUM, 10th and Fallon Sts., is of concrete finished in California granite, and divided into the Arena, the Theater, and the Art Gallery. Conventions and boxing and wrestling matches are held in the Arena; opera, road shows, and lectures are given in the Theater; the Art Gallery (*open 1-5 daily*) houses a permanent collection of painting, sculpture, and prints, and conducts annual exhibitions. The EXPOSITION BUILDING, Fallon St. between 9th and 10th Sts., similar in design to the Auditorium, is used for athletic and civic events.

9. The ALAMEDA COUNTY COURTHOUSE, Fallon St. between 12th and 13th Sts., a concrete building of neo-classic design, with terra cotta and granite trim, was completed by PWA in 1936 at a cost of $2,000,000. The HALL OF RECORDS is on the general floor. The COUNTY FREE LIBRARY (*open 9-5 Mon.-Fri., 9-12 Sat.*), and mosquito control exhibit are in the basement.

10. POSEY TUBE, entrance Harrison and 6th Sts., a $4,500,000 subway, 4,436 feet long, under the estuary connecting Oakland with Alameda, was opened to traffic in 1928. Its lighting, ventilation, drainage, fire protection, and traffic control systems have brought it to the attention of engineers the world over. The inside diameter of the tube is 32 feet, the walls are 2½ feet thick, and it is claimed to be earthquakeproof. The tube is named for George A. Posey, its designer and builder.

11. FIRST AND LAST CHANCE SALOON, 50 Webster St., is noted as a place frequented by Jack London. The saloon, built about 1880, retains an early western atmosphere. One block away at Webster and First Sts., JACK LONDON SQUARE commemorates the author. It fronts on the Estuary and is a center for waterfront restaurants.

12. ST. JOHN'S EPISCOPAL CHURCH, SW. corner Grove and 8th Sts., a shingled building with a square Gothic tower, built in 1860, is the oldest Episcopal church in Oakland. Hand-carved plaques adorn the walls.

13. LINDA VISTA PARK, Oakland and Olive Aves., is a landscaped area containing the eight-acre MUNICIPAL ROSE GARDENS. Some of the 100,000 rose bushes of more than 3,000 varieties are in bloom continuously.

14. CALIFORNIA COLLEGE OF ARTS AND CRAFTS, 5212 Broadway, a coeducational institution founded in 1907, is set on a high hill, behind an ivy-clad red stone wall. The landscaped four-acre campus with buildings of wood and stucco includes two fine specimens of *Sequoia gigantea* (big tree). The institution presents a full course in the arts and crafts, leading to a bachelor of arts degree. In 1964 it enrolled 760 students and 50 instructors.

15. THE HIGHTS (JOAQUIN MILLER PARK), NE. on Joaquin Miller Road, so spelled by Miller, was the home of the "Poet of the Sierras," where he and his friends planted 75,000 eucalypti, pines, cypresses, and acacias. The city bought the tract in 1917, granting a life tenure in it to the poet's widow and daughter, each of whom occupies a cottage on the grounds. The ABBEY (*open by appointment*), built in 1886, where the poet lived until his death in 1913, consists of three one-room frame structures connected to form a single unit, each room roofed by a shingled peak. Here he wrote "Columbus" and other poems. The poet claimed he could not write without rain on the roof; he had pipes installed to sprinkle water on the roof when he wanted inspiration. On the eminence to the north he built a stone foundation intended as his funeral pyre (never used); native rock towers dedicated to Gen. John C. Frémont and Robert Browning; and a pyramid to Moses.

16. In SEQUOIA PARK, adjoining The Hights to the E., a wooded area of 182 acres, is the OAKLAND ZOO (*always open*), Robinson Drive and Joaquin Miller Road, housing 30 specimens.

17. CHABOT OBSERVATORY, 4917 Mountain Blvd. (*open 1-4 p.m. and 7-10 p.m. Tues.-Sat., except during school holidays and vacations*), a two-story stucco building with a dome at either end, occupies 12 acres on a landscaped hill and contains 8- and 20-inch refracting telescopes.

18. MILLS COLLEGE, Trenor St. and Seminary Ave., oldest college in the West exclusively for women, was founded in 1852, in Benicia, as the Young Ladies' Seminary. It reached full collegiate standing and became known as Mills College in 1885. The college is nonsectarian and enrolled 727 in 1964. It confers bachelor and master degrees in arts and sciences, and is particularly distinguished in music and art. The more modern buildings on the campus are designed in the Mediterranean style of architecture. The CAMPANILE, in mission style, has ten bells, originally cast for the World's Fair in Chicago in 1893. The design of the MUSIC BUILDING is based upon the church

architecture of the Spanish Renaissance, with an elaborate arch-canopy doorway embellished with twisted columns, decorative finials and a sculptured lunette. It contains nearly 60 soundproof practice rooms. ETHEL MOORE HALL, one of the six residence halls, is built on 16 different levels, with five patios. The ART GALLERY (*open 2-5 Wed., Fri., Sun.; group visits by arrangement other days*) contains a permanent American collection of painting, sculpture, and art objects, including a group of Chinese paintings, an extensive art library, and a notable collection of the works of Robert Browning. Student painting and sculpture is exhibited in May and June. The LIBRARY (*private*) has a large collection of early western literature and books by California writers.

SKYLINE BOULEVARD—north approach from Berkeley, south approach from Foothill Boulevard, Oakland—from the tourists' standpoint the most distinctive feature of Oakland, is a winding road high above the city, which affords a magnificent panorama of the East Bay, the harbor, and San Francisco and Marin County across the bay. By means of a tunnel through the Berkeley Hills into Contra Costa County (and by a low-level tunnel at the head of Broadway) the driver can pass from 65° F. to 100° F. Oakland has quick access to the highly desirable residential areas of the unincorporated communities of ORINDA and MORAGA. The ridge that forms the boundary between Alameda and Contra Costa counties held back the fogs of San Francisco Bay, thus making the hills popular with well-to-do commuters who wanted acreage for swimming pools and vistas. When the rush of population started in 1950 Orinda had 4,712 people; in 1965 local authorities counted 17,230. Moraga had 2,156 in 1950; 5,690 in 1965. The small valley of Las Trampas Creek in the hills of Moraga is the site of ST. MARY'S COLLEGE a four-year denominational institution founded 1863, with an enrollment of 820 in 1964.

# Pasadena

*Transportation:* Santa Fe, Union Pacific and Southern Pacific Railways. Greyhound Bus Lines, American Trailways, Continental Trailways, Santa Fe Bus Lines. Airport Service, Inc.

*Community Facilities:* There are 11 hotels and 23 motels (1965); 4 general hospitals with 713 beds; 24 banks; 118 churches; 21 public parks; 3 golf courses, one private; 78 public tennis courts; 2 public plunges; 2 riding academies; 12 shuffleboard courts; 2 lawn bowling courts.

*Higher Education:* California Institute of Technology, Pasadena College (Nazarene), Ambassador College (Radio Church of God), Pasadena City College.

*Annual Events:* Tournament of Roses, Jan. 1. Football game between winning teams representing East and West, Rose Bowl, Jan. 1. Pasadena Flower Show, April and October. Pasadena Kennel Club Show, February and July.

PASADENA (700 to 1,200 ft. alt., north to south; 116,407 pop., 1960. 123,381 est. 1965) is located about 10 miles northeast of downtown Los Angeles. Described as "the city Los Angeles grew up around" it accepts the title of home of the affluent society, where its citizens "do very well indeed." Its metropolitan area takes in half a dozen sizable communities and some unincorporated places, with a population of 267,200 (1964) with a higher-than-average proportion of professional, clerical and sales workers. Pasadena ranks fifth in size among the 76 incorporated cities of Los Angeles County, down from fourth position in 1962. It is a retail trade center for the entire San Gabriel Valley and in July, 1964, 25,000 were engaged in wholesale and retail trade and 18,450 in manufacturing, chiefly electronics, food products and precision instruments. The *Star-News* stated that metropolitan Pasadena in 1960 had 5,413 families earning $25,000 a year or more and 15,185 earning more than $15,000; the average household taking home $10,660 in income annually.

Pasadena lies in the foothills of the Sierre Madre, overlooking the San Gabriel Valley. To the north are Altadena (42,060 pop.) and the pineclad heights of Mount Wilson and Mount Lowe. On the south are South Pasadena (20,978 pop.) and Alhambra (59,940 pop.). It is served by Colorado Freeway and Pasadena Freeway (US 66). On the east it stretches for several miles along broad Colorado Street, and ends abruptly in the west along the curving Arroyo Seco (dry watercourse).

From a vantage point in the hills, the city looks like a lumpy sea of green trees, from which rise church spires, the boxlike procession of business buildings along Colorado Street, and the massive resort hotels. An air of prosperity—the unhurried tenor of a Sunday afternoon—is engendered by the substantial buildings, the pretentious homes, generous foliage, and the winding, flower-edged streets.   The center of the small business district is the intersection of Colorado Street and Fair Oak Avenue.   Here the streets are lined with smart shops, lighted at night with a restrained display of neon lights.   There is no large-scale industry in Pasadena; business is mostly restricted to retail trade and stores that supply the wants of good living.

In the residential section, surrounding the business district, are homes in carefully tended gardens, mansions in estates with sunken gardens, swimming pools, and tennis courts.   Resort hotels spread their wings and terraces over grounds well back from the street, their lawns spotted with gay garden furniture.   The Huntington-Sheraton is the city's largest hotel.

Pasadena is headquarters for the Pacific Crest Trail System Conference (125 S. Grand Ave.), which sponsors the Pacific Crest Trail System, which affords hikers the satisfying experience of traversing 2,265 miles of unspoiled nature.

On Christmas Tree Lane (Santa Rosa Avenue, Altadena), giant deodars, planted as seedlings from the Himalayas in the 1890's, have stretched their branches across the street and almost conceal the houses. Each Christmas the trees are festooned with thousands of colored lights, creating a festive effect that attracts thousands of visitors.

On New Year's Day the city stages the Tournament of Roses, inspired by the flower fetes in Nice, and introduced in 1890 as a simple village festival to celebrate the midwinter flowering season.   Residents decked their buggies with roses, went picnicking, sent pictures back home, and connected roses with New Year's Day so effectively that Pasadena has been called "the town that roses built."

On this day young girls elected for their beauty are carried through the streets in floats of elaborate design, where they sit pelting the crowds with flowers.   Today the parade, widely televised, has its support of many national corporations.   Floats represent every prominent city in California.   The floral decorations follow a single theme, and floats bearing 100,000 to 300,000 fresh flowers are not uncommon.   The holiday became more elaborate each season; for twelve years the climaxing feature of the day was a thundering, ripsnorting chariot race, finally displaced in 1916 by the football game between picked eastern and western teams in the Rose Bowl.

Pasadena is staid—a city with an unusual number of churches for its size—but it supports an excellent small theater and several art and music associations.   The former Pasadena Community Playhouse, now the State Theater of California, is one of the leading little theaters in the country.   The city's educational institutions are relatively long established and rank high.   The California Institute of Technology, famous for its roster of great physicists, has made important contributions to scientific theory, notably Robert A. Millikan's study of cosmic rays and researches into the nature of the electron.   The Institute has also aided in advancing aeronautics, and by virtue of several foundations has carried forward cancer and other medical research.

The San Pasqual ranch of 4,000 acres was sold by John S. Griffin to the San Gabriel Orange Grove Assn., a land colonizing group, in 1873. It was named Pasadena in 1875 by combining Chippewa words meaning valley between hills or key to the valley. Most of the early settlers were well-to-do families from Indiana.

The site of Pasadena, once part of the lands of the San Gabriel Mission, has changed owners with perplexing frequency. The Rancho San Pasqual was first granted by the mission fathers to an aged mission housekeeper in 1826, and passed from her hands when she married at nearly 100 years of age. Her stepson sold his interest in 1839 to two dons who later abandoned the property.

Governor Micheltorena, looking about for a suitable present in 1843, granted the land to Don Manuel Garfías, a Mexican army officer. Garfías had his title validated by the United States Land Commission in 1854 and was sent a patent signed by Lincoln in 1863. Meanwhile Garfías sold his interest to Benjamin D. Wilson, a Yankee, who has given his name to a mountain, a canyon, a lake, a trail, an avenue, and a school. Wilson and his associates swapped, traded, and borrowed from each other, with the land as security, until in 1873 the land was divided between Wilson and Dr. John S. Griffin, who came to California as chief medical officer with the American Army. Griffin's share was approximately 4,000 acres and included the original site of Pasadena.

The story now moves East. The winter of 1872-73 was cold in Indiana. Dr. Thomas B. Elliott, of Indianapolis, and his friends "to get where life was easy," formed the "California Colony of Indiana," and sent a scouting committee to spy out the promised land. It looked as if it would be easy. The colony bought Griffin's land for $25,000, and that was the beginning of the exodus of wealthy men from the Middle West and East that resulted in the present millionaires' retreat.

## POINTS OF INTEREST

The CIVIC CENTER, Garfield Ave., between Walnut and Green Sts., is a harmonious group of modified Spanish and Italian Renaissance buildings, dominated by the CITY HALL, 100 N. Garfield Ave., an impressive domed three-story concrete structure occupying an entire block. The large red- and gold-topped dome rises above the entrance pavilion on an arcaded and pinnacled drum, the lower stage of which is adorned with Ionic columns. At the upper end of the Civic Center is the PUBLIC LIBRARY (*open 9-9 Mon.-Sat.*), 285 E. Walnut St., a rambling buff stucco building with walled forecourt, planted with palms. The library has more than 200,000 volumes.   The circulation hall, in the main section of the building, is decorated with a coffered ceiling and oak paneling; the children's room in the left wing and the periodical room in the right wing have outdoor reading rooms in frescoed cloisters that flank the forecourt.   At the lower end of the Civic Center is the CIVIC AUDITORIUM (*open 2-4 Wed.*), 300 E. Green St., that seats 3,000.

BROOKSIDE PARK, Arroyo Blvd. between Holly St. and Devil's Gate Dam, is a city recreational preserve of more than 500 acres, with a picnic and playground section, swimming pool, and municipal golf course.   Trails and bridle paths run through forests of oak and pine. Within its grounds is the ROSE BOWL (*open free, except during performances*), Arroyo Blvd. at Salvia Canyon Rd., a concrete stadium of elliptical shape, seating some 85,000.   It is used for other football games besides the annual Rose Bowl game, and for political and civic events.

LA MINIATURA, 645 Prospect Crescent, is a studio-residence built by Frank Lloyd Wright for Mrs. George M. Millard in 1923. Framed by eucalyptus trees, at the end of a ravine, its two-story facade is reflected in a pool of the sunken gardens.   The double walls of concrete blocks are stamped with a radical cross design.   Also forming a part of the house plan are the garage with its tall castle-like doors and the Little Museum of the Book designed by Wright's son.

CALIFORNIA INSTITUTE OF TECHNOLOGY (CAL-TECH), devoted to scientific teaching and research of the highest order, has a 22-acre campus on California Blvd., and several outlying laboratories.   Founded 1891 by Amos G. Throop, it bore his name until 1920. Independent and privately endowed, it normally has about 700 undergraduates, 800 graduate students and 550 faculty members.   Influential in its growth were George Ellery Hale, first director of Mt. Wilson Observatory; Arthur Amos Noyes and Robert Andrews Millikan. Hale obtained for Caltech ownership and supervision of the 200-inch reflecting telescope in the observatory on Palomar Mountain, now operated jointly with Mt. Wilson in agreement with Carnegie Institution of Washington, D. C.   Cal-tech is the site of a syncroton (atom smasher) capable of 1.5 billion electron volts.   During World War II more than 24,000 students were enrolled in courses relating to aeronautics, meteorology and ordnance.   The Air Force Reserve Officer Training Corps program is a four-year course in military air science leading to a commission in USAF.   Caltech is the site of Guggenheim Graduate School of Aeronautics, W. K. Kellogg Radiation Lab. (nuclear physics), Firestone Flight Science Lab., Karman Lab. of Flight Mechanics & Jet Propulsion, Willis H. Booth Computing Center.   Among many new facilities is BECKMAN AUDITORIUM, erected 1964.   Off-campus are KRESGE SEISMOLOGICAL LAB. and DONNELLEY SEISMOLOGICAL LAB. both on San Rafael Ave., Pasadena; KERKHOFF MARINE BIOLOGICAL LAB., Coronoa del Mar; OWENS VALLEY RADIO OBSERVATORY, Bishop, Calif.

The FLORES ADOBE (*private*), Garfield Ave. and Foothill St., was built in 1839 for Doña Eulalia Perez de Guillen, original owner of the Rancho San Pasqual.   The house, greatly restored, has reddish plaster walls and red tile roofs.   The original beams of rough-hewn timber still protrude beneath the eaves.   After the battle of La Mesa in January, 1847, the decisive fight in the conquest of California, Gen. José Mariá Flores, defeated commander of the Californian lancers, took refuge here.

PASADENA ART MUSEUM, 46 N. Los Robles Ave., in a building that makes use of Chinese ornamentation, has collections of oriental art and prints, and American and European art, especially German, of this century.   It holds about thirty exhibitions annually.

PASADENA PLAYHOUSE, 39 El Molino Ave., a U-shaped group of two-story, white-plastered Spanish Colonial buildings surrounding a rough-flagged forecourt, is one of the few nationally known little theaters.   In the right wing is the School of the Theater, and the Laboratory Theater, a workshop in which the plays of new authors are given test productions.   The theater was built in 1925, and seats 820.   It is now the State Theater of California.

MEMORIAL FLAGPOLE, at Colorado St. and Orange Grove Ave., is a lofty pole with a bronze sculptured base, designed by Bertram Goodhue and Lee Lawrie, and dedicated in 1927 as a memorial to Pasadena men who fell in World War I.

## POINTS OF INTEREST IN ENVIRONS

Huntington Library and Art Gallery, San Marino, 11.5 *m.;* Mount Wilson Observatory, 25.7 *m.* (*see TOUR 12c*).

Six miles northwest of Pasadena at the base of the San Gabriel Mountains is LA CANADA, a residential community of 20,000 pop. (1965) governed by the County of Los Angeles.   It is the site of the 140-acre Descanso Gardens of the Los Angeles Dept. of Arboreta and Botanic Gardens, with 600 varieties and 100,000 specimens of camellias, 800 bushes of roses exemplifying the evolution of the rose; azaleas, orchids, begonias and many other plantings.   Tram tours daily except Mondays, also bird study walks. (*free*)

# Sacramento

*Information:* Sacramento City-County Chamber of Commerce, 917 7th St. and 2717 Marconi Ave. Convention Bureau, 1515 J St. Better Business Bureau, 2003 J St.

*Transportation:* Southern Pacific and Western Pacific Railways, with Santa Fe connection via Central California Traction Co. Sacramento Northern Ry. freight service, Oakland to the Valley. Greyhound Bus Lines and Continental-American Trailways with downtown terminals. Sacramento Transit Authority bus lines in city and Suburban Transit Lines to suburbs. Sacramento Municipal Airport, 7 *m.* from center, has daily flights by United, Pacific, Western and West Coast Lines. Metropolitan Airport of County ready in 1967. Deep water channel gives direct access to sea.

*Freeways:* Two major east-west highways, US 40 and US 50, intersect with principal north-south highway, US 99W, freeway to Los Angeles. US 40 (Interstate 80) is a freeway to San Francisco and over the Sierra to Reno. US 50 to Lake Tahoe is freeway for 38 *m.* State 16 and 160 enter the center of Sacramento.

*Recreation:* Public golf in Ancil Hoffman Park, Haggin Oaks, Bing Maloney, William Land Park. Three membership clubs. Swimming at Lake Folsom, Nimbus Lake and 7 public pools. Water skiing and boating on Sacramento River and Folsom Lake. Sailing on Folsom Lake and Nimbus Lake. All boats must be registered with County Assessor. Fresh-water fishing year around (blue gill, perch, king salmon, bass, sturgeon, shad, catfish, steelheads and other trout). Licenses: $3 for resident; $4 for 10 days for nonresident; otherwise nonresident or alien, $11. Military personnel not exempt. Licenses for hunting: resident, $4; nonresident, $25; alien, $50. Additional fees for deer, pheasant, duck, bear. For tennis and other sports consult Recreation Dept., 442-5041.

*Special Events:* California State Fair & Exposition, 12 days beginning last week in August. Sacramento Music Circus, mid-June. JayRob Productions, plays, fall and spring. Camellia Festival, 10 days in March. Camellia Bowl Festival of Sports, December.

SACRAMENTO (17–30 alt., 191,667 pop. 1960; 249,300, 1964 est., State Dept. of Finance) is the capital of California and seat of Sacramento County, which coincides largely with its metropolitan area, with 612,500 pop. (est.) in 1964. Since 1960 it has annexed North Sacramento, which reported 12,922 in 1960. Its principal activity, the work of the State, employs 26,525 persons; close second are the space system industries, Aerojet-General Corp. and Douglas Aircraft Co., employing about 16,700 at peak times, followed by McClellan Air Force Base (aircraft maintenance), with more than 12,900. The city is the hub of a network of interstate and state highways, with arterial freeways, and since 1963 has been a deep-water port, with access to Suisun Bay and San Francisco, 90 *m.* southwest.

Sacramento is the center of a large wholesale and retail market. It is the gateway to the historic sites where gold was found and the great gold rush of 1849 began. It lies in the heart of the Central Valley Water Project, at the confluence of the American and Sacramento Rivers, and close to the great recreation areas of the Sierras and National and State parks and forests.

In 1964 Sacramento County had agricultural income of $72,601,440, of which field crops accounted for nearly $22,000,000, livestock and dairy products, $19,805,000, and fruit crops, $10,836,000. Emphasizing its success in horticulture Sacramento calls itself the Camellia Capital of the World, and annually in spring observes a 10-day Camellia Festival.

The PORT OF SACRAMENTO became a reality in 1963, when the deep water channel to Suisan on San Francisco Bay was completed and provided a new, cheap water route for the big agricultural output of the opulent Sacramento Valley. The Port has facilities for five deep-sea freighters. Barge canal and lock connections to the navigable Sacramento River enable shallow-draft barges with products from far inland to reach the Port from embarkation points to the north. Commodities moving through this channel include canned and dried fruits and vegetables, rice, grain and sorghums. Timber also is being moved. Industrial products to be imported are steel manufactures, petroleum products, fertilizers, vegetable oils and processed woods.

The domed Capitol dominates the city. The legislature meets biennially in odd years, holding two sessions broken by a recess. Epic struggles have been waged here, among others the long fight against the railroad stranglehold on the valley, ending in the reforms under Governor Hiram Johnson; and the bitter contest over Japanese immigration, which ended with exclusion.

Flat stretches of unclaimed land, the navigable river, which was named Sacramento in honor of the sacrament, by Jose Moraga, comandante of the presidio of San Jose, and tractable Indians for workers drew the attention of Capt. John Augustus Sutter, the pioneer settler, in 1839. The Swiss ex-army officer took up a 50,000-acre grant by swearing allegiance to the Mexican flag, and built a principality named "New Helvetia" in memory of the old country. He ruled in baronial splendor, with Indians as his subjects, and a fort of timber and adobe brick as his castle, with twelve guns mounted on the ramparts. Sutter built forges and shops, grazed herds on his lands, trapped for furs, and carried on a lively trade. The spot was a haven for settlers in the tide of overland emigration in the early 1840's. In 1848 the town of Sacramento was laid out on Sutter's farm, and the first lots were sold in January, 1849.

It was Sutter's boss carpenter, James W. Marshall, who, on January 24, 1848, found the first gold flake while building a mill for Sutter near Coloma (*see TOUR 4a*) on the South Fork of the American River, which resulted in the great gold rush of 1849 and the 1850's and in California's admission to the Union as a State. It also led to Sutter's ruin. Trampling hordes from the East overran his hospitable fort, stole his cattle, drove off his Indians, disputed his rights to the land. His white retainers deserted for the mines. Meantime, millions of dollars in gold dust passed over Sutter's landing. He moved to Pennsylvania in 1873, with only a small pension from California, and died at Washington, D.C., in 1880, after vainly beseeching Congress for the restoration of his property.

The settlement became the supply center for the northern mines of the mother lode. Thousands of gold-hungry men came pouring in to outfit for the diggings. The 1850 census showed 6,820, and the population soon jumped to 10,000, with gold seekers camped along the river bank in tents, frame houses, and even under trees—a packing box or a strip of canvas was considered good housing. Bearded men from the mines flashed pokes of gold dust with assumed indifference, and spent grandly in saloons, fandango halls, and gambling houses. The most profitable mining was done by entrepreneurs, who took it out of the miners' pockets. Bitter struggles took place between squatters and men who claimed titles to farmlands.

Three disastrous floods came between 1849 and 1853, and in 1852 a fire wiped out two-thirds of the town. In 1849 Sacramento had offered $1,000,000 for the honor of being the State capital. The Legislature met in 1852, sitting on hot ashes, and when it officially became the capital in 1854, flood debris was still in evidence. The floods caused epidemics, and corpses were shoved into the swollen river to drift away. Levees were finally built, and the town pulled itself up out of the foot-deep dust of summer and the hub-deep mire of the rainy season. For many years the water remained unpalatable for those who had the temerity to drink it. Few did.

In 1856 Sacramento was the terminus of the first railroad in California, built as a short line to Folsom by Theodore Dehone Judah, the young engineer who planned the first transcontinental railroad through the passes of the Sierra Nevada. Four years later came the Pony Express, which ran until 1861, when the transcontinental telegraph went through.

The Central Pacific Railroad joined East and West in 1869. Judah's financial sponsors were all Sacramento storekeepers: Collis P. Huntington, Mark Hopkins, Charles Crocker, and Leland Stanford, the "Big Four." The Central Pacific branched out and became the Southern Pacific, the "octopus" of Frank Norris' novel, which for 40 years practically controlled the State. Large-scale wheat growing and cattle raising soon after lost their lead to more lucrative fields of fruit, vineyards, cotton, and vegetables. Land prices rose, and Sacramento's prosperity with them.

Sacramento's position as the capital was challenged by Berkeley in 1907, and more recently by San Jose and Monterey, but with little effect. The river channel was dredged in 1911, and seagoing vessels could reach the city when the river stage was high. The early years of depression saw several State hunger marches, and in 1938 refugees from the labor troubles in Nevada City camped for a week outside the fairgrounds.

## POINTS OF INTEREST

OLD SACRAMENTO is an area along the Sacramento River that was designated in 1965 by the Redevelopment Agency for restoration to conditions of the Gold Rush days.   It extends from the river to Interstate 5 Freeway and includes the localities where John A. Sutter had his wharf and pioneers built stores, hotels, and a stage depot.   The area retains 53 buildings erected in the busy decades when thousands entered Sacramento on the way to the gold fields.   Here took place the first-spade ceremonial of the Central Pacific Railroad, the western start of the Pony Express and the development of the California Stage Co., which eventually employed 66 Concord coaches and 125 wagons.   Historic buildings from other areas will be moved to the site.   The optimistic planners estimate that Old Sacramento will attract as many as 2,500,000 visitors who annually will drop about $20,000,000 there by 1970.

1. CAPITOL PARK is an area of 40 acres in the heart of Sacramento dominated by the CAPITOL, a monumental structure of Graeco-Roman design completed in 1874.   The basement and first floor are of California granite, the three upper stories of brick, painted white.   The building is surmounted by a gilded dome reaching up 237 ft. from the ground.   In the Park are trees of many varieties and from far places.   The Park is the nucleus of the Capitol complex of buildings, many of which have been erected in the last twenty years.

In 1959 the Legislature created the Capitol Building & Planning Commission and ordered the development of a master plan.   The 69 acres now used by the State will be expanded to 138, streets will be closed to create a plaza and malls, and new structures will conform to patterns intended to expedite business and create uniformity and architectural harmony.   In order to retain the Capitol as a dominating landmark the new structures around Capitol Park will be restricted to six stories (75 ft.).   Office buildings farther removed will have 16 to 26 stories.

The Capitol is flanked by OFFICE BUILDING NO. 1 and the STATE LIBRARY AND COURTS BUILDING.   On Capitol Mall are the EMPLOYMENT BUILDING (1955, cost $6,923,000), PERSONNEL BOARD BUILDING (1955, cost $1,932,000) and the FEDERAL BUILDING.   South of the Park are the PUBLIC WORKS BUILDING (1937) and two annexes (1952, 1962, total cost $8,399,000); the ARCHIVES (1922, $365,000); the VETERANS' AFFAIRS BUILDING (1957, $2,240,500) and OFFICE BUILDING NO. 2.   Other State buildings in the general area include the AGRICULTURAL BUILDING and two annexes (1937, 1955, 1962, total cost $3,507,000); the BUSINESS & PROFESSIONS BUILDING and annex (1939, 1949, $2,557,000); the EDUCATION BUILDING (1953, $2,941,000); the EMPLOYMENT BUILDING (1955, $6,923,000); the CIVIL DEFENSE BUILDING (1953, $298,500); the MOTOR VEHICLES BUILDING NO. 1 (1953, $5,757,000); the MOTOR VEHICLES BUILDING NO. 2 (1963, $12,295,500); the HIGHWAY PATROL BUILDING NO. 1 (1953, $808,-

000, with No. 2 ready in 1967 at a cost of $2,132,000; the RESOURCES BUILDING (1964, $14,404,000); the FRANCHISE TAX BUILDING and annex (1927, 1947, $1,002,000).

The Office of Architecture and Construction of the Department of General Services reported an investment of $91,664,000 in existing office buildings, $20,473,000 in existing institutional facilities (Sacramento State College and the Northern California Reception Center and Clinic); and new facilities under way costing $43,316,500. A 1966 estimate of the State's investment in official buildings and facilities in Sacramento was placed at $170,252,000.

The Resources Building is the largest in the Capitol Complex. The second-largest is the Employment Building, 683 ft. long, which extends on the south side of the Mall between 7th and 9th Sts. and all floors above the second story level extend over 8th St., forming a bridge 70 ft. wide and 88 ft. long. The building, in contemporary style, has simple concrete surfaces. Office Buildings No. 8 and 9, scheduled for completion in 1968, will be twin 17-story towers on the block bounded by P, Q, 7th and 8th Sts. In the same area the Central Heating and Cooling Plant, to be ready in 1969 and cost $11,330,000, will serve all the State buildings.

2. The STATE OFFICE BUILDING and the STATE LIBRARY AND COURTS BUILDING (*open 8-5 Mon.-Fri., 9-12 Sat.; 8-4 July and Aug.*), 10th St. between L and N Sts., extending to 9th St., are twin five story buildings of neo-classic design, adorned with Ionic porticoes and colonnades, built in 1925. The State Building houses State government departments; the library, across a terraced garden, contains about 1,000,000 volumes, including rare items of Californiana, 65,000 volumes of law, and a large braille collection. The library was begun in 1850 with a collection of books donated by John C. Frémont. GILLIS HALL, at the entrance to the reference room, contains murals by Maynard Dixon depicting a Spanish-Mexican and an American migration pageant. The octagonal APPELLATE COURT ROOM, also in this building, is finished in Roman Corinthian style. The room has gilded walls and columns, bronze-embedded windows, and a gold and alabaster chandelier.

3. The MEMORIAL AUDITORIUM, 15th St. between J and I Sts., and extending to 16th St., of Italian Romanesque design, is a massive dark red brick building with colonnaded loggia and stone trim. It was completed in 1927, as a memorial to World War veterans. The main auditorium seats 3,200; the Little Theater in one wing seats 300, and the Memorial Hall in the other wing 200. The auditorium contains a huge stage, a movable floor and a great organ. Chimes above the building strike each quarter hour, and every evening at 6 o'clock play "The Star Spangled Banner."

4. The CITY PLAZA, corner of 9th and I Sts., was given to the city by Sutter in 1849. On the south side of the park, facing J Street, is a statue by Albert Weiner, erected "by his co-workers" in 1899 to A. J. Stevens, "a friend of labor," and a prominent railroad man of the

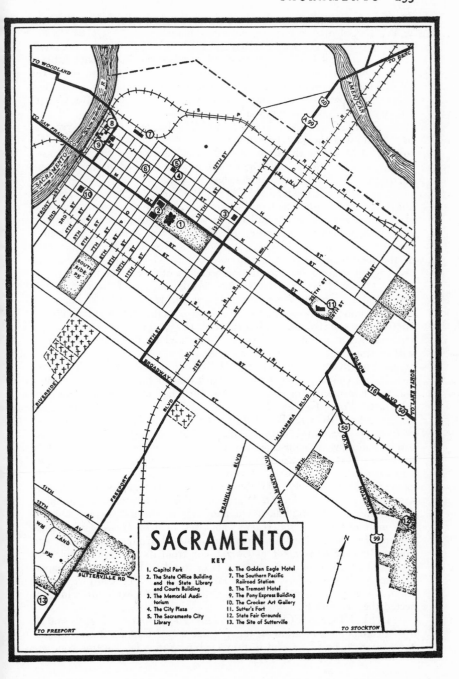

# SACRAMENTO

### KEY

1. Capitol Park
2. The State Office Building and the State Library and Courts Building
3. The Memorial Auditorium
4. The City Plaza
5. The Sacramento City Library
6. The Golden Eagle Hotel
7. The Southern Pacific Railroad Station
8. The Tremont Hotel
9. The Pony Express Building
10. The Crocker Art Gallery
11. Sutter's Fort
12. State Fair Grounds
13. The Site of Sutterville

1870's.  A fountain in modernist style by Ralph Stackpole is a memorial to W. T. Coleman, a pioneer real estate man.

5. SACRAMENTO PUBLIC LIBRARY (*open 9-9 weekdays*), corner of 9th and I Sts., dates from 1857, when the Sacramento Library Association was formed, among its founders being the railroad "Big Four," then all young men.  The main building has 400,000 volumes. There are five branches and two bookmobiles.  Sacramento County Library has 130,000 volumes and 30 branches.

6. The GOLDEN EAGLE HOTEL, located for many years at 627 K St. was the first headquarters of the Republican party in California.  Just across the street was the headquarters of the Democratic party.  In the 1860's and 1870's there were pitched battles between partisans.  The hotel was demolished in 1962.

7. The SOUTHERN PACIFIC RAILROAD STATION, 4th and I Sts., has a monument to Theodore D. Judah at the main entrance, erected by employees of the railroad in 1930.  It is a massive stone structure adorned with a bas-relief of Judah, below which is inserted a wooden tie from the old Central Pacific Railroad.  On the east wall of the waiting room is a mural by Arthur McQuarry depicting the breaking of ground for the first transcontinental railroad in 1863.

8. The VERNON-BRANNAN HOUSE, 112 J St., is a State Historical Landmark, erected in 1853 as a three-story brick hotel and operated under various names, best-known being the Vernon House, 1856-1866; the Brannan House, 1866-1873; Tremont Hotel, 1876-1918; Hotel Espanol, 1918-1960.  Now used as a Rescue Mission, it will be restored as part of Old Sacramento.

9. The PONY EXPRESS MUSEUM (*open 10-4 daily*), 1015 2nd St., a two-story brick structure with cement facing erected in 1860, was for eight months in 1860 and 1861 the office and relay station of the celebrated Pony Express from Sacramento to St. Joseph, Missouri.

10. The CROCKER ART GALLERY MUSEUM (*open 9-5 daily except Mondays*), corner 2nd and O Sts., consists of two large Victorian buildings in landscaped grounds.  The gallery was donated to the city in 1885 by the widow of Judge E. B. Crocker, brother of Charles Crocker of the "Big Four."  Its collection includes studies by Leonardo da Vinci, Michelangelo, and Rembrandt.  In the late 1930's priceless drawings by Holbein, Dürer, Watteau, and other masters were found in the basement.  Among the noted paintings in the gallery are Dürer's *St. Joseph and the Virgin Mary*, Van Dyck's *Christ Healing the Blind*, Rubens' *Portrait*, Murillo's *Gypsy*, a Claude Lorraine Landscape, and Guido Reni's *Entombment of Christ*, cut from its frame and stolen in 1923, but returned by mail ten days later to a San Francisco newspaper. Crocker built the gallery as a separate building.  The California Museum Association later bought the Crocker home next door and connected the two buildings.

11. SUTTER'S FORT (*open daily 10-5*), stands at 26th and L Sts., a complete restoration on the original site of Captain Sutter's ranch house, workshops, home, and fort, erected in 1839.  Ivy-covered concrete

walls, 18 ft. high, surround the fort.    Immediately inside the gate is the bell of Young America Engine Company No. 6, which rang for Lincoln's election and tolled for his assassination.    Near the bell are the cannon that guarded the fort when it was first erected.

The buildings are in a hollow square, one story high; the central museum, which was Sutter's quarters, is raised to two stories by a low raftered basement.    The original adobe bricks are protected by stucco, but the covering is removed in places so they can be seen.    The original pine door frames were from Fort Ross, which Sutter bought from the Russians when they left California in 1841; they were brought from Norway around the Horn.    The basement and main floor are filled with relics of early California days—furniture, clothes, printing presses, guns, letters from gold seekers to their families back home, mining pans and rockers, and saddles and spurs of Pony Express riders.

The INDIAN MUSEUM, just outside Sutter's Fort, contains more than 40,000 articles illustrative of the life and crafts of California Indians.

12. STATE FAIR GROUNDS, 2nd Ave. and Stockton Blvd., are the scene of the California's State Fair.    The extensive grounds include a race track, where running and trotting races are held.

13. The site of SUTTERVILLE, the town first projected by Captain Sutter in 1844, is S. of WILLIAM LAND PARK, across Sutterville Rd. The first brick house in California was built here in 1847.    The Park contains the Zoo, a golf course, an archery range, picnic facilities and the Police Academy.

SACRAMENTO STATE COLLEGE, near the Elvas Freeway, established 1947, one of the booming state colleges, has new buildings and a campus of 265 acres.    In 1964 it enrolled 8,107 students.

AMERICAN RIVER JUNIOR COLLEGE has a campus of 153 acres at College Oak and Myrtle Ave., 8 m. from the center of the city. In 1964 it enrolled 7,631 students.

McCLELLAN AIR FORCE BASE, 10 m. northeast of Sacramento covers 2,460 acres.    Over 5,000 military personnel are stationed here and 14,000 civilian employees.    Sacramento Air Materiel Area (SAMA) here monitors overall support for thousands of North American and Lockheed-built jet fighter aircraft of USAF.    This is hq for 552nd Airborne Early Warning and Control Wing, 55th Weather Reconnaissance Squadron and 2049th Airways and Air Communications Service Group.

MATHER AIR FORCE BASE, east of Folsom Blvd., (US 50) and north of Jackson Blvd., (State 16), estab. during World War I provides advanced navigator training to the USAF.    Is hq for 3535 Navigator Training Wing and 320 Bombardment Wing of Strategic Air Command.

SACRAMENTO ARMY DEPOT, estab. 1942, on Fruitridge Road in southeastern Sacramento serves the U. S. 6th Army Area, the Far East Command and other large units.

# San Diego

*Automobile Routes:* San Diego's freeways provide easy access to all parts of the city and unimpeded driving for miles around. Interstate 8, US 80, provides 18 *m.* of straight driving from US 101 east through El Cajon. Eight lanes of the Crosstown Freeway run 7½ *m.* from Palm St. to a connection with Montgomery Freeway at 18th St. in National City, runs all the way to the Mexican border. Cabrillo Freeway, California's first, runs north to Mission Valley and becomes US 395, which continues as a freeway through Linda Vista and across Kearny Mesa past the Miramar Naval Air Station. Another freeway, State 94, leads east to a connection with Interstate 8 at Grossmont Summit.

*Transportation:* Railroads—Atchison, Topeka & Santa Fe, San Diego & Arizona Eastern. Airlines—Lindbergh Field, Pacific Hwy. & Laurel St., for American, Bonanza, Delta, National, Pacific, Pacific Southwest, United and Western. Bus lines—Continental and Greyhound. Street cars—San Diego Transit System serves metropolitan San Diego, including Chula Vista, National City, Lemon Grove, La Mesa, El Cajon, Coronado and Imperial Beach.

*Information:* San Diego Convention & Visitors Bureau, 924 Second Ave.; San Diego Chamber of Commerce, 499 W. Broadway.

*Sports and Recreation:* Baseball—San Diego Padres (Pacific Coast League, Westgate Park, Mission Valley. Deep Sea Fishing—Boats operate all year from Imperial Beach, Municipal Sportfishing Pier, Mission Bay. Sport fishing from Mission Bay eligible for prizes in derby, April through November; registration required; also prizes are given in Yellowtail Derby from San Diego Bay, March 27 through September. Boating—Sailboat races every weekend in Mission Bay and San Diego Bay; speedboat races in Mission Bay Floodway Channel. Freshwater fishing in reservoirs and lakes, beginning March and April. Model Yacht Regatta, Mission Bay Aquatic Park, June. Surfing Contest, Santa Monica to San Diego, for prizes, July. Midsummer Regatta, Pacific Coast Yacht Assn., last days of July. Golf—San Diego has 60 golf courses; Municipal Courses in Balboa Park. Horses—National Horse Show during San Diego County Fair, Del Mar, 11 days, June-July. Del Mar Turf Club, 42 days of racing July-September. Tennis—Municipal grounds open year around; Junior Tennis Championship, Balboa Park, August. Rodeo—U.S. Marine Coast base, Camp Pendleton, June.

To Tijuana, Baja California, Mexico, via freeways (US 101) from Palm St., 16 *m.* El Toreo de Tijuana, bullfights every Sunday at 4 p.m., May 30 to Sept. 5 (or thereabouts). Information at phone 239-4711 San Diego. Also museum, chapel, corrals. Horse racing at Caliente Track, Sat. and Sun., 12 noon. Greyhound racing, Caliente Track, Wed. through Sat., 7:45 p.m., Sun., 7:15 p.m. Jai Alai, Fronton Palacio, Thurs. through Sun., 7:30 p.m.

Passports are not needed. Identification should be carried. Persons under 21 must have notarized permission from parent or other responsible person. On returning to U. S. visitor must declare merchandise bought at price paid. Total worth $100 is duty free, once in 31 days. Those traveling farther south of the border than 75 miles or staying longer than 72 hours must have a Mexican tourist card from Consulate of Mexico, 901 Bank of America Bldg., San Diego.

*Tours:* Harbor Excursion, 25-mile trip to Coronado, North Island, Embarcadero, South Bay area, etc., 2 hours daily, foot of Broadway. Tanner Tours, sightseeing buses, San Diego city and county, Tijuana, Mexico, from U. S. Grant Hotel. See and Do Tours, San Diego and Tijuana, 4 tours daily from hotels.

Mission Bay Excursion departs hourly from Islandia Hotel and Quivera Basin. R Bus weekdays to La Jolla and Scripps Cove Park, Kellogg Park, Aquarium of Scripps Institution of Oceanography, La Jolla Art Center.

Vista-Palomar Mountain Ride, to top of Palomar Mountain, usually held last week in June, has barbecue on third day at Doane Meadows, on the mountain, in which the public may participate.

SAN DIEGO (0–822 alt.) had 334,387 pop. in 1950, 573,224 in 1960, and an estimated 644,835 in 1965. Located in the extreme southwest corner of continental United States, it dates its discovery back to 1542, when Juan Rodriguez Cabrillo took possession for the King of Spain but, as the present-day San Diegoans put it, made the mistake of not staying there.  He tarried for six days in the famous bay that is now one of San Diego's avenues to fortune.  For centuries Spanish, Portuguese and Italian fisherman have made it the base of their voyaging; it is responsible for the location of the Eleventh U. S. Naval District and the anchorage of the Pacific fleet; headquarters also of the U. S. Marine Corps, First Division, and the U. S. Coast Guard.

Historically, three flags have flown over the San Diego territory— Spanish of the discoverers until 1825, when Mexico broke the hold of Spain; United States after 1846.  San Diego was within easy reach of the adventuresome Spanish explorers—navigators like Don Sebastian Viscaino, who camped on Ballast Point in 1602, and Franciscan fathers with holy zeal for converting the heathen Indians.  The padres arrived with Fra Junipero Serra and established the first of the California missions, San Diego de Alcala, July 18, 1760, 227 years after Cabrillo's landfall, in what is now Presidio Park.  Some say Fra Marcos came from the desert side in 1539, but this lacks exactitude.  Portola, sent by the Spanish to govern this settlement, erected the Presidio for protection; today only rolling mounds in Presidio Park tell where the first walls stood. Within six years Fra Serra found his mission church too remote from the Indian tribes he wished to convert, so he moved into Mission Valley, eight miles up the San Diego River.  There the Indians killed Fra Jaume and burned the church in November, 1775; five years later a new mission had been erected on the site.  Here the padres had the first irrigation system in California. (*See Index for Mission San Diego de Alcala*)

Hides were the chief stock in trade during these early years and Spanish settlers were the traders.  The English sloop *Discovery* touched the port in 1793 without disturbance, but the Yankee vessel *Lelia Byrd* was caught smuggling out otter skins and exchanged volleys with the Spanish battery at Ballast Point.  Cattle, originally introduced by the padres, roamed the hills and their useful hides were called California banknotes. A busy adobe village with men who carried the hides, as well as the usual horde of men in uniform who attended the governor—San Diego was a capital now—grew up in what is today called Old Town.  The first Mexican governor of Alta California was General Jose M. Echeandia, who arrived in October, 1825.  In 1846 American Marines from the sloop of war *Cyrano* landed, took over the stockade of the Presidio and called it Fort Dupont after the ship's captain.  Mexicans organized as the California Rangers threw them out; Commodore Robert F. Stockton returned, defeated the Rangers and rebuilt the Presidio as Fort Stockton. In December Brig. General Stephen W. Kearny, U.S.A., marched from Fort Leavenworth with a troop and suffered defeat by the Mexicans under General Andres Pico at San Pasqual. He moved on to San Diego and the American flag has flown there ever since.

On March 21, 1850, San Diego was incorporated as a city. To the hide business was added something else—trading in whale oil. There were so many whales in San Diego harbor at certain seasons that small boats were in danger of capsizing while crossing. The gray whales from the Arctic came to Baja California to bear their young, and even today, when their numbers have been greatly reduced by man, they still put on a show passing Cabrillo National Monument on Point Loma during the winter. But the principal provender of San Diegoans was fish—of which the seas were full—and the vast hauls of tuna by Portuguese and Italian fishermen have made the city a great canning center. A new town grew up, in competition with the Old Town, and was nicknamed Davis' Folly for its promoter, William Heath Davis. A fire burned down a lot of the old houses of the Old Town, but the adobes survived. In 1885 the Santa Fe railroad made San Diego its western terminus. By 1887 it had 40,000 people, then the boom collapsed and by the 1890 count there were only 17,000. The halt was temporary; by 1910 expansion set in again, industries flourished and San Diego became an important manufacturing center and shipping port. Stimulated by the building of Lindbergh's *Spirit of St. Louis* and Glenn Curtis' first seaplane flight it pioneered in the aerospace age. But if one asks San Diegoans what is the principal asset of their city they will reply: the climate.

San Diego has known great prosperity and industrial expansion since World War II, besides gaining many retired persons attracted by the comfortable climate, which had an average temperature of 62.1° in 1964 and only 87 days completely clouded. Within the last few years large-scale building construction has been changing the city's profile as tall office structures have risen, major industries have come and educational institutions and churches have multiplied. In 1964 San Diego issued construction permits for 95 public buildings, 66 churches, 774 commercial and industrial buildings, 5,222 apartments and 7,004 houses.

The new COMMUNITY CONCOURSE began taking shape in 1965, with the City Hall, the Convention Hall, the Civic Theater and the Civic Garage as the major units. The Civic Theater seats 3,500. The 11-story parking garage is considered an unusual example of municipal enterprise, costing $21,000,000. The skyline is changing with the erection of the United States National Bank Bldg., 25 stories; the First National Bank Bldg., 25 stories; the Electronics Capital Corp., 24 stories, and Home Tower, 18 stories.

General Dynamics Corp., with more than 17,000 employees, is San Diego's largest industry, its divisions including the Astronautical, employing 3,300 scientific engineers; the General Atomic, the Corvair and the Electronics. General Atomic Division maintains the large JOHN JAY HOPKINS LABORATORY for nuclear research south of Del Mar and west of US 101. Other large industries are the Ryan Aeronautical Co., the Rohr Corp., the Solar Division of International Harvester Co., and National Steel & Shipbuilding Co. A Navy Supply Ship, 581 ft. long, 17,500 tons, was in the recent output of the shipbuilders. The Lindbergh plane, *Spirit of St. Louis,* was built by Ryan. The SAN DIEGO AEROSPACE MUSEUM was opened in the Municipal Bldg. in 1961.

In addition to industrial expansion San Diego has become a major educational center, with nine college campuses. The development of the UNIVERSITY OF CALIFORNIA unit at La Jolla, is expected to embrace 12 distinct colleges. CALIFORNIA WESTERN UNIVERSITY, opened 1952, had 2,014 students in 1964. The UNIVERSITY OF SAN DIEGO, opened 1954 by the Roman Catholic Church on a 221-acre campus at Alcala Park, has a College for Women, a College for Men and a Law School. The oldest institution, SAN DIEGO STATE COLLEGE, founded 1897, had 16,299 students in 1966. There are five junior colleges, four opened since 1960.

The Eleventh U. S. Naval District also has helped prosperity of city and county. The growth of naval installations is credited to the equable climate, the location at the southwest point of continental United States, and the magnificent land-locked harbor. Here are located the Naval Electronics Laboratory, the Naval Radio Station, the Recruiting Depot of the U. S. Marine Corps, the Naval Air Station of North Island, the Naval Air Station of Miramar, the Naval Amphibious Base, the Naval Training Center, the Naval Sonar School, the Naval Hospital of Balboa Park and the Supply Depot. Camp Pendleton of the Marine Corps is located in the county. The fleet adds to the attractiveness of San Diego as a tourist center, since naval units, including aircraft carriers, are open to visitors on weekends.

## POINTS OF INTEREST

BALBOA PARK, entrance Laurel St. and Sixth Ave., cultural and recreation center, was the site of the expositions of 1915-16 and 1935-36. Its principal attractions are the FINE ARTS GALLERY and the SAN DIEGO ZOO. The Gallery, a Spanish Renaissance building has canvasses by El Greco, Murillo, Sorolla, Rubens, Goya, Zuloaga, Matisse, Henri and Bellows. *Open weekdays except Mondays, 10-5; Sundays, 1-4.* The ZOO occupies 100 acres and exhibits 4,500 animals of 1,200 species, many of them free behind moats. *Guided bus tours take 40 min.* The CHILDREN'S ZOO is a special attraction. Other features of Balboa Park:

AEROSPACE MUSEUM, in the Food & Beverage Bldg. ALCAZAR GARDEN, with Moorish-style fountains. The BOWL, home of Summer Symphony, Starlight Musicals and Ballet. CABRILLO BRIDGE over Canyon, 450 ft. long, 110 ft. high. HALL OF CHAMPIONS, in the House of Charm, memorabilia of athletes. MUSEUM OF MAN, anthropological, esp. Indian exhibits. MUSEUM OF NATURAL HISTORY, fossils,

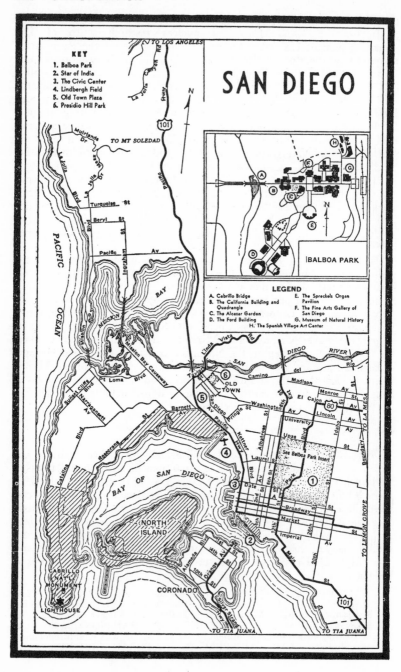

# SAN DIEGO

### KEY

1. Balboa Park
2. Star of India
3. The Civic Center
4. Lindbergh Field
5. Old Town Plaza
6. Presidio Hill Park

### LEGEND

A. Cabrillo Bridge
B. The California Building and Quadrangle
C. The Alcazar Garden
D. The Ford Building
E. The Spreckels Organ Pavilion
F. The Fine Arts Gallery of San Diego
G. Museum of Natural History
H. The Spanish Village Art Center

BALBOA PARK

mounted birds and mammals, shells, water colors. OLD GLOBE THEATRE, home of Community Theatre and National Shakespeare Festival, June-September. PHOTOGRAPHIC ARTS BLDG. SPRECKLES ORGAN PAVILION, open-air amphitheater. SPANISH VILLAGE ART CENTER, workshop of artists.

CIRCLE ARTS THEATRE, Clairemont Mesa Blvd. at Highway 395, a theater in the round, annually produces six musicals, *June-September*. In a recent season it produced *West Side Story, Oklahoma!, Camelot,* and *Most Happy Fella.*

LINDBERGH FIELD, Pacific Highway between Laurel and Sassafras Sts., a 287-acre airport dredged from the Bay, commemorates Lindbergh's famous flight in the *Spirit of St. Louis,* made by Ryan in San Diego.

OLD TOWN PLAZA, Calhoun and Wallace Sts. is the original center of town. At the Art Fiesta in June artists exhibit their work here. Old houses include:

CASA DE CARRILLO, 4136 Wallace St., an adobe of 1820. CASA DE BANDINI, 2660 Calhoun St., an adobe built 1829, enlarged 1869, headquarters of Commodore Robert Stockton, 1846-47. The Bandini daughters made the American flag that was raised on the plaza in 1846. CASA DE ESTUDILLO, Mason and Calhoun Sts., 1825, restored, now a museum. Used by Helen Hunt Jackson in her novel, *Ramona,* and called Ramona's Marriage Place. CASA DE LOPEZ, 3890 Twiggs St., a replica, now a museum. ADOBE CHAPEL, Conde St. near Congress, a restored adobe of 1850, originally Church of the Immaculate Conception, 1858.

PRESIDIO HILL PARK, Presidio. Fort Stockton was occupied by Commodore Stockton in 1846. The SERRA MUSEUM (*open 9-5, except Mondays*), 2727 Presidio Drive, of Spanish mission architecture, exhibits local historical relics. On the river flats below the hill stands the SERRA PALM, supposedly planted in 1769. EL PRESIDIO REAL (the royal garrison), bisected by Presidio Drive, the area of the original settlement in 1769, is the oldest part of San Diego.

MISSION BAY is a body of water from the Pacific Ocean covering 4,600 acres of San Diego near the outlet of the San Diego River. With MISSION BEACH it forms a recreation area and is devoted to aquatic and other sports. Sail and power boats can be rented. SEA WORLD offers entertainment with whales, porpoises, Japanese pearl divers and a Polynesian oceanarium. (*South Shores Drive off Midway Drive. Open daily from 10 a.m.*) VACATION ISLAND has model yacht basin, helicopter rides, water ski-ing. BELMONT PARK has Mission Bay Plunge, indoor heated salt water swimming pool, beach and amusement devices. Steamer *Bahia Belle* makes regular trips on Mission Bay from 7:30 p.m. on, for dancing.

NAVAL TRAINING CENTER has weekly parades open to the public. The MUSEUM near Gate 3 shows a 5-ton model of Nelson's *Victory.* Ships of the U. S. Navy, moored at Broadway and Navy piers, are open to visitors on weekends (*Harbor Drive, foot of Broadway*). San Diego Bay and the Embarcadero are the homes of the

Navy's ships, active and in mothballs. Here is the ferry to Coronado, across the Bay, and to North and West Shelter islands, Yacht Harbor and Commercial Basin.

STAR OF INDIA is a maritime museum on board a full-rigged iron sailing ship, built 1863 on the Isle of Man and docked at Embarcadero, north of B St. Pier. It carried emigrants from England to New Zealand for thirty years. (*Open 10 a.m. to 8 p.m. daily.*)

CABRILLO NATIONAL MONUMENT is near the southern tip of Point Loma, the arm of land that forms the west side of San Diego Bay. It is 10 miles from downtown San Diego and can be reached by following Pacific Blvd. (US 101) to the highway junction at U. S. Marine Corps base, thence to the monument. (*Open daily, 9 a.m. to 5:30 p.m.*) The 81 acres are administered by the National Park Service. It commemorates the discovery of the coast by Juan Rodriquez Cabrillo, September 28, 1542, and his landing in San Diego Bay, which he called San Miguel Bay. Cabrillo was a Portuguese navigator sailing for Spain. His two vessels, *San Salvador* and *Victoria,* remained here until October, when he proceeded up the coast. He died February 3, 1543, presumably on San Miguel, one of the Channel Islands. The STATUE OF CABRILLO was donated by Portugal to California September 28, 1949, the 407th anniversary of Cabrillo's landfall.

SAN DIEGO LIGHTHOUSE, on Point Loma, first lighted November 15, 1855, has tiles originally made for Fort Guijarros, built by the Spaniards on Ballast Point. The light tower, 462 ft. tall, has been reduced in height. The view from Point Loma (400 ft. alt.) over the Bay and the Pacific is most imposing.

A whale watching station here enables visitors to observe the migration of gray whales from the Arctic to the bays of Baja California, November through February.

POINT LOMA is the site of experiments by the Office of Saline Water of the U. S. Dept. of the Interior to convert sea water into fresh water. The first station was dedicated March 10, 1962, and operated successfully, providing fresh water to the city of San Diego. When the Communist regime of Cuba threatened to cut off the water supply of the U. S. Naval Station at Guantanamo, the plant was moved to Guantanamo. In March, 1966, the Office of Saline Water published specifications for a new plant at San Diego, capable of distilling 1,000,000 gallons a day. The original plant made fresh water at a cost of $1.16 per 1,000 gallons. It used the flash evaporation process, in which sea water is boiled, the steam collected and condensed and passed through thirty-six evaporators, each at lower air pressure, to recover the heat of boiling for secondary use.

# San Francisco

*Airport and Terminals:* San Francisco International Airport, 12 *m.* south of Post Office on US 101 Alt. Southern Pacific and Western Pacific Rys., Ferry Bldg., foot of Market St. Southern Pacific Coast Route and Peninsular commuting service, Third & Townsend Sts. San Francisco-Oakland Bay Bridge terminal, Fifth & Mission Sts. Electric interurban to San Mateo, Fifth & Market Sts. Greyhound Bus Lines, Fifth & Mission Sts. Greyhound Bus Lines, Peninsula and Marin County, Seventh & Jessie Sts. Northwestern Pacific Ry., same. Greyhound Bus Lines, Marin County commuting service, Sansome & Sacramento Sts. Santa Fe Passenger Terminal, Fourth & Mission Sts.

*Beaches:* Aquatic Park, foot of Van Ness Ave.; Baker's Beach, foot of 25th Ave.; China Beach, foot of 27th Ave.; Ocean Beach, Great Highway; Gilman Beach, foot of Gilman Ave. Fleishhacker Pool, Great Highway and Sloat Blvd., open daily 9 to 5; swimming pool, 1,000 ft. long, 150 ft. wide, warm salt water.

*Bridges:* Golden Gate Bridge. Approaches at Marina Blvd., Richardson Ave., and Park Presidio Drive. San Francisco-Oakland Bay Bridge, passenger terminal at Mission, First & Fremont Sts.; Automobile approaches at Fifth and Bryant Sts., and Fremont and Harrison Sts. Motor car toll 25¢.

*Cable Car Routes:* (1) Start at Powell and Market, takes in Fisherman's Wharf and Nob Hill. (2) Powell-Hyde line, starts at Powell and Market, takes in Aquatic Park. (3) California St. line, starts at California and Market, takes in Chinatown and Nob Hill to Van Ness Ave.

*Customhouse:* Battery, Washington & Jackson Sts.

*Freeways and Expressways:* From the East, US 40 and 50 and Interstate 80 cross the San Francisco-Oakland Bridge and pass through the heart of the city. From the North US 101 crosses the Golden Gate Bridge, follows Richardson Ave., Lombard St. and south on Van Ness Ave., and after connecting with Interstate 80 turns south as the James Lick Freeway to the International Airport. Also 101 connects near the Presidio with Park Presidio Blvd., which becomes 19th Ave., after passing through Golden Gate Park and State 1. The Great Highway, which runs along the Coast from Golden Gate Park south to Sloat Blvd., becomes Skyline Blvd. and State 5.

*Golf, Public:* Lincoln Park, 33rd Ave. and Clement St. Harding Park, Sunset Blvd. Sharp Park, Skyline Blvd. Greens fees: weekdays, $1; Saturdays, Sundays and holidays, $1.25; monthly, $5.

*Museums and Hours:* M. H. de Young Memorial Museum, Golden Gate Park, open daily 10 a.m. to 5 p.m. California Palace of the Legion of Honor, Lincoln Park, open daily 10 a.m. to 5 p.m., organ recitals Saturdays and Sundays 3 p.m. San Francisco Museum of Art, fourth floor of Veterans' Building, Van Ness Ave. and McAllister Sts., open weekdays 12 m. to 10 p.m., Sundays 1 to 5 p.m. Pioneer Hall, 456 McAllister Street, open 12:30 p.m. to 4:30 p.m., Saturdays 10 a.m. to 12 m. California State Mining Bureau, Ferry Building, open Monday-Friday 8:30 a.m. to 5 p.m., Saturdays 9 a.m. to 12 m. Junior Recreation Museum, 600 Ocean Ave., open 10 a.m. to 5 p.m. (closed Sundays). Wells Fargo Historical Collection, Wells Fargo Bank & Union Trust Company, 14 Montgomery St., open 9 a.m. to 5 p.m., Saturdays 9 a.m. to 12 m.

*Official Buildings, Civic Center:* City Hall, Van Ness Ave., Polk, McAllister and Grove Sts. Civic Auditorium, Grove St., between Polk and Larkin Sts. Main Library, McAllister and Larkin Sts. Health Center Bldg., Polk & Grove Sts. Municipal Opera House, Van Ness Ave., betw. Grove and Fulton Sts. Veterans'

War Memorial Bldg., Van Ness Ave., betw. Grove and Fulton Sts. State Bldg., McAllister St. betw. Larkin and Polk Sts. Federal Office Building, Leavenworth, Hyde, Fulton and McAllister Sts.

*Post Office, Main:* Seventh and Mission Sts.

*Stadiums:* Golden Gate Park, north of South Drive opp. 34th Ave. Kezar, Golden Gate Park, Stanyan and Waller Sts. Seals (San Francisco Baseball Club), 16th and Bryan Sts. Candlestick Park, Bayshore Freeway, San Francisco Giants baseball. Cow Palace, Geneva Ave. and Rio Verde, football, hockey.

*Veterans' Administration Diagnostic Center:* Fort Miley, Seal Rock Drive and 45th Ave.

*Yachting:* Municipal Yacht Harbor, Marina Blvd., Scott and Lyon Sts. St. Francis Yacht Club, private. Model Yacht Club, Spreckels Lake, Golden Gate Park.

*Annual Events:* Shrine East-West football game, Kezar Stadium, Jan. 1; Chinese New Year celebration, one week between Jan. 20-Feb. 20; Parilia Artists' ball, Feb.; National Open Matchplay golf championship, Feb.-Mar.; Army Day, Apr. 2; Livestock and Baby Beef Show, first and second weeks in Apr.; California Spring Blossom and Wildflower Show, Apr.; Spring Yachting Reg.tta, fourth week in Apr.; Children's Festival, Golden Gate Park, May 1; Rowing Regatta, July 4; Harbor Day, third week in Aug.; Dahlia Show, Aug.; Columbus Day Festival, Oct. 12; International Livestock Exposition, fourth week in Oct.; Pacific Auto Show, Civic Auditorium, Oct. 30-Nov. 6; Opera Season, War Memorial Opera House, Nov.-Dec.; Grand National Livestock Exposition, Nov. 27-Dec. 5; Symphony Season, War Memorial Opera House, Dec.-May.

SAN FRANCISCO (6 to 933.6 alt.) the central city of the great Bay Area lies at the northern end of a narrow peninsula that has the Pacific Ocean on one side and San Francisco Bay on the other, with the Golden Gate as the only sea level entrance through the coastal mountains to the Bay. The City occupies all of San Francisco County and with islands is 56,550 sq. mi. in extent. It had a population in 1940 of 634,536; in 1950 of 775,357; by the 1960 census it had receded to 740,316 as residents moved into the smaller, less confined cities of the Bay Area. The 1965 estimate noted an increase to 755,122. The boundaries of the city have not changed in more than 100 years. On the other hand, the population of contiguous communities in San Mateo County to the south has zoomed; San Mateo County had 444,387 in 1960, including such cities as San Mateo (69,870); Daly City (44,791); Redwood City (46,290) and South San Francisco (39,418). San Francisco has a shoreline of 30 miles and includes the following islands: Yerba Buena, Treasure, Alcatraz and the Farallon group, the latter 32 miles west. About 125,000 persons living in the Bay Area outside San Francisco work in that city, 56,000 of them from San Mateo County, while 15,000 San Franciscans commute daily to places outside their city.

San Francisco is cosmopolitan. It has 10.6% of the State's foreign-born, and a history of exploration, trading, violence, enterprise, rich living; finally, it is a mighty oasis of culture. Of the foreign-born and natives of foreign or mixed parentage, Italy leads as country of origin followed, in order, by Germany, Ireland and the United Kingdom, with Europe contributing 204,201 and Asia 61,530 (1960 census).

BUILDING THE CITY SKYWARD. Although many who

work in San Francisco live in the attractive suburbs on both sides of the Bay the concentration of business activities in the heart of the city is pushing buildings skyward. San Francisco is headquarters of the great BANK OF AMERICA, which leads the nation's commercial banks with deposits of more than $13 billion, several billions ahead of the next largest, Chase Manhattan Bank and First National City Bank of New York. It is appropriate that the Bank of America should plan to have the tallest office building in the city, 52 stories, to stand on the block bounded by California, Montgomery, Pine and Kearny Sts. Its 750 ft. will make it one of the tallest in the United States. Cost was estimated at $85,000,000.

Before the Bank of America building was started the new WELLS-FARGO BUILDING, Sutter and Montgomery Sts., reached its 45th story in 1966 and became the tallest building on the West Coast.

A complex of new buildings takes the place of the old wholesale produce market on the Embarcadero, where 45 acres were allotted to the GOLDEN GATEWAY PROJECT, including 2,294 unit apartments, a 1,300 car garage and a 25-story ALCOA OFFICE BUILDING above the garage.

Rebuilding of residential areas that have outlived their usefulness began in 1959. The principal developments include: Western Addition Area One, 108 acres, a former densely-populated area of 19th century type buildings, giving way to high-rise and garden apartment buildings containing 2,187 dwelling units. Three blocks were set aside for the JAPANESE CULTURAL CENTER, first of its kind in the United States, with shops, a hotel and a Kabuki theater. There also was rebuilding of 330 acres on Diamond Heights, on the southeast slope of Twin Peaks, where unsystematic streets have been replaced by a more convenient pattern using Red Rock, Gold Mine and Fairmount Hills, for 2,427 new units of detached and apartment dwellings.

WHOLESALE MARKET FACILITIES. San Francisco is a huge wholesale market, with facilities that include 250 warehouses; 30 are public; 25 for dry merchandise, and four with more than 4,600,000 cu. ft. for cold storage, regulating the supply of perishable products from farms and orchards. The WESTERN MERCHANDISE MART, largest wholesale market center for home goods on the Coast, has more than 3,100 lines of merchandise represented and more than 100,000 registered buyers annually. The SAN FRANCISCO FLOWER TERMINAL, erected 1957 at a cost of more than $1,000,000, was the first of its kind and transacts $50,000,000 worth of business annually. Another growing business center is JACKSON SQUARE, a collection of 33 remodeled early-type buildings with 76 showrooms devoted to the work of decorative home furnishings. It is open only to buyers, designers, decorators and architects, and its exhibitors represented more than 500 manufacturers from the United States and abroad. Even more modern in its facilities is the new SAN FRANCISCO PRODUCE TERMINAL, at Islais Creek Channel, Toland, Jerrold and Selby Streets, opened in September, 1963. This complex of eleven buildings is the center for distribution of produce from the West Coast states and Hawaii. It covers 25 acres and cost more than $6,000,000. It is easily accessible from the Bay and the freight lines of three railroads. Nearby is the large U. S. MARINE CORPS SUPPLY DEPOT.

San Francisco is a major center for manufactures of the Bay Area, despite the expansion of industries to outlining areas. Its plants employ more than 55,000, second only to Alameda County, which has 68,000. The largest expansion since 1960 in the Bay Area has been in food processing, petroleum industries, electrical machinery and equipment, paper and allied products and fabricated metals. In San Francisco the largest number of employees are in manufacturing, government, services, and retailing, in that order.

HIGH SPEED TRAVEL FOR COMMUTERS. The movement of motor cars in and out of San Francisco and its sister cities of the Bay Area prompted the building of the freeways, which move traffic through the heart of the city. To provide faster means of travel San Francisco and other cities have issued bond issues to build the BAY AREA RAPID TRANSIT SYSTEM, a high speed subway. In cost and extent this almost is a counterpart of the California Water Plan. The System, in various stages of construction (1966) calls for 75 miles of track, and equipment costing nearly $1 billion. The first segment, Richmond and Hayward, 27 miles, was scheduled for 1968. The most difficult piece of engineering encompassed construction of the east-west line, under downtown San Francisco, the Bay and downtown Oakland, and through the Oakland-Berkeley hills to Concord in Contra Costa County. This includes a 3.3 mile twin-bore tunnel through the hills and a 4-mile tube under the Bay. The System when completed will include 16 miles of subways and tunnels, 24 miles of surface lines and 31 miles of elevated lines. Three counties of the Bay Area—San Francisco, Alameda and Contra Costa—are cooperating in the construction of the System. The bulk of the cost is financed by a bond issue of $792,000,000. The State has assumed cost of the transbay tube, $133,000,000, to be repaid from vehicle tolls.

From the days of '49 San Francisco has been a great banking center, the largest west of Chicago. But since the first white man came, the city's prosperity has been founded on its maritime trade. San Francisco, a port of entry since 1849, possesses one of the finest land-locked harbors in the world, 3 to 12 miles wide, with 30 miles of frontage and 15 miles of wharfage. It pulsates with activity as ships from the Orient and the South Seas disgorge pungent and aromatic cargoes, and freighters from the East Coast creakily unload steel and heavy crates of machinery. A luxury liner disembarks her fashionable cargo as a tramp steams west through the Golden Gate, bound for strange places on the seven seas. Small but self-assertive tugs toot their shrill whistles as they run in and out among the ferries plying to Oakland and other cities; occasionally a gray man-of-war rides at anchor in the Bay.

The Chinese are the most identifiable minority, although more than half of them are native-born. In San Francisco's Chinatown, the largest

Chinese settlement outside the Orient, pagoda roofs and iron-grilled balconies appear side by side with American tin roofs and straight fronts; a Chinese graduate of an American medical school practices modern surgery in competition with a native herb doctor; men and women in the dress of old China rub elbows with those in the latest occidental fashions. The old Chinatown died in the great fire of 1906. Today, it is an orderly section, where old men quietly read the latest news bulletins, laboriously printed by hand in Chinese word-signs. It is a section of restaurants catering to those who know and enjoy Chinese cuisine; of shops and bazaars selling porcelains, lacquer-work, silks, jewelry, and trinkets of every kind; of Chinese theaters and joss-houses, or temples, in which the Chinese worship as their ancestors have for thousands of years. Chinatown is at its best during the Chinese New Year's celebration; the streets are lined with flower stands, the shrines in every shop are lavishly decorated, visitors throng the many restaurants and a spirit of goodwill and revelry prevails.

The Latin Quarter, a densely populated area around Telegraph Hill, is a gourmet's paradise. Of the many nationalities in the district the Italians are the most numerous, although there is a generous sprinkling of French, Spanish, and Portuguese. In some blocks not a single sign is written or printed in English. To this section, dotted with restaurants, San Franciscans turn for a variety of foods, for embedded in the local *mores* is the custom of dining out. Another popular area for dining is at or near Fisherman's Wharf, where sea food and a view of the Bay are attractions. Italian cooking is at its best here. Nearby are available sightseeing boats that make daily tours of the upper Bay.

The Cable Cars, picturesque examples of 19th century transportation, were installed in 1873 and are prime attractions to tourists. They are propelled by a cable that runs in a slot between the tracks and is gripped by a clutch operated by the "gripman." One line begins at Powell and Market Sts. and goes to Fisherman's Wharf, Nob Hill, Russian Hill and Bay St. A second line starts at Powell and Market Sts. and reaches Aquatic Park. A third line starts at California and Market Sts., takes in Chinatown and proceeds to Van Ness. There are two turntables, where the cars are turned around by the gripman's pushing, one at Powell and Market Sts. and the other at Aquatic Park. Fare, 15¢; unlimited one-day tickets with transfer privileges, Thursday through Sunday, 50¢.

The first men known to have visited the site of San Francisco were Tamal Indians from present Marin County, north of the Gate, who braved treacherous bay tides in frail canoes to obtain salt in the marshes here. For years the Spanish sought to find a good harbor in this region to serve as a stop on the long voyage from Mexico to the Philippines, but three expeditions between 1542 and 1602 failed of their purpose. A century and a half passed before the great harbor here was discovered, quite by accident, and not by sea but by land, when in 1769 an expedition was led northward from San Diego by Don Gaspar de Portolá. A reconnoitering party was detached under the command of

Sgt. José Ortega, who with his handful of men reached the shores of San Francisco Bay in November, 1769.

Settlement began seven years later when Don Juan Bautista de Anza, with his "army" of 30 soldiers and their families, marched some 200 colonists overland to the tip of the peninsula, where they began erecting shelters in 1776. A presidio and a mission were immediately laid out; the latter was established by Father Junípero Serra and named San Francisco de Asís, later known as Mission Dolores.

For seventy years the new colony of Yerba Buena was no more than an isolated outpost, occupied largely by the military. Its few civilians and priests carried on sporadic trade in tallow and hides, sea otter and seal pelts. For the most part they lived in tents and adobe huts. The first house, it appears, was erected in 1835 by an Englishman, Capt. William A. Richardson, for whom Richardson's Bay was named. Jacob Primer Leese, an American, opened the first store in the following year; Jean Vioget, a Swiss, made the first attempt to lay out streets in the straggling settlement, which had been named Yerba Buena (good herb), for a grass that grew thickly on the sand dunes.

By 1840 the Spanish-Americans of Yerba Buena were threatened with foreign invasion by Anglo-Americans from the East. In July, 1846, within three months of the outbreak of the Mexican War, Capt. John B. Montgomery landed marines from the *Portsmouth* on the plaza, hoisted the Stars and Stripes, and took possession of the town in the name of the United States. Soon the plaza was Portsmouth Square; the street passing along it was rechristened in honor of Captain Montgomery; and Yerba Buena became San Francisco.

Some 20 nationalities and races were represented in the population of the settlement when, in 1846, a group of thrifty and energetic Mormon artisans arrived under the leadership of Samuel Brannan, who had tried unsuccessfully to induce Brigham Young to abandon Utah and settle in California. For twenty years Brannan was a powerful figure in San Francisco; in January, 1847, he established its first newspaper, the *California Star,* and later was the principal organizer of the first vigilantes. Brannan and Brigham Young continually bickered over the disposition of tithes collected by Brannan from the Mormons in California; on several occasions Young sent his Destroying Angels to seize them by force, but they were never successful. Although he amassed a fortune, Brannan became a drunkard and died in poverty.

When news reached San Francisco that on January 24, 1848, James W. Marshall had picked up a gold nugget on the South Fork of the American River, its first effect was to depopulate the town. Almost every able-bodied man hurried off to the diggings. Ships lay abandoned in the harbor as crews and, in some cases, their officers turned from the sea to dig feverishly for gold. Communications were slow, and it was autumn before the East had first account of the discovery. The news trickled north, south, and into the Middle West, setting thousands of fortune-seekers in motion toward the Golden Gate, augmented by throngs from Central and South American countries. By 1850 the city had a more or less settled population of almost 25,000, of every race, creed, and color. Those that remained in San Francisco probably profited more than miners at the diggings. Lodgings were scarce; rooms rented from $200 to $300 a month; washing cost $20 for a dozen pieces; an apple brought $5, an egg $1, a loaf of bread 75¢. Many huge fortunes had their inception in San Francisco during this era of profiteering. In the last nine months of 1849, 549 vessels dropped anchor.

Portsmouth Square became the city's amusement center. In the streets spreading fanwise from it, dozens of gambling houses opened, some in lean-tos or tents. In the early days of the rush women were so few that the passage of one down the street emptied the ubiquitous saloons and gambling dens. Theatrical performances and other amusements were rare; gambling and drinking were the sole diversions left to the miners.

Six great fires devastated the town within four years; one in 1850 consumed 18 blocks of frame houses in 10 hours. Necessity directed attention to fireproofing of buildings and paving of streets, for in the rainy season the latter were quagmires into which horses, wagons—and fire engines—sank.

After the fires came the days of vice and extensive gambling. Dozens of saloons studded Portsmouth Square and environs, each a gambling hall and a recruiting station for the brothels of the world-notorious Barbary Coast on Pacific Street, from Sansome Street to Grant Avenue. This area was closed in 1917. Those were the days of laissez-faire, of easy-come-and-go, of goodnatured tolerance, not unnatural in a city where fortunes were made and lost overnight, where a bartender one day might be a nabob the next. San Francisco has always appreciated its eccentrics.

In nearly half a century afterward changes have given Portsmouth Square a respectability consonant with its historic importance. Memories other than those of violence and depredations now cluster around it. It has been the scene of public meetings and parades. A monument in the form of a bronze galleon dedicated to Robert Louis Stevenson now stands in the Square.

The city might smile at the gambling and the Barbary Coast, but it could not condone gangsterism married to crooked politics. The first Vigilance Committee was formed in June, 1851, an organization that at the height of its influence had several thousand members, who took the law into their hands, hanged the worst offenders, and inspired a general exodus among the others. A grand jury indicted nine of the vigilantes, but they stood high among the "respectables" and the serious charges against them were dropped. During the relatively peaceful years between 1852 and 1854 the Committee disbanded.

By the summer of 1855 the city was again swarming with swindlers, thieves, highwaymen, and thugs. A few months later U. S. Marshal George W. H. Richardson was shot and killed by Charles Cora, an Italian gambler, with powerful political supporters. A demand for his immediate trial and conviction was led by thundering editorials in the

*Bulletin,* established in October, 1855, under the editorship of James King of William, who signed his name thus to distinguish himself from other James Kings. He was bitterly opposed by James Casey, rival editor and local politician, who, exhausting his verbal weapons, shot King down as he emerged from the office of the *Bulletin* in May, 1856. Confident of protection, Casey immediately gave himself up to the authorities.

A crowd began to collect at the police station, summoned by the tolling of a fire bell. As it grew, confederates rushed Casey to the county jail, where a large force of armed deputies and militia was mustered to defend him from the mob. Before nightfall a new Vigilance Committee was begun, and during the night it enrolled some 2,000 members, all sworn to absolute secrecy, under the leadership of William T. Coleman and other members of the Vigilance Committee of 1851. An executive committee of thirty-three was formed; all vigilantes, soon numbering almost 10,000, were equipped with arms and organized into military companies; headquarters were established in a mercantile building on Sacramento Street, which was fortified with cannon as "Fort Gunnybags." Unlike its predecessor, the committee of 1856 was a deliberately planned and well-knit organization.

Four days after the shooting of King, the vigilantes surrounded the jail and demanded Casey and Cora, both of whom were surrendered without a struggle. They were tried, found guilty, and hanged from a window in Fort Gunnybags on May 22, two days after the death of King, whose large funeral procession was directed down Sacramento Street past the dangling bodies. A cleansing and reform of the local government was instituted, with salutary effects for years to come, and the Vigilance Committee disbanded in August, 1856. San Francisco continued to be a lively and lighthearted city, but with less physical and moral violence.

An era of expansion followed, broken by brief excitement during the Civil War, when California heatedly debated whether to support the Union cause or set itself up independently as the Pacific Republic. Oratory waxed loud and feeling ran high in the city until the State legislature voted against secession. During these years Bret Harte contributed to the *Golden Era* and in 1864 became secretary of the U. S. branch mint; Mark Twain paused momentarily, one jump ahead of his creditors; a dozen newspapers were established, and as many weeklies, some of which are still extant. From the fabulous Comstock and Mother lodes, from the Central Pacific Railroad, came the vast fortunes that Leland Stanford, Charles Crocker, Collis P. Huntington, Mark Hopkins, James Flood, William S. O'Brien, John W. Mackay, James G. Fair, William C. Ralston, "Lucky" Baldwin, and others spent on ornate Victorian palaces on Nob Hill, Lucullan banquets, enameled carriages with liveried footmen, great country estates, and on the fabrication and lubrication of political machines as relentless as steam rollers. There were frequent scandals and occasional duels. Dennis Kearney addressed large crowds of workers on the sand lots; the base of San

Francisco's development as a union town had been laid previously with the formation of the Working Men's Trade and Labor Union.

In 1873 the lumbering horsecars and the unique round "balloon cars" were supplemented with and later superseded by Andrew Hallidies' cable cars. The city's population doubled in two decades, and San Francisco celebrated in 1894, with the Midwinter Exposition, its first great carnival, in "Opal City," Golden Gate Park. Weathering the depression of 1893-96 and its attendant strikes, it became increasingly the railroad and maritime center of the Pacific Coast. In those days a traveler from any point along the coast between the Mexican and Canadian borders simply asked for a ticket to "the City" with complete assurance that he would be routed to San Francisco. Although Seattle profited most, the Klondike gold strike brought new wealth and residents; by 1903 the city had a population of 425,000, and plans were laid for immediate improvements and future expansion.

Steps were being taken for rezoning, for the creation of additional public parks, for the elimination of slum areas, when at 5:16 o'clock on the morning of April 18, 1906, the great San Andreas fault, extending up and down the coast, settled violently. The greatest earthquake ever to strike California shook San Francisco to its foundations. With the breaking of gas and water mains, fire broke out and for three days roared through the city unchecked; it was finally brought under control by dynamiting buildings along Van Ness Avenue. An early edition of a Los Angeles newspaper, so it is said, carried a huge headline, "San Francisco Punished!" In New York, Will Irwin, an adopted son, sat down and wrote sadly of "the city that was."

But the city's decease, like Mark Twain's, was greatly exaggerated, although it had suffered a staggering blow. Casualties included 500 dead and missing; four square miles, including virtually all of the business district, were destroyed—an area of 497 blocks, some 30,000 buildings. Damage was estimated at 500 million dollars, of which 200 millions remained a net loss after payment of insurance. Food and clothing for the thousands of homeless were rushed from all parts of the United States; Europe and Asia contributed millions to relieve suffering.

The ruins were still smoking when plans for reconstruction were started. The first contract for a new building was signed six days after the disaster. "Don't talk earthquake, talk business," read placards on the streets. New building and fire laws insured that no catastrophe of such proportions could occur again. Within three years, in spite of graft scandals and civic turbulence, 20,000 new buildings had been constructed. Within seven, a new City Hall and a new Public Library were under way, and electric tramways had replaced the cable lines except on the hills.

For four years before the fire the government of San Francisco had been dominated by the notorious Ruef-Schmitz machine. Masquerading as the Union Labor Party, the ring was financed by gambling houses, saloons, the brothels of the Barbary Coast—but principally by the city's traction and utility corporations. The attack on the machine was launched by Hearst and followed up by Fremont Older of the San Francisco *Bulletin,* Rudolph Spreckels, and James D. Phelan. The newspaper campaign was interrupted by the earthquake and fire, but shortly after was resumed and the charges against Ruef and Schmitz led to their indictment. Other figures prominent in promoting public utilities were named codefendants. Francis J. Heney was appointed special prosecutor and detective William Burns was retained. The trials dragged on for two years amidst considerable violence, in the course of which Older was kidnapped, Heney was shot (to be replaced by Hiram Johnson), and the residence of an important witness was dynamited. The trials ended with the conviction of Ruef, and the cases against his codefendants, the utility promoters, were not pressed.

In 1914 the city acquired control of the Hetch Hetchy watershed, near Yosemite, ultimately to supply 400,000,000 gallons of water daily. The opening of the Panama Canal on August 15, 1914, was of immense benefit to the city's maritime trade. In 1915 the Panama-Pacific International Exposition at "Rainbow City," built beside the Presidio on the Marina was inaugurated. At its close, the exposition presented the city with funds to build the Municipal Auditorium.

The history of the years from 1915 to the building of the bridges and the planning of the Golden Gate International Exposition for 1939, has been in part a story of labor unrest, particularly during World War 1 and the depression of the 1930's.

The bombing of the Preparedness Day Parade made the year 1916 a black one. The conviction of Tom Mooney and Warren K. Billings for the bombing on questionable evidence inspired a world-wide protest that was not allayed until 1939, when Governor Olson unconditionally pardoned Mooney. On the following day Mooney led a large parade up Market Street, lined for miles on both sides with cheering crowds. Above the cheers screamed the siren on the Ferry Building, opened full blast, as it had been to announce the bombing 23 years before.

In 1936 the Pan-American Airways initiated weekly passenger service from San Francisco to the Orient by means of giant flying "clipper ships," but the crowning accomplishment of 1936 and 1937 was the completion of the two great bridges—the San Francisco-Oakland Bay Bridge in November, 1936; the Golden Gate Bridge in May, 1937. The site of the Golden Gate International Exposition of 1939 was Treasure Island, created by dredging the bay near Yerba Buena Island.

San Francisco has been associated in larger or smaller measure with the careers of many who have made names for themselves in the arts, notably, Jack London; Isadora Duncan, the dancer; George Sterling, the poet; Bret Harte; Henry George, founder of the single tax movement and at one time managing editor of the local *Times.* It has been the subject of innumerable stories, novels, and non-fiction works. First described as an unlovely Spanish settlement by Richard Henry Dana in *Two Years Before the Mast,* the city has been pictured in Frank

Norris' *McTeague,* Gertrude Atherton's *Rezanov,* Stewart Edward White's *The Rose Dawn* (vigilante days), Dashiell Hammett's *The Maltese Falcon,* and William Saroyan's stories. From the days when audiences showered gold nuggets and pouches of gold dust at a popular performer's feet, when a theater was built and given to Edwin Booth to keep him from deserting his public, when "road shows" skipped from Chicago to Salt Lake City and San Francisco and back East again without a stop, the city has been stage-struck and music-mad. It has a club founded by artists and art lovers, which has grown and prospered until it possesses massive quarters on a downtown street, and it has coteries of poets, who read their works in bookshops.

Perhaps some of San Francisco's glamor has been drowned under a flood of neon lights; skyscrapers have replaced some of the rambling buildings mellowed by time and weather; and old-timers lament the happy-go-lucky days "before the fire." But it is still a gay city, convivial and dignified, for its gaiety has always worn a silk hat; and it heatedly objects to the nickname " 'Frisco," used by unsuspecting outsiders. San Francisco has granite qualities as well; fogs cannot dampen its ardor; earthquakes, political scandals, and labor wars have failed to impede its progress as a great financial and industrial center, of major importance in world trade.

## POINTS OF INTEREST

### MARKET STREET AND DOWNTOWN

The FERRY BUILDING, at foot of Market St., completed in 1903, has a 240-foot central tower topped with a four-faced clock and a set-back "belfry" and cupola in four stages. Each dial of the clock is 22 feet in diameter, with numerals 3 feet long. The clock was stopped at 5:16 a.m., April 18, 1906, by the earthquake, and remained so for more than a year until repairs were completed. The building is occupied by the WORLD TRADE CENTER, headquarters of San Francisco's vast international business, with offices for consulates, brokers, import-export firms. The Board of State Harbor Commissioners and the library of the State Fish & Game Commission are located here and the State Division of Mines maintains a GEOLOGICAL MUSEUM. Along the entire second floor corridor is a huge relief map of California.

The EMBARCADERO, formerly called East St., is a crescent-shaped street lined with piers and wharves paralleling the bay shore for three and one-half miles. For all the years of the city's history, until 1963, this was the location of the wholesale produce market. This has been moved to new quarters at Islais Slip Channel. The cleared 45 acres have been allotted to the GOLDEN GATEWAY PROJECT of apartment buildings and the 25-story ALCOA OFFICE BUILDING.

The SAN FRANCISCO-OAKLAND BAY BRIDGE, San Francisco approach from Bryant and 5th Sts., was completed in 1937 and reconstructed in 1964-1965, by the State Dept. of Public Works. Spanning the broad waters of the East and West Bay, this magnificent steel and concrete bridge serves as a giant traffic artery between San Francisco and the neighboring towns in Alameda County. It stretches its lofty spans from the anchorage in San Francisco to Yerba Buena Island, and continues at an oblique angle to the eastern approaches of Berkeley and Oakland. The bridge proper, including the island crossing, is approximately 4.5 miles long; with approaches, 8 miles.

The bridge is a double-deck structure. In 1965 improvements costing $35,000,000 were completed, increasing its capacity over the 40,-000,000 vehicles using it annually, with separate decks for one-way traffic. Rails were removed from the lower deck. The western section of the bridge, 216 feet above the water, consists of two suspension spans, fastened midway between San Francisco and Yerba Buena to a steel and concrete anchorage, the latter rising 502 feet from the rock floor of the bay. The two center spans on each side of the anchorage are 2,310 feet in length. The bridge is illuminated at night with strings of yellow sodium vapor lights, the brilliant rays of which can penetrate any fog.

The Port of San Francisco has the advantages of the finest harbor on the West Coast. It is located on the Bay, which ships enter by the Golden Gate, an opening 4,200 ft. wide. The Port has 42 piers and terminals, including terminals specially adapted for handling cotton, grain, bananas, copra and paper. It handles more general cargo than any port on the Pacific Coast, the preeminence in tonnage held by Richmond, Los Angeles and Long Beach being based on petroleum products. Sixty miles of belt railway serve transport needs and 102 berths are available for ships.

The Immigration & Naturalization Services of the Dept. of Justice reported 155,866 persons arrived and departed at San Francisco harbor in 1964; 87,330 were United States citizens and 68,536 were aliens. In 1963 imports reached 6,446,000 short tons and exports 2,961,000. Coastwise receipts were 11,946,000 tons and shipments 8,472 tons.

Japan is the largest customer of the city and Bay Area, buying 28% of all the exports of the Port in a typical year. It also is the largest

---

LOCATION OF BUILDINGS ON MAP OF
DOWNTOWN SAN FRANCISCO

1, 2. To Ferry Building and Embarcadero. 3. To San Francisco-Oakland Bay Bridge. 4. San Francisco Terminal. 5. Donahue Monument. 6. Wells Fargo Collection. 7. Lotta's Fountain. 8. Sheraton-Palace Hotel. 9. Telephone Building. 10. Pacific Coast Stock Exchange. 11. Russ Building. 12. St. Patrick's Church. 13. Cable Car Turntable. 14. Native Sons Monument. 15. Union Square. 16. St. Francis Hotel. 17. 415 Sutter Building. 18. Native Sons Building. 19. The Olympic Club. 20. The Bohemian Club. 21. Mark Hopkins Hotel. 22. Fairmont Hotel. 23. Pacific Union Club. 24. Grace Cathedral. 25. Kong Chow Temple. 26. Sun Sung Theater. 27. Chinese Hospital. 28. Bank of Canton. 29. Tin How Temple. 30. Old St. Mary's Church. 31. St. Mary's Square. 32. Portsmouth Square. 33. Montgomery Block. 34. Golden Era Building. 35. Hotaling Building. 36. Stevenson and Booth Houses. 37. Pioneer Park, Coit Tower. 38. SS. Peter and Paul Church. 39. San Francisco Art Institute. 40. Fisherman's Wharf.

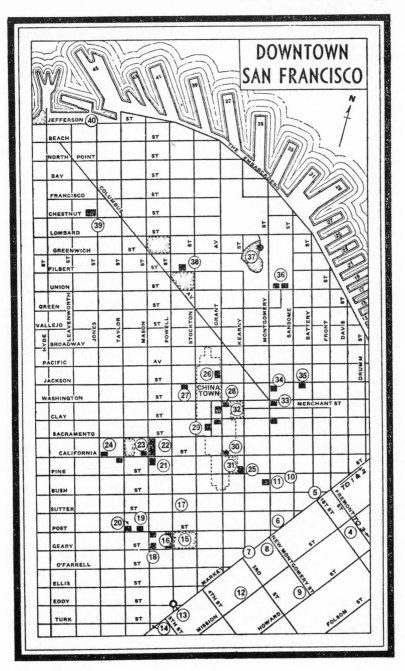

DOWNTOWN
SAN FRANCISCO

N

exporter to the Port, 25% of the total. Exports to Japan were industrial machines, steel scrap, raw cotton, tallow, chemicals, oil seeds, hides, residual fuel oil and iron ore. Imports from Japan were radio and television parts, electrical machinery, wool products, rubber goods, textile and steel mill products. The second largest customer for exports is the Republic of the Philippines. Five international shipping corporations have home offices in San Francisco.

YERBA BUENA ISLAND a U. S. Government reservation of 140 acres, now a depot of the Lighthouse Service, the roadway passes through a double-deck tunnel, 76 feet wide by 50 feet high, the largest bore tunnel in the world, and emerges on the east sector of the Bay bridge. The main cantilever span of 1,400 feet has 510-foot anchor arms. East of this span are five truss spans, each 509 feet in length, and 14 truss spans, 291 feet long.

The SAN FRANCISCO TERMINAL BUILDING, at 1st and Mission Sts., completed in 1939, the final unit of the Bay Bridge Electric Railway facilities, was constructed under the jurisdiction of the California Toll Bridge Authority by the State Department of Public Works. This building is virtually an enclosed system of ramps and stairs connecting the elevated tracks of the Interurban Electric (S.P.), the Key System, and the Sacramento-Northern Railways, which enter the terminal over a looping viaduct from the bridge to the streetcar concourse and the street. There are six railway tracks on the upper level, arranged in pairs, with long 700-foot platforms between. The tracks and platforms are 164 feet wide, roofed over with large skylights. From these platforms spacious ramps and stairs lead to a mezzanine concourse.

The DONAHUE MONUMENT, intersection of Market, Bush, and Battery Sts., locally known as the Mechanics' Monument, is the work of Douglas Tilden, noted deaf-mute sculptor. Executed in bronze and dedicated to Peter Donahue, founder of one of the city's first iron works, it consists of a fountain surmounted with a group of three artisans struggling to force the blade of an enormous mechanical punch through plate metal. A tablet set in the pavement at the foot of the monument marks the 1848 shoreline of Yerba Buena (San Francisco).

The WELLS FARGO HISTORICAL COLLECTION is in the Wells Fargo Bank, 420 Montgomery St. Among the relics are a stagecoach shipped around the Horn in the 1850's; the massive scales used in the Wells Fargo office at Columbia, Tuolumne County, and said to have weighed 55 of the 87 million dollars worth of gold mined in the Mother Lode; the mining tools used by James W. Marshall, gold discoverer.

The WELLS FARGO BUILDING, Sutter and Montgomery Sts., built by the Dillinham Corp., with the Wells Fargo Bank as its principal tenant, was the tallest on the West Coast, 43 stories, when erected in 1965-66.

LOTTA'S FOUNTAIN at intersection of Market, Kearny, and Geary Sts., transformed from a watering trough for horses to a drinking fountain for people, is of bronze, in the ornate style of the 1870's. It was presented to the city in 1875 by Lotta Crabtree, the beloved actress of gold rush days. Here on Christmas Eve, 1910, Luisa Tetrazzini sang carols to great throngs.

The SHERATON-PALACE HOTEL, the former Palace Hotel, Market and New Montgomery Sts., has figured in history and romance. The original was destroyed by the fire of 1906 and the present building was erected on its framework in 1910. At one time guests arrived by carriage in its Palm Court. President Warren G. Harding died here Aug. 2, 1923. Maxfield Parrish's Pied Piper mural is in the Buffet. A modern hotel recently built is the SAN FRANCISCO HILTON, O'Farrell and Mason Sts., at the Airlines Terminal, a house of 1,200 rooms.

PACIFIC COAST STOCK EXCHANGE, San Francisco Division, corner of Pine and Sansome Sts., consists of a one-story structure, housing the trading room, and an adjoining ten-story office building, both designed in the neo-classic style. Flanking the Doric entrance loggia of the trading room are heroic sculptures by Ralph Stackpole. Above the entrance to the office on Sansome St. is a bas-relief figure by the same sculptor. The interior of the trading room is adorned with concrete bas-reliefs by Robert Boardman Howard, while in the luncheon club room are frescoes by Diego Rivera, representing the growth of California's agriculture, mining, and industry.

The RUSS BUILDING, Montgomery St. between Bush and Pine Sts., is an imposing 31-story skyscraper of stone and terra cotta facing, with modified Gothic detail. Before the fire of 1906 this site was occupied by the Russ House, once San Francisco's finest hostelry, built by Christian Russ, a pioneer of 1847 and proprietor of an immensely popular beer garden and concert hall in the early days. The building was designed by George Kelham.

ST. PATRICK'S CHURCH, Mission St. between 3rd and 4th Sts., is sometimes called "the most Irish church on this continent." Constructed of brick, with a slender tower and steeple, it is the fourth building and the third site of this parish, established in 1851 by Father Maginnis, then the only English-speaking priest in San Francisco. The interior of the church is finished in green translucent Connemara marble and Caen stone, for which the late pastor, Father Rogers, searched Ireland. On the floor is a mosaic, *The River of Life*. The crucifix and vestments are by Mia Cranwill, Irish artist, after designs of the sixth and eighth centuries.

The NATIVE SONS MONUMENT, at intersection of Market, Turk and Mason Sts., by Douglas Tilden, is a tall granite shaft surmounted by a bronze figure holding an open book inscribed "September 9, 1850," the date of California's admission to the Union; below stands a male figure holding a flag with a new star for California. The column was presented to the city in 1897 by Sen. James D. Phelan, then mayor.

UNION SQUARE, on Post St. between Stockton and Powell Sts., extending to Geary St., originally a huge sandbank known as O'Farrell Mountain, was presented to the city in 1850 by John W. Geary, first mayor of the American City. The plot, leveled and landscaped, was given its present name because of pro-Union meetings held here before and during the Civil War. In 1864 the Mechanics' Institute held a fair in the pavilion on the square; after the 1906 disaster the square was dubbed "Little St. Francis" because of the temporary building erected here to house guests of the St. Francis Hotel. In the center of the square is the VICTORY MONUMENT, by Robert Ingersoll Aitken, commemorating Dewey's victory in Manila Bay, a 96-foot granite shaft. Under the Square is a four-story garage for 1,500 cars.

The ST. FRANCIS HOTEL, SW. corner of Post and Powell Sts., a gray stone structure, is one of San Francisco's largest and best-known hotels. Almost destroyed by the 1906 fire, its walls were scarcely cold when a banquet was held in the White and Gold Room to celebrate the beginning of reconstruction. The rebuilt hotel has a Borgia Room, a replica of the room of that name in the Vatican at Rome. Farther up on Powell St. the SIR FRANCIS DRAKE adds to the hospitality of this area.

The 450 SUTTER BUILDING, at 450 Sutter St., is a modern 25-story skyscraper of steel, glass, and terra cotta, designed by Miller and Pflueger. Light buff in color, it has windows set flush with the outside walls, accentuating the vertical mass. Ancient Mayan hieroglyphs and stylized ornament carry out the decorative motif in both exterior and interior detail.

The NATIVE SONS BUILDING, at 414 Mason St., a red brick building with terra cotta facing, is the headquarters of the Native Sons of the Golden West, an organization of native-born Californians. Around the two entrances are tile plaques representing California explorers and pioneers. The building has an auditorium seating 1,300, frequently used for lectures.

The OLYMPIC CLUB (*private*), at 524 Post St., is a buff brick building with the club's "winged O" symbol carved over the white stone entrance. The club was organized in 1860 and claims to be the oldest amateur athletic club in existence. In the club is a large swimming pool supplied with salt water directly from the Pacific Ocean. Annually on New Year's Day it holds a modified beach marathon along the ocean shore, after which participants take their first plunge of the new year.

The BOHEMIAN CLUB (*private*), NE. corner Post and Taylor Sts., a massive dark red brick building, houses one of San Francisco's best known artistic organizations. Originally, its membership was limited to distinguished artists and writers, but others interested in the arts are now permitted to join. Every January the club sponsors a free exhibition of paintings by its members, one of the rare occasions when women are admitted to any part of the building, and during its "Midsummer Jinks" at Bohemian Grove on the Russian River (*see TOUR 2a*) holds an annual Grove Play, with text, music, and performance by members. On the Post Street facade is a bronze bas-relief memorial to Bret Harte, the work of Jo Mora.

The MARK HOPKINS HOTEL, SE. corner California and

# The Natural Setting

CALIFORNIA TREE, 231 FEET TALL, MARIPOSA GROVE

WINDBLOWN CYPRESS, MONTEREY PENINSULA

COVE AND BEACH AT LA JOLLA

MOUNT SHUCKSUN AND PICTURE LAKE

CUFFY'S COVE, NORTH OF SAN FRANCISCO

JOSHUA TREE (YUCCA) JOSHUA TREE
NATIONAL MONUMENT, NEAR PALM SPRINGS

PALMS ON ROAD NEAR REDLANDS,
WITH MOUNT SAN JACINTO

AERIAL TRAM MOVES UP TO SAN JACINTO
NEAR PALM SPRINGS

TWIN LAKES, MAMMOTH LAKES AREA

DEVIL'S
POSTPILE
(BASALT) ON
MIDDLE FORK,
~~SAN JACINTO~~
~~RIVER~~
SAN JOAQUIN
RIVER

POINT ARENA LIGHTHOUSE, MENDOCINO COUNTY

SEA ELEPHANTS
DOZING,
SAN NICOLAS
ISLAND

YOSEMITE FALLS, WITH ICE FORMING

Mason Sts., a buff brick skyscraper, combines baronial French and Spanish Renaissance styles. The hotel, perpetuating the name of Mark Hopkins, one of the railroad "big four," occupies the site of the old Hopkins residence, a "magnificent monstrosity" destroyed in 1906. The Room of the Dons contains murals of early California history by Maynard Dixon and Frank van Sloun. The Peacock Court has a lunette of *Leda and the Swan,* by Ray Boynton, done by the ancient method of encaustic painting. The Top of the Mark is a nationally famous rendezvous.

The FAIRMONT HOTEL, NE. corner of California and Mason Sts., was built in 1906, by Mrs. Herman Oelrichs, daughter of James G. Fair, one of the bonanza kings of the Comstock Lode. In this massive granite hostelry are the TERRACE PLUNGE (*open 10 a.m.-10 p.m. daily*); the CIRCUS ROOM, with murals by Esther Bruton; and two rare sixteenth century Florentine mirrors, the only examples of this type in America, brought from the Castello de Vincigliata, Florence, by Mrs. Oelrichs. The hotel contains a theater seating 20 .

The PACIFIC UNION CLUB, NW. corner of California and Mason Sts., the only one of the brownstone Nob Hill mansions little damaged by the great fire, was formerly the home of James C. Flood, bonanza king who began his career as a saloonkeeper.

GRACE CATHEDRAL, NE. corner of California and Jones Sts., is an uncompleted gray stone building of modified Gothic design, the work of Lewis P. Hobart. The spire will rise 560 feet above sea level, and in size its nave will exceed that of any English cathedral. The carillon, donated by Dr. N. T. Coulson, was used in the Golden Gate International Exposition before being installed in the bell tower. Off the south nave, the Chapel of Grace, a delicate structure in Gothic style and the gift of Ethel Sperry Crocker, contains a tenth century stone altar from Brittany and a fourteenth century carved stone table used as a credence table. The cathedral stands on the site of homes built by Charles Crocker, the "hurry-up man" and hard driver of the "big four," and his son, William H. Crocker, a banker. Heirs of the family donated the land to the Protestant Episcopal Diocese of California in 1910.

## CHINATOWN AND OLD SAN FRANCISCO

The KONG CHOW TEMPLE (*open 10 a.m.-1 a.m. daily; voluntary offering*), 520 Pine St., is the largest Chinese joss house in America and is one of two in San Francisco open to the white public. Dedicated to the hero Quan Dai, it has two altars; before one tea is served every morning; on the other are paper and pencil for recording worshipers' requests. On the balcony, overlooking the courtyard, is the "prayer tree" in which written prayers may be placed.

The SUN SUNG THEATER, 1021 Grant Ave., is the current name for what was once the Mandarin Theater, first in the United States to give Chinese plays. Today it presents motion pictures. When an occasional Chinese play is performed the stage is devoid of curtains or scenery, and "props" are brought on and removed throughout the performance by nonchalant stagehands; there are no actresses, for all female roles are played by males; the musicians, when not playing, sit on the side of the stage and sip tea; meanwhile, the audience comes and goes, interrupts the players at will, and chews watermelon seeds continuously.

The CHINESE HOSPITAL, on Jackson St. between Stockton and Powell Sts., a four-story stone building, is the only one in the United States. It is completely modern in equipment and procedure and largely staffed by Chinese doctors and nurses. There are 57 beds, including a small maternity ward. White patients are welcome.

The BANK OF CANTON, 743 Washington St., occupies a highly ornate building with a three-tiered pagoda roof bright in vermillion, green and gold. The structure formerly was occupied by the Chinese Telephone Exchange.

The TIN HOW TEMPLE (*open 10 a.m.-1 a.m.; voluntary offering*), 125 Waverly Pl., the oldest Chinese joss house in San Francisco, is situated on the fourth floor of the building (*ring for priest or assistant*), because no human creation but a roof is allowed to stand above the gods. This joss house was established by Day Ju, one of the first three Chinese to arrive in San Francisco. The altar to Tin How, Queen of the Heavens and Goddess of the Seven Seas, was installed on their ship for daily worship and later removed to the temple. The present main altar, covered with gold leaf and intricate carvings representing the life of Confucius, is many centuries old. In the temple are ceremonial wands resembling ancient battle-axes; massive bronze urns containing prayer sticks; and Yuen Bo Pon, a fireplace in which written messages to the gods can be burned and thus recorded in the ether.

OLD ST. MARY'S CHURCH, at NE. corner Grant Ave. and California St., in the heart of Chinatown, is a red brick structure of Victorian Gothic design. Material for the structure was brought both from China and around the Horn; in 1855 bells arrived, were hung, and blessed. The church, the main part of which was built by Archbishop Alemany in 1854, later became the Roman Catholic Cathedral, and in 1894 was transferred to the Paulist Fathers. The congregation is still white although there is a Chinese branch of the church at Stockton and Clay Streets. The clock in the California Street tower bears the inscription, "Son, observe the time and flee from evil."

ST. MARY'S SQUARE, opposite Old St. Mary's Church, formerly explained the inscription on the church tower, for it was once St. Mary's Alley, a part of the old red-light district. This grass-covered municipal square is a favorite romping place for Chinese children. In the center is a stainless steel and concrete STATUE OF SUN YAT SEN by Beniamino Bufano.

PORTSMOUTH SQUARE, at Kearny St. between Washington and Clay Sts., the birthplace of San Francisco, was Candelario Miramontes' potato patch in 1833; then it became the Spanish and Mexican Plaza. A plaque in the NW. corner commemorates the raising of the American flag there July 9, 1846, by Capt. John B. Montgomery of the

U.S.S. *Portsmouth,* for which the square is named.    In the square also is a BRONZE GALLEON, mounted on granite, "to remember Robert Louis Stevenson."

The MONTGOMERY BLOCK, at 628 Montgomery St., built in 1853 by Gen. H. W. Halleck with bricks and cement brought in clipper ships from England and France, is the oldest of San Francisco's "fireproof" buildings.    Once the home of the Stock Exchange, the rambling structure, affectionately nicknamed the "Monkey Block," is now the heart of the city's Bohemia; many artists and writers have had studios in the building.    During the fire of 1906 it narrowly escaped dynamiting by the Army.

In 1938 the revived "Order of E Clampus Vitus," the gold miners' burlesque fraternity, placed a commemorative plaque on the site of Parker's Bank Exchange Saloon, at the Washington Street corner of the block, where Duncan Nichol invented the celebrated drink, Pisco Punch.    This saloon was frequented by the mad "Emperor" Norton and the reform editor, James King of William, who was brought here after being shot by Casey.

Joshua A. Norton, the "Emperor," was born in England in 1819. At the age of 30 he arrived in San Francisco with $40,000, which he pyramided to a quarter of a million.    Attempting to corner the rice market, he and his colleagues lost their fortunes.    Norton went into seclusion for several years; when he reappeared, his mind was unbalanced, and he soon became the favorite ward of the city.    Clad in an old uniform and military cap, with a small sword dangling at his side and a stick or umbrella in his hand, trailed always by two mongrel dogs, Bummer and Lazarus, he was a familiar figure on the downtown streets.    Norton declared himself Emperor of the United States and Protector of Mexico: one of his frequent proclamations dissolved the Democratic and Republican parties in the interests of peace; another dissolved a steamship company because a purser, violating imperial privilege, had summarily put him ashore; a third called the public's attention to the duty of replenishing his wardrobe.    He was the first to "propose" a bridge across the bay.    He was permitted to eat, drink, and amuse himself gratis, and to draw checks up to 50 cents on San Francisco banks. These checks were always honored, and Norton added to his cash by selling 50-cent bonds and by collecting "taxes."    He dropped dead on the street in 1880 and was given an elaborate funeral by the city.

The GOLDEN ERA BUILDING, 718-20 Montgomery St., is a three-story stone and brick building of which the interior has passed through various stages and is now a decorator's showroom.    It is Victorian in style, painted white, with high narrow upper windows above a dentate molding.    It is the last of San Francisco's noted ship buildings. These odd structures were built around abandoned ships drawn up and fastened at what was then the waterfront.    Bret Harte worked as a compositor on the *Golden Era* and wrote his earliest works here.

The HOTALING BUILDING, at 451 Jackson St., a three-story stone and brick building designed in the style of the French Second

Empire, was occupied for many decades after 1866 by a wholesale liquor concern. The Hotalings sold it in 1945. Some of the original furniture is still in use—desks, chairs, and bookcases of beautiful hardwood in excellent condition. After the earthquake and fire of 1906, a popular ditty by Charles K. Field ran:

> If, as they say, God spanked the town
> For being over-frisky,
> Why did He burn all the churches down
> And spare Hotaling's Whiskey?

The STEVENSON AND BOOTH HOUSES, at 287 and 289 Union St. between Sansome and Montgomery Sts. (*accessible only on foot*), are pointed out as the former homes of the author and the actor. Actually, the decrepit little frame house at 287, with steeply pitched roof and gingerbread trim, was the home of Edwin Booth's hostler (Booth himself lived on Pine Street), and the modernized stucco studio building next door was Booth's stable. Robert Louis Stevenson, however, did live at 289 during the early 1870's.

In PIONEER PARK, on the crest of Telegraph Hill, stands the COIT MEMORIAL TOWER (*elevator service 9-4 daily; adm. 25¢*), erected in 1933 with a legacy left by Mrs. Lillie Hitchcock Coit. It is a cylindrical concrete structure 210 feet high, affording a fine view of the city and bay. The frescoes on the walls of the ground floor, depicting life and labor in California, are by the Public Works Art Project. A plaque at the main entrance marks the site of "the inner signal station—1849, and the first Western Telegraph Station—1853."

SS. PETER AND PAUL CHURCH, at 650 Filbert St., facing Washington Square, is of Romanesque design, with two 191-foot turreted towers of terra cotta. It was built in 1924 by Charles Fantoni. Two mosaics at the front entrance depict Columbus disembarking on American soil and Dante at work on the "Paradiso." In the heart of San Francisco's Italian section, this church is known locally as the "Church of the Ten Commandments," because part of the motion picture of that name was filmed here.

SAN FRANCISCO ART INSTITUTE, 800 Chestnut St., of modified Italian Renaissance design was constructed in 1926 of unpolished concrete, with a campanile. Founded 1871, it comprises its College, Gallery, Art Bank of the work of West Coast artists, headquarters of the Artist Association and the Anne Bremer Memorial Library of more than 9,000 volumes. The College (1874), known as the Mark Hopkins Institute of Art when housed in the Hopkins mansion on Nob Hill, and later as the California School of Fine Arts, is an affiliate campus of the University of California and offers the degrees of bachelor of fine arts and master of fine arts. It is the oldest art school west of the Mississippi and enrolls more than 700 students. In the gallery a huge fresco by Diego Rivera illustrates the painting of a mural. After World War II the school became the West Coast birthplace of abstract expressionism. Faculty members at that time included

Clyfford Still and Mark Rothko and among their students were Richard Diebenkorn, Frank Lobdell, John Hultberg and James Weeks, all of whom later taught at the school. During the same period Ansel Adams started the first course in photography as a fine art offered in an American college. In the 1950's the school, with Diebenkorn, Weeks, Elmer Bishcoff, Nathan Oliveira and David Park on the faculty, became known as the center of San Francisco figurative painting.

FISHERMAN'S WHARF, on Taylor St. at the Embarcadero, is the embarking and landing point for the city's many Italian fishermen. Brightly painted fishing boats, mostly in blue, the Virgin's color, lazily tug at their anchors or mooring lines as weather-beaten old men, wearing large gold earrings, mend nets with wooden needles on the wharf. When vessels arrive with their day's catch, the wharf seethes with activity as dealers and fishermen haggle over prices. Along Taylor Street are sidewalk stands displaying shellfish, and at the curb big iron cauldrons boil large freshly caught crabs to be eaten there or carried away by the purchaser. East of Fisherman's Wharf at Pier 43 is moored the three-masted sailing vessel BALCLUTHA, a veteran of many voyages around Cape Horn, now restored as a maritime museum, open daily.

## MARINA AND PRESIDIO

ST. BRIGID'S CHURCH, at SW. corner Van Ness Ave. and Broadway, probably the only church in the world built of old paving blocks, is constructed of slabs of hewn granite that served as pedestrian crossings in the days of cobblestone streets. It is of Romanesque design, with a terra cotta entrance carved with liturgical symbols. Henry A. Minton was the architect.

OCTAGON HOUSE, 2645 Gough St., is headquarters of the California chapter of the Colonial Dames of America and has an exhibit of Colonial furnishings. Built 1864, it is two-storied with a cupola and eight sets of double windows on each floor. The rooms are square, with the angles taken up by closets.

AQUATIC PARK (*open daily*), at foot of Polk Street and Van Ness Ave., San Francisco's marine recreation center, was built by the WPA and opened in January, 1939. The landscaped park spreads along a semicircle of beach on a cove in the lee of Black Point. The municipal pier, circular in shape, encloses a half-mile stretch of water for swimming, boating, and racing. Inland rises the white Casino, four stories high toward the sea, with ends rounded like a ship's stern, and stories, or decks, semielliptical in shape. Its seaward face is almost entirely of glass. On the lowest floor are bathing facilities to accommodate several thousand persons a day. In the Polk Street entrance is a large slate sculpture executed by the Federal Art Project; the central lounge room on the second floor is decorated with murals by the Federal Art Project, picturing marine and undersea life; elsewhere are statues of St. Francis and Sun Yat Sen. Opening from the main lounge is a glass-enclosed dining salon in yacht club motif. Above, on the smaller floors or decks, are other lounges and dining rooms, with windows like portholes on the land side, and wide expanses of glass toward the sea. On each side of the Casino are stone bleachers and a promenade running the length of the beach. At the eastern and western extremities of the playground are 50-foot towers in modernistic style, containing loud-speakers to broadcast sporting events and music.

FORT MASON, at Van Ness Ave. and Bay St., is an Army Sup-ply Depot and contains the residences of the commanding general and ranking staff officers of the Ninth Corps Area. This 67-acre reserva-tion was once the home of John C. Frémont, who built a house here in 1853, since occupied by 36 commanding officers.

The ARMY TRANSPORT DOCKS, northwest shore of the reservation, are three in number, one 500 feet long, the others 650 feet; each year they receive and ship to and from Pacific and Far East posts about 45,000 officers and enlisted men.

YACHT HARBOR, at Divisadero St. and Marina Blvd., is pro-tected on the north by a narrow spit, Marina State Park. Hundreds of pleasure craft are berthed here, from small speedboats and sailboats to palatial private yachts. The ST. FRANCIS YACHT CLUB (*private*) is on the eastern tip of Marina State Park. To the south of the harbor is MARINA PARK, fronting the bay, a long grass-covered strip, popular on Sundays with promenaders.

The PALACE OF FINE ARTS, last surviving building of the PANAMA-PACIFIC INTERNATIONAL EXPOSITION of 1915, stood near Marina Blvd. between Jefferson and Baker Sts. until 1964, when it was demolished. It had a Roman rotunda that in recent years was used for indoor tennis. It is to be rebuilt.

The PRESIDIO (*open: night parking prohibited*), entrance gate at Baker and Lombard Sts., once the garrison of Spanish soldiers protecting the mission, is a U. S. military reservation of 1,542 acres, and the head-quarters of the Sixth U. S. Army. Within the reservation is the LETTER-MAN HOSPITAL for service men and their families. The CEMETERY is the second largest national cemetery in the United States. One woman interred here is not a veteran's wife—Pauline Cushman Tyler, a young actress, who was a Union spy during the Civil War and later commis-sioned an honorary officer of the Army. At the southern anchorage of the Golden Gate Bridge stands FORT WINFIELD SCOTT, on a site fortified since 1776, but from which a hostile shot has never been fired. It was originally known as the Castillo de San Joaquin. In 1846 Frémont stole over from the Sausalito and spiked its guns, and the American flag was hoisted over the Presidio on July 9 of that year. In 1854, the bluff at Fort Point was graded to the water's edge, and the present fort, somewhat similar to Fort Sumter, was completed in 1860. The OFFICERS' CLUB, once the Spanish comandante's headquarters and the oldest building standing in San Francisco, is a long low adobe structure built about 1776; the Presidio MARKER nearby records its history. In front of the marker stand two old Spanish guns, named "Poder" and "San Pedro," bearing the Spanish coat-of-arms and inscribed, "Lima, Peru—1673."

On August 27, 1915, in a destructive fire at the Presidio, the wife and three daughters of Gen. John Pershing lost their lives.

The GOLDEN GATE BRIDGE, the main San Francisco approach from the Presidio, was designed by Joseph B. Strauss, and completed in May, 1937 at a cost of $35,500,000. The huge web-like span, illuminated at night with strings of yellow sodium vapor lights, suspended high above the water, links northern California to the peninsula of San Francisco. Two enormous steel towers, erected on concrete piers, act as props and hold up the giant "clothes line" cables from which the bridge is hung. The massive steel framework of these towers consists of two soaring steel legs which rise in five tapering stages, with heavy diagonal and horizontal cross braces or struts to the cable saddles at the top. The legs of the tower, each 32 feet by 53 feet, rise 746 feet above the water (the height of a 65-story building). The skeleton superstructure of the towers, together with the steel framework of the bridge floor and the sweeping cables, forms an impressive silhouette.

The main central span, 4,200 feet in length, is the second longest span in the world. The minor spans at either end are each 1,125 feet in length. Above are the two sagging cables, each more than a yard in diameter and fastened at both shores to huge concrete anchorages. The suspended floor structure is 90 feet wide and 25 feet deep, and supports a reinforced concrete six-lane roadway and sidewalks. The center of the span clears water by 220 feet. It is crossed by US 101 (*toll 25¢*).

At the south end of the bridge proper are a large steel arch passing over Fort Winfield Scott, four 125-foot truss spans, and finally the Toll Plaza, from which lead two roads, one to the northeastern section of San Francisco and the other southward. The Marin County end of the bridge has five 175-foot truss spans and is in Fort Baker, a U. S. Army reservation.

TEMPLE EMANU-EL, Arguello Blvd. (First Ave.) between Lake and Clay Sts., erected in 1925, is a huge, cream-colored concrete edifice of modified Byzantine design with a red tile dome. Standing in the Pacific Heights residential district, this temple is the home of the largest Jewish congregation in San Francisco.

## MIDTOWN

The UNITED STATES POST OFFICE, NE. corner of 7th and Mission Sts., one of the few public buildings to withstand the fire of 1906, is Italian Renaissance in design. Constructed of granite, it was built in 1905 under the direction of James Knox Taylor, then supervising architect of the Treasury Department. The first floor corridors, decorated by skilled artisans brought from Italy, are of Pavonezza marble trimmed with glass mosaic; the floors and ceiling are of mosaic tile.

The CIVIC CENTER, just off Market St. and roughly bounded by McAllister, Franklin, Hayes, and Leavenworth Sts., has a number of municipal and Federal buildings designed in Italian Renaissance style grouped about it.

The FEDERAL OFFICE BUILDING, McAllister St. between Leavenworth and Hyde Sts., extending to Fulton St., is a five-story colonnaded structure built around a central court, with entrances at the north and south ends. The building was erected in 1936 and houses practically all the Federal offices of San Francisco except the Post Office, and those in the Appraisers Building.

The SAN FRANCISCO PUBLIC LIBRARY (*open 9 a.m.-10 p.m. Monday through Friday; 9 a.m. to 6 p.m. on Saturday; 1:30-5 Sun.*), SE. corner McAllister and Larkin Sts., is on the site of the old City Hall and Public Library destroyed in the 1906 fire. Designed by George Kelham, the new granite structure was completed in 1917, the Carnegie Foundation donating a third of the cost. The principal facade is designed with a colonnaded loggia at the second story, adorned with coupled Ionic columns and sculpture. The entrance hall and staircase, and the main delivery room on the second floor are finished in travertine marble. Along the second floor corridor are low-toned murals of California scenery by Gottardo Piazzoni; in the reference and reading rooms are murals by Frank Vincent DuMond, depicting various phases of the State's history. In addition to the Main Library, there are a business library and 26 branches. Collections total more than 1,000,000 volumes, more than half of them in the Main Library. They include the Nat Schmulowitz Collection of wit and humor, 16,000 volumes; the Max Kuhl collection of fine printing and binding; an important collection of Californiana; the Phelan Collection of California Authors; the Richard Harrison Collection of Calligraphy and Lettering and the Eric Hoffer Papers.

The STATE BUILDING, McAllister St. between Larkin and Polk Sts., is a five-story granite structure of neo-Classic design, housing the San Francisco offices of the State government, chambers of the California Supreme Court, and the Hastings College of Law of the University of California. The LAW LIBRARY (*open only to students and alumni, 9-1, 2-5 daily*) contains about 46,000 volumes.

The CIVIC AUDITORIUM, facing Grove St. between Polk and Larkin Sts., is constructed of granite in the Italian Renaissance style. Its main hall seats 9,000 and smaller halls seat 1,600. A $6,000,000 renovation was completed in 1965. Adjoining is Brooks Hall, an underground exhibit hall, and the 1,500-car Civic Center Garage, also underground.

MARSHALL SQUARE, Hyde St. from Fulton to Grove Sts. and extending to Larkin St., used frequently for open-air meetings, is the city's nearest approach to a "Hyde Park." The PIONEER MONUMENT, at the southeastern corner, was donated in 1894 by James Lick, founder of the Lick Observatory. The work of Frank Happersberger, it is really a group of five monuments, the central figure representing California and the others characterizing significant periods in the State's history.

The HEALTH CENTER BUILDING, SW. corner Polk and Grove Sts., constructed of granite and marble, is designed in harmony with the civic group and contains the Central Emergency Hospital, a detention hospital, and the offices of the city health department.

The WAR MEMORIAL GROUP, facing Van Ness Ave., consists of twin buildings erected as a unit in 1932—the MUNICIPAL OPERA HOUSE, the first owned by a municipality, and the VETERANS WAR MEMORIAL BUILDING—both constructed of granite, and designed in modified Italian Renaissance style, with arched and rusticated first story walls, Doric colonnaded loggias and ribbed metal roofs. The Opera House seats 3,285 and possesses the most modern equipment. The basement has an emergency hospital and a buffet. The War Memorial Building, commemorating San Franciscans killed in the World Wars, is headquarters for numerous veterans' organizations. In the SOUVENIR AND TROPHY GALLERY (*open 9-9 daily*) on the first floor stands a granite shaft with sod from a soldier's grave inside it and a perpetual light burning over it. The gallery contains relics of the Civil, Spanish-American and World Wars. The fourth floor of the building is occupied by the GALLERIES OF THE SAN FRANCISCO ART ASSOCIATION (*open 1-10 daily*), in which permanent and traveling exhibitions of all schools and periods are presented.

The CITY HALL, facing Polk St. between McAllister and Grove Sts., is modeled after the U. S. Capitol, its dome being 13½ feet higher. Designed by Bakewell and Brown in the Italian Renaissance style, it is constructed of granite; the interior is finished with carved sandstone and marble. Its two main facades have central Doric pedimented pavilions, flanked by long two-story colonnades. The high drum of the central dome is adorned with a colonnade of the same order, and topped with an elaborate cupola. In the interior, winding stairs lead up from the center of a vast rotunda, with balconies on the four upper floors looking down into the lobby. Facing the building is a formal French garden with flower beds, fountains, tiled walks, and flocks of pigeons. Left of the Polk Street entrance is a bronze STATUE OF LINCOLN by Haig Patigan, while at the McAllister Street side is a MONUMENT TO HALL MCALLISTER, a distinguished lawyer of early days; it is the work of Robert Aitken.

The LIBRARY OF THE CALIFORNIA HISTORICAL SOCIETY (*open 12:30-4:30 Mon.-Fri.; 10:12 Sat.*), 456 McAllister St., opened in 1938 and conducted in conjunction with the Society of California Pioneers, contains rare prints and other material illustrating the State's history, including "State documents" by "Emperor" Norton, a notice of an exhibit of "the head of the renowned bandit, Joaquin Murrieta, and the hand of three-fingered Jack, notorious robber and murderer"; solid ivory poker chips used by the bonanza kings in their $75,000 games at the old Palace Hotel; the watch of Luis Antonio Arguello, first Mexican governor of California; and the whiskey flask that Jack London carried on his celebrated voyage on the *Snark*.

ST. MARY'S CATHEDRAL, NW. corner of Van Ness Ave. and O'Farrell St., a brick building of Victorian Gothic design, dates from 1891 and is the seat of the Roman Catholic diocese of San Francisco. The church narrowly escaped destruction in 1906 when flying brands ignited the belfry. Two priests climbed to the roof and extinguished the blaze by means of buckets and a garden hose.

In LAUREL HILL CEMETERY, entrance at Bush St. and Presidio Ave., dating back to 1854, are the graves of Senator David C. Broderick, William C. Ralston, James King of William, Senator James G. Fair, Senator William Sharon, and many other pioneers and mining kings. Samuel Woodworth, author of "The Old Oaken Bucket," has a tombstone here, although his body has been removed. On the tombstone of Judge Sanderson, an early jurist, is the inscription, "Final Decree."

The MEMORIAL COLUMBARIUM (*open 9-5, daily*), entrance, 1 Loraine Court, is a cream-colored building constructed entirely of stone, metal, and glass. The structure has a metal dome and is adorned with mosaic ornaments and stained glass windows. The only columbarium in San Francisco, its niches contain the ashes of many thousand persons.

The SAN FRANCISCO COLLEGE FOR WOMEN, at Turk St. between Parker and Masonic Aves., opened in 1932, is a Roman Catholic institution offering a four-year arts course to girls of any denomination. The buildings, of Gothic design, are finished in pale pink stucco, and the campus occupies the whole arc of Lone Mountain, one of the city's major hills. Enrollment, 1964, was 570.

The UNIVERSITY OF SAN FRANCISCO, at Fulton St. between Clayton St. and Parker Ave., founded as St. Ignatius College in 1855, was granted a State charter in 1859. In 1930, on the 75th anniversary of the founding, the name was changed to the University of San Francisco. After the acquisition of the present 20-acre campus, the cornerstone of the first of its pinkish concrete buildings was laid in 1920. The university, coeducational and with an enrollment of 4,701 in 1965, consists of a day school for men, and a law school and night school for both men and women. Although the institution is controlled by the Jesuits, its faculty and student body are nonsectarian.

ALAMO SQUARE, on Fulton St. between Steiner and Scott Sts., and extending to Hayes St., was part of the squatter's stronghold held by Charles and Jack Duane in the 1850's. Charles P. (Dutch Charlie) Duane, a lieutenant in the political army of Senator Broderick and chief engineer of the fire department, narrowly escaped hanging by the vigilantes in 1851 after he shot and killed a theater manager who had refused him free admission. The second Vigilance Committee "deported" him from the city, and the municipality finally gained possession of the property in 1877 after nine separate suits.

SAN FRANCISCO STATE COLLEGE, at 124 Buchanan St., has rebuilt its campus in recent years and favors one-story buff-colored concrete buildings in the Mediterranean style. On the campus are tennis and basketball courts, and the Roberts Stadium. This was originally a teachers' college, being distinguished in the field by the pioneer work of Dr. Frederick Burk; authorized in 1937 to offer a B.Ed. degree, in 1965 it had a faculty of 1,000 and 14,630 students.

The UNITED STATES MINT, NW. corner of Duboce Ave. and Buchanan St., completed in 1937, replaced the old mint at 5th and Mission Streets, where Bret Harte once worked. The present structure, designed by Gilbert Stanley Underwood, has walls of reinforced concrete and granite. The severity of the walls is relieved by a row of medallions below the fourth floor, representing all coins issued by the United States. Precautions against robbery include electrically controlled doors, a gun tower, and tear gas lines. The Mint stands on a 100-foot cliff, with foundations set deep into solid rock, and was considered impregnable until January, 1939, when two schoolboys by daylight scaled a wall by means of a drain pipe, slipped through a window opened for ventilation, and threw out a copper plate, "just to see if it could be done." The original Mint (1876) a classical adaptation with a portico and six fluted columns, has been stripped of insecure ornamentation and shelters the U. S. General Services Administration.

The SPANISH WAR MONUMENT, just below Market St. in

the parkway that intersects Dolores St., a Tilden sculpture, erected in honor of California's volunteers in the Spanish-American War, represents an equestrian Victory of heroic size, with a young soldier marching beside her.

The MISSION DOLORES (*open 9-5 daily, May-Nov.; 9:30-4:30, Nov.-Apr.*), Dolores St. between 16th and 17th Sts., was founded in 1776 by Father Junípero Serra. First named in honor of St. Francis of Assisi, common usage soon gave it the name of Misión de los Dolores from a nearby marsh known as Laguna de Nuestra Señora de los Dolores (Lagoon of Our Lady of Sorrows). The first mass was sung five days before the Declaration of Independence was signed at Philadelphia. The adobe building was begun in 1782 and is an unusual example of Spanish mission architecture. Due to the angle of the coping line on the façade, the original roof line is believed to have been changed. This rectangular structure is constructed of stone covered with plaster. The façade is designed with a simple arched entrance and a superimposed surface colonnade of crudely shaped Doric columns. A thin iron railing once extended along the cornice above the doorway. The side and rear walls have been covered with clapboards. No nails were used in its construction; the wooden beams of the arched roof were tied with leather thongs by Indian workmen. The Indians painted the interior walls with vegetable colors that are still bright after more than 150 years. The high hand-carved altar covered with gold leaf was brought from Mexico in 1870. The earthquake of 1906 damaged the building, but failed to raze it.

Behind the mission in the high-walled, flower-covered GRAVEYARD are buried many of the famous dead of San Francisco's early days, including Don Luis Arguello, a native San Franciscan and the first governor of California under Mexican rule. Argüello was a brother to Concepción Argüello, famed in California legend and stories because of a romantic love affair with Rezanov, the Russian plenipotentiary. The graves of Casey and Cora, hanged by the vigilantes in 1856, are a reminder of lawless days. Many of the graves are unmarked.

MOUNT OLYMPUS, 17th and Clayton Sts., is crowned with the LIBERTY MONUMENT, the work of the Belgian sculptor, Antoine Wiertz, and a gift of Adolph Sutro in 1887. Sometimes called "The Triumph of Light," it portrays a woman symbolizing Liberty, with a male figure, representing Despotism, cowering at her feet. The figure's torch and sword, it is said, were removed by ship masters because the statue threw them off their course to the Golden Gate.

TWIN PEAKS (910 alt.), at Twin Peaks Blvd., appear in legends of the Tamal Indians, and were called by the Spanish Los Pechos de la Choca (the breasts of the Indian maiden). The figure-eight drive around the peaks affords a wide view from all vantage points. At night the lights of the city twinkle far below. The long tunnel constructed under Twin Peaks by the Municipal Railway, leading from Market Street to the St. Francis Wood and Ingleside districts, stimulated the development of these residential districts.

MEDICAL CENTER OF THE UNIVERSITY OF CALIFORNIA, Parnassus Ave. between Arguello Blvd. and 4th Ave., encompasses teaching, research and health services.   In 1964 it had 1,993 students and a staff of 1,750, plus several thousand employees.   There are schools of medicine, dentistry, nursing and pharmacy.   The principal buildings are the Medical Sciences Bldg. (1958); the Herbert C. Moffitt Hospital (1955), 465 beds; the University of California Hospital; the Clinics Bldg. (new addition 1965); the Medical Research Bldg. (1951); the Health Sciences Instruction and Research Bldg. (1965) and the Postgraduate Dental Center.   There is also a Student Union. The Langley Porter Neuropsychiatric Institute is operated by the California Dept. of Mental Health and School of Medicine.   Also in the Center are eight research organizations and a library of 220,000 volumes.   The Center's fifty clinics have about 125,000 patient visits annually.

PRESBYTERIAN MEDICAL CENTER, which traces its history back to the first medical school of 1858, took over the facilities of Stanford University Hospital and Medical School when the latter moved to Palo Alto in 1960.   A new Research Bldg. was completed in 1964 and a School of Dentistry begun.   Plans for expansion include a new medical school and hospital.

SUTRO FOREST, a large wooded tract NW. of Twin Peaks was planted by Adoph Sutro in the 1870's and has been enlarged by additional plantings by school children.   Mount Sutro, 909 feet high, occupies the center of the area.

## ALONG THE OCEAN

LINCOLN PARK, entrance at 33rd Ave. and Clement St., extends northwest almost to the ocean.   A flagpole in the park marks the western terminus of the Lincoln Highway (US 30-40).   Here at one time were the city's cemeteries, each segregated according to nationality. The old Chinese Cemetery is now the Municipal Golf Links, on which the first hazard is the sacrifice stone, a stone oven used for roasting pigs to propitiate the gods.   Near the 15th green is a 25-foot bronze monument to Mrs. Rebecca H. Lambert, founder of the Ladies' Seamen's Friend Society.

The PALACE OF THE LEGION OF HONOR (*open 10-5 daily; free organ recitals 3-4, Sat. and Sun.*), adjacent to the golf links, is designed in the manner of the Legion of Honor Palace in Paris.   The entrance to the classic U-shaped building is through an impressive forecourt in form of an Ionic peristyle with a massive central arch.   It was constructed as an art museum and presented to San Francisco in 1924 by Mr. and Mrs. Adolph B. Spreckels as a memorial to the California soldiers who lost their lives in World War I.   The palace has 19 galleries exhibiting permanent and loan collections of paintings, sculpture, porcelain, tapestry, antique furniture and prints; it also has a little theater, two enclosed gardens, and a pipe organ used for recitals.

LAND'S END, a precipitous promontory reached by a path leading northeast from Lincoln Park along the route of the former "Scenic Route" streetcar line, has long been a favorite haunt of lovers of the sea. From here is a fine view of Mile Rock Lighthouse, a few hundred feet offshore. A section of the bridge of the U.S.S. *San Francisco* is part of a memorial commemorating the sailors who died in the battle of Guadalcanal, Nov. 12-13, 1942. Beyond Mile Rock, toward the Marin shore, is an area of ocean known as the Potato Patch, usually covered with whitecaps, which mark a navigable channel through the dangerous shoals near Golden Gate.

SUTRO GARDENS, on Sutro Heights, Point Lobos and 48th Aves. (*open daily, 9 to 5 p.m.*), was the property of Adolph Sutro, Nevada capitalist and former mayor of San Francisco. The house, built in 1879, is gone. The 20-acre garden was donated to the city by Sutro's daughter, Dr. Emma Sutro Merritt; the shrubbery is dotted with marble statues from Belgium, carried to San Francisco in ships as ballast.

The CLIFF HOUSE, on Great Highway opposite Sutro Heights, has been a noted restaurant since the first house of that name was built in 1858. The original Cliff House, bought by Adolph Sutro in 1883, was destroyed by fire in 1894, and its successor likewise in 1907. The present house, erected in 1907, was remodeled and reopened after being vacant a number of years. The building has a dining room overlooking the ocean, and a redwood cocktail bar. From the lookout platform by the Cliff House is a view offshore of the sharply pointed SEAL ROCKS, on which hundreds of "seals" (actually California sea lions) disport themselves, being protected by State law. Binoculars can be rented for a close-up view. On clear days the Farallon Islands are visible.

OCEAN BEACH, extending from the Cliff House to Golden Gate Park, is not much used for bathing at this end because of a strong undertow, but the Esplanade flanking the beach affords a broad view of the Pacific Ocean and is crowded with sun bathers on warm days. On the east side of the Great Highway below Sutro Heights is a miniature Coney Island, with restaurants and the usual attractions.

The FLEISHHACKER POOL (*open 10-5 daily*), STORY-LAND (*open 10-5 daily*), and ZOO (*open 10-5 daily*), Great Highway and Sloat Blvd., occupy a 128-acre tract. The open-air pool is 1,000 by 100 feet, with a 150-foot offset in the center for races, and contains 6,500,000 gallons of water. It has locker accommodations for 5,000, and 20 lifeguards are on duty.

On the Playground are tennis courts, a baseball field, sand boxes, a miniature steam railway, and a wading pool.

The Zoo uses the cageless plan, under which animals live in a reproduction of their natural environment with deep moats between them and the public.

MOUNT DAVIDSON (956 alt.), in Mount Davidson Park and accessible only on foot, is the highest point in the city. On the summit stands the Easter Cross of concrete and steel, 103-feet high, before which Easter sunrise services are held, attended by 60,000 persons and broadcast from coast to coast.   During Easter Week floodlights illuminate the cross.   At its base is a crypt containing relics from Palestine; the crypt is sealed with concrete mixed with water from the Holy Land. Northeast of Mt. Davidson are TWIN PEAKS, 904 and 910 ft. tall, with a panoramic Observation Point.

## GOLDEN GATE PARK

GOLDEN GATE PARK, at Stanyan St. between Fulton St. and Lincoln Way, extending to the ocean, contains 1,013 acres.   A half mile wide and more than four miles long with its "Panhandle" to the east, the park was created from bare sand dunes in the 1870's by John McLaren, a Scotsman, who was superintendent from 1887 to 1943. The park is noted for its rhododendrons; the Midwinter Fair of 1894 was held here.

KEZAR STADIUM, Frederick St. between Stanyan St. and Arguello Blvd., is a concrete bowl accommodating 60,000 spectators.   Municipally owned, it is the scene of the annual All-Star East and West football game on New Year's Day sponsored by the Shrine.   During football season the stadium is used by college teams that are not members of the Coast League.

The CONSERVATORY has a collection of rare orchids and begonias, and many varieties of ferns.   In front of the Conservatory is a large flower bed on which various messages adapted to the season or special events are spelled out with flowers.   The building, similar to the conservatory in Kew Gardens, London, was bought by popular subscription.

The M. H. DEYOUNG MEMORIAL MUSEUM houses many important art and historical collections and is expanding annually.   It is rich in Aztec, Mayan, Inca and pre-Columbian American art; has rooms devoted to the French 18th century; Flemish tapestries from the William Randolph Hearst Foundation; valuable donations by the Kress Foundation and Avery Brundage, the latter's gift necessitating a $2,275,000 bond issue for galleries.   Among the masters represented are Rembrandt, Franz Hals, Rubens, Van Dyck, Poussin, Boucher, Titian, El Greco, Velasquez, Goya, Raeburn and many others of their stature; sculptures, decorative arts and period rooms are also notable.   Near the museum, among other statues, are the ROBERT BURNS STATUE, by Earl Cummings, the JUNIPERO SERRA MONUMENT, by Douglas Tilden, and the CERVANTES MONUMENT by Jo Mora, depicting Don Quixote and Sancho Panza kneeling before their creator.

A stone BANDSTAND, the gift of Claus Spreckels, is an open-air shell in the Music Concourse; the Municipal Band presents concerts here.

The JAPANESE TEA GARDEN, an authentic reproduction of an original in Nippon, includes a *zashiki,* or Japanese home; a granite shrine with an altar; and an arched bridge built in the shape of a drum.   In and around the thatched tea houses, rice cakes and tea are sold by girls dressed in native costume.

The CALIFORNIA ACADEMY OF SCIENCES conducts a number of large scientific enterprises in the park. They include the NATURAL HISTORY MUSEUM, the SIMSON AFRICAN HALL, the STEINHART AQUARIUM and the MORRISON PLANETARIUM.

The NATURAL HISTORY MUSEUM (*open 10-4 weekdays, 10-5 Sundays and holidays*) contains departments of ornithology, herpetology, and paleontology, but visitors are mainly attracted by its mammal groups, mounted animals in social or family assemblage against natural backgrounds.   Other exhibits include flowers, semiprecious stones, butterflies, herbariums, and Indian baskets. Set in the pavement at the main entrance of the academy building are four old millstones, the oldest of which was brought around the Horn for use in a local flour mill in 1851.

SIMSON AFRICAN HALL (*open 1-5 Sun., 1-4 Wed.*), was built in 1932 to house a number of habitat groups of African mammals collected by Leslie Simson and mounted by Frank Tose, who spent many years in Africa. In the basement is an exhibit of fish, and on the second floor one of insects, neither of which is specifically African.

The STEINHART AQUARIUM (*open 10-5 daily, 1-4 in winter*), approached through an open court in which are five large pools, was named for Ignatz Steinhart, who donated $240,000 for its foundation. The large reinforced concrete aquarium contains one of the most colorful collections of live fish in the world, including many Hawaiian and Oriental specimens. Outside the aquarium is a tank in which California sea lions swim.

MORRISON PLANETARIUM is associated with the Hall of Science. Its May Treat Morrison auditorium seats 450 and presents hourly programs about the stars, displaying its views on the inside of a 650 ft. dome. The projector cost $140,000. *Closed on Mondays.*

The PRAYER BOOK CROSS, a gift of George W. Childs, Philadelphia publisher, is an Iona cross of Colusa marble, 57 feet high, designed by Ernest Coxhead and erected under the auspices of the Protestant Episcopal Diocese of Northern California. It commemorates the first Christian service held in English on the Pacific Coast, in 1579, by Sir Francis Drake's chaplain on the shore of Drake's Bay (*see Tour 1a*).

On Lloyd Lake, beyond Lindley Meadow, is the celebrated PORTAL OF THE PAST, a classic marble doorway from the A. N. Towne home destroyed in the fire of 1906. A plaque describes its history.

The DUTCH WINDMILLS, facing the ocean, at the northwestern and southwestern corners of the park, are operated by electric pumps. The water enters a reservoir two miles away to feed the park lakes.

To the left of the northern windmill is the ship *GJOA* (pronounced Yoah), presented to the city of the late Roald Amundsen, the Norwegian explorer. This tiny vessel in 1905 was the first craft to navigate the Northwest Passage, the objective of many of the early voyages to the New World.

# SOUTHEAST AND IN THE OUTSKIRTS

CANDLESTICK PARK on Candlestick Point, southeast of SAN FRANCISCO NAVAL SHIPYARD near the Bayshore Freeway (US 101) is the base of the San Francisco Giants baseball team of the National League. One of the most modernly equipped of ball parks it seats 45,000 and has six acres for parking.

The GRAND NATIONAL LIVESTOCK PAVILION, widely known as the COW PALACE, Geneva Ave. and Rio Verde St., west of US 101, is used for exhibitions, rodeos and political conventions. It seats 12,000. It is 400 ft. long, 300 ft. wide and 104 ft. high, with a rounded roof.

SAN FRANCISCO INTERNATIONAL AIRPORT, one of the largest and busiest in the nation, is located on US 101 (alt.), on the Bay Shore 14 *m.* south of San Francisco and 5 *m.* north of San Mateo. Originally built on part of the 1,376 acres of the Mills estate, it has expanded to 3,722 acres. The airport ranks fourth in volume of passenger traffic in the U. S., with 171,431 scheduled arrivals and departures and 6,414,-620 passengers in 1963. Its garage facilities (1964) are believed the largest in the world.

ALCATRAZ ISLAND (Sp. pelican) is a 22-acre site known locally as The Rock, 62 to 136 ft. above sea level. It was used until 1963 as a Federal penitentiary for the incarceration of the most dangerous and hardened criminals. It was so strongly guarded that escape was considered impossible, but two men are believed to have made an effort to escape by swimming. The island was discovered by the Spanish in 1545. In 1775 they named it Isla de Alcatraces. When the Americans took over California in 1846 the governor of California gave it to Julian Workman, who sold it to the United States government for $5,000. In 1850 it was reserved for military purposes. A lighthouse was built in 1854 and the island was fortified at a cost of $2,000,000. It was first used as a prison for military offenders in 1868 and Indian leaders were later confined there. After the Spanish-American War it became a convalescent center for soldiers arriving from the Philippines. After the earthquake of 1906 it housed prisoners from the San Francisco jails. The Dept. of Justice took over in 1934 when gangsters were terrorizing the Midwest. Among its most notorious prisoners were Al Capone, Alvin Karpis, George (Machine-gun) Kelly and Basil (The Owl) Banghart. More than 1,500 unruly prisoners were transferred there from other Federal prisons.

The Dept. of Justice has given up use of the island. The Senate authorized a Commission to determine its disposition, members being Sen. Edward V. Long of Missouri, Glenn Anderson, Lieut. Governor of California, Rep. Jeffery Cohelan of California, J. Eugene McAteer, California State Senator, and James F. Thatcher, San Francisco lawyer. The Commission has recommended that the island be administered by the National Park Service, with the right of the State to use part of it for public purposes if needed and to accept the offer of the San Francisco chapter of the American Assn. for the United Nations to contribute funds for demolishing present structures and raise a monument commemorating the founding of the United Nations at San Francisco in 1945.

ANGEL ISLAND (*Government boats make free trips from Fort Mason and Pier 5, Ferry Building, daily, 7 a.m.-12 p.m.*), N. of Alcatraz and the largest island in the bay, is the district headquarters and detention barracks of the Immigration and Naturalization Service; here immigrants arriving via the Pacific are received, and deportees to the Orient and the Antipodes are shipped out. It is also the quarantine station of the Public Health Service, and an overseas replacement depot.

The first white visitor to the island was Juan Manuel de Ayala, who came in 1775 and gave the island its name. In 1851 a prison brig was anchored near it, but escape proved too easy and the prisoners were removed to San Quentin, which was completed in 1854. Angel Island was the scene of many duels, the most famous being the Johnston-Ferguson encounter in 1858, over the slavery question. Senator William I. Ferguson was killed, and his antagonist, George P. Johnston, clerk of the U. S. Circuit Court, was tried and acquitted.

The FARALLON ISLANDS (*closed*) consist of three groups of small islands in the Pacific, 26 miles west of the mainland, and visible on clear days from the Cliff House and other points. They are a constituent part of San Francisco, yet no county or city official may set foot on them without the permission of the lighthouse superintendent. The bare waterless islands are inhabited by four lighthouse keepers, seven Navy men in charge of the Radio Beam Compass Station, and their families. The light, one of the most powerful on the coast, stands 358 feet above water at high tide. The islands are a bird refuge.

# San Jose

*Transportation:* Southern Pacific and Western Pacific Railroads; Southern Pacific operates 25 passenger trains daily between San Jose and San Francisco. All coastal and transcontinental bus lines have terminals in the city. The new Municipal Airport offers 25 daily passenger and freight service flights.

*Accommodations:* Three major hotels in city, 650 rooms; 62 modern motels and 2 motor hotels, total more than 3,000 rooms. Motels chiefly near State 82.

*Theaters:* San Jose has 12 theaters and 7 outdoor theaters. The San Jose Civic Auditorium offers many programs in music and entertainment, with national artists participating. The San Jose Symphony Orchestra, the San Jose Municipal Chorus and the Light Opera Assn. give regular performances.

*Recreation:* In the eastern foothills overlooking San Jose and the Santa Clara Valley is the San Jose Country Club with a picturesque 18-hole golf course. There are 15 other 18-hole and five 9-hole golf courses in the San Jose area. The South Bay Yacht Club is located in Alviso, 7 miles north of San Jose on San Francisco Bay. Swimming pools, baseball parks, playgrounds and recreation centers and a 7½-acre Happy Hollow Playpark for children are located within the city. Redwood Parks are nearby; the surrounding mountains furnish good hunting in season; marsh lands lear the southern tip of San Francisco Bay furnish duck hunting; good trout fishing is found in the foothills, seaside and mountain resorts are less than an hour's drive away. Fishing, boating, swimming, water skiing, picnicking facilities are available at the ten water conservation resorvoirs. There are 43 parks, including Alum Rock Park in the foothills, 776 acre municipal playgrounds, with barbecue pits, 22 mineral springs (sulphur, soda, iron and iodine content) a natatorium, deer paddocks, junior museum. In Kelley Park 7½ acres are devoted to children's playground.

*Annual Events:* Maximum bloom of 100,000 roses in Municipal Rose Garden, Naglee and Dana Aves., early May; Fiesta de las Rosas Golf Tournament, Hillview Public Golf Course, September; Santa Clara County Fair, September.

SAN JOSE (*San Ho-say;* 80 alt.; 95,280 pop., 1950; 204,196, 1960; 310,200, 1964 est.). The metropolis of Santa Clara Valley is located at the southern end of San Francisco Bay, 50 *m.* from San Francisco and 42 *m.* from Oakland. The city itself is eight miles from the waters of the bay, separated by low ground and marshlands. Mountains are visible from almost any point in the city; brown, bare foothills merge into the peaks of the Mount Hamilton Range to the east and to the west is the green and thickly wooded Coast Range. These mountains trap rains and fogs generated over the ocean and give San Jose a semi- arid climate with no rain at all during the summer months. The Guadalupe and Coyote Rivers run through the city, but water flows in their channels only in early spring.

San Jose is a major packing center; one-third of the world's supply of

prunes comes from Santa Clara County.    Its office buildings, department
stores, hotels, theaters, and shops are grouped along First and Santa
Clara Streets.    The geographical center of town is the crossing of these
two streets.    West of First Street, business buildings merge into an
industrial district of shops, warehouses, garages, and factories.

San Jose is the core of the thickly populated Santa Clara County,
where many families from the Bay area are finding new homes.    It is
served by Bayshore Freeway (US 101), El Camino Real (State 82),
State 9 and 207, and the newly constructed Junipero Serra Freeway
(Interstate 280) and is soon to be served by the West Valley Freeway,
which will parallel the Southern Pacific.    Most of these roads also serve
Santa Clara (city), which had 58,880 pop. in 1960.

The SAN JOSE PARK CENTER PROJECT is a cooperative
effort of public and private interests to modernize a large area at an
initial investment of $45,000,000.    Land was being acquired in 1965-66
for the project, which includes plans for a 350-room hotel, shop and office
structures, underground and multi-story parking facilities, a library, theater, concert hall and cultural center.    About 900 dwelling units are a
part of the plan.    The SAN JOSE CIVIC AUDITORIUM houses the programs of the San Jose Symphony Orchestra, the San Jose Municipal
Chorus and the Light Opera Assn.

Santa Clara (*see TOUR 2b*) is a separate city northwest of San
Jose, but connected with it by solid blocks of houses and stores.    The
main artery between the two cities is The Alameda, a broad avenue
lined with willow trees originally planted as windbreaks and for protection against wild cattle.    Along The Alameda were some fine examples
of the gingerbread school of architecture: large Victorian frame mansions with tall windows, towers and turrets, stained glass, intricate fret-
work decorations, built by wealthier citizens during the city's first agricultural prosperity, nearly all replaced since.

San Jose was California's first town, as distinguished from forts and
missions, and was the first capital of the State following American occupation.    It is the seat of Santa Clara County, and has a State College,
which was the first and for many years the only normal school in California.

First known inhabitants of this section were the Olhone Indians,
who painted themselves with cinnabar ore from New Almaden and wor-
shiped the sun.    Mission life and white men's diseases and ways gradually exterminated them.    An anthropologist in San Jose has a standing
offer of $500 to anyone who will bring him a full-blooded Olhone.

The population now includes a few descendants of early Spanish
settlers, such as the Bernals, Ortegas, Peraltas, and Berryessas; a solid
core of "old families" descended from Americans who settled after 1840;
farmers, workers, business and professional men, students, and teachers,
all largely of native American stock; and groups of Italians, Mexicans,
Portuguese, and Slavs, attracted by farming and industry.    These groups
retain only a few of their folk ways, chiefly manifested in religious
festivals.

On November 29, 1777, in response to orders from the viceroy of Mexico, nine soldiers, five *pobladores* (settlers) with their families, and one cowboy, were detailed to found the Pueblo de San José de Guadalupe, named in honor of St. Joseph. This was the first of a series of towns established in Alta California to foster agriculture and handicraft and make the territory self-supporting. Each man was allotted two cows, two oxen, two mules, two sheep, two goats, seed, necessary implements for cultivation of the soil, and was promised monthly stipends of about $10 during his first years. The missions were not pleased by this encroachment, but could do nothing about it. The first settlers built their small huts about a mile north of the present business section. In later years the town was moved to higher ground because of seasonal floods from the Guadalupe River.

Mexico broke from the Spanish Crown in 1821, and the Mexican flag was raised over Monterey, the capital, the next April (1822); but it was not until May 10, 1825, that San Jose got around to acknowledging Mexican rule. Then there was a three-day public celebration, complete with music and dancing.

In 1831 the town had only 524 residents (Indians were not counted). The chief industry was stock raising; only enough crops were grown to satisfy local needs. The main interest of the young bloods was the bull and bear fights; bears were lassoed in the foothills and brought back to town in a bullock cart. The bear and bull were tied together and the fight continued—one bear usually being good for three or four bulls—until a fresh bull finally gored the tired bear to death.

In the 1840's, with the beginning of mass emigration from the East on the overland route, San Jose began to grow. Descendants of such noted expeditions as the Bidwell-Bartleson, the Donner, and the Murphy parties still live in San Jose, some of them grown rich through mining and real estate operations.

When Capt. Thomas Fallon, with 19 men, entered San Jose on July 14, 1846 and raised the United States flag over the town hall, he found a sleepy pueblo, its population composed mostly of Mexicans, Peruvians, Chileans, Spanish Californians, and Indians. The gold rush changed all that. San Jose became one of the supply cities for men on their way to and from the mines in the Sierra foothills. It grew so fast that in 1849 it was the logical choice for State capital.

The first California Legislature convened in San Jose on Dec. 15, 1849. It was known as "the legislature of a thousand drinks." Because of the shortage of local women, the countryside was "raked for señoritas," who, at the appointed time, made their appearance at the Assembly Hall and danced and imbibed with the solons of the region. "The legislators were good drinkers—they drank like men. If they could not *stand* the ceremony on any particular occasion, they would *lie* down to it with a becoming grace." Drinking and gaiety did not end with the first grand ball. A fandango usually cheered the weary legislators each evening after strenuous hours of deliberation. But accommodations were poor in San Jose and in February 1851, the capital was moved to Benicia.

Meanwhile the city was incorporated in 1850, with a population of 3,000. Stage and boat connections were established with San Francisco, but were discontinued in 1864 when the first railroad came through. In the 1880's the steady growth of the city was stimulated by a real estate boom which came to a climax in August 1887. Land sales zoomed to a high of $2,000,000 a day, and then collapsed. After the Civil War, when the gold fever had run its course, experiments in prune and apricot growing were made in the fertile regions around the city. Growth of apricots, prunes, and grapes promised to be profitable.

Since World War II industries have been attracted to Santa Clara County and San Jose has developed two large industrial parks. It remains a major canning center, especially of beans, peas, raspberries, strawberries, sweet corn, cherries and walnuts, and helps give California first place in the nation in processing. Since 1945, 550 industries have moved into Santa Clara County, crowding into the fields. San Jose has a substantial number of employees in durable manufacturing.

## POINTS OF INTEREST

CITY HALL PARK, a double landscaping of S. Market St. between San Carlos and W. San Fernando Sts., is the civic center of San Jose. The CIVIC AUDITORIUM, San Carlos and South Market Streets, is a yellow concrete building, erected in 1936. Besides offices, it contains the Main and Little (Dunn) Theaters. CITY HALL, at the south end of the park, a four-story red brick building, contains city offices. North of City Hall is a plaque commemorating the site of California's first State capitol. The actual site is at San Antonio and South Market Streets.

ST. JAMES PARK, N. 1st St. between St. John and St. James Sts., is planted with shrubs and flowers and is distinguished for its tall palms and elm trees. In 1933 two men accused of kidnaping and murdering the son of a wealthy merchant were dragged from jail and hanged to trees in the park. The country rang with details of the lynching, and James Rolph, Jr., then Governor, caused further reverberations by approving the mob's action. The trees, stripped of bark and twigs by souvenir hunters, had to be cut down.

SAN JOSE STATE COLLEGE, S. Fourth and San Antonio Sts., oldest public educational institution in California, was opened July 18, 1862. In the 1965 school year it had 19,250 registered students and 1,200 faculty members. The Library has 225,000 volumes. The college owns the Edwin Markham house, 430 S. Eighth St., where the poet in 1898 wrote "The Man with the Hoe," which won him national fame. SAN JOSE CITY COLLEGE enrolls nearly 8,000 students and has 335 teachers. SAN JOSE BIBLE COLLEGE has a four-year course in religious studies. The UNIVERSITY OF SANTA CLARA is located on The

Alameda in Santa Clara, a short distance from the northwestern limits of San Jose. In 1964 it had 3,772 students.

The PUBLIC LIBRARY, at Market and San Fernando Sts., is the hub of an extensive library service that circulates more than 2,000,000 volumes annually. The Library has five branches, in East San Jose, Willow Glen, Rosegarden, Cambrian and West Valley, and a bookmobile service for outlying areas. Also in the city are the Santa Clara County Free Library, the County Law Library, and the Medico-Dental Library.

ROSICRUCIAN PARK, MUSEUM AND UNIVERSITY, 1342 Naglee Ave., is headquarters for the Ancient and Mystical Order of the Rosy Cross. It maintains an Art Gallery, Egyptian Temple, Oriental Museum, and Science Museum, with Planetarium. The buildings follow the Egyptian style of architecture.

WATER CONSERVATION. San Jose profits by an abundant water supply impounded by ten dams that can hold back 170,040 acre-feet of water. (An acre-foot is water covering one acre one foot deep). Largest is Leroy Anderson Reservoir, with a capacity of 91,300 acre-feet; cost was $2,980,000. Other dams and reservoirs are Coyote, Lexington, Uvas, Calero, Chesbro, Stevens Creek, Guadalupe, Almaden, and Vasona, which distribute water in over 50 miles of canals and conduits in the Santa Clara Valley. Electrical power reaches the city from hydroelectric stations in the Sierra Nevada Mts.; natural gas comes from the Kettleman Hills, Rio Vista and Tracy Fields, as well as from Texas in a 34-inch pipe line.

SAN JOSE MUNICIPAL ROSE GARDEN, Naglee and Dana Avenues, is a tract of 5½ acres filled with 5,000 varieties of roses old and new. Represented are roses from the old gardens of the Missions, old-fashioned climbing and hedge roses and modern hybrids and prize-winners of international renown. *Open daily.*

FIRST STATE CAPITOL of California is reproduced on the Santa Clara County Fair Grounds and contains the CAPITOL MUSEUM, which exhibits items of historical interest.

## POINTS OF INTEREST IN ENVIRONS

Right from San Jose on State 17 (San Carlos St.) 2 *m.* to the junction with San Jose-Los Gatos Rd. Straight ahead here on Stevens Creek Rd. 2 *m.* to the WINCHESTER MYSTERY HOUSE (*adm. $1.50*), a crazy-quilt, 6-acre, 160-room mansion resembling a small city more than a house. It was the home of Mrs. Sarah L. Winchester, widow of a son of the firearms manufacturer. Arriving in California in the 1880's she bought the 17-room mansion, then under construction, and assumed command of a corps of 16 or more carpenters and artisans. It was destined never to be finished, for Mrs. Winchester, who had become a spiritualist following the death of her husband and two children within a short space of time, was informed by a medium's message that as long as she kept on building, death would never overtake her. As the rambling mansion began to take on gargantuan proportions, she bought more land to accommodate it. Every weekday for 38 years the structure resounded with the noise of hammering and sawing, as she poured the Winchester fortune into operations that finally reached a reported cost of several millions. In 1922 death came to Mrs. Winchester and the hammering stopped.

The mansion stands in parklike grounds, hidden from prying eyes by dense hedges, an unscalable fence, and secure iron gates. The reception room scintillates with thousands of prisms amid silver and gold leaf. The ballroom is a vast maple-paneled chamber equipped with a pipe organ and fireproof vaults, but no social function has ever been held in it. The "white satin chamber," its walls, ceiling and floor covered with the sumptuous fabric, was entered by no one but Mrs. Winchester. The oldest part of the house was damaged in the 1906 earthquake.

So labyrinthine are the miles of corridors that a stranger is in danger of losing his way completely. The house is a fantastic patchwork of trapdoors, crooked halls, steps leading nowhere, doors opening into space. Forty stairways twist in and out, up and down; 2,000 doors open at unexpected places; there are reportedly thousands of windows. The house has acquired much tourist publicity and is visited annually by many.

# Santa Barbara

*Transportation:* Santa Barbara is served by the coast line of the Southern Pacific Railroad between Los Angeles (92 *m.*) and San Francisco (337 *m.*). The Greyhound Bus lines operate twenty-one schedules daily with more than fifty arrivals and departures. United Air Lines and Pacific Air Lines provide a daily service. There are truck lines, sightseeing buses and city and suburban transit lines of all kinds.

*Accommodations:* More than 90 motels and 26 hotels have 5,000 available rooms.

*Theaters:* There are eight theaters including three major movie houses (Arlington, Granada and State), a Spanish-speaking theater (Mission), an Art Theater (Riviera). The Lobero, 33 E. Canon Perdido, is a legitimate theater where road shows and local repertory companies play. The Santa Barbara Film Society shows foreign films every other Monday night at the Granada.

*Fishing and Yachting:* The Yacht Harbor between the breakwater and Stearns Wharf has a protected area of 84 acres, with fishing fleets and accommodations for 850 boats. Deep sea fishing is available.

*Recreation:* There are five golf courses, including a municipal course open to the public. The Polo Club presents matches every Sunday. There are accommodations for all spectator and participant sports and a Children's Zoo and numerous facilities for swimming, wading and pony riding for children.

*Special Events:* La Fiesta (Old Spanish Days) August, 2nd week. Semana Nautica (Summer Sports Festival) week of July 4. Garden Tours, Fridays, April–Sept., except June. Casa Tour, Sunday before Fiesta, August. Channel City Horse Show, Earl Warren Show Grounds, March. National Horse Show, same grounds, July. International Cymbidium Orchid Show, April. Geranium Show, Museum of Natural History, May. Kennel Club Dog Show, Polo Field, July. Easter Relays, La Playa Stadium, Easter Week. A picturesque annual custom is the Rancheros Visitadores, when cavaliers in costume make an eight-day ride visiting ranches in the environs.

SANTA BARBARA (37 to 850 alt., 59,768 pop., 1960; 69,800 est. 1964) lies on a coastal shelf that rises into the southern slopes of the Santa Ynez Mountains. With its extensive landscaped estates, and the predominant Spanish flavor of its architecture, Santa Barbara has long maintained a reputation of ease and leisure, principally because of its large proportion of wealthy residents. The earthquake of 1925 created the opportunity to condense within a few years the rebuilding of a city in harmony with the dominant architectural motif. As a result, it has an air of spaciousness and quiet comfort; even the railroad roundhouse is disguised, and looks like a Spanish bull ring.

Santa Barbara has carefully preserved the beauty of its waterfront. From the foot of State Street a broad strand stretches for several miles to the east, a large section of it operated by the city as a public bathing beach. The paralleling highway is landscaped, and an area of marshland near the beach's eastern extremity has been converted into a bird refuge. Oil drilling has been forbidden on shore and in the ocean opposite the city by a prohibition that the city hopes to maintain in perpetuity. East and west of the city and a few miles off shore are located oil platforms for drilling. These operations help support the economy of Santa Barbara, as also does the great expansion of building construction. The city is often chosen for conventions; in 1964 there were 136, with 21,000 delegates, who spent nearly $1,600,000. Industrial development is chiefly by firms in research engineering; there were 156 concerns in this field in 1964 with an annual payroll of $40,574,000.

The city is bisected by its main thoroughfare, State Street, which carries a steady stream of coastwise motor traffic. It is flanked by residential sections, the more restricted areas being to the north. Upper State Street is lined with swanky shops and motion picture theaters; the lower end is a district of second-hand stores, drinking places, and a small Mexican quarter. State Street proceeds northwest to connect with US 101.

During the 1870's the city overcame a temptation to number and letter its streets, which commemorate ancient Spanish families (De la Guerra, Carillo), the Indians (Yanonali), and even an outlaw (Valerio). Episodes in Santa Barbara's history are recalled by Canon Perdido (Lost Cannon), Salsipuedes (get out if you can) and Indio Muerto (dead Indian).

The proximity of Santa Barbara to the cooling trees of Los Padres National Forest proved no advantage in September, 1964, when fires swept over the dried-out areas and with a 45 mph wind swept into the city and destroyed fine homes. The fires were contained by the efforts of fire apparatus from Santa Barbara City and County, Los Angeles City and County, and Montecito.

For three days during the full moon in August the city returns to its past in "Old Spanish Days," a fiesta inaugurated in 1924. It commences with a reception and pageant held on the steps of the old Mission, where Franciscan padres welcome the participants beneath chiming ancient bells. The following afternoon thousands line the main streets for the parade, depicting the city's past from Indian times to the arrival of American troops. Squealing *carretas* (carts) carry old Spanish families, and scores of fine horses mounted by distinguished visitors pass between red and gold banners along the line of march. Gaily caparisoned serenaders stroll the streets singing songs of Spanish days, and descendants of pioneer families dance the folk dances of their forefathers. There is a pageant on the site of a Canalino village, street dances every night, and a variety of free entertainment.

In 1542, when the navigator Cabrillo came up the coast, he was met in the channel by a fleet of Canalino (channel) Indians, who greeted him from great canoes. Cabrillo's account states that "most of the Indian chiefs were men, but the ruler of one of the villages was a very wrinkled old woman, which seemed very queer to us." Cabrillo was fatally injured in a perilous landing and lies in an undiscovered grave on one of the Channel Islands. Vizcaino entered the channel on Saint Barbara's Day, December 4, 1603, and named the region Santa Barbara.

In 1768, rumor reached Spain that Russia intended to explore and claim the territory south of Alaska, and King Charles III ordered the Viceroy of Mexico to establish presidios and missions in California. Spanish colonization had already begun when Capt. José Francísco Ortega, accompanied by Governor Neve, Father Junípero Serra, and fifty men, entered Santa Barbara on April 21, 1782, and founded the presidio.

Indians, paid in food and clothing, brought fish and game and assisted in hewing timbers and making adobe bricks for the fort. After their conversion to the Catholic faith, they were set to work, under supervision of the padres, constructing dwellings, building the mission, cultivating large acreages, and raising cattle. After secularization of the Missions in 1834 the presidio officers became barons of wide estates and prolific herds, and the Indian population waned. (The last survivor of the Canalino tribe died in 1930.) The presidio "dons" were of a proud heritage, many bearing noble names, and they indulged their traditions of urbanity and social grace. Mexico shook off the yoke of Spain in 1821, Yankee trade developed, and the exchange of New England wealth for hides and tallow greatly enriched them.

The Barbareños enjoyed this productive economy for three decades. "My house is your own, Señor," was the greeting, and *mañana* was the philosophy. An occasional revolution was staged, bloodless and courteous as a tennis match.

But the influx of the Yankees foretold a change. The serene existence of the Californios had led many a Yankee sea captain to desert his calling for marriage with a wealthy señorita; American trappers had been drawn by the rich hauls of seal and otter at the Channel Islands. Commodore Stockton landed in Santa Barbara Bay in August 1846, ran up the American flag, and left a small garrison. Several weeks later the garrison was attacked, and given the choice of surrender or flight. It fled, but in Christmas week of the same year Lt. Col. John C. Frémont, after dodging an ambush in Gaviota Pass, re-entered Santa Barbara and held it. Three weeks later California was ceded to the United States.

Under the new American regime the town prospered. Great herds of cattle were driven north to feed the miners. "Every bullock was a skinful of silver and his marrow as fine as gold." Luxurious furnishings filled adobe dwellings, and fine silks trailed on clay floors. The civilization of the dons reached its apex, with gay Castillian cavalcades, the gallantries of caballeros and fan-wielding señoritas, cock-fighting and gambling.

The decay of all this glory began with a drought in 1864. There were 200,000 cattle in the county in 1863; only 5,000 gaunt creatures were alive the following year. A primitive wharf built two years later put an end to landings in small boats through the surf such as those described in *Two Years Before the Mast*. In 1872 a more elaborate wharf was completed to which ships and side-wheel steamers could tie. The real estate boom of the early 1870's collapsed in 1877 because of another drought, and Santa Barbara dozed in gentle dignity until the Southern Pacific Railroad entered the city from the south in 1887. In 1901 the line was extended to San Francisco; Santa Barbara took its place on the tourist map and began its metamorphosis into a wealthy residential community.

## POINTS OF INTEREST

The SANTA BARBARA COUNTY COURTHOUSE, Anapamu and Anacapa Sts., is a rambling, white stucco structure with wide arches and towers, resembling the palace of a Spanish prelate. The assembly room (*open 8-5 weekdays*) on the second floor has murals by Dan Sayre Groesbeck portraying the arrival of Cabrillo, the building of the mission, and the coming of the American troops.

The SANTA BARBARA HISTORICAL SOCIETY MUSEUM occupies a new building at De la Guerra and Santa Barbara Sts. It contains Indian relics, saddles, branding irons, and the like, and the *cañón perdido* (lost cannon), which was cast ashore on the wreckage of the American brig *Elizabeth,* lost off the coast of Santa Barbara during the winter of 1847-48. The 12-pound brass cannon was found by a group of native Californians, who hid it in the vicinity of the present Canon Perdido Street. Fearing that the natives might use the gun against the Americans, Governor Mason levied a fine of $500 on the town of Santa Barbara, and sent soldiers from Los Angeles to collect it. Tradition relates that the State returned the money to the town to build a jail. Local officials, dissatisfied with the amount, sought to increase it to $1,000 by staking it in a game of Yankee poker. They lost the whole $500, and shamefacedly gave up their plan for a jailhouse.

UNIVERSITY OF CALIFORNIA, SANTA BARBARA, is located in Goleta, a few miles west of the city limits of Santa Barbara on a promontory overlooking the ocean. It was located in midtown from 1891 and moved to this campus in 1954. Some structures dating from the Marine Air Base are still in use, but a dozen new buildings have enlarged its facilities, which served 7,879 students in the 1964-65 year. The School of Engineering graduated its first class in 1965. It has departments of electrical, mechanical and chemical-nuclear engineering. Laboratories in electronics, control systems, computer engineering and solid state devices have been provided and laboratories in fluid mechanics and heat transfer were installed in the fall of 1965.

HOPE RANCH ESTATES, about 2,000 acres, is the newest residential development, intended for luxurious living. It lies immediately beyond the western limits of Santa Barbara between the shore and US 101.

EL PASEO DE LA GUERRA, 15 E. De la Guerra St., called the historical center of Santa Barbara, is built around the house of Don José de la Guerra, comandante of the Presidio a century ago. Courtyards and passageways simulating streets in old Spain, with small shops and a restaurant opening into them, have been built around the original adobe. Another notable house on this street is 29 E. De la Guerra.

The COVARRUBIAS ADOBE, 715 Santa Barbara St., built about 1817, and still in excellent repair, is a notable example of Spanish-Colonial architecture.

The YACHT HARBOR, bordering W. Cabrillo Blvd. SW. from the foot of State St., is a placid 84-acre shelter for transient and resident craft, protected by an L-shaped breakwater 2,364 feet long. The municipal West Beach, also protected by the breakwater, attracts summer bathers to its restrained surf.

ANDREE CLARK BIRD REFUGE (*open 9-5 weekdays*), E. end of E. Cabrillo Blvd., is a landscaped preserve of 49½ acres with an island-dotted lake in the center, where geese, swan, and other wild fowl live; the land was reclaimed from a swamp and is maintained by the city. There are bridle paths among the trees, and a large parking space on the east shore.

SANTA BARBARA COUNTY BOWL, E. end of E. Anapamu St., completed in 1937, is a 4,000-seat amphitheater where a historical play is produced annually as part of the city's "Old Spanish Days" festival. Its large revolving stage—75 by 40 feet—holds two sets at once. Cut stone seats follow the natural contour of the canyon in which the bowl is built. The bowl is also used for concerts and other programs.

LOBERO THEATER, 33 E. Canon Perdido St., was founded 1872 by Jose Lobero, an innkeeper with musical ambitions. He produced grand opera at a loss. The original adobe has been rebuilt and the Community Arts Assn. sponsors plays and concerts there.

SANTA BARBARA MISSION (*open 8-5 weekdays, 11-5 Sun.*), Los Olivos St. between Garden and Laguna Sts., called Queen of the Missions in the days when it was rich and powerful, is the best preserved and architecturally one of the finest missions. A blending of old Spanish and Moorish architecture, it was constructed in 1815 by the padres, using Canalino Indian labor, to replace the building destroyed in the 1812 earthquake. The original mission chapel was made of boughs in 1786. Damage to mission buildings by the 1925 earthquake was promptly repaired.

The church, designed by Padre Riptoll, is constructed of native sandstone, painted ivory. It is rectangular in plan with massive square front towers of solid masonry and arcaded and domed belfries. The towers are flanked by heavy buttresses. The design of the classic facade, with its engaged columns of modified Ionic order, its dentiled cornice and frieze adorned with a heavy fret motif and its crowning pediment, is based upon the detail of a plate of the classic orders, appearing in a Spanish volume of Citruvius, still in the Mission library. In the tympanum of the pediment is a niched figure of Saint Barbara. Surmounting the pediment are three seated figures and a stepped gable cresting topped with a cross.

Across the entire width of the facade is a traditional broad-stepped platform. The deeply recessed arched entrance with its simple classic trim has double paneled doors. Above the entrance is a circular "rose" window with deep splayed reveal. At the left is the long, low arcaded mission house with red-tile roof, enclosing one side of the rear patio.

The interior of the long narrow nave is lighted by small splayed windows in the side walls. It is finished in plaster with Ionic pilasters painted in imitation of veined marble rising in support of a painted dentil cornice and has a flat wooden ceiling, embellished with painted and carved rosettes. The structural roof timbers are concealed.

At the left of the entrance is a door leading to the Mission House and a spiral stairway in the left tower. The walls of the nave are flanked by side altars with religious paintings above. In the first bay, left and right, are chapels, recessed in the deep side walls. The main altar is screened by a painted and paneled reredos, adorned with Roman Doric columns, painted floral festoons and figures. On the Epistle side of the main altar is the tomb of Father Francisco García Diego y Moreno, first Bishop of California, flanked by Ionic columns and topped with a pediment. A doorway to the left of the sanctuary leads to the sacristy and the choir room. The stations of the cross were brought from Mexico in 1797.

Two small side doors near the center of the nave lead to the patio or Monks Garden, on the left, and the Mission Cemetery on the right. The patio is landscaped with trees, flower beds, and radiating walks around a central well. Two sides are enclosed by the rooms and arcaded corridors of the Mission House. Especially notable are the deeply recessed windows with their turned wooden grilles and the unstilted arches of the arcades, supported by heavy square piers.

This is the only California mission in which the altar light has not been extinguished since the founding. Bodies of Franciscan friars are interred in crypts set in the thick walls of the building, and 4,000 Indians are buried in trenches across the garden. Art and relics of the Canalino tribe are exhibited in the curio rooms. The mission has old paintings, creased in their journey from Spain and the pack-trip across Mexico, and a copy of Murillo's *Assumption of the Virgin*.

The MUSEUM OF NATURAL HISTORY (*open 9-5 week-days, 1-5 Sun.*), Puesta del Sol Road and Mission Creek, its one-story stucco Spanish-Colonial type buildings grouped upon two acres of sycamore and live-oak studded grounds, has pavilions with permanent exhibitions of the flora and fauna of the region, natural habitat groups of animals from all parts of the world, artifacts of the Hunting People and the Oak Grove and Canalino Indians, and a library on natural science. Lectures and motion pictures on natural science are presented.

SANTA BARBARA BOTANIC GARDEN (*open 9-5 weekdays, 10-5 Sun.*), 1212 Mission Canyon Rd., is a 50-acre creekside tract planted with trees, shrubs and flowers indigenous to California. Specimens are labeled and arranged in ten sections to show characteristic flora of the desert, foothill, canyon, waterside and other plant associations. Literature on plants and birds in the garden is available near the entrance.  Experimental culture here has added to existing knowledge on the habits of native plants and their adaptability to home-gardening.

MORETON BAY FIG TREE, Chapala and Montecito Sts., a native of Australia, is considered the largest fig tree in North America.

## POINTS OF INTEREST IN ENVIRONS

LOS PADRES NATIONAL FOREST covers more than 1,749,-000 acres in Santa Barbara and Ventura Counties.  In September, 1964, fires swept over 65,500 acres of the Forest and 4,500 acres of private lands leading into Santa Barbara.  Headquarters are in the Federal Bldg.

CHANNEL ISLANDS NATIONAL MONUMENT consists of Anacapa and Santa Barbara, two of the eight Channel Islands lying 10 to 70 miles off the southern coast from the latitude of Los Angeles to that of San Diego.  They are administered by the National Park Service. Santa Barbara Island lies 38 miles out opposite San Pedro and is 1¼ miles long.  Anacapa, 10 miles offshore, is 40 miles from Santa Barbara Isl. and five miles long.  The islands are frequented by sea lions and visited occasionally by the giant sea elephant and the Guadalupe fur seal. The giant coreopsis blooms in such profusion in the spring that it is visible ten miles away.  Transportation is available daily to Anacapa in the summer and on weekends in other seasons (Channel Islands Transportation Co., Port Hueneme, Calif.)  There are no facilities of any kind on the islands.

# Stockton

*Transportation:* Santa Fe, Southern Pacific and Western Pacific Railways. Western Greyhound, Lincoln Village and Stockton City Bus Lines. Stockton Metropolitan Airport: Pacific and United Air Lines. Bridgeport Flying Service.

*Information:* Stockton Chamber of Commerce, 1105 N. El Dorado St.

*Recreation:* A multiplicity of waterways connecting Stockton and San Francisco Bay afford many miles of navigation for yachting, cruising, outboard-motor boating, canoeing, houseboating and water sports such as ski-ing. Boats of all kinds are available. The lagoons formed by dredging the marsh lands give sportsmen access to inland waters frequented by game of all kinds. For fishermen there are black bass, striped bass, crappie, perch and catfish.

Golf is available at Swenson Park, Van Buskirk Park and Elkhorn Golf Course, all open to the public. There is trap and skeet shooting at Waterloo Gun Club. Weekly wrestling bouts are held at Stockton Civic Auditorium. Baseball games between the Stockton Ports and members of Class A, California League are held during the season in Billy Hebert Field, Oak Park.

*Annual Events:* A Fantasy in Flowers, April. Pacific Music Camp, Port Stockton Regatta, Sports Car Races, San Joaquin Valley Rangers Play Day and Blue Ribbon Horse Show, June. Captain Weber Days Sports Spectacular, last two weeks, July. San Joaquin County Fair, Water Show, August. Stockton Civic Theater, 4 performances, November-May. "Messiah" by University of Pacific Music Dept., December.

STOCKTON (23 alt., 86,321 pop. 1960; 156,480 in Metropolitan Area, 1960) at the head of tidewaters on the San Joaquin River, is California's major inland seaport, 78 nautical miles from San Francisco Bay. It is the principal shipping point for the agricultural products of San Joaquin County (pop. 249,989), of which it is the county seat, with diversified products led by asparagus, tomatoes, Tokay grapes, potatoes, celery and sweet cherries. The San Joaquin River and the Calaveras River border the city and the Stockton Channel cuts through the city and stops at its center. The Channel on the San Joaquin River has a minimum width of 300 ft. and is 32 ft. deep at mean low water.

The Port of Stockton, which handles up to 4,000,000 tons annually, is the major factor in the tremendous development of Stockton since World War II. More than 85 percent of the grain exported by California moves through the Port, where the elevators have a capacity of 4,500,000 bu. for grain and an additional capacity of 500,000 bu. for bulk rice. It is the home port of the *Angelo Petri,* the largest bulk wine tanker, which can carry 2,500,000 gallons of wine in its stainless steel tanks to Jersey City, N. J.

Only 800 yards distant from dockside is the 257-acre industrial park. The seven largest plants are Fibreboard Products, Diamond Walnut Growers, Stockton Box Co., International Harvester Co., American Can Co., Johns-Manville Corp. and Libby-Owens-Ford Glass Co.

The business district radiates from Courthouse Plaza, Weber Avenue and Hunter Street. The tall office buildings, modern shops, metropolitan stores, and Civic Center reflect the new Stockton, starting point for trips to such places as the Bret Harte country, Lake Tahoe, and Yosemite Valley, while only a few blocks west, along Main and El Dorado Streets, stand the aged landmarks of the pioneer days, when Stockton was a wide-open gold rush town, the jumping off place for the Mother Lode country. Twenty-six tracts are set aside as parks, playgrounds, and squares, including Victory Park, a 27½-acre landscaped area in the heart of the northwest residence district.

Ten per cent of Stockton's population is Mexican. It is also a center for Basque sheepherders. There are many Basque restaurants, where wine is poured Basque fashion in a stream from the leather flask into the drinker's open mouth. There was at one time a considerable number of Hindus in California's Central Valley, brought into the State for their knowledge of irrigation; in recent years many of them have returned to India with money they managed to accumulate. Bearded, turbanned Sikhs, grave and dignified, may still, however, occasionally be seen in the streets of Stockton.

Capt. Charles M. Weber, a native of Germany who came to California with the Bidwell-Bartellson party in 1841, is generally recognized as the founder of Stockton. Weber first settled in San Jose, where he met William Gulnac, a naturalized Mexican citizen. The two men formed a partnership to establish a colony in the San Joaquin Valley: and to this end Gulnac obtained a tract from the Mexican government, about 50,000 acres, including the site of Stockton. Gulnac led the first group of settlers to the area, which they called El Campo de los Francesces (Sp. French Camp), but in 1845 he became discouraged and sold out to Weber for a $60 grocery bill.

Weber remained in San Jose, though in 1847 he founded the town of Tuleburg on the site of the present levee of that name. He built corrals, planted wheat, and set up houses for ranchers. After discovery of gold in 1848, Weber moved to Tuleburg, which he planned to promote as a supply post for miners. He surveyed the town in 1849, renaming it Stockton for his friend Commodore Robert Stockton.

The Gold Rush took Stockton by storm. Bayard Taylor, noted author and traveler, found it in 1849 "a canvas town of a thousand inhabitants, and a port with twenty-five vessels at anchor! The mingled noises of labor around—the click of hammers and the grating of saws —the shouts of mule drivers—the jingling of spurs—the jar and jostle of wares in the tents—almost cheated me into the belief that it was some old commercial mart. . . . Four months had sufficed to make the place what it was." One of a dozen new wholesale firms already had done $100,000 worth of business. A lot 80 by 100 feet sold for $6,000; a common, one-story clapboard house cost $15,000 to build.

In 1850 Stockton became the county seat, and within three years the population grew from a few hundred to 5,000. Between the time he became an outlaw in 1851 and his death in 1853, the Mexican bandit Joaquin Murrieta ranged as far north as Stockton. On one occasion he rode into town, noticed a sign offering a reward for his capture, wrote underneath it "I will give $10,000—Joaquin!" then galloped off through the crowd, unmolested.

The settlers of Stockton built churches and schools as early as 1850, despite the gold rush. The introduction of irrigation after the 1860's and the decline of the gold mines turned attention once again toward agriculture. Grain poured into the city's warehouses to await shipment by the railroad which first reached the city in 1869. This increased the demand for farm implements, and Stockton began production of tractors, harvesters, and other farm machinery. The caterpillar tractor, first machine to use the track-laying traction principle, originated in Stockton; the device employed in these tractors was later applied to the military tank in World War I.

In June, 1934 the last of the Pony Express riders, William Campbell, died at Stockton. He was on the 95-mile run from Fort Kearney to Fort McPherson. Chased once for miles by a pack of wolves, on his return he left a poisoned ox on the trail for their benefit. His reward was a dozen dead wolves whose hides brought $50.

## POINTS OF INTEREST

SAN JOAQUIN COUNTY COURTHOUSE, Main and Hunter Sts., designed in 1890 by E. E. Myers & Son of Detroit, is built in classic style, with a lofty, gilded dome bearing a figure of justice.

The two-story brick SIKH TEMPLE (*open*), 1930 S. Grant St., is said to be the only temple of this sect in the United States. The building has high stained-glass windows and an ornate mosaic entrance framed by a horseshoe of electric lights. The first floor contains a library and a meeting room. Visitors must take off their shoes and leave them on the veranda before entering the temple proper.

The FORTY-NINE DRUGSTORE, Main and El Dorado Sts., a two-story building of gray stone with gingerbread trim, has been used continuously for the same purpose since 1850, when E. S. Holden built it and opened Stockton's first pharmacy. The main room, with its vaulted ceilings, is the same one in which bearded miners of the boom days purchased their medicines.

CITY HALL, on Civic Center Square, is a stone structure of modern design. This site is called Lindsay's Point for Thomas Lindsay, one of the company that came here in 1844 under the leadership of Gulnac. The tule hut Lindsay erected on the point just back of the City Hall was the first house built by a white man within the city limits. A smallpox scare drove out most of the settlers soon after their arrival, and in the spring of 1845 a band of Indians killed Lindsay, set fire to his hut, and drove off the cattle. He is buried on the Point.

The HAGGIN MEMORIAL GALLERY AND PIONEER HISTORICAL MUSEUM in Victory Park was given by Louis Terah Haggin, who dominated stock raising in pioneer days. Haggin, of Turkish descent, was an art collector and his collection of 300 nineteenth century European and American paintings forms the nucleus of the gallery.

There are also on exhibit numerous relics of early California, among them the weapons of a party that came over the Oregon Trail, old wagons, fire engines, porcelains and silverware.

The UNIVERSITY OF THE PACIFIC was projected by the Methodist Church in San Jose, January, 1851, and became California's first chartered institution of higher education.   In 1924 it moved from San Jose to Stockton.   Its academic structure has three liberal arts colleges (COLLEGE OF THE PACIFIC, RAYMOND COLLEGE and ELBERT COVELL COLLEGE), five professional schools (Music, Education, Pharmacy, Engineering, Dentistry) and the Graduate School.   The College of the Pacific is a school of arts and sciences that preserves the name utilized by the university from 1911 to 1961.   In 1964 the university had 2,673 students.   In 1962 it established the "cluster college" concept. Each college is a residential unit limited to 250 students, following both traditional and experimental methods.   Elbert Covell College is the first Spanish-speaking liberal arts college in North America, English being taught as a foreign language.   The School of Dentistry is located in San Francisco; its new building at Sacramento and Webster Sts. is costing $8,500,000.   A 12-year development program is in force at Stockton.

# PART III
## Up and Down the State

# *Tour 1*

Westport—Fort Bragg—Point Arena—San Francisco—Santa Cruz—
Monterey—Carmel—San Simeon—Morro Bay—San Luis Obispo—
Las Cruces; 554.5 *m.* State 1.

Roadbed winds continuously, with frequent sharp turns; occasional slides during
rainy season.
Southern Pacific Lines parallel route between Davenport and Pacific Grove.
Accommodations limited except in larger towns.

State 1 skirts closely the waters of the Pacific. It swings outward
around headlands and inland past sandy-edged coves in a succession of
hairpin curves; it climbs barren slopes and dips into brush-choked
ravines. At times it edges along sheer bluffs high above the surf. Eastward, wind-swept hills, wooded only in patches, rise to the timbered
crests of the Coast Range. After the first rains these hills are briefly
green; at other times their slopes are brown with dried grass, close-
cropped by grazing sheep.

Walled off by mountains, the narrow coastal shelf is sparsely settled
except around San Francisco and Monterey Bays. The half-primitive
ways of the seventies and eighties, when lumbering, fishing, and sheep
raising flourished, linger on in the isolated villages and farms. The
region now affords only a meager living to its hard-working inhabitants.
Along the northern section, where redwoods grow down to the sea in
forest-choked ravines, the lumber towns at the mouths of rivers, once
shipping points for logs hauled by narrow-gage railways from the forested hinterland, are sinking into decay beside abandoned mills.

Fishing is still a gainful pursuit at such points as Noyo, Tomales
Bay, Monterey, and Half Moon Bay. Flocks of sheep roam over the

hills up and down the coast and great herds of dairy cattle over the
knolls and hollows around Tomales Bay.   Berries and peas are grown
around Fort Bragg; brussels sprouts and artichokes, in the foggy strip
near Half Moon Bay; and apples in the Pajaro Valley; but most of
the country is too rough, too bleak for farming.   The occasional
weather-beaten farm buildings huddle behind ragged, protective files of
wind-battered cypress or eucalyptus trees.

The coastal strip between the mouth of the Russian River and Big
Sur attracts increasing numbers of vacationers every year.   It is a
picturesque stretch, indented with rocky, islet-studded coves where
crescent-shaped beaches of white sand lie between bold promontories.
Along the highway in this area are a succession of resort towns and
camps that offer bathing and fishing in the surf, clam and abalone hunting along the shore, and riding and hiking in the forested hinterland.

### Section a.   WESTPORT to SAN FRANCISCO; 205.4 m.

On the maps the northern end of State 1 is extended to a junction
with US 101 not far south of Eureka, with feeders from US 101 north
of Westport; but these connections are barely passable even in good
weather.

WESTPORT, 0 m. (50 alt.), is at the beginning of *Westport Landing State Park*.   First named Beal's Landing for Lloyd Beal, who arrived in 1864, the town was renamed Westport at the instigation of
James T. Rogers, a native of Eastport, Maine.   After construction of
two wharves in 1878, it became for a while an important lumber-shipping
point.

> North from Westport on a poor road (the sketchy continuation of State
> 1), past ROCKPORT, 11.5 m., a small lumber camp with bleak, weather-
> beaten shacks, to the junction with a narrow, ungraded dirt road, 14.5 m.
> Right here, up a long, steep forested grade to a summit, 25.5 m., then
> downward to a junction with US 101, 30.1 m. (*see TOUR 2a*).

South of Westport State 1 winds over close-cropped pasture lands
sloping to the sea.   Crossing the marshy bottoms of sluggish Ten Mile
River, 7.8 m., it strikes through an eerie wilderness of storm-blasted
pine and cypress groves, edged at intervals by sand dunes.   Patches of
farm land and orchard, crisscrossed by files of cypress windbreaks, hedge
the road.

FORT BRAGG, 61.2 m. (60 alt., 4,433 pop.), spreads over a sloping coastal shelf to the edge of a wild and rocky coast line.   A settlement of wooden buildings—false-front stores, steepled churches, and
gabled frame houses in fenced yards—it has a weather-worn, settled air.
Fort Bragg's chief stock in trade is lumber, but it also ships farm and
truck-garden crops (especially berries), poultry and dairy products, and
fish.   Its racial make-up is mixed: Finns and Swedes predominate; after
them, Germans and Italians.

In June 1857 Lt. Horatio Gates Gibson was ordered to establish a
military post within the boundaries of the Mendocino Indian Reserva-

tion. The fort he set up here and named for Gen. Braxton Bragg of Mexican War fame covered a 10-acre clearing. The land was thrown open for purchase in 1867, when the reservation was abandoned, and a lumber town grew up. It was damaged by the earthquake of April 18, 1906, but rebuilt at once.

The heart of the town's industrial life is the UNION LUMBER COMPANY PLANT, a large redwood sawmill with a capacity of 350,000 to 400,000 board feet a day. Its red-painted mill buildings, lumberyards, and log pond lie along the railroad yards at the edge of the rocky bluffs. The UNION LUMBER COMPANY REFORESTATION AND ORNAMENTAL NURSERY (*open workdays 8-5*), on Main Street (R) near the southern outskirts, established in 1922, raises redwood and other seedlings for systematic reforestation of cutover lands.

NOYO (*boats for ocean fishing rented*), 17.9 *m.* (sea level, 93 pop.), lies at the mouth of placid, winding Noyo River, crowded with small fishing craft tied up alongside tumble-down warehouses. Noyo was the name given by Northern Pomo Indians to their village at the river's mouth. The village escaped the fate of most former lumber towns along the Mendocino coast by turning to fishing for a living. Settled largely by Italian fishermen, it is now the center of the area's commercial fishing industry. It has fish-canning and drying plants and a deep-water harbor protected by a breakwater.

CASPAR, 22.3 *m.* (52 alt., 250 pop.), on the edge of high bluffs at the mouth of Caspar Creek, is a collection of old frame houses amid weed-grown vacant spaces, dirt paths, and picket fences. The lumber mill beside the log pond and chute, occasionally operated, was built in 1861.

At 25.2 *m.* is the junction with a dirt road.

> Right on this road 0.3 *m.* to RUSSIAN GULCH STATE PARK HEAD-QUARTERS (*nominal fee a day per car for camping or picnicking*). The park contains more than 1,000 acres of second-growth redwood. Along the fern-banked canyon bottom, deep among redwoods, alders, and Douglas fir, are scattered camp sites and picnic grounds.

MENDOCINO, 27.3 *in.* (41 alt., 500 pop.), ranges over the northern shore of a half-moon-shaped bay at the mouth of Big River—a jumble of weathered, gabled wooden buildings fronting dirt streets, edged by the gloomy pine woods of encircling hills. It was named for Cape Mendocino, which Juan Rodríguez Cabrillo discovered in 1542 and named for Don Antonio de Mendoza, first viceroy of New Spain (Mexico).

Intermittent lumbering provides Mendocino's main support. A party sent out from Bodega in 1851 to salvage tea and silk from a vessel wrecked nearby carried back information of the country's rich timber resources to Alderman Harry Meiggs of San Francisco, lumberman and mill owner. On July 19, 1852, the brig *Ontario,* chartered by Meiggs, arrived with sawmill machinery imported from the East. Meiggs, finding that one William Kasten had staked out a claim to the water-front, purchased the claim with the first lumber from his sawmill —the first on the Mendocino coast—as part payment.

The architecture of Mendocino's well-preserved buildings (there has been only one serious fire) reflects the New England origin of most of its early settlers. Notable remnant of a bygone era is the MASONIC HALL (R), on Main Street. A buff-colored, gable-roofed structure, the hall bears on its cupola a piece of sculpture carved from a single block of redwood. It represents the Masonic emblem and the symbolic figures of Masonic lore: the broken pillar, the maiden beside it with a sprig in her hand, and Father Time dallying with her wavy locks.

At 30.1 m. is the junction with a graveled road.

> Right on this road 0.3 m. to VAN DAMME BEACH STATE PARK HEADQUARTERS (camping and picnicking fees as at Russian Gulch). This 1,800-acre tract fronting a lagoon with a sloping bathing beach stretches 4 miles up the forested canyon of the Little River. The chief attraction for visitors is the fishing: trout are caught in the Little River; red, blue, and China cod in the surf; leaf cod and salmon in the bay.

ALBION, 34.3 m. (37 alt., 75 pop.), a village of brightly painted, shingle-roofed cottages, overlooks the cove at the mouth of the Albion River, where an abandoned lumber mill decays amid half-ruined company shacks. A sawmill was erected here in 1852-53 and operated until 1928. Today the inhabitants subsist chiefly by fishing and berry picking.

At 38.6 m., in a deep valley where the broad Navarro River winds over marshy bottoms and through a sand bar into the sea, is the junction with paved State 128.

> Left on State 128, which runs along the riverbank, shadowed by a forest of second-growth redwood, 8.4 m. to DIMMICK MEMORIAL PARK (picnicking), a 12-acre reserve. The Navarro River offers fine swimming, and is one of the best trout and bass streams in the State.
>
> On State 128 at 14.8 m. is NAVARRO. Many of its gray, weathered houses stand empty, reminders of its lively past as a lumber town.
>
> The road enters Anderson Valley, a fertile basin given over to apple growing, and reaches BOONVILLE, 30.2 m. (pop. 315). Named in 1868 for an early settler, W. W. Boon, the settlement today furnishes supplies to ranchers and travelers. It celebrates an annual County Fair and Apple Show in October.
>
> Southwest of Boonville the highway climbs over a succession of hills, winds past rolling sheep pasturage, and joins US 101 (see TOUR 2a) at 57.5 m.

ELK, 44.6 m. (200 pop.), also known as Greenwood, lying along the highway skirting the very edge of steep bluffs—is a string of frame store buildings, most of them left to sag and gather cobwebs since lumbering operations stopped in 1931. In its heyday, when two or three boats anchored offshore every week to load lumber brought from inland by railroad, Elk had nearly a dozen saloons and half as many hotels. The loading trestle remains, flung from the edge of the bluffs to a jagged islet in the surf. In the debris-littered gravel bottoms just south of town lie the remains of the mill, rusted and rotting.

State 1 winds between fences over sheep ranges and strips of farm land that roll upward from the narrow coastal shelf to forest-fringed hills. A vast sweep of surf-scalloped shore line appears at intervals, curving off in the long promontory of Point Arena (*see below*). A far stretch of rolling country sweeps to timbered hills (L) as the highway strikes inland from the shore.

MANCHESTER, 58.8 *m.* (300 pop.), a handful of buildings widely scattered among farms and pastures, lies in a farming, dairying, and sheep- and cattle-raising region, one of the few sections along the northern coast level enough to permit extensive farming.

At 62.6 *m.* is the junction with a paved road.

Right on this road 2.5 *m.* to POINT ARENA LIGHT STATION (*visitors 1-3 Mon., Wed., Fri.*), where gray, red-roofed frame houses cluster around the tall cylindrical white light tower. On November 10, 1792, Capt. George Vancouver spent the night off this promontory in his ship *Discovery,* en route from Nootka to San Francisco. He named it Punta Barro de Arena (Sp., point sand bar). A brick light station erected here in 1870 was replaced, after its destruction in the 1906 earthquake, by the present 115-foot tower, which has a light of 380,000 candle power.

POINT ARENA, 64.5 *m.* (39 alt., 596 pop.), has scattered cottages in cypress-sheltered gardens and trim, stuccoed business buildings, churches, and schools. It traces its history to the opening of a store here in 1859. Although it was said to be the most thriving town between San Francisco and Eureka at the height of lumbering operations, it was not incorporated until 1908. Today it is a trading center for a dairying region.

South of Point Arena State 1 again skirts the coast, running through dense patches of dwarf-pines and dipping into gulches choked with undergrowth. Ten miles south is ANCHOR BAY.

GUALALA, 79.6 *m.* (sea level, 15 pop.), is on a curving beach at the mouth of the broad, forest-bordered Gualala River. Its name (pron. Wah-lá-la), is probably the Spanish spelling of the Pomo Indians' "wala'li" or "wa'lali," meaning a meeting place of waters. Gualala had its lumbering boom in the 1860's and 1870's—although its sawmill, abandoned now at the river's mouth, was operated until 1920. Its life centers today around the two-story, white frame GUALALA HOTEL (1903), with veranda and balcony. The fishing season attracts many visitors.

STEWART'S POINT, 91.3 *m.* (20 alt., 30 pop.), named for a pioneer lumberman and settler, is a handful of frame houses around a general store. On the rocky point at the edge of the cove, hidden by trees, are the abandoned sheds and trestle from which lumber was once shipped.

As State 1 winds southward, through rolling stretches thickly wooded with dwarf pines and littered with boulders, the coast becomes more and more rugged—saw-toothed with jutting promontories and rocky inlets where the surf crashes on kelp-strewn crags. The route makes a short swing inland through the KRUSE RHODODENDRON RESERVE, 99.3 *m.,* maintained in its natural state, where the rhododendrons, growing 20 to 30 feet high, blossom in late May and early June.

FORT ROSS, 107 *m.* (100 alt.), once chief outpost of Russian civilization in California, stands on a high shelf sloping from wooded hills to the edge of the cove. At this place, in the spring of 1812, the Russian-American Fur Company's vessel, the *Chirikov,* deposited a party of fur traders and Aleut hunters under command of Ivan Alexander Kuskof. Since 1806, when the Tsar's chamberlain, Nikolai Rezanof, had visited the San Francisco Presidio (*see SAN FRANCISCO*) in quest of food for the starving Russian settlement at Sitka, Alaska, the Russian-American Company had planned to establish settlements in California as sources of food supply for its fur-trading posts in the north. On May 15, 1812, Kuskof's party began building a fortress; three months later, on August 30, they dedicated it with ceremony, naming it Rossiya (Russia).

The settlement, laid out in a rectangle, was enclosed by a 14-foot stockade of hewn timbers and guarded by two-story blockhouses with portholes for cannon at the north and south corners. There were 59 buildings. Inside the enclosure were the chapel, the commandant's house, barracks, two warehouses, blacksmith and other shops, and a jail. Outside clustered the redwood huts of the Aleut hunters, a windmill, several farm buildings, and a tannery. At the foot of the steep bluffs were a small wharf, a workshop for shipbuilding, a blacksmith shop, a bathhouse, and sheds for the bidarkas (skin boats) of the Aleuts and for storing lumber.

Despite the efforts of apprehensive Spanish officials to check the growth of La Fuerte de los Rusos (the fort of the Russians), the colonists began a thriving trade with the San Francisco Presidio and mission, exchanging tobacco, sugar, kitchen utensils, iron, cloth, and wax candles for grain, peas, meat, tallow, flour, and hides. When Missions San Rafael and San Francisco Solano (*see TOUR 2a*) were founded to halt Russian expansion southward the Russians extended their trade to the missions themselves.

The Russian settlement began to face economic difficulties, however, when the revenue from sea-otter hunting diminished with the rapid extermination of the otter along the coast. Unable to make a living from farming, the colonists turned to shipbuilding; they used the green timber of oak to construct four vessels, two of 160 and two of 200 tons, between 1819 and 1824; but the timber decayed so rapidly that this activity was abandoned. The settlement was in the end a failure. Restrained from expanding southward by the Spanish, Russia agreed in 1824 to limit its future settlements to Alaska.

The man into whose hands Fort Ross finally passed, when in 1841 the Tsar ordered withdrawal of his subjects, was Johann August Sutter, founder of New Helvetia (Sacramento). The price agreed on for the entire property—buildings, chattels, livestock, and even the 20-ton schooner *Constantine*—was $30,000; of this Sutter agreed to pay $2,000 in cash and the rest in yearly installments of produce, chiefly wheat. Sutter dismantled fort and buildings and shipped everything he could carry on his schooner to New Helvetia. The transferred property included 1,700 head of cattle, 940 horses and mules, 9,000 sheep, agricultural implements and industrial machinery, and an arsenal, including brass pieces, cannon, and muskets—all French weapons picked up in 1813 in the path of Napoleon's retreat through the snow from Moscow. Even a 20-foot-square conservatory, with glass windows and doors, was removed in sections to Sacramento; Madame Rotchev, the Russian governor's wife, had begged Sutter (he wrote) "not to destroy the garden house which she had built and in which she had spent so many happy hours. . . . However . . . my men . . . could not put it together because they did not understand the workmanship of the Russian carpenters . . ."

The few remaining buildings were neglected until in 1906, after damage by the earthquake, the State began restoration. The original stockade has been rebuilt with heptagonal blockhouses at either corner as it appeared when Sutter acquired it from the Russians. At the eastern corner is the restored GREEK ORTHODOX CHAPEL (*open 8-5 except Tues.*), a crude structure 20 feet wide and 25 long, with a squat, dull yellow belfry and dome on its weather-worn red-gabled roof. The RUSSIAN COMMANDANT'S HOUSE, a spacious edifice with a shingled roof sloping over a wide veranda, preserves remnants of the original structure—including the fireplace and the log finish between the doors and windows of the facade—reinforced by later additions. Here is a small museum.

South of Fort Ross State 1 winds tortuously around brush-grown, rocky hillsides and through twisting ravines, on a narrow ledge overhanging the boiling surf. At 118.8 *m.* it swings up the broad valley of the Russian River (*see TOUR 2a*), which finds its way to the ocean through a narrow strait in the great sand bar that holds back its waters in a wide, placid lagoon.

JENNER-BY-THE-SEA, 119.7 *m.* (0 alt., 160 pop.), is a resort with peaked-roofed white and green cottages hugging the steep slopes above the river.

At 120.8 *m.*, where State 1 crosses Russian River on a giant concrete and steel bridge, is the junction with State 116.

At 121.7 *m.* is the junction with a dirt road.

Right on this road 0.2 *m.* to BODEGA-SONOMA COAST STATE PARK, which stretches along 5 miles of picturesque ocean shore from the mouth of the Russian River to Bodega Bay. The shore waters abound with shellfish and abalones and the surf with fish that can be caught by line from the rocks or by net in the breakers.

At 122.9 *m.* on State 1 is the junction with an oiled road.

Right on this road 0.2 *m.* to SHELL BEACH in Bodega-Sonoma Coast State Park.

WRIGHT'S BEACH is at 124.3 *m.* and ARCH ROCK BEACH at 127 *m.* Both are wide sandy strands sheltered in rocky coves in the State park.

SALMON CREEK BEACH, 128.5 *m.,* rimmed by great sand dunes, lies at the mouth of Salmon Creek, where a sand bar impounds a lagoon below scattered cottages.

BAY, 130.4 *m.,* a string of frame houses sheltered by a lane of eucalyptus trees overlooking a row of small wharves where fishing smacks are moored, lies along the curving shore of BODEGA BAY.

Bodega Bay is now a shallow, sand-choked inlet, rimmed by mud flats at low tide; its egress to the sea on the south is blocked, except for a narrow strait, by a sandspit stretching from the mainland on the east to Bodega Head at the tip of the long promontory on the west. The bay was named for its discoverer, Lieut. Juan Francisco de la Bodéga y Cuadra, who anchored his schooner, the *Sonora,* off Bodega Head October 3, 1775. In 1809 the Russian-American Fur Company's agent, Ivan Kuskof, landed with a party from Sitka. They sowed wheat, and in August, with the harvested grain and a catch of 2,000 sea-otter skins, returned to Alaska. In 1811 the Russians returned to found the settlements of Port Roumiantzoff on the bay and Bodega (*see below*) and Kuskof in the hinterland. They cultivated land toward the tip of the Bodega peninsula and erected two warehouses.

First Yankee settlers at Bodega Bay were three sailors. In 1835 Gen. Mariano G. Vallejo gave them large land grants on condition that they settle at the border of the Russian claims to check Russian expansion. In 1843 Capt. Stephen Smith was granted the land formerly occupied by the Russians. Five years later he erected a small warehouse and in 1852 a hotel. By 1860 the port was alive with people and business, its harbor crowded with sails. The warehouses lining the shore overflowed with potatoes—a variety known as Bodega Reds for the bright maroon coat beneath their rough skins—raised on great ranches roundabout. Regular freight and passenger boats from San Francisco anchored in the open roadstead outside the sandspit, where they were loaded from small lighters. In the 1870's the bay began to fill with sand. In time, potato raising was supplanted by dairying, the chief industry of the region ever since. Vessels no longer call here—nor have they for a generation past.

State 1 winds inland over rolling farm lands where cattle graze in fenced pastures, bordered by lanes of eucalyptus trees and patches of orchards.

BODEGA, 136.4 *m.* (40 alt., 100 pop.), clusters amid cypress patches around a red-roofed schoolhouse and two white-spired churches.

Beside the road (R) at 138.4 *m.* stands the WATSON DISTRICT SCHOOL, built in 1856, a white clapboarded building with a bell tower jutting from its peaked red roof. It was named for James Watson, an immigrant of 1853, who acquired so many thousand acres of land from the yield of bumper crops of the high-priced Bodega Reds that he became a land baron, entertaining the whole countryside with horse racing at his private course.

VALLEY FORD, 142.3 *m.* (45 alt., 200 pop.), with old brick and frame stores, is among gently rolling pasture lands dotted with gracious white farmhouses, roomy barns, and corrals. It lies at the head of tidewater on the Estero Americano (American Creek), which empties into Bodega Bay; it was named for the "valley ford," where an ancient Indian and Spanish trail crossed the Estero. This is a dairying town: when the bank was organized in 1893, it was called The Dairymans Bank.

TOMALES, 149.3 *m.* (75 alt., 450 pop.), a trim looking town, rambles over the slopes of a hollow. The countryside is noted for its butter, cheese, and milk. Tomales' first house was built in 1850 by John Keyes, who operated a small schooner between Bodega Bay and San Francisco and opened a trading post here in the spring of 1854.

State 1 winds through the shallow gully of San Antonio Creek to its mouth in a delta of mud flats at TOMALES BAY, 151.9 *m.,* and then runs for 13 miles along the shore. (Tomales is a Spanish corruption of the Coast Miwok Indian word *tamal,* bay.) The bay is a long, narrow, fingerlike inlet, resembling a firth in the Scottish Highlands. On the east bare brown hills slope down to the shore; on the west, low, tumbled peaks densely forested with green. In the shallow water offshore, oyster beds are fenced in by a long file of slender stakes.

At POINT REYES STATION, formerly a busy shipping point for dairy products, a road going west connects with US 101.

At 166.7 *m.* is the junction of State 1 with Sir Francis Drake Highway. This extends west to INVERNESS PARK, whence Drakes Summit Road leads southwest to DRAKE'S BAY. The main highway continues along the Inverness area west of Tomales Bay, serving INVERNESS. James Black, a native of Inverness, Scotland, settled here in 1832; the town was incorporated in 1908. The highway then enters TOMALES BAY STATE PARK, after which it enters the national park and extends to the coast and the U. S. LIGHTHOUSE.

POINT REYES NATIONAL SEASHORE is a unit of the National Park System authorized September 13, 1962, when the United States chose 53,000 acres for conservation and recreational development. About 25,000 acres are privately-owned cattle and dairy ranchland. The name is traced to Sebastian Vizcaino, who in 1602 called the anchorage Puerto de los Reyes or Port of Kings. Point Reyes peninsula is divided into four topographic sections: (1) a depression occupied by Tamales Bay, Olema Valley and Bolinas Lagoon; (2) Inverness Ridge; (3) rolling middle ground west of the ridge and (4) Point Reyes promontory.

Part of the peninsula extends along the San Andreas Fault, which is believed to move northward about 2 inches a year. A number of beaches are open for public use the year around but facilities are limited, pending development of swimming, fishing, camping and other recreational improvements. Park headquarters are at Bear Valley Ranch, 1 *m.* west of Olema on Bear Valley Road; the Superintendent is at Point

Reyes, Calif., 94956. Tomales Bay separates the north end of the Peninsula from the mainland. A depressed land surface beneath this 13-mile bay continuing southward through Olema Valley under Bolinas Lagoon delineates a short segment of the fault. The Peninsula's total contact with the mainland is along this fault. Its slow movement north makes it an "island in time."

Southeast of this point the main side route follows the bleak, wind-swept slopes of POINT REYES. The half-mile distant wide beach (R) extends north in an unbroken straight line toward the hazy bluffs of Tomales Point and Bodega Head. The low-growing vegetation on the hill slopes is brightened in spring with myriads of tiny red, yellow, and purple flowers.

At 11 m. is the junction with a dirt road; R. here 0.7 m. to the UNITED STATES RADIO COMPASS STATION, which broadcasts compass bearings to ships at sea.

At 15 m. on the main side route, south of a barnyard gate near a farmhouse, is the junction with a dirt road; L. here 1.3 m. to the UNITED STATES COAST GUARD LIFE-SAVING STATION, facing DRAKE'S BAY from a cove in the lee of Point Reyes. The white-faced bluffs fringing the bay in an immense crescent-shaped sweep suggested the white cliffs of the English coast near Dover to Sir Francis Drake on June 17, 1579, when he took refuge here in the *Golden Hinde*. The Drake company, in the last of the five vessels with which it had sailed from England nearly two years earlier, was searching southward along the coast for a haven from the wind, the fog, and the bitter cold that had plagued them for weeks. In this sheltered bay, its waters as smooth as a mill pond, they found a "convenient and fit harborough." For nearly six weeks Drake and his men remained, reconditioning their boats and causing wonderment among awe-struck Indian visitors from villages for miles around (*see INDIANS*).

A small party led by Drake made a journey inland, where they found, as chaplain Francis Fletcher wrote, "a goodly country and fruitful soyle, stored with many blessings fit for the use of man." Drake named it Nova Albion (Lat., New England). On July 23, after religious ceremonies, they set sail again while Indians watched from the hilltops. But before "we went from thence," wrote Fletcher, "our generall caused to be set up a monument of our being there, as also of her maiesties and successors right and title to that Kingdom; namely, a plate of brasse, fast nailed to a greate and firme post, whereon is engrauen her graces name, and the day and yeare of our arrival there, and of the free giving up of the province and Kingdom, both by King and people, into her maiesties hands; together with her highnesses picture and armes, in a piece of sixpence current English monie, shewing itself by a hole made of purpose through the plate . . ."

Late in 1933 a chauffeur, on a hunting expedition with his employer at the Laguna Ranch, just east of Drake's Bay, picked up a slab of blackened metal near the roadside and wiping it off, uncovered in one corner what looked like the word "Drak." He placed the metal in the side pocket of the car.

A week later, as he drove past a point near the mouth of Corte Madera Creek, where the southern shore of Point San Quentin reaches away from the mainland (*see TOUR 2a*), he threw the plate away. On April 6, 1937, a motorist, stopped by a flat tire, picked up the plate near the highway. For months it lay unnoticed among his effects until one day, using it to tinker with his automobile, he noticed its crude engraving and took it to the head of the University of California history department.

Carefully cleaned, the plate revealed the inscription:

Bee It Knowne Vnto All Men By These Presents
Ivne 17 1579
By The Grace Of God And In The Name Of Herr
Maiesty Queen Elizabeth Of England And Herr
Successors Forever I Take Possesson Of This
Kingdome Whose King And People Freely Resigne
Their Right And Title In The Whole Land Vnto Herr
Maiesties Keepeing Now Named By Me And To Bee
Knowne Vnto All Men As Nova Albion
Francis Drake

After exhaustive investigation by metallurgists, chemists, museum cura-
tors, archeologists, and geologists, the plate was finally accepted in America
as the real "plate of brasse" left by Drake, though British scientists still
question the authenticity.

The main side route turns westward to POINT REYES LIGHTHOUSE (*open*),
19.9 *m.*, at the verge of a cliff on the tip of a knifelike headland, one of
the windiest points on the coast. The light was established in 1870. Its
white pyramidal tower is 294 feet above water. Throughout the summer,
when dense fog blankets the coast, the fog signal blasts almost constantly.
Back of the lighthouse are a storm-warning display and telegraph station.
So many ships have piled up on the treacherous rocks off Point Reyes that
the San Francisco newspapers are said to keep set up the headline, "Ship
Aground at Point Reyes." At dawn of November 29, 1938, a Seattle-
Oakland airliner off its course and hours overdue, landed on the water
1,000 yards offshore and was battered on the rocks by crashing surf, with
the loss of 5 lives.

OLEMA (Ind., Olemaloke: coyote valley), 168.8 *m.* (67 alt., 150
pop.), consists of three or four old frame buildings gathered around an
old-fashioned two-story frame hotel and a little steepled white church.

The moss-grown, masonry RUINS OF A LIME KILN occupy a
ravine near the roadside (R) at 172.8 *m.*, where lime from an outcrop
on Olema Creek was fired in the early 1850's. Against a cut in the
slope of the ravine tower the kiln's three chimneys—two of them still
standing and a third in ruins—resembling giant beehives in shape.

State 1 runs southeast to the junction, at 177.5 *m.*, with a paved
road.

Right on this road, along the western shore of a landlocked lagoon, to
the head of crescent-shaped Bolinas Bay, in the lee of cliff-edged Bolinas
Point, probably named for Francisco Bolaños, pilot of the Vizcaíno expedition in 1602. The SITE OF THE BOLINAS LIGHTER WHARF (L), 0.4 *m.*, is
marked by a few piles. During the 1850's ox-drawn wagons with wooden
wheels—crosscut sections of huge tree trunks—hauled lumber to the wharf.
From this point their loads were carried by flat-bottomed lighters to cargo
vessels anchored in the bay.

At 1.7 *m.* is the junction with a paved road; R. here 2.6 *m.* to the RCA
COMMUNICATIONS, INC. STATION on a 1,500-acre tract on the western shore
of the Bolinas peninsula. RCA's San Francisco radio-telegraph terminal
has its sending station here for transmitting short-wave messages across
the Pacific. The transmitting equipment includes 49 antennae—about half
of them of the high-power short-wave directive type.

BOLINAS, 2.1 *m.* (10 alt., 125 pop.), circles the base of the headland.
A miniature church, parsonage, and houses built a half century ago are
neighbors of the shingled summer homes of San Franciscans. Low tide
brings out dozens of rubber-booted clam diggers. First settler here was
Gregorio Briones, owner of the 8,911-acre cattle domain of Baulinas Rancho,

whose daughter Maria's marriage to Francisco Sebrean, celebrated May 20, 1850, with feasting on a barbecued fat bullock and dancing on a floor of whip-sawed lumber, was Bolinas' first.

At Bolinas is a UNITED STATES COAST GUARD LIFE-SAVING STATION. The jagged rocks of Duxbury Reef, stretching seaward 100 feet below the cliff-edged tableland of Duxbury Point, west of the town, have been the grave-yard of many ships. The Panama-San Francisco propeller steamer *Lewis* was battered to pieces here April 9, 1853, with the loss of all its freight and baggage and the narrow escape of 400 passengers.

STINSON BEACH (*accommodations; boats, tackle, and bait for surf fishing*), 182.1 *m.* (sea level, 130 pop.), a family resort thronged on holidays by vacationers, fronts a 3-mile white sand beach curving around Bolinas Bay; the surf is warm enough for bathing all year. The winters are so mild that swarms of big brown Monarch butterflies immigrate from the high Sierra. The settlement has evolved from a campground beside a grove of willows and alders near the beach at the end of the Dipsea (Lone Tree) Trail ("Dipsea" is an Indian corruption of "deep sea"); from the slopes of Mount Tamalpais (*see TOUR 2a*) to the beach, the trail is followed every year by cross-country hikers in the Dipsea Trail Race from Mill Valley (*see TOUR 2a*).

At 182.4 *m.* is the junction with the dirt Mount Tamalpais Road (*see TOUR 2a*).

State 1 twists upward, high above the crashing breakers. At 187.1 *m.* it winds along the crest of a knifelike ridge overlooking the timbered hollows of Muir Woods (*see TOUR 2a*) on one hand and ocean expanses on the other.

At 188.6 *m.* is the junction with the Muir Woods Road (*see TOUR 2a*).

At 188.8 *m.* is the junction with a dirt road.

> Right on this road 0.7 *m.* to MUIR BEACH (*swimming and fishing*), a sandy strip curving around the shores of Big Lagoon.

At 194.6 *m.* is the junction with US 101 (*see TOUR 2a*), with which State 1 unites into SAN FRANCISCO, 205.4 *m.* (*see SAN FRANCISCO*).

*Section b.   SAN FRANCISCO to MONTEREY; 133.1 m.   State 1*

The rugged flanks of the Peninsula ridge south of San Francisco crowd State 1 to the edge of blunt-faced mesas battered by the waves. The highway dips to wide, sandy beaches and climbs to tumbled heights above the surf. Swinging inland around the great curve of Monterey Bay, it crosses the fertile Pajaro Valley's apple orchards. Its way back to the shore leads through low, rolling land, fringed with sand dunes. Along the whole route the countryside—early, but thinly, settled—has a look of age about it, except where seaside resorts have replaced the whaling stations, the old fishing villages, the abandoned schooner landings.

Along this forbidding coast line in the autumn of 1769 struggled the first white men to come by land into California—"that small company of persons, or rather say skeletons, who had been spared by scurvy, hunger and thirst," as their commander, Don Gaspar de Portolá, described them. They were searching for the "fine harbor sheltered from all winds" of Monterey, over enthusiastically and misleadingly described by Sebastián Vizcaíno in 1602—there to found a military port and a mission. The expedition included Portolá's aides, Capt. Don Fernando de Rivera y Moncada, Lt. Don Pedro Fages, and army engineer Ensign Miguel Constanso; the two Franciscan friars, Fray Juan Crespi and Fray Francisco Gómez; Sgt. José Francisco de Ortega, with his 27 soldiers; and a troop of servants and Christian Indians from Lower California. The soldiers wore leather jackets fashioned of seven thicknesses of deerskin and carried bullhide shields, lances and broad-swords, and short muskets. At the head of the expedition, with its four pack-train divisions of mules each, rode Portolá; at the rear, behind the spare horses and mules and their guard, Rivera.

On September 30, two and a half months after leaving San Diego, they came to the coast at the mouth of the Salinas River on Monterey Bay. The open gulf so little resembled the "fine harbor sheltered from all winds" for which they were looking that they went on—now with 17 men on the sick list, 11 so ill that they had to be carried on litters fastened with long poles to the mules. As they continued northward in 5- and 10-mile stages, toiling up steep grades and across deep arroyos, often cutting their way through brush, they had to ration their rapidly diminishing store of food. Finally on October 31 they climbed to the heights above San Pedro Point and saw the Gulf of the Farallones and Point Reyes far to the north. Forced to the unhappy conclusion that they had overshot their mark, they turned eastward and then southward down the Peninsula—having in the meantime discovered San Francisco Bay—and retraced their steps to Monterey Bay. Once more failing to recognize the object of their search, they went on south to San Diego, where Portolá reported his expedition a failure.

West from Van Ness Ave. in SAN FRANCISCO, 0 *m.*, on Hayes St. to Franklin St.; R. to Fulton St.; L. to Funston (13th) Ave.; L. through Golden Gate Park into Nineteenth Ave. and south into Junipero Serra Blvd.

At 6.1 *m.* is the junction with Sloat Blvd.

Right on Sloat Blvd. to the junction with Sunset Blvd., 6.7 *m.* and L. around Lake Merced to the SITE OF THE TERRY-BRODERICK DUEL, 9.6 *m.*, at the southern tip of the lake, marked by two granite shafts, one bearing the name "Broderick" and the other "Terry" in bronze letters. At dawn on September 13, 1859, a United States Senator and a California Supreme Court Chief Justice took their positions here with duelling pistols, 30 paces apart. They represented opposing factions in the struggle on the issue of slavery which was tearing the Democratic Party in California apart—Broderick the anti- and Terry the pro-slavery side. Broderick was the son of an Irish stone mason, schooled in politics by Tammany Hall; Terry, a Kentucky-born aristocrat, aligned with the "Chivalry" Democrats. Terry had publicly attacked Broderick and the Douglas Democrats for sailing under "the banner of the black Douglass, whose name is Frederick, not Stephen." When Broderick replied in kind, Terry resigned from the bench and demanded a retraction; Broderick refused. Broderick was no match for his opponent; his shot, fired first, entered the ground only 9 feet from where he stood. Terry's shot entered his breast. He died three days later. A crowd of 30,000 people gathered at Portsmouth Square in San Francisco to hear the funeral oration.

State 1 turns southwest on Alemany Boulevard through neat truck gardens toward the ocean.

At 9.8 *m.* is the junction with Skyline Boulevard (State 35).

Left on Skyline Boulevard, up from gently rolling hill country to the crest of the forested Sierra Morena and down the ridge of the Peninsula. The highway skirts the western shore of long, narrow, fingerlike SAN ANDREAS LAKE, 10.3 *m.*, and CRYSTAL SPRINGS LAKE, 14 *m.*, along which the Portolá expedition traveled November 4 and 5, 1769 on their way southward.

Near the northern end of Crystal Springs Lake is the JEPSON LAUREL, 55 feet high and 22 feet 4 inches in circumference. It is called the Deathshead Tree because of the skull and crossbones carved in its fork in the days when the Spanish held barbecues beneath its branches.

State 35 crosses SKYLINE DAM, 15.4 *m.*, at the head of San Mateo Creek, and strikes westward from Crystal Springs Lake.

At 25 *m.* is the junction with King's Mountain Road; L. here 5 *m.* to the WOODSIDE STORE, the first opened between San Francisco and Santa Clara. It was built in 1854 by Dr. R. O. Tripp. It is a two-story structure with a peaked, shingled roof; the posts upholding the wide veranda, where horses were once hitched, are well-worn. The wooden sign over the porch was put up before the Civil War. Inside are the post office pigeon-holes, the old-fashioned counters, the oil lamps with their tin reflectors, the tin signs advertising plug chewing tobacco. As many as a thousand lumberjacks from the dense redwood forests roundabout—where 15 sawmills operated in a radius of 5 miles—called here for mail, food, and liquor.

Skyline Boulevard continues to the SKYLINE METHUSELAH REDWOOD (L), 26.2 *m.*, a lone giant dominating the countryside. More than 1,500 years old, it measures 55 feet in circumference. Its trunk is blackened by the repeated fires that long since felled its neighbors.

At 31.1 *m.* is the junction with the paved La Honda (the deep) Canyon road; R. on this road that winds down the slopes in a flicker of sun and shadow through clumps of redwoods and madrones 7 *m.* to LA HONDA (403 alt., 150 pop.), a mountain resort center (*cabins, campgrounds*) in the La Honda Grove of redwoods. In the winter of 1861-62, John L. Sears settled here and built the LA HONDA STORE, employing two newcomers to the vicinity, Jim and Bob Younger. Their stay was brief, for they left suddenly to rejoin the James gang in the Midwest for a bank robbery at Northfield, Minnesota, that landed them in the penitentiary.

Left from La Honda on a paved road 1 *m.* to the junction with a paved road; R. here 5 *m.* to the SAN MATEO COUNTY MEMORIAL REDWOOD PARK, a 310-acre grove.

At 38.4 *m.* on State 35 is the junction with a dirt road; R. here 4 *m.* and L. to ISLAM SHRINE PARK, 7 *m.*, a 1,400-acre redwood grove.

State 35 continues down the east slope of the Sierra Morena to its junction with State 9 (*see TOUR 2b*) 45 *m.*

State 1 skirts hills velvety with matted chaparral that slope steeply to the water's edge, where flocks of sea birds perch on the crags.

SHARP PARK, 14.7 *m.*, a resort hamlet facing a wide, sandy beach, clusters near the northern edge of SHARP PARK MUNICIPAL

GOLF COURSE, 15.2 *m.*, part of the 480-acre park given the city of San Francisco by Mrs. Honora Sharp.

PACIFICA, 16 *m.* (50 alt., 25,000 pop.), one of the newest of California cities, was incorporated 1957 by several small communities.

The road cuts across the mouth of Pedro Valley to SAN PEDRO CREEK, 17.8 *m.*, guarded by lofty SAN PEDRO POINT. Near the mouth of the creek, by an Indian village, the Portolá expedition camped on October 31, 1769 and feasted on mussels pried from the rocks. After mass the next morning, Portolá sent Sgt. José Francisco de Ortega with a party to scout eastward. As they climbed to the top of the ridge, the vast expanse of San Francisco Bay, never before seen by white men, appeared in the distance. Before they could report their discovery, however, another party that went out November 2 to hunt and returned before nightfall had brought tidings of the "great arm of the sea, extending to the southeast farther than the eye could reach." On the morning of November 4, the expedition broke camp. Abandoning their trek in search of Monterey Bay, they climbed the ridge to the east, looking for the "port and a ship therein" only two days distant of which Indians had told Ortega.

The ragged leaves and green globes of row on row of silvery-green artichoke plants carpet fertile Pedro Valley, thriving here—and near Half Moon Bay—as nowhere else. Much of the United States supply of artichokes is grown in this fog-moistened coastal strip, where the first commercial planting was made in 1900. The plants are trimmed to the ground in the spring and watered and cultivated in summer to force the buds to mature in the fall and winter, although they mature naturally in June and July. The harvest season, beginning in August or September, reaches its peak in February, March, and April. About half the crop is hauled to market in California by truck and the rest shipped to the East in refrigerator cars. The plants, spaced four to six feet apart in rows, produce from three to four dozen buds apiece by the end of their third year, and up to twice that number in succeeding years, until their sixth year, when they are usually replaced.

On the south bank of San Pedro Creek is the junction with a graded road.

> Left on this road 1.3 *m.* to the restored two-story SANCHEZ ADOBE, the balconied ranch house of Rancho San Pedro, built by Don Francisco Sánchez in 1842. It stands on the site of an older house, which is said to have been rebuilt in 1817 with timbers from a ship wrecked on San Pedro Point.

State 1 climbs over the hump of MONTARA MOUNTAIN; on the summit above San Pedro Point, Portolá's men at noon of October 31, 1769, sick and hungry and exhausted from the tortuous climb through matted brush up the southern slope, looked out over a vast sweep of sea and land—Twin Peaks and Mount Tamalpais rising to the north, Point Reyes curving out to sea far beyond, and the rocky Farallon Islands jutting from the misty horizon. The road dips to the spot where the Portolá party stopped the night of October 30, 1769, in despair, their way northward blocked by the steep slopes.

The rolling land east of MONTARA, 22 m. (300 pop.), is checkered with fields that supply large quantities of everlasting-flowers. The blossoms are cut from their stems, mounted on fine wire, and dried for about 36 hours. The industry, begun in 1925, has achieved a production of 20,000,000 or more blossoms in recent years.

As State 1 continues past plots of artichokes and brussels sprouts, the stout tower of POINT MONTARA LIGHT and the wire-webbed steel masts of a UNITED STATES NAVAL RADIO COMPASS STATION appear (R) at 22.7 m. on Point Montara, near a half-submerged circle of upstanding rocks.

MOSS BEACH, 23.3 m. (75 alt., 300 pop.), is a tiny cluster of weather-beaten houses sheltered by wind-battered cypresses. From the rocks along the shore delicate sea mosses can be gathered. The strangely beautiful marine gardens offshore are famous for their flora.

The highway rounds gently curving HALF MOON BAY, 25.5 m., whose blue waters stretch southward, breaking in hissing foam on a long white beach guarded by the rocky headland of PILLAR POINT, which navigator Francisco de Gali sighted from his galleon in 1585. He reported: ". . . we passed by a very high and fair land with many trees, wholly without snow; there likewise we found great store of seals; whereby it is to be presumed and certainly to be believed, that there are many rivers, bays and havens along by those coasts . . ." The harbor, protected by a submerged reef off the point, became a port of call for whalers and traders—and, more recently, for rum runners.

The town of HALF MOON BAY, 30.3 m. (10 alt., 1,957 pop.), now populated largely by Italians and Portuguese, is a quiet farm village surrounded by neatly laid out fields of artichokes and brussels sprouts. The weary men of the Portolá expedition pitched camp near the mouth of Pilarcitos Creek, at the northern edge of town, on the rainy night of October 28, 1769, and spent a wet and miserable weekend—their medicine gone and their food running low—before they could gather enough strength to move on. The creek, extending up Pilarcitos Valley, was later the boundary between Tiburcio Vásquez' (no relative of the bandit) part of Rancho El Corral de Tierra (the enclosure of earth) and Candelario Miramontes' Rancho Miramontes. The two *rancheros* built their low-roofed, rambling adobe houses on opposite banks of the creek in the 1840's, affording each other company at a time when the region was a wilderness roamed by grizzly bears. Around their houses grew up a settlement that went by the name Spanishtown for 40 years or more after it was platted in 1863.

State 1 continues past small farms where large whitewashed barns and small weather-beaten farmhouses are sheltered from the wind by lines of dark, ragged cypresses. The rising hills curve gently, splotched in the hollows with dusky chaparral.

The village of PURISIMA (purest), 34.5 m. (46 alt.), once a lively town on José María Alviso's Rancho Cañada de Verde y Arroyo de la Purísima, is ghostly and deserted now. Its weathered gray buildings stand among mosshung cypresses and eucalyptus trees, their windows broken, their stairs falling in, their facades rudely stuck with gay circus posters.

From a VIEWPOINT at 38.6 *m.*, tawny bluffs bordered by surf stretch south. The highway descends to the beach at TUNITAS GLEN, 38.8 *m.* (*25¢ a car for camping*).

The farm hamlet of SAN GREGORIO (St. Gregory), 42.1 *m.* (100 alt., 107 pop.), in a valley where suave hills sweep up to the Sierra Morena crest, is near the mouth of San Gregorio Creek. The place so enchanted Fray Crespi of the Portolá expedition that he proposed it for a mission site, naming it Santo Domingo—but others called it the Valley of the Curses of the Soldiers, for "they were sick and tired and hungry," as diarist Miguel Costanso wrote. They stayed two days to rest.

Although PESCADERO (fishing place), 49.5 *m.* (56 alt., 979 pop.), was named for Pescadero Creek's once plentiful supply of speckled trout, the town's predominantly Portuguese inhabitants neither catch nor sell fish. Pescadero's cluster of prim white buildings give it the appearance of a New England village. It was long the whitest town in the State; when the *S.S. Columbia* was wrecked near Pigeon Point, most of her cargo of white paint drifted ashore and, salvaged by the inhabitants, was used lavishly.

At 50.5 *m.* is the junction with a dirt road.

Right here 2 *m.* to PEBBLE BEACH, famous for its polished pebbles—small agates, jaspers, opals, moonstones, moss agates, and water-drops (white pebbles with drops of water in their centers).

South of Pescadero State 1 crosses low mesas that break off abruptly in bluffs, jagged with deep caves and gulches created by the waves. The PIGEON POINT LIGHTHOUSE, 55.8 *m.* (*open 2-4 Tues., Fri., Sat.*), overlooks a rock-bound coast, on whose headland the Boston clipper *Carrier Pigeon* was wrecked May 6, 1853. The tower was built in 1872. The powerful lens was used first on the New England and later on the South Atlantic coast, where it was buried in the sand during the Civil War—according to one story, to keep it from falling into Confederate hands.

The road curves inland from PUNTA DEL ANO NUEVO (New Year's Point), stretching out to sea at 63.5 *m.*, the NEW YEAR'S POINT LIGHTHOUSE at its tip. This was the first important spot sighted by Sebastián Vizcaíno's crew when they sailed from Monterey January 3, 1602; they named it for the season of the year.

The pine-forested mountainsides slope steeply to the sea, crowding the highway to the edge of a narrow bench. Then State 1 drops to a cove to travel along a roadway carved from the cliffs. The wide beach here, where the long rollers arch in transparent blue-green hues and crash in a welter of foam, was once the greatest hazard on the Santa Cruz to Pescadero stage line. Since the coaches could travel along the hard-packed, sandy strip only at low tide, a delay in schedule was apt to prove disastrous. The more adventurous drivers enjoyed timing the trip down to the last second so that they could race the tide to safety, much to the consternation of their passengers.

The countryside around DAVENPORT, 75.5 m. (90 alt., 600 pop.), a company town near a large cement plant, is liberally powdered with lime dust. In the 1850's Davenport Landing was the site of whaling operations, directed by Capt. John P. Davenport, who devised a stay-at-home method of hunting. The whalers lived in cabins on the shore, from which they sallied forth in whaling boats when a whale was sighted. They towed their catch to the beach and there fried the blubber in huge pots. Portuguese from the Azores built lookouts and stationed watchmen to sound bells when they sighted whales.

SANTA CRUZ, 86.8 m. (15 alt., 25,596 pop., 1960; 28,000 est. 1964) is favorably situated at the north end of Monterey Bay, in the center of fine beaches, state parks with recreational features, and within a few miles via State Route 9 of the finest redwoods in BIG BASIN REDWOOD STATE PARK and HENRY COWELL STATE PARK.

Numerous beaches line the county shore, and nine state parks invite recreation activities. Boating and deep-sea fishing in Monterey Bay are available. There is daily trolling for salmon and albacore fishing during September, October and November. Pismo clams are dug in the beaches at low tide. Fishing from any public wharf is free. A Pacific Ocean license for California residents costs $1 for three days; non-residents may buy a ten-day license for $3.

Annual events in Santa Cruz include the state finals for Miss America Pageant in June and the County Horse Show in the summer.

The UNIVERSITY OF CALIFORNIA SANTA CRUZ opened its first unit, COWELL COLLEGE, in 1965 on the former Cowell Ranch, northwest of the city. The 2,000-acre forested site overlooks the city and Monterey Bay. Cowell College was designed for 600 students and 40 faculty, with its own houses of residence, dining room, library and classrooms. The plan calls for additional colleges, with a School of Engineering to open 1967. South Pacific studies, conservation and regional development will be primary topics at Santa Cruz.

Santa Cruz expected a 10% rise in population after 1965 as a result of the opening of the university. The population had an annual increase of 3% in the 1960's, aided by the shift in the county from farm to non-farm pursuits. Santa Cruz' best known industry was the plant of the Wrigley chewing gum corporation. Defense industries have come into the area and in nearby Watsonville.

When the expedition of Don Jasper de Portolá planted a cross on the bank of the river which they named the San Lorenzo, on October 17, 1769, they noticed redwoods and "roses of Castille" but—to Fra Crespí's disappointment—no Indians. Only 22 years later, however, a fellow Franciscan, Fra Fermín Francisco de Lasuen, said mass to consecrate the site of a mission. Misión la Exaltación de la Santa Cruz (the elevation of the holy cross) became the new foundation that was formally founded two months later, September 25, 1791, when Don Hermenegildo Sal, *comandante* of the Presidio of San Francisco, took the name of King Carlos IV. Fathers Alonzo Salazar and Baldomero López began their work, equipped with an image of Our Father Saint Francis, a painting of Our Lady of Sorrows, and gifts from nearby missions—including barley for seed, cows, sheep, oxen, horses and mules. For more than two years they baptized the heathen without even the roof of a church above their heads, for the first church was not completed and dedicated until March 10, 1794.

On May 12, 1797, the schooner *Concepción* anchored in the bay with a boatload of colonists for the Villa de Branciforte, the Spanish Government's third, last, and least successful experiment in pueblo founding. The instructions of Governor Diego de Borica for the pueblo, named in honor of the Mexican Viceroy, the Marquis de Branciforte, had been sensible and to the point: "An adobe house to be built for each settler so that the prevalent state of things at San José and Los Angeles, where the settlers still live in tule huts, being unable to build better buildings without neglecting their fields, may be avoided; the houses not to cost over $200." The government had promised each colonist a musket, a plow, a few animals, and a loan of 116 pesos. Unfortunately, the farmers, mechanics, artisans, and sailors for whom Borica had called proved to be a tatterdemalion crew of vagabonds and ex-convicts. Futhermore, none of the houses was ready when they arrived. Don Alberto Córdoba, a Spanish Army engineer, arrived in August to supervise digging an irrigation canal, erecting public buildings, and building houses—all according to plans laid out in Mexico— but he got little further than submitting estimates for the work, since funds failed to arrive.

The model village across the river was a sore trial for the mission padres, who regarded it with suspicious anxiety—justifiably, as it turned out. When the Buenos Aires privateersman Hippolyte de Bouchard sacked Monterey in November, 1818, the padres retired in haste to Mission Santa Clara, leaving the mission in the hands of Branciforte's inhabitants for safekeeping. The protectors found the stock of aguardiente in the padres' cellar pleasantly useful for bolstering their morale. The damage to the church and its furnishings was considerable. Unfortunately, since Bouchard never appeared for his scheduled raid, they could not blame him for the depredations as they had planned.

The mission, secularized in 1834, fell into decay, while Branciforte survived. By 1840, when twenty ranchos had been granted in the vicinity, whalers were finding it a good place to buy fresh vegetables for scurvy-ridden crews. A new town grew up around the mission plaza, borrowing the mission's name. Under the Yankee regime it developed a fine trade, shipping lumber from the redwood-forested hinterland. One of its first industrial plants was Elihu Anthony's foundry, which in 1848 was turning out light-weight iron picks for the mines and cast-iron plows, the first made in California. In 1866 the city of Santa Cruz was granted a charter by the State. Meanwhile neighboring Bran-

ciforte preserved the easy-going ways of old.   As late as July, 1867, the
bull ring was gay with red flags and noisy with firecrackers on bull
fight days—"Admission and seats—$1.00.   Standing room on the sunny
side—50 cents."   Finally in 1907 Branciforte, now a mere suburb of
its former rival, was incorporated in Santa Cruz.

A reproduction of MISSION SANTA CRUZ (*adm. 50¢*), on Emmet
St. facing the Upper Plaza, was built in 1931 about 75 yards from the
old site.   The original structure built in 1793 suddenly collapsed with
a loud crash a month after an earthquake had weakened its walls on
January 9, 1857.   About one-half the size of the original but identical
in proportions, the mission has a square bell-tower topped with a dome,
overlooking one-story porticoed living quarters at one side and a rear
garden court.   It houses old relics—richly ornamented vestments, a
candle chandelier, and a statue of Our Lady of Sorrows brought from
Monterey on muleback.   The brick CHURCH OF THE HOLY CROSS,
facing the Plaza, was built in 1858 and rebuilt in 1889.   Back of the
mission, on the brow of the hill, the ancient headstones of the eucalyptus-shaded graveyard are half hidden by tangled myrtles.   The adobe
NEARY HOUSE, R. from the mission on School St., was formerly the
headquarters of the corporal of the mission guard.   The adobe ROD-
RIGUEZ HOUSE, joined to it by a 5-foot adobe wall, has been in the
possession of descendants of José Antonio Rodríguez ever since 1838.

The SANTA CRUZ MUNICIPAL PIER, at the foot of Pacific Ave.,
projects into the surf from the half-mile strip of smooth white sand
bordering the bay.   At the western end of the boardwalk is the Casino,
and nearby are a bathing pavilion and pleasure pier.

Right from Pacific Ave. into 2.8-mile West Cliff Dr.   On the
drive are the SANTA CRUZ LIGHT STATION (*open 2-4 Tues., Thurs.*);
the 565-acre expanse of the municipal recreation ground, LAVEAGA
PARK, still in its natural state; and NATURAL BRIDGES STATE PARK,
in a sandy, cliff-edged cove where jutting rocks have been carved into
natural bridges by the waves.

Santa Cruz is at the junctions with State 9 (*see TOUR 2b*) and
State 17 (*see TOUR 2b*).

East of Santa Cruz State 1 passes through farms and nurseries to
SOQUEL, 91.1 *m.,* in a canyon on Soquel Creek, now among bulb
gardens, orchards, and vineyards, but a booming lumber town in the
days when the hills roundabout were forested with redwoods.   Marching toward Soquel Creek October 10, 1769, Portolá and his men saw
"low hills well forested with high trees of a red color, not known to
us.   They have a very different leaf from cedars, and although the
wood resembles cedar somewhat in color, it is very different, and has not
the same odor; moreover, the wood of the trees that we found is very
brittle.   In this region there is a great abundance of these trees and
because none of the expedition recognizes them, they are named redwoods from their color."   Awe-struck Pedro Fages wrote: "Here are
trees of girth so great that eight men placed side by side with extended
arms are unable to embrace them."

Right from Soquel on a paved road to CAPITOLA, 1.5 *m.*, a long-established resort facing NEW BRIGHTON BEACH STATE PARK in sheltered Soquel Cove.

Over the route of State 1 on their way to Santa Cruz by way of San Juan (*see TOUR 2b*) ran the mail stages from San Jose. The most daring driver on the line in the 1860's was swaggering "Cock-eyed Charley" Parkhurst, outstanding even among teamsters for his profanity. A naturally truculent expression, enhanced by a black patch over a missing eye and tobacco-juice stains on mouth and chin, made Charley the toughest looking fellow in the region. Not until Charley's death in 1879 was it discovered that "he" was a woman. Born Charlotte Parkhurst in New Hampshire in 1806, "Charley" had turned up in California in 1848. More than 50 years before introduction of woman suffrage, this enterprising Amazon had voted, "his" name appearing on the Santa Cruz Great Register for 1866.

At 94.2 *m.* on State 1 is the junction with a paved road.

Right on this road 0.5 *m.* to SEACLIFF STATE PARK, where the beach affords fine surf bathing and clamming. At the end of a pier stands an old hulk, one of the concrete ships built during World War I, anchored here by an enterprising night club owner as a dance hall. Although a large crack yawned in the hull—and signs reading "DANGER" were numerous—fishermen cast their lines from the prow interested only in the results of the catch.

APTOS (Ind., the meeting of the streams), 94.6 *m.* (100 pop.), at the base of oak- and chaparral-clad hills, was long a fashionable resort, but its OCEAN VIEW HOTEL (L) is deserted today. Late in the nineteenth century Claus Spreckels, founder of the State's first sugar dynasty, who built a great sugar beet refinery near Watsonville, bought up most of Don Rafael Castro's Rancho Aptos. His estate—with its race track and its mansion containing an elevator, the first south of San Francisco—became the wonder of the countryside, especially when Spreckels welcomed as a visitor the King of the Hawaiian Islands.

From the hill country east of Aptos, State 1 descends across the broad, level Pajaro Valley, watered by the river that the Portolá expedition named the Río del Pájaro (river of the bird) because they found on its banks a great eagle stuffed with straw by the Indians. The Pajaro Valley is a vast sweep of apple orchards—in springtime snowy with blossoms, whose petals eddy in fragrant showers on the breeze. In the summer, when the orchards are luxuriantly green, the trees—bellflowers and pippins—drooping under their burden of fruit, are propped up to prevent their branches breaking. Along the way are stands selling cold cider.

The orchard hamlet of FREEDOM, 104.4 *m.* (115 alt., 4,206 pop.), went by the name of Whiskey Hill—up until the era of sobriety inaugurated by prohibition.

The brisk modern trade center of the apple country, WATSONVILLE, 106.4 *m.* (25 alt., 13,700 pop.), on both sides of the Pajaro River, is called the world's strawberry capital. This fruit distributor was laid out in 1852 by Judge John H. Watson and D. S. Gregory on land purchased from Don Sebastián Rodríguez' Rancho Bolsa del Pájaro. Many other settlers dispensed with the formality of purchase, squatting on the rest of Rodríguez' land before his numerous heirs could claim it after his death in 1855. Jesse D. Carr's success with his apple orchard in 1853 led others to plant trees. Today Watsonville ships as many as 6,500,000 boxes of apples in a year—as well as vast quantities of strawberries, apricots, lettuce, and garden crops. The town has more than 75 packing houses and numerous evaporating plants, canneries, and cider and vinegar factories.

Watsonville's Plaza in the center of town was the scene of bull and bear fights and horse races were held on its main street in the days when the townsmen spent their Sundays—after dutiful attendance at early mass—gambling, dancing, and racing. The small cannon in the square is the one fired from the Pacific Mail steamship *Oregon* as it steamed into San Francisco Bay in October, 1850, announcing California's admission into the Union.

Watsonville is at the junction with State 152 (*see TOUR 2b*).

Right from Watsonville on paved Beach Road 5 *m.* to SUNSET BEACH STATE PARK, a broad sandy strip bordering Monterey Bay.

At the foot of the hill on the stretch of road south of Watsonville the stages from Natividad and Monterey used to meet and race into town—the drivers hunched forward, whipping their four-horse teams to a gallop, the lumbering coaches swaying and careening while the cheering male passengers made bets and the ladies fainted quietly away.

On the edge of a bluff overlooking the Pajaro Valley (R), 109.3 *m.*, is the site of the so-called HOUSE OF GLASS, the Casa Materna (mother house) of the history-making Vallejo family, once the wonder and envy of the countryside because of its glass windows. The mansion was built, supposedly about 1824, by Don Ignacio Vincente Ferrer Vallejo, on the Rancho Bolsa de San Cayetano (pocket of St. Gaetan). The two-story structure had walls 20 inches thick, joists and window frames of hewn redwood, and a shingle roof upheld by a single beam; the floor of its two downstairs rooms was of hard-packed earth. According to legend, the upper veranda was glassed-in—at a time when glass windows were all but unknown in California—because Vallejo received a shipment of twelve dozen windows instead of the one dozen he had ordered. The Vallejo family consisted of eight daughters and five sons—of whom the most distinguished was Mariano, the founder of Sonoma.

From the Vallejo ranch the young rebels, Juan Bautista Alvarado and José Castro, led an army of 75 armed with antiquated muskets on Monterey in November, 1835, bound to overthrow Gov. Nicolás Gutiérrez and proclaim the "free and sovereign State" of Alta California. The army set out to the martial strains of a fife and drum corps recruited from San Juan. On the way they were joined by 50 daredevil Yankee riflemen, led by the reckless Tennesseean, Isaac Graham, who had turned from trapping and hunting to the more profitable business of operating a whisky distillery in the Pajaro Valley. A single shot was enough to capture Monterey—one cannon ball, fired by a lawyer who had to consult a book to learn how to fire it; it struck the Governor's house, reducing him to such abject terror that he surrendered forthwith. Young Alvarado wrote to Vallejo: "It is wonderful, Uncle, with what order our expedition has been conducted. Everybody shouts *vivas*, for California is free."

The rancho of 1847 was described by young Lt. William T. Sherman, who called early one morning on one of the sons, Juan Antonio: "It was on a high point of the plateau, overlooking the plain of the Pajaro, on which were grazing numbers of horses and cattle. The house was of adobe, with a long range of adobe huts occupied by semi-civilized Indians, who at that time did all the labor of a ranch, the herding and marking of cattle, the breaking of horses, and cultivating the little patches of wheat and vegetables which constituted all the farming of that day. Everything about the house looked deserted, and, seeing a small Indian boy leaning up against a post, I approached him and asked him in Spanish, 'Where is the master?' 'Gone to the Presidio.' 'Is anybody in the house?' 'No.' 'Is it locked up?' 'Yes.' 'Is no one about who can get in?' 'No.' 'Have you any meat?' 'No.' 'Any flour or grain?' 'No.' 'Any chickens?' 'No.' 'Any eggs?' 'No.' 'What do you live on?' "Nada' (nothing)."

As the forested hills retreat to the foot of distant mountains, the way lies through rolling fields and pastures where white-faced cattle graze.

The warm-colored marsh grasses of ELKHORN SLOUGH, 114.6 *m.*, crossed by a concrete bridge usually lined with fishermen (*tackle, bait, boats for rent*), are the haunt of wild fowl. A peculiar form of marine algae colors the water red.

At 115.1 *m.* is the junction with an oiled road.

Right on this road is MOSS LANDING, 0.1 *m.* (10 alt., 100 pop.), a whaling station and schooner landing established about 1865 by Capt. Charles Moss. So large was its shipping business that at times wagons from the Salinas Valley farms were lined up for 5 miles, waiting their turn to unload. Up until 1920 as many as five whales a week were handled here, despite the complaints of inhabitants for miles around when the wind blew its odors inland; the Board of Health finally declared it a public menace. The fish reduction plant that took its place was scarcely an improvement in an olfactory sense.

CASTROVILLE, 117.7 *m.* (2,838 pop.), was founded in 1864 by Juan B. Castro on his father's rancho, which bore the curious name of Bolsa Nueva y Morro Coyo (new pocket and lame Moor)—in reference, according to one conjecture, to a lame black horse, and according to another, to the black soil (since the Spaniards used the word *morro* to mean anything black). Once predominantly Portuguese in population, it is today mostly Swiss-Italian.

State I, turning seaward, crosses the SALINAS RIVER, 120.7 *m.*, which the Portolá expedition followed to the coast in its search for

Monterey Bay. Arriving near its mouth on September 30, the men spent a week exploring the shores of the bay, but—as Sgt. Ortega wrote —"not finding the shelter and protection ascribed . . . to the port caused us doubt, since we saw a gulf . . . large enough to hold thousands of vessels, but with little protection from some winds." After consultation, they resumed their weary journey northward. As the highway skirts sand dunes along the shore, the hazy blue Santa Lucia Mountains loom ahead above Monterey on its curved sweep of bay, gleaming in the sun.

At 132 m. are the spacious grounds and gardens of the former HOTEL DEL MONTE, now a professional training school for officers of the United States Navy. The original hotel was erected in 1880 and replaced in 1887, and the present structure was erected in 1924. It obtained a reputation for the finest hospitality and cuisine on the Pacific Coast, and gained an exclusive clientele. In 1948 it closed and was taken over by the Navy. At one time *Pravda* of Moscow "exposed" it as the U. S. training center for spies. In the surrounding forest are bridle trails, a race track, steeplechasing and cross-country racing courses, skeet and trapshooting grounds, archery and badminton courts, and swimming pools, golf courses, and polo fields where championship matches are played.

MONTEREY, 133.1 m. (0-600 alt., 22,618 pop.) (*see MONTEREY*).

### Section c. MONTEREY to LAS CRUCES, 217 m. State 1.

In 1897 young Dr. John Roberts tended the sick on the isolated ranches south of Monterey, riding long, slow miles on horseback over the narrow wagon road that twisted in and out of the foothills and canyons of the Santa Lucia Range. Later he traveled along the coast from San Luis Obispo to Monterey on foot, sketching—planning the road in which he tried for years to arouse interest. Roberts estimated that $50,000 would pay for its construction. When he could raise only half that sum, he carried his fight to the State Legislature. One ardent legislator—Senator James Rigdon—was largely responsible for the passage of the bill in 1919 that authorized construction of the road. In 1920 the first surveys were made and the work was begun. Hundreds of men—free and convict—labored for 18 years; not $50,000 but $10,000,000 was spent; lives and equipment were lost in the sea; and in June 1937, the section of State 1, known as the Carmel-San Simeon Highway, was opened to the public.

In MONTEREY, 0 m. is the junction of Del Monte Avenue and Washington St.

Right from Monterey on Washington St.; R. on Lighthouse Avenue; R. on First Street; and L. on Ocean View Avenue along the shore to HOPKINS

Marine Station of Stanford University (R), 1.7 *m.*, on Cabrillo Point, founded by Timothy Hopkins in 1892. Its studies of oceanic biology include a hydrobiological survey of Monterey Bay. It has a collection of marine life for the observation of students and visitors.

In a pine forest by Monterey Bay is PACIFIC GROVE, 2.3 *m.* (47 alt., 12,121 pop.), a family recreation and residential community. The site of the first Chautauqua in the West, it was founded by Methodist Episcopal Church members in 1874, as a center for conferences, meetings, and outings; it still, by deed restriction, forbids the sale of liquor within its boundaries. The Municipal Museum (*open 2-5 daily except Mon.; free*), on Forest Ave., displays collections of California butterflies and Monterey Bay marine life among other exhibits. The salt-water Municipal Plunge is near the bathing beach, fishing pier, and bath house. Glass-bottomed boats afford a view of underwater plant and animal life in the Marine Gardens offshore.

Left from Pacific Grove on Asilomar Boulevard 0.5 *m.* to the Butterfly Trees, two pines that serve as the refuge every fall for thousands of huge brown, red, and white butterflies (*amosiae plexippus*) from east of the Rocky Mountains. Children have a butterfly parade in October. The city imposes a $500 fine for injury to the butterflies.

As the road continues westward round POINT PINOS at the southwestern extremity of Monterey Bay, the rocky coastline, lashed by foaming breakers, grows more and more rugged.

At 3.5 *m.* is the junction with a paved road; L. here 0.3 *m.* to Point Pinos Lighthouse (*open 1-4 Tues., Thurs.*), built in 1872, which guards the coast with a white oscillating light and an electric fog siren.

The snowy crests of sand dunes fringe the beach at ASILOMAR (Ind., a place of retreat), 6.2 *m.*, the 60-acre resort opened by the Young Women's Christian Association when the growth of Pacific Grove crowded religious conventions out of the city.

The toll gate to the Seventeen-Mile Drive, 6.4 *m.* (*$1.50 per car*) opens on a dirt road winding through Monterey pines and scrub oaks, their branches hung with long streamers of Spanish moss. In a filled-in lake bed (R) at 6.9 *m.* is the Sand Plant of the Del Monte Properties Company, only one of its kind on the Pacific Coast, which washes and dries sand for bathing beaches. The Seventeen-Mile Drive skirts MOSS BEACH, running along a wide mesa between dazzling white sand dunes, to POINT JOE 8.6 *m.*, named for a Japanese squatter who lived here many years. It overlooks the surging deep indigo currents of the RESTLESS SEA, where three large vessels have foundered.

At 11.5 *m.* is the junction with a paved road; R. 0.1 *m.* to CYPRESS POINT, commanding crescent-shaped CARMEL BAY. Along the cliffs grow Monterey cypresses. Once widely distributed over this section of the coast, they now make their last stand in the limited area between Cypress Point and Point Lobos (*see below*). Robert Louis Stevenson compared them to "ghosts fleeing before the wind." Clutching at precarious footholds in the face of ocean gales, they lift their gnarled and twisted branches, hung with rags of yellow moss, in grotesque postures.

A lone cypress, the most painted and photographed in the forest, crowns MIDWAY POINT (R), 12.4 *m.* The strangely contorted Ghost Tree, 13.1 *m.*, worn white by spray and wind, appears as the road rounds PESCADERO POINT.

The Seventeen-Mile Drive curves through the spacious homes and gardens of PEBBLE BEACH, 13.8 *m.*, a socially exclusive playground with its Del Monte Lodge, sport field, and golf course.

At 14 *m.* is the junction with a paved road; R. 0.3 *m.* to STILLWATER COVE, with its arch rock offshore, its fishing club and bathing beach, yacht harbor and marine gardens (*glass-bottom boats*).

At 15.9 *m.* is the junction with a paved road; L. here, past the forest sheltered homes of CARMEL WOODS, to another toll gate at the junction with State 1, 17.4 *m.*

From Del Monte Ave. and Washington St. in Monterey, 0 *m.*, State 1 follows Washington St., turns L. on Abrego St., and cuts across the Monterey Peninsula to the junction with Seventeen-Mile Drive (*see above*), 2.3 *m.* At 2.8 *m.* is the junction with Carmel Road.

Right on Carmel Rd. is CARMEL, 1 *m.* (220 alt., 4,580 pop.), art center of the Monterey Peninsula, affectionately termed "The Village," facing the dazzling white beach of Carmel Bay from pine- and oak-forested slopes. The village dates from about 1904, when Mary Austin, James Hopper, George Sterling and other young writers and artists built small shacks in the woods. Determined to keep out modern inventions, they fought introduction of paved streets, gas and electricity, and jails. As dilettantes, charlatans, and idlers flocked in after them, the town grew. The divergence of point of view between artists and non-artists led to sharp local battles. By and large the "artists" have won, for Carmel still has no public utilities of its own, no house numbers, no mail delivery; and it forbids cutting down of trees without a police permit. The business buildings bordering the main street with its pine-dotted parkway and the dwellings along the residence streets meandering through untidy flower patches are a weird conglomerate of Spanish, Italian, French, and English styles, built according to the individual taste of each owner. The community supports a little theater, small art galleries, a forum for visiting lecturers, a music society that presents winter concerts and an annual Bach festival. Among the better-known residents have been the scientist David Starr Jordan; photographers Arnold Genthe and Edward Weston; artists Maynard Dixon, Jo Mora, Armin Hansen, Rollo Peters, William Ritchel; writers Ambrose Bierce, Don Blanding, Martin Flavin, Lincoln Steffens, Jesse Lynch Williams, Rhys Williams, and Harry Leon Wilson. The Forest Theater, in a grove of trees on Mountain View Ave., founded in 1919, is said to have been California's first open-air community theater. A village showplace is Tor House with its tower rising from Carmel Point, the home of the poet Robinson Jeffers (1887-1962) built by his own hand from natural rock.

At 4.2 *m.* on State 1 is the junction with an oiled road.

Left on this road through the farms, orchards and pastures of CARMEL VALLEY, along the Carmel River between the chaparral-clad Santa Lucia Mountains. The valley was the setting for Mary Austin's *Ysidro*, an idyll of mission days. Beyond the San Clemente Dam (R), 15.5 *m.*, built (1921) to impound the Carmel River, the road climbs through lonely cattle ranches into more rugged country.
At 24 *m.* is the junction with a dirt road; R. on this road is JAMESBURG, 27.1 *m.* (*cabins available*), founded in 1867 by John James, but now little more than a country store.
The road climbs up jagged forested mountain slopes to MADRONE FLATS, 31 *m.*, which provides a splendid view. It drops sharply downward through chaparral dotted with yucca trees, sycamores, and maples.
In a heavily wooded canyon is TASSAJARA (Ind., meat curing place) SPRINGS, 41.3 *m.* (1,700 alt.), hot mineral springs (160° F) flowing from boulders beside a rushing stream. Under one of the present bath houses is a crude tub hollowed out of a large rock by Indians, who believed the waters to have magic qualities. The resort has a large hotel, built in the 1890's of sandstone quarried nearby; two large sanitary bath houses, 14 private bathrooms, tubs and showers, and natural vapor baths; two plunges, a swimming pool, an outdoor dance floor, and stables.

At 4.5 *m.* on State 1 is the junction with an oiled road.

Right on this road 0.6 *m.* to MISIÓN SAN CARLOS BORROMEO DEL RIO CARMELO (Mission St. Charles Borromeo of the Carmel River), on the cypress-dotted slopes overlooking Carmel Bay. To the three Carmelite priests of Sebastián Vizcaíno's expedition who visited the site in 1602, it so closely resembled the landscape around Mount Carmel in Palestine that they named it for the birthplace of their order. The mission, second in California, was founded in 1770 by Junípero Serra at Monterey and moved to its present site the following year. It remained the home of Serra, who was buried here beside his devoted co-worker, Padre Juan Crespi, at his death in 1784. The present church was founded July 7, 1793 by Serra's successor as *Padre-presidente* of the missions, Fermin Francisco de Lasuen. The mission reached the height of its prosperity in 1794, when its Indian population numbered 927. After its secularization it fell rapidly into ruin, overrun by birds and squirrels. The restoration of the mission was begun in the 1880's, when the ruins of the fallen roof were cleared off the graves of Serra and Crespi. The roof, shingled at that time, was later replaced by one of tile. The walls of the church, five feet thick, built of sandstone blocks cemented with lime made by the Indians from abalone shells, remain standing on their granite foundation; they curve in a parabolic arch to the ceiling, which is supported by stone and wooden pillars. To the left of the main entrance are the baptistry and font, carved by neophytes, and the modern mortuary chapel (1924) with its beams and murals reproducing the original decorations and its monument to Serra (Jo Mora, sculptor). To the right of the entrance, hollowed sandstone steps lead to the balcony, lighted by an irregular star-shaped window. The interior has many of its original paintings and statues. In the sanctuary are buried Serra, Crespi, Lasuen, and López. Serra's grave is marked by the simple wooden cross placed on it at the time of his death by an Indian convert. The mission is the setting today of the annual Serra Pageant in August.

From its crossing of the CARMEL RIVER, 5.1 *m.,* State 1 climbs out of the valley, past the CARMELITE MONASTERY (L), 6.2 *m.,* where the Discalced Nuns of Our Lady and Saint Therese live in absolute seclusion.

Just beyond the boundary of POINT LOBOS STATE PARK is the entrance (R) to POINT LOBOS RESERVE, 7 *m.* (*adm. 50¢ per car; picnicking, no camping*), a wildly rocky promontory fringed with wind-blown trees. The sea lions that congregate on the rocks gave rise to the Spanish name, Punta de los Lobos Marinos (point of the sea wolves). The point is the northernmost habitat of the brown pelican and the southernmost of the Monterey Cypress. The visits of Robert Louis Stevenson in 1879 have given rise to the legend that Point Lobos was the inspiration for Spyglass Hill in *Treasure Island.* The somber battle of the elements waged here inspired Robinson Jeffers to make it the setting for his poem *Tamar.*

State 1 follows the coast, alternately dipping to the mouths of creeks and climbing over promontory ridges, to the ruins of NOTLEY's LANDING (R), 16.2 *m.,* where timber and tanbark brought by muleback from the canyons were once loaded by cable on waiting vessels.

Above the surf-beaten cove at the mouth of Bixby Creek arches the single concrete span of RAINBOW BRIDGE, 17.8 *m.,* 718 feet long and 260 feet high. On the cliff edge (R) are the ruins of BIXBY's LANDING, the setting for Robinson Jeffer's poem *Thurso's Landing,* where in the early 1900's lime from inland quarries was carried in great buckets over a 3-mile aerial tramway down the canyon to the pier.

At 23.1 *m.* is the junction with a narrow, winding road.

Right on this road 0.5 *m.*, scaling a great rock, to the POINT SUR LIGHT-HOUSE (*open 1-4 Mon., Wed., Fri.*), perched 270 feet above the surf at the tip of POINT SUR. When the S. S. *Los Angeles* ran aground here in 1873, young Dr. John Roberts rode the 30 miles from Monterey in 3½ hours to find 150 victims, alive and dead, clinging to the shore or washed up on the beach. From miles around came the ranchers in 1879, when the *Ventura* went down, to salvage its cargo of fine linens and knock-down wagons. Old men on the lonely ranches still boast to their grand-children of having helped build in 1889 the lighthouse and its buildings, the former stairway with its 395 wooden steps, and the water system. When the light intended for Pigeon Point, brought from France and shipped around the Horn, was delivered here instead, there was mighty rejoicing among the mountain folk. Only dissenter was old Choppy Casuse, who commented: "Good light, but she no work. Go all the time sad, 'Boo-Boo,' but the fog, she creep in just the same." Off Point Sur in 1935 the United States Navy dirigible *Macon* went down in a dense fog, with the loss of two lives.

State 1 turns inland up the valley of the BIG SUR RIVER, past the white buildings and orchards of Rancho El Sur (R), 26.3 *m.*, claimed in 1852 by the region's first settler, sea captain Juan Bautista Roger Cooper, a Yankee trader who had been in the habit of landing cargoes here to evade customs duties at Monterey. The bleak Big Sur Country provided a meager living to the homesteaders who settled it in the 1870's. The few who have remained live far off the road in isolated ranches. The inbreeding, passion, moroseness, and suspicion engendered by their primitive, lonely lives have been well interpreted by Robinson Jeffers, who has made this country the background of many of his poems.

The highway continues along the river bank, fringed with oaks, sycamores, and young redwoods, into PFEIFFER REDWOOD STATE PARK, 30 *m.* (*picnic grounds, swimming pools*), a resort where CCC boys have constructed an outdoor theater and winding lagoons. It is named for Michael Pfeiffer, who settled here in November, 1869, and brought up a family whose descendants homesteaded roundabout. In the park is BIG SUR, 30.5 *m.* (*post office, cabins, lodge, restaurant; saddle horses*).

Climbing abruptly from the canyon, State 1 emerges on high bluffs above the ocean at 32.9 *m.* Soon it gains spectacular heights, cut from sheer cliffs. Ahead rise hills, rumpled and scarred—some smooth and brown, some mantled in green, some mottled with the hues of red clay and white granite. The road twists in around creek mouths, out around headlands, rising and falling. The almost ever-present fog drifts in and out, drawn up the funnel-like canyons, swept back to reveal long vistas of coastline. Off-shore the crags are girdled by floating forests of seaweed, greenish-brown, red-purple, and black.

ANDERSON'S CANYON, 41.7 *m.*, is the site of the road-con-struction camp for convicts, established here with few safeguards against the escape of prisoners beyond the offer· of a $200 reward, chargeable against the wages of the convicts, for the capture of a runaway. One of many stories about the convicts tells how, one winter night when slides had blocked the road, the word spread that the wife of a man in the freemen's camp, about to give birth to a child, needed a doctor; of their own free will, men from both camps poured out to work in pouring rain and pitch darkness, blasting open with dynamite a road to the Community Hospital.

The DOLAN CREEK BRIDGE, 45.8 *m.,* largest timber-arch bridge in the State, carries the highway 150 feet above the canyon. Its carefully fitted redwood sections are held together by hinges.

At wide intervals are schoolhouses, small farm clearings, or the buildings of cattle ranches, isolated in the midst of unsettled lands. For a long time there were no facilities for travel for many miles in that unsettled area.

The mountainsides are too steep in most places for human habitations —so steep at some spots, in fact, that it was literally necessary to move mountains to make room for the road. At the curve around LIME KILN POINT, 56 *m.,* 163,000 yards of solid rock had to be excavated in 1,000 feet; one blast of 70,000 pounds of dynamite moved 95,000 yards, blowing 75,000 yards into the sea 300 feet below. Southward State 1 continues over a cliff-edged tableland to the house and gas station comprising GORDA, 66.8 *m.* The canyon below SALMON CREEK BRIDGE, 74.7 *m.,* which affords a glimpse of a waterfall (L), is the southernmost stand of the redwood tree.

From sharp windings high above the sea, the highway descends to SAN CARPOJO CREEK, 79.8 *m.,* where the mountains retreat inland from meadows dotted with grazing cattle. Over a difficult trail up the creek, Gaspar de Portolá and his expedition (*see TOUR 1b*) turned inland on their march north September 16, 1769, when they found the way up the coast blocked by precipices. Southward State 1 skirts Rancho Piedra Blanca (Sp., white rock), first of the three ranchos that comprised William Randolph Hearst's 240,000-acre San Simeon Ranch, stretching for 50 miles southward. Rancho Piedra Blanca, nucleus of the estate, was acquired by his father, Senator George Hearst, for 70¢ an acre and stocked with prize cattle.

At 87.1 *m.* is the junction with a dirt road.

Right on this road 0.2 *m.* to the PIEDRAS BLANCAS LIGHTHOUSE (*open 2-4 Mon., Wed., Fri.*), rising from a low point guarded by two large white rocks offshore, its conical tower and white, red-roofed buildings neatly silhouetted against the sea.

At 92.8 *m.* is the junction with a dirt road.

1. Right on this road is the village of SAN SIMEON, 2 *m.* (20 alt., 50 pop.), overlooking a wide bay from San Simeon Point, where Portuguese whalers made their home between 1865 and 1890. A handful of the old frame buildings remain. Beyond the village Senator George Hearst built his great frame ranch house, later owned by his son William Randolph Hearst, who bought most of the village. For years its warehouses were crammed with unpacked art treasures.

Left 5 *m.* from State 1 to HEARST SAN SIMEON STATE HIS-
TORICAL MONUMENT, the former private estate of William Randolph Hearst (1863-1951), begun in 1919 on a hilltop of the Santa Lucia
range and called by its owner La Cuesta Encantada—the Enchanted Hill.
Topped by La Casa Grande, an immense Spanish castle, are numerous subsidiary buildings, gardens and pools, built with materials imported from
their original sites, and furnished with costly treasures of other centuries.

> The estate was given to the State of California by the Hearst Corpora-
> tion as a memorial to Hearst and his mother Phoebe Apperson Hearst.
> For many years Hearst poured millions into erecting the buildings and
> furnishing them with rare antiques. The three guest houses are elaborate
> Italianate palaces. The white marble Neptune pool holds 250,000 gallons
> of water, is bordered by colonnades leading to a classical temple to Neptune.
> The assembly room in the castle is 84 ft. long and 35 ft. wide and the ceil-
> ing is 23 ft. from the floor. It is decorated with a rare mantelpiece, tapes-
> tries and marble medallions. The first floor vestibule is paved with
> Pompeiian mosaic dating from 60 B. C. Carved woodwork from foreign
> palaces adorns walls and ceilings and some of the furnishings of the refectory
> came from European monasteries. The library extends the length of the
> second floor. The house has 100 rooms of which 38 are bedrooms, 31 bath-
> rooms, and 14 sitting rooms.

The public may view the first floor and the grounds under direction
of guides daily except Thanksgiving, Christmas and New Year's Day
for a fee. Reservations are made by the Public Tours Reservation
Office, Division of Beaches and Parks, P. O. Box 2390, Sacramento 11;
telephone 445-8828 Sacramento.

From the moss-draped pine forest surrounding the resort of CAM-
BRIA PINES, 100.2 *m.*, State 1 turns inland through dairy farm pastures to CAMBRIA, 101.2 *m.* (59 alt., 2,000 pop.), a farming and
dairying center, continues down a narrow valley edged by brown hills,
past HARMONY, 106.3 *m.* and returns to the coast.

On ESTERO BAY are ESTERO BEACH STATE PARK and
the village of CAYUCOS, 115.9 *m.* (34 alt., 260 pop.), named for the
canoes paddled by the Indians who dwelt here when Juan Rodríguez
Cabrillo named the bay in 1542. A small pleasure pier replaces the
wharf built in 1870 by James Cass, who laid out the town in 1875.

At 120.4 *m.* is the junction with US 466 (*see TOUR 12b*).

On a bluff commanding land-locked MORROW BAY are the summer cottages of MORRO, 122.4 *m.* (72 alt., 5,500 pop.), named for
immense MORRO (Sp., headland) ROCK, sometimes called the "Gi-
braltar of the Pacific," which rises 576 feet above a shallow lagoon impounded by sand dunes. From the rock, a great pile of trachyte (volcanic rock) covering 40 acres, thousands of tons of building material
have been blasted. Right from Morro 1.5 *m.* to MORRO STATE PARK.

State 1 turns sharply inland, passing (R) the chain of volcanic
cones to which Morro Rock belongs—CERRO ALTO (1,415 alt.), CERRO
ROMUALDO (1,310 alt.), and BISHOPS PEAK (1,510 alt.), for which
San Luis Obispo is named.

SAN LUIS OBISPO (*see TOUR 2b*), 135.8 *m.*, is at the junction
with US 101 (*see TOUR 2b*), with which State 1 unites for 12.2 *m.*

Branching southward from US 101 at PISMO BEACH (*see TOUR 2b*), 148 *m.* State 1 crosses vegetable and flower-seed farms to their shipping center, OCEANO, 151.6 *m.* (19 alt., 1,317 pop.). Its beach, fringed by sand dunes, invites vacationers with a preference for seclusion. The dunes, piling up to surprising heights, are at their best in the late afternoon when the sun casts long shadows accenting their undulating lines. Here at one time was a group of shacks and tents inhabited by artists and others escaping high rents. When the tide is out, the sandy beach in this region is hard-packed, a natural race track often used by automobiles.

Across a broad mesa checkered with fields and flower beds, State 1 continues to GUADALUPE, 163.8 *m.* (80 alt., 2,614 pop.), an ancient community whose population is as jumbled as its streets and houses. The two-story ARELLANTES ADOBE and the one-story OLIVERA ADOBE, Third St. near State 1, built in 1843 by the grantees of 30,048-acre Rancho Guadalupe, Teodoro Arellantes and Diego Olivera, recall the past.

At 164.9 *m.* is the junction with a hard-surfaced road. Left on this road to the junction with a hard-surfaced road, 1 *m.;* R. here at 2.7 *m.* to BETTERAVIA, 5 *m.* (185 alt., 125 pop.), a settlement dominated by a sugar refinery.

ORCUTT, 173.4 *m.* (314 alt., 1,414 pop.), born with the discovery of oil in the hills in 1900, is still a petroleum shipping point. From Orcutt a side road runs to CASMALIA south of which along the Coast are 65,000 acres used by the VANDENBERG AIR FORCE BASE, home of First Strategic Aerospace Division. On April 3, 1965, it launched the first nuclear reactor to operate in outer space.

Through rolling hills State 1 winds southward into LOMPOC VALLEY, 184.5 *m.,* said to be the nation's largest flower seed-growing center. Among fields of mustard, beets, beans, and potatoes are interspersed beds of nasturtium, delphinium, larkspur, poppy and marigold. In June the annual FLOWER FESTIVAL of the city of LOMPOC draws thousands to the Valley. Lompoc, 194.9 *m.* (95 alt., 24,150 pop. est. 1965) originated as California's first successful land colonization project in October, 1874, when the California Immigrant Union purchased and subdivided Ranchos Lompoc and Misión Vieja. So successful was the venture that one week's sale of land aggregated $700,000, including $70,000 in town lots. The deeds of sale, forbidding sale of liquor on the land, lend documentary support to Lompoc's claim of pioneering prohibition in California. Here mining and processing plants make use of diatomite found in the Valley. This comes from fossilized remains of tiny water plants and can be used for clarifying drugs, filtering and purifying, processing metals, oils and chemicals and polishing metals.

From Lompoc on State 246 to the Coast and SURF. South of it is CAMP COOKE and the POINT ARGUELLO MISSILE TEST CENTER of the U. S. Navy. Continuing down the Coast a side road from State 1 runs to JALAMA and JALAMA BEACH PARK. At POINT CONCEPCION the coastline turns a right angle and lies north of the Santa Barbara Channel, bordering the Santa Ynez Mountains. State 1 joins US 101 at Las Cruces (*Tour 2c*) 217 *m*.

At 196.1 *m*. on State 1 is the junction with a paved road.

> Left on this road 2.6 *m*. to MISION LA PURISIMA CONCEPCION (Sp., the immaculate conception), eleventh of the 21 missions, founded December 8, 1787 by Padre Fermín de Lasuen. Following destruction of the first church by earthquake in 1812, the present one was built. Between 1815 and 1823 it was the seat of mission government in California. In 1824 the Indian neophytes seized the mission and held it for nearly a month before soldiers came to disperse them. La Purísima, with all its lands and buildings, was sold in 1845, 11 years after its secularization, to Don Juan Temple for $1,100. Acquired by an oil company in 1903, it was donated to Santa Barbara County. The present buildings, with their mellow cream-colored walls and red-tile roofs, have been restored by the Civilian Conservation Corps under direction of the National Park Service. The RESIDENCE BUILDING, 318 feet long and 65 feet wide, with walls 4½ feet thick, has a cloister with a colonnade of 20 fluted columns, notable for their design, supporting a low, red-tile room. The church still has part of its original tile flooring. Under the floor, before the altar, is the grave of Padre Mariano Payeras, under whose direction it was built. The area, now a State Historical Monument, has been enlarged to 980 acres and the original water supply system has been uncovered. Fiesta Days come in May.

This coastal area has one of the State's biggest oil pools. In 1965 operators negotiated leases with the State government covering 312,940 acres of tidelands extending three miles offshore north of Point Concepcion.

# *Tour 2*

(Brookings, Ore.)—Crescent City—Eureka—Santa Rosa—San Francisco—San Jose—Santa Barbara—Los Angeles—San Diego—San Ysidro (Mexican border); US 101.
Oregon Line to Mexican Border, 980.8 *m*.

Paved roadbed throughout; open all seasons; small landslides during heavy rains; snow in higher elevations during winter months.
Excellent route for trailers.
Route paralleled by Northwestern Pacific R.R. between Eureka and Sausalito, by Southern Pacific between San Francisco and Los Angeles, and by Santa Fe between Los Angeles and San Diego.
Accommodations plentiful; many camps and resort hotels.

## *Section a. OREGON LINE to SAN FRANCISCO; 392.5 m. US 101.*

This section of US 101 in natural beauty is one of the most diversified routes in the State. In the north, where it parallels the Pacific Ocean, the highway traverses farm and forest, climbing from surf-bordered meadows to skirt high crags overlooking the sea. South of Crescent City the road is called the Redwood Highway, taking its name from the giant redwoods through which it passes. It gradually ascends to a high plateau cut by numerous fertile valleys; descending, it traverses a wine-grape and orchard area—a region converted each spring into a wonderland of white blossoms. Nearing sea level once more, the road reaches into the heart of the State's poultry-raising district; but even here fringes of the blue Coast Range are always in sight.

US 101 crosses the State Line, 0 *m.*, 6.5 miles south of Brookings, Ore., and follows the coast of Pelican Bay to PARADISE VALLEY, 1 *m.*, where sheep and cattle graze on broad terraced meadows that slope from forested hills to foam-bathed rocky promontories. Isolated farm buildings and an occasional white-steepled country schoolhouse blend into the farmland and forest.

SMITH RIVER, 7.6 *m.* (50 alt., 300 pop.), on Rowdy Creek, is a trading center for a small dairying country and headquarters for sportsmen during the fishing and hunting season.

Salmon and steelhead trout are plentiful in the wide, green waters of SMITH RIVER, 11 *m.*, named for Jedediah Smith, adventurer and trapper, who explored the region in 1828. In December, 1964, Smith River flooded the towns of Gasque and Fort Dick and ruined roads and public utility facilities north of Crescent City.

South of FORT DICK, 13 *m.* (46 alt., 75 pop.), the broad grazing lands are interspersed increasingly with wooded areas, until at 13.4 *m.* the highway enters the WEBBER GROVE, northernmost of the redwood groves. Here on a thick carpet of green clover and luxuriant fern, these coast redwoods (*Sequoia sempervirens*) stand straight and tall, dwarfing the lesser trees that grow beneath their heavy shade.

At 21.4 *m.* is the junction with US 199.

CRESCENT CITY, 21.9 *m.* (7-35 alt., 2,958 pop.), seat of Del Norte County, facing a shallow harbor edged by arc-shaped Crescent Beach, ships lumber and shingles, dairy products, and fish by boat and truck. It was laid out in 1852, the year after discovery of the harbor by a party of treasure-seekers hunting gold hidden by a legendary prospector. A town of 800, with its own newspaper by 1854, it grew so fast that by 1856 it was enjoying its first drama—a presentation of *The Toodles* and *Paddy Miles, the Limerick Boy* by the Crescentonian Club. Crescent City was at first the seat of the former Klamath County, and so jealous were Crescentonians of the honor, that when the seat was moved to Orleans Bar, they angrily forced formation of a new county, Del Norte, in order to make their city its seat. Before construction of the pier in the 1860's, passengers arriving on the *Oregon* were transferred to surf boats and then to horse-drawn carts—to be hauled ashore over the shallow tidal flats—for a $2 fee.

Just north of the beach is POINT ST. GEORGE, which protects the city from heavy north winds. It was on St. George Reef that the sidewheeler, *Brother Jonathan,* was wrecked in the 1860's. A LIGHT-

HOUSE and RADIO STATION are maintained on BATTERY POINT, on the north arm of the bay. A light and fog signal station, SEAL ROCK LIGHT, on a small reef about 7 miles off-shore, was completed in 1891 after four years of labor.

At 24.1 m. is a junction with a narrow road. Left on this road to JEDEDIAH SMITH REDWOODS STATE PARK, 9,539 acres. Facilities include 104 campsites, 40 picnic sites, laundry and showers. Trailers permitted. Unit of park was the 44-acre FRANK A. STOUT MEMORIAL GROVE (1929). In 1944 the 6,708-acre Mill Creek Redwood Grove was bought with funds of the Save-the-Redwoods League.

US 101 begins the slow ascent of low foothills, 26 m., to climb high above the sea. There is evidence of the work of lumber companies that chose only the best of the trees and burned off the rest; denuded, blackened hillsides alternate with thinly wooded slopes. The road follows a high ridge, through whose trees the ocean (R) intermittently appears in the distance. To the left are miles of blue-green treetops, a section of DEL NORTE COAST PARK. From KNAPP POINT, 35 m., overlooking the Pacific, the highway descends almost to the surf, shortly to enter another of the small valleys whose meadows stretch from forest to sea. SIX RIVERS NATIONAL FOREST, 896,165 acres, occupies a large part of Del Norte County. At 41 m. is a graded dirt road.

Right on this road is REQUA (Ind., rek-woi: mouth of the river), 0.5 m. (sea level, 108 pop.), on the north bank of KLAMATH RIVER, near its mouth, where a schooner arrived in 1851 with prospectors who founded Klamath City. The camp grew rapidly. Frames of houses, ready to assemble, arrived in sailing vessels from San Francisco, and a small iron building was erected, probably as a guard house for gold and protection against Indians. But the town declined as rapidly as it had grown; the men left to explore up river, and the iron house was shipped back to San Francisco. When Requa was on the old route of US 101, travelers crossed the Klamath by ferry, a motor-driven barge attached trolley fashion to a cable, but in 1925 the construction of a bridge upstream eliminated the crude ferry service and isolated the town. A law enacted in 1934 prohibited commercial fishing in the tidewater, and the population declined. Near Requa's large modern inn are the scattered, vine-covered shacks of Klamath Indians who compose the bulk of the population. Half of the bridge carrying US 101 was demolished by the river flood of December, 1964, and Requa was badly damaged.

The word Klamath is thought to be a derivation from *maklaks* (Lutuami Ind., people), translated as "the encamped." According to Indian tradition, the river once met the sea at Wilson Creek, about 6 miles north, where it was kept in its course by high parallel bluffs. When Po-lick-o-quare-ick (the Wise One)—the Indian equivalent to Christ—had completed his mission on earth, he gathered his possessions and prepared to depart. His grieving people watched him paddle toward the mouth of the river and began to follow him seaward, whereupon the Wise One commanded the bluffs to separate, forming a breach through which the river could flow quickly to the ocean. When the followers reached the shore they glimpsed the Wise One fading into the setting sun. Since then the Klamath has followed that course.

Close to the river mouth, on the northern bank, stands a Family House of weather-beaten planks, said to be at least 150 years old. The house sheltered only the women and children of a family; the men and boys slept in the underground chambers used as sweathouses.

KLAMATH, 43 *m.* (40 alt., 75 pop.), on the site called Hah-Paew by the Indians, is at the northern end of the DOUGLAS MEMORIAL BRIDGE over Klamath River.   During August and September, when the town's hotels and camps are crowded, the river is so densely dotted with fishing craft that one can cross the stream by leaping from boat to boat.   But the townspeople themselves, many of whom are Indians, are forbidden to earn their livelihood by fishing.   Klamath folk blame mining companies operating on the upper Klamath and Trinity Rivers for the anti-fishing laws.   It is said that when commercial fishermen objected to pollution of the stream by debris from hydraulic mining, mining interests retaliated by obtaining the support of sportsmen anglers for a law designating Klamath River as a recreational stream, on the premise that commercial fishing would deplete the supply of fish.   Mining operations proceed unchallenged except during the sportsmen's fishing season.

Klamath and Klamath Glen lost all their dwellings in the Klamath River flood of December, 1964.

The SHAKERS' CHURCH is a small, unpainted, barnlike structure (L) at the southern end of town.   The congregation is composed of Indians, whose services consist mainly of violent shaking and shouting; their sect has no relation to that founded by Mother Ann Lee.   On evenings when "the Shakers are at it" the townspeople are kept awake late by the clamor attending the devotions.   The ghost dance, a principal rite of the sect, is a whirling performed before the congregation by one or two persons.   The sect was brought to Klamath from the State of Washington by a local Indian, Jimmie Jacks.   The medicine man, Smohalla, chief of the Columbia River Indians, founded the religion. When his tribe was crushed by the whites, Smohalla became a wanderer, his travels taking him as far south as Mexico.   In 1860, he devised a religious ceremony showing the influence of his observation of Roman Catholic, Mormon, and Protestant rituals.

A sudden turn in the road, 47.4 *m.*, reveals a wide sweep of surf in the distance below, and the highway climbs high above the shore into PRAIRIE CREEK STATE PARK (*fishing, swimming, horseback riding, camping*), 50.9 *m.*, a reserve of 6,467 acres.   At the park's lower end are the last surviving herd of Roosevelt elk in California, about 150 in number.   These elk, a rich dark brown in color, are larger than other animals of the species.

ORICK, 63 *m.* (75 alt., 250 pop.), trade center of a prosperous dairy region, has a milk products plant.

LOOKOUT POINT, 65.4 *m.*, affords a view of the ocean in three directions.   At the foot of the cliff is FRESHWATER LAGOON, separated from the Pacific by a narrow sand bar; its waters, always fresh, are believed to be fed by an underground stream.   STONE LAGOON, 68.2 *m.*, and BIG LAGOON, 72.2 *m.*, overflow into the ocean during the winter when rainfall is heavy, permitting steelhead and salmon to enter both lagoons to spawn.   In the vicinity of DRY LAGOON PARK (*motorboat regattas in summer*), 77.3 *m.*, are many small summer cabins. (*Warning: dangerous, powerful undercurrent.*)

In TRINIDAD, 83 *m*. (200 alt., 289 pop.), scattered business buildings offer little reminder of the town of 3,000 of 1851-52, when the settlement was the distribution point for the Trinity County mines. In close proximity are TRINIDAD BEACH STATE PARK and PATRICK'S POINT STATE PARK, the latter noted for its Agate Beach.

> Right from Trinidad on a narrow graveled road to TRINIDAD HEAD, 1.7 *m*., a large promontory. The white granite memorial cross at the summit replaces the Spanish cross of pine erected there June 11, 1775, by Capt. Bruno Heceta and Lt. Juan Francisco Bodéga y Cuadra. The original wooden marker bore the inscription "Carolus III Dei G. Hyspaniarum Rex," signifying that the explorers took possession of the territory in the name of Charles III of Spain. The Spaniards named the region Trinidad because they took possession on the day following the feast of the Holy Trinity.

At the mouth of LITTLE RIVER, 86 *m.*, northern boundary of LITTLE RIVER BEACH STATE PARK, an exploration party of nine men headed by Dr. Josiah Gregg reached the coast in December, 1849, after weeks of hardship. They had left Weaverville, about 100 miles inland, the month before, in search of a harbor described by the Indians as "a large bay with fertile land and tall trees, eight suns to the west." Their supplies gave out, and before they reached the coast, they were near starvation.

CLAM BEACH (*auto camps nearby*), 87.9 *m.*, is a popular clam-digging and picnicking spot. One mile up Mad River Road off Highway 101 is the AZALEA STATE RESERVE, 30 acres.

At 95.7 *m.* is the junction with US 299 (*see TOUR 8b*).

ARCATA (Ind., where boats land), 100 *m*. (100 alt., 5,235 pop.), on the western shore of Humboldt Bay, is built around a plaza. Many of the dwellings on the town's wide streets have broad lawns and flower gardens. Lumber, shingles, wool, and milk compose the bulk of exported products. Uniontown—as the place was named by its founders April 10, 1850—was a shipping point and until 1856 the seat of Humboldt County. Bret Harte is said to have written his first newspaper story here, while working as compositor and assistant to S. G. Whipple, editor of the *Northern California,* as well as agent for Wells, Fargo & Co., from 1857 to 1859. HUMBOLDT STATE COLLEGE, established 1913, had 2,846 students in 1965.

> Right from Arcata on a paved road that traverses a narrow, sandy peninsula to SAMOA (97 alt., 600 pop.), 5 *m.*, a company town around an extensive redwood mill (*open to visitors*). The ocean lies just beyond the sand dunes behind the town. About one mile south is the HULK OF THE U.S.S. MILWAUKEE, grounded in 1917 while attempting to free a submarine that had run aground. Bids had been submitted to haul the submarine to land and to refloat it, but they were rejected as too high. The Navy Department then sent the cruiser *Milwaukee* from San Francisco to rescue the submarine. After the *Milwaukee* grounded, one of the original bids was accepted.

US 101 curves around the southern shore of HUMBOLDT BAY, a landlocked inlet so well guarded from the sea by its two narrow peninsulas of sand that it eluded discovery until Capt. Jonathan Winship, hunting seals and sea otter along the coast for the Russian-American Fur Company in 1806, steered the *O'Cain* through the narrow entrance. The search for a safe harbor along the northern coast prompted its rediscovery on December 20, 1849 by the Josiah Gregg party of Government-employed traders and explorers. On April 9 of the following year the United States revenue cutter *Laura Virginia* sailed into the bay, which the expedition's second officer, Capt. Hans Buhne, named for the German naturalist, Baron Alexander von Humboldt. The harbor's usefulness has been menaced, ever since its discovery, by the shifting sand bars at its mouth. To keep the channel open, construction of rock jetties and constant dredging have been required.

EUREKA, 105.7 *m*. (30 alt., 28,500 pop.), seat of Humboldt County, on the shore of Humboldt Bay, owes its name—as well as the surveying of its first town lots in 1850—to James Ryan, who drove his vessel onto the mud flats, shouting jubilantly "Eureka!" (Gr., I have found it!). The largest California town north of Sacramento, Eureka is in the center of a most popular fishing and redwoods recreation area. Its principal activities are lumber and plywood manufacturing, and fish processing and canning. Tours are conducted to plywood and timber plants during the summer.

Eureka was settled by men from New England and Nova Scotia, seafarers and woodsmen, the latter recruited for lumbering operations. It developed a busy saloon and dance hall section on the waterfront.

SEQUOIA PARK is an area of forty-six acres within the city limits filled with huge redwoods. Peter B. Kyne made this the locale for his story, "Valley of the Giants," which also was made into a motion picture. There are facilities for picnics.

On a high plateau overlooking the bay near the southern city limits is FORT HUMBOLDT, where troops were garrisoned for protection against Indians between 1853 and 1865. Ulysses S. Grant was stationed here in 1854 as captain of the Fourth United States Infantry. The life of the lonely post was so dreary that, according to legend, he spent much of his time drinking in Ryan's saloon at Eureka. In the end he resigned from the army out of sheer discouragement. Of the string of offices and barracks that lined the parade ground on three sides, only one, the headquarters of the commissary department, remains today.

Most violent episode of the Indian warfare that prompted establishment of Fort Humboldt was the massacre of a band of Indians by whites, on INDIAN ISLAND, largest of several small isles in the bay near the waterfront. The remnants of two or three tribes were encamped on the island. On the night of February 25, 1860, when the warriors were away hunting and fishing, white settlers killed all the women and children, the old and infirm. The husbands, fathers, and brothers returning to burned homes and mutilated dead, swore vengeance; and months of bitter warfare followed. When Bret Harte, temporarily in charge of the Uniontown paper, denounced the outrage, he was compelled to return to San Francisco because of threats against his life. The island—also called Gunther's Island for the man who later settled on it—was thereafter protected from salt water by dikes and turned into farmland. Gunther deeded it to someone, then changed his mind and demolished the dikes by night, allowing the water of the bay to pour over the island and swamp the fields.

Eureka's Chinese, like its Indians, were hounded out of town. In 1885 Eureka's Chinatown housed several hundred; as in most small California towns, anti-Chinese prejudice was strong. When, on the evening of February 6, 1885, a Eureka councilman was killed by a stray bullet during an outbreak between warring tongs, feeling was inflamed to the point of mob violence. Cooler heads among the whites assumed command, and at a meeting held in Centennial Hall a committee was appointed to order members of the Chinese colony to leave the county within 24 hours. A scaffold was erected on Fourth Street, and a hangman's noose warned of the intention of the citizens, should their order be disregarded. When rough weather delayed the sailing of ships chartered to take the Chinese to San Francisco, the whites took advantage of the delay to go through the county and issue the same command to the entire oriental population. The Chinese properties were appropriated by Eurekans. A suit was subsequently brought against the city of Eureka for $132,820 but the case never went to trial. Today Humboldt County is one of the few California counties that have no oriental residents. When vessels with Chinese crews dock at Eureka, the sailors do not attempt to go ashore.

The CARSON MANSION, Second and M Sts., sometimes called "the most photographed house in America," is an example of flamboyant Victorian architecture, the peak of the woodworker's art. It was built in 1886 by William Carson, lumber magnate, and is now the home of the Ingomar Club, an organization of business men formed to preserve the historic house. It is constructed of redwood with fir timbering on the exterior and has redwood, oak, Philippine mahogany and South American primavera in the interior. The STUMP HOUSE, on Broadway (US 101), an edifice built of the log and stump of a giant redwood, is likewise a monument to Eureka's chief industry; it houses a collection of articles fashioned from redwood burl and grotesque formations found in redwood forests.

LOLETA, 119.7 m. (50 alt., 885 pop.), first named Swauger for a settler and renamed when it became a shipping point for a prosperous dairying region, has a milk condensing plant. Many of the dairymen were Portuguese who came here as milkers and later bought farms. The December, 1964, flood of the Eel and Van Duzen Rivers created much damage.

Right from Loleta on a paved road to the TABLE BLUFF RADIO STATION and LIGHTHOUSE, 5 m. The radio station, co-operating with the Coast Guard, has been instrumental in saving many ships.

Along the valley of the EEL RIVER, visible (R) at 120.8 *m.*, the highway winds through pastures. It was discovered by the Gregg party, which came upon a small band of Indians laden with eels from the river and named the stream accordingly. At this point the party divided. Gregg and three others followed the coast south, and the other four, led by L. K. Wood, returned inland by way of Eel River. Both parties met disaster. Doctor Gregg died of starvation, and Wood was mangled by bears. He begged his companions to shoot him, but they carried him to a ranch.

FERNBRIDGE, 121.7 *m.* (35 alt.), is a settlement at the approach to FERN BRIDGE, a graceful concrete span over Eel River. On Dec. 21-25, 1964, the Eel River, swollen by heavy rains, became a raging torrent wrecking bridges used by US 101.

FERNDALE (35 alt., 1,320 pop.) four *m.* west of the Fernbridge Interchange on Redwood Highway, has cultivated its nickname, Victorian Village, by preserving its period architecture. It is the seat of Humboldt County Fair and in the center of sheep and cattle raising.

FORTUNA, 124.7 *m.* (23 alt., 3,523 pop.) in the center of the dairy industry, holds an annual pioneer rodeo. About 18 *m.* southwest of Fortuna on State 36 is GRIZZLY CREEK REDWOOD STATE PARK, 149 acres, opened 1941, with swimming and fishing in the Van Duzen River.

The Sandy Prairie Levee Project at the junction of the Eel and Van Duzen Rivers near Fortuna was damaged in the December, 1964, flood.

Another Eel River bridge carries US 101 into SCOTIA, 136.2 *m.* (101 alt., 1,122 pop.), named by its settlers, woodsmen from Nova Scotia, called "Blue Noses." Here is the large PACIFIC LUMBER COMPANY REDWOOD LUMBER MILL (*visitors admitted*) established in 1886.

RIO DELL (3,222 pop., 1960) on the Eel River opposite the Pacific Lumber Co. mill, is near fossil beds that provide new attractions for tourists. Here the Eel River flood of December, 1964, carrying millions of board feet of timber, wrecked the north abutment and 62 ft. of North Scotia Bridge.

About 10 *m.* south of Scotia near DYERVILLE begins HUMBOLDT REDWOODS STATE PARK, 37,923 acres, which stretches along US 101 for more than 20 *m.* This is the largest of the redwoods parks, containing about fifty memorial parks and some of the tallest redwoods known. Near the northern end of the park is ROCKEFELLER REDWOOD FOREST, noted for FOUNDER'S TREE, 364 ft. tall and 47 ft. circumference at the base. The Avenue of the Giants is the old highway, running parallel with US 101. Numerous campsites and picnic facilities are available throughout the park.

The redwood belt extends from extreme southwestern Oregon to the Santa Lucia Mountains over an area 450 miles long and from 1 to 40 miles wide. The *Sequoia sempervirens,* the earth's tallest trees, are exceeded in girth only by the *Sequoia gigantea* of the Sierra Nevada. The trees were named for the Cherokee chief, Se-quo-yah, who perfected a phonetic alphabet of 86 symbols for his tribe. The *sempervirens* are between 500 and 1,300 years old and the *gigantea* between 900 and 2,100. The two varieties of redwood are similar in appearance; the bole of each tapers gently from a heavily buttressed base, free of branches for a full third of the height. The branches are short, and the evergreen foliage, of small, stiff, sharp-pointed leaves, is usually a deep but brilliant yellow green. The thick, cinnamon-brown bark is deeply furrowed, giving the tree a sharply ribbed appearance. The redwood matures at a height exceeding 200 feet, when about 10 feet in diameter, and it may grow half again as high. Although a remarkable feature of the redwood is its resistance to disease and fire—because of the thick bark, the small amount of resin, and the soft spongelike quality of the wood, which absorbs water easily—fires occur almost every year in the scrub areas and in deforested sections among fallen logs, dead trees, and waste from cuttings. During the fall a heavy pall of blue-gray smoke often hangs over the entire region.

West of Humboldt Redwoods State Park on the Mattole River is PETROLIA, near which the first California oil well was drilled in 1861-62. First oil was shipped in June, 1865.

From WEOTT, 154.5 *m.* (168 alt., 150 pop.), among the redwood stands, the road climbs to skirt the sheer bluffs of the narrow gorge (R) of the south fork of Eel River, occasionally glimpsed below. South of MIRANDA, 165 *m.* (187 alt., 44 pop.), where the woods are interspersed with small clearings in which sheep graze, the highway closely follows the bank of the river.

The country around GARBERVILLE, 181.9 *m.* (225 alt., 1,000 pop.), on a high, terraced bluff overlooking Eel River, was chosen by pioneer J. C. Garber as a potential stock-raising area. The Iowan's foresight was good, for this town is a shipping point for sheep ranches.

At BENBOW, 185 *m.,* summer homes are scattered near a resort hotel in lush green mountain meadows where the waters of the Eel River, flowing here around two great bends, are backed up in a placid lake by a "summer dam."

Below RICHARDSON GROVE STATE PARK, 190.6 *m.* (*cabins, campgrounds, swimming pool, dance floor*), US 101 climbs the high rim of a narrow canyon. LILLEY REDWOOD PARK (*private*), 198.3 *m.,* is the home of the QUADRUPED TREE, called by Robert L. Ripley "the tallest one-room house in the world." This hollow 250-foot tree, used as a shop for redwood novelties, has a ground circumference of 101 feet. Four openings have been made, one in each of the huge, footlike roots. It has been used as a barn, a blacksmith shop, and, during the construction of the highway, as sleeping quarters for 32 convicts. US 101 descends from the high rim of the gorge among redwoods interspersed with Douglas and lowland fir, alder, madroña, coast hemlock, and tanoak—the latter festooned with yellow-green elk moss.

At COOLIDGE REDWOOD PARK, 206.4 *m.,* southernmost of the State redwood parks, an archway has been cut in one of the redwoods through which an automobile can pass (*25¢ per car*).

From a small, broad valley, US 101 now climbs rugged mountains where seemingly illimitable miles of blue-green forest reach in every direction.

LAYTONVILLE, 229.1 *m.* (1,600 alt., 116 pop.), is the trading center for cattle and sheep ranches.

> Left from Laytonville on a narrow dirt road to DOS RIOS (Sp., two rivers), 11.8 *m.* (924 alt., 20 pop.), a resort at the junction of the Middle and South Forks of the Eel River. COVELO, 27.8 *m.* (1,397 alt., 600 pop.), in the ROUND VALLEY INDIAN RESERVATION, is a trading center for the valley and an outfitting point for sportsmen and vacationists. The reservation's productive farming land is coveted by white farmers who have encroached steadily on it. The Indians here, excellent farmers, choose to live in brush huts rather than wooden houses.

The former lumber community of WILLITS, 254 *m.* (1,360 alt., 3,410 pop.), a division point on the Northwestern Pacific R.R., was once Willitsville, so named for the Indiana immigrant, Hiram Willits, who purchased the store opened here in 1865. The center of a hay, stock, and poultry raising region, it pays homage to the past at its yearly Frontier Days Celebration.

BLACK BART ROCK, 265.2 *m.,* commanding a clear view of southbound traffic from a slight incline (R), is so-named for the robbery of a mail stage here by the elusive road agent, "Black Bart," a lone highwayman, traveling on foot, who robbed 27 coaches in the Sierra and Coast Range mountain country between 1875 and 1883. Always polite, fastidiously dressed in a linen duster and mask, he used to leave behind facetious rhymes signed "Black Bart, Po—8," in mail and express boxes after he had finished rifling them. A laundry mark on a handkerchief dropped near the scene of one robbery in Calaveras County eventually led pursuers to San Francisco, where "Black Bart" was discovered to be the highly respectable Mr. Charles C. Bolton, ostensibly a mining engineer who frequently made trips to the mines. A stay in San Quentin from 1883 to 1885 cut short his career.

The highway descends to CALPELLA, 271 *m.* (623 alt., 300 pop.), named for an Indian chief whose name meant "Shell Bearer," a slow-moving country town in the center of an area producing large, black grapes that make an excellent dry wine. There are three wineries (*open to visitors*), with a combined annual capacity of 200,000 gallons, one of them very old, and built of heavy stones that keep the interior cool and dark. Laid out in 1858, Calpella in 1873 rivaled Ukiah in importance, but as the latter town grew it fell into decay.

US 101 cuts through vineyards to a junction with State 20 (*see TOUR 2A*) at 274.1 *m.* To the south is Mendocino Lake.

UKIAH (Ind., Yo-Ka-Ya, deep valley), 276 *m.* (650 alt., 9,900 pop.), seat of Mendocino County, is in long, narrow, mountain-flanked Ukiah Valley, where pears, prunes, grapes, and hops flourish. Ukiah celebrates the valley's important occupation of stock raising at its yearly rodeo in June. The first settler was Samuel Lowry, who built a log cabin here in 1856. Although Mendocino County was one of the 27 counties created in 1850, so few people lived in it that neighboring Sonoma County administered its affairs until a county seat was established here in 1859. This is redwood country and scene of much commercial lumbering.

Ukiah's INTERNATIONAL LATITUDE OBSERVATORY (*open in daytime*), near US 101 (R) at the end of town, is one of five in the world, widely distributed in longitude but all situated on the same parallel of latitude (39° 8′ north). They were established by the International Geodetic Association, beginning in 1898, to derive from observation of selected stars the harmonic analysis of the latitudes, which are shifting constantly, as is the North Pole. The other observatories are situated in Gaithersburg, Maryland, Sardinia, Russian Turkestan, and Japan.

    1. Left from Ukiah on an oiled road, which becomes a dirt road, 3.9 *m.* to VICHY SPRINGS, a resort noted for its "champagne baths."
    2. Left from Ukiah on a graveled road 8 *m.* to THE TERRACES, mountainside gardens of Carl Purdy, who in 1900 started a project for propagation of native western bulbs, shrubs, wild flowers, and trees. Although not the first to gather native seeds and flowers—the Royal Horticultural Society of London had sent David Douglas to California for the purpose as early as 1830—Purdy was the first to start many California wild flowers on foreign migrations. Besides gathering native plants—which he collected at elevations up to 10,000 feet—he acclimatized in his mountain garden many foreign species—from Morocco morning-glories to Scotch harebells.

The trellised green tendrils of hop vines shade the fertile fields around HOPLAND, 290 *m.* (488 alt., 860 pop.), center of the Sanel Valley's rich farmlands along the upper reaches of the Russian River. The village that grew up here around the adobe ranch house of the Mexican Fernando Felix stands on the site of a populous Indian settlement, called "Sanel" by the aborigines. The first hops were planted in 1858 by Stephen Warren Knowles, who sold his first crop, dried in the loft of his barn, for 30¢ a pound. During the growing season, the hop vines—burgeoning at the rate of 10 or 12 inches a day—are trained along strings until they cover the fields with leafy, tent-like bowers. The migratory hop pickers, arriving at harvest time in their dilapidated autos piled high with dogs, babies, pots, pans, and bedding, camp in the fields round about. The fresh-picked hops are hauled in trucks to the weather-stained drying kilns that dot the countryside—odd-looking shingled, peak-roofed structures with chimney-shaped wooden towers. The hops are dumped into the dryers and dried out by means of wood-and-sulphur fires built under each kiln.

At 302.6 *m.* is the junction with a narrow graveled road.

Left on this road to THE GEYSERS, 14.5 *m.* (1,500 alt.), where, in a small canyon, jets of steam shoot high in the air from hissing fumaroles and 35 mineral springs, no two of them alike, bubble from the earth. The Devil's Inkstand emits a black water which can be used for writing purposes. The springs early acquired fame for therapeutic qualities, and in 1851 a hotel was built.

At 303.2 *m.* is the junction with State 128 (*see TOUR 1a*).

CLOVERDALE, 304.8 *m.* (318 alt., 2,848 pop.), has a residential area with wide streets shaded by maple and eucalyptus trees; picket fences and well-tended lawns front neat frame houses. The town lies in an orange grove belt at the head of Santa Rosa Valley; it celebrates an annual citrus fair; also ships wines.

ASTI, 309.3 *m.* (264 alt., 100 pop.), is the home of an Italian-Swiss colony established in 1881 by a group of San Francisco Italians as a commercial venture to employ Italians and Swiss of that city. Today Italian-Swiss Colony wines are nationally known. Beside the highway (L) is the CHURCH OF OUR LADY OF MOUNT CARMEL, built by the vineyardists in the shape of half an enormous wine barrel. For miles vineyards stretch along the highway, dotted with old stone wineries, in one of which is a large wine vat with a capacity of 500,000 gallons, cut out of solid rock and lined with a special glass-surfaced cement. Wine is shipped from this area in tank cars.

In the spring the region south of Asti is one of exquisite beauty. Yellow mustard and golden poppies brighten a countryside of hundreds of acres of plum and pear trees, whose soft blossoms form a sea of white reaching to green foothills.

GEYSERVILLE, 314.8 *m.* (250 alt., 629 pop.), a shipping point for great quantities of apples, pears, and plums, was settled in 1852.

Hot springs tapped 700 to 5,000 ft. below ground send up scalding steam that is piped to generators of the Pacific Gas & Electric Co.

Right from Geyserville on a paved road to SKAGGS SPRINGS, 9 *m.* (800 alt., 30 pop.), a resort town, where Samuel Brannan attempted to settle Mormons in 1847.

HEALDSBURG, 323.3 *m.* (101 alt., 4,816 pop.), a trade center, was founded by Harmon G. Heald in 1852 as a trading post. Many of its inhabitants are Italian grape-growers.

At 334.5 *m.* is a junction with an oiled road (*see TOUR 2A*).

SANTA ROSA, 338.7 *m.* (150 alt., 31,027 pop.), seat of Sonoma County, is said to owe its name to Padre Juan Amarosa of Mission San Rafael, who baptized an Indian girl of the region in 1829, calling her Rosa because it was the feast day of St. Rose of Lima. The main distributing center for the ranches of Sonoma Valley, it also has been developing industries.

The rich soil and gentle climate of the Santa Rosa Valley so delighted Luther Burbank (1849-1926) that he chose this as the best place for his experiments in plant breeding. For half a century he worked here, experimenting with thousands of kinds of plants, developing a long series of what he called "new creations." Uninterested in proving special scientific theories, Burbank aimed solely to produce more and better varieties of cultivated plants. Among his achievements were the Burbank potato; thornless cactus; edible cactus; the Santa Rosa, climax, Wickson, apple, gold, and other plums; a new fruit, the plumcot; the giant, sugar, and stoneless prunes; the Burbank cherry; the Burbank, Santa Rosa, and peachblow roses; Shasta daisies; giant and fragrant callas; and many other new flowers, fruits, vegetables, ferns, grasses, trees, and nuts. He lies buried under a tall deodar, a few steps from his charming greenhouse, where his tools are still stacked against the wall. The LUTHER BURBANK HOUSE AND GARDENS (open), Santa Rosa Ave. at Tupper St., were given by his widow to the Santa Rosa Junior College botanical department.

SANTA ROSA JUNIOR COLLEGE established 1918, is under district direction and draws students from the Valley. In the 1965-66 school year it enrolled 6,916 students and had a faculty of 220.

1. Right from Santa Rosa on State 12 is SEBASTOPOL, 4.2 m. (68 alt., 2,694 pop.), trade center for vineyard- and orchard-growers, lying in the heart of an area known as the Gold Ridge which is famous for its early Gravenstein apples. It derived its name from a fight between two men in 1855; when one barricaded himself inside Dougherty's store, besieged by the other, onlookers dubbed the store Hibbs' Sebastopol, in reference to the Crimean War siege then taking place. The town helped itself to the name. On the outskirts is the LUTHER BURBANK EXPERIMENTAL GARDEN, established here in 1885 when Burbank's 4-acre garden in Santa Rosa proved too small. Not a show garden, the tract has none of the formal air of a landscaped plot about it; it was planted for working purposes.

State 12 cuts across vineyards and orchards to the RUSSIAN RIVER, which once drained into San Francisco Bay, until geological changes forced it to seek a new channel through the Coast Range to the sea. The river, which the Indians called Shabaikai or Misallaako (Ind., long snake) and the Russians, Slavianka (Russ., charming little one), is named for the Russian occupation (1812-1841). Capt. L. A. Hagermeister, writing to the Russian-American Fur Company in 1817, praised the fertile fields along this river, protected from wind and fog, as being suitable for wheat growing and cattle raising, but the Russians never settled there. The Russian River today is a famous fishing stream; in its fresh-water pools, small-mouth black bass abound, and in the lower river near the sea, striped bass. During the winter steelhead and salmon are caught in great numbers. For nearly 25 miles inland from its mouth, the river is bordered by an almost unbroken line of summer resorts, where from 100,000 to 150,000 people spend their vacations.

State 12 crosses the river to GUERNEVILLE, 18.2 m. (52 alt., 800 pop.), trade center of a dairying, fruit growing and lumbering region, especially noted for its apples. Its population expands in summer to about 10 times its winter size. The environs are thronged with tent colonies and camping grounds by the river's brink. The town is named for George Guerne, its founder, who built a large mill here in 1865.

Right from Guerneville on a paved road 2.8 m. to ARMSTRONG REDWOODS STATE PARK, a 400-acre grove where outdoor plays and festivals were presented during the summer in rustic ARMSTRONG FOREST THEATER, seating 1,000.

At 23.1 m. on State 12 is the junction with a paved road; L. on this road, which bridges the river, to MONTE RIO, 0.2 *m.* (41 alt., 320 pop.), a summer resort by the river where redwoods shadow a thicket of rock maples and wild grapevines.

Right from Monte Rio 0.9 *m.* to BOHEMIAN GROVE, a 2,437-acre grove of virgin redwoods extending from the river bank. The grove, owned by the Bohemian Club of San Francisco, is open to members only; it contains a large outdoor theater seating 1,200 with seats of bark-covered logs and a bark-covered cement structure housing a pipe organ. At the annual two-week summer encampment of the club, celebrations called High Jinks have been presented ever since 1878.

At 26.1 *m.* is the junction with a paved road; R. on this road, 6.4 *m.* through a redwood belt, thick with summer camps and cabins, to CAZA-DERO (87 alt., 300 pop.), a resort center in a dairying district.

State 12 continues to DUNCAN MILLS, 28.1 *m.* (26 alt., 37 pop.), a summer resort in the center of a small dairying region along the banks of the Russian River.

At 32 *m.* is the junction with State 1 (*see TOUR 1a*).

2. Left from Santa Rosa on State 12 around the northern end of a foot-hill spur and southeastward down long, narrow Sonoma Valley between wooded hills. The name Sonoma is probably of Indian origin, derived from the words *tso* (earth) and *noma* (village) of the Yukian Wappo dialect, although Jack London popularized the fanciful translation "Valley of the Moon" in his novel of that name. Sun-drenched for long months—but cooled by ocean fogs in summer—the vineyard-mantled slopes grow some of the State's best wine grapes.

At 14.6 *m.* is the junction with the Valley of the Moon Highway; R. on this road 1 *m.* to GLEN ELLEN (131 alt., 100 pop.), in the shade of ancient oaks and maples.

Right from Glen Ellen 0.4 *m.* to the entrance of JACK LONDON RANCH, a State Historical Monument, overlooking the valley from orchard-clad knolls, where the author of *The Call of the Wild* spent his last years in a fling at running an experimental model farm which his widow operated as a "dude" ranch. During London's life on the ranch, his daily schedule began with a gallop around the estate; after lunch, having finished his 1,000-word writing stint for the day, he spent the afternoons supervising ranch operations from horseback. In the white ranch house where the Londons lived, his library is preserved. All that remains of the costly Wolf House, which London built but never lived in, are its bare stone walls; the unfinished building was razed by fire, supposedly set by an incendiary. Only a short time later London died at the ranch on November 22, 1916—by his own hand, according to his latest biographer. On "Little Hill" near the ruins of his unfinished house, a rough boulder, unmarked, shelters his ashes.

South of Glen Ellen, the Valley of the Moon Highway follows Sonoma Creek, through a quiet countryside fragrant in season with acacia blossoms and new-mown hay, to the SONOMA STATE HOME, 2 *m.*, a group of red-roofed buildings on extensive lawns, established in the late 1880's. Although it is one of the largest hospitals for the mentally deficient in the State, it was badly overcrowded until additions were built in 1939.

The once-thriving farm and poultry center of EL VERANO (Sp., the summer), 6.2 *m.* (103 alt., 200 pop.), suffered a sharp decline when the railroad discontinued service to its station here, as a huge, empty hotel, windowless stores and homes, and rusting railway tracks attest.

At 7.2 *m.* the Valley of the Moon Highway rejoins State 12.

South of its northern junction with the Valley of the Moon Highway, State 12 continues through AGUA CALIENTE, 18.3 *m.* (75 alt., 150 pop.), FETTERS SPRINGS, 18.7 *m.*, and BOYES SPRINGS, 19.4 *m.* (129 alt., 2,462 pop.)—all resorts with cabins, hotels and swimming pools around hot mineral springs.

SONOMA, 21.9 *m.* (97 alt., 3,023 pop.), sprawls over the flat valley floor, with low-lying frame and adobe buildings, typically Californian in their second-story Spanish balconies, along wide streets around a plaza. Established as a frontier post, Sonoma has survived threatened invasion by Russians from the north, raids by horse thieves, and rebellion by *Americanos,* and still pursues its leisurely ways, untroubled by bustle and scurry, amid pleasant acres of farm, vineyard, and cattle land.

The straggling Russian settlements along the northern coast (*see TOUR 1a*) worried Gov. Luís Argüello so much that he urged Padre José Altimira to move Missions San Francisco de Asís and San Rafael Arcángel northward without delay. Too impatient to wait for the sanction of church authorities, the young priest set out in June 1823 to find a site. On July 4, 1823, he dedicated his chosen spot with rites before a cross of tree limbs and an altar of woven willow twigs and named it Misión San Francisco Solano for the saint known as the Apostle to the Indies. The mission authorities were so outraged by Padre Altimira's precipitous action that at first they forbade him to continue. By April 24, 1824, however, this, the last and most northerly of the missions, had been finished and dedicated —a crude structure of whitewashed boards—and by the end of the year a long, low tile-roofed adobe with overhanging eaves, a priest's house and guards' houses, and a granary had been added. During the 11 years before it was secularized in 1834, the mission grew rich from its vineyards, orchards, and herds of stock.

Still plagued by the Russian menace, Gov. José Figueroa ordered the commissioner for the mission, young Alferez Mariano Vallejo, Comandante of the Line of the North, to found a pueblo on the northern frontier. In 1835, having failed to establish successful colonies at Santa Rosa and Petaluma because of the hostility of the Indians, he laid out the Pueblo de Sonoma around a plaza—the largest in all California—and built his own two-story *palacio* on the northern side. As other adobe dwellings— including those of his brother Salvador on the northern side and his brother-in-law, Jacob P. Leese, at the southwestern corner—were erected, the pueblo took on the shape of a quadrangle bordered with backyard gardens. By 1839, the population included more than 25 families, over whom Vallejo reigned like a feudal baron. In the plaza he drilled his Mexican soldiers, augmented by Indians paid out of his own pocket. From the four-story watch tower of his *palacio* he used field glasses to survey his lands, ranged by vast herds of cattle and horses. To guarantee the security of his domain—and of the northern frontier—he formed an alliance with the chief of the Suisun, Sem-Yet-Ho (Mighty Arm), baptised Solano, through whose powerful friendship he won the allegiance of Indian groups whom the missions had never touched.

The drowsy pueblo was awakened to sudden life before dawn of June 14, 1846, by a villainous-looking band of three dozen armed gringoes. A rapid "change in the political affairs of Sonoma" took place, as one of the gringo leaders, William B. Ide, put it. The invaders were Yankee trappers and settlers, led by rough, rawboned Ezekiel Merritt; they were acting on orders from Capt. John C. Frémont, encamped nearby with his purported scientific expedition. Uneasy at the threat of expulsion from the province by the Mexican authorities, they were ready to begin a struggle to bring California under the American flag—unaware that the United States had already declared war against Mexico. As Ide told the story in a letter to Commodore Robert Stockton: ". . . we charged upon the Fortress of General Guadaloupe Vallejo, and captured eighteen prisoners (among whom were three of the highest officers in the Californian Government and all the military officers who reside in Sonoma) eight field-pieces, two hundred stand of arms, a great quantity of cannon, canister, and grape-shot, and a little less than one hundred pounds of powder (quite too little to sustain us against an attack by the use of cannon) . . . the soldiers were set at liberty, and the said officers were escorted by ten armed men to an asylum under the generous protection of Captain Frémont. This day we proclaim California a Republic, and our pledge of honor that private property shall be protected . . . Destined as we are to certain destruction should we prove unsuccessful, we have the honor to be your *Fellow Countrymen* . . ." He signed himself "Commander-in-chief at the Fortress of Sonoma," having been elected president of the new "California Republic."

A flag was hastily improvised from a yard-wide strip of unbleached homespun and a 4-inch strip of red flannel. With brown paint William L. Todd, Mrs. Abraham Lincoln's nephew, painted a star in one corner—in memory of the Lone Star Republic of Texas—a grizzly bear, and the words "California Republic." Said Benjamin Dewell, one of the revolutionaries: "A bear stands his ground always, and as long as the stars shine we stand for the cause." The bear, however, was so fat and clumsily drawn that the Sonomans laughed and called it a pig. The flag was run up the high flag pole in the plaza, where it fluttered until the flag of the United States replaced it on July 9.

After the Yankee occupation, when a military garrison was stationed here, Sonoma grew into a prosperous town, with Vallejo, who soon adjusted himself to American rule, as one of its leading citizens. In 1856 the Hungarian nobleman Col. Agaston Haraszthy, called the father of wine making in California, purchased land east of town. By 1858 he had planted 85,556 vines in his Buena Vista Vineyard. When he wrote an article on viticulture and wine making in the latter year, Sonoma was deluged with a flood of inquiries; overnight it became the State's chief center for distribution of viticultural knowledge and nursery cuttings of foreign vines. From Col. Haraszthy's vineyard, cuttings of the Zinfandel, Flame Tokay, Black Morocco, Seedless Sultana, and Muscat of Alexandria were distributed throughout the State.

Sonoma's plaza, once a dusty square carelessly littered with the skeletons of slaughtered beeves, is green with lawns and shrubs today. It surrounds the stone COURTHOUSE AND CITY HALL, dedicated in 1908. At the northeastern corner is the BEAR FLAG MONUMENT, a bronze figure (John MacQuarrie, sculptor) of a pioneer waving the Bear Flag from a 40-ton granite chunk; it was unveiled on the sixty-ninth anniversary of the Bear Flag Revolution.

MISSION SAN FRANCISCO DE SOLANO, at the northeastern corner of the plaza, now a State Monument (*open 10-4*), was restored in 1910-1914, after the chapel had served since 1880 as storehouse for cattle feed and the cloisters as wine cellars. The chapel (1824) and a tile-roofed one-story wing belong to the early days. The original mission bell, green with age, hangs near the door. In the cool, dim interior, old heavy unpainted beams support an adobe ceiling. More than 60 water colors of the California Missions painted by Chris Jorgensen in 1903-1904 are exhibited here.

The BLUE WING INN, 217 Spain St. East, a long, shabby, shingle-roofed adobe building with a balcony, was reputedly the first hotel north of San Francisco at the time of its erection in the early 1840's. It houses an old music box that still tinkles when fed coins, and Sonoma's first fire engine, decorated with faded birds and flowers. The SONOMA BARRACKS, Spain St. East and First St. East, a two-story adobe with a balcony (1836), has served as headquarters for Mexican troops, for the Bear Flag rebels, and for U. S. Army officers. The VALLEJO HOME, next door, the two-story adobe Palacio where Sonoma's overlord ruled his little principality, is still in use, although the tall tower from which he surveyed his holdings has disappeared. The two-story HOTEL EL DORADO, Spain St. West and First St. West, with balconies across the front of two long wings, consists of a first story of adobe—which in 1848-49 housed a noted hostelry—and a second story of wood, added in the 1860's. Vallejo's brother-in-law, Jacob P. Leese, erected the FITCH HOUSE, southwest corner of the plaza; both it and the RAY HOUSE, Main St. West and Second St. West, a two-story frame and adobe house with an overhanging roof, sheltered U. S. Army officers.

Left from Sonoma on paved Third St. West into a tree-lined avenue leading 0.5 *m.* to the VALLEJO HOME STATE HISTORICAL MONUMENT in a tree-shaded 17-acre tract. The two-story, ten-room frame mansion with its white fret-work dripping from the eaves was built by Vallejo in 1851 in the gabled and bracketed vogue of the period. In the front and back yards are white cast-iron fountains—one fashioned in the likeness of a fat swan with raised neck and open red bill spouting water. Vallejo called his place Lachryma Montis (Lat., tears of the mountain) because its first water supply came from a mountain spring. Near the house is the Swiss chalet, now the VALLEJO MUSEUM (*open 10-4*), a long, narrow edifice with a second-story overhang, built in 1850 of buff-colored brick and timbers supposed to have been brought around the Horn in sailing ships as ballast. Among the exhibits are the general's Spanish-embroidered christening robe, his derby and silk top hat, and his wife's enamel and silk jewel case.

South of Sonoma, State 12 continues to its junction with State 37 at SHELLVILLE, 25.5 *m.* (10 alt., 84 pop.); R. from Shellville on State 37 to the junction with US 101, 41.5 *m.*

ROHNERT PARK (3,675 pop.), near Cotati, incor. 1962, is the seat of SONOMA STATE COLLEGE.

COTATI, 346 *m.* (113 alt., 1,852 pop.), trade center of a poultry and farming area, is within the bounds of the former Rancho Cotati.

The roads leading into PETALUMA (Ind., beautiful view), 354.7 *m.* (100 alt., 16,000 pop.), are often clogged by trucks heavily loaded with crates of eggs and white leghorns. The slopes around town echo with the cackle of hundreds of thousands of chickens, for Petaluma produces eggs on a mass scale. Although the Mexican colony here dated from 1833 and the Yankee settlement from 1852, Petaluma rose to prominence only with the founding of its major commercial activity by a young Canadian, Lyman Ryce, who decided in 1878 that the region was adapted to poultry raising and sent to Canada for some white leghorns. Conceiving the idea of artificial incubation, he lived to see his incubators and brooders used throughout the world.

More recently Petaluma has added many diversified industries, including the manufacture of fishing and other specialty lines and twines on a large scale, as well as oil and heating units.

Left from Petaluma on an oiled road 1.5 *m.* to the junction with a dirt road; L. here 1.8 *m.* to brown-roofed CASA GRANDE (*caretaker*), largest adobe structure in northern California, standing in wide, level fields. Gen. Mariano Vallejo in 1833-34 built the casa as headquarters of his 75,000-acre Rancho Petaluma. Here he farmed successfully with the aid of his Indian laborers—probably for several years before the land was formally granted to him in 1834. The adobe walls of the massive, fort-like structure are 4 feet thick. The heavy beams used in its framework—hewn from trees brought by ox-cart from Mendocino County—are bound with tough rawhide thongs. Wide, second-story balconies run the length of the three facades, enclosing the rear patio.

NOVATO, 365 *m.* (12 alt., 700 pop., 1940; 17,881, 1960), is a trade center of a fruit-raising and dairying region.

At 368.5 *m.* is the junction with State 37 (*see above*).

At 370.5 *m.* is a junction with a paved road.

Left on the Point San Pedro Road to the new MARIN COUNTY CIVIC CENTER, designed by Frank Lloyd Wright, with the Administration Bldg., an example of architectural originality.

SAN RAFAEL, 376.3 *m.* (10 alt., 20,460 pop., 1960; 24,000 est. 1965), tripled its population in 20 years and is largely populated by commuters to San Francisco. It is the seat of Marin County, named for a Lacatuit Indian chief. It grew up around the MISSION SAN RAFAEL ARCANGEL, twentieth in the chain of California missions, founded by Father Ventura Fortuni September 18, 1817. The present buildings are restorations. In 1834 the mission had 1,250 Indians (Jouskionme), 3,000 head of cattle, 500 horses, 4,500 sheep, goats, and hogs, and a harvest of 1,500 bushels of grain. In 1842, 8 years after the decree secularizing all the missions, only 20 Indians remained. Today the DOMINICAN COLLEGE OF SAN RAFAEL, founded 1890, enrolls more than 700 students annually.

At 720 Fourth St. is the ANGELOTTI HOUSE; built by prison labor for the pioneer family, it remains as originally built. A restaurant at 1339 Fourth St., built in 1886, was long a training place for pugilists, among them James J. Corbett, Joe Gans, Jimmie Britt, Battling Nelson, and Young Corbett. Another restaurant, at 603 Lincoln Ave., was the HOUSE OF PETER DONAHUE, early railroad builder and capitalist; the spacious halls bear murals and gold leaf; the latter was especially favored by wealthy men during part of the 19th century.

US 101 gives San Rafael a direct route across the Bay to Contra Costa County. It moves down toward Point San Quentin and the SAN RAFAEL-RICHMOND BRIDGE, which carries State 17. This is a cantilever bridge completed in 1957 and has a main span of 1,070 feet.

Left from San Rafael on a paved road to POINT SAN PEDRO, 5.9 *m.*, where three Spaniards—Francisco and Ramón de Haro of San Francisco, and José de los Reyes Berryessa, an aged rancher from Santa Clara—were shot and killed by Kit Carson on June 28, 1846, during the Bear Flag revolt, while Capt. John C. Frémont was temporarily in possession of Mission San Rafael. Seeing a boat approaching from San Pablo, Frémont, it is said, ordered Carson to intercept the passengers. The three men disembarked at the point. A witness, Jasper O'Farrell, said that Carson asked Frémont whether he should make prisoners of the strangers, and that the general waved his hand and replied, "I have no room for prisoners."

At GREENBRAE, 379 *m.* (32 alt., 100 pop.), where houseboats are anchored along Corte Madera Creek, is a junction with a paved road.

Left here, to the tip of Point San Quentin reaching eastward into San Francisco Bay, to SAN QUENTIN PRISON, 2.5 *m.* (*relatives and persons with legitimate reasons to see prisoners admitted weekdays 9-2:30*). The approach to San Quentin is barred by gates; only automobiles of prison officials are permitted to pass. Within the gates, a concrete walk leads past guards' cottages and the prison fire department (of which Norman Selby—"Kid McCoy"—was once a member) to the prison wall. Construction of San Quentin, one of the largest and most overcrowded State prisons, was started in 1852. It holds about 5,000 prisoners. About 1935 the dungeons, in use since 1852 as prison disciplinary quarters, were abolished; now transgression of prison rules results in confinement in "solitary," where the prisoner is fed only one meal each day and loses his privileges (visitors, tobacco, mail, or reading matter). Execution for capital offenses committed since August 1937 is by lethal gas.

In recent years the prison has been much improved. The so-called Old Spanish Prison, a stone structure of 1854, was torn down in 1959 and replaced by a special house for offenders hard to control. A new Chapel has been built and other new buildings have been erected in a simple functional style. There is now a well-supplied cafeteria with modern appliances. There are 19 vocational shops where prisoners learn trades and make articles for prison use, from textiles to furniture. Visitors often ask to see the death house where Caryl Chessman died. Other well-known prisoners have been Tom Mooney, the labor leader who was there 22 years before Governor Olson pardoned him in 1939 and Abe Ruef, San Francisco mayor sentenced for corruption.

At 380.8 *m.* is a junction with a paved road.

Right on this road to MILL VALLEY, 2.1 *m.* (57 alt., 10,411 pop.), a residential community at the base of MOUNT TAMALPAIS (Ind., bay mountain country). The mountain rises 2,608 ft. above the Golden Gate and offers the spectator one of the finest panoramas of the work of nature and man in all California. From the summit the view embraces the tapestry of San Francisco and the Bay communities and extends to Mt. Diablo, Mt. Hamilton and the Santa Cruz mountains on the south and the Sierra Nevada in the east.

The land on which Mill Valley stands was once part of the Rancho Saucelito (little willow). A mortgage on the property was foreclosed in 1891, and the land auctioned off in lots to form the town named for the sawmill built here by Juan Read in 1834. The heavy redwood frame of the mill stands in OLD MILL PARK, on Throckmorton Ave., on the bank of the stream that formed the boundary between the Rancho Saucelito and Read's Rancho Corte Madera del Presidio (cut wood for the army post). The latter grant was named from the fact that timber cut from the land went into the construction of the presidio at Yerba Buena (San Francisco).

The route continues L. from Throckmorton Ave. in Mill Valley on Cascade Ave. and climbs to a junction with paved Muir Woods Road, 4.6 *m.;* L. here 1.6 *m.* to an entrance (R) to MUIR WOODS NATIONAL MONUMENT (*picnicking facilities*), a 485-acre grove of redwoods in Redwood Canyon. The grove, named in honor of John Muir, the naturalist, contains redwoods as much as 2,000 years old and as tall as 250 feet, frequently growing in great circles around the fire-blackened stumps of trees burned in the remote past. An unusual feature of the grove is the albino redwood sapling, about 6 feet tall; containing no chlorophyll, it cannot manufacture its own food and therefore depends on the root of the nearby parent tree for sustenance. Among the other trees found in the woods are California laurel, tan-bark oak, Douglas fir, alder, madrone, nutmeg, and buckeye. Ferns and wild flowers grow in abundance. The park owes its existence to William Kent, an ardent conservationist, who purchased the nucleus—295 acres—and donated it to the Government in 1907 to save the grove from destruction by a water company which had filed condemnation proceedings to secure Redwood Canyon for a reservoir. The grove became a National Monument in 1908. South of the entrance the side road traverses Frank Valley and joins State 1 (*see TOUR 1a*) at 5.7 *m.*

From the junction with Muir Woods Road the main side route swings sharply R.; at 6.4 *m.* it crosses a trestle built over the abandoned road-bed of the old Mount Tamalpais and Muir Woods Railway, a steam-operated road known as "The Crookedest Railroad in the World," constructed in

1896. The line had 281 curves. The chief engineering feature was the Double Bow Knot, where the track negotiated a 100-foot rise by paralleling itself five times within 2,000 feet.

At PANORAMA GATE, 9.4 m., the route turns R. on a toll road (toll 50¢).

Left from Panorama Gate on West Point Road 3.5 m. to the junction with State 1 (see TOUR 1a).

At 10.3 m. on the toll road is the MOUNTAIN THEATER, a natural amphitheater with terraced stone seats on the lower western side of Mount Tamalpais, more than 2,000 feet above sea level in a forest of redwoods, madrones, and mountain oaks. The backdrop of the natural stage is a sweeping stretch of San Francisco Bay and the Pacific Ocean. Since its inception in 1913, the Mountain Play Association has presented a play here annually on the third Sunday in May. Past presentations have included *Rip van Winkle, The Pied Piper, Robin Hood, As You Like It, Peer Gynt,* and *Androcles and the Lion.*

The toll road winds along the slopes of Mount Tamalpais' three crests— West Peak (2,605 alt.), Middle Peak (2,570 alt.), and East Peak (2,586 alt.)—to the MOUNT TAMALPAIS TAVERN, 12.4 m. From the tavern's broad windows is a far view on clear days. Mount Tamalpais appears much higher than it is because it rises almost from sea level. Myriads of ferns and wild flowers grow in the forest shade. The entire mountain is a game refuge, with hundreds of deer grazing on its slopes.

RICHARDSON BAY, bridged by US 101 at 383.1 m. for many years held the rotting hulks of German sailing vessels seized during World War I. In the distance is the graceful San Francisco-Oakland Bay Bridge.

At 383.2 m. is a junction with State 1 (see TOUR 1a), which unites with US 101 into San Francisco.

At 383.7 m. is a junction with a paved road.

Left on this road to SAUSALITO, 1 m. (8 alt., 5,331 pop), whose first permanent English-speaking settler was Captain William Richardson, a shrewd and active business man, who although as a foreigner he had no such rights, engaged quite openly as a pilot for trading and whaling ships anchoring off the Marin shore and appropriated the fees for his services; he claimed this as his privilege, since he officially represented the Mexican Government on the San Francisco shore. Sausalito (corruption of Sp. *salcedo,* willow) was so named because of the abundance of willows in early times growing about its spring, from which in early days, all the fresh water used in San Francisco was transported in barrels on rafts. The place is a strange combination of fishing village, residential suburb, and literary art colony, with a polyglot population. It is divided into Old Town and New Town; local humor divides the residents into "Wharf Rats" and "Hill Snobs." The vicinity of the SAUSALITO YACHT HARBOR in Old Town is called Hurricane Gulch despite the attempts of realtors to rename it Shelter Cove; it is a natural funnel through which strong winds blow from the hills. Whalers first began to use the cove around 1800 and later came here in large numbers. On the western shore is FORT BAKER, with high batteries. Still farther south near POINT BONITA is FORT BARRY.

South of the Sausalito junction US 101 climbs through low, windswept hills, in sight of numerous craft on the broad bay.

The 3.6 mile Golden Gate Bridge (see SAN FRANCISCO), 386.1 m., spans the entrance to San Francisco Bay. From the toll house

389 *m.,* the island of Alcatraz is visible: No longer a Federal prison, it is expected to become a public park.

SAN FRANCISCO, 392.5 *m.*

*Section b.*  *SAN FRANCISCO to SAN LUIS OBISPO, 243.3 m.*
*US 101*

South of San Francisco US 101 follows California's oldest road—El Camino Real (the king's highway), the life line that linked Spanish California's 21 missions, her straggling pueblos, and isolated presidios. In the days when it was just wide enough for an oxcart, it was used by the soldiers of the Spanish king, clad in leather cuirasses and helmets and armed with swords and smoothbore muskets. Brown-robed Franciscans plodded along it on their way between the missions, spaced a day's journey apart.

"Down the peninsula"—as local inhabitants say—the way is now a tree-lined boulevard in a country-club domain populated largely by San Francisco commuters. Here latter-day millionaires following in the steps of the mid-Victorian "bonanza kings" have laid out estates, golf links, racetracks, and polo fields. US 101 cuts across saucer-like Santa Clara Valley's prune and apricot orchards—in early spring a fragrant sea of white blossoms—dotted with fruit canneries and packing plants. It winds into Salinas Valley, a narrow trough checkered with lettuce fields and orchards and dairy farm alfalfa patches, stretching southeastward a hundred miles between bare rolling hills where cattle have ranged since the Mexican rancho era. From the southern tip of the valley the highway crosses the oak-dappled Santa Lucia Mountains.

Van Ness Ave. and Fell St., 0 *m.,* in SAN FRANCISCO, is the junction with US 101-Alt.

East from Van Ness Ave. on Fell St., which curves (R) into Tenth St.; R. on Potrero Ave. and L. on Bayshore Highway (US 101-Alt.), a speed road skirting the marshy flats along San Francisco Bay.

About 8 *m.* south and west of US 101 stands the COW PALACE, or Grand National Livestock Pavilion. *See San Francisco.*

At the southern edge of hills that wall San Francisco's outskirts is SOUTH SAN FRANCISCO, 10.5 *m.* (11 alt., 39,418 pop.), a closely built conglomeration of steel mills, foundries, smelters and refineries, machine shops and lumber yards, stockyards and packing plants.

SAN FRANCISCO INTERNATIONAL AIRPORT is on the Bay Shore, 14 *m.* formerly Mills Field. *See San Francisco.*

A cement industry grew up in this area when oyster shells were dredged up from the bottom of the Bay and converted into cement by a pulverizing process.

MOFFETT FIELD, 36 m. (visitors 7-5), a U. S. Army aviation base (acquired from the Navy in 1935 in exchange for three Army air fields), has a dirigible hangar almost a quarter of a mile long that housed the ill-fated *Macon,* a mooring mast, helium tank, airplane runway, barracks, and shops. In SAN JOSE (*see below*), 46.9 m. US 101-Alt. rejoins US 101.

South of Van Ness Ave. and Fell St., 0 m., in San Francisco, US 101 follows Van Ness Ave. into Mission St.

From the hills around DALY CITY, 5.6 m. (190 alt., 44,791 pop.), named for dairyman John D. Daly and expanded in 1936 to include the former town of Colma, hundreds of people from the Peninsula watched San Francisco burn in 1906. When speculators who bought up the land here attempted in 1859 to drive settlers off the site, the squatters built a fort and armed themselves with muskets and a cannon loaded with grapeshot. Chased away by pluguglies, they went to court and recovered their land in 1866, when the Supreme Court upheld their rights. The fields and slopes are covered with fields of lettuce, artichokes, brussels sprouts, pansies, marigolds, and violets.

Smooth green burial grounds dotted with marble headstones comprise LAWNDALE, 8.1 m. (113 alt., 369 pop.), a town populated with cemetery employees. Nurseries, florists' establishments, marbleworks, and tombstone shops border the highway.

The soldiers of the San Francisco Presidio once pastured their cattle on the site of TANFORAN RACE TRACK (L), 11.7 m. Named for the Mexican rancher, Torbirio Tanforan, it was opened by the San Francisco Jockey Club in the late '90's; but racing scandals involving jockeys, trainers, and owners evoked so much hue and cry that betting was made illegal in 1912, forcing it to close. The track was the scene of a race between an automobile and a Wright pusher biplane in aviation's pioneer period. The pilot, Lincoln Beachey, was the victor, thrilling watchers by scraping the earth with wingtips as he cut corners and narrowly cleared his rival's head as he swooped over the automobile. One of his stunts—seldom attempted even today—was to fly between two trees, where the opening was narrower than his wingspread, by tilting his plane. Beachey was killed soon afterward while stunting at the Panama-Pacific Exposition (1915). The track was reopened when betting was legalized in 1933.

On the site of SAN BRUNO, 12.7 m. (20 alt., 34,000 pop.), a community shipping vegetables and poultry, was a roadhouse where travelers by stagecoach down the Peninsula used to change horses and young bloods from San Francisco practiced target shooting.

The tree-shaded avenues of MILLBRAE, 14.6 m. (8 alt., 17,500 pop.), a nursery and dairy trade center, extend toward the bay shore over the former estate of Darius Ogden Mills. His was one of the baronial country retreats where San Francisco's "bonanza kings" set themselves up as country gentlemen. The great two-story, mansard-roofed MILLS HOUSE, built in 1866, stands in the shade of Himalayan cedars on lawns where cast-iron shepherd-maids pose with flower baskets. The garish iron and wooden grillwork that once festooned the exterior is gone—but not the carved grandfather clock, the chandeliers and the full-length mirrors, the marble mantlepieces and the red plush canopies over walnut bedsteads that graced the interior. On the oak-dotted acres sloping toward the bay, reclaimed with levees built by Chinese coolies in 1872, Mills pastured dairy cattle, built an up-to-the-minute dairy and a glass-domed conservatory with a white marble fountain. The fortune that he poured into the estate had begun accumulating in 1850, when he made his stake with a cargo of miners' supplies sold in Stockton; it had grown rapidly after he opened a bank at Columbia, a Sacramento merchandising house, and eventually—with William C. Ralston—the Bank of California. It grew even more rapidly as he acquired vast holdings in the Comstock mines. The fortune passed to his son, Ogden L. Mills, Secretary of the Treasury under President Hoover.

Ragged eucalypti—grown from seed brought from Australia by Mills—interlace in a green arch high overhead for 3 miles south of Millbrae. In the summer the trees give forth a pungent scent as the sun draws out the resinous sap; in autumn bonfires of the fallen branches and peeling bark fill the air with a spicy tang and bluish haze.

The first center of country-club life in the West was BUR-LINGAME, 17.3 m. (30 alt., 26,000 pop.), a spacious town laid out with long avenues running from the hills to the bay shore. The pseudo-Spanish stucco villas of commuters and the great rambling mansions of the rich stand in the shade of eucalypti, pepper-trees, and oaks among golf links and polo fields. Burlingame was the product of banker William C. Ralston's ambitious dream of a colony where—as Gertrude Atherton later wrote—". . . San Franciscans could have charming summer homes not too far apart for social gatherings; with small grounds, but houses spacious enough for entertaining . . . In those days everybody in society was more or less intimate, and of course no outsider would be able to buy an acre in this sacrosanct colony." The dream had already prompted Ralston to buy the site when "His Excellency, the Honourable Anson Burlingame, High Minister Plenipotentiary and Envoy Extraordinary to the Court of Pekin," came to Ralston's estate with members of the Chinese Imperial Embassy to be wined and dined. Full of enthusiasm for his project, Ralston drove his visitor, an imposing gentleman with luxuriant Dundreary whiskers, to the tract and christened it in his honor. Ralston cut his land into 5-acre lots, built roads and planted trees, drilled wells and installed water mains—and sold the plots for exorbitant prices. But the colony grew slowly; not till after establishment (1893) of the BURLINGAME COUNTRY CLUB, first in the State, did it become the city of "charming summer homes" that he had envisioned.

The millionaires' community of HILLSBOROUGH (40-700 alt., 7,554 pop.), southwest of Burlingame, climbing hills that command sweeping views, now contests Burlingame's long-unchallenged social supremacy. Its founders decreed that it should have no post office, no telegraph or express office, no stores, saloons, hotels, boarding houses, newspapers—and no sidewalks. In summer Hillsborough's WOODLAND THEATER is the scene of Sunday afternoon symphony concerts.

SAN MATEO, 19.2 *m.* (22 alt., 75,000 pop.), is at the western approach to the new San Mateo-Hayward Bridge, where US 101 (Freeway) connects with State 92 to cross the bridge. The bridge cost $70,000,000. The region looked like a "nobleman's park" to officers of the British naval vessel *Blossom,* on their way to Monterey in 1827; "herds of cattle and horses were grazing upon the rich pasture, and numerous fallow deer, startled at the approach of strangers bounded off to seek protection among the hills." But they could trace the resemblance no further. "Instead of a noble mansion in character with so fine a country," they found on the banks of San Mateo Creek "a miserable hut dwelling before the door of which a number of half naked Indians were basking in the sun," surrounded with litter that "sadly disgraced the park-like scenery." The building, a long, low adobe, was a hospice where friars, officials, and soldiers broke their journey between Mission Dolores and Mission Santa Clara. The roof tiles, all that remained after the earthquake of 1868, were used on the Burlingame railroad station.

The first San Mateo settler, John B. Cooper, a deserter from the British Navy in 1833, took up his adobe in 1851 in a brush booth beneath an oak. The town, platted in 1863, was eventually encompassed by the estates of San Francisco rich men—W. D. M. Howard and Frederick Macondray, the merchants; John Parrott, shipping and financial magnate; and Alvinza Hayward, mine operator and financier.

The COLLEGE OF SAN MATEO, largest Junior College in California, in 1963 moved to College Heights, 153 acres with 12 major buildings, 19th Ave. Freeway. It served 5,600 day students in 1964 and had more than 9,000 in evening classes.

The stands of BAY MEADOWS RACE TRACK (L), 20.7. *m.* are filled with 25,000 horse fans during the winter racing season.

The wooded hills sloping steeply to BELMONT, 23 *m.* (32 alt., 15,996 pop.), delighted Capt. George Vancouver's appreciative eye when he paused here for lunch November 20, 1792, on his way to Mission Santa Clara with a military escort from the anchorage near the San Francisco Presidio of the British warship *Discovery,* first non-Spanish vessel to enter the Bay. On "a very pleasant enchanting lawn situated amidst a grove of trees at the foot of a small hill, by which flowed a stream of most excellent water," the party had their noontime refreshments "with some grog we had brought from the ship, spirits and wine being scarce articles in this country." For Vancouver, the countryside could properly be described only with eighteenth-century grandiloquence: "The stately lords of the forest were in complete possession of the soil, covered with luxuriant herbage and beautifully diversified with pleasing eminences and valleys; which, with the range of lofty, rugged mountains that bounded the prospect, required only to be adorned with the neat habitations of an industrious people to produce a scene not inferior to the most studied effects of taste in the disposal of the grounds."

Only "the most studied effects of taste" would do for William Chapman Ralston—the gambling financial genius of the Bank of California who poured his Comstock mining millions into countless enterprises—when he purchased Count Lussetti Cipriani's modest hillside villa in the Cañada del Diablo at Belmont and began transforming it into the Peninsula's most extravagant showplace. Architects, artisans, and gardeners changed the villa into what Gertrude Atherton called "an immense, rambling, French-looking structure," thrusting out guest wings in all directions. By 1867 it had accommodations for 30 guests; by 1868, for 120. The floors were of parquetry, the walls panelled with mirrors, the ceiling hung with chandeliers. Europe and the Orient were plundered for rugs, hangings, vases, furniture, glassware and napery to furnish the spacious, high-ceilinged chambers. Outside the mansion were brick-and-glass greenhouses; a bowling alley and gymnasium with a Turkish bath; a "Little Belmont" for the Chinese servants, the grooms and hostlers; and stables with walls of redwood outside and carved mahogany inlaid with mother-of-pearl inside, and with a glass-enclosed harness room having solid silver pegs for the silver-monogrammed trappings of Ralston's thoroughbreds. To illuminate his country seat, Ralston erected a gas-works; to irrigate his far-reaching gardens, he built a dam and reservoir in the hills.

At the great white mansion's long porte-cochère an almost continuous stream of carriages began discharging actresses, ambassadors, generals, and statesmen, the great and near-great from Mark Twain to Baron Ikakuri of the first Japanese delegation to visit America. One of the sights of the time was Ralston's four-in-hand, crowded with guests and drawn by spirited steeds, with Ralston himself cracking the whip. He usually managed to arrive with new guests just after dark when the house was a blaze of light against the black of the canyon. Often Ralston used to sit in his royal box, watching his guests dance in the dazzling chandelier-lighted ballroom, reflected in its great mirrors. As many as a hundred dinner guests used to be escorted to the library, there to wait until suddenly "the opposite wall gave a sort of shiver, then rose slowly like the curtain of a theatre, revealing an immense banqueting-hall laden with the most splendid plate, china and glass that had been imported to California at that period . . . As motionless as an army about to salute stood the pigtailed Chinese servants . . ." The San Francisco *Call* once described what appeared on the table before them: "Glorious was the grand salmon stuffed with brook trout and baked in rose leaves . . . the pyramid of skewered frogs *a la mode* Huguenots . . . But these were as nothing beside the grand course

. . . humming-bird filled with baked almonds, surrounded by a Spring linnet, which, in turn, was enveloped by an English snipe. These the carcass of a stuffed goose surrounded, covering which were two canvasback ducks . . . the whole placed within the bosom of a Chicago goose. Soaked in raisin wine for six days, then larded, and smoked three weeks over burning sandalwood, it was at last placed on the spit and roasted with pig-pork drippings."

The day after Ralston's Bank of California closed its doors on clamoring investors, August 26, 1875, in a financial scandal that rocked the State, Ralston's body was found floating in the Bay. The estate passed to his partner, William Sharon, whose daughter's marriage was the last of Belmont's social flings. The great mansion became successively a young ladies' seminary, a private insane asylum, and finally, the COLLEGE OF·NOTRE DAME, opened here in 1923 by the Sisters of Notre Dame de Namur.

SAN CARLOS, 24.2 m. (21 alt., 21,370 pop.), a town of homes among oaks, named for Lt. Juan Manuel de Ayala's *San Carlos*, first vessel to enter the Golden Gate, was the seat of Rancho de las Pulgas (the fleas). "The ranch had been well-named by the matter-of-fact Spanish," wrote Gertrude Atherton in later years. "I may add that it was no breach of decorum to speak of fleas in California, nor even to scratch."

The flower beds in the neighborhood supply eastern markets with carloads of chrysanthemums, asters, roses, violets, lilies, irises, anemones, gardenias, acacia, heather, and peach blossoms.

REDWOOD CITY, 26.2 m. (10 alt., 50,000 pop. est.), seat of San Mateo County, spreads over land some miles eastward from the docks and piers, canneries, and salt works of its deep-water bay frontage. Redwood Slough once extended inland to the mouth of Redwood Creek, now the center of town, where the Mexican rancheros shipped from the Embarcadero de las Pulgas. As shipment of redwood lumber hauled from the forested ridges to the west began in 1850, Embarcadero became a busy shipbuilding, wagonmaking, and blacksmithing center. Each time that San Francisco burned to the ground the demand for lumber swelled. The redwood business prompted the renaming of the town in 1858, despite founder S. M. Mezes' attempts to substitute his own name for the more euphonious Embarcadero.

The country estates of ATHERTON, 28.7 m. (52 alt., 7,717 pop.), are so heavily wooded that little of the town beyond its shady lanes winding under great live oaks can be seen from the highway. Besides its mansions, it has the old railroad station where the Peninsula's first steam carriages stopped.

The first estate here was Faxon Dean Atherton's mile-square Valparaiso Park, laid out in 1860. The family mansion (no longer standing) was later described by his daughter-in-law, Gertrude, as "a large comfortable house with two bath rooms—few houses boasted more than one —and a wing for the servants . . . About the house was a continuous

bed of Parma violets whose fragrance greeted one when passing the
deer park. (The deer generally died, homesick for their forests on the
mountains.)" Faxon Atherton, "in his early youth, had adventured as
far as Chile in search of his fortune. He made it in hardware. Not
long after his arrival he married Dominga de Goni . . ." Mrs. Atherton, her daughter-in-law wrote, "had hopes of making a true Atherton
out of me, and I sometimes wonder she did not . . . 'Ladies in Spain
do not write,' she said to me when I began to betray symptoms; and
it was quite twelve years after I published my first novel before the
painful subject that I wrote at all was mentioned by any of the family
in my presence . . ." Life in Valparaiso Park for Gertrude Atherton
seemed to be a long series of summer afternoons spent with neighbors
"on the wide verandah, sewing, embroidering, exchanging recipes, gos-
siping. I often wondered if life anywhere else in the whole wide world
were as dull."

When James L. Flood, the former San Francisco saloonkeeper who
rose to sudden riches by speculation in Virginia City mines, began in
1878 to build the scrollwork-festooned extravaganza of gables, cupolas,
and porticos that he called Linden Towers, "the impertinent invasion
of . . . the Bonanza millionaires" threw the country aristocracy into
a furore, and "for weeks the leading topic on the verandah was whether
or not the Floods should be called upon when they moved in." The
"colossal white house . . . looked more like a house on a wedding cake
than something to live in." In the end, "for business reasons, impressed
upon them by their husbands, the women did call." When the Floods
returned the call at Valparaiso Park—Mrs. Flood wearing "a flowing
dark blue silk wrapper, discreetly ruffled, and 'Miss Jennie' a confec-
tion of tourquoise-green flannel trimmed with deep flounces of Valen-
ciennes lace!"—Gertrude Atherton fancied "they went away . . . with
the pleasant feeling of superiority that only multi-millions can give."
The trappings of Linden Towers—the sterling silver soap dishes ini-
tialed J.F., the statues and tapestries, the marble fireplaces and carved
rosewood panels—went on the auction block in 1934 when the mansion
was torn down; all that remains of the JAMES L. FLOOD ESTATE on
Middlefield Rd. are the lodge, iron gateways, and a wall.

MENLO PARK, 29.9 m. (63 alt., 26,957 pop.), on US 101 connects with State 84, which crosses the Upper Bay on Dumbarton
Bridge to Newark (9,884 pop.) in Alameda County. It developed in
1863 around an estate named by two Irishmen for their home in Ireland, was chosen in 1871 by Milton S. Latham, Governor and U. S.
Senator, for his stately, pillared mansion. When the Duke of Manchester passed through on his way around the world, he was escorted
here by train to meet the country fashionables. The company was
gathered in the drawing room—the women in their Paris gowns and
the men in their evening best eagerly awaiting their first sight of a real
duke when the English butler announced him. "And then," as Gertrude
Atherton told the story, "the duke strode in, and they nearly fainted.
He wore boots that reached his thighs and a red flannel shirt! . . .

# *History*